T0234963

Lecture Notes in Artificial Intelligence 13087

Subseries of Lecture Notes in Computer Science

Series Editors

Randy Goebel
University of Alberta, Edmonton, Canada

Wolfgang Wahlster
DFKI, Berlin, Germany

Zhi-Hua Zhou
Nanjing University, Nanjing, China

Founding Editor

Jörg Siekmann
DFKI and Saarland University, Saarbrücken, Germany

More information about this subseries at https://link.springer.com/bookseries/1244

Bohan Li · Lin Yue · Jing Jiang · Weitong Chen ·
Xue Li · Guodong Long · Fei Fang ·
Han Yu (Eds.)

Advanced Data Mining and Applications

17th International Conference, ADMA 2021
Sydney, NSW, Australia, February 2–4, 2022
Proceedings, Part I

Springer

Editors
Bohan Li
Nanjing University of Aeronautics
and Astronautics
Nanjing, China

Jing Jiang
University of Technology Sydney
Sydney, NSW, Australia

Xue Li
University of Queensland
Brisbane, QLD, Australia

Fei Fang
Carnegie Mellon University
Pittsburgh, USA

Lin Yue
University of Queensland
Brisbane, QLD, Australia

Weitong Chen
University of Queensland
Brisbane, QLD, Australia

Guodong Long
University of Technology Sydney
Sydney, NSW, Australia

Han Yu (iD)
Nanyang Technological University
Singapore, Singapore

ISSN 0302-9743   ISSN 1611-3349 (electronic)
Lecture Notes in Artificial Intelligence
ISBN 978-3-030-95404-8   ISBN 978-3-030-95405-5 (eBook)
https://doi.org/10.1007/978-3-030-95405-5

LNCS Sublibrary: SL7 – Artificial Intelligence

© Springer Nature Switzerland AG 2022
This work is subject to copyright. All rights are reserved by the Publisher, whether the whole or part of the
material is concerned, specifically the rights of translation, reprinting, reuse of illustrations, recitation,
broadcasting, reproduction on microfilms or in any other physical way, and transmission or information
storage and retrieval, electronic adaptation, computer software, or by similar or dissimilar methodology now
known or hereafter developed.
The use of general descriptive names, registered names, trademarks, service marks, etc. in this publication
does not imply, even in the absence of a specific statement, that such names are exempt from the relevant
protective laws and regulations and therefore free for general use.
The publisher, the authors and the editors are safe to assume that the advice and information in this book are
believed to be true and accurate at the date of publication. Neither the publisher nor the authors or the editors
give a warranty, expressed or implied, with respect to the material contained herein or for any errors or
omissions that may have been made. The publisher remains neutral with regard to jurisdictional claims in
published maps and institutional affiliations.

This Springer imprint is published by the registered company Springer Nature Switzerland AG
The registered company address is: Gewerbestrasse 11, 6330 Cham, Switzerland

Preface

The 17th International Conference on Advanced Data Mining Applications (ADMA 2021) was held in Sydney, Australia, during February 2–4, 2022. Researchers and practitioners from around the world came together at this leading international forum to share innovative ideas, original research findings, case study results, and experienced insights in advanced data mining and it's applications. With the ever-growing importance of appropriate methods in these data-rich times, ADMA has become a flagship conference in this field.

ADMA 2021 received a total of 116 submissions. After a rigorous review process, 61 regular papers were accepted to be published in the proceedings. Of these, 26 were selected to be delivered as oral presentations in the conference, and 35 were selected as poster presentations. This corresponds to a full oral paper acceptance rate of 22.4%. The Program Committee (PC), composed of international experts in relevant fields, did a thorough and professional job of reviewing the papers submitted to ADMA 2021, and each paper was reviewed by at least three PC members. With the growing importance of data in this digital age, papers accepted in ADMA 2021 covered a wide range of research topics in the field of data mining, including machine learning, text mining, graph mining, predictive data analytics, recommender systems, query processing, analytics-based applications, and privacy and security analytics.

There are a number of important aspects to the ADMA 2021 conference worth mentioning. First, due to the impact of COVID-19, the conference date was postponed from December 2021 to February 2022 to allow for in-person gathering and networking. Second, the submission system was switched from EasyChair to CMT, which provided a smoother submission process. Third, we have witnessed an overwhelming trend of deep learning that has profoundly influenced or reshaped many research and application domains, thus, many submissions to ADMA 2021 explored deep learning technology to solve various data mining problems. Fourth and finally, the organizing committee was composed of an international team from prestigious universities and research institutes, such as Carnegie Mellon University (USA), Stanford University (USA), the University of Washington, (USA), Nanyang Technological University (Singapore), the University of Queensland (Australia), the University of Technology Sydney (Australia), the University of Western Australia (Australia), and the University of Alberta (Canada).

We would like to express our gratitude to all individuals, institutions, and sponsors that supported ADMA 2021. We also thank the PC members for completing the review process and providing valuable comments within tight schedules. The high-quality program would not have been possible without the expertise and dedication of our PC members. Moreover, we would like to take this valuable opportunity to thank all authors who submitted technical papers and contributed to the tradition of excellence at ADMA. We firmly believe that many colleagues will find the papers in this proceedings exciting and beneficial for advancing their research. We would like to thank Microsoft for providing the CMT system that is free to use for conference organization, and thank Springer for the long-term support and sponsorship of the conference.

We are grateful for the guidance of the steering committee members, Xue Li and Jianxin Li, and the great support from the general co-chairs, Fang Chen, Osmar Zaiane, and Mohammed Bennamoun. With their leadership and support, the conference has run smoothly in a well-organized manner.

We also would like to acknowledge the support of the other members of the organizing committee. All of them helped to make ADMA 2021 a success. We appreciate local arrangements from the local co-chairs, Jing Jiang and Weitong Chen, the time and effort of the publication co-chairs, Lin Yue and Bohan Li, and the effort on advertising the conference by the publicity co-chairs, Lu Liu, Miranda Li, Yanjun Zhang, and Sonali Agarwal. We would like to give very special thanks to the web chair, Xueping Peng, for creating a beautiful website and maintaining the information. We also want to thank Chiyu Wang for her contribution in managing the registration system. Finally, we would like to thank all other co-chairs who have contributed to the conference organization.

November 2021   Guodong Long
                                                                      Fei Fang
                                                                      Han Yu

Organization

General Co-chairs

Fang Chen	University of Technology Sydney, Australia
Osmar Zaiane	University of Alberta, Canada
Mohammed Bennamoun	University of Western Australia, Australia

Program Committee Co-chairs

Guodong Long	University of Technology Sydney, Australia
Fei Fang	Carnegie Mellon University, USA
Han Yu	Nanyang Technological University, Singapore

Steering Committee

Xue Li	University of Queensland, Australia
Jianxin Li	Deakin University, Australia

Tutorial Co-chairs

Franck Vidal	Bangor University, UK
Tao Shen	University of Technology Sydney, Australia
Tianyi Zhou	University of Washington, USA

Publication Co-chairs

Lin Yue	University of Queensland, Australia
Bohan Li	Nanjing University of Aeronautics and Astronautics, China

Publicity Co-chairs

Lu Liu	University of Technology Sydney, Australia
Miranda Li	University of New South Wales, Australia
Yanjun Zhang	University of Queensland, Australia
Sonali Agarwal	Indian Institute of Information Technology, Allahabad, India

Workshop Co-chairs

Huaxiu Yao   Stanford University, USA
Sunil Aryal   Deakin University, Australia

Local Co-chairs

Jing Jiang   University of Technology Sydney, Australia
Weitong Chen   University of Queensland, Australia

Volunteer and Virtual Co-chairs

Xianzhi Wang   University of Technology Sydney, Australia
Qin Zhang   Shenzhen University, China
Xuyun Zhang   Macquarie University, Australia

Web Chair

Xueping Peng   University of Technology Sydney, Australia

Program Committee

A. M. Kayes   Swinburne University of Technology, Australia
Bin Zhao   Nanjing Normal University, China
Bo Ning   Dalian Maritime University, China
Bohan Li   Nanjing University of Aeronautics and
                                    Astronautics, China
Chang-Dong Wang   Sun Yat-sen University, China
Chee Keong Wee   Department of Health, Australia
Chun Wang   University of Technology Sydney, Australia
Debajyoti Bera   IIIT-Delhi, India
Dong Huang   South China Agricultural University, China
Farhana Choudhury   University of Melbourne, Australia
Guangyan Huang   Deakin University, Australia
Haiyan Zhao   University of Technology Sydney, Australia
Han Zheng   University of Technology Sydney, Australia
Hongzhi Wang   Harbin Institute of Technology, China
Indika P. K. Dewage   Tilburg University, The Netherlands
Jiajie Xu   Soochow University, China
Jianxin Li   Deakin University, Australia
Jie Ma   University of Technology Sydney, Australia
Jing Zhang   Changchun University of Science and
                                    Technology, China

Ke Niu	Beijing Information Science and Technology University, China
Ke Deng	RMIT University, Australia
Krzysztof Goczyta	Politechnika Gdańska, Poland
Lei Li	University of Queensland, Australia
Li Li	Southwest University, China
Lin Guo	Changchun University of Science and Technology, China
Lina Yao	University of New South Wales, Australia
Lu Chen	Swinburne University of Technology, Australia
Lu Liu	University of Technology Sydney, Australia
Lukui Shi	Hebei University of Technology, China
Manqing Dong	University of New South Wales, Australia
Md. Musfique Anwar	Jahangirnagar University, Bangladesh
Meng Wang	Southeast University, China
Ningning Cui	Anhui University, China
Noha Alduaiji	Majmaah University, Saudi Arabia
Peiquan Jin	University of Science and Technology of China, China
Peng Yan	University of Technology Sydney, Australia
Philippe Fournier-Viger	Shenzhen University, China
Priyamvada Bhardwaj	Otto von Guericke University Magdeburg, Germany
Qin Zhang	Shenzhen University, China
Quan Z. Sheng	Macquarie University, Australia
Quoc Viet Hung Nguyen	Griffith University, Australia
Saiful Islam	Griffith University, Australia
Sayan Unankard	Maejo University, Thailand
Shan Xue	Macquarie University, Australia
Shuiqiao Yang	University of Technology Sydney, Australia
Tao Shen	University of Technology Sydney, Australia
Tarique Anwar	Swinburne University of Technology, Australia
Tong Chen	University of Queensland, Australia
Wei Chen	University of Auckland, Australia
Weiwei Yuan	Nanjing University of Aeronautics and Astronautics, China
Xiangmin Zhou	RMIT University, Australia
Xianzhi Wang	University of Technology Sydney, Australia
Xiaowang Zhang	Tianjin University, China
Xueping Peng	University of Technology Sydney, Australia
Xuming Han	Jinan University, China
Xuyun Zhang	Macquarie University, Australia

Yajun Yang	Tianjin University, China
Yanda Wang	Nanjing University of Aeronautics and Astronautics, China
Yang Li	University of Technology Sydney, Australia
Yanjun Zhang	University of Queensland, Australia
Yanmei Hu	Chengdu University of Technology, China
Ye Yuan	Beijing Institute of Technology, China
Ye Zhu	Deakin University, Australia
Yucheng Zhou	University of Technology Sydney, Australia
Yue Tan	University of Technology Sydney, Australia
Yuhai Zhao	Northeastern University, China
Yunjun Gao	Zhejiang University, China
Yurong Cheng	Beijing Institute of Technology, China
Yuwei Peng	Wuhan University, China
Zhi-Hong Deng	University of Technology Sydney, Australia
Zhuowei Wang	University of Technology Sydney, Australia
Zonghan Wu	University of Technology Sydney, Australia

Contents – Part I

Others

Contents – Part II

Text Mining

Multimedia and Time Series Data Mining

Healthcare

Deep Learning Based Cardiac Phase Detection Using Echocardiography Imaging

Moomal Farhad$^{(\boxtimes)}$, Mohammad M. Masud, and Azam Beg

College of Information Technology, United Arab Emirates University,
P.O.Box 15551, Al Ain, UAE
{201990108,m.masud,abeg}@uaeu.ac.ae

Abstract. Echocardiography is a widely used, affordable, and high-throughput test to evaluate heart conditions. There are two cardiac phases known as end-systolic (ES) and end-diastolic (ED), which are observed by cardiologists and technicians during echocardiography. These phases are used to perform critical calculations during echocardiography, such as calculating heart chamber size and the calculation of ejection fraction. Typically, ED and ES phase detection is performed manually by a technician or cardiologist, which makes echocardiography interpretation time-consuming and error-prone. Therefore, it is crucial to develop an automated and efficient technique to detect the cardiac phases and minimize diagnostic errors. In this paper, we propose a deep learning model, namely DeepPhase, for accurate and automated interpretation of the ES and ED phases to assist cardiology personnel. Our proposed convolutional neural network (CNN) is designed to learn from echocardiography images and identify the cardiac phase from the given image without segmentation of left ventrical or the use of electrocardiograms. We have performed an extensive evaluation on two-real world echocardiography image datasets, namely, the benchmark Cardiac Acquisitions for Multistructure Ultrasound Segmentation (CAMUS) dataset and a new dataset (referred to as CardiacPhase) that we collected from a cardiac hospital. The proposed model outperformed relevant state-of-the-art techniques by achieving 0.98 and 0.92 area under the curve (AUC) on the CAMUS dataset, and the CardiacPhase dataset, respectively. We have proved the generalizability of our proposed work by training and testing with different cardiac views.

Keywords: Deep learning · Echocardiography · Convolutional neural network · Artificial intelligence · Medical imaging

1 Introduction

Cardiac imaging has a vital role in the assessment of heart structure and functionality. The standard cardiac imaging tests include chest X-ray, cardiac computed

This work is funded in part by United Arab Emirates University collaborative team grant number 31R239.

© Springer Nature Switzerland AG 2022
B. Li et al. (Eds.): ADMA 2021, LNAI 13087, pp. 3–17, 2022.
https://doi.org/10.1007/978-3-030-95405-5_1

tomography (CCT), cardiac magnetic resonance imaging (CMR), electrocardiogram (ECG), and transthoracic echocardiography, also known as echo. Echocardiography has gained popularity as a safe, affordable and non-invasive heart diagnostic test [1], which is recommended by the cardiologist as a first response, in conjunction with ECG, to the patient with any heart-related symptoms. It is a screening tool for diagnosing various cardiac conditions such as including valvular insufficiency, aneurysms, septal hypertrophy, etc. An echocardiogram, which is the result of the echocardiography test, is generated by the reflections of a high-frequency sound wave propagating through a transducer. Echocardiogram images can be collected during one of the two phases of the cardiac cycle and from multiple viewpoints. The two phases of the cardiac cycle are end-systolic (ES) and end diastolic (ED). During the ED phase, the isovolumetric contraction and ventricular diastolic filling occur. In the ES phase, isovolumetric relaxation and blood ejection performed by the heart. A detailed heart examination via echocardiography involves observing the heart from multiple viewpoints. The examples of viewpoints are parasternal, apical, subcostal, suprasternal and the viewpoints are defined by the transducer position on the heart. In order to perform certain calculations such as stroke volume and cardiac output during echocardiography, the radiologist has to capture recommended cardiac viewpoint and phase.

The computer-assisted echocardiography analysis is a booming area of research. Precise and accurate segmentation of left ventricle (LV) in every echocardiogram is required for different applications such as wall motion abnormality detection and ejection fraction estimation. The ground truth annotation for the LV region is only available for the two end-diastolic and end-systolic frames and the recommended viewpoints are apical two-chamber and four-chamber. Here ground truth annotations refer to the labels given by experts of the field such as cardiologists and echocardiography technicians. Therefore accurate detection of ES and ED frames is the primary step for cardiac anatomy localization, landmark detection, and segmentation.

The motivations behind our work are multifold. First, echocardiographers manually identify the ED and ES phases by visually observing each frame during the echocardiography test for changes in the LV dimension and left sided valves in relation to the ECG tracing. This process can be time consuming and depends on the expertise of the interpreter. Our primary motivation is to propose an approach that caters for these shortcomings and decreases inter and intra-observer variability, and improves automation and diagnostic throughput. Second, we are motivated by the fact that cardiologists misdiagnose a problem when they are overworked, as suggested in the literature. A survey conducted by Rao et al. [11] reported that out of 1882 cardiologists, 45.6% reported a high level of burnout symptoms due to overwork. Our automatic phase detection approach can help cardiologists to avoid misdiagnosis in the diagnostic process. Finally, we are motivated to automate the primary step of the echocardiography test because of the quality of the echocardiograms. Echocardiograms contain speckle noise and their distribution is highly dependent on the underlying local tissue structure. The quality of the echocardiograms has a direct correlation with the boundaries in a given standard viewpoints and the visibility of desired anatomical markers. Therefore computerized detection of ES and ED phases can support and help the medical personnel in the given circumstances.

Studies have applied various image-processing techniques to interpret echocardiography automatically, e.g., velocity spectrum envelopes [13]. Recently, deep learning (DL) has revolutionized visual object recognition in many fields, e.g., medicine and sports. DL techniques learn and recognize patterns from data requiring less preprocessing and achieving better accuracy compared to traditional methods such as hand-crafted features and image processing techniques [7].

LV segmentation is performed by many researchers to identify LV hypertrophy and cardiac views from echocardiogrpahy [9] . LV segmentation is also one of the methods used by researchers [2,4] to classify ES and ED frames. Segmentation-based methods identify the ES and ED frames based on the speculation that the smallest and largest LV segmented cross-sections in a cardiac cycle represent the ES and ED frames respectively. LV segmentation methods require complex preprocessing and are prone to error due to the noisy nature of echocardiograms. In this paper, we have utilized the power of CNN-based image recognition to identify the ES and ED frames from echocardiography images.

In this paper, we propose a technique to automatically classify the ED and ES phases in the two-chamber and four-chamber view from the echocardiography modality without manual measurement or automated segmentation of the left ventricle. We named our approach as DeepPhase which represents 'Deep learning based cardiac Phase detection using echocardiography imaging'. To the best of our knowledge, this is first such attempt at phase detection. Our primary contributions are summarized as follows. First, we propose an effective CNN model for the ES and ED classification task. Second, we present a custom loss function that enriches the CNN model with high prediction accuracy and showed its effectiveness over traditional loss functions. Third, we introduce a new dataset annotated by two expert cardiologists. Forth, We have shown the effectiveness of our approach by training with two-chamber view and testing with four-chamber view and vice versa. Finally, we evaluate the efficacy of the DeepPhase model in extensive experiments on a benchmark dataset (CAMUS) and the newly introduced dataset. Results demonstrate better performance than relevant state-of-the-art techniques.

2 Related Work

Leclerc et al. [7] introduced the Cardiac Acquisitions for Multistructure Ultrasound Segmentation (CAMUS) dataset, the largest publicly available dataset comprising ED and ES images and video sequences of 500 patients. They applied UNet, an anatomically constrained neural network, an encoder-decoder, stacked hourglasses, the B-spline explicit active surface model framework, and structured random forest to segment the LV endocardium and myocardium. Other researchers [8,9] have applied different deep learning algorithms such as UNet and CNN for LV segmentation and view classification. Badcaro et al. [2] classified ES and ED frames as an initial step for the segmentation of the LV cavity and the computation of the LV ejection fraction in echocardiographic images. The classification of ES and ED frames was carried out by LV segmentation using Otsu's threshold. Dezaki et al. [14] explored DL techniques for ED and ES phase detection from the four-chamber view of the echocardiography cine series. They proposed a custom loss function based on mean squared error. Their framework comprised CNN and recurrent neural network modules, and their dataset comprised 3087 cine series. They achieved an error measurement of 0.49 for ED and 1.33 for ES.

The current study is motivated by Dezaki et al. [14]; however, our study differs in several aspects. First, we classify ED and ES cardiac phases from echocardiography images rather than cine series. Second, we formulate ES and ED detection problems as a classification problem, contrary to Dezaki et al. work, where they dealt with this as a regression problem. We select echo images for several reasons. Advancements in communication technologies and the emergence of advanced image- and video-compression standards have enabled efficient storage of medical images and videos. A comparison of the storage and transmission resources required by medical images and videos reveals that images would obviously use less system memory and transmission bandwidth than videos. Moreover, for physicians in underdeveloped areas, accessing and storing medical images is easier than processing videos because videos may require additional resources. Some studies [5,6] have employed echo images to develop a cardiac diagnostic and analysis system because echo images are sufficient to enable cardiologists and computer systems to make accurate diagnoses.

This study is expected to provide a foundation for achieving impressive results for cardiac phase detection in the apical two-chamber view and apical four-chamber view. Unlike previous research works, we carried out the task without LV segmentation, using only a custom CNN architecture and a dataset of 1000 images.

3   Methodology

We divided the methodology into two phases: model training and model testing. There are several substages in each phase, e.g., preprocessing and data augmentation, optimizing and testing the DeepPhase model, and calculating results. The high level architecture of DeepPhase is given in Fig. 1.

3.1   Phase I: Model Training

Training Dataset: We used the CAMUS dataset, which was introduced by Leclerc et al. in 2019 [7], to train and validate the DeepPhase model. The lack of publicly available and comprehensive data for echocardiography motivated Leclerc et al. to develop the CAMUS dataset, which contains the reports of 500 patients with ED and ES frames in four-chamber and two-chamber views.

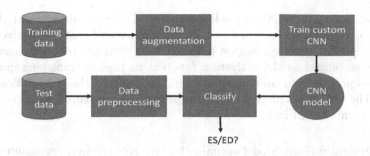

Fig. 1. High level architecture of the DeepPhase

The patient reports were acquired from St. Etienne hospital in France, and the dataset reflects daily clinical practice data. The full dataset was acquired using GE Vivid E95 ultrasound scanners with a GE M5S probe (GE Healthcare, US). The dataset contains good-, poor-, and medium-quality images. The labeling was performed by three cardiologists.

Data Augmentation: Data augmentation is one of the techniques for improving the generalization of the CNN network and for reducing overfitting. Multiple variants of every training image were generated. For each augmentation, we vary the augmentation hyperparameters across their specified ranges. These ranges were chosen such that a single transformation in the range preserves the class while a transformation outside of the range is not guaranteed to be class-preserving. We employed four augmentation methods which are as follows:

Rescale: Every gray-scale image is formed by a pixel having a value in range 0–255. 0 is black and 255 is white. Since 255 is the maximum pixel value, a rescale factor of 1/255 is used to transform every pixel value from the range $[0, 255] \rightarrow [0, 1]$.

Shear: We set shear intensity to 0.2. Shear intensity implies that the image will be distorted along an axis, mostly to rectify or create the perception angles. The shear method is used to augment images to model to show how human beings see things from different angles.

Zoom: We set the zoom range as 0.2. Zoom augmentation randomly zooms the image and adds new pixels for the image.

Horizontal Flip: As the name implies, the augmented images are generated by flipping the original image horizontally.

DeepPhase Model: Typically, the CNN architecture comprises convolutional, pooling, and fully connected layers [15], where the neurons in one layer are not necessarily connected to all neurons in the next layer. In this study, we propose a 9-layer CNN architecture including the input, convolutional, pooling, fully connected, and output layers. The structure of the CNN architecture comprises three convolutional layers, three pooling layers, and a single fully connected layer. Each convolutional layer creates a (3,3) convolution kernel that is convolved with the layer input to generate feature maps. In addition, the rectified linear unit (ReLU) is employed as the activation function to prevent vanishing gradients during backpropagation and introduce nonlinearity (to the convolution layer output). The detailed structure of the DeepPhase architecture for cardiac phase detection is shown in Fig. 2.

Model Optimization: Model optimization involves the hyperparameter selection and loss function construction substages, which are described below.

i) Hyperparameter Selection: Refer to Sect. 4.3 and Fig. 2 for a description of the hyperparameter settings.

ii) Loss Function: The loss function is employed to approximate the loss of the model so that the weights can be adjusted to reduce the loss in the next epoch. For our loss function, we employed regularization techniques to reduce training loss. Regularization efficiently decreases the variance of the model without a considerable increase in its bias. The proposed loss function is based on the mean squared error (MSE) and comprises two parts given by Eqs. 1 and 2.

$$MSE(\chi, M) = \frac{1}{n} \sum_{i=1}^{n} (\tau(x_i) - M(x_i))^2 \tag{1}$$

$$mean(\chi, M) = \frac{1}{n} \sum_{i=1}^{n} (\tau(x_i) - M(x_i)) \tag{2}$$

where χ is the set of n instances $(x_1, x_2, ..., x_n)$ and M represents the prediction model. In addition, $\tau(x_i)$ is the actual label of x_i, where $\tau(x_i) \in (0, 1)$, $M(x_i)$ represents the label of x_i predicted by the model, and n is the total number of instances. The proposed loss function is given below.

$$L(\chi, M) = MSE(\chi, M) + \beta.mean(\chi, M) \tag{3}$$

where $L(\chi, M)$ is the loss function. The formula in Eq. 3 indicates that after taking the mean difference of the true and predicted labels, the number is multiplied by a hyperparameter $\beta > 0$. The result is then added to $MSE(\chi, M)$; this adds an extra term to the traditional MSE loss function, which further penalizes the model for incorrect classifications. We have empirically shown the effectiveness of the proposed loss function over MSE and other traditional loss functions in Sect. 4.

3.2   Phase II: Model Testing

Dataset: In this study, we evaluated the performance of the DeepPhase model on two datasets. First, we used 100 images from the CAMUS dataset as a test set (already divided by the authors of the dataset). Second, we used a fully annotated dataset that we developed, which we refer to as the **CardiacPhase** **Dataset** as described below.

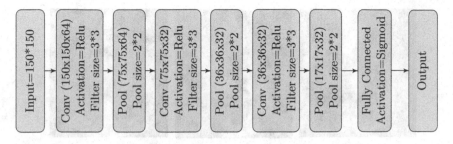

Fig. 2. Architecture of the DeepPhase.

CardiacPhase Dataset: The CardiacPhase dataset includes the echocardiograms of 35 patients acquired at CardioLife diagnostic center, Hyderabad, Pakistan. To incorporate the clinical realism, no particular data selection technique was employed. Consequently, some of the images were blurry and of poor quality. The dataset includes a wide variety of acquisition settings. This produces a highly heterogeneous dataset in terms of both pathological cases and image quality, which is typical of routine clinical practice data. The participants include 20 male and 15 female patients, in the age range of 30–45 years). The collected echocardiography data were acquired between June and September 2020, and two cardiologists annotated the data in this dataset. The CardiacPhase dataset comprises only 70 images; therefore, we used it as a testing dataset to evaluate the DeepPhase model's performance. The complete dataset was acquired using Philips EPIQ CVx ultrasound scanner. No additional protocol other than that used in clinical routine was considered. For each patient, the ED and ES phases were captured in the two-chamber view. The gathering of data was carried out following the principles of the Declaration of Helsinki.

Preprocessing. As both datasets were acquired using different scanners and probes, there was a difference in the frame quality. Another reason for the dissimilarity was caused by differences in the expertise of the technician and the protocols used in different countries. To make the images from both the datasets appear similar, we applied several preprocessing techniques. First, the images were cropped to remove unwanted labels and lines, and the image size was adjusted to 150 × 150 × 1. The cropping step is also necessary for maintaining data anonymity. Second, several image-denoising techniques were applied, such as linear and mean filters, to suppress noise and improve image quality. Figure 3 shows three frames (all images show the ED phase of the cardiac cycle) from the two datasets, where the first frame is an unprocessed image from the CardiacPhase dataset, the second frame is the same image after postprocessing, and the final frame is an image from the CAMUS dataset.

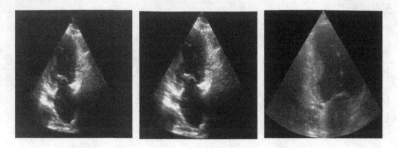

Fig. 3. Left: an unprocessed image from CardioPhases dataset; middle: the same image after applying preprocessing; right: an image from the CAMUS dataset

4   Experiments

4.1   Datasets

We used the CAMUS and CardiacPhase datasets (discussed in Sect. 3).

4.2   Competing Approaches

In this study, we evaluated and compared the following competing approaches.

DeepPhase: The proposed method comprises a CNN and the custom loss function. The architecture of the DeepPhase model is shown in Fig. 2, and the custom loss function is described in Sect. 3.

CNN Proposed by Siddiqi [12]: The DeepPhase model was compared with the Siddiqi's [12] model, which was used to diagnose pneumonia from X-ray images. Although Dezaki et al. [14] work is relevant to ours, as discussed in Sect. 2, it is not directly comparable to DeepPhase. Firstly because they have used cine series of echocardiography imaging and secondly they dealt with the problem as regression and not classification.

The key differences between the DeepPhase model and Siddiqi's [12] CNN model are summarized below. In Siddiqi's [12] proposed architecture, a pair of convolution layers are inserted at the start and after every dropout layer. By contrast, DeepPhase model utilizes a single convolution layer at the start and after every pooling layer to reduce resource consumption, e.g., storage and computation time. Further, a pooling layer is employed after each pair of convolutional layers in the architecture proposed by Siddiqi [12]. We employed max pooling in the DeepPhase model because this technique is superior in terms of selecting invariant features; thus, generalizability is improved. The max pooling operation also converges significantly faster during training (compared with other pooling operations). Here, a pool size of (2, 2) was used, which is the most frequently used configuration for pooling layers. With these setting, each pooling layer discarded 75% of the activations. In Siddiqi's proposed architecture, a dropout layer (with a dropout rate of 0.2) is used after each pooling layer. In our proposed architecture, we did not use dropout layers. The main purpose of a dropout layer is to prevent the model from overfitting. We employed several techniques to avoid overfitting in the DeepPhase model, e.g., the regularization of the loss function and data augmentation. Finally, we employed a single dense layer. By contrast, Siddiqi's model employs two dense layers.

DeepPhase-MAE: This is the DeepPhase using the mean absolute error (MAE) loss function (instead of custom loss function).

DeepPhase-CrossEntropy: This is the DeepPhase model using the cross entropy loss function (instead of custom loss function).

DeepPhase-MSE: This is the DeepPhase model using the mean squared error (MSE) loss function (instead of custom loss function).

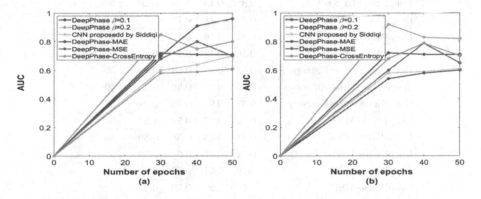

Fig. 4. (a) Performance of the competing approaches on CAMUS dataset (b) Performance of the competing approaches on CardiacPhase dataset

4.3   Parameter Configuration

The CAMUS dataset was divided into training and testing sets by the publishing authors. There are 900 frames or images (two images per patient) in the training set and 100 frames in the testing set. From the 900 images of the training set, we allocated 90 images as a validation set. The validation set helps avoid overfitting and assists in parameter selection. The model was optimized for other hyperparameters such as learning rate, batch size, and optimizer using the randomized grid search method. Here, the Adam optimizer was used with a batch size of 10 and learning rate of 0.00001.

4.4   Hardware and Software Configuration

The compared models were coded in Python (version 3.6.5; 64-bit) using the open-source Keras (version 2.1.5) library as the backend and open-source Tensor-Flow (version 2.5.0) library for the CNN algorithms. The models were executed using the GPU runtime setting of Google Colab on the Google cloud.

5   Evaluation

5.1   Evaluation Metrics

Table 1. Summary comparison among competing approaches

Competing methods	CAMUS		CardiacPhase		Epochs
	AUC	Loss	AUC	Loss	
DeepPhase ($\beta >= 0.2$)	0.85	0.18	**0.92**	**0.14**	30
DeepPhase ($\beta >= 0.2$)	0.75	0.19	0.83	0.17	40
DeepPhase ($\beta >= 0.2$)	0.8	0.14	0.82	0.16	50
DeepPhase ($\beta >= 0.1$)	0.7	0.18	0.72	0.2	30
DeepPhase ($\beta >= 0.1$)	0.91	0.16	0.7	0.27	40
DeepPhase ($\beta >= 0.1$)	**0.96**	**0.08**	0.7	0.26	50
DeepPhase-CrossEntropy	0.63	0.9	0.68	0.90	30
DeepPhase-CrossEntropy	0.6	0.8	0.80	0.4	40
DeepPhase-CrossEntropy	0.58	0.9	0.70	0.94	50
DeepPhase-MAE	0.72	0.27	0.54	1.13	30
DeepPhase-MAE	0.71	0.29	0.58	0.89	40
DeepPhase-MAE	0.71	0.31	0.6	0.79	50
DeepPhase-MSE	0.76	0.21	0.60	0.49	30
DeepPhase-MSE	0.7	0.2	0.79	0.21	40
DeepPhase-MSE	0.72	0.35	0.65	0.32	50
CNN propsoed by Siddiqi [15]	0.6	0.81	0.58	0.85	30
CNN propsoed by Siddiqi [15]	0.64	0.7	0.59	0.79	40
CNN propsoed by Siddiqi [15]	0.7	0.31	0.61	0.83	50

The performance of each model in all experiments was evaluated based on the area under the receiver operating characteristic curve (AUC) and loss.

5.2   Comparison Among Competing Approaches

The comparisons of each model's performance in Fig. 4 demonstrate that the DeepPhase model outperformed Siddiqi's model [12] on the CAMUS dataset. The performances of all competing models on both CAMUS and CardiacPhase dataset at epoch 30, 40, and 50 are given in Table 1.

In the experiment, we explored the best results on CAMUS when the value was set to 0.1 at epoch 50 i.e., testing AUC = 0.96 and testing loss = 0.08. The model also performed well for $\beta >= 0.1$, epochs = 40 and $\beta >= 0.2$, epochs = 30. Note that the CardiacPhase dataset was used as a test dataset for the model trained on the CAMUS dataset. The highest AUC of 0.92 was achieved at epoch 30 with $\beta >= 0.2$. This high AUC was achieved despite CAMUS and CardiacPhase datasets having different frame quality and distributions. This demonstrates the flexibility of the DeepPhase model and custom loss function. It can be observed that the performance of DeepPhase-MSE was consistent for both the dataset. On the other hand, DeepPhase-MAE performance was better on CAMUS dataset than on CardiacPhase dataset. DeepPhase-CrossEntropy and Siddiqi [12] model gave comparable performance on CAMUS dataset but DeepPhase-CrossEntropy outperformed Siddiqi [12] model in CardiacPhase dataset.

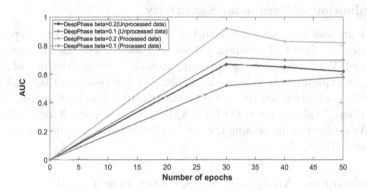

Fig. 5. Performance of DeepPhase on unprocessed and prepossessed CardiacPhase dataset

5.3 Effect of Image Preprocessing

As discussed in Sect. 3, we applied several image-processing techniques to remove noise and improve the quality of the images in the CardiacPhase dataset. To observe the effect of image processing on the CardiacPhase dataset, we compared the results of our obtained with the DeepPhase on the unprocessed and preprocessed CardiacPhase datasets. Figure 5 displays the performance of the DeepPhase model on the unprocessed and preprocessed CardiacPhase datasets. The graph clearly shows an improvement in AUC when the preprocessed images were used. The highest AUC obtained on the unprocessed test set was 0.67, while on the preprocessed dataset, the highest obtained AUC was 0.92.

Table 2. Performance of DeepPhase with different β values

	CAMUS		CardiacPhase	
	AUC	Loss	AUC	Loss
DeepPhase ($\beta = 0.05$)	0.85	0.18	0.65	0.35
DeepPhase ($\beta = 0.1$)	0.96	0.08	0.7	0.26
DeepPhase ($\beta = 0.15$)	0.76	0.22	0.8	0.19
DeepPhase ($\beta = 0.2$)	0.8	0.14	0.92	0.14
DeepPhase ($\beta = 0.3$)	0.81	0.18	0.8	0.17
DeepPhase ($\beta = 0.4$)	0.85	0.16	0.75	0.12
DeepPhase ($\beta = 0 .5$)	0.84	0.17	0.74	0.19
DeepPhase ($\beta = 0.6$)	0.85	0.12	0.7	0.10

5.4   Evaluation of Parameter Sensitivity

In our custom loss function, shown in Eq. 3, β played the role of a hyperparameter. Finding the effect of different values of β was crucial for the performance of our model. We carried out the experiment with different β values as shown in Table 2. It is evident from Table 2 that when β value reaches at 0.5 and 0.6, the values of the evaluation metrics became undeviating. The best testing AUC was achieved when β value is set at 0.1 for CAMUS dataset and 0.3 for CardiacPhase dataset. As we kept on increasing the value, the evaluation values goes down and then became static.

5.5   Performance Analysis of the Custom Loss Function

To further evaluate the performance of the custom loss function, we performed following two experiments.

Weights: Deep learning models with smaller weights result in more stable training and are less likely to overfit [3]. A model with large weights can be a sign of an unsteady network where small changes in the input can lead to large changes in the output [10]. This will result in poor performance when making a prediction on new data. Our custom loss function results in smaller weights and simpler model. Figure 6(a) shows that the model trained with the custom loss function results in the lowest weights as compared to the other models which are trained using MSE, MAE and binary crossentropy.

Convergence: In order to show the effectiveness of the custom loss function, we compared its convergence rate with other traditionally used loss functions such as MSE, MAE and binary crossentropy. Figure 6(b) visualizes the training procedure and convergence of the aforementioned DeepPhase models. From this figure, we observe that the proposed custom loss function not only converged faster than other counterparts but also achieved lower loss value. DeepPhase with β =0.3 converged slower than $\beta = 0.1$ and 0.2.

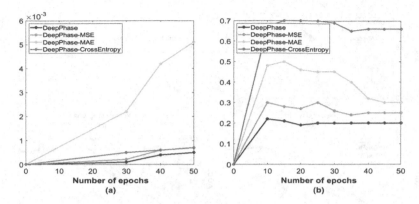

Fig. 6. (a) Average weights of the DeepPhase model using different loss function (b) Convergence of different loss functions

5.6 Evidence of Generalization of DeepPhase

In this experiment, we evaluate the performance of our model when trained with two-chamber and tested with four-chamber viewpointss (and vice-versa). We utilized the data from CAMUS dataset and hyper-parameters have been adopted from the above apical two-chamber view experiments.

Figure 7(a) shows results of experiment 01 where the model is trained and tested over apical four-chamber viewpoint of CAMUS dataset for 30, 40 and 50 epochs. We have kept the value of $\beta = 0.1$ as the model is performing well on this value (faster convergence and lowest weights). The DeepPhase model achieved highest training AUC of 0.98 at epoch 50 while the DeepPhase-MAE and model proposed by Siddiqi achieved the highest AUC of 0.88 and 0.87 respectively. Figure 7(b) shows experiment 02 where the DeepPhase model is trained over apical two-chamber view and tested over apical four-chamber view of the CAMUS dataset. The model proposed by Siddiqi and DeepPhase-MAE achieved the highest AUC of 0.85 and 0.77 respectively. Figure 7(c) visualises experiment 03, where the DeepPhase model is trained over apical four-chamber viewpoint and tested over apical two-chamber viewpoint of CAMUS dataset. The DeepPhase model achieved the highest AUC of 0.9 at epoch 50 with loss=0.08. The performance of the DeepPhase-MAE was closely comparable in both experiments. The DeepPhase performance declined from 0.97 to 0.9 when trained over apical two-chamber view. It is noticeable here that the DeepPhase model performed consistently well when trained over apical four-chamber view. After learning over this viewpoint, the model was successfully able to identify ES and ED frames from another viewpoint. This observation can be useful in the circumstances when no or less data is available for one of the viewpoints. In experiment 04, we trained the model over apical four-chamber viewpoint and tested over CardiacPhase dataset which contains apical two-chamber ES and ED frames. Figure 7(d) shows that the highest AUC achieved by the DeepPhase model is 0.72 while the other two models achieved 0.62 and 0.65 at epoch 50. All of

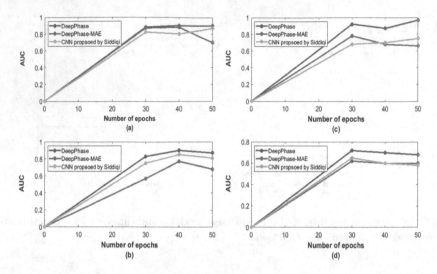

Fig. 7. The performance of competing approaches when (a) trained and tested over apical four-chamber viewpoint (CAMUS) (b) when trained over apical two-chamber viewpoint (CAMUS) and tested over apical four-chamber viewpoint of CAMUS dataset (c) trained over apical four-chamber viewpoint (CAMUS) and tested over apical two-chamber viewpoint (CAMUS) (d) when trained over apical four-chamber viewpoint (CAMUS) and tested over apical two-chamber viewpoint (CardiacPhase)

the above experiments confirmed the performance consistency of the DeepPhase model not only on daily clinical data but also on another clinically important cardiac view.

6   Conclusion

In this paper, we proposed a method to solve the ES and ED phase detection problem directly without the need for LV segmentation. The DeepPhase model could successfully classify frames from unseen data. In addition, the experimental results confirm that the proposed MSE-based loss function outperformed other standard loss functions. To mitigate the lack of publicly available data for echocardiography, we also introduced a dataset of 70 images and used it as a test set in our experiments. To test the generalizability of the DeepPhase model, we also experimented with the apical four-chamber view and obtained comparable results. However, the results presented in this paper can be improved if the DeepPhase model can be trained on a larger dataset. Thus, in the future, we plan to develop a larger dataset for echocardiography views and train the DeepPhase model using transfer learning techniques to improve performance.

Acknowledgement. This work is funded in part by United Arab Emirates University collaborative team grant number 31R239.

References

1. Abdi, A.H., et al.: Automatic quality assessment of echocardiograms using convolutional neural networks: feasibility on the apical four-chamber view. IEEE TMI **36**(6), 1221–1230 (2017)
2. Barcaro, U., Moroni, D., Salvetti, O.: Automatic computation of left ventricle ejection fraction from dynamic ultrasound images. Pattern Recogn. Image Anal. **18**, 351–358 (2008)
3. Brownlee, J.: Better deep learning. Machine Learning Mastery (2020)
4. Darvishi, S., Behnam, H., Pouladian, M., Samiei, N.: Measuring left ventricular volumes in two-dimensional echocardiogra-phy image sequence using level-set method for automatic detection of end-diastole and end-systole frames. Cardiovasc. Med. **1**, 39 (2012)
5. Ghorbani, A., et al.: Deep learning interpretation of echocardiograms. bioRxiv (2019)
6. Kusunose, K., Haga, A., Inoue, M., Fukuda, D., Yamada, H., Sata, M.: Clinically feasible and accurate view classification of echocardiographic images using deep learning. Biomolecules **10**, 665–671 (2020)
7. Leclerc, S., et al.: Deep learning for segmentation using an open large-scale dataset in 2D echocardiography. IEEE Trans. Med. Imaging **38**(9), 2198–2210 (2019)
8. Madani, A., Ong, J.R., Tibrewal, A., Mofrad, M.R.K.: Deep echocardiography: data-efficient supervised and semi-supervised deep learning towards automated diagnosis of cardiac disease. NPJ Dig. Med. **1**(1), 21–30 (2018)
9. Moradi, S., et al.: MFP-UNET: a novel deep learning based approach for left ventricle SEG in echocardiography. Physica Medica **67**, 58–69 (2019)
10. Nielsen, M.A.: Neural Networks and Deep Learning. Determination press, San Francisco (2015)
11. Rao, S., et al.: Physician burnout, engagement and career satisfaction in a large academic medical practice. Clin. Med. Res. **18**, 3–10 (2020)
12. Siddiqi, R.: Automated pneumonia diagnosis using a customized sequential convolutional neural network. In: Proceedings of the 2019 3rd International Conference on Deep Learning Technologies, ICDLT 2019, pp. 64–70. ACM, New York (2019)
13. Sulas, E., Urru, M., Tumbarello, R., Raffo, L., Pani, D.: Automatic detection of complete and measurable cardiac cycles in antenatal pulsed-wave doppler signals. Comp. Methods Prog. Biomed. **190**, 105336–105345 (2020)
14. Taheri Dezaki, F., et al.: Cardiac phase detection in echocardiograms with densely gated recurrent neural networks and global extrema loss. IEEE TMI **38**(8), 1821–1832 (2019)
15. Yang, L., Zeng, S., Zhou, Y., Pan, B., Feng, Y., Li, D.: Design of convolutional neural network based on tree fork module. In: 2019 18th International Symposium on Distributed Computer and Applications for Business Engineering and Science (DCABES), pp. 1–4 (2019)

An Empirical Study on Human Flying Imagery Using EEG

Yichen Tang[1] , Wei Chen[1,2] , and Xuyun Zhang[3]([:envelope:])

[1] The University of Auckland, Auckland, New Zealand
[2] The University of Tokyo, Tokyo, Japan
[3] Macquarie University, Sydney, Australia
xuyun.zhang@mq.edu.au

Abstract. Traditional electroencephalography (EEG) based brain computer interface (BCI) systems for performing three-dimensional (3-D) movement control used motor imagery paradigm, where the participants had to be trained to imagine certain combinations of movements of parts of their body such as hands, feet, and tongue to control the movements in separate dimensions. In the present work, we propose a new mental imagery - flying imagery - where the participants imagine flying in certain directions in the 3-D space surrounding them. As an empirical study, the present work used machine learning methods to classify flying imagery under two stages (preparation and execution) in six directions (forward, backward, left, right, up, and down) along with a control state where no movement was imagined. We also performed classification-based time-frequency analyses in identifying the significant frequency bands, time windows, and EEG features associated with flying imagery that differ between classes and contribute to the classification. We obtained classification results significantly better than chance levels, showing that the direction of flying imagery can be decoded from the EEG signals. Our results also suggest that the spatial information of flying imagery might be encoded mainly in alpha band activities over the parietal lobe, likely originated from the posterior parietal cortex (PPC).

Keywords: Machine learning · BCI · EEG · Mental imagery · Flying imagery

1 Introduction

The brain-computer interface (BCI) directly translates brain activities to instructions understandable by a computer. It provides a communication channel for computers to understand one's intentions directly. There are many techniques to gather information from the brain, among which non-invasive electroencephalography (EEG) has been a popular choice due to its convenience, and efficiency [8]. By placing electrodes outside of the scalp, it allows the use

---

Y. Tang and W. Chen—Contributed equally to the paper as co-first authors.

© Springer Nature Switzerland AG 2022
B. Li et al. (Eds.): ADMA 2021, LNAI 13087, pp. 18–32, 2022.
https://doi.org/10.1007/978-3-030-95405-5_2

of BCI systems without surgical implementation. For people with motor impairments, BCI systems could be used to enhance their abilities to interact with electrical devices. For example, many studies have attempted to decode participants' intentions of moving a computer cursor in a two-dimensional (2-D) space using EEG [4,7,12,16]. These studies have shown applications of EEG-based BCI systems for supporting motor-impaired people to operate computers and other devices.

A natural extension for the 2-D cursor control would be controlling object movements inside a three-dimensional (3-D) space. A few studies have attempted to build EEG-based BCI systems in controlling the movement of a physical or simulated device, often a drone, inside a 3-D space [11,15,18,21]. The motor imagery BCI paradigm was applied in all of these studies, wherein motor imagery paradigms, participants run a mental simulation of performing specific movements, resulting in different activation patterns on the motor cortex and corresponding changes in EEG signals, then the BCI system decodes these brain activities for various applications [1]. In 2010, McFarland et al. developed the first EEG-based BCI system to perform 3-D movement control. The participants were trained to imagine a combination of both hands and feet movements to control a cursor in a 3-D computer space over three independent dimensions. Royer et al. also achieved 3-D movement control of a virtual helicopter using EEG [21]. Royer et al. made the helicopter move forward at a constant speed, and asked participants to control the rotation and the vertical movement of the helicopter by imagining different movements of the left and right hands. The work was further extended with added imagery of feet and tongue to achieve independent control of the rotation, forward/backward speed, and vertical speed of the helicopter [11]. In a later work, LaFleur et al. further extended the work by Royer et al. into controlling a quadcopter in the physical world [15]. More recently, Meng et al. incorporated spatial attention paradigm besides motor imagery in the 3-D movement control EEG-based BCI system, where the participants were asked to pay attention to objects located at different spatial positions while performing motor imagery tasks at the same time to move a virtual ball to one of the bars placed on the edges of a 3-D virtual space [18]. The imagery tasks performed by the participants in these studies were complicated and involved combined movements of both hands, feet, and sometimes the tongue.

Could a more intuitive imagery task be used for controlling 3-D movements of objects using EEG based BCI systems? In the current work, we propose a new mental imagery practice which we call "flying imagery", where one's imagery of flying to certain directions is directly mapped into movements in the 3-D space along the corresponding dimensions. Many studies have shown encoding of spatial information in various brain regions, and sensory experiments have also provided evidence that spatial coordinates are encoded in the brain activities and can be extracted using brain imaging methods [14]. However, to the best of our knowledge, the present work was the first in studing human imagery of flying in a 3-D space. The present work focused on proving the concept of flying imagery decoding and analysing EEG features associated with flying imagery.

This empirical study performed classification of flying imagery in six directions (forward, backward, left, right, up, and down) along with a control state where no movement was imagined, and analysed EEG features associated with flying imagery using classification-based time-frequency analysis.

The remaining parts of this paper are organized as follows. Section 2.1 introduces an experiment we designed for participants to perform flying imagery in multiple directions and the method we used to gather multi-channel EEG data. Section 2.2 describes the machine learning method and evaluation framework used for classifying the EEG data, as well as the EEG feature analysis procedure. Finally, Sect. 3 presents the classification and EEG feature analysis results.

2 Method

2.1 Experiment and EEG Recording

Experiment Design and Participants. The experiment comprises 630 trials of flying imagery tasks that broke into two experiment sessions over two different days. An illustration of an experiment trial is shown in Fig. 1.

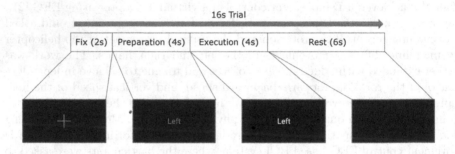

Fig. 1. An illustration of a single experiment trial.

Each trial began with a white fixation cross presented in the centre a black screen. After two seconds, we replaced the fixation cross with a stimulus word in grey, notifying the start of the preparation stage. The word was randomly chosen from "Left", "Right", "Forward", "Backward", "Up", "Down", or "Stay". The first six word options indicated six directions in a 3-D space. "Stay" was used as a control state, where the participants were asked to do nothing in this trial. If a direction was presented instead, the participants were asked to pay attention to the given direction and prepare for imagining flying. After four seconds, we changed the colour of the stimulus word from grey to white, notifying the participant to start imagining flying in the given direction. After another four seconds, we cleared the word from the screen and then gave the participants six seconds to rest and wait for the next trial to begin. We instructed the participants to fix their eyes on the centre of the screen and minimise their head and eye movements during the experiment. Breaks were given to the participants every 20 min to half an hour. The experiments were done inside a small, sound attenuated, electrical noise-blocking faraday room, where the participants were sitting at the centre of the room.

For the imagination of flying, we asked the participants to imagine a state where their body is flying or floating to a specific direction without movements of any part of the body, as if traction exists that causes the body to naturally move to the given direction. The experiment procedure was approved by the University of Auckland Human Participants Ethics Committee. Two participants P1 and P2 (both male; between 20 to 25 years old) participated in the experiment.

EEG Data and Preprocessing. During the experiments, 128 channel EEG was recorded using the 300 series Geodesic EEG system at a sampling frequency 1000 Hz (GES 300; EGI, Eugene, USA). The EEG data was bandpassed between 0.5 Hz and 40 Hz using an FIR filter, then sliced into epochs of 5 s, starting from 1 s before the presentation of the stimuli at the beginning of the preparation and the execution stages, to the end of the stages. Epochs with large artefacts were removed manually. Independent component analysis (ICA) was then used to remove EOG artefacts. The baseline for each epoch was set to be 200-0 ms before the stimulus onset, and the average voltage during this baseline period was calculated and subtracted from the epoch on each individual channel. The earlier 800 ms before the baseline in each epoch was left for reducing the edge effect when applying further bandpassing as described below in Sect. 2.2. In total, 1228 usable epochs were gathered for participant P1, and 1260 usable epochs were gathered for P2. Roughly an equal amount of epochs were recorded for each of the seven classes ("Left", "Right", "Forward", "Backward", "Up", "Down", or "Stay") and two stages (preparation and execution).

2.2   Classification and Feature Analysis

We summarised the classification and feature analysis procedures in Fig. 2. The classification framework involved performing a stratified 5-fold cross-validation (CV) and obtaining an averaged f1-score on classifying the preprocessed EEG data, using the Riemannian geometry-based classification method described below. Then, we performed permutation tests by randomly permutating the labels of the data and obtaining chance-level f1-scores using the same CV framework. The f1-score obtained using the real labels was compared with the chance-level scores and a p-value was calculated. The feature analysis procedure reused the classification framework by applying various temporal and spectral filters on the preprocessed data, then feeding the filtered data into the classification framework. The f1-scores and p-values obtained from the classification framework indicated the significance of the EEG features in the corresponding time and frequency windows.

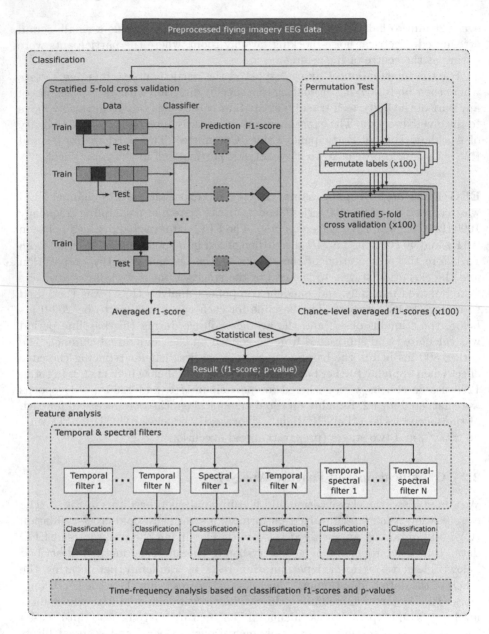

Fig. 2. Overview of the classification and feature analysis procedure.

Classification Tasks and Performance Metric. We used machine learning methods to classify EEG epochs into one of the seven classes - "Left", "Right", "Forward", "Backward", "Up", "Down", and "Stay". The classification was done within participant, and within stage (either preparation or execution). To measure the performance of the classification method, we used weighted f1-score as the metric, as shown below in Eq. 1:

$$f1 = \frac{2}{w_{total}} \sum_{c \in C} w_c \cdot \frac{precision(c) \cdot recall(c)}{precision(c) + recall(c)}, \tag{1}$$

where C is the set of all classes $\{c_1, c_2, ..., c_n\}$; $precision(c)$ and $recall(c)$ are the precision and recall of the prediction on class c; w_c is the weight of class c, corresponding to the number of true instances for class c; while w_{total} is the sum of weights for all classes, which is equal to the total number of instances.

Cross-validation. We used 5-fold cross-validation frameworks to evaluate the performance of our classification method. We randomly shuffled and divided the data into five equally sized parts, where the relative proportions of the classes were kept the same for each part. For each fold, we used four parts to train the machine learning method, and the remaining one to test the method. We calculated an f1-score for each fold from its testing set, and the mean of the five f1-scores, which represents the performance of the method (the higher the better).

Permutation Test. We performed permutation tests with 100 random permutations to test the significance of the obtained f1-score. In each permutation, we randomly shuffled the labels for the data, and applied the same 5-fold CV to obtain an f1-score for the given permutation. With the set of 100 permutated f1-scores F and the observed f1-score from the original data set f_o, we can obtain a p-value using Eq. 2:

$$p = \frac{|\{f : f \in F, f \geq f_o\}| + 1}{n_{perm} + 1}, \tag{2}$$

where $n_{perm} = 100$ permutations. A p-value less than 0.05 indicates that the observed f1-score for the method was significantly greater than the chance level.

Classification Model. We used the Riemannian geometry-based classification method to classify the EEG epochs. Since being developed in 2010 by Barachant et al. [6], the Riemannian geometry-based methods have shown state-of-art performances in various EEG-based BCI paradigms and competitions [10,17]. This paper adopted a simple variation of the Riemannian geometry based methods.

Firstly, for each epoch, we obtained the EEG data from time 0 s at the stimulus onset to the end of the epoch. Then, using this data, we calculated a covariance matrix of size 128 by 128 for each epoch by calculating the covariance between every pair of channels. The covariance matrix of an EEG epoch captures the variance between EEG channels as well as within each channel over 4 s from the stimulus onset. It provides information about how the channels are related to each other and how the channels themselves vary over this period of time. It thus provides insight in how the brain regions beneath the channels activate and change over time and how the different brain regions activate and change with each other.

As a type of symmetric positive definite (SPD) matrices, these covariance matrices are located on a Riemannian manifold [9]. The geometric distributions of these covariance matrices on the Riemannian manifold could then be used to perform classifications. However, to allow a conventional classifier that works in the Euclidean space, the covariance matrices need to be vectorised while keeping the geometric distribution. To do so, we obtained a tangential space of the manifold at the geometric mean of all covariance matrices in the training set of the CV fold. Then we mapped covariance matrices from the complete data set onto the tangent space. The mapped values on the tangent space were in the form of vectors, and the positions of these vectors on the tangent space estimated the locations of the covariance matrices on the Riemannian manifold. The tangent space transformation was done using the pyRiemann python library [5]. We then used the training set tangent vectors to train a logistic regression classifier (l2-regularized) implemented in scikit-learn [20]. Finally, we used the trained classifier to predict the associated classes for the samples in the testing set by classifying their corresponding tangent vectors.

Classification-Based Time-frequency Analysis on EEG Features. To identify the important time and frequency windows for the EEG features to differ between classes, we performed time-frequency analysis using various temporal and spectral filters along with the above classification framework. On the original epochs, we applied four different bandpass FIR filters corresponding to the five well-known brain rhythms to obtain EEG activities specific to the five frequency bands - the delta band (1 to 4 Hz), theta band (4 to 8 Hz), alpha band (8 to 13 Hz), beta band (13 to 30 Hz), and gamma band up to the low-pass cut off in the original data (30 to 40 Hz). For EEG signal filtered into each of the five frequency bands, we performed the same CV framework and permutation test as described above to obtain an f1-score and a p-value for this specific frequency band. Then, on the original data, we used a sliding window of 1-second length with 50% overlapping to select data at different time windows: 0–1 s, 0.5–1.5 s, 1–2 s, 1.5–2.5 s, 2–3 s, 2.5–3.5 s, and 3–4 s. Again, we obtained an f1-score and a p-value for each time window. Further more, we also applied the sliding window on the frequency band filtered data and calculated f1-scores and p-values for the specific time-frequency bins.

Finally, we identified the most significant time-frequency bins for both stages (preparation and execution) and both participants and analysed the EEG patterns in the corresponding bins. To do so, we first applied bandpass filters on the original data corresponding to the bins. Then, we applied Hilbert transformations on the filtered data and obtained the envelope of the analytic signal, representing the instantaneous amplitude of the EEG signals at the given frequency band. Then, we calculated the average of the analytic signal envelope at the corresponding time windows. These values were then averaged over classes for each stage and each participant to obtain an averaged EEG pattern map for each class.

3   Results

3.1   Overall Classification Results

On the original data, the classification results for the preparation stage on participant P1 ($f1 = 0.186$, $p = 0.020$) and for the execution stage on participant P2 ($f1 = 0.183$, $p = 0.010$) were significantly higher than their chance levels ($f1 = 0.143$ for both cases). The classification results for the execution stage on P1 ($f1 = 0.164$, $p = 0.119$) and for the preparation stage on P2 ($f1 = 0.165$, $p = 0.069$) were however, not significantly higher than the chance levels ($f1 = 0.141$ and $f1 = 0.145$ correspondingly).

3.2   Frequency Band Specific Classification Results

The classification framework has, however, produced f1-scores signifantly higher than chance-levels for all classification tasks using EEG signals filtered with bandpass filters, and there was consistency in both participants, as plotted in Fig. 3. For both preparation and execution stages on both participants, the alpha band EEG activities had the greatest contribution to the classification ($f1 = 0.268$, $p = 0.0099$, Preparation, P1; $f1 = 0.216$, $p = 0.0099$, Execution, P1; $f1 = 0.295$, $p = 0.0099$, Preparation, P2; $f1 = 0.291$, $p = 0.0099$, Execution, P2). This result suggests major differences in alpha band brain activities for different flying imagery tasks. Besides, for both participants, it also appears that the significant frequency windows extended lower 4 Hz in the preparation stage compared 8 Hz in the execution stage, suggesting significant low frequency activities specific in the preparation stage.

3.3   Time Window Specific Classification Results

The time window specific analysis also revealed significant time windows for classification on both stages and on both participants, as shown in Fig. 4. Again, consistencies were shown for both stages across participants.

In the preparation stage, the important features appeared to be contributed after the first second of EEG recording. The f1-score obtained from the first time window (0–1 s) was not significant for either participant, indicating that it is unlikely that differences in event-related potentials (ERPs) evoked by different visual stimuli (presentation of the word) contributed to the classification result. The f1-score then rapidly increased to a peak at the time window 1–2 s after the stimulus onset, which might have resulted from the cognitive attention shifting and formation of the flying movement plan that differs for different

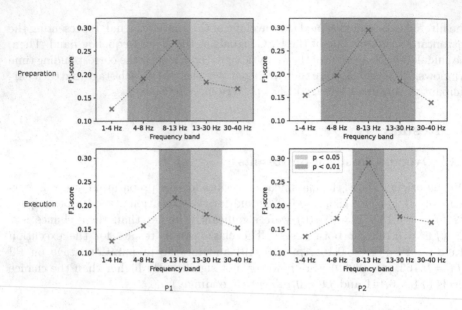

Fig. 3. F1-scores and permutation test results for frequency band specific analysis.

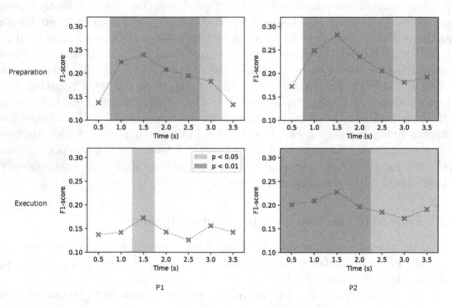

Fig. 4. F1-scores and permutation test results for time window specific analysis. Each time window is represented by its middle point on x axis. For example, 1.5 s represents time window 1–2 s.

directions. Starting from the 1.5–2.5 s time window, the f1-score began to drop slowly, though maintaining above chance-level for most of the time. This slow declining slope indicates a gental reduction in the level of EEG features that differ between classes, suggesting a maintainance stage in the participants' brains for sustaining the spatial attention and planned flying movement. This slope could also be observed in a visual memorisation task in work done by Harrison and Tong [13].

For the execution state, we observed a similar pattern. The f1-score increased from the first time window (0–1 s) to the peak at the third time window (1–2 s), and then the f1-scores showed a slow decreasing trend. Similarly, this increasing slope in the first 1.5 s might have represented the cognitive execution of the flying imagery and the following decreasing slope might have represented the process of sustaining the imagery. The statistical significance of the classification results indicated direction-specific brain activation patterns during execution of the flying imagery, resulting in EEG features contributing to the classification.

3.4   Time-frequency Specific Classification Results

The time-frequency analysis showed similar results as described above (Fig. 5). The peak f1-scores were observed at the alpha band (8–13 Hz) and at around 1.5 s after the stimulus onset in the preparation stage, indicating the existence of direction-specific flying imagery planning brain activities centralised at the alpha band at around 1.5 s after the stimulus onset. The sustained plan of flying imagery may also be centralised in the alpha band, given that the significant time windows at this band extended to the end of the preparation stage and the time windows at the surrounding bands (theta and beta) became insignificant earlier after the peak at 1.5 s. This planned flying imagery was then executed in the execution stage, again centred at the alpha band. The peak f1-score also appeared to be occurring around 1 to 2 s in the execution stage, but this peak did not seem to be as prominent as in the preparation stage. Although the theta band (4–8 Hz) was not recognised as a significant frequency band in the frequency band-specific analysis above, here it has shown that there might also be some minor differences at this band at around 1 and 1.5 s. However, the differences in the theta band were again not as prominent as those in the alpha band, and these differences might be specific to participant P2. Moreover, surprisingly, for preparation stage classification on participant P2 specifically, the results showed high significance at delta band in the first time window ($f1 = 0.187$, $p = 0.0099$). It requires further studies to identify the sources for this significant time-frequency bin.

3.5   EEG Activity Patterns in Most Significant Time-frequency Bin

We calculated the averaged maps of EEG patterns for the seven classes from the alpha band as described above (Fig. 6). The maps were averaged over 1–2 s after stimulus onsets for preparation stages, and were averaged over 0.5–2.5 s after stimulus onsets for execution stages. Because the amplitudes of the analytic signals obtained from the two participants were significantly different from each

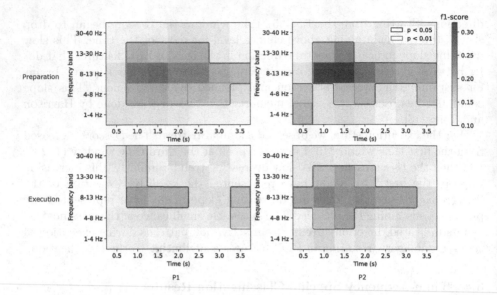

Fig. 5. F1-scores and permutation test results for frequency band and time window specific analysis. Each time window is represented by its middle point on x axis. F1-scores without statistical significance are masked into greyscale. F1-scores with $p < 0.05$ are contoured by black edges. F1-scores with $p < 0.01$ are contoured by red edges. The deepness of the color at each bin represents the f1-score obtained for the bin. (Color figure online)

other, the colour bars were scaled differently for the two participants. Participant P2 showed stronger analytic signals than P1 overall, where the maximum amplitude reached 13 μV on P2, but only reached 8 μV on P1. We can see a cluster of higher analytic signal amplitudes concentrated over the parietal lobes for both participants, and the corresponding areas were consistent between the preparation and execution stages. On participant P1, these areas were more centralised to the right parietal lobe, while for P2, the regions were more equally distributed on the two sides of the centerline. There also appeared to be a cluster at the frontal central part of the scalp, though the amplitude of the analytic signal over this area was not as large as the other cluster over the parietal lobe. These areas with high analytic signal amplitudes represented high activities in the alpha band at the parietal areas on the cortex over the given time windows.

The differences between classes were more evident in the preparation stage on participant P2, but many of these pattern differences could also be observed in the execution stage and both stages on P1. We can see the following pattern differences on P2. The activities appeared to be at the lowest when imagining flying forward and at the highest when imagining flying downward. These two patterns differed from the control state, while the other directions were associated with moderate activities closer to the control state. In the preparation stage on P2, it appeared that the activities at backward flying imagery might also be higher

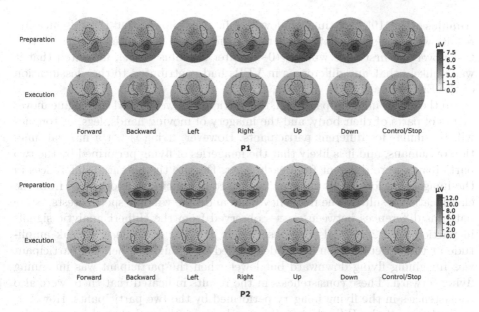

Fig. 6. Topo maps of EEG patterns for different flying imagery tasks for participants P1 and P2. Map values are the amplitudes of Hilbert analytic signals at 128 channels computed from the alpha band EEG signals, averaged over 1–2 s for the preparation stage, and over 0.5–2.5 s for the execution stage.

than the other classes apart from downward flying imagery. The left and right flying imagery had the same level of activities. However, the balance between the left and right hemispheres appeared to be different. When imagining flying to the left, activities were more concentrated on the left parietal area. When imagining flying to the right, activities were more focused on the right parietal area. These differences in the EEG patterns would have contributed to the classification of the EEG epochs, representing differences in the underlying brain activities among different flying imagery tasks, especially at the parietal lobe. Further studies are required to reveal the mechanisms under the scalp causing these differences.

4   Discussion

In our experiment, word stimuli were used to cue the participants either the direction to imagine flying to or to stay still. The differences between the visual stimuli would have introduced differences in the visual evoked potentials (VEPs) - the ERPs evoked by visual stimuli - evoked immediately after these visual stimuli. However, the differences in the visual patterns presented to the participants due to the different lengths and shapes of the words were small, and it is unlikely that the VEPs evoked by the different word stimuli were vastly different from each other. Besides, VEPs occur within the first few hundred milliseconds after the stimulus onset [19]. Our time window specific tests showed that the classification results were not significantly higher than the chance level in most classification tasks over the first time window (0–1 s after stimulus onset), indicated that it was unlikely that any differences in VEPs had contributed to the classification of the EEG signals.

In the motor imagery paradigm, the participants were asked to imagine movements of parts of their body, and the imagery of moving hands, legs, or tongues will be similar for different participants. However, flying is not a natural function of humans, and it is likely that the imageries of flying performed by the two participants were different from each other. Despite the potential differences in the imagery performed by the participant, consistencies were observed from the classification results in the frequency band and time window specific tests. Some patterns differences between classes observed from the Hilbert analytic signals in participant P2 were also be observed in P1. For example, the peak amplitude at the parietal region electrodes tended to be higher when the participant was imagining flying downward but lower when the participant was imagining flying forward. These consistencies in the results indicated that there were also consistencies in the flying imagery performed by the two participants. However, the patterns of the Hilbert analytic signals also indicated that there were also inter-person differences in the underlying brain activities, especially the regions been activated, when performing flying imagery in general.

Though with differences in the left-right hemisphere balance in the peak analytic signal regions between the two participants. The peak regions were over the parietal lobe for both participants. The high alpha band analytic signal amplitudes over these areas might have reflected the activities from the posterior parietal cortex (PPC). The PPC is believed to subserve high-level cognitive functions related to actions such as intentions and early plans for movements [2]. It was also found that spatial locations of goals for movements are also likely encoded in the PPC [3]. The flying imagery tasks involved attention to certain directions or locations in the space corresponding to the head location, which might have caused a higher activation in PPC. Although no movements of certain body parts were imagined, an abstract, high-level movement of whole-body displacement was likely still planned in the PPC and contributed to the higher activation in the region.

5   Conclusion and Future Work

In the present work, we proposed a new mental imagery paradigm - flying imagery - for EEG based BCI systems to perform 3-D movement control. We performed experiments and obtained multi-channel EEG data on two participants with flying imagery tasks under two stages (preparation and execution) in six directions (forward, backward, left, right, up and down) plus a control state where no flying imagery was performed, in total seven classes. We used machine-learning methods to perform within-subject and within stage classifications on the seven flying imagery tasks and obtained classification results significantly higher than chance level guessings, using 5-fold, 100-permutation test frameworks. We also performed frequency band and time window specific classification analysis and obtained the most significant frequency bands and time windows where the EEG signals differed between classes and contributed to the classification. We identified the alpha band and the 1–2 s time window after stimulus onset as the most significant bin where the differences in EEG signals between classes reached their maximum. With this time-frequency bin, we used Hilbert analytic signal to show that the EEG activities and differences were concentrated over the parietal lobe, most likely reflecting activities from the PPC.

The present work contributed to the community by proposing a novel and intuitive flying imagery paradigm with potential applicability in EEG based BCI systems for performing 3-D movement control of objects. The work also contributed in analysing the time and frequency courses of EEG features that differ by classes, using classification-based time-frequency analysis. The work has also performed a deeper analysis in the EEG patterns at the most significant time-frequency bins and targeted a potential cortex region (PPC) that involved in flying imagery and worked differently on various directions and the control state. However, the flying imagery paradigm is still in its initial stage and the application of the classification framework used in the current work is still limited. More researches are required to further understand how the spatial information is encoded in the EEG signals, and to develop methods in retrieving the intended direction or location of flying in continuous scales instead of discrete options from the EEG signal.

Acknowledgements. We thank Prof. Ian James Kirk (The University of Auckland) for providing insightful advice in EEG preprocessing and analysis; we thank Dr. Veema Lodhia (The University of Auckland) for providing technical support in using the GES 300 EEG system and the EEG lab. Dr Xuyun Zhang is the recipient of an ARC DECRA (project No. DE210101458) funded by the Australian Government.

References

1. Abiri, R., Borhani, S., Sellers, E.W., Jiang, Y., Zhao, X.: A comprehensive review of EEG-based brain-computer interface paradigms. J. Neural Eng. **16**(1), 011001 (2019)
2. Andersen, R.A., Buneo, C.A.: Intentional maps in posterior parietal cortex. Ann. Rev. Neurosci. **25**(1), 189–220 (2002)
3. Andersen, R.A., Snyder, L.H., Bradley, D.C., Xing, J.: Multimodal representation of space in the posterior parietal cortex and its use in planning movements. Ann. Rev. Neurosci **20**(1), 303–330 (1997)
4. Aydemir, O., Kayikcioglu, T.: Decision tree structure based classification of EEG signals recorded during two dimensional cursor movement imagery. J. Neurosci. Methods **229**, 68–75 (2014)
5. Barachant, A.: Pyriemann. https://github.com/pyRiemann/pyRiemann/tree/v0.2.6

6. Barachant, A., Bonnet, S., Congedo, M., Jutten, C.: Riemannian geometry applied to BCI classification. In: Vigneron, V., Zarzoso, V., Moreau, E., Gribonval, R., Vincent, E. (eds.) LVA/ICA 2010. LNCS, vol. 6365, pp. 629–636. Springer, Heidelberg (2010). https://doi.org/10.1007/978-3-642-15995-4_78

7. Bascil, M.S., Tesneli, A.Y., Temurtas, F.: Spectral feature extraction of EEG signals and pattern recognition during mental tasks of 2-D cursor movements for BCI using SVM and ANN. Aust. Phys. Eng. Sci. Med. **39**(3), 665–676 (2016). https://doi.org/10.1007/s13246-016-0462-x

8. Bell, M.A., Cuevas, K.: Using EEG to study cognitive development: issues and practices. J. Cogn. Dev. **13**(3), 281–294 (2012). https://doi.org/10.1080/15248372.2012.691143

9. Bhatia, R.: Positive Definite Matrices. Princeton University Press, Princeton (2009)

10. Congedo, M., Barachant, A., Bhatia, R.: Riemannian geometry for EEG-based brain-computer interfaces; a primer and a review. Brain-Comput. Interf. **4**(3), 155–174 (2017)

11. Doud, A.J., Lucas, J.P., Pisansky, M.T., He, B.: Continuous three-dimensional control of a virtual helicopter using a motor imagery based brain-computer interface. PloS one **6**(10), e26322 (2011)

12. Fabiani, G.E., McFarland, D.J., Wolpaw, J.R., Pfurtscheller, G.: Conversion of EEG activity into cursor movement by a brain-computer interface (BCI). IEEE Trans. Neural Syst. Rehabil. Eng **12**(3), 331–338 (2004)

13. Harrison, S.A., Tong, F.: Decoding reveals the contents of visual working memory in early visual areas. Nature **458**(7238), 632–635 (2009)

14. Herweg, N.A., Kahana, M.J.: Spatial representations in the human brain. Front. Human Neurosci. **12**, 297 (2018)

15. LaFleur, K., Cassady, K., Doud, A., Shades, K., Rogin, E., He, B.: Quadcopter control in three-dimensional space using a noninvasive motor imagery-based brain-computer interface. J. Neural Eng. **10**(4), 046003 (2013)

16. Li, Y., et al.: An EEG-based BCI system for 2-D cursor control by combining Mu/Beta rhythm and P300 potential. IEEE Trans. Biomed. Eng. **57**(10), 2495–2505 (2010)

17. Lotte, F.: A review of classification algorithms for EEG-based brain-computer interfaces: a 10 year update. J. Neural Eng. **15**(3), 031005 (2018)

18. Meng, J., Streitz, T., Gulachek, N., Suma, D., He, B.: Three-dimensional brain-computer interface control through simultaneous overt spatial attentional and motor imagery tasks. IEEE Trans. Biomed. Eng. **65**(11), 2417–2427 (2018)

19. Odom, J.V., et al.: Visual evoked potentials standard (2004). Documenta ophthalmologica **108**(2), 115–123 (2004)

20. Pedregosa, F., et al.: Scikit-learn: machine learning in python. J. Mach. Learn. Res. **12**, 2825–2830 (2011)

21. Royer, A.S., Doud, A.J., Rose, M.L., He, B.: EEG control of a virtual helicopter in 3-dimensional space using intelligent control strategies. IEEE Trans. Neural Syst. Rehabil. Eng. **18**(6), 581–589 (2010)

Network Graph Analysis of Hospital and Health Services Functional Structures

David Ben-Tovim[1], Mariusz Bajger[2] (iD), Viet Duong Bui[2], and Shaowen Qin[2(✉)] (iD)

[1] College of Medicine and Public Health, Flinders University, Bedford Park, Australia
[2] College of Science and Engineering, Flinders University, Tonsley, SA 5042, Australia
shaowen.qin@flinders.edu.au

Abstract. Hospitals and health services are complicated places that generate large quantities of data focusing on individual patient care. That care is the product of multiple interactions between patients and the many differently staffs within a hospital or health service. It is hard to use the data produced by hospitals and health services to adequately represent those interactions and use them to identify how services work in practice. We present a set of proof-of-concept studies that represent health systems as networks, analysed by contemporary network graph theory, to look for interpretable patterns of interactions that reveal modular functional structures at multiple levels within large general hospitals.

Keywords: Graph analysis · Modularity · Healthcare services provision · Decision support · Patient flow

1 Introduction

A Hospital of any size will have an organisation chart identifying the administrative and reporting structure of the different groups that make the hospital's workforce. Professional groups such as doctors, nurses, and allied health professionals will each have separate, parallel, management and reporting systems alongside the formal managerial structures. But none of these are of great interest to patients. From their perspective, hospitals and health services are provided by teams whose members undertake different, but important, roles. Enormous scientific and technical resources have gone into identifying appropriate biomedical interventions that will prevent or remedy disease states. However, as reports into problems with the safety, quality, and access to, healthcare across the world, have made clear [1], delivering a healthcare intervention is not only a matter of access to resources. It requires mastery of the relevant, albeit broadly defined, operational processes. Here, we use the term functional structure [2] to represent a description of healthcare services work in practice, acknowledging that those functional structures are not isomorphic with either their physical or administrative structures. The complexity of the interactions involved means that the functional structures underpinning the delivery of care may not always be apparent even to the participants involved, let alone to others more external to the systems concerned.

© Springer Nature Switzerland AG 2022
B. Li et al. (Eds.): ADMA 2021, LNAI 13087, pp. 33–44, 2022.
https://doi.org/10.1007/978-3-030-95405-5_3

There is no shortage of data generated by health services. A general hospital of any size may have hundreds of thousands of unique interactions with patients over the course of a year. The volume of data produced from those encounters is very substantial. The challenge is to find new ways to use existing data sources to visualise the underlying structures through which care is delivered. Furthermore, the increasing pace of digitisation in healthcare emphasises the need for an analytic framework for describing and identifying functional structures that is applicable both to existing services, and their extension into new environments as digitisation expands in scope.

Like many complicated systems [3], healthcare services naturally fall into a hierarchical modular structure [4]. The end-to-end (arrival to discharge) activities associated with each episode of care divide into parts that interoperate according to defined interfaces, which, in a manner that is familiar in areas such as software design, enables the complexity of the activities within each component to be 'hidden' from the participants in other modules. Physicians may order an MRI scan by a request form that is submitted digitally or manually. It is not necessary for the physician to understand the physics behind MRI scans, nor how to set up the scan, the work of radiographers and radiologists. The physician will make a decision based on receiving the scan images and a report on its content, trusting to the expertise of the imaging team. Psychiatrists and surgeons get on best when they do not interfere with each other's expert work, and doctors and nurses collaborate most effectively when they acknowledge the importance of each other's roles in the delivery of care. Embedding a modular structure that acknowledges this diversity, within a scientific framework that does justice to the underlying complicated nature of the interactions is still at a relatively early stage.

Increasingly sophisticated, simulation-based models for analysing resource intensive settings such as hospital inpatient services have been developed that represent healthcare services in terms of patient agents with variable characteristics, moved through simulated modular physical resources by varying therapeutic processes [5, 6]. However, those models are based on assumed patterns of care, and contain predetermined structural assumptions. It is challenging to relate those simulation models to the more nuanced functional structures required for a full description of functional structures within a complicated health system. In this regard, health systems provide an important opportunity for exploring the capacity of data mining techniques to reveal underlying patterns of care.

In this paper, we propose that representing healthcare services as networks [7] and analysing the characteristics of the underlying systems by way of network graph analysis [8], is a technique that has the potential to provide a unifying framework within which to consider the interactions between the parts that make up a functioning healthcare system.

Studying healthcare systems as networks is not uncommon [9], but network graph theory analyses that make use of contemporary techniques to identify the structural characteristics of health systems hardly exist in the peer-reviewed literature. We have undertaken a series of proof-of-concept studies of resource intensive components of several general hospitals, as a test of the hypotheses (i) that network graph analysis can be used to identify the underlying multi-level functional structures within a working general hospital, and (ii) that those functional structures are likely to be modular in nature [8].

The proof-of-concept work is a step towards laying the foundation for the development of a Healthcare Connectome [10] – a visual representation of a living structure with a common scientific language that will enable hospitals and health services to not only identify the key features of interactions among units in their own organisation and develop improvement strategies, but also enhance communication and bigger-picture understanding, and reduce resistance to change.

2 Subjects and Methods

A general hospital of any size is a very complicated place. Individual patients may present with one of over 14,000 diagnostic conditions, each of which can be either a primary disorder, or act as a complication of another condition identified as the condition of primary concern. The individual social and personal circumstances of patients may further complicate the provision of care. We are particularly interested in the potential graph theory network analysis has to operate at multiple levels within such organisations, identifying patterns that relate to varying aspects of the interactions between patients' needs and institutional demands. It is also clear that interpreting the structures that can be identified by graph theory analysis requires a close collaboration between data analysts and domain specialists who can relate patterns of interactions to real-world phenomena of direct interest. Using a biomedical analogy, we see network graph analysis as a kind of microscope that can be used to expose structural characteristics at different levels of magnification but using the basic technology.

The identification of a measurable modularity parameter has been an important innovation in graph theory. It measures the extent to which identified structures differ from a graph of the same nodes linked to each other at random [14]. It is effectively a test of the extent to which the identified structure differs from the null state. Modularity scores vary from −1 to 1. The closer to 1, the more confidence there is in the robustness of the solution. Nevertheless, it is necessary to cross-check the combinatorically derived graph parameters against expert opinion to ensure that the graph analysis reflects identifiable real-world system characteristics.

A series of studies were undertaken using data obtained from healthcare institutions in an Australian metropolitan area. The hospitals are well resourced and adequately staffed, and representative of health services across Australia.

Hospital 1 is a teaching general hospital that provides a comprehensive (neonatal to end-of-life care) hospital service to a de-facto catchment population of around 300,000 plus. Hospital 2 is also a large teaching general hospital that provides a comprehensive medical and surgical service to patients over the age of 18. It does not provide paediatric, gynaecological or obstetrics services. As well as being the primary resource for a 200,000 plus community, Hospital 2 is also a centre for a range of state-wide specialised medical and surgical services.

All Australian hospitals have well developed administrative patient-related data systems that follow detailed national guidelines [11]. The universal patient related administrative data sets contain demographic, admission (emergency or elective, location of care and treating clinical team) and discharge data, and detailed diagnostic information. Hospital 1 has also developed a searchable patient journey database that incorporates administrative information with a computerised time and location stamp process that automatically records every occasion that a patient is moved between locations within the hospital.

For both Hospital 1 and Hospital 2, anonymised data sets of a series of hospital wide snapshots of all patients present in hospital at midnight of the 15th day of the month were accessed. For Hospital 1 this was from the patient journey database described above. For Hospital 2, the snapshots relied on the administrative database. In Hospital 1, an additional extract was analysed, described further below.

The snap-shot data enabled creation of datasets representative of the most resource intensive services in hospitals, overnight stay inpatients. It is those services that are most demanding in terms of the staffs involved, and the intensity of interactions required. The snapshots for both hospitals included the whole of 2019 and up to September in 2020, and in the case of Hospital 2, the whole of 2020. The patient's location in a ward, and the clinical team responsible for the patient's treatment, were recorded in the snapshot. In the case of Hospital 1, they were as at the time of the snapshot. For Hospital 2 the ward and clinical unit information included in the database were those recorded on the date of discharge.

3 Network Graphs

We used the healthcare databases to develop network graphs and analyse them by network graph theory-based techniques. Patients do not interact with each other, and their use as nodes is thereby limited. But a hospital or a health service without patients makes no sense. The patient facing components of western style hospitals are bipartite. Nurses manage the minute-by-minute care of patients. Medical practitioners make clinical diagnoses and formulate and monitor treatment plans, and head clinical units. Both groups will implement various aspects of those treatment plans. Nurses' roles mean that, in general, they are allocated to specified locations (wards, clinics, et cetera) and do not follow patients when they move. The day-by-day practice of doctors, and the clinical units that they head, may involve dealing with patients in various settings within institutions. The same clinical unit may follow patients between locations. There are many exceptions to these generalisations, and Allied Health staff will vary in their relationships to teams and locations, but the basics of a bipartite structure of the human resources required for patient care are universal in western-style hospitals and health services.

Accountability requirements in healthcare mean that a location is provided (wards, or other location identifier labels) for every patient in an administrative data set, as is the patient's designated clinical unit or individual medical practitioner. A bipartite graph [12] is a graph whose nodes fall into two separate sets. Edges only connect nodes between sets. A bipartite graph with clinical units and wards as nodes, and patients connecting the wards and units that are related to their care in the data sets, exactly reproduces the linkages through which care is provided, as the wards stand for the nursing groups involved. In the bipartite graphs that are used in our proof-of-concept studies, the node sets are wards (or other geographic settings) and clinical units. The edges are the patients that connect specific ward and unit nodes. The edges can be weighted by the number of patients involved, and both nodes and edges can be further analysed in various ways.

For hospitals 1 and 2, an adjacency matrix was developed for each monthly snapshot, and for the snapshots combined for 2019, and for 2020. Ward and unit identifiers were the nodes, and weighted edges recorded the number of patients for each connection. The data was analysed using open-source software Gephi (Version 0.9.2). The Louvain algorithm [13] for detecting modules was applied, and the graphs were displayed using the Force Atlas algorithm. The Louvain algorithm is fast, appropriate, and capable of handling large data sets. Various graph parameters, were computed, including the modularity score [14]. Graphs were constructed of the whole dataset for both Hospitals, and a variety of sub-graphs were constructed for Hospital 1, looking for patterns of interactions at a level below that of the whole population of patients, but using the same bipartite structure.

4 Results

Figure 1 is a complete bipartite graph of the accumulated interactions between wards and units in Hospital 1, using merged data from 12 monthly snapshots in 2019. The size of the nodes represents variations in the numbers of adjacent edges, not their edge weights. The modularity value for Fig. 1 is 0.714, confirming the modularity of the bipartite graph and the underlying functional structure. Figure 2 is a similar graph for Hospital 2 over a comparable time, with a modularity of 0.734. The graphs as shown are taken from a series of graphs of individual monthly and composite snapshots for 2019 and 2020. The graph series were reviewed by multi-disciplinary groups of senior health professions both from Hospitals 1 and 2, and other health services. The graphs were found to be interpretable and to provide a credible and useful representation of underlying functional structures. As one senior clinician, put it, "it is one thing to know something. It is quite another to see it".

In Figs. 1 and 2, the wards are represented as rectangles, and the clinical units as ovals. Networks graphs exhibit their own topological characteristic, with bipartite graphs being a subclass having its own unique properties. The colours, shapes and layout of the graphs are arbitrary and can be structured for clarity of presentation without misrepresenting the interactions. Figure 1 identifies 13 communities, or modules, within the graph, and Fig. 2, 12 modules. The graphs demonstrate the modular nature of the underlying structures, that is, nodes within modules interact extensively with each other, and to a lesser, but still present, extent link to nodes in other communities.

The graphs demonstrate that there are only a limited number of one-to-one relation-ships between clinical units and healthcare wards (and therefore to the kinds of patients within those wards and staff assigned to treat them). In general, the inter-relationships are many-to-many. However, the ward-unit interactions are not random, as confirmed by the distribution of nodes between communities, where the weighted degree of the nodes aligns to an exponential type of distribution. Figure 3 show the histogram of nodes degree distribution and the corresponding graph in logarithmic scales. The straight line clearly indicates an exponential distribution of the degrees. Analytical calculations using Matlab confirm that the exponential function is a preferable fit. Specifically, the MSE (mean square error) for an exponential type of distribution (Weibull type) was 0.00006, while the error for fitting a normal distribution was 0.0001.

Whilst the potential number of combinations of primary and secondary conditions for individual patients is beyond immediate computation, in practice a much more restricted range of clinical and social problems present for care. In Fig. 1, several of the large modules are relatively self-contained and the ward and unit structure closely align to the specific biomedical characteristics of the patients being treated. This includes a tightly structured module for neonatal (units identified by one of the unit acronyms NNU), a module for obstetric and gynaecological wards and clinical units; a module for mental health wards and units (FMH); an one-to-one ward and unit module for the assessment of elderly patients with complex care needs (GEMSA); and one to one ward and unit modules for paediatric (PAED) and stroke care (STROKE). By contrast, there are large modules with much looser internal structures and extensive cross-modular interactions that relate to the provision of multi-diagnostic surgical (COLREC, ORTHO and VASC) and medical services, including both general (GMF) and specialised medical care (RESP), including cardiology (CARACS). The general structures hold true for monthly as well as merged data sets, although the modular values are slightly smaller in the monthly graphs.

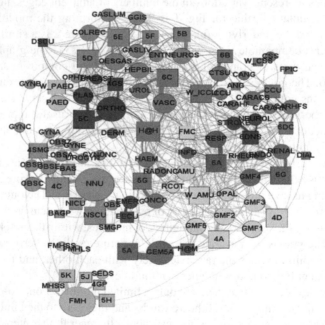

Fig. 1. Graph showing modular structures with modules distinguished by colours. Vertices corresponding to wards are indicated by rectangles while clinical units by ovals. Acronyms are used on each vertex corresponding to its original name in Hospital 1

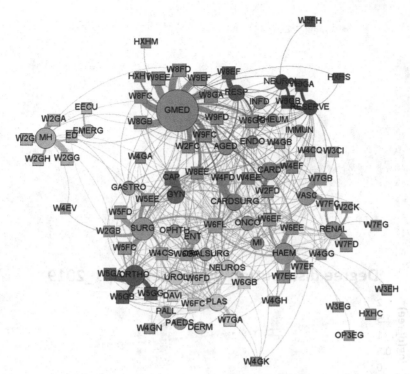

Fig. 2. Graph showing modular structures with modules distinguished by colours. Vertices corresponding to wards are indicated by rectangles while clinical units by ovals. Acronyms are used on each vertex corresponding to its original name in Hospital 2

In Fig. 2, as in Fig. 1, the mental health unit services (MH) and wards (W2G, W2GA, etc.) form a relatively self-contained module, as do neurosurgical and stroke services (STROKE). The various medical (includes GMED, CARD) and surgical (includes ORTHO, SURG) services interact extensively, but with a slightly better modularity score than that of Hospital 1.

Both hospitals were in Australian cities where COVID related health care demands were, up until the time of writing, concentrated in the first half of 2020, and in that year never reached the extremes seen in many other countries. In both hospitals, elective admissions were limited during 2020 but Hospital 2 was a nominated COVID centre whilst Hospital 1 continued its community responsibilities. Figure 4 compares the monthly modularity scores of the two hospitals over 2019 and 2020. It shows an increase of modularity in Hospital 2 over 2020. In Hospital 1, there was a brief increase in homogeneity before the underlying structure returned to the status quo ante.

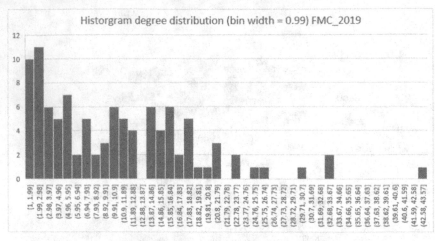

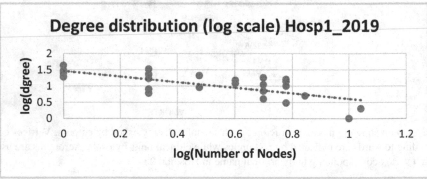

Fig. 3. Histogram of nodes degree distribution and the corresponding graph in logarithmic scales

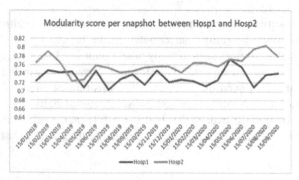

Fig. 4. Comparison of Modularity scores between two hospitals (the upper one is Hosp 2 while the lower is Hosp 1)

So far, we have been considering graphs related to the functional structures of the whole hospitals. It is possible to use a bipartite graph analysis approach to look at various sub-graphs within the complete bipartite graphs. Two examples are provided, both drawn from analyses of Hospital 1.

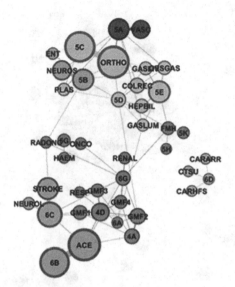

Fig. 5. Graph shows unit modularity structure for patients with extended hospital stays due to psycho-social difficulties with discharge.

Over several years, Hospital 1 focussed on a hospital-specific method for identifying a common, but poorly documented, healthcare issue. In many public hospitals, there are a limited number of patients whose hospital stay, for psychosocial reasons, is prolonged beyond the point at which the clinical condition has been stabilised. Figure 5 is a sub-graph of all those patients in Hospital A in 2019. The ward-unit modules identified by the Louvain algorithm [13] are mostly drawn from larger modules within the general graphs, but with many ward-unit linkages missing and a different structure of intensity of edge adjacency. The distribution of nodes and edges is not random, but neither is it identical to that of the complete graphs. Serial graphs (not shown here) enable observers to identify whether interventions in relation to patient choice have made an impact on the status of the modules involved.

Figure 6 is a more restricted sub-graph showing the provision of care to emergency and elective patients by clinical units.

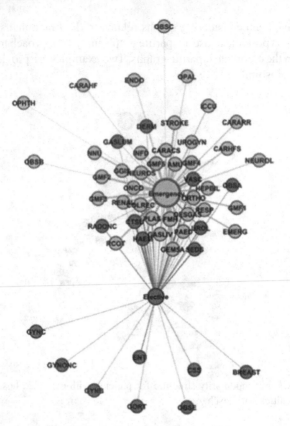

Fig. 6. Emergency and elective modules

5   Discussion

We set out to assess whether the functional structures by which healthcare services are delivered in the most resource intensive components of general public hospitals can be represented by network graphs and then analysed by network graph theory. Our proof-of-concept studies of two general public hospitals that are representative of those hospitals across Australia have confirmed that they can be so represented, and that the underlying functional structure is modular in nature. The hospitals studied were placed under considerable stress in 2020 during the COVID 19 pandemic. The modular functional structure proved to be flexible, resilient, and adaptable, as is the case for many other large systems. In particular, as the pandemic took hold in 2020, the modular structure in both hospitals was maintained, with the functional structure in a COVID lead hospital reflecting the narrowing of functions during that time.

There are a number of features of interest in the graphs presented here. They show a mixture between tightly interconnected ward and unit pairs that are responsible for limited, and quite specialised areas of clinical care. Much of the remainder of the in-patient services are taken up with a range of medical and surgical services that are predominantly influenced by the need to undertake emergency procedures and treatments in adult patients admitted as an emergency. The advantage of tightly structured services is that specialised knowledge is accessed in a cost, and time-efficient manner. The dilemma is that if specialised services are allowed to grow without regard to more general services, the point will come when hospitals become seriously over-crowded because the more numerous the general medical and surgical services are, the less flexible it is for patient placement. Network graphs provide graphic reminders of the issues involved, and we are currently working on developing metrics to reflect the extent to which overcrowding is reflected in (and possibly preceded by) periods when the internal functional structures become more random and less well structured.

Network graph theory can be seen as having a place in describing how hospitals work at a variety of levels. As previously stated, we see network graph theory as being analogous to a microscope with a variety of magnifying lens systems. We can adjust the magnification and penetration of network graph theory to shed a light on issues at various levels, from whole of institution graphs to sub-graphs illuminating a variety of areas of healthcare processing that might otherwise be hard to understand 'at a glance'.

The computational requirements for network graph analysis are such that specialised software and data preparation are required. But the basic methods are now established. The graphs that are produced identify patterns that would be hard to visualise without graph theory. Although only a limited number of more detailed analyses have been undertaken (at levels below the whole institution), it seems evident that existing administrative and clinical data sets can be used to identify meaningful patterns at varying levels within institutions through network graph analysis.

6   Conclusion and Future Work

Network graph theory is a major area of scientific and technical advance, and we are hopeful that using network graph theory analyses, the rich and varied data sets produced by health care services will be able to be mined for information that will increase the safety, quality, and accessibility of health services, a vital task as nations and their health services confront the challenge of current, and future, pandemics.

References

1. Dixon-Woods, M.: How to improve healthcare improvement. BMJ **367**, l5514 (2019)
2. Joellerendon: Healthcare Organizational Structural Analysis. https://n415son21.wordpress.com/2014/02/18/healthcare-organizational-structural-analysis/. Accessed 14 July 2021
3. Pan, R.K., Sinha, S.: Modular networks with hierarchical organization: the dynamical implications of complex structure. Pramana J. Phys. **71**, 331 (2008)
4. Simon, H.A.: The Architecture of Complexity. Facets of Systems Science, pp. 457–476. Springer, Boston (1991)
5. Ben-Tovim, D., Filar, J., Hakendorf, P., Qin, S., Thompson, C., Ward, D.: Hospital Event simulation model: arrivals to discharge-design, development and application. Simul. Model. Pract. Theory **68**, 80–94 (2016)

6. Mackay, M., Qin, S., Clissold, A., Hakendorf, P., Ben-Tovim, D., McDonnell, G.: Patient flow simulation modelling–an approach conducive to multi-disciplinary collaboration towards hospital capacity management. In: Piantadosi J., Anderssen R.S., Boland J. (eds.) MODSIM2013, 20th International Congress on Modelling and Simulation. The Modelling and Simulation Society of Australia and New Zealand, The 20th Inter-national Congress on Modelling and Simulation, pp 50–56. Adelaide, Australia (2013)
7. Newman, M.: Networks: An Introduction. Oxford University Press, Oxford (2010)
8. Fortunato, S.: Community detection in graphs. Phys. Rep. **486**(3–5), 75–174 (2010)
9. Brunson, J.C., Laubenbacher, R.C.: Applications of network analysis to routinely collected health care data: a systematic review. J. Am. Med. Inform. Assoc. **25**(2), 210–221 (2018)
10. Sporns, O., Tononi, G., Kötter, R.: The human connectome: a structural description of the human brain. PLoS Comput. Biol. **1**(4), e42 (2005)
11. Australian Government Department of Health, Hospital Data Collections. https://www1.health.gov.au/internet/main/publishing.nsf/Content/health-casemix-data-collections-about. Accessed 14 July 2021
12. Pavlopoulos, G.A., et al.: Bipartite graphs in systems biology and medicine: a survey of methods and applications. GigaScience **7**, 1–31 (2018)
13. Blondel, V.D., Guillaume, J.-L., Lambiotte, R., Lefebvre, E.: Fast unfolding of communities in large networks. J. Stat. Mech: Theory Exp. **2008**(10), P10008 (2008)
14. Newman, M.E.: Modularity and community structure in networks. Proc. Natl. Acad. Sci. **103**(23), 8577–8582 (2006)
15. Fornito, A., Zalesky, A., Bullmore, E.: Fundamentals of Brain Network Analysis. Academic Press, Cambridge (2016)

Feature Selection in Gene Expression Profile Employing Relevancy and Redundancy Measures and Binary Whale Optimization Algorithm (BWOA)

Salim Sazzed[✉]

Old Dominion University, Norfolk, VA 23529, USA
ssazz001@odu.edu

Abstract. The presence of a large number of genes in the gene expression profiles imposes a computational challenge for cancer classification. To deal with the high-dimensional feature space, in this paper, we present a 3-step feature selection framework, RRO (Relevancy-Redundancy-Optimization). In the first step, RRO identifies top-ranked class-relevant genes utilizing the analysis of variance (ANOVA) and F-test. In the second step, class correlated but redundant genes are removed by employing the Kendall rank correlation coefficient (Kendall's τ). Finally, we utilize a metaheuristic optimization algorithm, binary whale optimization algorithm (BWOA), with the support vector machine (SVM) classifier to select an optimal gene subset. The comparisons with thirteen state-of-the-art methods in ten gene expression datasets show that RRO yields better or comparable accuracy.

1 Introduction

The microarray gene expression profiles contain a large number of genes with a limited number of samples. Feature selection plays a crucial role in cancer classification as it allows researchers to identify the most substantial genes that provide insight into the mechanisms responsible for cancer. Furthermore, it decreases the computational costs associated with the classification by excluding non-informative and redundant genes. Moreover, it yields a simpler classification model, which refers to more interpretable results.

Researchers mainly utilized three approaches for gene selection: filter, wrapper, and hybrid approaches. The filter-based methods estimate the relevance scores of every feature by computing statistical measures and then remove the statistically non-significant features. The wrapper methods examine various combinations of gene subsets and determine the best subset by integrating them into a classifier. Although they are usually more accurate than the filter-based methods, they require extensive computational resources and are more prone to overfitting. The hybrid methods usually apply one or multiple filter-based methods in the first step to reduce the feature space. Afterward, a wrapper-based method is employed to select the optimal feature subset.

© Springer Nature Switzerland AG 2022
B. Li et al. (Eds.): ADMA 2021, LNAI 13087, pp. 45–60, 2022.
https://doi.org/10.1007/978-3-030-95405-5_4

The proposed methodology, RRO, starts with distinguishing the top-class discriminative genes using the filter-based ANOVA method. The Kendall rank-order correlation coefficient (Kendall's τ) is employed to eliminate class-correlated but redundant genes. Then, we apply the binary whale optimization algorithm (BWOA) with the SVM classifier to identify an optimized feature subset. Finally, we feed the selected gene subset to the SVM classifier to determine cancer types. We compare RRO with thirteen state-of-the-art methods on ten gene expressions datasets considering both best and average accuracy. The results demonstrate that RRO yields comparable or better accuracy than most of the existing methods.

1.1   Objective and Contributions

The main objective of this study is to demonstrate the efficacy of the combination of several feature selection methods (i.e., ANOVA, Kendall, and BWOA) and the SVM classifier for gene selection and cancer classification. The main contributions of this paper can be summarized as follows:

- We show that the combinations of ANOVA and Kendall's τ can effectively remove irrelevant and redundant genes in gene expression datasets.
- We demonstrate that the SVM classifier with the BWOA feature selection algorithm can effectively identify cancer subtypes (or presence).

2   Related Work

A number of univariate feature selection methods such as Chi-square [21], Information Gain (IG) [13,19], Laplacian score (L-score) [37] and Fisher score (F-score) [11] have been employed for gene selection in literature. Besides, researchers also studied multivariate filter methods such as Minimal Redundancy Maximal Relevance (mRMR) [28], Random Subspace Method (RSM) [18], and Relevance Redundancy Feature Selection (RRFS) [12] which considers the dependencies among features.

Due to the high computational cost associated with wrapper-based feature selection methods, they are often combined with a filter-based method. The hybrid methodology initially employs a filter-based method to exclude non-informative genes to reduce search space. Mundra et al. [25] hybridized two of the most popular feature selection approaches, namely SVM-RFE and mRMR. Shreem et al. [34] proposed RM-GA approach that combines ReliefF, mRMR, and genetic algorithm (GA). In [9], the authors introduced a hybrid method named CFS-TGA, which utilizes correlation-based feature selection (CFS), Taguchi-Genetic Algorithm (TGA), and K-NN classifier. In [5], the authors proposed a feature selection algorithm, mRMR, and combined it with the Artificial Bee Colony (ABC) algorithm to select informative genes. The performance of the mRMR-ABC algorithm was evaluated on six binary and multiclass gene expression microarray datasets. Lee and Leu [20] presented Genetic Algorithm Dynamic Parameter (GADP) that produces every possible subset of genes and ranks the genes using their occurrence frequency. Yassi and Moattar [38] proposed a feature selection approach for microarray data that fuses both ranking and wrapper-based methods.

MIMAGA-Selection [22] is a hybrid feature selection algorithm that combines Mutual Information Maximization (MIM) and Adaptive Genetic Algorithm (AGA). CLA-ACO [31] is a hybrid approach that employs Cellular Learning Automata (CLA) and Ant Colony Optimization (ACO). CLA-ACO consists of three phases: filter-based Fisher criterion method, cellular learning automata, and ant colony optimization.

Shreem et al. [33] combined Symmetrical Uncertainty (SU) with the Harmony Search Algorithm (HSA) for gene selection. The authors first eliminated non-essential genes using the SU method. In the second stage, HSA was employed as a wrapper method to find the most informative genes. Two classifiers, IB1 and NB, were utilized to assess the performance of SU-HSA. The authors applied SU-HSA to 10 microarray datasets and achieved 100% accuracy in four of them.

Salem et al. [29] proposed an Information Gain (IG) and Standard Genetic Algorithm (SGA) based method, IG/SGA, for feature selection. IG was applied at the initial step for feature reduction. Then, a genetic algorithm was applied to select the optimal features, and finally, Genetic Programming (GP) classifier was employed. Their method was evaluated on seven cancer microarray datasets and achieved 100% accuracy in two datasets. A GA and Intelligent Dynamic Genetic Algorithm (IDGA) based method for gene selection was proposed in [10]. The authors applied Laplacian and Fisher scores independently in the first phase to select the top 500 genes. In the second phase, the reinforcement learning-based IDGA method was applied. Support Vector Machine (SVM), Naïve Bayes (NB), and K-Nearest Neighbour (KNN) were employed as classifiers on five microarray cancer datasets. It was observed that when combined with the IDGA, the Fisher score outperformed the Laplacian score on four datasets.

A hybrid framework that employs both extraction and wrapper gene selection methods was presented by Aziz et al. [8]; as an extraction method, the authors used ICA, while as a wrapper method, ABC was utilized. Their experimental results utilizing the NB classifier yielded better performance compared to other gene selection algorithms. A Gene Selection Programming (GSP) method was proposed in [2] to select relevant genes for cancer classification. The authors adopted the SVM with a linear kernel as a classifier for the GSP. A neighborhood entropy-based feature selection algorithm was introduced in [35]. At first, the neighborhood entropy-based uncertainty measures were utilized to assess the uncertainty and exclude the noise present in gene expression datasets. In the subsequent steps, the neighborhood credibility degree and coverage degree were applied. The authors employed a heuristic reduction algorithm to decrease the computational complexity and to improve the classification performance.

A hybrid method that employs Adaptive Elastic Net (AEN) with Conditional Mutual Information (CMI) was introduced in [36]. AEN-CMI obtained better performance compared to L1-SVM, Elastic Net, Adaptive Lasso, and classic Adaptive Elastic Net algorithms on two cancer microarray datasets. In [1], an unsupervised two-stage feature selection technique was presented. In the first stage, three filter-based methods techniques were applied. A genetic algorithm was utilized in the second stage. Finally, three ML classifiers, SVM, k-NN, and random forest (RF) were employed for classification.

Several variants of Particle Swarm Optimization (PSO) algorithm have been proposed in the literature for cancer classification [15,16,24,30]. HPSO-LS [24] embedded a local search strategy within the PSO to reduce the feature space before applying PSO. The authors also used the Pearson correlation coefficient to identify correlation among features. As a classifier, the k-NN classifier was used. In another PSO-based work [16], k-NN with PSO was utilized for feature selection and classification. However, their work focused more on selecting the best k value for the k-NN classifier to achieve better accuracy. In [15], the correlation-based feature selection (CFS) algorithm and iBPSO were applied for identifying the best feature set, and then NB classifiers were employed for classification. In [30], ANOVA, Spearman rank-order correlation (SRC), and BPSO were employed for feature selection.

3   Proposed Methodology

The RRO starts with normalizing the gene expression values. Afterward, the feature selection process consisting of three phases, relevance analysis (ANOVA), redundancy analysis (Kendall's τ), and feature set optimization (BWOA-SVM) are employed. Finally, the SVM classifier is applied for classification. The flow diagram of the proposed methodology is shown in Fig. 1.

3.1   Feature Scaling

The value of each feature (i.e., gene expression value) is scaled to fit within a range between 0 and 1. The following equation is used to normalize the d'th value (i.e., value for the d'th instance) of feature i in set X,

$$X_{id}.scaled = \frac{(X_{id} - X_i.min)}{X_i.max - X_i.min} \tag{1}$$

where, $X_i.max$ and $X_i.min$ are the maximum and minimum gene expression values of gene i acorss all the instances, respectively.

3.2   Phase 1 Feature Selection: Relevance Analysis

In phase 1, ANOVA, a statistical method, is applied to reduce the feature search space by identifying top class-correlated genes. ANOVA F-test determines the variance between and within the groups, calculates F-value, and utilizes it to identify informative genes. This step selects a set of top class-correlated genes. The number of genes in the set is either 200 genes or 5% of the genes present in the dataset, whichever is minimum. The selected top class-correlated genes are then forwarded to the redundancy measure step.

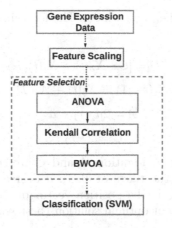

Fig. 1. Flowchart of the proposed methodology

3.3 Phase 2 Feature Selection: Redundancy Analysis

As univariate filter-based feature selection methods do not consider the interaction among features, they may select class-correlated but redundant genes. In phase 2, we employ Kendall's τ coefficient to remove redundant genes identified in phase 1. The Kendall rank correlation coefficient (often called Kendall's τ coefficient) is a non-parametric measure of the correspondence between two rankings. A value close to +1 indicates strong agreement, a value around −1 indicates strong disagreement, and a 0 value indicates no correlation.

Let $(x_1, y_1), ..., (x_n, y_n)$ be a set of observations of the joint random variables X and Y such that all the values of x_i and y_i are unique (assume their is no tie). Any pair of observations (x_i, y_i) and (x_j, y_j) , where i < j, are said to be concordant if the sort order of (x_i, x_j) and (y_i, y_j) agrees; otherwise they are said to be discordant. The Kendall τ coefficient is defined as:

$$\frac{(\#num\ concordant\ pairs\ -\ \#num\ disconcordant\ pairs)}{\frac{n(n-1)}{2}}$$

The redundancy threshold value is selected as 0.5 to identify the redundant genes. When two genes show a Kendall's τ correlation coefficient above the redundancy threshold, the lower class-relevant gene is removed.

3.4 Phase 3 Feature Selection: Meta-heuristic Optimization

Phase 3 of the feature selection step leverages binary whale optimization algorithm (BWOA) and SVM classifier. Whale Optimization Algorithm (WOA) [23] is a nature-inspired optimization algorithm that imitates the social behavior of humpback whales. The WOA optimization algorithm assumes that the present best candidate solution is the target prey or is close to the optimum solution. The other search agents (i.e., whale) gradually change their positions towards the current best solution (i.e., best whale). The following equations describe this behavior of i'th whale:

$$D = |C * X_b(t) - X_i(t)| \tag{2}$$

$$X_i(t + 1) = X_b(t) - A * D \tag{3}$$

$$A = 2a * r_1 - a \tag{4}$$

$$C = 2 * r_2 \tag{5}$$

where t indicates the current iteration, A and C are coefficient values, r_1 and r_2 are random vectors in the range of $[0, 1]$; a decreases linearly through the iterations from 2 to 0. X_i is the position vector of the i'th whale. X_b is the position vector of the current optimal solution (best search agent position).

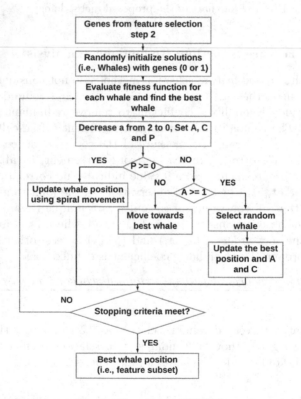

Fig. 2. The steps of BWOA

The two phases of bubble-net attacking behaviour of whales are the exploitation and exploration phases.

Exploitation Phase

Shrinking Encircling Mechanism: This behavior is achieved by decreasing the value of a. The fluctuation range of A decreases as a is reduced from 2 to 0 gradually over the course of iterations. By setting random values for A in $[-1, 1]$, the updated position of each agent can be defined anywhere in between the position of the current best agent and the original position of the agent.

$$X_i(t+1) = X_b(t) - A * D \tag{6}$$

Spiral-Based Position Update: In this step, for each whale i, the distance to current best solution is computed. To imitate the helix-shaped movement of the humpback whale, a spiral equation is used, which is shown below-

$$X_i(t+1) = D * e^{bl} * cos(2\pi l) + X_b(t) \tag{7}$$

where $D = |X_b(t) - X_i(t)|$ indicates the distance of the prey (i.e., best solution) to i'th whale, b is the logarithmic spiral shape constant, l is a random number in $[-1, 1]$.

The Exploration Phase

The exploration phase searches randomly instead of moving towards the current best solution. The position of a search agent is updated respect to a randomly chosen search agent instead of using the best search agent found so far. This strategy is employed when $|A| > 1$, it emphasizes exploration and allow the WOA algorithm to perform a global search. The mathematical model is described as follows:

$$D = C * X_{rand} - X_i \tag{8}$$

$$X_i(t+1) = X_{rand} - A * D \tag{9}$$

where, X_{rand} is the position vector of a randomly chosen search agent.

3.5 Binary Whale Optimization Algorithm (BWOA)

For feature selection, we use a modified version of WOA, called binary WOA (BWOA) [14], that finds the candidate solution with a binary value (i.e., not-selected (0) or selected (1)) of individual genes. We use the S-shaped sigmoid function in each dimension to map the continuous-valued velocity given by Eq. 2 to the range $[0, 1]$, as shown in Eq. 10.

$$sig(v_{id}) = \frac{1}{1 + exp(-v_{id})} \tag{10}$$

The feature (i.e., gene) states in the solutions are changed based on the Eq. 11. For example, the state of the d'th gene in solution i at time t is determined by,

$$x_{id}(t) = \begin{cases} 0 & \text{if } \rho_{id} \geq sig(v_{id}) \\ 1, & \text{otherwise} \end{cases} \tag{11}$$

where ρ_{id} is a random number with uniform distribution within the range of $[0.0, 1.0]$.

3.6   BWOA for Gene Selection

The BWOA optimization process involves several steps, as shown in Fig. 2. The BWOA algorithm initially starts with a set of random solutions. Each solution represents an d-dimensional feature (i.e., gene) set, where $g_i = 1$ means the gene i is selected as a feature, while 0 value means it is not selected (an example provided in Fig. 3). At each iteration, candidate solutions update their positions towards either the best solution obtained so far or a randomly chosen solution. The parameter a is decreased from 2 to 0 to support exploration and exploitation. A random solution is chosen when $|A| \geq 1$, while the current best solution is selected when $|A| < 1$ for updating the position of the candidate solutions. Depending on the value of p, BWOA can switch between either a circular movement or spiral. The BWOA algorithm terminates when the maximum number of iteration is reached. We use 300 as a maximum limit for the iterations.

Optimization Goal
In RRO, the optimization goal of the BWOA is set to identify a gene subset that provides the highest accuracy for cancer classification. The optimization functions of BWOA only consider accuracy to find the best solution; minimizing the number of genes is not considered in the optimization step, as irrelevant and redundant genes are discarded in the earlier phases.

Training and Testing Data Splitting
The SVM classifier is used to assess the accuracy of a candidate solution. We use 90% data for training and the remaining 10% data are used to asses the accuracy of the candidate feature set. The data split is performed randomly and in a stratified fashion. We use the BWOA implementation of [17].

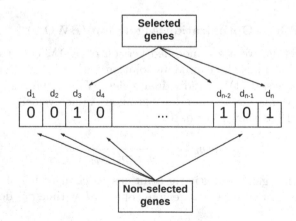

Fig. 3. Representation of a candidate solution of BWOA with a gene set with n number of genes $(d_1, d_2, \ldots, d_n)$

3.7   Classification

In the classification stage, the SVM classifier is utilized for determining the types (or presence) of cancer leveraging the informative genes identified in the feature selection stages. The default parameters settings of scikit-learn [27] implementation of the SVM classifier (with class-balanced weights) are used. The results are reported based on the 10-fold cross-validation.

Table 1. Description of gene expression datasets

No.	Dataset	#Gene	#Sample	Class distribution	Smallest class	Largest class
1	Colon	2000	62	2 (22/40)	35.48%	64.51%
2	CNS	7129	61	2 (21/40)	34.42%	65.58%
3	DLBCL	7128	77	2(19/58)	24.67%	75.32%
4	Leukemia	7129	72	2(25/47)	34.72%	65.27%
5	Lung	12533	181	2(31/150)	17.12%	82.87%
6	Prostate	10509	102	2(50/52)	49.01%	50.98%
7	SRBCT	2308	63	4(8/12/20/23)	12.69%	36.50%
8	Ovarian	15154	253	2 (91/162)	35.96%	64.03%
9	Leukemia-3	7129	72	3 (28/24/20)	27.77%	38.88%
10	Lymphoma	4026	66	3 (9/11/46)	13.63%	69.69%

4   Datasets and Baselines

4.1   Gene Expression Datasets

We report the performance of RRO on ten gene expression benchmark datasets[1,2], shown in Table 1. The datasets represent gene expression profiles of different types of cancers, such as Colon, Central Nerve System (CNS), DLBCL, Leukemia, Lung, Prostate, SRBCT, Ovarian, Leukemia-3 and Lymphoma shown in Table 1.

The Colon dataset is a binary dataset consisting of gene expression profiles of 40 cancerous and 22 normal colon tissues. The CNS dataset comprises 61 examples from two classes. The DLBCL dataset consists of 77 gene expression samples from two classes, DLBCL and Follicular Lymphoma (FL) morphology. In the Leukemia dataset, 25 samples belong to AML and 47 samples belong to ALL. Lung cancer consists of 181 samples, 31 from Malignant Pleural Mesothelioma (MPM) and 150 from Adenocarcinoma (ADCA). The Prostate and SRBCT datasets contain 102 and 63 samples, respectively. The four classes of the SRBCT dataset are neuroblastoma (NB), rhabdomyosarcoma (RMS),

---

[1] https://github.com/kivancguckiran/microarray-data.
[2] http://csse.szu.edu.cn/staff/zhuzx/Datasets.html.

non-Hodgkin lymphoma (NHL), and the Ewing family of tumors (EWS). The three classes of the Lymphoma-3 dataset are DLBCL, FL, and CLL. The Ovarian dataset represents cancer and normal class.

4.2 Performance Metrics

The precision, recall, macro F1 score, accuracy, and the number of genes used are provided to demonstrate the efficacy of the RRO. The recall (R_c), precision (P_c), and F1 score ($F1_c$) of a class c is calculated as follows:

$$R_c = \frac{TP}{TP + FN} \tag{12}$$

$$P_c = \frac{TP}{TP + FP} \tag{13}$$

$$F1_c = \frac{2 * R * P}{R + P} \tag{14}$$

The TP_c, FP_c, FN_c of a class c is defined as follows:

TP_c = Both prediction and true label refer to the same class c
FP_c = Prediction indicates class c, while true label is different (i.e., not class c)
FN_c = Prediction indicates any of the other classes (i.e., non c-class) while true class is c

Finally, the macro F1 score is calculated by taking the average of F1 scores of all the classes.

Besides, the accuracy of RRO is reported in various gene expression datasets to compare it with state-of-the-art methods. The accuracy is defined as follows:

$$Accuracy = \frac{Number\ of\ samples\ correctly\ classified\ \ in\ a\ dataset}{Total\ number\ of\ samples\ present\ in\ the\ dataset}$$

Besides, we investigate the number of genes different methodologies use for classification. The number of genes utilized is a critical indicator of the efficacy of various methods since the fewer number of genes usually makes the results more interpretable and less prone to over-fitting.

Table 2. State-of-the-arts methods

Harmony Search Algorithm (HSA), Markov Blanket (MB), NB [32]
Hidden Markov Models (HMMs), Modified Analytic Hierarchy Process (AHP) [26]
Independent Component Analysis (ICA), Artificial Bee Colony (ABC), NB [8]
Laplacian and Fisher score, Intelligent Dynamic Genetic Algorithm, SVM, KNN, NBY [10]
Information Gain (IG), Standard Genetic Algorithm (SGA), Genetic Programming (GP) [29]
Neighborhood Entropy-based Uncertainty Measures [35]
Adaptive Elastic Net, Conditional Mutual Information (AEN-CMI) [36]
PCA, Correlation and Spectral-based Feature Selection, Genetic Algorithm (GA), SVM, K-NN, RF. [1]
Artificial Bee Colony (ABC), SVM [7]
Minimum Redundancy Maximum Relevancy (MRMR), Bat-inspired Algorithm (BA), SVM [4]
PSO, adaptive K-nn [16]
CFS, improved-Binary PSO (iBPSO), Naive-Bayes (NB) [15]
FF-SVM (FIREFLY FEATURE SELECTION) [3]

4.3   Baseline Methods

The efficacy of RRO is shown by comparing it with thirteen state-of-the-art methods. The summary of each method is provided in Table 2. The comparative performances of RRO and the state-of-the-art methods are shown in terms of accuracy and the number of genes utilized.

5   Results and Discussion

Table 3 shows the precision, recall, F1 score, and accuracy of RRO. Among the 10 datasets, RRO obtains a perfect F1 score of 1.0 in 5 datasets (DLBCL, Leukemia, SRBCT, Lymphoma, and Ovarian). In two datasets, Lung and Prostate, it achieves almost perfect F1 scores (0.994 and 0.990).

Table 3. Precision, Recall and Macro F1 scores of RRO in ten gene expression datasets

No.	Dataset	#Selected genes	Precision	Recall	F1 Score
1	Colon	22	0.933	0.896	0.913
2	CNS	67	0.983	0.988	0.985
3	DLBCL	38	1.0	1.0	1.0
4	Leukemia-2	35	1.0	1.0	1.0
5	Lung	8	0.996	0.992	0.994
6	Prostate	24	0.955	0.975	0.964
7	SRBCT	15	1.0	1.0	1.0
8	Leukemia-3	69	0.992	0.989	0.990
9	Lymphoma	21	1.0	1.0	1.0
10	Ovarian	4	1.0	1.0	1.0

Table 4 shows the comparison results of RRO with thirteen state-of-the-art methods. Both accuracy (Acc.) and the number of genes (#G) used by various methods are provided (except [1,26], which did not report the number of genes utilized). Note that existing works used distinct sets of evaluation datasets in their experiments; thus, they may not have experimental results for all the datasets used in this study (indicated by '-').

The comparisons with the state-of-the-art methods demonstrate that RRO provides better accuracy than most of the existing methodologies. We notice, in several datasets, such as Lung, Ovarian, and SRBCT datasets, RRO achieves the perfect (i.e.,100%) accuracy using less than seven genes. In three other datasets, it also attains 100% accuracy. In other datasets such as Colon, Leukemia-3, and Prostate, it is noticed that RRO shows better performance compared to most of the existing methods; Although, yields a bit less accurate results than [4,15] in Colon and [29] in Prostate datasets, respectively. When the average accuracy is considered, RRO yields better results than other methods (which reported average accuracy) in CNS and Prostate datasets (shown by non-integer values for the number of genes).

The running time could be a limiting factor of the applicability of evolutionary algorithms for feature selection; especially, with the presence of thousands of features in the dataset. RRO utilizes two filter-based approaches in early steps to reduce the feature search space, thus, keeps the running time feasible.

Table 4. The comparison of accuracy and genes utilized by various methods in ten gene expression datasets (bold texts represent highest accuracy in a dataset)

Ref.	Metric	Dataset									
		Colon	CNS	DLBCL	Leu-2	Lung	Prost.	SRBCT	Ovari	Lymph	Leu-3
[36]	Acc	0.89	–	–	0.91	–	–	–	–	–	–
	#G	(25.20)	–	–	(26.85)	–	–	–	–	–	–
[10]	Acc	–	–	**1.0**	**1.0**	–	0.96	**1.0**	–	–	–
	#G	–	–	**(9)**	**(15)**	–	(14)	**(18)**	–	–	–
[26]	Acc	0.89	–	0.99	0.98	–	0.92	–	–	–	–
	#G	–	–	–	–	–	–	–	–	–	–
[8]	Acc	0.92	–	–	0.94	0.84	0.89	–	–	–	0.973
	#G	(4)	–	–	(6)	(4)	(4)	–	–	–	15
[1]	Acc	0.85	0.85	0.98	0.90	0.99	0.99	–	–	–	–
	#G	–	–	–	–	–	–	–	–	–	–
[32]	Acc	0.90	0.84	–	0.99	0.96	–	0.99	1.00	1.00	0.99
	#G	(4.16)	(7.43)	–	(5)	–	–	(8.9)	(5.73)	3.75	5.84
[29]	Acc.	0.85	0.87	0.95	0.97	–	1.0	–	–	–	–
	#G	(60)	(38)	(110)	(3)	–	(26)	–	–	–	–
[35]	Acc	0.84	–	0.93	0.93	0.99	–	0.94	–	–	–
	#G	(3)	–	(11)	(9)	(8)	–	(9)	–	–	–
[6]	Acc	0.92	–	–	–	0.93	0.92	–	–	–	–
	#G	(20)	–	–	–	(8)	(10)	–	–	–	–
[4]	Acc.	0.93	0.94	–	1.0	–	–	1.0	–	–	–
	#G	(8.13)	(19.2)	–	(4.3)	–	–	(12.83)	–	–	–
[16]	Acc	–	–	–	0.97	–	–	0.96	–	–	–
	#G	–	–	–	(2.7)	–	–	(8.5)	–	–	–
[15]	Acc	**0.95**	0.96	–	1.0	1.0	–	1.0	1.00	100	–
	#G	**(4.2)**	(10.5)	–	(4.3)	((6)	–	(34.1)	12	24	–
[3]	Acc	0.93	–	–	0.99	–	–	–	–	–	0.93
	#G	19	–	–	11	–	–	–	–	–	19
[7]	Acc	0.92	–	–	0.92	–	–	–	–	–	0.93
	#G	20	–	–	14	–	–	–	–	–	20
RRO	Acc	0.92	**0.98**	1.0	1.0	1.0	0.98	1.0	1.0	1.0	0.99
(Best)	#G	(41)	**(67)**	**(38)**	**(35)**	**(6)**	(20)	**(15)**	(4)	21	69
RRO	Acc	0.89	0.97	0.98	0.98	0.99	0.96	1.0	0.99	0.99	0.98
(Avg.)	#G	(18.3)	57.6	(27.8)	(32.3)	(9.6)	(25.4)	(24.2)	5.5	18.5	59.5

The efficacy of RRO is shown on datasets of distinct characteristics. We use 2-class, 3-class, and 4-class gene expression datasets (Table 1). Besides, the datasets used in the experiment have distinct class distribution ratios. The results reveal that RRO yields fairly good performances across different types of datasets.

The comparison results reveal that the efficiency of various methods depends on the dataset, the number of genes utilized, and the parameter settings. It is noticed that none of the methods (including the proposed RRO) is constantly better than others.

6   Summary and Conclusions

In this study, a hybrid feature selection framework RRO is proposed for cancer classification. RRO utilizes ANOVA for selecting the initial set of class-discriminative genes. In the subsequent step, redundant genes are eliminated using Kendal's τ correlation. Finally, BWOA and SVM are employed to identify an optimized feature set for classification. It is observed that among the ten gene expression datasets, RRO reaches a perfect F1 score of 1.0 in five datasets. Besides, RRO realizes 100% classification accuracy in six datasets using a varied number of genes. The comparisons with the thirteen state-of-the-art methods on ten microarray datasets demonstrate that RRO exhibits better or comparable performance in terms of classification accuracy and the number of genes utilized. The results demonstrate that RRO is a highly effective approach for feature selection in the microarray dataset. The comparative analysis also reveals that the performances of various feature selection and classification methods are not consistent across datasets. The future work will involve investigating the performance of RRO in other types of gene expression datasets, such as the RNA-Seq dataset.

References

1. Al-Obeidat, F., Tubaishat, A., Shah, B., Halim, Z., et al.: Gene encoder: a feature selection technique through unsupervised deep learning-based clustering for large gene expression data. Neural Comput. Appl. **788**, 1–23 (2020)
2. Alanni, R., Hou, J., Azzawi, H., Xiang, Y.: A novel gene selection algorithm for cancer classification using microarray datasets. BMC Med. Genomics **12**(1), 10 (2019)
3. Almugren, N., Alshamlan, H.: FF-SVM: new firefly-based gene selection algorithm for microarray cancer classification. In: 2019 IEEE Conference on Computational Intelligence in Bioinformatics and Computational Biology (CIBCB), pp. 1–6. IEEE (2019)
4. Alomari, O.A., Khader, A.T., Al-Betar, M.A., Abualigah, L.M.: Gene selection for cancer classification by combining minimum redundancy maximum relevancy and bat-inspired algorithm. Int. J. Data Min. Bioinform. **19**(1), 32–51 (2017)
5. Alshamlan, H., Badr, G., Alohali, Y.: MRMR-ABC: a hybrid gene selection algorithm for cancer classification using microarray gene expression profiling. Biomed. Res. Int. **2015** (2015)
6. Alshamlan, H.M., Badr, G.H., Alohali, Y.A.: Genetic bee colony (GBC) algorithm: a new gene selection method for microarray cancer classification. Comput. Biol. Chem. **56**, 49–60 (2015)

7. Alshamlan, H.M., Badr, G.H., Alohali, Y.A.: ABC-SVM: artificial bee colony and SVM method for microarray gene selection and multi class cancer classification. Int. J. Mach. Learn. Comput. **6**(3), 184 (2016)
8. Aziz, R., Verma, C., Srivastava, N.: A novel approach for dimension reduction of microarray. Comput. Biol. Chem. **71**, 161–169 (2017)
9. Chuang, L.Y., Yang, C.H., Wu, K.C., Yang, C.H.: A hybrid feature selection method for DNA microarray data. Comput. Biol. Med. **41**(4), 228–237 (2011)
10. Dashtban, M., Balafar, M.: Gene selection for microarray cancer classification using a new evolutionary method employing artificial intelligence concepts. Genomics **109**(2), 91–107 (2017)
11. Dudoit, S., Fridlyand, J., Speed, T.P.: Comparison of discrimination methods for the classification of tumors using gene expression data. J. Am. Stat. Assoc. **97**(457), 77–87 (2002)
12. Ferreira, A.J., Figueiredo, M.A.: An unsupervised approach to feature discretization and selection. Pattern Recogn. **45**(9), 3048–3060 (2012)
13. Gao, L., Ye, M., Lu, X., Huang, D.: Hybrid method based on information gain and support vector machine for gene selection in cancer classification. Genomics Proteomics Bioinform **15**(6), 389–395 (2017)
14. Hussien, A.G., Hassanien, A.E., Houssein, E.H., Bhattacharyya, S., Amin, M.: S-shaped binary whale optimization algorithm for feature selection. In: Bhattacharyya, S., Mukherjee, A., Bhaumik, H., Das, S., Yoshida, K. (eds.) Recent Trends in Signal and Image Processing. AISC, vol. 727, pp. 79–87. Springer, Singapore (2019). https://doi.org/10.1007/978-981-10-8863-6_9
15. Jain, I., Jain, V.K., Jain, R.: Correlation feature selection based improved-binary particle swarm optimization for gene selection and cancer classification. Appl. Soft Comput. **62**, 203–215 (2018)
16. Kar, S., Sharma, K.D., Maitra, M.: Gene selection from microarray gene expression data for classification of cancer subgroups employing PSO and adaptive k-nearest neighborhood technique. Expert Syst. Appl. **42**(1), 612–627 (2015)
17. Khurma, R.A., Aljarah, I., Sharieh, A., Mirjalili, S.: EvoloPy-FS: an open-source nature-inspired optimization framework in python for feature selection. In: Mirjalili, S., Faris, H., Aljarah, I. (eds.) Evolutionary Machine Learning Techniques. AIS, pp. 131–173. Springer, Singapore (2020). https://doi.org/10.1007/978-981-32-9990-0_8
18. Lai, C., Reinders, M.J., Wessels, L.: Random subspace method for multivariate feature selection. Pattern Recogn. Lett. **27**(10), 1067–1076 (2006)
19. Lai, C.M., Yeh, W.C., Chang, C.Y.: Gene selection using information gain and improved simplified swarm optimization. Neurocomputing **218**, 331–338 (2016)
20. Lee, C.P., Leu, Y.: A novel hybrid feature selection method for microarray data analysis. Appl. Soft Comput. **11**(1), 208–213 (2011)
21. Liu, H., Setiono, R.: Chi2: feature selection and discretization of numeric attributes. In: Proceedings of 7th IEEE International Conference on Tools with Artificial Intelligence, pp. 388–391. IEEE (1995)
22. Lu, H., Chen, J., Yan, K., Jin, Q., Xue, Y., Gao, Z.: A hybrid feature selection algorithm for gene expression data classification. Neurocomputing **256**, 56–62 (2017)
23. Mirjalili, S., Lewis, A.: The whale optimization algorithm. Adv. Eng. Softw. **95**, 51–67 (2016)
24. Moradi, P., Gholampour, M.: A hybrid particle swarm optimization for feature subset selection by integrating a novel local search strategy. Appl. Soft Comput. **43**, 117–130 (2016)

25. Mundra, P.A., Rajapakse, J.C.: SVM-RFE with MRMR filter for gene selection. IEEE Trans. Nanobiosci. **9**(1), 31–37 (2009)

26. Nguyen, T., Khosravi, A., Creighton, D., Nahavandi, S.: Hidden Markov models for cancer classification using gene expression profiles. Inf. Sci. **316**, 293–307 (2015)

27. Pedregosa, F.: Scikit-learn: machine learning in python. J. Mach. Learn. Res. **12**, 2825–2830 (2011)

28. Peng, H., Long, F., Ding, C.: Feature selection based on mutual information criteria of max-dependency, max-relevance, and min-redundancy. IEEE Trans. Pattern Anal. Mach. Intell. **27**(8), 1226–1238 (2005)

29. Salem, H., Attiya, G., El-Fishawy, N.: Classification of human cancer diseases by gene expression profiles. Appl. Soft Comput. **50**, 124–134 (2017)

30. Sazzed, S.: ANOVA-SRC-BPSO: a hybrid filter and swarm optimization-based method for gene selection and cancer classification using gene expression profiles. In: Proceedings of the Canadian Conference on Artificial Intelligence (2021). https://caiac.pubpub.org/pub/hay53dvq, https://caiac.pubpub.org/pub/hay53dvq

31. Sharbaf, F.V., Mosafer, S., Moattar, M.H.: A hybrid gene selection approach for microarray data classification using cellular learning automata and ant colony optimization. Genomics **107**(6), 231–238 (2016)

32. Shreem, S.S., Abdullah, S., Nazri, M.Z.A.: Hybridising harmony search with a Markov blanket for gene selection problems. Inf. Sci. **258**, 108–121 (2014)

33. Shreem, S.S., Abdullah, S., Nazri, M.Z.A.: Hybrid feature selection algorithm using symmetrical uncertainty and a harmony search algorithm. Int. J. Syst. Sci. **47**(6), 1312–1329 (2016)

34. Shreem, S.S., Abdullah, S., Nazri, M.Z.A., Alzaqebah, M.: Hybridizing RELIEFF, MRMR filters and GA wrapper approaches for gene selection. J. Theor. Appl. Inf. Technol. **46**(2), 1034–1039 (2012)

35. Sun, L., Zhang, X., Qian, Y., Xu, J., Zhang, S.: Feature selection using neighborhood entropy-based uncertainty measures for gene expression data classification. Inf. Sci. **502**, 18–41 (2019)

36. Wang, Y., Yang, X.G., Lu, Y.: Informative gene selection for microarray classification via adaptive elastic net with conditional mutual information. Appl. Math. Model. **71**, 286–297 (2019)

37. Xiaofei, H., Deng, C., Partha, N.: Laplacian score for feature selection. In: Advances in Neural Information Processing Systems, pp. 507–514 (2005)

38. Yassi, M., Moattar, M.H.: Robust and stable feature selection by integrating ranking methods and wrapper technique in genetic data classification. Biochem. Biophys. Res. Commun. **446**(4), 850–856 (2014)

Hand Bone Age Estimation Using Deep Convolutional Neural Networks

Antoine Badi Mame and Jules R. Tapamo(✉)🄳

Discipline of Electrical, Electronic and Computer Engineering, University
of KwaZulu-Natal, Durban 4041, South Africa
tapamoj@ukzn.ac.za

Abstract. Bone age is an indicator of skeletal maturity and is widely
used by doctors to diagnose patients with growth disorders. Bone age
estimation is predominantly determined by a human rater comparing an
X-ray image with a set of standards plates (GP) or a set of stages (TW).
In both methods, the process is tedious and highly error-prone. This
paper presents a novel approach that uses a U-net and a deep convolutional neural network to predict bone age from a hand radiograph. First,
background objects are discarded from an X-ray, which is the combined
with sex information to predict a bone age in months. The proposed
model achieves a mean absolute error of 8.04 months when tested on
1259 X-rays of both sexes, comparable to state-of-the-art performance.

Keywords: Bone age assessment · Machine learning · Convolution
neural networks · Deep learning

1 Introduction

Bone age is a measure of skeletal maturity. During a person's life, from birth to
adulthood, their bones undergo some changes. These changes can be measured
by the degree of ossification in various areas of bone development. The main areas
which change significantly are the primary ossification areas (Epiphysis), and the
secondary ossification areas (Diaphysis) [2]. Since skeletal development ends at
adulthood, at about 19 years of age, bone age is used to estimate chronological
age in infants and young adults.

It is known that clinicians such as pediatricians and endocrinologists use bone
age in diagnosing diseases that affect children's skeletal growth [10]. Discrepancies between a person's chronological age and bone age can indicate retarded
growth or other health issues. Another important use of bone age is to estimate a person's chronological age where supporting documents are lacking. This
makes bone age assessments very useful in parts of the world, such as Europe,
where asylum seekers below the age of 18 years are to be granted special rights
like access to health care and education [2].

Bone age assessment (BAA) is a set of steps followed by a clinician to determine the bone age of an individual from their hand-wrist radiograph. BAA

© Springer Nature Switzerland AG 2022
B. Li et al. (Eds.): ADMA 2021, LNAI 13087, pp. 61–72, 2022.
https://doi.org/10.1007/978-3-030-95405-5_5

is predominantly performed using the Greulich and Pyle (GP) [6] or Tanner-Whitehouse (TW) [16] methods. The GP method compares the X-ray with standard plates found in an Atlas, which represents healthy persons. After comparison, the standard which fits most closely is picked and its age allocated. The TW method is based on a set of numerical scores given to 20 selected regions of interest (ROI) in a hand radiograph. Each numerical score represents the level of maturation of each bone. The scores are later summed up to give a total maturity score, which is correlated with a bone age. The maturity score is given according to the stage of development (lettered A, B, C,..., I), which is detailed in TW.

Recent research has shown that computer vision and machine learning can be used to automate bone age assessment and obtain significant results. In this paper, we present a novel approach to performing bone age assessment that is both simple to implement and achieves state-of-the-art performance.

2   Background and Related Works

An important consideration for automatic BAA is the pre-processing step, which involves enhancing the X-ray and removing background objects. This enables the age prediction model to use the right regions of interest when making predictions. In [5], Giordano et al. propose a method for obtaining skeletal age from X-rays by extracting Epiphysial and Metaphysial Regions of Interest (EMROI). Hand-crafted features are extracted from these regions, and a process similar to TW2 [16] classification is used to determine the bone age. One drawback of this method is that it strongly depends on user input, introducing subjectivity to the process.

More recent solutions treat the whole hand-wrist as a region of interest. An input image is segmented using a classification neural network, which assigns a class (or label) to each pixel in an image. The hand pixels are labeled as one class, and all other pixels are labeled as another class. This allows the removal of background objects from an X-ray image. For instance, in [9], Lee et al. develop a fully automated deep learning system for performing BAA. The system uses deep CNNs to segment a region of interest, and a classification neural network is used to predict bone age.

In [1], a system is developed to provide a second opinion to inexperienced doctors performing BAA. The solution consists of an optimized regression network using residual separable convolutional models that predict a bone age using three modules of the Xception network. It is reported that model's accuracy is limited by the lack of gender information.

More recent implementations of automatic BAA use CNNs alongside fully-connected layers to perform either classification or regression to predict a bone age. Most of these solutions use trained deep CNN architectures like AlexNet [14], GoogLeNet [14], and VGG-16 [13]. These CNNs are pre-trained on a dataset (ImageNet) of images of different classes. They are known to effectively extract discriminative features from biomedical images by applying transfer learning theory [17]. The 2017 Paediatric Bone Age Challenge winning solution [7] uses a pre-trained InceptionV3 [15] network to extract features from an image and three fully-connected layers to predict a bone age.

A common limitation in existing approaches is the limited amount of data, and the race imbalances in the dataset. As noted in [1], sex and ethnicity are significant factors that could improve future deep-learning models.

3   Materials and Methods

Figure 1 gives the proposed BAA approach. The method uses a patient's hand X-ray image and gender information. It starts by pre-processing an X-ray using normalization techniques in image processing. Next, a U-net is used to detect a hand and a vision pipeline is applied to remove background objects from the image. Finally, a pre-trained convolutional neural network predicts a bone age from the pre-processed image and gender. The method's performance is evaluated using mean absolute error, which is a commonly used metric.

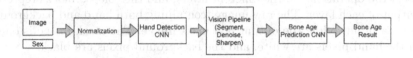

Fig. 1. Proposed method of bone age assessment

3.1   Normalization

Standard X-ray images are supposed to be in grayscale. Therefore, an input image must first be converted to grayscale. Next, the image should be scaled down and then padded with black margins to give it a fixed resolution (i.e., 224×224 pixels). Finally, the image needs to be enhanced because some images appear washed out or have low contrast.

Images are enhanced using Contrast Limited Adaptive Histogram Equalization (CLAHE). Histogram equalization is an image processing technique used to improve the contrast in images by spreading the most frequent intensity values. It allows for areas of lower contrast to gain a higher contrast. CLAHE is a variant of histogram equalization where equalization is applied to small patches or small tiles rather than the entire image.

Let I be an image represented by $M \times N$ matrix of integer pixel intensities, L is the number of possible intensity values, p is the normalized histogram of I. The histogram equalized image g will be defined as

$$g_{i,j} = \left\lfloor (L-1) \sum_{n=0}^{I_{i,j}} p_n \right\rfloor \tag{1}$$

where $n = 0, 1, \ldots, L - 1$, $0 \leq i \leq M$, $0 \leq j \leq N$, and

$$p_n = \frac{\text{number of pixels with intensity n}}{\text{total number of pixels}}$$

3.2 Hand Detection

This step involves the classification of pixels belonging to the hand in an X-ray. Each pixel in the image must be labeled as being either hand or not hand. Pixels that are not hand (or background) are later removed through a bitwise operation. A Convolutional neural networks module can be used for this task because they can capture spatial and temporal dependencies in an image [12]. A U-net is an effective architecture for performing semantic segmentation, and image classification tasks [11]. The architecture consists of a contracting path to capture context and a symmetric expanding path that enables precise localization. The model in Fig. 2 is used to detect hand pixels in an X-ray image. The arrows represent the operations on the different layers, and the colored blocks represent the output of each layer. The raw image (containing both hand and background) is the data input, while the output is a mask image. The mask image is one in which the hand pixels are white, and the background pixels are black.

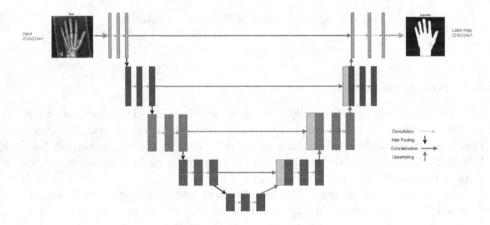

Fig. 2. Hand detection U-Net

The previous step outputs an array of values between 0 and 1. These values must be converted to either 0 or 1 by applying binary thresholding. If the value is greater than 0.5, it is replaced by 1, otherwise, it is set to 0. The result is a mask image. Let I denote an $M \times N$ array output by the CNN module in the hand detection unit. The mask image J obtained is defined as

$$J(x, y) = \begin{cases} 1 & \text{if } I(x, y) \geq 0.5 \\ 0 & \text{otherwise} \end{cases} \tag{2}$$

where $0 \leq x \leq M$ and $0 \leq y \leq N$.

The U-net is trained using an iterative procedure called positive mining [8]. The process begins with annotation, where a handful of X-rays are labeled pixel-by-pixel. Annotation is performed using an online tool from Supervise.ly [3]. Each pixel is labeled as either hand or background, producing a label map containing the class of each pixel. The label maps are then used alongside the original images to train the U-net.

Figure 3 depicts this procedure where a raw image (A) is taken from the dataset and annotated to produce a mask (B). The raw images and masks are then used to train the hand detector (U-net). After training, the model is used to obtain the mask of a test image (C). The model predicts (D), which on visual inspection may contain some incorrectly classified pixels. The mask is then corrected, and this produces the correct mask (E). The mask and raw images are then added to the training data set, and the U-net is trained once more, and the cycle repeats until all training data has been masked.

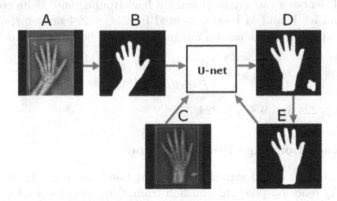

Fig. 3. Training the hand detector using positive mining (adapted from [8])

The network is trained by minimizing the binary cross-entropy for 25 epochs. A call-back function that implements early stopping is used so that if the model does not improve for three consecutive epochs, the training is stopped. The model is evaluated using an accuracy metric and mean intersection over the union. The Accuracy is the number of correct predictions divided by the total number of predictions, given by

$$\text{Accuracy} = \frac{1}{n} \sum_{i=1}^{n} \sum_{x}^{M} \sum_{y}^{N} G_i(x, y) \tag{3}$$

where

$$G_i(x, y) = \begin{cases} 1 & \text{if prediction equals ground truth} \\ 0 & \text{otherwise} \end{cases}$$

Intersection over union (IoU) measures the degree of overlap between the predicted and true masks. It is calculated by finding the true positives, false positives and false negatives, then the average of IoU is defined as

$$\text{Average(IoU)} = \frac{1}{n} \sum_i^n \frac{\text{TP}_i}{\text{TP}_i + \text{FP}_i + \text{TN}_i} \tag{4}$$

where $\text{TP}_i, \text{FP}_i, \text{TN}_i$ are numbers of True positives, False positives, and False negatives for the ith prediction, respectively.

3.3   Vision Pipeline

The vision pipeline is a series of steps which completes the pre-processing of an X-ray image. First the mask and the X-ray are combined through a bitwise operation. Thereafter, denoising and sharpening operations are applied to the X-ray. Let R denote a raw image (having a background) and M its corresponding mask, and let R and M be represented by 224×224 arrays, the following operation is applied to produce an image J (without background), defined as

$$J(x, y) = \begin{cases} 0 & \text{if } M(x, y) = 0 \\ R(x, y) & \text{if } M(x, y) = 1 \end{cases} \tag{5}$$

where $0 \leq x \leq 224$ and $0 \leq y \leq 224$.

3.4   Proposed Bone Age Prediction Model

Two deep networks are designed to perform bone age predictions. The first network (M1) relies on pixel information from X-ray images, while the second network (M2) relies on both pixel and sex information. M1 is constructed with an input layer that receives a 3-channel image that feeds into an InceptionV3 network. The InceptionV3 network produces a 3-dimensional array, which passes through a global average pooling layer reducing the dimensionality to a linear array. The linear array then goes through two fully connected layers and an output layer. The output layer uses the rectifier linear unit (ReLU) activation function to give a bone age in months. Figure 4(a) gives the structure of the first network (M1). The second network (M2) is designed similarly to the first with a sex input, a fully connected layer, and a concatenation layer. As shown in Fig. 4(b), the sex input is a single value passed to a fully-connection layer of 16 neurons then concatenated with the output of the global average pooling layer. The rest of the network is the same as M1.

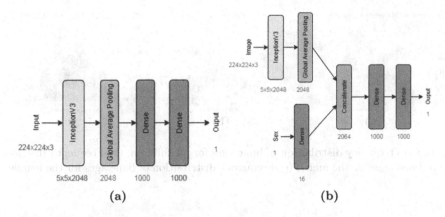

Fig. 4. (a) Network structure for M1, (b) Network structure for M2.

Transfer learning is used during the training process, where pre-trained weights from ImageNet are loaded into the InceptionV3 network. The network layers are unlocked from the top (output layer) to bottom (input layer), thus fine-tuning the network to learn features of bone age development. Then the rest of the layers shown in Fig. 4(b) are added. Then, the model is trained with learning rate of 0.0001, batch size of 16 and 20% of the data is used for validation after each epoch. One of the challenges faced during training is overfitting, which is addresssed by changing the learning rate and increasing the number of images used for training.

The proposed model is evaluated using the mean absolute error (MAE) metric. MAE (see Eq. 6) measures the average of magnitude of the difference between predicted bone age (y_i) and the true bone age ($\hat{y}_i$) for all the examples in the test set.

$$\text{MAE} = \frac{1}{n} \sum_{i}^{n} |y_i - \hat{y}_i| \tag{6}$$

3.5   Dataset

Dataset is the most crucial part of machine learning because the model's performance depends on the dataset's quality. The data used for this research is obtained from the Radiological Society of North America (RSNA) Challenge of 2017. The training dataset contained 11328 examples, while 1259 examples are used for testing, each example made of up an image file, a sex value, and a bone age in months. The gender distribution is as follows: 6100 males and 5228 females. After inspection, 24 images are discarded because they are either very blurred or did not contain a left-hand X-ray. Figure 5(a), 5(b), and 5(c) give the frequency distributions for all children, for males only and females, respectively. Most of the samples have bone ages between 70 and 180 months, which is the pre-adolescent period.

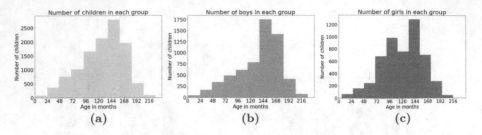

Number of children in each group   Number of boys in each group   Number of girls in each group

(a)   (b)   (c)

Fig. 5. (a) Frequency distribution of bone ages for all children, (b) Frequency distribution of bone ages for the males, (c) Frequency distribution of bone ages for the females.

Typical images found in the dataset are shown in Fig. 6. The images generally contain a left hand wrist on a black background, with lead marks holding the initials of the radiologist. Some images like no. 13 have low contrast, making it difficult to see the flesh and bones distinctly. Also, though most hands are upright, some are tilted like no. 21. A few images like no. 11 have colors inverted, i.e., white background with black bones. The images also vary in width and length.

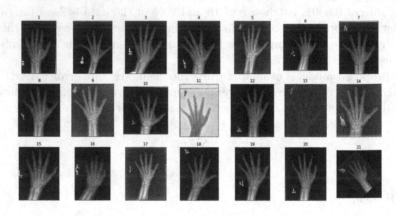

Fig. 6. Typical images in the RSNA dataset

4   Experimental Results and Discussion

The dataset used to train the models contains 12611 examples (each example comprising an image, sex, and bone age in months). After inspection, some images need to be discarded because they are either blurred, do not contain a left hand, or contain a different body part. All images are pre-processed by resizing them into square images with dimensions 224 × 224 and applying a contrast equalization filter. As a result, the dataset's storage size is reduced from 9 GB to under 300 MB. This pre-processing step speeds up the loading and training process without compromising on pixel data.

Using the smart annotation tool from Supervisely [3] we generate label maps from each X-ray at 100 X-rays per hour, which is faster than manual annotation. Also, the data augmentation tools from Supervise.ly allow us to generate 2200 images and corresponding label maps, which are used to train the hand detection U-net. After growing the training dataset to 3194 examples through data mining (discussed earlier), the U-net gives predictions with an accuracy of 0.9803 and a mean intersection over the union of 0.9537. These results are comparable to those obtained in [8], in which a similar training method is used.

After constructing the U-net, it is used to make predictions for masks for the remainder of the X-rays. The masks generated by the U-net are saved to the hard drive and then manually corrected if required. After annotation, each X-ray is segmented by combining it with its mask, and then the pre-processing is finalized. Figure 7 shows the result of the segmentation of a X-ray image; the first row shows some resized and enhanced images, the second row gives the masks generated through data mining and the third row gives the segmented X-ray, having a hand on a black background.

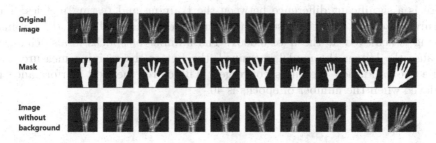

Fig. 7. Quality assessment of pre-processed images

After background removal (through segmentation), all the X-rays are used to train the age regression models. The model (M2), which uses sex input alongside image input, gives the highest performance with a mean absolute error of 8.04, 8.11, and 7.97 months on all sexes, male and female test cohorts. The model (M1), which uses only image input, performed lesser, with a MAE of 10.43, 10.93 and 9.80 months on all sexes, males, and female cohorts. The performance for M2 is comparable to the results obtained by Iglovikov et al. [8] in their regression solution, achieving MAE of 8.08, 6.67, and 7.12 months on all sexes, males and female cohorts, respectively. Figure 8 shows the MAE performance of all three models, showing that M2 gives similar results to the BAA model proposed in [8] when tested on all sexes. Since M1 and M2 are trained and tested under similar conditions, the difference in performance suggests that sex information is a helpful factor for improving the accuracy of bone age predictions.

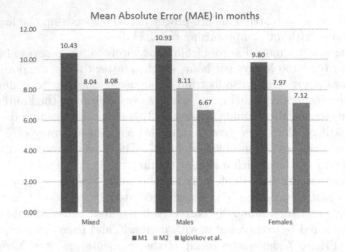

Fig. 8. Evaluation of models

During training, a high amount of overfitting is seen in both models since there is a significant difference between the training and testing metrics. The learning rate (lr) is initially set to 0.01 and then decreased until the optimal setting is achieved at the lr of 0.0001. The number of epochs is also changed because the longer the model is trained, the better the training measures are while the validation measures converged. Therefore, the best performance is achieved when the number of epochs is 40.

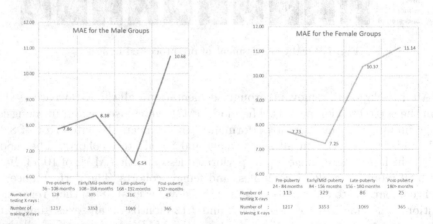

(a) MAE results on the males cohorts   (b) MAE results on the females cohorts

Fig. 9. MAE results per gender.

We further evaluate our solution on age groups: infancy, toddlers, pre-puberty, early/mid-puberty, late-puberty, and post-puberty. These groups are formed based on significant differences in skeletal maturity from one group to the following [4]. Each group is again divided into male and female cohorts since their boundaries are different for each sex. Four cohorts (infancy and toddlers for both sexes) are excluded from the tests because they have too few examples (less than 20 examples per cohort).

As shown in Fig. 9(a), the best performing male group is Late-puberty, giving a MAE of 6.54 months. On the other hand, the best performing female group is Early/Mid-puberty, giving a MAE of 7.25 months. Iglovikov et al. obtained similar results for the males, showing that the best performance is obtained in the Late puberty group. However, for the females, our results do not agree. Overall, we note that the groups with over 1000 training examples give better results, with MAEs in the range from 7 to 8 months (rounded to the nearest integer). The examples which have less than 1000 training examples performed with MAEs above 11 months. This suggests that an imbalance in age distribution caused an uneven performance of the model across age groups. However, the number of examples used during testing is too small to draw firm conclusions.

Finally, we picked individual X-rays from each test group and compared their rated bone age against the predicted value. In Fig. 9(b), we observe that the predictions are within a year (12 months) of the ground truth. Overall, the best prediction is made with an error of 2 months, while the worst prediction is made with an error of 9 months.

5 Conclusion

In this paper, a fully automated deep learning system for hand bone age assessment is proposed. When tested on 1259 new examples, the proposed bone age model gives a mean absolute error of 8.04 months on all predictions. The U-net is able to detect hand pixels in an X-ray with a mean intersection of over the union of 0.98 when evaluated on 3914 images. Results show that the performances of both models are comparable to state-of-the-art solutions for automatic BAA using deep neural networks. The model performs better when predicting certain age groups than others because of the number of training examples in each age group.

References

1. Chen, X., Li, J., Zhang, Y., Lu, Y., Liu, S.: Automatic feature extraction in x-ray image based on deep learning approach for determination of bone age. Future Gener. Comput. Syst. **110**, 795–801 (2020)
2. Dallora, A.L., Anderberg, P., Kvist, O., Mendes, E., Diaz Ruiz, S., Sanmartin Berglund, J.: Bone age assessment with various machine learning techniques: a systematic literature review and meta-analysis. PloS one **14**(7), e0220242 (2019)
3. Drozdov, D.: What's supervisely (2020). Accessed Dec 2020, https://docs.supervise.ly/

4. Gilsanz, V., Ratib, O.: Hand Bone Age: A Digital Atlas of Skeletal Maturity. Springer, Heidelberg (2005). https://doi.org/10.1007/b138568
5. Giordano, D., Leonardi, R., Maiorana, F., Scarciofalo, G., Spampinato, C.: Epiphysis and metaphysis extraction and classification by adaptive thresholding and dog filtering for automated skeletal bone age analysis. In: 2007 29th Annual International Conference of the IEEE Engineering in Medicine and Biology Society pp. 6551–6556. IEEE (2007)
6. Greulich, W.W., Pyle, S.I.: Radiographic Atlas of Skeletal Development of the Hand and Wrist. Stanford University Press, Palo Alto (1959)
7. Halabi, S.S., et al.: The RSNA pediatric bone age machine learning challenge. Radiology **290**(2), 498–503 (2019)
8. Iglovikov, V.I., Rakhlin, A., Kalinin, A.A., Shvets, A.A.: Paediatric bone age assessment using deep convolutional neural networks. In: Stoyanov, D., et al. (eds.) DLMIA/ML-CDS -2018. LNCS, vol. 11045, pp. 300–308. Springer, Cham (2018). https://doi.org/10.1007/978-3-030-00889-5_34
9. Lee, H.: Fully automated deep learning system for bone age assessment. J. Dig. Imaging **30**(4), 427–441 (2017)
10. Mughal, A.M., Hassan, N., Ahmed, A.: Bone age assessment methods: a critical review. Pak. J. Med. Sci. **30**(1), 211 (2014)
11. Ronneberger, O., Fischer, P., Brox, T.: U-Net: convolutional networks for biomedical image segmentation. In: Navab, N., Hornegger, J., Wells, W.M., Frangi, A.F. (eds.) MICCAI 2015. LNCS, vol. 9351, pp. 234–241. Springer, Cham (2015). https://doi.org/10.1007/978-3-319-24574-4_28
12. Saha, S.: A comprehensive guide to convolutional neural networks-the eli5 way (2020). Accessed 15 Dec 2018, https://towardsdatascience.com/a-comprehensive-guide-to-convolutionalneural-networks-the-eli5-way-3bd2b1164a53
13. Simonyan, K., Zisserman, A.: Very deep convolutional networks for large-scale image recognition. arXiv preprint arXiv:1409.1556 (2014)
14. Szegedy, C., et al.: Going deeper with convolutions. In: Proceedings of the IEEE Conference on Computer Vision and Pattern Recognition, pp. 1–9 (2015)
15. Szegedy, C., Vanhoucke, V., Ioffe, S., Shlens, J., Wojna, Z.: Rethinking the inception architecture for computer vision. In: Proceedings of the IEEE Conference on Computer Vision and Pattern Recognition, pp. 2818–2826 (2016)
16. Tanner, J.M., Whitehouse, R., Cameron, N., Marshall, W., Healy, M., Goldstein, H., et al.: Assessment of skeletal maturity and prediction of adult height (TW2 method). WB Saunders London (2001)
17. Yosinski, J., Clune, J., Bengio, Y., Lipson, H.: How transferable are features in deep neural networks? arXiv preprint arXiv:1411.1792 (2014)

An Interpretable Machine Learning Approach for Predicting Hospital Length of Stay and Readmission

Yuxi Liu$^{(\boxtimes)}$ ⓘ and Shaowen Qin ⓘ

College of Science and Engineering, Flinders University, Tonsley, SA 5042, Australia
{liu1356,shaowen.qin}@flinders.edu.au

Abstract. Length of stay (LOS) and risk of readmission of patients are critical indicators of the quality and operation efficiency of hospitals. Various machine learning (ML) approaches have been applied to predict a patient's hospital LOS and risk of readmission, but those with more accurate predictions are often the so called 'black-box' approaches. This study aims to add interpretability in predicting LOS and the risk of readmission in 30-day among all-cause patients admitted through the emergency department (ED) while improving the accuracy and parsimony of the ML approach. Several state-of-the-art ML models were applied to our prediction tasks and their predictive power reported and compared. The CatBoost model outperformed the rest, hence is chosen as the baseline for this study. For interpretability, we introduced Shapley values and analyzed, at both aggregated and individual levels, the prediction results from the CatBoost model. Lower dimension models were further developed following the guidance of Shapley values. Our results show that the lower dimension model can robustly predict hospital LOS and risk of readmission, indicating that Shapley values are not only useful for adding model interpretability, but also effective for creating a lower-dimensional model amenable to implementation.

Keywords: Machine learning · Interpretability · Emergency department · Readmission · Length of stay

1 Introduction

ED crowding continues to be a challenging healthcare issue in large government-funded hospitals [1]. Significant research efforts towards resolving this issue can be found in the literature. In addition to recognizing the increased demand for healthcare services associated with the changing demographics of modern societies, attention has been paid to analyze hospital resource utilization with the aim to improve its operational efficiency. One longitudinal study found that ED crowding was correlated to increased hospital admission of return ED visitors [2]. Moreover, [3] was found that increased LOS is both the cause and the result of ED crowding. Further, the prolonged LOS and increase in readmission both

© Springer Nature Switzerland AG 2022
B. Li et al. (Eds.): ADMA 2021, LNAI 13087, pp. 73–85, 2022.
https://doi.org/10.1007/978-3-030-95405-5_6

have a significant impact on patients' experience as well as the performance of healthcare providers [4] and [5]. Therefore, patients' LOS and readmission rates have been considered as vital indicators for assessing a hospital's operation capacity and efficiency in the Council of Australian Governments (COAG) [6] and US Medical Center (Medicare and Medicaid Services) [7].

Increased availability of electronic health records (EHRs) offers an unprecedented opportunity for both exploration and development of data-driven solutions to advance healthcare [8]. In developing predictive models, ML techniques have been established recently as the most widely used approach and proving invaluable across disciplines. As a result, research on the LOS and readmission predictions has seen a renewed interest due to increased availability of data and ML techniques. For healthcare providers, predictive tools based on ML algorithms can be employed in hospital management. Two of the most common algorithms for predicting LOS and risk of readmission are logistic regression and Naive Bayes [9–12].

Although standard ML algorithms have achieved a certain level of success in terms of their predictive power, such simplistic models cannot account for the complicated interactions among clinical characteristics, demographic baseline information, and experiences of healthcare providers [13]. To tackle these issues, several previous studies have applied more complicated algorithms such as support vector machines (SVM) [14], random forests (RF), gradient boosting trees (GBM) (such as Adaboost [15] and XGBoost [16]), and deep neural networks (DNN) [17]. Although GBM and DNN are quite robust for predictive modeling [18], both models have demonstrated poor or even non-applicable interpretability in predicting the LOS and readmission to date. A major drawback of GBM and DNN is the lack of transparency and interpretability to healthcare providers (clinicians/medical experts). Healthcare providers expect the proposed algorithms to include the clinically relevant variables in a more explicit manner so that the final predictive model makes logical sense, leads to new insights and practices. Rather than supplanting human inputs completely, interpretable ML algorithms can be used as a supporting tool to help clinicians making better decisions. A ML algorithm would be considered more desirable when it makes understandable predictions by identifying the relative importance of clinically relevant variables and their contributions.

In this paper, we conducted two case studies on the predictions of inpatient LOS and 30-day readmission rates, using a patient journey dataset from a metropolitan hospital in Australia. Building on recent advances and emerging analytical opportunities, we first applied several state-of-the-art ML models to train on demographics and clinical characteristics. The CatBoost model [19] consistently outperforms most of the other ML baselines. However, as a black box ML model, CatBoost does not offer interpretability. We then looked into interpretations at aggregated and individual levels by employing Shapley values [20]. All suboptimal features were estimated and interpreted by using the Shapley values as well. Lastly, we reselected the impactful features based on parsimony, accuracy, and interpretability and built low-dimensional models. We reported the predictive power of each model for LOS and 30-day risk of readmission.

2   Methods

Data. The patient flow data set being used is the administrative part of the EHRs from the Hospital for the whole of 2018 and 2019. It contains demographic, admission (emergency or elective, location of care and treating clinical team) and discharge data, and detailed diagnostic information. It also contains time and location stamp information that records every occasion a patient was moved between locations within the hospital. Ethics approval was obtained for access to the dataset.

Study Design: Hospital LOS and 30-Day Risk of Readmission. In the dataset, each admitted patient is assigned a unique URN (patient ID). Multiple admissions (e.g., readmissions) of a patient are identified by the same URN. We examined the number of days between the current admission and the previous discharge for a given patient and checked if it is less than 30 days. For LOS, our data contains inpatient days for a given patient. The goal of the two case studies is to learn variables from given data and predict the class label Y. For LOS, the class label Y is LOS in days. For readmission prediction, the class label Y is likely to be readmitted within 30-day (=1) vs not likely to be readmitted within 30-day (=0).

Data Preprocessing. To learn the common patient behaviors, we selected disease codes with more than 100 visits from the dataset, which included 181 diseases and 61264 rows of data (about 83% of the total data). Patient features were organized into two sets: (i) Demographics characteristics; (ii) Clinical characteristics, as shown in Table 1. Moreover, we utilized the undersampling approach [21] to address the label imbalance problem.

Clinical Characteristics. The admission date was divided into two parts, including the day of a week and the time of a day. Specifically, the week includes seven categories: Monday-Sunday; the time of a day is divided into three categories: 10 pm − 2 am (2 h before and after midnight), 2:00 am ≤ − 12 noon, and 12 noon ≤ − 10 pm.

ARDRG6 (Australian Refined Diagnosis Related Groups Version 6.0) [22] is a collection of diagnosis codes. Additionally, our EHRs data also includes the description of comorbidity diseases or complexity of patients (described by DRG feature). Motivated by [23], we categorized the DRG feature into seven subgroups as follows: Cat1: comorbidity complication; Cat2: catastrophic or severe comorbidity complication; Cat3: catastrophic or severe; Cat4: without comorbidity complication; Cat5: without catastrophic or severe; Cat6: minor complexity;

Cat7: major complexity. The aim is to fully utilize all the comorbidity and complexity of patients because these information may have impacts on the final prediction.

Table 1. Overview of the feature groups

Demographic characteristics
AGE
SEX
USUALACCOM (Type of usual accommodation)
RACF (Residential aged care facilities)
ATSI (Aboriginal and torres strait islander)
Clinical characteristics
SAAS (Arrival mode: ambulance or not)
PRIORITY (Emergency severity index)
AREA
TIME
WEEKDAY
FIRST_BED
UNIT
DIVISION
ED_HOURS
OUTCOME
FINAL_WARD
FINAL_UNIT
NOS (Nature of separation)
IP_DAYS (Length of stay)
ARDRG6 (Australian Refined Diagnosis Related Groups Version 6.0)
DRG (the description of comorbidity diseases or complexity of patients)

Feature Selection. This study identified determining features to build two low-dimensional models based on parsimony, accuracy, and interpretability. Parsimony means the use of a small number of variables. Accuracy means the best prediction performance based on the selected features. Interpretability means that healthcare providers can clearly understand the contributions of selected features. Unlike automated feature extraction such as principle component analysis (PCA) and autoencoder-based methods, we used Shapley values to represent feature interpretability [20], meaning that the selected features can provide direct information (e.g., importance score) about the specific prediction, which would allow clinicians to understand the predictions made by ML-based systems.

Specifically, we first obtained the best prediction performance from 100 training iterations of the full feature CatBoost model. We then selected the features based on the Shapley values. Thirdly, we estimated the average information gain [24] for each feature based on the corresponding training iterations. Lastly, we trained two lower dimensional CatBoost models and used two subsets of features with high information gain to test whether the model can robustly predict the hospital LOS and readmission rate as a full model.

Predictive Modeling. A tree ensemble model such as random forests and GBM may be well suited than a linear model because EHRs data usually involves a large number of categorical variables and nonlinear combinations. We employed CatBoost, a branch model from the GBM family, as the predictive model. To overcome the problem of model overfitting, we used training, validation, and testing sets and practiced early stopping at 200 iterations. We divided the cohort of admission patients into three groups for study: 80% for model training, 10% for testing, and 10% for validation. Moreover, we also used the Bayesian hyperparameter optimization, as available in the Python package hyperopt [25], to select hyperparameters for the main predictive targets. To evaluate model performance, we applied several state-of-the-art methods such as logistic regression and DNN to the same dataset. Lastly, we conducted ten-fold cross-validation to generate confidence intervals.

Model Interpretation. As mentioned earlier, such complicated models (e.g., random forests and GBM in particular) are difficult to provide interpretability outputs. The SHAP packages (https://github.com/slundberg/shap) provide utilities for computing Shapley values for ML algorithms and optimize algorithms hyperparameters. The core idea of Shapley value stems from the classical game theory and is the only additive feature attribution method that yields local accuracy, consistency, and allowance for missingness. It can provide interpretability at aggregated and local levels. At the aggregated level, it examines the average contribution of a given feature to the model output. At the local level, it examines the most important variables for a given prediction. Further, it can also examine the interactions between variables.

Performance Evaluation. The root mean square error (RMSE) is used to evaluate the numeric outcomes (regression outcome: LOS in days). The area under the receiver operating characteristic curve (AUROC), F1 score, Brier score loss (BSL), and other metrics are used to evaluate the binary outcomes (at risk for readmission or not). All analyses were carried out using ScikitLearn v0.24.1 and Python v3.7.0.

3   Results and Discussion

Prediction Results. The results obtained from the predictive models are summarized in Table 2. As can be seen from Table 2, the CatBoost significantly outperforms other ML models for the same tasks. Specifically, the LOS was predicted with the RMSE of 3.1225, and one standard deviation of 0.207. A low-dimensional CatBoost built on AGE, DIVISION, ED_HOURS, OUTCOME, FINAL_UNIT, NOS, ARDRG6, and DRG yielded the RMSE of 3.1265, and one standard deviation of 0.194. Thirty-day risk of readmission was predicted with a ROC AUC of 0.8516, and one standard deviation of 0.010. The average precision was 0.8431. The BSL was 0.1559. A low-dimensional CatBoost built on AGE, USUALACCOM, ED_HOURS, FINAL_UNIT, NOS, and ARDRG6 yielded the AUC of 0.8497, and one standard deviation of 0.010. The average precision was 0.8406. The BSL was 0.1568.

Table 2. Performance of predictive models

Algorithm	RMSE	ROC AUC	Average precision	Precision
Catboost	3.1225(0.207)	0.8516(0.010)	0.8431(0.011)	0.7748(0.013)
Generalized linear model	3.9346(0.232)	0.7593(0.012)	0.7240(0.016)	0.6881(0.014)
Support vector machine	3.9721(0.241)	0.7565(0.012)	0.7223(0.017)	0.6677(0.013)
Random forest	3.9435(0.231)	0.8209(0.011)	0.7958(0.014)	0.7443(0.015)
Deep neural network	3.5482(0.222)	0.7776(0.014)	0.7461(0.018)	0.6971(0.036)
Adaboost	17.0006(3.528)	0.8158(0.011)	0.7930(0.014)	0.7361(0.014)
Explainable boosting machine	3.2103(0.220)	0.8319(0.010)	0.8123(0.014)	0.7528(0.014)
Algorithm	Recall	Accuracy	F1 score	BSL
Catboost	0.7476(0.016)	0.7759(0.010)	0.7608(0.011)	0.1559(0.005)
Generalized linear model	0.6909(0.019)	0.7031(0.012)	0.6894(0.014)	0.1996(0.005)
Support vector machine	0.7257(0.018)	0.6968(0.012)	0.6954(0.013)	0.2003(0.005)
Random forest	0.7364(0.017)	0.7535(0.012)	0.7402(0.013)	0.1723(0.005)
Deep neural network	0.6933(0.094)	0.7059(0.017)	0.6893(0.038)	0.1963(0.009)
Adaboost	0.7291(0.018)	0.7460(0.012)	0.7325(0.013)	0.2463(0.000)
Explainable boosting machine	0.7457(0.016)	0.7618(0.011)	0.7492(0.012)	0.1664(0.005)
Algorithm	RMSE	ROC AUC	Average precision	Precision
Catboost (low-dimensional)	3.1265(0.194)	0.8497(0.010)	0.8406(0.011)	0.7752(0.014)
Algorithm	Recall	Accuracy	F1 Score	BSL
Catboost (low-dimensional)	0.7469(0.015)	0.7759(0.010)	0.7607(0.011)	0.1568(0.005)

Aggregated Level Interpretability. Figures 1 and 2 present the distribution of the impacts of each feature on the model output. For numeric features, the red color represents the variables with larger contributions and blue for ones with smaller contributions. Positive Shapley values (extending to the right) show an increased probability of increasing LOS and readmission risk. Negative Shapley values (extending to the left) show a decreased probability of reducing LOS and readmission risk. For categorical features, the grey shadow represents specific possible values such as ARGRG6 (diagnosis code). A certain diagnosis can significantly increase or decrease the model's output.

The observation to emerge from the data comparison was the difference in the importance of demographic features in Figs. 1 and 2. Comparatively, demographic characteristics such as age, usualaccom, and sex have a relatively high ranking in 30-day readmission. Obviously, age was observed to be the most impactful feature in 30-day readmission. Specifically, the advanced age increases the likelihood of readmission (Shapley value between 0 and 0.75), while young age tends toward a Shapley value between roughly 0.5 and 0, corresponding to reduced probability. Figures 1 and 2 show that extended ED hours increases LOS and the likelihood of readmission, while shorter ED hours reduces LOS and the likelihood of readmission.

Local Level Interpretability. Figures 3, 4, 5 and 6 show the relative importance of all variables incorporated in the CatBoost model using Shapley values. For ease of visualization, we present only the most important variables in these figures, but other variables can be queried from the model results. For LOS, the predicted value is LOS in days, and the baseline value is the predicted mean value. For readmission, the predicted value is a probability, and the baseline value is the predicted mean probability.

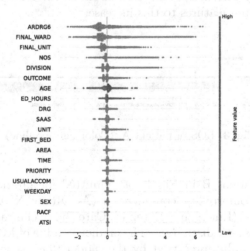

Fig. 1. The most impactful features for LOS prediction based on Shapley value. (Color figure online)

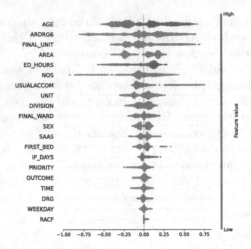

Fig. 2. The most impactful features for 30-day readmission prediction based on Shapley value. (Color figure online)

For example, patient A in Fig. 3 was admitted for kidney and urinary tract disease with catastrophic or severe (ARDRG6: L67A), his NOS is 7 (other hospital-down transfer). The predicted value of LOS (13.15) was five times the baseline value (2.5). The size of the red bars shows the relative amount of contributions of the listed features to this increase.

Fig. 3. LOS of patient A. (Color figure online)

For example, patient B in Fig. 4 was admitted for injuries without catastrophic or severe comorbidity complication (ARDRG6: X60B), clinical ward (final ward) is EECU (Emergency Extended Care Unit), clinical division is emergency, and NOS is 8 (self-discharge). The predicted value of LOS (0.17) was well below the baseline value predicted by the model (2.8). The major contributors to this low value were the diagnosis, followed by the nature of the clinical ward, and finally by the clinical division and NOS. The most interesting aspect of patient B is his NOS, which is self-discharge without following the doctors advice. Apparently, self-discharge is causally associated with short LOS.

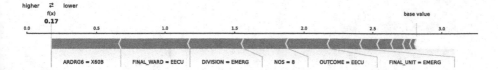

Fig. 4. LOS of patient B.

For example, patient C in Fig. 5 was admitted for heart failure and shock without catastrophic comorbidity complication (ARDRG6: F62B). The predicted probability of 30-day readmission was 0.85, higher than the baseline value (≈0.5). The size of the red bars shows the relative amount of contributions of the listed features to this increase.

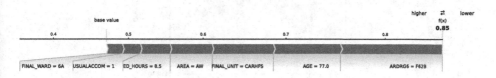

Fig. 5. 30-day readmission risk of patient C. (Color figure online)

For example, patient D in Fig. 6 was admitted for syncope and collapse without catastrophic or severe comorbidity complication (ARDRG6: F73B). The model predicted the patient 30-day readmission probability is 0.21, which is about half of the baseline prediction. The major contributor to this low probability was the relatively young age followed by relatively short ED hours.

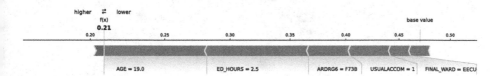

Fig. 6. 30-day readmission risk of patient D.

Variable Interactions. For each task, we give two examples of variable interactions. Specifically, the SHAP algorithm can automatically calculate the interactions of any two variables. The results obtained from the calculation of the SHAP algorithm are displayed in Figs. 7 and 8. The positive and negative Shapley values represent the forces that drove an increase or decrease from the average prediction. For ease of visualization, we show only the top ten subcategories based on their proportions.

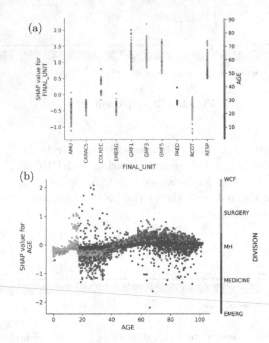

Fig. 7. Sample Shapley value based variable interaction diagrams for LOS prediction. a): the interaction between age and final unit; b): the interaction between division and age.

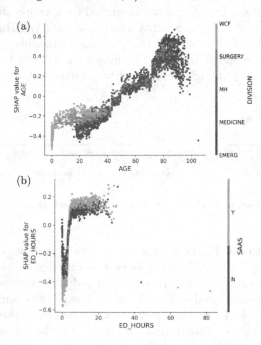

Fig. 8. Sample Shapley value based variable interaction diagrams for 30-day readmission. a): the interaction between division and age; b): the interaction between saas and ED hours.

In Fig. 7a, the color bar represents AGE. For FINAL UNIT, a certain number of subcategories have decreased the average LOS, such as AMU, CARACS, EMERG, PAED, and RCOT. Contrastively, COLREC, GLM1, GLM13, GLM15, and RESP have increased the average LOS. PAED is only involved with young patients. The elderly patients have mainly focused on RCOT, GLM1, GLM3, and GLM5. For RESP, the older the age, the greater the LOS. In Fig. 7b, the color bar represents DIVISION. Most of the young patients were focused on WCF and SURGERY. With the increase of age, patients tend to focus on MEDICINE and EMERG. Moreover, there is no clear indication that age has a significant positive or negative effect on the average LOS.

In Fig. 8a, the color bar represents DIVISION. The elderly patients are focused on MEDICINE and EMERG. The older the patient, the higher the probability of readmission. The young patients are most seen in the WCF and SURGERY. Most of the younger patients have less than average readmission probability. In Fig. 8b, the color bar represents SAAS. Most Y category (the arrival mode is ambulance) patients have an above-average value probability for readmission. The larger the ED HOURS, the greater the readmission probability.

4 Conclusion

In this paper, we generate an interpretable ML model, which not only reliably predicts a patient's LOS and probability of 30-day readmission, but also offers insight as to what features contribute the most to a prediction. The key lies in using Shapley values to evaluate the impact of each feature on prediction outcomes. By selecting the impactful features with a balanced consideration of parsimony, accuracy, and interpretability, we were able to train lower-dimension models that can robustly predict patient's hospital LOS and risk of readmission. These findings confirm the benefit of interpretable ML in healthcare data analysis and provide a basis for further research.

References

1. Morley, C., Unwin, M., Peterson, G.M., Stankovich, J., Kinsman, L.: Emergency department crowding: a systematic review of causes, consequences and solutions. PloS one **13**(8), e0203316 (2018)
2. Jo, S., et al.: Emergency department crowding is associated with 28-day mortality in community-acquired pneumonia patients. J. Infect. **64**(3), 268–275 (2012)
3. Chaou, C.H., et al.: Predicting length of stay among patients discharged from the emergency department-using an accelerated failure time model. PloS one **12**(1), e0165756 (2017)
4. Baek, H., Cho, M., Kim, S., Hwang, H., Song, M., Yoo, S.: Analysis of length of hospital stay using electronic health records: a statistical and data mining approach. PloS one **13**(4), e0195901 (2018)
5. Upadhyay, S., Stephenson, A.L., Smith, D.G.: Readmission rates and their impact on hospital financial performance: a study of Washington hospitals. INQUIRY J. Health Care Organ. Provision Finan. **56**, 0046958019860386 (2019)

6. Authority, N.H.P.: Hospital performance: length of stay in public hospitals in 2011–12 (2013)
7. CMS: Hospital readmissions reduction program (HRRP). https://www.cms.gov/Medicare/Medicare-Fee-for-Service-Payment/AcuteInpatientPPS/Readmissions-Reduction-Program, Accessed 4 July 2021
8. Wiens, J., Shenoy, E.S.: Machine learning for healthcare: on the verge of a major shift in healthcare epidemiology. Clin. Infect. Dis. **66**(1), 149–153 (2017). https://doi.org/10.1093/cid/cix731
9. Peck, J.S., Benneyan, J.C., Nightingale, D.J., Gaehde, S.A.: Predicting emergency department inpatient admissions to improve same-day patient flow. Acad. Emerg. Med. **19**(9), E1045–E1054 (2012)
10. Combes, C., Kadri, F., Chaabane, S.: Predicting hospital length of stay using regression models: application to emergency department. In: 10ème Conférence Francophone de Modélisation, Optimisation et Simulation-MOSIM'14 (2014)
11. Sun, Y., Heng, B.H., Tay, S.Y., Seow, E.: Predicting hospital admissions at emergency department triage using routine administrative data. Acad. Emerg. Med. **18**(8), 844–850 (2011)
12. Leegon, J., Jones, I., Lanaghan, K., Aronsky, D.: Predicting hospital admission for emergency department patients using a bayesian network. In: AMIA Annual Symposium Proceedings, vol. 2005, p. 1022. American Medical Informatics Association (2005)
13. Hilton, C.B., et al.: Personalized predictions of patient outcomes during and after hospitalization using artificial intelligence. NPJ Dig. Med. **3**(1), 1–8 (2020)
14. Artetxe, A., Beristain, A., Graña, M., Besga, A.: Predicting 30-day emergency readmission risk. In: Graña, M., López-Guede, J.M., Etxaniz, O., Herrero, Á., Quintián, H., Corchado, E. (eds.) SOCO/CISIS/ICEUTE -2016. AISC, vol. 527, pp. 3–12. Springer, Cham (2017). https://doi.org/10.1007/978-3-319-47364-2_1
15. Baig, M.M., et al.: Machine learning-based risk of hospital readmissions: predicting acute readmissions within 30 days of discharge. In: 2019 41st Annual International Conference of the IEEE Engineering in Medicine and Biology Society (EMBC), pp. 2178–2181. IEEE (2019)
16. Morel, D., Kalvin, C.Y., Liu-Ferrara, A., Caceres-Suriel, A.J., Kurtz, S.G., Tabak, Y.P.: Predicting hospital readmission in patients with mental or substance use disorders: a machine learning approach. Int. J. Med. Inf. **139**, 104136 (2020)
17. Roquette, B.P., Nagano, H., Marujo, E.C., Maiorano, A.C.: Prediction of admission in pediatric emergency department with deep neural networks and triage textual data. Neural Netw. **126**, 170–177 (2020)
18. Hong, W.S., Haimovich, A.D., Taylor, R.A.: Predicting hospital admission at emergency department triage using machine learning. PloS one **13**(7), e0201016 (2018)
19. Dorogush, A.V., Ershov, V., Gulin, A.: Catboost: gradient boosting with categorical features support. arXiv preprint arXiv:1810.11363 (2018)
20. Lundberg, S.M., et al.: From local explanations to global understanding with explainable AI for trees. Nature Mach. Intell. **2**(1), 2522–5839 (2020)
21. Lemaître, G., Nogueira, F., Aridas, C.K.: Imbalanced-learn: a python toolbox to tackle the curse of imbalanced datasets in machine learning. J. Mach. Learn. Res. **18**(1), 559–563 (2017)
22. Authority, I.H.P.: Australian refined diagnosis related groups version 6.x addendum, https://www.ihpa.gov.au/publications/australian-refined-diagnosis-related-groups-version-6x-addendum, Accessed 10 July 2021

23. Pereira, M., Singh, V., Hon, C.P., McKelvey, T.G., Sushmita, S., De Cock, M.: Predicting future frequent users of emergency departments in California state. In: Proceedings of the 7th ACM International Conference on Bioinformatics, Computational Biology, and Health Informatics, pp. 603–610 (2016)

24. Guyon, I., Elisseeff, A.: An introduction to variable and feature selection. J. Mach. Learn. Res. **3**(Mar), 1157–1182 (2003)

25. Bergstra, J., Yamins, D., Cox, D.D., et al.: Hyperopt: a python library for optimizing the hyperparameters of machine learning algorithms. In: Proceedings of the 12th Python in Science Conference, vol. 13, p. 20. Citeseer (2013)

STCT: Spatial-Temporal Conv-Transformer Network for Cardiac Arrhythmias Recognition

Yixuan Qiu[1], Weitong Chen[1(✉)], Lin Yue[1], Miao Xu[1], and Baofeng Zhu[2]

[1] University of Queensland, Brisbane, QLD 4072, Australia
{y.qiu,w.chen9,l.yue,miao.xu}@uq.edu.au
[2] Neusoft Research of Intelligent Healthcare Technology, Co Ltd., Shenyang, China
zhubf@neusoft.com

Abstract. Cardiac arrhythmia, one of the primary causes of death, can be diagnosed using the electrocardiogram (ECG), a visual representation of heart activity. Existing methods can annotate ECG signals and achieve satisfactory results. However, they usually require prepossessing the ECG signals by extracting individual heartbeats before being fed into the recognition model. Then, the data is typically processed as a one-dimensional signal that leads to the loss of information. In this context, we propose a Transformer-based Spatial-Temporal Conv-Transformer (STCT) Network that deals with raw ECG data. The STCT considers the raw ECG signal as two-dimensional features by utilising the spatial and temporal information for more accurate identification of irregular heartbeat. Additionally, the model identifies parts of the feature space that are especially relevant and filters out the remainder, ensuring that STCT performance can be enhanced. To demonstrate the effectiveness and efficiency of the proposed method, four separate open ECG datasets, MIT-BIH, EDB, AHA, and NST, were used for the benchmarking. Ultimately, this method achieved 98.96%, 99.29%, 99.88% and 99.13% of accuracy and outperformed the state-of-art methods when compared.

Keywords: ECG · Deep learning · RNN · Cardiac arrhythmia

1 Introduction

Cardiac arrhythmia refers to an abnormal heart rhythm. It is considered one of the leading causes of cardiovascular diseases (CVDs) and death. Electrocardiogram (ECG) is a non-invasive medical diagnosis tool that detects cardiac (heart) abnormalities by measuring the electrical activity it generates as it contracts.

This research is supported by the Shenyang Science and Technology Plan Fund (No. 20-201-4-10), the Member Program of Neusoft Research of Intelligent Healthcare Technology, Co. Ltd. (No. NRMP001901)).

© Springer Nature Switzerland AG 2022
B. Li et al. (Eds.): ADMA 2021, LNAI 13087, pp. 86–100, 2022.
https://doi.org/10.1007/978-3-030-95405-5_7

Given this feature, ECG is widely adopted as an effective and low-cost cardio-vascular disease diagnosis method. Moreover, ECG signals contain a sequence of waves representing the electrical activity generated by the heart over time. Each heartbeat indicates one period of heart activity that includes a P wave followed by a QRS complex and a T wave [27]. The abnormality of the P-QRS-T waveform can establish solid evidence for cardiac arrhythmia diagnosis, such as Premature Ventricular Contraction (PVC), a type of cardiac arrhythmia that presents peaked T waves and QT prolongation [9]. To data, extensive efforts have been invested into the automatic diagnosis of cardiac diseases using different machine learning approaches that have achieved satisfactory results [25].

In recent years, deep learning has succeeded across many domains, such as computer vision, Natural Language Processing (NLP) and recommendation systems [36]. Moreover, deep learning frameworks have been explored in the medical domain[37,39], including intention recognition [4–6,35,38], cancer analysis [13] and the analysis of electronic health records (EHRs) [21,31,32]. Similarly, considerable work has been done on the diagnosis of ECG based diseases using deep learning methods [3,25]. Although such methods have been adopted for ECG classification, they require pre-processing the ECG data before being fed into the neural networks. Despite achieving satisfactory outcomes, several improvements could be incorporated into these methods. Firstly, most approaches extract heartbeats for arrhythmia recognition, which requires locating the R-peak. As a result, the performance of the model heavily depends on the heartbeat extraction process. Secondly, the existing methods only consider the spatial or the temporal features without considering the spatial-temporal fusion information. Finally, numerous techniques have required manual feature engineering. While ECG feature extraction is key to improving the accuracy of ECG heartbeat classification, manual selection may result in the loss of information.

To address these issues, we proposed the Spatial-Temporal Conv-Transformer (STCT) based framework. It can process the raw ECG signal in a sliding window segment faction instead of heartbeats, delivering a possible end-to-end process. Subsequently, the Conv-Transformer framework processes ECG signals as two-dimensional features instead of a one-dimensional signal. More spatial-temporal information can be employed to increase the accuracy of recognition tasks. Lastly, the transformer identifies parts of the feature space that are especially relevant and filters out the remainder, further improving STCT performance. In the original transformer, the three vectors map from the output of the previous step encompasses Query, Key and Value, respectively. They are calculated using the position-wise linear project, then encoded into the attention module. In this paper, the positional-wise linear projection is replaced by the convolutional projection used to extract more spatial features. The contribution of this work is briefly summarised as follows:

- A novel spatial-temporal Conv-transformer network is proposed for cardiac arrhythmia recognition using convolutional projection. It calculates the Query-Key-Value pairs instead of the position-wise linear projection.

- The model simultaneously utilises the spatial feature of the morphological waveform and the temporal feature of heart rhythm for a more accurate cardiac arrhythmia recognition, which was largely overlooked by previous works.
- Extensive experiments were conducted for the benchmarking of the proposed STCT model with six state-of-the-art models using four publicly available datasets. The findings demonstrate that the STCT outperforms the latter and achieved accuracy levels of 98.96%, 99.29%, 99.88% and 99.13% across the four datasets for benchmarking.

2   Related Works

Cardiac arrhythmias recognition can be regarded as a classification task. Diagnosing the heart's physiological state is based on the abundant information provided by the ECG signals, including waveform morphology and rhythm changes. Although much effort has been put into automatic ECG diagnosis, these techniques have not fulfilled specific clinical standards.

2.1   Diagnosis of Cardiac Arrhythmias

The traditional automatic diagnosis of cardiac arrhythmias is divided into three essential tasks: signal pre-processing, feature extraction, feature selection and training classifier. As an example, Minami et al. [15] extracted QRS-wave features from the frequency domain using the Fourier transform method. Their study fed them into a neural network (NN), discriminating three kinds of rhythms and ultimately achieving high sensitivity and specificity. Additionally, Huang et al. [12] achieved a sensitivity of over 90% for the ventricular ectopic beats (VEB) and supraventricular ectopic beats (SVEB) by extracting features from R-R interval and training a support vector machine (SVM). Similar to Huang et al., Venkatesan et al. [29] extracted the various features of heartbeat using the discrete wavelet transform (DWT) and employed the SVM classifier to detect irregular heartbeats. Furthermore, Wang et al. [1] adopted a heartbeats classification scheme consisting of the combination of principal component analysis (PCA), linear discriminant analysis (LDA) and a probabilistic neural network (PNN) classifier to identify eight types of arrhythmia. As a result, they achieved an average accuracy of 99.71%. Equally important, Perlman et al. [20] proposed a model that involves the noise removal process and QRS detection. Their study utilised a decision tree for clinical decision analysis to classify specific supraventricular tachycardia (SVT). Shi et al. [23] extracted six categorical features, including temporal and morphological features, which were used to train an extreme gradient boosting (XGBoost) classifier that achieved an overall accuracy of 92.1%. Overall, these traditional methods yielded satisfactory results. However, the procedure involved in the traditional methods is cumbersome, and in particles, the performance of those models significantly depends on the QRS block extraction since inaccurate QRS pre-processing will distort the final result.

2.2   Deep Learning-Based Cardiac Arrhythmias Diagnose

In recent years, deep learning has provided effective techniques for ECG feature extraction. Compared to the traditional methods, deep learning can directly process ECG without the excessive use of feature engineering. Besides, the deep learning model exploits the informative features on deep layers that are suitable for cardiac arrhythmia recognition. Inspired by the success of deep learning in various applications, Rajendra et al. [3] trained a network composed of 11 layers 1D convolutional neural network (CNN). It aims to recognise arrhythmic heartbeats under five categories, reaching 95.11% classification accuracy. Wang et al. [30] proposed a model consisting of a 33-layer ResNet followed by a non-local convolutional block attention module that achieved an average F1-score of 96.64% on the MIT-BIH dataset. Both works still required detecting QRS waves and extracted heartbeats at the pre-processing stage. To address this problem, Rajendra et al. [2] constructed a long-duration segment dataset and fed it into a 9-layer CNN network, yielding 94.03% accuracy. However, this model identified the ECG segments by only using the local features extracted in CNN, which does not consider the features on temporal dimensionality. Following these efforts, Ribeiro et al. [22] achieved the state-of-the-art results using the residual neural network (ResNet) based method that considers the pre-post sequence simultaneously. It was trained on a large dataset and was not suitable for smaller datasets. Yao et al. [34] yielded an overall accuracy of 81.2% on the 1st China Physiological Signal Challenge dataset using an attention-based time-incremental convolutional neural network (ATI-CNN). It combined spatial and temporal features through a 13-layer CNN network and a 2-layer LSTM with a similar attention mechanism. They evaluated the model using one dataset.

Unlike the numerous existing methods, this paper proposes the STCT model that processes raw ECG data using the sliding window fashion without the need to extract heartbeats. Moreover, the spatial-temporal cascade framework takes into account the individual ECG segments as a two-dimension feature. Both morphology and rhythm characteristics of the ECG signal are considered. More importantly, the transformer can filter irrelevant information to boost the performance of the STCT.

3   Methodology

In this section, we will first illustrate the data segmentation process and discuss the detailed architecture of STCT. The STCT consists of two major components, a convolutional neural network and a convolutional-transformer network, for the extraction of spatial and temporal features.

3.1   Data Segmentation

In the signal segmentation process, we initially used the discrete wavelet transform (DWT) [14] to remove the noise in the raw signal, which was generated during the collection process. The denoised ECG signal was then segmented using a sliding window and 1250 sample points to acquire the ECG segment as shown in Fig. 1. More specifically, each ECG segment is a 5-second long ECG reading. The specified sliding window length (l) depends on the sampling rate (f), $l = 5f$. We controlled the moving forward stride variable to balance the number of samples with each type of arrhythmia by controlling the forward stride variable. The below equation was used to calculate the variable strides:

$$vs = round\left(S \cdot \frac{n}{N}\right) \tag{1}$$

where vs is the variable step size, S is the initial stride, N is the largest category, and n is the category that requires to be balanced. In this work, we used the sliding window method to clip the ECG signal with 60% of the length of l as the initial overlapping. In other words, the initial moving stride was 40% of the length of l. Typically, an ECG database can be represented as $X = [x_1, x_2, x_3, \cdots, x_i]$, where x donates as a raw ECG series, and i is the number of the records in the database. After processing with the sliding window, the new dataset for each record becomes $S_i = [s_t^i, s_{t+1}^i, s_{t+2}^i, \cdots, s_{t+N}^i]$, $r_t \in \mathbb{R}^{1250}$, where s donates a the long duration segment clipped by the sliding window. Each dataset can be written as: $R = [S_1; S_2; \cdots; S_i]$.

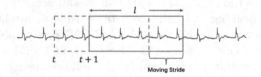

Fig. 1. The illustration of the sliding window

3.2   the Proposed Model

The proposed model is primarily comprised of spatial feature extractor and a convolutional transformer module. Figure 2(a) illustrates the workflow of the model.

Spatial Feature Extractor. One of the most challenging issues when dealing with the cardiac arrhythmia recognition is the complexity of ECG features. To address this problem, we designed a CNN network inspired by the VGGNet [24] and extracted the local spatial features. More broadly, CNN networks had significant achievements across multiple fields, contributing to its extraordinary feature extraction ability. As the network deepens, more abstract information is extracted, which means more detailed features are exploited. Figure 2(b) presents the VGGNet network made of 13 convolutional layers. It starts the first convolutional layer with 64 feature maps and doubles the feature maps following the

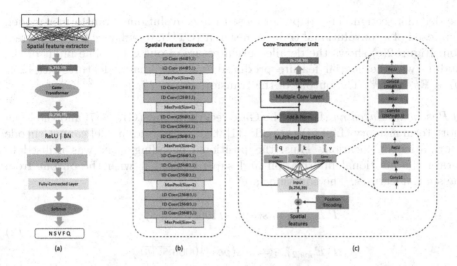

Fig. 2. (a) The workflow of the proposed model; (b) The VGGNet structure and the parameters; (c) Convolutional transformer unit that consisting of the positional encoding layer and the convolutional projection layer to calculate the values of q, k and v.

convolutional layer when it passes through the first two pooling layers. All convolutional layers have a kernel size of 3 with a stride of 1, and the zero-padding technique is used with 1. Moreover, each convolutional layer follows a rectified linear unit (ReLU) active function and a batch normalisation layer. ReLU is a widely used active function that prevents the vanishing gradient problem and enhances the sparsity of data. All pooling layers have a kernel size of 2 with a stride of 2, which can select significant features and reduce the dimensionality, mitigating the risk of over-fitting. Subsequently, the input of the first convolutional layer is the pre-processed ECG signals, $s_t \in \mathbb{R}^{B \times 1 \times 1250}$, where B is the size of the mini-batch. After a series of convolutional operations and pooling operations, the output of the last pooling layer is $f_k \in \mathbb{R}^{B \times 256 \times 39}$.

Convolutional Transformer Module. The spatial feature extractor acquires features that cannot characterise the variability of the heart rhythm on a global scale. In this case, it would only work within the local range. Therefore, the transformer network was designed to exploit the global features that cover a broader range. Transformer [28] is an attention mechanism-based model that relies on the weights of each element in the entire series to pay more attention to crucial and relevant information, thus considering the connection between local and global features. The original transformer network was first used in natural language processing (NLP) [28], consisting of the encoder layer and decoder layer like other end-to-end networks. On top of that, some researchers modified the transformer network and applied it to computer vision [8]. Unlike NLP tasks, the transformer networks are used in classification tasks that do not require the decoder section. This paper proposed the convolutional transformer model, composed of a convolutional transformer unit (CTU), to enhance feature extraction. Figure 2(c) shows the detailed architecture of our CTU. The input of the module was the spatial feature produced from the spatial feature extractor, $sf_k \in \mathbb{R}^{B \times 256 \times 39}$. The output of the transformer was $tf_k \in \mathbb{R}^{B \times 256 \times 39}$.

1) Positional Encoding. Unlike the Gate recurrent unit (GRU) [7] and the Long short-term memory (LSTM) network [11], the transformer model cannot encode information on location. Thus, the positional encoding layer was utilised to obtain the positional information and superimposed it with the output from the spatial features. The equations are:

$$P.E_{pos,2j} = sin(pos/10000^{\frac{2j}{d_{model}}})$$

$$(2)$$

$$P.E_{pos,2j+1} = cos(pos/10000^{\frac{2j}{d_{model}}})$$

where pos is the position, and j is the dimension. The wavelength forms a geometric progression from 2π to $10000 \times 2\pi$ [28].

2) Convolutional projection. This was inspired by [33] and introduced the convolutional projection layer instead of the position-wise linear projection in the original transformer model. Additionally, the convolutional layer was designed for capturing local spatial features. Figure 2(c) illustrates the implementation in our transformer unit. The convolutional projection has three separate 1D convolutional layers with a kernel size of 3 and a stride of 1 to calculate the query (q), key (k) and value (v), respectively.

3) Multi-head Attention module. The transformer is an attention-based mechanism model. The core part of the network is the attention module with inputs known as *query*, *key* and *value* that are mapped from the input of the CTU with the convolutional projection. Typically, the similarity between query and key is calculated using the dot-product attention, then divided by $\sqrt{d_k}$, which scales the value of dot products. This approach avoids getting extremely small gradients after encoding the dot-products into a Softmax function, where d_k donates the dimensions of q, k and v. Equation 3 presents the computation of the self-attention:

$$Attention(Q, K, V) = Softmax\left(\frac{Q \cdot K^T}{\sqrt{d_k}}\right) \cdot V$$

$$(3)$$

where Q, K and V are a set of q, k and v packed together, respectively.

In order to extract the most relevant information, multiple attentions are combined to form a multi-head attention module. Each attention function gets a global feature subset, and all the features captured by multi-head attention are concatenated together to form an information-abundant feature set.

4) Multiple Convolutional layers. Instead of using a multilayer perception layer, two convolutional layers are used. Moreover, each layer follows the ReLU active function to maximise more detailed features from the most relevant information extracted from the attention module. Figure 2 exhibits the details. Moreover, σ is the scale coefficient, which was set to 2 in this paper.

4   Experiment

We focused on four publicly available mainstream datasets, particularly MIT-BIH Arrhythmia datasets, European ST-T datasets, AHA and NST. The objective was to evaluate the STCT network for cardiac arrhythmias recognition under the AAMI standard. Meanwhile, we compared our proposed model against the previously published state-of-the-art methods. The source code is available on GitHub[1].

4.1   Datasets and Model Implementation

Various ECG databases have been established to address various kinds of ECG-related tasks, such as MIT-BIH Arrhythmia [16], European ST-T (EDB) [26], American Heart Association (AHA) [10], CU Ventricular Tachyarrhythmia [18], which are all publicly available on PhysioNet. In this study, we used the MIT-BIH, EDB, AHA and Noise Street Test (NST) [17] datasets to train and evaluate our model, substantiating generalizability and robustness of our method.

In the analysis, the ECG signals from the entire databases were categorised into five groups following the recommendation of the Association for Advancement of Medical Instrumentation (AAMI) that is specified in ANSI/AAMI EC57: 1998/(R)2012 [1]. Table 1 itemises the details of the classification criteria. The description of each database used in this work will be listed below:

- MIT-BIH Arrhythmia: The MIT-BIH Arrhythmia database is most commonly used in handling ECG-related tasks. It consists of 48 records with 30 min of individual annotations by cardiovascular specialists, sampling with the frequency 360 Hz from 2 leads.
- European ST-T: The datasets developed by the European Society of Cardiology have been widely used for ST and T waves detection. It includes 90 records, 2 h long each, with a sampling 250 Hz from two leads.
- AHA: The AHA database contains 155 records. However, only two are available on the PhysioNet repository, consisting of the normal beats (N) and Ventricular ectopic beat (VEB). The records were collected 250 Hz from two leads, and each record was three hours long. The last few minutes of each record were annotated.
- NST: The MIT-BIH Noise Street Test database includes 12 half-hour records and three half-hour records of noise typical in ambulatory ECG recordings. This database was employed to assess the model's capacity to process ECG signals with noise.

---

[1] https://github.com/yixuanqiu/STCT.

Table 1. The categorised group by ANSI/AAMI EC57:1998/(R)2012 Standard

Group	Annotations	Category
Non ectopic heartbeat (N)	N	Normal beat
	L	Left bundle branch block beat
	R	Right bundle branch block beat
	e	Atrial escape beat
	j	Nodal (junctional) escape beat
Supraventricular ectopic heartbeat (SVEB)	A	Atrial premature beat
	a	Aberrated atrial premature beat
	J	Nodal (junctional) premature beat
	S	Supraventricular premature beat
Ventricular ectopic heartbeat (VEB)	V	Premature ventricular contraction
	E	Ventricular escape beat
Fusion heartbeat (F)	F	Fusion of ventricular and normal beat
Unknown heartbeat (Q)	P	Paced beat
	f	Fusion of paced and normal beat
	U	Unclassifiable beat

In order to investigate the performance of the proposed model in terms of effectiveness and robustness, we evaluated it using comparison methods on four open datasets. First, we resampled the MIT-BIH arrhythmia dataset and NST dataset (360 Hz) to the same frequency with the EDB and AHA (250 Hz) for data pre-processing. Then we applied the proposed sliding window method with a length of 5 s or $l = 1250$ sample points. Then, 70% of the data for each dataset were used for training, and the proportions of the validation set and testing set were 10% and 20% of the whole dataset, respectively. Table 2 shows the details of the four datasets.

Table 2. The details of datasets

Dataset	Sampling rate	Re-sampling	Class
MIT-BIH	360 Hz	250 Hz	[N,S,V,F,Q]
EDB	250 Hz	No	[N,S,V,F,Q]
AHA	250 Hz	No	[N,V]
NST	360 Hz	250 Hz	[N,S,V]

All neural networks were implemented with the Pytorch framework (1.9.0 + cu102) on the Colaboratory platform using Nvidia Tesla V100 GPU. In the experiments, the STCT model was trained through the Adam optimiser. It aimed to update the cross-entropy loss function with an initial learning rate of 1e–3 and applied scheduler, which reduced the learning rate multiplied by a factor of 0.1 when the validated loss further decreased for 10 rounds. The minimum learning rate was 1e–8. The probability of the dropout rate with 0.1 was applied to ignore the features randomly, which prevented overfitting. To accelerate the training process, the group comprised of 128 data samples was packed. Afterwards, the Dataloader randomly selected the group of data for each round.

4.2   Comparison Model

We implemented five innovative methods through the suggested setting. These models were evaluated under the same setting. The selected comparable methods are as follows:

- Singh et al. [25] adopted the RNN based model (LSTM and GRU) for multiple classifications.
- Oh et al. [19] used a model that employs a combination of CNN and LSTM for multi-classification.
- Ribeiro et al. [22] utilised a residual neural network-based (ResNet) method for multiple classifications.
- Yao et al. [34] employed an attention-based time-incremental convolutional neural network (ATI-CNN), which consists of the CNN network and LSTM with the attention module for the multiclass arrhythmia classification.
- Wang et al. [30] applied the multiple classification network based on a convolutional neural network with a non-local convolutional block attention module (NCBAM).

4.3   Experimental Results

This section presents the results of cardiac arrhythmia recognition.

Table 3 reports the results of the models for comparison and the STCT model. The findings of our proposed method exceeded the former on almost all of the evaluation criteria. Moreover, the accuracy of our model reached 98.96% on the MIT-BIH dataset. Meanwhile, the LSTM and GRU models only focused on extracting temporal features. Therefore, we were not surprised that our model performed better. The CNN-LSTM method only uses three convolutional layers. Consequently, the model cannot capture deeply informative local features and does not consider relationships on a global scale. Meanwhile, ATI-CNN also implements the VGGNet as the spatial features extractor. However, its attention module is unable to achieve better performance.

The ROC curve is used to evaluate the discriminative capability of a classifier by plotting the true positive rate against the false-positive rate over a range of threshold values. Moreover, the x-coordinate is the proportion of the samples predicted to be positive but turned out to be negative for all the negative cases, and the y-coordinate donates as the proportion of the samples that are predicted to be true turned out to be the case for all the positive cases. Figure 3, including 4 ROC curves evaluated on four datasets, shows the ROC curves of those above 99.9%. This highlights that our model achieved a robust and considerably high performance. Figure 4 depicts that the accuracy improved as the epochs increased. It also demonstrates that the performance of the proposed model

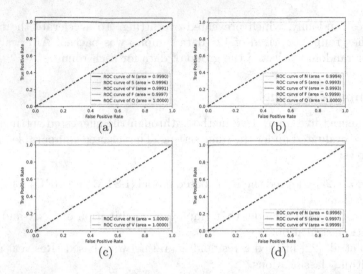

Fig. 3. The ROC curves of the STCT network on four different datasets. Panels (a), (b), (c) and (d) show the ROC curves on MIT-BIH, EDB, AHA and NST, respectively.

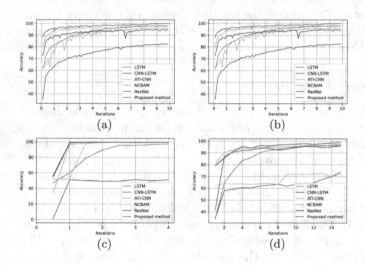

Fig. 4. Accuracy vs Iteration diagram of STCT and five comparison methods evaluated on four datasets. Panels (a), (b), (c) and (d) illustrate the diagram of Accuracy vs Iteration on MIT-BIH, EDB, AHA and NST, respectively.

exceeded 95% after the 1st Epoch on the MIT-BIH dataset. On top of that, the training accuracy was very close to 100% after 9 epochs on the MIT-BIH and EDB datasets, indicating our model's significant improvement in speeding convergence.

Table 3. The results of the cardiac arrhythmia recognition for all methods

Dataset	Model	Accuracy (%)	Recall (%)	Precision (%)	F1-score (%)	AUC (%)
MIT-BIH	SVM	67.37	43.79	74.58	55.18	73.00
	Xgboost	80.24	80.63	84.13	82.34	87.56
	CNN	92.56	92.52	92.60	92.54	99.20
	LSTM [25]	80.96	83.35	80.84	80.84	95.50
	GRU [25]	82.09	82.00	81.98	81.96	96.04
	GRU-Attention	83.12	87.96	85.57	86.74	96.91
	CNN-LSTM [19]	87.35	87.23	87.60	87.32	98.02
	ATI-CNN [34]	97.37	98.11	97.61	97.86	99.86
	NCBAM [30]	96.09	94.27	98.74	96.45	99.76
	ResNet [22]	95.89	97.06	97.16	97.11	99.72
	STCT	98.96	99.42	99.19	99.31	99.96
EDB	SVM	84.04	44.51	80.71	51.55	65.70
	XGboost	87.30	26.30	89.22	40.63	72.62
	CNN	96.53	89.53	93.00	91.06	99.20
	LSTM [25]	89.49	89.49	88.66	88.98	94.63
	GRU [25]	89.64	54.99	75.90	73.09	94.34
	GRU-Attention	91.08	62.42	73.59	67.55	96.31
	CNN-LSTM [19]	94.57	70.58	83.02	76.30	98.52
	ATI-CNN [34]	98.20	84.22	96.11	89.77	99.79
	NCBAM [30]	96.81	70.68	86.31	77.72	99.34
	ResNet [22]	97.99	88.52	95.41	91.83	99.81
	STCT	99.29	96.10	96.95	96.52	99.96
AHA	SVM	96.02	94.08	96.83	95.90	96.00
	XGboost	96.60	95.34	97.67	96.49	96.58
	CNN	99.70	99.70	99.71	99.71	99.98
	LSTM [25]	93.62	93.67	93.62	93.62	98.24
	GRU [25]	91.71	89.84	91.77	91.70	96.65
	GRU-Attention	93.47	96.43	90.81	93.53	98.52
	CNN-LSTM [19]	99.47	99.04	99.88	99.46	100.00
	ATI-CNN [34]	99.47	99.16	99.76	99.46	99.72
	NCBAM [30]	99.65	99.28	100.00	99.64	99.61
	ResNet [22]	99.59	99.52	99.64	99.58	99.97
	STCT	99.88	99.76	100.00	99.88	100.00
NST	SVM	91.03	85.42	90.11	87.70	93.21
	XGboost	96.99	97.91	97.42	97.66	97.75
	CNN	96.19	96.17	96.19	96.18	99.64
	LSTM [25]	96.33	96.33	96.34	96.34	99.59
	GRU [25]	95.68	96.65	95.69	95.68	99.48
	GRU-Attention	97.85	98.16	98.97	98.56	99.81
	CNN-LSTM [19]	90.93	86.15	92.00	93.11	98.73
	ATI-CNN [34]	96.48	96.90	94.68	95.78	99.77
	NCBAM [30]	76.38	70.73	64.77	67.62	90.96
	ResNet [22]	97.49	99.95	93.63	96.68	99.95
	STCT	99.13	99.19	98.69	98.94	99.97

Table 4. Results of the baseline model and STCT network evaluated on MIT-BIH dataset

Model	Accuracy (%)	Recall (%)	Precision (%)	F1-score (%)	AUC (%)
VGGNet-Transformer	97.51	98.17	98.71	98.44	99.80
STCT	98.96	99.42	99.19	99.31	99.96

Table 5. The evaluation results of the STCT model for all classes on four datasets

Dataset	Class	Accuracy (%)	Recall (%)	Precision (%)	F1-score (%)	AUC (%)
MIT-BIH	N	98.47	98.47	98.97	98.72	99.91
	SVEB	99.15	99.15	98.91	99.03	99.97
	VEB	97.76	97.77	98.71	98.24	99.93
	F	99.66	99.66	98.45	99.05	99.98
	Q	99.83	99.83	99.71	99.77	100.00
EDB	N	99.66	99.66	99.61	99.63	99.94
	SVEB	95.62	95.62	96.59	96.10	99.93
	VEB	97.17	97.17	97.82	97.49	99.93
	F	99.05	99.05	98.26	98.65	99.99
	Q	100.00	100.00	99.78	99.89	100.00
AHA	N	100.00	100.00	99.77	99.89	100.00
	VEB	99.76	99.76	100.00	99.88	100.00
NST	N	98.69	98.69	98.83	98.76	99.99
	SVEB	99.19	99.19	98.64	98.91	99.97
	VEB	99.53	99.53	99.91	99.72	99.99

Table 4 presents the results of the baseline method, the VGGNet-Transformer model compared with our proposed STCT model. Our model has improved by almost 1.5%. Table 5 lists the evaluation results that underscore the competence of our model in the classification of each category. Then, Table 4 details that STCT consistently outperformed all the methods on four publicly available datasets. These pieces of evidence significantly prove that the STCT network works well for the cardiac arrhythmia recognition task. Meanwhile, our model exhibited strong generalisability and robustness.

5   Conclusion

This paper proposed a novel spatial-temporal convolutional transformer network (STCT) for the cardiac arrhythmia recognition task. The recommended model is composed of a 13-layer CNN network inspired by VGGNet and a convolutional transformer network. Additionally, the transformer network is an attention-based module that can capture the significant features on a global range over a long period. We applied the sliding window method to simplify the pre-processing procedure and balance the number of samples for each class. Finally, a comparative evaluation of the STCT model against five state-of-the-art methods on four public benchmark datasets reported the model with accuracy rates of 98.96%, 99.29%, 99.88% and 99.13%, respectively.

References

1. Aami, A.E.: Testing and reporting performance results of cardiac rhythm and ST segment measurement algorithms (2012)

2. Acharya, U.R., Fujita, H., Lih, O.S., Adam, M., Tan, J.H., Chua, C.K.: Automated detection of coronary artery disease using different durations of ECG segments with convolutional neural network. Knowl.-Based Syst. **132**, 62–71 (2017)

3. Acharya, U.R., et al.: A deep convolutional neural network model to classify heartbeats. Comput. Biol. Med. **89**, 389–396 (2017)

4. Chen, W., Long, G., Yao, L., Sheng, Q.Z.: AMRNN: attended multi-task recurrent neural networks for dynamic illness severity prediction. World Wide Web **23**(5), 2753–2770 (2020)

5. Chen, W., et al.: EEG-based motion intention recognition via multi-task RNNs. In: Proceedings of the 2018 SIAM International Conference on Data Mining, pp. 279–287. SIAM (2018)

6. Chen, W., Yue, L., Li, B., Wang, C., Sheng, Q.Z.: DAMTRNN: a delta attention-based multi-task RNN for intention recognition. In: Li, J., Wang, S., Qin, S., Li, X., Wang, S. (eds.) ADMA 2019. LNCS (LNAI), vol. 11888, pp. 373–388. Springer, Cham (2019). https://doi.org/10.1007/978-3-030-35231-8_27

7. Cho, K., et al.: Learning phrase representations using rnn encoder-decoder for statistical machine translation. arXiv preprint arXiv:1406.1078 (2014)

8. Dosovitskiy, A., et al.: An image is worth 16x16 words: transformers for image recognition at scale. arXiv preprint arXiv:2010.11929 (2020)

9. Farzam, K., Richards, J.R.: Premature ventricular contraction (pvc) (2018)

10. Goldberger, A.L., et al.: Physiobank, physiotoolkit, and physionet: components of a new research resource for complex physiologic signals. Circulation **101**(23), e215–e220 (2000)

11. Hochreiter, S., Schmidhuber, J.: Long short-term memory. Neural Comput. **9**(8), 1735–1780 (1997)

12. Huang, H., Liu, J., Zhu, Q., Wang, R., Hu, G.: A new hierarchical method for inter-patient heartbeat classification using random projections and RR intervals. Biomed. Eng. Online **13**(1), 1–26 (2014)

13. Kourou, K., Exarchos, T.P., Exarchos, K.P., Karamouzis, M.V., Fotiadis, D.I.: Machine learning applications in cancer prognosis and prediction. Comput. Struct. Biotechnol. J. **13**, 8–17 (2015)

14. Martis, R.J., Acharya, U.R., Min, L.C.: ECG beat classification using PCA, LDA, ICA and discrete wavelet transform. Biomed. Signal Process. Control **8**(5), 437–448 (2013)

15. Minami, K.I., Nakajima, H., Toyoshima, T.: Real-time discrimination of ventricular tachyarrhythmia with Fourier-transform neural network. IEEE Trans. Biomed. Eng. **46**(2), 179–185 (1999)

16. Moody, G.B., Mark, R.G.: The impact of the MIT-BIH arrhythmia database. IEEE Eng. Med. Biol. Mag. **20**(3), 45–50 (2001)

17. Moody, G.B., Muldrow, W., Mark, R.G.: A noise stress test for arrhythmia detectors. CIC **11**(3), 381–384

18. Nolle, F., Badura, F., Catlett, J., Bowser, R., Sketch, M.: Crei-gard, a new concept in computerized arrhythmia monitoring systems. CIC **13**, 515–518 (1986)

19. Oh, S.L., Ng, E.Y., San Tan, R., Acharya, U.R.: Automated diagnosis of arrhythmia using combination of CNN and LSTM techniques with variable length heart beats. Comput. Biol. Med. **102**, 278–287 (2018)

20. Perlman, O., Katz, A., Amit, G., Zigel, Y.: Supraventricular tachycardia classification in the 12-lead ECG using atrial waves detection and a clinically based tree scheme. IEEE BHI **20**(6), 1513–1520 (2015)

21. Rajkomar, A., et al.: Scalable and accurate deep learning with electronic health records. NPJ Dig. Med. **1**(1), 1–10 (2018)

22. Ribeiro, A.H., et al.: Automatic diagnosis of the 12-lead ECG using a deep neural network. Nature Commun. **11**(1), 1–9 (2020)
23. Shi, H., Wang, H., Huang, Y., Zhao, L., Qin, C., Liu, C.: A hierarchical method based on weighted extreme gradient boosting in ECG heartbeat classification. Comput. Methods Prog. Biomed. **171**, 1–10 (2019)
24. Simonyan, K., Zisserman, A.: Very deep convolutional networks for large-scale image recognition. arXiv preprint arXiv:1409.1556 (2014)
25. Singh, S., Pandey, S.K., Pawar, U., Janghel, R.R.: Classification of ECG arrhythmia using recurrent neural networks. Procedia Comput. Sci. **132**, 1290–1297 (2018)
26. Taddei, A., et al.: The European ST-T database: standard for evaluating systems for the analysis of ST-T changes in ambulatory electrocardiography. Eur. Heart J. **13**(9), 1164–1172 (1992)
27. Tso, C., Currie, G.M., Gilmore, D., Kiat, H.: Electrocardiography: a technologist's guide to interpretation. JNMT **43**(4), 247–252 (2015)
28. Vaswani, A., et al.: Attention is all you need. In: ANIS, pp. 5998–6008 (2017)
29. Venkatesan, C., Karthigaikumar, P., Paul, A., Satheeskumaran, S., Kumar, R.: ECG signal preprocessing and SVM classifier-based abnormality detection in remote healthcare applications. IEEE Access **6**, 9767–9773 (2018)
30. Wang, J., et al.: Automated ECG classification using a non-local convolutional block attention module. Comput. Methods Prog. Biomed. **203**, 106006 (2021)
31. Wang, Y., Chen, W., Pi, D., Yue, L.: Adversarially regularized medication recommendation model with multi-hop memory network. Knowl. Inf. Syst. **63**(1), 125–142 (2020). https://doi.org/10.1007/s10115-020-01513-9
32. Wang, Y., Chen, W., Pi, D., Yue, L., Wang, S., Xu, M.: Self-supervised adversarial distribution regularization for medication recommendation (2021)
33. Wu, H., et al.: CVT: Introducing convolutions to vision transformers. arXiv preprint arXiv:2103.15808 (2021)
34. Yao, Q., Wang, R., Fan, X., Liu, J., Li, Y.: Multi-class arrhythmia detection from 12-lead varied-length ECG using attention-based time-incremental convolutional neural network. Inf. Fusion **53**, 174–182 (2020)
35. Yue, L., et al.: Exploring BCI control in smart environments: intention recognition via EEG representation enhancement learning. ACM Trans. Knowl. Disc. Data (TKDD) **15**(5), 1–20 (2021)
36. Yue, L., Sun, X.X., Gao, W.Z., Feng, G.Z., Zhang, B.Z.: Multiple auxiliary information based deep model for collaborative filtering. J. Comput. Sci. Technol. **33**(4), 668–681 (2018)
37. Yue, L., Tian, D., Chen, W., Han, X., Yin, M.: Deep learning for heterogeneous medical data analysis. World Wide Web **23**(5), 2715–2737 (2019). https://doi.org/10.1007/s11280-019-00764-z
38. Yue, L., Tian, D., Jiang, J., Yao, L., Chen, W., Zhao, X.: Intention recognition from spatio-temporal representation of EEG signals. In: ADC, pp. 1–12 (2021)
39. Yue, L., Zhao, H., Yang, Y., Tian, D., Zhao, X., Yin, M.: A mimic learning method for disease risk prediction with incomplete initial data. In: Li, G., Yang, J., Gama, J., Natwichai, J., Tong, Y. (eds.) DASFAA 2019. LNCS, vol. 11448, pp. 392–396. Springer, Cham (2019). https://doi.org/10.1007/978-3-030-18590-9_52

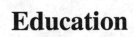

Education

Augmenting Personalized Question Recommendation with Hierarchical Information for Online Test Platform

Lu Jiang[1], Wanfei Zhang[1], Yibin Wang[1], Na Luo[1(✉)], and Lin Yue[1,2(✉)]

[1] Northeast Normal University, ChangChun 130117, JiLin, China
{jiangl761,zhangwf124,wangyb856,luon110}@nenu.edu.cn
[2] The University of Queensland, Brisbane, Australia
l.yue@uq.edu.au

Abstract. Personalized question recommendation for students is an important research topic in the field of smart education. Current studies depend on collaborative filtering based, cognitive diagnosis based, or cognitive diagnosis based on collaborative filtering methods. However, the above methods can only model the knowledge state for a single student and the common features of similar students while ignoring students' flat and hierarchical information. To solve the problems above, we propose an augmenting personalized question recommendation method(APQR) which combines flat and hierarchical information. Firstly, we propose a framework to capture student and question hierarchical information jointly. Secondly, we propose a cognitive diagnostic method that uses flat and hierarchical information to model students' proficiency on each question. Finally, we recommend questions based on students' performance by using probabilistic matrix factorization combined with students' proficiency. We apply APQR to personalized question recommendation to demonstrate the performance improvement via an online test platform dataset. The promising results show that the proposed APQR can recommend questions to students effectively.

Keywords: Personalized question recommender system · Hierarchical structure · Cognitive diagnosis

1 Introduction

In recent years, online test has gradually been witnessed into the smart education due to the development of the Internet. But the overwhelming tests cause the information overload issue, which jeopardizes students' study quality and efficiency. Therefore, to address the problem, in the paper, we propose to develop a recommender system for question recommendation based on personal knowledge, background and interests.

This research work has been supported by Project of Philosophy and Social Sciences of Jilin Province under Project No. 2019C70.

© Springer Nature Switzerland AG 2022
B. Li et al. (Eds.): ADMA 2021, LNAI 13087, pp. 103–117, 2022.
https://doi.org/10.1007/978-3-030-95405-5_8

Conventional recommendation methods divide into two parts, including collaborative filtering(CF) [17] and deep learning [21,22]. Although the above methods have achieved promising results, there are gaps in the application for deploying them to the study scenario. There are two main reasons. First, student and question features in hierarchical information are structured. Traditional recommendations cannot model the structured features. Second, the relationship between student, question and knowledge concept is difficult to model. Therefore, it highly desires a new framework to accommodate with recommending questions. We have three challenges addressed to achieve this goal: (1) How to capture the hierarchical information of students and questions? (2) How can hierarchical information be added to cognitive diagnostics? (3) How to recommend the personalized questions? Next, we will describe how to deal with these challenges.

The first challenge is that there are hierarchical structures in students and questions. It desires an appropriate framework to organize. For example, as shown in Fig. 1, the book *"College Computer Applications Course"* category, which reflects a hierarchical structure. Typically, a hierarchical structure can be represented by a tree. In this tree, the chapter *Number system and its conversion in computer* is a child node of chapter *Representation of information in the computer*, which can also be a parent node of chapter *Numeral system* in the next layer. We will give the detail in Sect. 3.

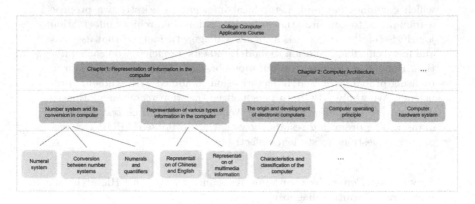

Fig. 1. Knowledge concept hierarchical structure

The second challenge is that learn a student performance on a question via the knowledge concept proficiency is difficult. In general, a test consists of two different kinds of questions: objective and subjective questions [12]. Objective questions are those with clear standard answers, while subjective questions are anything else. We need to consider how to handle data from both objective and subjective questions. In the traditional DINA-based cognitive diagnostic model, a student's mastery of a knowledge point is dichotomous-mastered (i.e., 1) and not mastered (i.e., 0) [1]. This applies to dichotomous objective questions, which are somewhat "absolute", while the scoring rules for subjective questions are different from those for objective questions. To compensate for this deficiency, we used a fuzzy cognitive diagnostic method that serializes students' mastery of knowledge concepts from 0 to 1 using a logistic regression model.

The third challenge is to recommend suitable question to student. In this work, we choose probability matrix factorization (PMF) as the basic recommendation method of APQR. Probability matrix decomposition is a classical scoring prediction algorithm that maps students and topics to low-dimensional potential factor space to achieve student cognitive modeling [18].

In summary, we propose a new framework for question recommendation to improve the study quality and efficiency. The main contributions of our work can be summarized as follows:

- First, we propose a unified framework to capture student and question hierarchical information jointly.
- Second, we propose a cognitive diagnostic method that uses flat and hierarchical information to model students' proficiency on each question.
- Third, we recommend questions to students based on students' performance by probabilistic matrix factorization combined with students' proficiency.
- Finally, we apply APQR to personalized question recommendation to demonstrate the performance improvement via a real-world dataset.

2 Preliminary

We introduce some important definitions and problem statement firstly. Then, the framework overview of the APQR is introduced. Besides, some important notations are summarized in Table 1.

Table 1. Some important notations

Notation	Description
H	Test number
P	Students' collection
P_{hu}	Student u in test h
T	Questions' collection
$\mathcal{R}$	Students' response matrix
$\mathcal{Q}$	Knowledge concept investigation matrix
S	Knowledge concepts' collection
α_u	The situation of student u to knowledge concept k
η_{uv}	Student u's mastery on question v
s_v, g_v	The slip and guessing factors of question v
φ_{uv}	Student u's latent responses on question v
M_u	Student u's latent feature vector
N_v	Question v's latent feature vector

2.1   Definitions and Problem Statement

We let $E = \{E_1, E_2, ..., E_H\}$ to be the set of H exams, $P_m = \{P_{h1}, P_{h2}, ..., P_{hU}\}$ to be the set of U students, $T_h = \{T_{h1}, T_{h2}, ..., T_{hV}\}$ to be the set of V questions for each exam $E_h(h = 1, 2, ..., H)$. We let $S = \{S_1, S_2, ..., S_K\}$ to be the set of K knowledge concepts have examined in the question set V.

Definition 1 Student-question scoring matrix R. Student-question scoring matrix R refers to the matrix of student scores on each of the test questions taken. We let matrix $R \in R^{U \times V}$ and if a student P_u has scored question T_v, $R(u, v) > 0$ denotes the score, otherwise, $R(u, v) = 0$.

Definition 2 Question-knowledge concept association matrix Q. Question-knowledge concept association matrix Q refers to the matrix of the situations of the knowledge concept examined in each question. We let matrix $Q \in Q^{K \times V}$ and if a question T_v has examined a knowledge concept S_k, $Q(v, k) = 1$, otherwise , $Q(v, k) = 0$.

Definition 3 Problem Statement. Given a target student and corresponding test records, the goal is to calculate the student's rate with knowledge concepts, and the student's rate with the recommend questions. More formally, given a matrix **R**, a matrix **Q**, and associated feature matrix **M** and **N** of students and questions, a recommend function $\hat{R} = f(\mathbf{R}, \mathbf{Q}, \mathbf{M}, \mathbf{N})$ denotes the predicted questions to students.

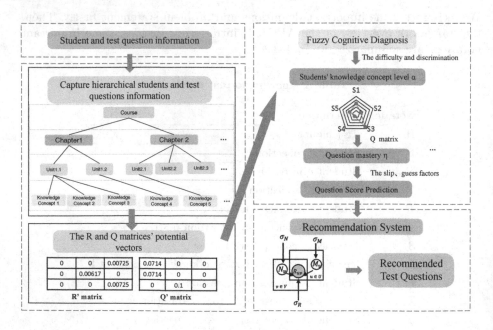

Fig. 2. Framework overview.

2.2   Framework Overview

Figure 2 shows the framework overview of APQR. The APQR includes four key components: (1) Input: student and test question information: matrix R, matrix Q, student feature matrix M and question feature matrix N; (2) Capture hierarchical information: a unified framework is proposed which can incorporate the student and question hierarchical information; (3) Student performance prediction: we used a fuzzy cognitive diagnostic method that handled both objective and subjective questions, then obtained the mastery degree of students' knowledge concepts, and modelled students' mastery level of questions according to the mastery degree of students' knowledge concepts; (4) Personalized question recommendation: combine with PMF method, considering the hierarchical information and student performance on questions to recommend questions to students.

3   Method

We present the major components of the proposed recommender system as follows: (1) incorporating the student and test hierarchical information; (2) student performance predicting; (3) the proposed framework APQR.

3.1   Incorporating the Student and Question Hierarchical Information

The test matrix $T \in R^{d \times v}$ gives the latent feature representation of v questions in a d-dimensional latent space. Because of the non-negative matrix T, we further decompose T into two non-negative matrices $T_1 \in R^{v_1 \times v}$ and $\hat{T}_2 \in R^{d \times v_1}$ to get a 2-layer hierarchical structure of tests as follows:

$$T \approx \hat{T}_2 T_1 \tag{1}$$

where v_1 is the number of latent sub-categories in the 2nd layer and T_1 indicates the affiliation of v tests to v_1 latent sub-categories. Therefore, T_1 denotes the parent-child relationship between the v_1 categories in the 2nd layer and the v categories in the 1st layer. $\hat{T}_2$ denotes the potential feature representation of the v_1 categories. So the potential feature representation T_j of a test j can be interpreted as the potential vector representation of this test's parent category with them: $T_j \approx \hat{T}_2 T_1$.

Suppose there are more than two layers of hierarchical relationships. In that case, we continue to break down $\hat{T}_2$, where $\hat{T}_2 \in R^{v_2 \times v_1}$ represents the parent-child relationship between the second layer and the third layer category. The potential representations of the first question can be expressed as $T_j \approx \hat{T}_3 T_2 T_1$ $(:, j)$. The structure can be repeated $p-1$ times to represent characteristics with p-layer structure:

$$T \approx T_p T_{p-1}...T_2 T_1 \tag{2}$$

where $T_i \in R^{v_i \times v_{i-1}}$, $(1 < i < p)$ and $T_p \in R^{d \times v_{p-1}}$.

The *parent-child* relationship are implicit by Eq. (2). However, the explicit hierarchy contains more structural information that can be used to guide the learning process of potential features. To achieve this, we will display the implicit hierarchy. In the APQR, the aggregation function selects the mean function. Thus, the question hierarchical structure information can be captured as follows:

$$min \sum_{i=2}^{p} \|T_p \cdots T_i - T_p \cdots T_{i-1} \mathcal{P}_{i-1}\|_{Fro}^2 \qquad (3)$$

Since a parent node can be represented by the average of its children, $\mathcal{P}_k$ is a normalized version of T_k and $\mathcal{P}_k(i,j) = \frac{I_k(i,j)}{\sum_{i=1}^{v_k-1} I_k(i,j)}$. In the same case, the student structure characteristics of q-layer can be expressed as:

$$P \approx P_1 P_2 ... P_{q-1} P_q \qquad (4)$$

where $P_i \in R^{u_i \times u_{i-1}}, (1 < i < q)$ and $P_q \in R^{d \times u_{q-1}}$. The student hierarchical structure information can be captured as follows:

$$min \sum_{i=2}^{q} \|P_q \cdots P_i - P_q \cdots P_{i-1} Q_{i-1}\|_{Fro}^2 \qquad (5)$$

where Q_k is the normalized version of $C_k \in R^u_{k-1} \times u_k$ and $Q_k(i,j) = \frac{C_k(i,j)}{\sum_{i=1}^{u_k-1} C_k(i,j)}$.

3.2   Student Performance Predicting

Based on the hierarchical information of students and test questions, we obtain the potential representations of students and test questions. In this subsection, we will show how to acquire specific mastery of knowledge concepts from the potential representations of students and questions. And predict the rates of the questions that the students have not done.

Modelling Knowledge Concept. To solve the problem of modelling subjective data, we introduced fuzzy set theory into student cognitive modelling by fuzzifying students' knowledge concept and ability mastery levels to simultaneously model objective and subjective data. "Fuzzify" [1] means redefining a deterministic binary variable (e.g., mastery or non-mastery) as a fuzzy variable with values in the interval [0, 1].

$$\alpha_{uk} = \mu_k(u) = \frac{1}{1 + exp[-1.7\alpha_{uk}(\theta_u - b_{uk})]} \qquad (6)$$

Students' proficiency in a given skill (α_{uk}) depends on students' high-level latent traits (θ_u) and the knowledge concept's properties: the difficulty (b_{uk}) and discrimination (a_{uk}) of knowledge concept k for student u.

Modelling Student Knowledge of Questions. An objective question will have a standard answer, and the question can only be answered correctly if all the required knowledge competencies are fully mastered. Therefore, the combined effect of knowledge and ability on objective questions is usually considered to be conjunctive. In contrast, subjective questions are generally open-ended, and students may include detailed steps for solving the problem. Thus, given a subjective question and its required knowledge, the more knowledge and skills one has, the higher one's score will be. Therefore, this chapter assumes that the subjective questions are compensatory because they are subject to a combination of knowledge and ability.

A formal definition of student topic mastery is given below. Given a Q-matrix of K knowledge concepts, the degree of mastery of student u on question v, $\eta_u v$, if based on the conjunctive assumption, can be defined as follows:

$$\eta_{uv} = \bigcap_{1 \leq k \leq S, Q'_{uk}} \mu_k(u) \tag{7}$$

where Q'_{uk} is the latent feature of the question-knowledge concept obtained by the hierarchical model, and is the Q-matrix after the continuum processing, Q'_{uk} takes the value of $[0,1]$.

Similarly, if based on the compensatory assumption, η_{uv} is defined as follows:

$$\eta_{uv} = \bigcup_{1 \leq k \leq S, Q'_{uk}} \mu_k(u) \tag{8}$$

We use standard fuzzy intersection and fuzzy concatenation to obtain students' question mastery:

$$\mu_{A \cap B(x)} = min\left(\mu_{A(x)}, \mu_{B(x)}\right) \tag{9}$$

$$\mu_{A \cup B(x)} = max\left(\mu_{A(x)}, \mu_{B(x)}\right) \tag{10}$$

By this method, both objective and subjective questions can blur the students' mastery of the topic (η_{uv}).

In the actual exams, students' answers do not only depend on their mastery of the knowledge concepts, but also two real situations may occur: (1) Students do not master the knowledge concepts and get the correct result by guessing the answer. (2) Students master the knowledge concepts but answer incorrectly due to slip. Therefore, we introduce a slip factor (s_i) and a guessing factor (g_i). Since objective and subjective questions were scored on different criteria, a Bernoulli distribution was used to model students' objective scores, and score data were normalized to handle subjective scores.

The actual level of objective question answers:

$$P\left(R'_{uv} \mid \eta_{uv}, s_v, g_v\right) = (1 - s_v)\,\eta_{uv} + g_v\,(1 - \eta_{uv}) \tag{11}$$

The real level of subjective question answers:

$$P\left(R'_{uv} \mid \eta_{uv}, s_v, g_v\right) = \mathcal{N}\left(R'_{uv} \mid [(1 - s_v)\eta_{uv} + g_v(1 - \eta_{uv})], \sigma^2\right) \quad (12)$$

In Eq. (11) and (12), R'_{uv} is the student-test latent features obtained through the hierarchical model, is the R-matrix after continuous processing, R'_{uv} takes the value of [0,1]. σ is the normalized variance of the subjective scores. s_v and g_v denote the slipping and guessing factors for question v. $(1 - s_v)\eta_{uv}$ indicates that the student u mastered the question and got the correct answer, while $g_v(1 - \eta_{uv})$ indicates that the student obtained the correct answer directly by guessing. That is, these are the two ways for a test to give a correct response. We put the true level of students' answers on the test questions into the X matrix.

3.3   The Framework APQR

The previous introduction to components aims to capture student and question hierarchical information into student cognitive diagnosis. Combining them, PMF decomposes the student-question scoring matrix R into the matrix M of students and the matrix N of test questions. In addition, $M \in R^{D \times U}$, $N \in R^{D \times V}$ are latent students, and questions feature matrices. The conditional distribution is defined as:

$$p(R|M, N, \sigma^2) = \prod_{u=1}^{U} \prod_{v=1}^{V} [N(R_{uv}|M_u^T N_v, \sigma^2)]^{I_{uv}} \quad (13)$$

$N(x|\mu, \sigma^2)$ is the probability density function of the Gaussian distribution. I_{uv} is the indicator function, if student u rated question v is equal to 1, otherwise, equal to 0. And, we place zero-mean spherical Gaussian priors on student and question embedding vectors:

$$p(M|\sigma_M^2) = \prod_{u=1}^{U} N(M_u|0, \sigma_M^2 I),$$

$$p(N|\sigma_N^2) = \prod_{v=1}^{V} N(M_u|0, \sigma_N^2 I) \quad (14)$$

Through Bayesian inference, the posterior probabilities of eigenvectors of students and questions are deduced as follows:

$$p(M, N|R, \sigma_R^2, \sigma_M^2, \sigma_N^2) \propto$$
$$p(R|M, N, \sigma_R^2)P(M|\sigma_M^2)P(N|\sigma_N^2)$$
$$= \prod_{u=1}^{U} \prod_{v=1}^{V} [N(R_{uv}|M_u^T N_v, \sigma^2]^{I_{uv}{}^R}$$
$$\times \prod_{u=1}^{U} N(M_u|0, \sigma_M^2 I) \times \prod_{v=1}^{V} N(M_u|0, \sigma_N^2 I)$$

After obtaining students' cognitive diagnostic information, it is used in the probability matrix factorization. Specifically, feature y_{uv} can be extracted from the student answer real level matrix X as prior information for the PMF:

$$y_{uv} = y_u + y_v \tag{15}$$

$$y_u = \frac{1}{V} \times \sum_{i=1}^{V} X_{ui} \tag{16}$$

$$y_v = \frac{1}{U} \times \sum_{i=1}^{U} X_{iv} \tag{17}$$

After adding the personalized features y_u and y_v of students and test questions, the cognitive diagnosis-based answer situation modeling method in our method is obtained, the latent answer situation φ_{uv} of students is obtained by the following equation:

$$\varphi_{uv} = \mu + \rho y_{uv} + (1 - \rho) M_u^\top N_v \tag{18}$$

where μ is the overall average score, ρ is the parameter that regulates the proportion of students' individual learning status and common learning status, $\rho \in [0, 1]$ indicates that the predicted score is influenced by the individuality of students' learning status. Conversely, it indicates that the predicted score is influenced by the commonality of students' learning status. By adding students' individualized learning states y_{uv} to the PMF decomposition, it can make the low-dimensional potential factors M, N from the PMF decomposition include students' individual representations when including the learning states common among students so that it can improve the accuracy of the score prediction and the interpretation of the results.

Mathematically, probability matrix factorization solves the following optimization problem:

$$\min_{P,T} I_{uv} (R'_{uv} - \varphi_{uv})^2 + \lambda_M \|M\|_{Fro}^2 + \lambda_N \|N\|_{Fro}^2$$

$$+ \min \sum_{i=2}^{p} \|T_p \cdots T_i - T_p \cdots T_{i-1} P_{i-1}\|_{Fro}^2 \tag{19}$$

$$+ \min \sum_{i=2}^{q} \|P_q \cdots P_i - P_q \cdots P_{i-1} Q_{i-1}\|_{Fro}^2$$

where, λ_M, λ_N are the regularization factors of the model.

In general, our method uses the hierarchical information of students and test questions. By combining the information on students performance prediction, we modelled jointly on the objective and subjective question, and excluded to the greatest extent the interference of students' guessing and slip in modelling the answer situation, which made the method has the interpretability of a cognitive diagnostic model.

4   Experiments

4.1   Online Test Dataset

We collect the dataset from Northeast Normal University(NENU) Online Test Platform, the platform is for the final computer science exams for first-year college students, including objective and subjective problems. We collect the students who enrolled the course from September, 2018 to December, 2018. We shows the statistics of the dataset after preprocessing in Table 2. The NENU online test dataset includes the score information of 1878 students on 672 test problems.

Table 2. Datasets summary

Students	Knowledge concepts	Problems			
1878	95	672			
		Obj.	Sub.		
		Multiple Choice	Word	Excel	Powerpoint
		602	48	10	12

4.2   Evaluation Metric

We evaluate the model performances over the personalized question recommendation in terms of the following metrics.

(1) **Recall:**

$$Recall = \frac{TP}{TP + FN} \tag{20}$$

(2) **F1:**

$$F1 = \frac{2TP}{2TP + FP + FN} \tag{21}$$

(3) **Mean Absolute Error(MAE):**

$$MAE = \frac{1}{n} \sum_{i=1}^{n} |\hat{y}_i - y_i| \tag{22}$$

(4) **Mean Square Error(MSE):**

$$MSE = \frac{1}{n} \sum_{i=1}^{n} (\hat{y}_i - y_i)^2 \tag{23}$$

where $\hat{y}_i$ is the set of predicted student scores, y_i is the set of true student scores. For metrics "Recall" and "F1", the larger the value, the better the performance. For metrics "MAE" and "MSE", the smaller the value, the better the performance.

4.3   Baseline Algorithms

We compare the performances of Augmenting Personalized Question Recommendation(namely "APQR") with the following baselines.

(1) **U-CF:** This is a method that user-based on the user similarity collaborative filtering approach [10].
(2) **PMF:** This is a method of using probabilistic matrix factorization to embedding students and questions [18].
(3) **FuzzyPMF:** This is a method of adding fuzzy cognitive diagnosis method to probability matrix factorization [23].
(4) **HIRE:** This is a method of exploring heterogeneous side information and hierarchical information for recommendations [11].

For the NENU online test dataset, we split it into a training set $x\%$ and a test set $1 - x\%$, and vary x as $\{40, 60, 80\}$. To prevent our method from overfitting during training [18], the regularization factor $\lambda_M = \lambda_N = 0.5$, and the parameter $\rho = 0.8$ in the model are set (the parameter ρ will be set in Sect. 4.4 through experiments).

Table 3. Results obtained with different models of different training sample sizes.

	Methods	40%	60%	80%
Recall	U-CF	0.00115	0.00121	0.00123
	PMF	0.00108	0.00119	0.00124
	FuzzyPMF	0.00150	0.00141	0.00147
	HIRE	0.00106	0.00111	0.00123
	APQR	**0.01489**	**0.01486**	**0.01486**
F1	U-CF	0.00230	0.00242	0.00244
	PMF	0.00215	0.00238	0.00248
	FuzzyPMF	0.00299	0.00281	0.00293
	HIRE	0.00211	0.00222	0.00246
	APQR	**0.00373**	**0.00535**	**0.00353**
MAE	U-CF	0.00010	0.00019	0.00036
	PMF	0.00169	0.00137	0.00118
	FuzzyPMF	0.00015	0.00012	0.00010
	HIRE	0.00167	0.00135	0.00118
	APQR	**0.00007**	**0.00006**	**0.00005**
MSE	U-CF	0.49225	0.83830	1.26547
	PMF	1.44880	1.42034	1.41685
	FuzzyPMF	0.01179	0.01090	0.01094
	HIRE	1.40445	1.38974	1.41245
	APQR	**0.00274**	**0.00275**	**0.00278**

4.4   Overall Performance

In experiment, we presented the results for "Recall", "F1", "MAE" and "MSE" of APQR on the personalized question recommendation problem compared to other baselines on NENU online test dataset. The results are reported in Table 3. Our method "APQR" higher than all baselines on "Recall" and "F1", and lower than all baselines on "MAE" and "MSE". In general, our algorithm shows significant improvement compared with baseline algorithms.

4.5   Parameter Analysis

In the APQR, the parameter $\rho \in [0, 1]$ is used as a weighting parameter to adjust the PMF and the FuzzyCDF. In the experiments on the setting of parameter ρ, we selected 40%, 60% and 80% of the test sets. From Fig. 3, it can be seen that the selection of ρ value has a significant effect on testing recommendation effect of our method. When $\rho \in [0.1, 0.7]$, the F1 values do not differ much, when $\rho \in [0.7, 0.9]$, we see that no fluctuations in performance at the beginning, after $\rho = 0.7$, the performance rose first then fell after $\rho = 0.8$, so choosing $\rho = 0.8$ can make the best test recommendation for APQR.

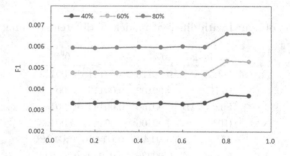

Fig. 3. Parameter Analysis with ρ

5   Related Work

In this section, we will introduce the related prior works, including recommender system and student performance modeling.

5.1   Recommender System

Recently, due to the explosive growth of information, research on recommender systems [2,3,30] has attracted more and more attention. Conventional recommendation methods divide into two parts: collaborative filtering(CF) and deep learning [4,5,16,19,26]. Specifically, Polyzou *et al.* proposed a course grade prediction method based on a regression model [15]. Zhang *et al.* proposed a hierarchical reinforcement learning method, which formalizes the revising of a user profile to be a hierarchical sequential decision process [28]. Yu *et al.* presented a two-level hierarchical reinforcement learning (HRL) machanism for knowledge concept expansion in MOOCs [24].

5.2 Student Performance Modeling

Classical student performance modeling approaches exploit existing deep learning models, including matrix factorization [8] and neural networks [9,20,25,27, 29] to modeling student's performance. Jiang *et al.* proposed a novel EduHawkes approach for modeling online study behavior patterns [7]. Hu *et al.* proposed a course Markov model for student grade prediction [6]. Okubo *et al.* proposed a RNN classifier, which uses data from various learning activity logs to predict student performance [14]. Morsy *et al.* modeled students' curriculum planning in order to study how to improve graduation rates [13].

6 Conclusion

In the APQR, we propose a hierarchical student and question embedding model for a personalized question recommendation task. Specifically, we first propose a framework to capture student and question hierarchical information. Then, we propose a cognitive diagnostic method that uses the obtained flat and hierarchical information to model students' proficiency on each question. Finally, we recommend questions to students based on students' performance by probabilistic matrix factorization combined with students' proficiency. The experiments on NENU online test dataset demonstrate the performance improvement for augmenting personalized question recommendations.

References

1. Liu, Q., et al.: Fuzzy cognitive diagnosis for modelling examinee performance. ACM Trans. Intell. Syst. Technol. **9**(4), 1–26 (2018)
2. Adomavicius, G., Tuzhilin, A.: Toward the next generation of recommender systems: a survey of the state-of-the-art and possible extensions. IEEE Trans. Knowl. Data Eng. **17**(6), 734–749 (2005)
3. Bobadilla, J., Ortega, F., Hernando, A., Gutiérrez, A.: Recommender systems survey. Knowl.-Based Syst. **46**, 109–132 (2013)
4. Chen, W., Long, G., Yao, L., Sheng, Q.Z.: AMRNN: attended multi-task recurrent neural networks for dynamic illness severity prediction. World Wide Web **23**(5), 2753–2770 (2020)
5. Chen, W., Yue, L., Li, B., Wang, C., Sheng, Q.Z.: DAMTRNN: a delta attention-based multi-task RNN for intention recognition. In: Li, J., Wang, S., Qin, S., Li, X., Wang, S. (eds.) ADMA 2019. LNCS (LNAI), vol. 11888, pp. 373–388. Springer, Cham (2019). https://doi.org/10.1007/978-3-030-35231-8_27
6. Hu, Q., Rangwala, H.: Course-specific Markovian models for grade prediction. In: Phung, D., Tseng, V.S., Webb, G.I., Ho, B., Ganji, M., Rashidi, L. (eds.) PAKDD 2018. LNCS (LNAI), vol. 10938, pp. 29–41. Springer, Cham (2018). https://doi. org/10.1007/978-3-319-93037-4_3
7. Jiang, L., et al.: Eduhawkes: a neural hawkes process approach for online study behavior modeling. In: SDM, pp. 567–575. SIAM (2021)
8. Koren, Y., Bell, R., Volinsky, C.: Matrix factorization techniques for recommender systems. Computer **42**(8), 30–37 (2009)

9. Liu, K., Wang, P., Zhang, J., Fu, Y., Das, S.K.: Modeling the interaction coupling of multi-view spatiotemporal contexts for destination prediction. In: SDM, pp. 171–179. SIAM (2018)

10. Na, L., Ming-xia, L., Hai-yang, Q., Hao-long, S.: A hybrid user-based collaborative filtering algorithm with topic model. Appl. Intell. **51**(11), 7946–7959 (2021). https://doi.org/10.1007/s10489-021-02207-7

11. Liu, T., Wang, Z., Tang, J., Yang, S., Huang, G.Y., Liu, Z.: Recommender systems with heterogeneous side information. In: The World Wide Web Conference, WWW 2019, San Francisco, CA, USA, 13–17 May 2019, pp. 3027–3033. ACM (2019)

12. Liu, Z., Jansen, B.J.: Subjective versus objective questions: perception of question subjectivity in social Q&A. In: Agarwal, N., Xu, K., Osgood, N. (eds.) SBP 2015. LNCS, vol. 9021, pp. 131–140. Springer, Cham (2015). https://doi.org/10.1007/978-3-319-16268-3_14

13. Morsy, S., Karypis, G.: A study on curriculum planning and its relationship with graduation GPA and time to degree. In: Proceedings of the 9th International Conference on Learning Analytics & Knowledge, pp. 26–35 (2019)

14. Okubo, F., Yamashita, T., Shimada, A., Konomi, S.: Students' performance prediction using data of multiple courses by recurrent neural network. In: 25th International Conference on Computers in Education, ICCE 2017, pp. 439–444. Asia-Pacific Society for Computers in Education (2017)

15. Polyzou, A., Karypis, G.: Grade prediction with models specific to students and courses. Int. J. Data Sci. Anal. **2**(3–4), 159–171 (2016)

16. Qi, L., Zhang, X., Li, S., Wan, S., Gong, W.: Spatial-temporal data-driven service recommendation with privacy-preservation. Inf. Sci. **515**, 91–102 (2019)

17. Ricci, F., Rokach, L., Shapira, B.: Recommender Systems: Introduction and Challenges. Recommender Systems Handbook (2015)

18. Salakhutdinov, R.: Probabilistic matrix factorization. Curran Associates Inc. (2007)

19. Umair, S., Sharif, M.M.: Predicting students grades using artificial neural networks and support vector machine. In: Encyclopedia of Information Science and Technology, pp. 5169–5182 (2018)

20. Wang, D., Wang, P., Liu, K., Zhou, Y., Hughes, C.E., Fu, Y.: Reinforced imitative graph representation learning for mobile user profiling: An adversarial training perspective. In: AAAI, vol. 35, pp. 4410–4417 (2021)

21. Wang, Y., Chen, W., Pi, D., Yue, L.: Adversarially regularized medication recommendation model with multi-hop memory network. Knowl. Inf. Syst. **63**(1), 125–142 (2020). https://doi.org/10.1007/s10115-020-01513-9

22. Wang, Y., Chen, W., Pi, D., Yue, L., Wang, S., Xu, M.: Self-supervised adversarial distribution regularization for medication recommendation (2021)

23. Wu, R., Qi, L., Liu, Y., Chen, E., Yu, S., Chen, Z., Hu, G.: Cognitive modelling for predicting examinee performance. AAAI Press (2015)

24. Yu, J., et al.: Expanrl: hierarchical reinforcement learning for course concept expansion in moocs. In: AACL/IJCNLP, pp. 770–780 (2020)

25. Yue, L., et al.: Exploring BCI control in smart environments: intention recognition via EEG representation enhancement learning. TKDD **15**(5), 1–20 (2021)

26. Yue, L., Tian, D., Chen, W., Han, X., Yin, M.: Deep learning for heterogeneous medical data analysis. World Wide Web **23**(5), 2715–2737 (2019). https://doi.org/10.1007/s11280-019-00764-z

27. Yue, L., Tian, D., Jiang, J., Yao, L., Chen, W., Zhao, X.: Intention recognition from spatio-temporal representation of EEG signals. In: ADC, pp. 1–12 (2021)

28. Zhang, J., Hao, B., Chen, B., Li, C., Chen, H., Sun, J.: Hierarchical reinforcement learning for course recommendation in MOOCs. In: Proceedings of the AAAI Conference on Artificial Intelligence, vol. 33, pp. 435–442 (2019)
29. Zhao, X., et al.: Simplifying reinforced feature selection via restructured choice strategy of single agent. In: ICDM, pp. 871–880. IEEE (2020)
30. Zhou, G., et al.: Deep interest network for click-through rate prediction. In: Proceedings of the 24th ACM SIGKDD International Conference on Knowledge Discovery & Data Mining, pp. 1059–1068 (2018)

Smart Online Exam Proctoring Assist for Cheating Detection

Mohammad M. Masud[1]([envelope]) [iD], Kadhim Hayawi[2] [iD], Sujith Samuel Mathew[2], Temesgen Michael[2], and Mai El Barachi[3]

[1] College of Information Technology, United Arab Emirates University, Al Ain, UAE
m.masud@uaeu.ac.ae

[2] College of Technological Innovations, Zayed University, Dubai, UAE
{Abdul.Hayawi,sujith.mathew}@zu.ac.ae

[3] Faculty of Engineering and Information Sciences, The University of Wollongong in Dubai, Dubai, UAE
MaiElbarachi@uowdubai.ac.ae

Abstract. Online exams are the most preferred mode of exams in online learning environment. This mode of exam has been even more prevalent and a necessity in the event of a forced closure of face-to-face teaching such as the recent Covid-19 pandemic. Naturally, conducting online exams poses much greater challenge to preserving academic integrity compared to conducting on-site face-to-face exams. As there is no human proctor for policing the examinee on site, the chances of cheating are high. Various online exam proctoring tools are being used by educational institutes worldwide, which offer different solutions to reduce the chances of cheating. The most common technique followed by these tools is recording of video and audio of the examinee during the whole duration of exam. These videos can be analyzed later by human examiner to detect possible cheating case. However, viewing hours of exam videos for each student can be impractical for a large class and thus detecting cheating would be next to impossible. Although some AI-based tools are being used by some proctoring software to raise flags, they are not always very useful. In this paper we propose a cheating detection technique that analyzes an exam video to extract four types of event data, which are then fed to a pre-trained classification model for detecting cheating activity. We formulate the cheating detection problem as a multivariate time-series classification problem by transforming each video into a multivariate time-series representing the time-varying event data extracted from each frame of the video. We have developed a real dataset of cheating videos and conduct extensive experiments with varying video lengths, different deep learning and traditional machine learning models and feature sets, achieving prediction accuracy as high as 97.7%.

Keywords: Online exam · Cheating detection · Video analysis · Deep learning

© Springer Nature Switzerland AG 2022
B. Li et al. (Eds.): ADMA 2021, LNAI 13087, pp. 118–132, 2022.
https://doi.org/10.1007/978-3-030-95405-5_9

1   Intruduction

The Guradian conducted a study [10] on 24 top ranking institutions in the UK, including Oxford and Cambridge University, and observed that cheating has grown by around 40% within three academic years, from 2014–15 to 2016–17. The current ongoing COVID-19 exacerbated this situation as all educational institutions have been forced to switch to online learning and assessments. Many academic institutes strived to quickly adapt to this situation by resorting to various online assessment monitoring tools. Many of these tools require the students to use webcam to record their activities during the assessment. However, these videos are not available in real time, rather they become available long after the exam is over. Besides, the videos may not clearly reveal cheating attempt because one webcam cannot record a 360 view of the environment.

Various approaches have been proposed to address this issue, for example, Bedford, et al. (2009) recommend using a remote proctor that combines a biometric authentication, blackboard site with software that blocks needless websites during online exams and a 360° camera. Another research conducted by Javed, A., & Aslam, Z. (2013) recommends an enhanced eye movement detection algorithm for improved surveillance during online exams. An alternative to proctoring examinees is to use double cameras, one placed on the computer to record the examinee and the other placed on the examinee's head to record the examinee's vision (Hsu, et al., 2015). Currently, the most prominent and well-known companies on providing proctoring services are ProctorU, Mettle, TestReach, ExamSoft, and Examity.

Educational institutions have applied several methods to catch and avoid cheating activities; however, the proctoring service providers have not come up with a fully efficient system (OReilly, G. & Creagh, J., 2016). In addition, the likelihood of students bypassing the methods implemented by universities is very high. There is also a possibility the implemented methods can have false positive results. Moten et al. (2013) have mentioned some of the common practices used by students to cheat on an online exam. The methods discussed in the article include receiving answers from students that have submitted the exam, questions about nonexistent errors to deceive professors, collusion, essay plagiarism, and buying answers online.

Therefore, none of them seems to bring a comprehensive solution to detect cheating. Besides, proctoring a large number of exams for large number of students would also involve a lot of resources and prove to be costly. Therefore, the cost of these tools may not be affordable by many. In this work we propose a technique to automatically detect cheating by analyzing the video recorded by webcam during the online exam. Our approach analyzes an exam video to track four types of events: eye movement, head movement, mouth opening, and face recognition for identity check. The datas from these events are extracted for every frame, and thus generates a multi-variate time series from each video. Thus, the problem is formulated as a time-series classification problem, which we address by training an appropriate machine learning model. We constructed our own real video dataset for this purpose, and conducted empirical study on varying scenarios and learning models.

Our main contributions to this work are as follow. First, we build a real video dataset consisting of both cheating and non-cheating videos. The videos are of varying lengths and represent different cheating activities. Second, we formulate the cheating detection problem as a two-step problem, address these problems. The first step is to identify characteristic features from a video to distinguish cheating from non-cheating, and thus transform a video into a multivariate time-series feature vector. The second problem is to train a classifier from the feature vector. Both the problems have been addressed systematically. Third, we address the challenge of training from variable-length videos by proposing video-length uniforming approach using frame oversampling and undersampling. Fourth, we propose a real time cheating indicator technique that is able to indicate the probability of cheating in real time, while the exam is ongoing. We believe this will help in early detection of cheating. Finally, we perform comprehensive evaluation on the dataset we built with various scenarios, such as varying video length, varying feature sets and classification models, and achieve accuracy as high as 97.5% in detecting cheating.

The rest of the paper is organized as follows. Section 2 discusses the related work, and Sect. 3 outlines the problem statement and high level architecture. Section 4 then explains the details of the proposed work. Section 5 discusses the experiments and analyzes the results. Finally, Sect. 6 concludes with directions to future work.

2   Related Work

Asep and Bandung [3] suggest the use of continuous user verification for online exam proctoring in remote learning platforms. The authors propose a method to improve the stability for pose and lighting variations by performing an incremental training process using the training data set obtained from the remote learning online lecture sessions. The authors claim to have a precise, inexpensive, convenient online exam proctoring for remote learning performed on smartphones. However, this algorithm's applicability is restricted by the memory and processing power constraints of smartphones.

Atoum et al. [4] propose a system that uses one webcam, one wear cam (a camera that is worn by an examinee to see his/her vision), and a microphone to proctor the visual and acoustic environment of the remote exam location. The suggested solution in this article has several components such as user verification, text detection, speech detection, active window detection, gaze estimation, and phone detection. To identify cheating behaviors, they created several cheating scenarios and stored the data in an Online Exam Proctoring (OEP) database. The suggested solution uses binary Support-Vector Machines (SVM) for classifier learning in order to appropriately classify behaviors as cheating and normal. From the OEP dataset, segments with no cheating are considered as samples of negative class. In another paper, Atoum et al. [5] suggest a CNN based solution for face anti-spoofing. To illustrate, it mentions that the suggested method works by fusing two CNN streams to identify face spoofing.

Marras et al. [9] aim at combining visual and audio data for user identification or verification during online examinations. The article mentions several training datasets for audio-visual identification. For face detection, each frame will be analyzed to identify the face area and landmarks using Multi-Task Cascaded CNN (MTCNN). The algorithm uses five facial points, two eyes, a nose, and two mouth corners, to detect a face in each frame. Kuin [7] recommends the use of convolutional neural networks (CNN) to automate the process of monitoring students during online exams. According to the paper, the results achieved an accuracy of 96.8% when categorizing frames into fraud and not fraud. The proposed solution uses a few thousand frames extracted from a 2-hour long video recording of an online exam. Furthermore, Garg et al. [6] propose combining Haar cascade and CNN to detect and recognize the face of an examinee during an exam. The paper claims that Haar cascade is fast but not accurate enough and CNN is slow due to a high detection rate. Therefore, they combine the two in order to achieve faster and more precise results during online exam proctoring.

Messerschmidt and Pleva [11] suggest the introduction of biometrics to authenticate examinees during an online examination. Some of the proposed biometric authentication methods in the paper include; fingerprint recognition, facial recognition, iris recognition, etc. The paper also plans on using some neural networks to detect facial expressions. Additionally, this paper also suggests the use of a non-neural network approach called Viola-Jones Algorithm for facial recognition. In addition, the solution proposed by Abisado et al. [1] mainly uses gesture recognition, face recognition and head pose estimation to proctor examinees during remote examinations. To test the system, they used 60-min videos from 75 participants. According to the researchers, the Convolutional Neural Network is appropriate for the facial and gesture recognition.

Our work is different from the above in that we not only use face recognition but also track three other types of events, the combination of which is not offered in any other work, to the best of our knowledge. Besides, the proposed technique is cost-effective, easily accessible (no extra hardware/biometric needed), and generalizable to variable length videos.

3   Proposed Technique Highlight

3.1   Problem Statement

We formulate the cheating detection problem from exam video as a time-series classification problem, as described here.

First, we will define a few terms to help developing the problem formulation. A video is defined as a sequence of image frames as follows.

Definition 1 (Video $\mathcal{V}^i$ and Frame $F^i(t)$). *Let each video $\mathcal{V}^i$ is composed of a sequence of T^i frames $\{F^i(t): 0 < t \leq T^i\}$ where each frame is a 2D image.*

We need to identify useful features from the videos to distinguish a cheating video from a non-cheating video. We define the video characteristics as follows.

Definition 2 (Video characteristic vector $\mathcal{X}^i$). *A video feature vector $\mathcal{X}^i$ is a k-dimensional multivariate time-series, which represents the time-varying features of the video $\mathcal{V}^i$:*

$$\mathcal{X}^i(T^i) = \{x^i(t)\}_{t=1}^{T^i} \tag{1}$$

where $x^i(t)$ is the k dimensional feature vector $[x_1^i(t), ..., x_k^i(t)]$, representing the frame $F^i(t)$, $1 \le t \le T^i$.

Therefore, the cheating detection from exam videos is a two-step problem. The first step is to identify k characteristic features x_t^i from each frame $F^i(t)$ of a video $\mathcal{V}^i$ and construct the corresponding multi-variate time series $\mathcal{X}^i$. The second step is to train appropriate classification model from the time series data.

Let $\mathcal{D} = \{\mathcal{V}^i, Y^i\}_{i=1}^N$ be a dataset of N videos $\mathcal{V}^i$, where each video is labeled with the binary label Y^i: $Y^i \in \{$'non-cheating','cheating'$\}$. We need to extract useful characteristics from the videos and thus transform each video $\mathcal{V}^i$ into a multivariate time series $\mathcal{X}^i$ as defined above. Thus the problem will be transformed into a time-series classification problem, which can be solved by training appropriate deep learning models. The following subsections explains the solution to these problems.

3.2 High Level Architecture

The proposed technique consists of several stages. Figure 1 shows the architecture. First, the video is recorded using webcam. Then four different types of video characteristics are extracted from each frame that capture four main events: the eye movement, head movement, mouth opening, and the identity of the examinee. The computed values are then organized as a feature vector. For training, the videos are labeled ('cheating' or 'no cheating') by experts, and supplied to a machine learning algorithm for training. Once the classification model is trained, it is used to classify new videos that are analyzed and vectored using the same analysis and vectorization technique used for training. Following subsections discuss the stages in more details.

4 Proposed Work Details

4.1 Exam Recording

The examinee joins the exam by first identifying himself to the user authentication system. After he is authenticated, the system performs face detection and other checks. The face recorded this time will be used later to validate the identity of the examinee at regular intervals, as explained in the 'identity tracking' activity in Sect. 4.2. Exam recording starts at this stage.

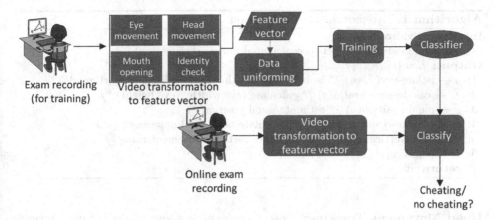

Fig. 1. Architecture of the proposed technique

4.2 Video Characteristic Analysis

The video recorded during the exam is analyzed for detecting cheating activity. Four types events are analyzed on each frame, as discussed below.

Eye Movement Tracking: The eye movement tracking activity analyzes movement of the pupil of the eye. A person can move his pupils in different directions without moving head, which can indicate a suspicious activity. Blinking of eye may also indicate a suspicious activity. Therefore, three readings are computed in this analysis: horizontal movement ratio, vertical movement ratio, and blinking ratio. The code for this tracking activity is adapted from [8]. Here we briefly describe each of them.

Horizontal Eye Movement Ratio: This ratio is calculated using the relative horizontal position of the pupil with respect to its center. The ratio can be between 0.0 to 1.0, where 0.0 indicates looking at extreme left, 1.0 indicates looking at extreme right and 0.5 indicates looking at the middle.

Vertical Eye Movement Ratio: This ratio is calculated using the relative vertical position of the pupil with respect to its center. The ratio can be between 0.0 to 1.0, where 0.0 indicates looking at extreme up, 1.0 indicates looking at extreme down and 0.5 indicates looking at the middle.

Eye Blinking Ratio: This ratio indicates whether an eye is closed or not. It is calculated by dividing the eye width with the eye height. Therefore, a higher ratio indicates eye is closing.

Algorthm 1 sketches the algorithm for tracking eye movement in a frame.

Algorithm 1. Eye-movement computation

Input: f: a video frame
    m: facial landmark model (precalculated during registration)
Output: $E = (e_h, e_v, e_b)$
 1: $g \leftarrow$ isolate-eye(f, m) /* isolate eye from the frame using landmark model */
 2: $e_b \leftarrow$ calc-blinking-ratio(g) /* calculate (eye width / eye height) */
 3: $p \leftarrow$ pupil-position(g) /* estimate pupil position */
 4: $e_h \leftarrow$ calc-horizontal-ratio(p) /* calculate horizontal movement ratio */
 5: $e_v \leftarrow$ calc-vertical-ratio(p) /* calculate vertical movement ratio */
 6: $E = (e_h, e_v, e_b)$
 7: **return** E

Head Movement Tracking: Head movement is a suspicious activity during exam. Therefore, it is important to track it. The head movement tracking attains facial landmarks from a user and computes the estimated angle between the 3D coordinates of the facial landmarks and the x-axis and y-axis. The computation results in two angles (between −90 to +90): horizontal angle and vertical angle. The code for this computation is adapted from Agarwal [2]. Algorthm 2 sketches the algorithm for tracking head movement in a frame.

Algorithm 2. Head-movement computation

Input: f: a video frame
    m: facial landmark model (precalculated during registration)
Output: $H = (h_x, h_y)$
 1: $R \leftarrow$ facial-marker-detection(f,m)) /* isolate facial markers from the frame using landmark model */
 2: $C \leftarrow$ calc-3D-coord(R) /* calculate 3D coordinates from markers */
 3: $h_x \leftarrow$ calc-horizontal-angle(C) /* calculate horizontal angle wrt axis */
 4: $h_y \leftarrow$ calc-vertical-angle(C) /* calculate vertical angle wrt axis */
 5: $H = (h_x, h_y)$
 6: **return** H

Mouth Opening Tracking: The height of the opening is calculated in this analysis. Mouth opening is suspicious because the examinee may be talking to a person who is not in the camera range. This type of activity will cause the mouth to be found as opened in several consecutive frames. The code for this computation is adapted from Agarwal [2]. The code computes mouth width and mouth opening using the facial landmarks.

Algorthm 3 sketches the algorithm for tracking mouth opening in a frame.

Identity Tracking: Identity tracking checks whether another person appears in the frame, which indicates a sure cheating activity. As mentioned earlier, The program takes the ID and username of the examinee at the beginning and takes

---

Algorithm 3. Mouth-opening computation

Input: f: a video frame
      m: facial landmark model (precalculated during registration)
Output: $M = (m_h, m_w)$
1: $R \leftarrow$ facial-marker-detection(f,m)) /* isolate facial markers from the frame using landmark model */
2: $m_h \leftarrow$ calc-mouth-height(R) /* calculate vertical distance between lips */
3: $m_w \leftarrow$ calc-mouth-width(C) /* calculate horizontal dist. between mouth ends */
4: $M = (m_h, m_w)$
5: **return** M

---

30 sample images for recognition. Then, it trains and associates the face with the username and ID of the examinee based on the sample images taken. After that it is able to recognize the face and identify when an "unknown" person is detected. The code that will be used in this part of the program is adapted from Rovai [12]. The code returns true if an unknown face is detected, and returns false otherwise.

Figure 2 shows different scenarios captured by the video analysis technique mentioned above.

Fig. 2. Example frames for video analysis. (a) Looking straight, no apparent cheating symptom detected. (b) Horizontal eye movement (to the left). (c) Vertical eye movement (down). (d) Horizontal head movement (to the right). (e) Vertical head movement (down). (f) Unknown identity detected. (g) Mouth open.

4.3 Videos Transformed to Feature Vector

Using the above technique mentioned in previous subsection, we extract different event-based features from each video $\mathcal{V}^i$, which in turn constructs a multi-variate time-series $\mathcal{X}^i$, addressing the first part of the problem. In particular, each feature vector $\boldsymbol{x}^i(t)$ extracted from each frame $F^i(t)$ of the video $\mathcal{V}^i$ is an eight dimensional vector (i.e., $k = 8$), and therefore, $\mathcal{X}^i$ can be expressed as:

$$\mathcal{X}^i = \{\boldsymbol{x}^i(t)\}_{t=1}^{T^i} = \{[e_h^i(t), e_v^i(t), e_b^i(t), h_x^i(t), h_y^i(t), m_h^i(t), m_w^i(t), ID^i(t)]\}_{t=1}^{T^i} \tag{2}$$

where $e_h^i(t)$ is the horizontal eye movement ratio in frame t of the i-th video
$e_v^i(t)$ is the vertical eye movement ratio in frame t of the i-th video
$e_b^i(t)$ is the eye blinking ratio in frame t of the i-th video
$h_x^i(t)$ is the horizontal angle of head in frame t of the i-th video

$h_y^i(t)$ is the vertical angle of head in frame t of the i-th video

$m_h^i(t)$ is the mouth height in frame t of the i-th video

$m_w^i(t)$ is the mouth width in frame t of the i-th video, and

$ID^i(t)$ is the identity (known/unknown) in frame t of the i-th video

Therefore, given a video dataset $\mathcal{D} = \{\mathcal{V}^i, Y^i\}_{i=1}^N$ of N videos $\mathcal{V}^i$, and their labels Y^i: $Y^i \in \{\text{'non-cheating','cheating'}\}$, the dataset is transformed into a labeled, multivariate time-series dataset $\{\mathcal{X}^i, Y^i\}_{i=1}^N$, where $\mathcal{X}^i$ is defined above.

4.4   Data Uniforming by Video Length Equalizing

The videos in the dataset $\mathcal{D}$ may not be of the same length, i.e., for any pair of videos $(\mathcal{V}^i, \mathcal{V}^j)$, it is possible that $T^i \neq T^j$. Therefore, these two videos, having different number of frames, generates different feature vector sizes. This will be problematic during training because the vector sizes of each training instance must be the same to train a machine learning algorithm. In order to solve this problem, we perform video length equalization using either frame undersampling or oversampling, thereby making all the videos in the dataset of uniform length. These techniques are described below.

Frame Oversampling: Assume that a video of length T needs to be over-sampled to a video of length N, where $N > T$. For this, we randomly choose one frame from the T frames, and repeat this N times. Then these frames are ordered (i.e., sorted by index), making a new video of N frames. Algorithm 4 sketches the oversampling algorithm.

Algorithm 4. Frame oversampling

Input: $\mathcal{V}$: a video of length T = sequence of T frames $\{F(1),...,F(T)\}$
   N: New length $(N > T)$
Output: $\mathcal{W}$: new video of length N after frame oversampling of $\mathcal{V}$
 1: $\mathcal{W} = \{\}$ /* empty list */
 2: **for** $i = 1$ to N **do**
 3:     $r \leftarrow$ Random(T) /* generate a random number between 1 ... T */
 4:     $\mathcal{W} \leftarrow$ insert$(\mathcal{W}, F(r))$ /* insert frame $F(r)$ in $\mathcal{W}$ in ordered fashion */
 5: **end for**
 6: **return** $\mathcal{W}$

Frame Undersampling: Assume that a video of length T needs to be under-sampled to a video of length N, where $N < T$. First, we calculate T/N to see if the video can be split into multiple videos of length N. For example, if $T/N = 2.8$, we take the floor $= 2$. This means we can split the video into at least two videos of length N. Then for each split, we randomly choose N frames from the original video, and sort them to get the new undersampled videos. Algorithm 5 sketches the undersampling algorithm.

Algorithm 5. Frame undersampling

Input: $\mathcal{V}$: a video of length T = sequence of T frames $\{F(1),...,F(T)\}$
   N: New length $(N < T)$
Output: $\mathcal{W}$: new array of videos of length N each after frame undersampling of $\mathcal{V}$
1: $m \leftarrow$ floor(T/N) /* the video will be split into m undersampled videos */
2: $\mathcal{W}$ = Video$[m]$ /* empty array of m videos */
3: **for** $i = 1$ to m **do**
4:    $\mathcal{W}[i]$ = {} /* empty video */
5:    **for** $i = 1$ to N **do**
6:       $r \leftarrow$ Random(T) /* generate a random number between 1 ... T */
7:       $\mathcal{W}[i] \leftarrow$ insert$(\mathcal{W}[i], F(r))$ /* insert frame $F(r)$ in $\mathcal{W}[i]$ in ordered fashion */
8:    **end for**
9: **end for**
10: **return** $\mathcal{W}$

4.5 Training

For training, video recordings are collected from exam sessions, where each session is identified as either 'cheating' or 'not cheating' by the participant, and the corresponding video is labeled as such. We have developed our own dataset with the help of several volunteers as described in Sect. 5.1.

Recall that the feature vector for each video is a 2D vector, and therefore, requires appropriate learning algorithm that can handle 3D training data (or tensor). There are mainly two main categories of deep learning algorithms that can learn from the 3D vector, namely, convolutional neural network (CNN), and recurrent neural network (RNN). Although CNN is mainly used for images, it has been used to learn from time series data as well. On the other hand, RNN is able to learn from the temporal relationships of time series data. We have used two special variant of RNN called long short term memory (LSTM), and bidirectional gated recurrent unit (BiGRU). We have used a combination of CNN, LSTM and BiGRU as well, which has been proven useful by some researchers. The five different types of deep learning models that we use are shown in Fig. 4, with the outline of their architectures. In addition to the deep learning models, we also use two traditional machine classification algorithms, namely, random forest and logistic regression. However, since both of these algorithms require 1D vector for each training/testing instance, we collapse the 2D vector for a video to 1D by taking the average of each column.

5 Experiments

This section describes the dataset, experimental setup, reports the results and analyzes them (Fig. 3).

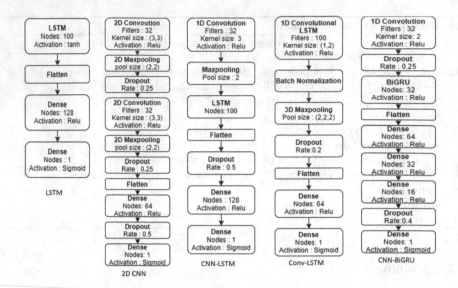

Fig. 3. Deep learning models used

5.1 Dataset

We build the video dataset by using several volunteers. Each volunteer is asked to record exam video, and either deliberately perform cheating activity, or perform no cheating. Each such video is then labeled by them accordingly. There are 43 such videos, 21 of them are cheating, and 22 of them non-cheating. The video lengths vary from 75 to 500 frames, with the average length being 330. Please recall that for training we had to make the video lengths uniform. We have chosen four different lengths to make them uniform: 75, 100, 150, 200, and 250. The resultant number of videos (due to splitting by undersampling) we got for each of these lengths are 162 videos (for 75 length), 127 videos (for 100 length), 93 videos (for 150 length), 60 videos (for 200 length) and 46 videos (for 250 length). We performed experiments considering each length set as a different dataset.

5.2 Competing Approaches

We compare five deep learning algorithms, namely, LSTM, 2DCNN, CNN-LSTM, Conv-LSTM, and CNN-BiGRU and two traditional machine learning algorithms, namely, random forest, and logistic regression. The architectures of the learning algorithms are introduced in Sect. 4.5.

5.3 Parameters, Hardware and Software

For all the learning algorithms, we use the following hyperparameters: Batch size = 16, Optimizer = Adam, Loss = Binary cross entropy, Early stopping =

yes (with validation loss monitor), Early stopping patience = 5. The parameters have been chosen by running the algorithms several times and selecting the best combination that is uniform across all the models. For random forest, the number of trees are set to 100, and for logistic regression the number of iterations is set to −1 (i.e., until convergence). We developed the code using Python on the Jupyter notebook environment. Tensorflow is used for deep learning algorithms. For the video analysis tasks, we mainly use the OpenCV API as well as the relevant open source modules as discussed in Sect. 4.2. All the experiments are run on Google Colab platform.

5.4   Evaluation

We evaluate the competing techniques using five-fold cross validation on the dataset. The evaluation metric is chosen to be 'Accuracy', as the dataset is balanced between two classes.

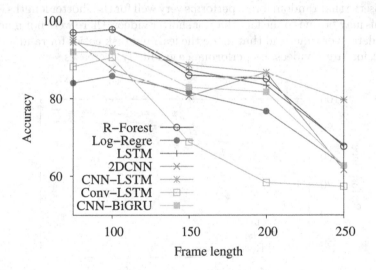

Fig. 4. Accuracy of different deep learning models and video lengths

Comparison Among Competing Algorithms and Video Lengths: Figure 4 shows the accuracy of 5-fold cross validation on the dataset for different learning algorithms and different video lengths. Table 1 reports the same in tabular format.

We observe that for any learning algorithm, the accuracy drops in general with increasing video length. This is expected because as we increase the video length, the dataset size decreases, as per statistics mentioned in Sect. 5.1. Also, it is noticeable that LSTM performs the best for video lengths 75 and 100, but CNN-LSTM performs the best for larger lengths. It can be justified by the fact that CNN-LSTM

Table 1. Summary result on different algorithms and video lengths

Learning algorithm	Video length				
	75	100	150	200	250
Random forest	96.9	**97.7**	86	85	67.6
Logistic reg.	84	85.8	81.6	76.7	62.7
LSTM	**96.91**	**97.7**	87.4	83.3	68.0
2DCNN	95.1	87.6	80.5	**86.7**	61.6
CNN-LSTM	94.47	92.9	**88.6**	**86.7**	**79.6**
Conv-LSTM	88.24	90.6	68.8	58.3	57.3
CNN-BiGRU	92.01	92.1	82.9	81.7	62.7

better captures the feature space separation between the two classes for longer videos because it possesses both the power of CNN and LSTM. It is also interesting to observe that random forest performs very well for the shorter lengths (75 and 100). This may be due to the fact that for shorter videos, there were not much variation in data over time, and that made the learning task easier for random forest. However, for larger videos, its performance gradually decreases.

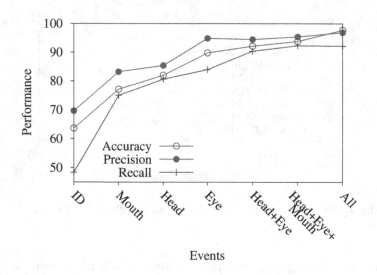

Fig. 5. Accuracy of different events, individual and combined

Individual and Combined Event-Based Feature Performance: In order to examine the performance of different event-based features, we conduct this experiment. This is done only with LSTM and 100 length videos as per the performance data from the previous experiment. The results are illustrated in Fig. 5 and Table 2.

Table 2. Individual and combined event-based feature performance

Event name(s)	Performance metric		
	Accuracy	Precision	Recall
Head movement	82	85.4	80.6
Eye movement	89.8	94.9	84
Mouth movement	77.1	83.2	75
Identity change	63.6	69.6	48.33
Head and Eye movement	92.2	94.5	90.4
Head, Eye and Mouth movement	93.8	95.4	92.3
All	**97.7**	**96.9**	**92.2**

We observe that among four events, ID change feature has the least accuracy (63.6%), and eye movement feature has the highest accuracy (89.8%). The head movement feature has the second highest accuracy, being at 82%. When the best two features are combined, we achieve 92.2% accuracy, improving about 2.5% from the individual best (i.e., eye). Combining these two with mouth movement feature increases the accuracy even further to 93.8%. Combining all four gives us the best accuracy, which is 97.7%. Therefore, we observe the importance of combining all these four event features for achieving the best performance.

6   Conclusion

Online exams are becoming a necessity nowadays due to widespread popularity and adaptation of remote teaching and learning. However, recent tools for exam proctoring are unable to provide a comprehensive solution for preventing and detecting cheating during online exam. In this work, we propose a cheating detection technique by analyzing the exam videos. We have identified several useful events that help to characterize a video as cheating or non cheating. We build our own dataset of videos and perform extensive experiments with different deep learning and machine learning models and validate efficacy the proposed technique. In future, we would like to enrich the video database with more videos of larger length, and incorporate other useful features into the learning model such as social behavior and past academic records of the examinees.

Acknowledgement. The research was funded by Zayed University, UAE, from the research initiative fund R19099.

References

1. Abisado, M., Gerardo, B., Vea, L., Medina, R.: Experimental facial expression and gesture training towards academic affect modeling. In: 2018 IEEE 10th International Conference on Humanoid, Nanotechnology, Information Technology, Communication and Control, Environment and Management (HNICEM), pp. 1–4 (2018). https://doi.org/10.1109/HNICEM.2018.8666415

2. Agarwal, V.: Real-time head pose estimation in python. https://towardsdatascience.com/real-time-head-pose-estimation-in-python-e52db1bc606a, Accessed 14 July 2021

3. Asep, H.S.G., Bandung, Y.: A design of continuous user verification for online exam proctoring on m-learning. In: 2019 International Conference on Electrical Engineering and Informatics (ICEEI), pp. 284–289 (2019). https://doi.org/10.1109/ICEEI47359.2019.8988786

4. Atoum, Y., Chen, L., Liu, A.X., Hsu, S.D.H., Liu, X.: Automated online exam proctoring. IEEE Trans. Multimedia **19**(7), 1609–1624 (2017). https://doi.org/10.1109/TMM.2017.2656064

5. Atoum, Y., Liu, Y., Jourabloo, A., Liu, X.: Face anti-spoofing using patch and depth-based CNNs. In: 2017 IEEE International Joint Conference on Biometrics (IJCB), pp. 319–328 (2017). https://doi.org/10.1109/BTAS.2017.8272713

6. Garg, K., Verma, K., Patidar, K., Tejra, N., Patidar, K.: Convolutional neural network based virtual exam controller. In: 2020 4th International Conference on Intelligent Computing and Control Systems (ICICCS), pp. 895–899 (2020). https://doi.org/10.1109/ICICCS48265.2020.9120966

7. Kuin, A.: Fraud detection in video recordings of exams using Convolutional Neural Networks. Master's thesis, Amsterdam, Netherlands (2018)

8. Lame, A.: Gaze tracking application. https://github.com/antoinelame/GazeTracking, Accessed 13 July 2021

9. Marras, M., Marín-Reyes, P.A., Lorenzo-Navarro, J., Castrillón-Santana, M., Fenu, G.: Deep multi-biometric fusion for audio-visual user re-identification and verification. In: De Marsico, M., Sanniti di Baja, G., Fred, A. (eds.) ICPRAM 2019. LNCS, vol. 11996, pp. 136–157. Springer, Cham (2020). https://doi.org/10.1007/978-3-030-40014-9_7

10. Marsh, S.: Cheating at UK's top universities soars by 40%. https://www.theguardian.com/education/2018/apr/29/cheating-at-top-uk-universities-soars-by-30-per-cent, Accessed 29 Apr 2018

11. Messerschmidt, M., Pleva, M.: Biometric systems utilizing neural networks in the authentication for e-learning platforms. In: 2019 17th International Conference on Emerging eLearning Technologies and Applications (ICETA), pp. 518–523 (2019). https://doi.org/10.1109/ICETA48886.2019.9040132

12. Rovai, M.: Real-time face recognition: an end-to-end project. https://towardsdatascience.com/real-time-face-recognition-an-end-to-end-project-b738bb0f7348, Accessed 14 July 2021

Design and Development of Real-Time Barrage System for College Class

Yuan-pan Zheng[1,2](✉) ⓘ, Bo-yang Xu[1,2] ⓘ, Yiqing Niu[1,2] ⓘ, Zhenyu Wang[1,2] ⓘ, and Ning Li[1,2] ⓘ

[1] College of Computer and Communication Engineering, Zhengzhou University of Light Industry, Zhengzhou 450001, Henan, China
[2] 136 Science Avenue, High-tech Zone, Zhengzhou, China

Abstract. In order to activate classroom atmosphere, enhance interaction between teachers and students, and to facilitate teachers to answer questions raised by students in a timely manner, a new real-time barrage class system was designed. To complete overall system design, C/S and B/S mixed-mode and MVC architecture were adopted. Our system is divided into a PC terminal function management module and a mobile terminal function management module. Through TCP protocol, mobile terminal data are communicated with server in form of JSON string. In addition to basic functions of each module, Highcharts technology was used on mobile terminal to realize visual display and analysis function of barrage data. Combined with web crawler technology and the DFA (Deterministic Finite Automaton) algorithm, a sensitive vocabulary filtering function was realized by us. Practice has proved that our real-time barrage class system can strengthen interaction between teachers and students in college classes, stimulate students' enthusiasm for learning, and improve students' participation and concentration in teaching process. Therefore, our system has feasibility and promotion value.

Keywords: College class · Barrage system · Mixed mode · Data visualization · DFA · Sensitive word filtering

1 Introduction

In university classrooms, interaction between teachers and students directly affects teaching quality of teachers and enthusiasm of students in learning. However, high-frequency interaction between teachers and students is not common in college classrooms. During class, teachers mainly teach courses based on PPT courseware. Students rarely speak, and there is very little communication between teachers and students. This teaching model is likely to cause students to lose their enthusiasm for learning, have low learning efficiency, and even affect assessment of courses. Problems presented by students in classroom gradually attracted attention of educators, so new teaching models were proposed to improve such problems. For example, Ye Donglian et al. [1] proposed a teaching model based on flipped classrooms to enhance interaction between teachers and students. However, this method has higher requirements for teachers and students

© Springer Nature Switzerland AG 2022
B. Li et al. (Eds.): ADMA 2021, LNAI 13087, pp. 133–143, 2022.
https://doi.org/10.1007/978-3-030-95405-5_10

in all aspects, and the limited class time cannot achieve expected results. Shi Yinghui et al. [2] analyzed interaction behavior of teachers and students in colleges in the smart classroom environment and found that interaction between teachers and students under smart classroom teaching mode was significantly improved by comparing with traditional multimedia teaching mode, and smart classroom teaching reduced the frequency of teachers' teaching at the same time. With increment of frequency of teacher-student interaction, students show a higher degree of initiative to participate in teaching practice. However, this model ignores students' autonomous learning and autonomous inquiry to a certain extent, and results in some students' lack of independent thinking, analysis, and problem-solving ability. So this mode is unable to cultivate innovative talents [3]. With the development of Internet technology, rise of barrage video has attracted more young people to explore this field. College students are the main representatives of this group of young people [4]. As a result, some teachers tried to introduce barrage technology in college classrooms and achieved some good results. Here are some barrage teaching samples. Dai Fangmei et al. [5] applied barrage technology to teaching of physical education theory in colleges. Zhang Chang et al. [6] applied barrage technology to teaching Chinese as a foreign language. Liu Shuang et al. [7] designed a micro course based on video barrage technology. Experiments have proved that students have a high degree of recognition of teaching model of this method. Interaction between teachers and students and enthusiasm of students in learning are improved. In one word, teaching and studying effects are both good. Therefore, barrage technology has gradually become one of the important ways of teaching reform. However, using pure barrage technology, there is room for improvement. For example, teachers cannot control contents of barrage and set barrage rules in class; feedback rate of barrage is low, and classroom teaching seems too entertaining. These problems will have an adverse effect on teaching content and classroom discipline to a certain extent. How to solve the above problems encountered by teachers in teaching process using barrage technology has become a key factor in development of barrage teaching in the future.

Based on this background, we decided to develop a real-time barrage teaching system for college classrooms after investigation and analysis. Firstly we designed the overall functional architecture of system and established a complete development process. Taking into account flexibility and scalability, system adheres to principle of independence in structural design. Browser-side function realization does not depend on any APP, and is realized by the mobile-side browser alone. Secondly, technical difficulties and typical algorithms in development process were introduced in detail. Finally, combined with test experiment, function realization of system was described detailedly.

2 System Design

2.1 System Framework and Function Design

Our barrage class system is mainly composed of three parts: PC end, mobile end and server end. This system adopted C/S and B/S mixed-mode architecture, combined with MVC architecture to complete overall system design, in which Server-side in C/S structure is the back-end Web server, and client-side in C/S structure refers to PC side. PC side uses Qt5 framework and C++ programming language to implement system visual interface. Server in B/S structure is the same as the Server in the C/S structure, using Nginx and uWSGI technology, and is mainly for data storage and calculation, and provides corresponding interface services. Client in the B/S structure mainly refers to mobile browser. Mobile terminal used Django framework and Python programming language for students to log in to system and launch barrage. In addition, client-side of system sets up two major functional modules, namely, teacher-oriented function management module and student-oriented function management module. In addition to providing basic function modules for teachers, the former also includes barrage data export and other functions and is convenient for teachers to analyze status of students in class after class, and to answer questions left by students in class. The latter mainly provides students with basic information management functions, including registration/login, personal information modification, data display and analysis, etc., so that students can review courses after class.

Barrage classroom system adopted MVC architecture and realizes data transmission between various ports through TCP/IP protocol [8]. This system could be mainly divided into application presentation layer, business logic layer and resource access layer. First, students and teachers access system through application presentation layer. After the user confirms his identity, he obtains the corresponding authority and enters the information into the system. Submission and processing of the information are realized by business logic layer. Then, business logic layer submits the input information to the resource access layer. At last, resource access layer matches the information with data in database, and feeds results back to presentation layer. The whole system architecture is shown in Fig. 1.

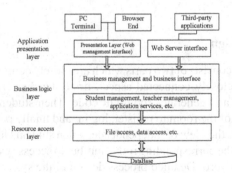

Fig. 1. System overall design architecture

Functional design of the barrage classroom was also divided into three parts: PC (teacher), mobile (student) and server. PC terminal is operated by teacher on teacher's computer, and its functions are basic system management, such as: setting barrage font, speed and transparency and whether to allow students to launch barrage, etc. It is convenient for teacher to deal with emergencies in the process of students using the system. In addition, barrage data export function can help teachers inquire about the speeches and questions of students in this section of the course, so that teachers can make a targeted analysis of courses and change teaching methods in time. Mobile terminal is operated by students through mobile browsers and does not need to rely on a specific APP, which is also different from other barrage classroom systems [9]. On mobile terminal, besides basic functional operations, such as login/registration, launching common/question barrage and setting barrage colors, the system also adds data analysis and sensitive word filtering functions to it. On one hand, it is convenient for students to query barrage information that has been launched, on the other hand, it plays a vital role in purifying classroom atmosphere. Server mainly provides data storage, exchange and information processing functions for PC and mobile terminals to ensure normal operation of system. Its concrete function structure is shown in Fig. 2.

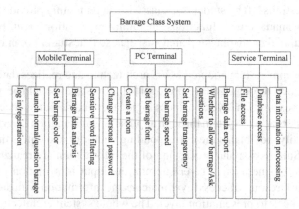

Fig. 2. System function structure

2.2 System Flow Design

System process design consists of two parts which are closely connected but independent of each other. As for closely connected aspect, firstly teacher creates a logical room on teacher's computer and generates room QR code. Then students use mobile phone browser scan QR code of the room to register, log in, and finally perform corresponding operations in system. In the view of independence, when students log in to system again, they only need to enter the corresponding room number to access system without entering account name and password. Detailed process design of the system is shown in Fig. 3.

It can be seen from Fig. 3 that PC and mobile terminals are connected through a QR code. First, teacher role transmits server address, room number, and built-in system login interface address to business logic layer of system through TCP protocol. Then we use QR code specification generation technology to encapsulate information into a QR code. Finally, through drawing function of Qt5, image is displayed on teacher's computer. Meanwhile, the QR code image is mapped to classroom screen through teaching aids such as projector. On mobile terminal, students use "scan" function that comes with mobile browser to scan and parse the QR code. Then the packaged information is obtained and system login/registration interface is displayed. Communication process between PC end and mobile end is shown in Fig. 4.

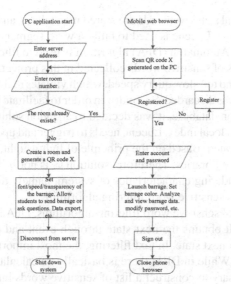

Fig. 3. System flow chart

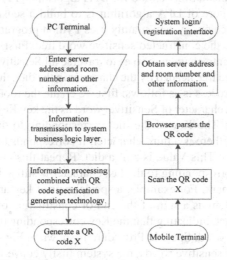

Fig. 4. Flow diagram of communication between PC and mobile

3 Analysis of Sensitive Word Filtering Algorithm

In order to prevent sensitive words from being used and projected on screen, our system defaults to sensitive word filtering function. We use crawler technology to collect the most frequently used sensitive words [10] on the Internet to create a sensitive word database. Then appropriate filtering algorithms is to be used to filter sensitive words. Our survey found that there are four commonly used filtering methods for sensitive words. ① After organizing sensitive words directly into Strings, the indexOf method is used to query and filter them. ② Traditional sensitive words are stored in database, and SQL statements are used to query and filter. ③ Lucene is used to build a word segmentation index to query. ④ Deterministic Finite Automaton (DFA) algorithm is used to filter sensitive words.

There are thousands of sensitive words collected in this project. Solution ① result in too long String length and too slow query speed, which violates real-time requirements of system. So solution ① was discarded. Secondly, in order to facilitate future scalability and minimize dependence on database, it was decided to abandon solution ②. Then Lucene itself is usually used as a local index. Lucene needs to trigger and update index again after sensitive words are updated. Based on the principle of lightweight, our system does not intend to introduce more libraries. Therefore, solution ③ is not suitable for this system. Comprehensively considering characteristics of system, namely the DFA algorithm, is selected as the system's sensitive word filtering algorithm.

In implementation of sensitive word filtering algorithms, DFA is a better implementation algorithm [11]. It obtains the next state through event and current state, that is, event + current state = next state. In text filtering, the most important goal is to reduce amount of calculation. While in DFA, there is basically no calculation but transition of state. When it is necessary to construct a list of sensitive words into a state machine, it is more troublesome to implement it with a matrix. However, tree structure provides a relatively simple implementation method for DFA algorithm [12].

In this project, the core of DFA algorithm is to build a sensitive word tree based on sensitive words. Since our system mainly uses Python programming language, dict function is used to store the constructed sensitive word tree. First, convert the collected Sensitive_word strings into characters so as to traverse all Sensitive_word characters. If there is no sensitive word tree headed by the character in the dict, then construct this tree. Specific construction process is as follows: first we create the root node of the sensitive word tree using the first character of Sensitive_word as the key Key, and the value Value is used as another dict. The Key of the dict corresponding to the value Value stores the second character. If there is a third character, it corresponds to the Value where the second character is Key. This Value is still a dict. Repeat this procedure until the last character. The Value corresponding to the last character is still a dict, but this dict only needs to store an end mark. For example, a special pair of key and value, i.e. {'\x00': 0} is stored in this system as a sign of the end of construction of sensitive word tree. This symbol is also a dict, indicating that the Key corresponding to this Value is the last character of a sensitive word. Specific Procedure is shown in Fig. 5.

When searching for sensitive words, the system firstly converts the input text string into characters, so that each character matches the constructed sensitive word tree. If the corresponding subtree cannot be matched, it will skip directly. When a certain character is detected and it is found that there is a corresponding subtree in the sensitive vocabulary, mark this subtree as tree_1. Then go on traversing and judge whether the next character is a child node of subtree tree_1. If it is, then system assesses whether the character is a leaf node of tree_1. If it is, this means that a sensitive word has been successfully matched. Based on sensitive words, system will block the input text and prompt students not to use of sensitive words.

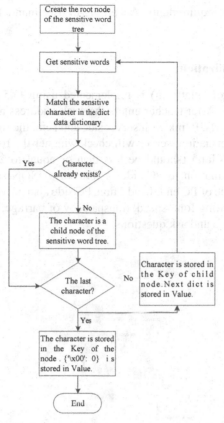

Fig. 5. Construction process of sensitive word tree

4 System Realization

In order to ensure normal operation of system, there are certain requirements for deployed hardware devices and they are listed in the below Table 1.

Table 1. Experimental environment configuration

Side	Component		
	CPU	Main memory	Secondary memory
PC	3.4 GHZ or faster	4 GB or more	100 GB or more
Mobile	1.5 GHZ or faster	2 GB or more	32 GB or more
Server	3.9 GHZ or faster	8 GB or more	1 TB or more

Our system was tested in a multimedia classroom of Zhengzhou University of Light Industry after the system was installed on teacher's computer which is qualified for the system deployment requirements. According to user manual, all kinds of system functions were tested.

4.1 PC Function Realization

PC terminal (teacher role platform) is implemented using Qt5 framework and C++ programming language. After teacher enters the server address and room number, PC terminal will establish a TCP link with server side and send the room number to server. Once receiving the information, server will check whether the room number provided already exists or is too long (should be less than or equal to 20 characters). Server will feedback the information to PC side in form of a JSON string. Figure 6 is the implementation interface of PC end. In addition, PC side also provides functions such as displaying QR code, setting font, speed, transparency of barrage, and whether to allow student to launch barrage and ask questions.

Fig. 6. PC terminal application interface

4.2 Mobile Function Realization

Mobile terminal (student terminal) was implemented by using Django framework and Python and JavaScript programming languages. Students can use browser based on Android, IOS and other mobile platform to scan the QR code generated by PC terminal to register or log in to system, modify personal passwords, etc.

Send General or Question Barrage
Students only need to enter content of barrage to be sent into web form, select corresponding barrage color, choose barrage type (normal or question), and finally click launch button to achieve this function. As shown in Fig. 7, Fig. 7(a) is mobile terminal barrage launch interface, and Fig. 7(b) is PC terminal implementation interface of the barrage.

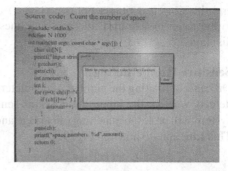

(a) Mobile terminal barrage launch interface   (b) PC terminal response of barrage

Fig. 7. Barrage launch interface

Barrage Data Analysis

In order to facilitate students to view information of barrage that has been launched, the system provides a visual query function for barrage data. Using High-charts technology, combined with barrage information, data is displayed in form of a chart. Highcharts is a chart library written in pure JavaScript. It is easy and convenient for Highcharts to add interactive charts to websites or web applications. Supported chart types include line charts, area charts, histograms, pie charts, and scatter point graph and comprehensive charts. This system uses Highcharts' histogram form to display data and its effect is shown in Fig. 8.

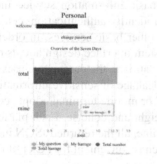

(a) Barrage information data display   (b) Question information data display

Fig. 8. Barrage data analysis

System defaults to display data information for the past seven days. As shown in Fig. 8(a), "Total" means total number of barrages launched by all students in the same room. The gray part indicates the total number of questions, and the blue part indicates total amount of ordinary barrage. "Mine" refers to the total number of individual barrages launched by the current student user. The brown part represents total number of personal questions, and the green part represents total number of individual ordinary barrage. In Fig. 8(b), the blue part represents percentage of individual questions to total question, and the gray part represents percentage of ordinary barrage launched by individuals to the total. In summary, the personal question information for the past seven days is displayed.

Sensitive Word Filtering

On basis of limiting the number of characters in the input text, system also automatically detects whether the input text contains sensitive words. If it contains sensitive words, system will prohibit launching of barrage and prompt students not to use sensitive words. This function is shown in Fig. 9.

Fig. 9. Sensitive word filtering

4.3 Server-Side Function Realization

System server is built on Window platform, using Apache HTTP Server and MySQL database. Background server provides system with basic information service interfaces, including basic information acquisition, unified identity authentication, centralized authority management, unified event record and other basic services. In order to ensure safety and convenience of each subsystem, system interface design adopts certain specifications. First, interface with sensitive information in the parameters uses the POST method instead of the GET method to prevent leakage of sensitive information. Secondly, data format returned by the interface to PC or mobile terminal adopts commonly used JSON format, which is relatively lightweight and concise. Each platform has a mature analysis solution for JSON. At the same time, all the returned JSON information conforms to a unified format specification, which is convenient for PC or mobile terminals to execute further processing.

5 Conclusion

The real-time barrage system designed and developed in this project for college classrooms has characteristics of simple operation, easy use and low requirements for hardware and software environment, which have significant positive support for classroom interactive teaching activities. Test showed that barrage system has a significant effect on activating classroom atmosphere and enhancing interaction between teachers and students. However, Due to fast update speed of network sensitive words, manual collection and use of sensitive words based on web crawlers has certain limitations. There are still many sensitive words that have not been collected in time, which makes the system's sensitive word filtering function suffer from certain deficiencies. In the future, our research and development work would combine neural network technology to realize online collection and detection of sensitive words, and further improve the system.

Acknowledgement. This work is supported by the key scientific research project plan of colleges and universities in Henan Province, grant no. 21A520049.

References

1. Ye, D., Wan, K., Zeng, T., et al.: Research on teacher-student interaction effect of participatory teaching mode based on flipping classroom. Mod. Educ. Technol. **24**(12), 77–83 (2014)
2. Shi, Y., Peng, C., Zhang, J., et al.: Analysis of interaction between teachers and students in colleges and universities in the context of smart classrooms. Mod. Educ. Technol. **29**(01), 45–51 (2019)
3. Ma, X., Zhao, G., Wu, T.: An empirical study of flipping classroom to promote the development of college students' self-learning ability——based on the practice of computer public courses in universities. China Electro-chem. Educ. (07), 99–106 (2016)
4. Zhang, J., Shui, S.: Analysis of barrage video in the internet age. Publishing Wide Angle (07), 70–72 (2016)
5. Dai, F., Yang, M.: Empirical study on the application of barrage technology in college physical education theory teaching. Hubei Sports Sci. Technol. (10), 919–921 (2017)
6. Zhang, C.: Research on the application of barrage technology in teaching Chinese as a foreign language. Asia-Pac. Educ. (24),129–131 (2016)
7. Liu, S., Zheng, Y.: Interaction design of micro-course based on video barrage technology. Modern Dist. Educ. (04), 64–69 (2015)
8. Aniche, M., Bavota, G., Treude, C., Gerosa, M.A., van Deursen, A.: Code smells for Model-View-Controller architectures. Empir. Softw. Eng. **23**(4), 2121–2157 (2017). https://doi.org/10.1007/s10664-017-9540-2
9. Wang, S.: Rain classroom: smart internet teaching tools in the background of mobile internet and big data. Mod. Educ. Technol. **27**(05), 26–32 (2017)
10. Zhu, H., Xue, X., Li, H., et al.: Distributed FP-Growth algorithm based on Hadoop under massive data. Acta Metall. Sin. **33**(05), 97–102 (2018)
11. Liu, L.: A DFA participle algorithm design and optimization in a keyword filtration system. Comput. Appl. Softw. **29**(01), 284–287 (2012)
12. Xu, L.: Algorithm research of rule combination based on DFA. Netw. Secur. Technol. Appl. (08), 38–40 (2019)

Recommendation for Higher Education Candidates: A Case Study on Engineering Programs

Bruno Mota da Silva[✉] and Cláudia Antunes

Instituto Superior Técnico, Universidade de Lisboa, Lisbon, Portugal
brunomotadasilva@tecnico.ulisboa.pt

Abstract. Over the years, there have been created new applications recurring to automatic discovery of information in educational data. The recommendation of undergraduate programs to high school students is one of these applications with little researching so far. This can be explained by the existence of a small data quantity in this context, and traditional recommendation systems demand a large number of items and users.

In this paper, we propose a hybrid approach, combining a collaborative filtering and content-based architecture, focused on programs and students. Our system suggest programs to the candidates that guarantee a high successful academic path by predicting their grades.

Keywords: Recommendation systems · Educational data mining · Feature generation from prediction

1 Introduction

Every year, thousands of high schoolers apply to higher education programs, and new degrees are created. These candidates have the difficult decision of choosing which program suits them. And if programs are significantly different from schools in a single university, sometimes the differences between programs in each one are more difficult to distinguish.

The problem of courses recommendation is very well-known in the field of Educational Data Mining, but programs recommendation puts some additional challenges to the recommendation task. One of them being that candidates are not users in the system. These engines use different approaches, like content-based or collaborative filtering recommendation systems. The last type is the most used due to the large amount of data community can give.

Considering all these aspects, we propose an architecture of a recommendation system that receives candidates personal data and academic records and

Supported by national funds by Fundação para a Ciência e Tecnologia (FCT) through project GameCourse (PTDC/CCI-CIF/30754/2017).

© Springer Nature Switzerland AG 2022
B. Li et al. (Eds.): ADMA 2021, LNAI 13087, pp. 144–155, 2022.
https://doi.org/10.1007/978-3-030-95405-5_11

it outputs the programs that best fit to their profile, comparing to the current Técnico's student community. Students and programs were the two studied entities. In one hand, we evaluated the best way to match the candidate to the students community, by computing his or her profile. On the other hand, we explored how programs and courses relate to each other and how we can implement these relations in our system to improve recommendation accuracy.

Since this type of systems demand a high validation study in order to be deployed, we applied it to Técnico students community. This way, we could see the strengths and weaknesses of the system, and make any required adjustments, considering our large domain knowledge about the way Técnico works.

This paper is divided in three more sections. Section 2 summarizes the actual scenario of Educational Recommendation Systems. Section 3 presents the proposed architecture, focusing on the two modules description and the detailed tasks to build it, and Sect. 4 explains how this work was evaluated, by presenting a Case Study based on Técnico students community. This paper ends with an overview of the performance of our system and the next steps to improve it.

2   Related Work

Recommendation Systems (RS) are software tools and techniques that provide suggestions for items to be of use to a user [8]. A RS can be exploited for different purposes, such as, to increase the number of items sold, to better understand what the user wants, or, in another point of view, to recommend a specific item to that user. A recommendation system is typically characterized by a set of users C, a set of items I and a rating function f that measures the utility of the item i to user c [3]. Hence, the aim of the RS is to recommend the item $i' \in I$ for each customer $c \in C$ that maximizes the user's rating.

Over the years, a large amount of educational data is being generated and there are being applied more collaborative filtering approaches than content-based methods in this area. Collaborative filtering approaches focus on community past behaviour [1,5,6] and in Portugal there were being developed educational many examples of these systems [2,9]

The topic around course and programs recommendations gained even more attention recently, with several published studies in the last years, following a variety of approaches [4,7].

3   ESTHER

The proposed rEcommendation SysTem for Higher Education pRograms (ESTHER) shall enlighten candidates about the degrees that are more compatible with their interests and that were chosen by successful students similar to them, following a hybrid approach. Our system architecture is composed of two main modules: Students Profiler and Programs Recommender.

Candidates start using our system by inputing their personal data that will be used to predict their profile. Current students data allow us to compute candidates profiles that will feed the second module. Programs Recommender uses the previous output to estimate a program success measure considering estimated grades, returning in the end a ranking of the most suitable programs to the candidates.

3.1 Students Profiler

There is a major difference between our recommendation system and the common ones, where the target user is inside the system among the others. Here, the target user candidate is not in the system, since he or she is not enrolled at a higher education degree yet, and therefore can not rate programs or take courses. Hence, it must be developed a strategy where we can compare users.

Students Profiler computes the candidate profile as if he or she was inside the system, by comparing him or her with the current students. Since candidates and students are people, they share personal variables that can be used to compute the similarity between them. Therefore, the first step is to collect these data and build a students profiling model.

During this model building, we performed data preparation and a feature selection study, where we tried to identify if there were useful variables for discriminating among different profiles. In order to build the Profiling Model, we applied the K Nearest Neighbors (KNN) method, after choosing the best similarity measure and number of neighbors, K. In the end, Students Profiler will return candidate profile that will be fed to the next module.

3.2 Programs Recommender

Programs Recommender module is a more complex one which aims at finding the ranking of the best programs to the candidates, considering their profile. This module has two models within: Grades Model, that will receive Candidate Profile and will estimate the candidate performance in each possible academic unit that is missing on the profile, and Ranking Model, that will be fed with Candidate Grades and will return the Programs Ranking, making it clear which programs are most suitable to the candidate.

Students Grades and Programs Data datasets will allow the building of the necessary models to implement this strategy. The first one is composed by the grades each student had in all the courses he or she took, and the second has the curricular plans of each program, and syllabuses and objectives of all courses.

After having Candidate Grades to all possible courses, we estimated the Grade Point Average that candidate would have for each program, recurring to Programs Data, composed by each curricular unit from its curriculum and the respective credits. Therefore, Ranking Model is only GPA computation and ranking the nineteen programs in descending order of their estimated GPA.

To add more complexity to ESTHER engine, Ranking Model was built on different levels, namely by implementing prediction methods. Hence, the second approach was implementing a Belief Network, where the probability of having success, knowing a course grades dataset, was computed for each program.

This strategy recurred to the notion of full joint probability and it follows the Eq. 1, which demanded the building of several data objects regarding the needed parameters and probabilities.

$$P(S|Courses) = \frac{\prod_{i=1}^{n} P(course_i = x|S) \times P(S))}{\prod_{i=1}^{n} P(course_i = x)} \tag{1}$$

Every element of the Eq. 1 is observable. The course grades probabilities can be computed assuming normal distributions and the success probabilities can be computed for each course and program after establishing a success measure.

A higher level of complexity can be achieved through the use of a content-based approach. Recommendation systems usually deal with a very large number of items, but the number of programs available in any university is just a few, when compared. Additionally, each student is enrolled on just one program, which means that our grades matrix would be very sparse, not contributing for a good recommendation. A third aspect is that programs share some courses (for example all engineering students study Physics and Maths, while all art students study Drawing and Geometry). But we can go a step further, and understand that courses cover some topics present in different areas. For example, several engineering courses study systems, their architecture and their dynamics.

Considering these aspects, we made use of the domain knowledge, and performed a thorough information retrieval operation from the syllabus of all existing courses, contained on every program available. This analysis was done using natural language processing (NLP) usual techniques, which were able to identify the terms present on all courses syllabus. In this manner, instead of describing each program by its generic description, we do it through a bag of words (terms) and their importance on the course, and consequently on the program. These terms are then the new features stored in the Feature Store, which is kind of a repository to save variables derived from some source, and the formula to derive them. These formulas, when applied to students grades stored, create new records, richer than the original ones, which feed the training of the Ranking Model. This strategy gave us the possibility of dealing with the academic units at different levels of granularity: we can aggregate everything to recommend programs, or we can simply identify a ranking of topics that are recommended for the candidate. This ability is very important to reach a new level of explainability, so needed in the field.

All the tasks and elements regarding Program Recommender module at its higher level of complexity are shown in Fig. 1 with all the tasks separated by the two modules. Note that most of them are done before the candidate uses our recommendation system, only the steps in bold are done during each system running.

3.3 System Dependencies and Limitations

As it was mentioned above, ESTHER architecture differs from a typical recommendation system, given that the target user is not among the other users inside

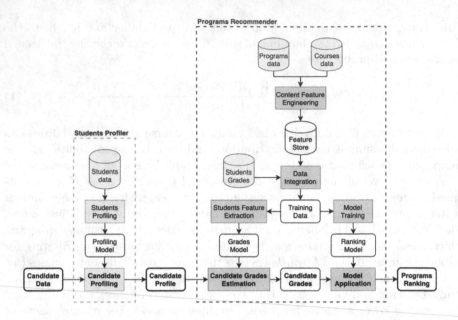

Fig. 1. Proposed architecture for ESTHER engine - Higher complexity level.

the system. We wanted to build a candidate profile based on a KNN approach to overcome this difficulty, but that can bring some errors to the recommendations.

The variables we considered to compute the nearest neighbors can not work as we wished, since they can not be sufficient to distinguish the students between programs. Since Students Profiler is the first ESTHER module, its errors will propagate through the system and affect the ranking of recommended programs.

Since courses are taught by different professors to different students, each course grades range can be very different. This can affect the programs with lower grades, which will be less recommended.

Despite the introduction of the content-based feature being a hard task to implement, since we depend on the NLP tools accuracy, this will allow us to see the system on different granularity levels.

With all above considered, we applied ESTHER engine to Técnico student community and explored all strengths and weaknesses of this architecture.

4   Case Study

Choosing a higher degree is a sensitive issue, since it will affect your life, therefore it is important to make this decision wisely, with all the available options in mind. Considering the delicacy of this choice, ESTHER engine must be extensively tested before being deployed to high school candidates. Hence, we applied our architecture on the students who have enrolled at Técnico from 2014 to 2019 to evaluate the performance of ESTHER engine.

Since our architecture has two modules with different components with deep implications between them, we validated ESTHER in two ways: first, analyzing each component's performance and exploring different approaches in each one, and evaluating our global system considering the different combinations of the relevant approaches of each component. Regarding the evaluation from a global point of view, we considered some performance measures. The first one is the percentage of candidates that enrolled at the recommended program. This measure derives from precision measure of classification algorithms, which we called precisionRS, showed in Eq. 2, where SEF means students who enrolled at the first recommended program.

$$precisionRS = \frac{no.\ of\ SEF}{Total\ no.\ of\ students} \tag{2}$$

The idea of creating this tool arose to help candidates deciding their future and we want to recommend programs where they will succeed. Therefore, we estimated a evaluation measure called successful outcome (SO), showed below in Eq. 3.

$$SO = \frac{no.\ of\ successful\ SEF}{no.\ SEF} \tag{3}$$

4.1   Students Profiler

Students Profiler module is responsible for computing Candidate Profile, by identifying which students are most similar to the candidate, and as it was mentioned before, personal data are the variables that make possible this match. In this section, we describe the studies that were done with personal data and the different effects on ESTHER performance.

Best K and Similarity Measure Study. The computation of candidate's profile demands a study to find the best pair (K, similarity measure) mimetizing a KNN performance study, but without focusing on the classification task.

First, we needed to define which condition must students achieve to have success on their program, based on their Grade Point Average (GPA), from a 0–20 scale. Since the average of students GPA is 12.99, we labeled as having success students which GPA was equal to 13 or more, and not having success otherwise. This way we guaranteed a balanced dataset, despite KNN does not be affected by balancing.

After the labeling, we computed ten trials of data train-test split for five similarity measures (chebyshev, correlation, cosine, euclidean, and cityblock) and for K between 5 and 155 in multiples of 5, considering both datasets. For each pair, we computed the average of KNN model accuracies along the ten training trials, since 70% train and 30% test datasets are random in each one.

The results for Complete dataset are shown in Fig. 2. The best pairs considering each similarity measure were: (90, chebyshev); (20, cityblock); (50, correlation); (40, cosine) and (20, euclidean). The best pairs for Reduced dataset considering each similarity measure were: (105, chebyshev); (20, cityblock); (60, correlation); (40, cosine) and (20, euclidean).

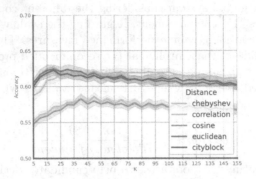

Fig. 2. Zoom of K and similarity measure study for complete dataset.

Since the pair (20, cityblock) was the one with higher accuracy in both studies, 62.5% for Complete dataset and 62.3% for Reduced dataset, we chose it as our measure to compute the candidate's nearest neighbors and estimate candidate's profile.

Choosing 20 neighbors for this step means that each candidate will receive the grades of twenty students that can be from different programs. Therefore, we made use of our test sample and explored if the computed neighbors and the candidate are from the same program. Those results suggested that the answers from NEP Survey do not distinguish students among different programs, since in 20 most similar students only 1 in average has the same program as the candidate.

After that, we tried to aggregate the nineteen programs into clusters, considering students' answers to the survey. We concluded that using all the answers does not lead to relevant clusters, since silhouette coefficient is below 0.2, which means there is not sufficient similarity between each student to the cluster he or she is in. However, for Reduced dataset, we have a silhouette coefficient higher than 0.6 for 5 clusters, which is satisfactory for this work, and it is similar to the one we obtained in the previous KNN Study.

Finally, considering all the aspects of this study, we decided to test two conditions in the global system: using Complete dataset, with cityblock similarity measure and 20 nearest neighbors, and using Reduced dataset, with the same KNN parameters.

4.2 Programs Recommender

Programs Recommender module is responsible for computing the ranking of recommended programs, considering the Candidate Profile outputted by the previous module. We could build this ranking using Students Grades and Programs

Data datasets, that lead respectively to Grades Model and Ranking Model. In this section, we describe the models that were implemented and the global performance of ESTHER engine.

NEP gave us access to a database of 216802 grades data for 918 courses taken by 7414 students. Students Grades dataset allowed us to compute the current GPA for each student and added to the previous mentioned dataset. We analyzed the distribution of students GPA, where 12.99 was the average, and we concluded that GPAs follow an approximated normal distribution. However, the average GPA varies in each program, which can affect ESTHER system, because programs with lower GPA are less likely to be recommended. Note that the distribution of students GPA is also distinct through different programs.

After merging both datasets, Students Personal Data and Students Grades, we keep 7288 students with 156544 grades for 353 courses that will be our case study population. Composed by 140406 course grades for training purposes, this merged dataset allowed us to build different Grades Models, and, by leveling up the complexity, distinct Ranking models as well, that will be described ahead.

Programs Data dataset is composed by the curricular plans of each one of the nineteen Bachelor programs offered by Técnico. For each course, we scraped its textual data about syllabuses and objectives from Técnico's website. We collected this data in order to characterize all the programs, by trying to find scientific terms that reveal what each course is about.

After data collection, we applied a Natural Language Processing technique called bag-of-words to the concatenation of both text objects for each course. This method counts the occurrences of each word in the text piece, and for each program we can sum the word vectors of all the courses that composes it. Since we wanted to obtain expressions that could define each program, we only keep words that were verbs or nouns recurring to a Part-of-Speech Tagger.

Considering the word vectors for each program, we applied a hierarchical clustering technique to aggregate programs with similar word expressions. Taking into consideration our domain knowledge on the scientific areas of Técnico's programs, we considered the results satisfactory. We applied a simple NLP technique for Portuguese language that was not optimized. If we had translated textual data in English and an accurate POS Tagger tool, we believe that this content based feature can improve substantially ESTHER system.

Grades Model. This model is the one responsible for estimating the grades each student would have in all programs at Técnico. As explained before, we used a collaborative approach to implement this estimation, where grades are ratings and students are users, using the Surprise library.

Surprise is a Python scikit for building and analyzing recommender systems that deal with explicit rating data[1]. This library offers several prediction methods to build recommendation systems: CoClustering, where users and items are assigned some clusters C_u, C_i, and some co-clusters $C_u i$; KNNBasic, KNNWith-Means and KNNWithZScore, which are prediction methods based on K Nearest

---

[1] http://surpriselib.com/.

Neighbors technique; SVD and SVDpp, that use matrix factorization techniques; and SlopeOne, which is a simple but effective recommender. Since each algorithm has different specifications, we tested all the above offered by Surprise library on ESTHER and we concluded that SVDpp was the algorithm that works worse with our data, with higher error measures and their respective standard deviations. All the other methods presented similar results. Singular Value Decomposition (SVD) algorithm, which is one of the most used matrix factorization techniques in recommendation systems, showed the lowest error measures, hence, we chose it as our prediction method for computing Candidate Grades.

To sum up, Grades Model receives Candidate Profile as input and it goes through a SVD matrix factorization technique, resulting into Candidate Grades, the object fed to the Ranking Model.

Ranking Model. Ranking model application is the end of ESTHER system, which returns a sorted list of the most suitable programs to the Candidate, according to his or her data. Since programs can be similar, we tested two types of recommendations: First 1, where the current program of our simulated candidate matches the first recommended program of the outputted ranking, and First 5, where the current program of our simulated candidate is in the first five recommended programs of the outputted ranking.

As we described in Sect. 3.2, Programs Recommender was implemented under different levels of complexity. In the simplest approach, our ranking was based on the computed GPA for each program (GPA Approach), and we developed a more complexed one, using a Belief Network (BN Approach). In this section, we will explore the differences in the results of both approaches, considering the two types of recommendations.

PrecisionRS, that was described on the beginning of this chapter, measures how many correct recommendations we made using ESTHER system. The results are shown in Fig. 3. Overall, our values for precisionRS are not promising, since, in First 1 approach, we never had more than 10% correct recommendations. However, if we consider to recommend 5 programs, our precisionRS is slightly better, reaching values of 30%. GPA Approach returns better outcomes than BN Approach, as well, using the Complete Dataset, instead of using the Reduced dataset. Since Belief Network was the only classification method applied and it was not sufficiently tuned due to time effort, there still is room for improvement. Regarding to the size of the datasets, the difference is not enough to automatically discard Reduced one, only considering precisionRS results.

Considering all the candidates who we gave a correct recommendation, we computed the mean absolute error of their current Grade Point Average and the one computed by ESTHER. The average of these results are showed in Fig. 4. As it can be seen on the bar chart, all methods and approaches had similar results, around 2 points of error. Since our Grading System is a 0–20 scale, we have an error of approximatedly 10%, which is satisfactory.

Taking into consideration that a program recommendation can have a huge impact into candidate's life, it is important to make proper recommendations

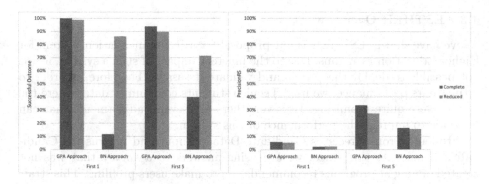

Fig. 3. PrecisionRS and sucessful outcome for each approach of ESTHER system.

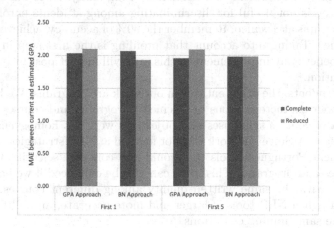

Fig. 4. Mean absolute Error between current and estimated GPA for each approach of ESTHER system.

that will lead to a successful academic path. Therefore, we evaluated the successful outcome of those candidates, again only considering the students enrolled in the recommended program. The results are shown in Fig. 3. By analyzing the bar chart above, we see that using BN Approach does not work well with Complete dataset in terms of successful outcome. Using Reduced dataset returns better results, but these outcomes highlight the need to tune this approach. However, we can conclude that the certainty of having success is very high, when using the GPA Approach. Using Complete dataset on this strategy guarantees 100% of success to students who follow our recommendation. Even, when we consider students who followed one of the first 5 recommended programs, successful outcomes are around 90%, which are very good results.

4.3   ESTHER Overview

As we have shown, ESTHER is our proposal for a Recommendation System for Higher Education Programs. Due to the inherent impact of such a system, it was not possible to deploy the system and validate its usage. Therefore, in order to estimate its performance, we used Técnico students community data, where the results were quite promising. However, there are several adjustments that can be made to improve the performance of this system.

Students Profiler receives Candidate Data as input and returns the Candidate's Profile. At this stage, we are using answers to a survey that was not created aiming at programs recommendation to make users profiling. This strategy was the only available to do this work, however, Técnico can work to develop a system to know its students and candidates community. As it was shown, the existing survey is not useful for discriminating among students enrolled in the different programs at Técnico. Remember the 60% of accuracy, achieved with the KNN classifier. Taking into account that profiling is the first step in ESTHER system, we believe any improvement in this task will impact positively programs recommendation.

Besides students, the other entities in our work are programs. We have failed to make proper characterizations of Técnico's programs and courses, since the textual data of courses syllabuses and objectives were not homogeneous and it was in Portuguese. Since our work was not focused at NLP strategies, we did not explore efficient Portuguese tools that could find correctly scientific terms that define courses and programs. This work can also be enhanced if we have english textual data with the same written quality among different courses, since the universe of English NLP tools is larger and more accurate, and all the courses will be in the same mining conditions.

When we overcome these two difficulties, we can think about improving our Ranking Model. The quite low precision of our system is due to the current lack of data to characterize the programs. This lack of data does not allow the training of accurate models for choosing the best programs for each candidate. We believe that the extraction of features from programs and curricular units descriptions will help on that characterization, which should improve those models, and consequently our system's precision. Additionally, we can also explore different success measures on those models, such as, measures based in quartiles and personalized to each program.

Despite these difficulties, we believe that ESTHER has very good results, considering all these disadvantages. This work can be the start of a major investment in a more personalized education.

5   Conclusions

The current educational context, even more after the beginning of the pandemic situation, demands new educational systems. Systems able to address the difficulties inherent to distance learning contexts, where students are far from educators, and plenty of times try to follow their path without any guidance.

Most of the times, online education tools deal with students in a 'one-fit-all' approach, that ignores each student's preferences.

We proposed a new architecture for a recommendation system, designed for suggesting programs to university candidates, taking into account their personal data. Our system benefits from an hybrid architecture, that combines collaborative filtering with a content-based philosophy, proposing to explore the full documentation of programs and courses available.

ESTHER showed so far promising results, suggesting programs that guarantee a successful academic path for those who follow our recommendations. We believe that the proposed architecture is adaptable to smaller contexts, for example for suggesting learning resources at any abstraction levels, such as exercises, and it can be scaled up to make recommendations in larger contexts, such as suggesting the most suitable school of a university.

References

1. Al-Badarneh, A., Alsakran, J.: An automated recommender system for course selection. Int. J. Adv. Comput. Sci. Appl. **7**, 166–175 (2016). https://doi.org/10.14569/IJACSA.2016.070323
2. Carballo, F.O.G.: Masters courses recommendation: Exploring collaborative filtering and singular value decomposition with student profiling (2014)
3. Jariha, P., Jain, S.K.: A state-of-the-art recommender systems: an overview on concepts, methodology and challenges. In: 2018 Second International Conference on Inventive Communication and Computational Technologies (ICICCT), pp. 1769–1774 (2018)
4. Ma, B., Taniguchi, Y., Konomi, S.: Course recommendation for university environment. In: EDM (2020)
5. Morsomme, R., Alferez, S.V.: Content-based course recommender system for liberal arts education. In: EDM (2019)
6. O'Mahony, M.P., Smyth, B.: A recommender system for on-line course enrolment: an initial study. In: Proceedings of the 2007 ACM Conference on Recommender Systems, RecSys 2007, pp. 133–136. Association for Computing Machinery, New York (2007). https://doi.org/10.1145/1297231.1297254
7. Polyzou, A., Nikolakopoulos, A.N., Karypis, G.: Scholars walk: a markov chain framework for course recommendation (May 2019)
8. Ricci, F., Rokach, L., Shapira, B.: Recommender Systems Handbook, vol. 1–35, pp. 1–35 (October 2010)
9. de Sousa, A.I.N.A.: Market-based higher education course recommendation (2016)

Web Application

UQ-AAS21: A Comprehensive Dataset of Amazon Alexa Skills

Fuman Xie, Yanjun Zhang[✉], Hanlin Wei, and Guangdong Bai

The University of Queensland, Brisbane, Australia
yanjun.zhang@uq.edu.au

Abstract. Various virtual personal assistant (VPA) services have become popular, due to the convenient interaction manner of voice user interface (VUI) they offer. Centered around them, an ecosystem involving service providers, third-party developers and end users, has started being formulated. The developers are enabled to create applications and release them through application stores, from which the users can obtain them and then run them on smart devices. This emerging ecosystem is still in its early stage, and a great deal of research effort is desired to make it on the healthy track to facilitate its development. Nonetheless, there is still a lack of comprehensive datasets for our research community to conduct research on relevant issues, e.g., the bug-freeness and quality of the applications, and users' security and privacy concerns on them. In this work, we aim to build such a dataset for research use. We target the Amazon VPA service, i.e., the Alexa, which is the most popular VPA service. We collect 65,195 Alexa applications (or *skills*), and extract comprehensive information about them, including invocation names, user reviews, among overall 16 attributes. We show the demographic details of the skills and their developers, and also conduct preliminary statistical analyses on the quality and privacy issues, to demonstrate the potential usage of our dataset. The dataset and analysis results are released online to facilitate future research: https://github.com/xie00059/Amazon-Alexa-UQ-AAS21-datasets.

Keywords: Alexa skills · Voice user interface (VUI) · Dataset

1 Introduction

The boom of the Internet of Things (IoT) in recent years has accelerated the integration of various smart devices into our daily life. They are reshaping the traditional way of graphics-based human computer interaction into the voice-based user interaction. Various AI (artificial intelligence)-backed virtual personal assistant (VPA) services are easily accessible on the smart devices, and serve people in a convenient interaction manner of voice user interface (VUI). They handle a wide range of user requests, from making phone calls, setting alarms, playing music, looking up weather forecasts, to controlling smart home devices. According to Statistics [4], VPAs have been deployed on billions of devices around the world, and this number is estimated to reach 8.4 billion by 2024.

© Springer Nature Switzerland AG 2022
B. Li et al. (Eds.): ADMA 2021, LNAI 13087, pp. 159–173, 2022.
https://doi.org/10.1007/978-3-030-95405-5_12

Besides the embedded capabilities, the VPA services enable third-party developers to provide applications as an enrichment of their functionalities. The developers create applications and publish them through application stores. The users can then activate an application verbally on their smart speakers and interact with it through oral commands, in place of the traditional mouse movement or screen tapping. Through this model, an ecosystem similar to the Android one that is centered around the Google play market [6], is gradually formulated. Take Amazon's VPA service, i.e., Alexa, as an example. The number of its applications has gone within three years from 130 to over 100,000 around all its stores as of September 2019 [8]. As another example, the number of applications for Google Assistant, Google's VPA service, has risen 2.5 times within 2018 [16].

Due to this rapid growth, the VPA ecosystem has also attracted much attention from various research communities. Some studies have been conducted to analyze VPA users' behaviors [10,20,24], and security implications [23,29] and privacy concerns [15,18,22] of the VPA services. When a dataset is needed, the researchers tend to crawl one on their own. This is however a burdensome and time-consuming process. In addition, the dataset maintenance is troublesome. If an application, or some field of an application, e.g., a piece of user review, is not well kept, it may have become unavailable online when it is needed. Therefore, a comprehensive, well-organized, and publicly available dataset is desirable.

In this work, we aim to build such a dataset named UQ-AAS21. As the first step, we target Amazon Alexa [1], the most popular VPA service at present. We browse through all accessible Alexa applications (or *skills*) in the Amazon Skill store, and download the raw data on the webpage of each skill. We also download all links available on the webpage, so that rigorous information of the skills can be taken into record. This enables our dataset to include useful information that may have overlooked by previous studies, such as the privacy policies and user review comments. Overall, we have included 65,195 skills in our dataset, and comprehensive information about them is incorporated, including invocation names, developers, user reviews, among a total of 16 attributes. All these data are pre-processed and well-formatted to be easily accessible.

We explore the comprehensiveness and usability of our dataset with two preliminary studies. First, we conduct a demographic study on the skills and their developers. Our dataset enables us to reveal several enlightening facts. For example, the analysis of the top popular skills reveals their distribution among the categories. We summarize the quality of a skill from its user rating, and this allows us to explore the potential correlation between a skill's popularity and its quality. Our preliminary semantic analysis of user reviews, taking two popular skills as case studies, shows users' negative attitude towards the in-skill purchase. Our statistical analysis of the developers shows that high productivity may not imply high quality. Also, the skills provided by third-party developers could be susceptible to malicious attacks.

Second, we conduct a study on the availability of skills' privacy policies and terms of use. It reveals that the coverage of developer privacy policy (DPP) and developer terms of use (DTOU) is low. This should raise an alert to all

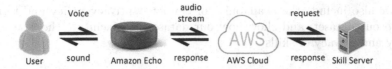

Fig. 1. Interaction flow of an Alexa skill application

stakeholders in the VPA ecosystem, especially in the context that many countries around the world start imposing strict administrative procedures on the user data protection, such as the EU General Data Protection Regulation (GDPR) [5].

Contributions. In summary, this work makes the following contributions.

- **A comprehensive and highly usable dataset.** We build a dataset that includes 65,195 Amazon Alex skills and their rigorous information. It is demonstrated to be highly usable. We have released it to the public to facilitate future research.
- **Two studies based on our dataset.** We conduct two studies on the skills and their developers, revealing some enlightening findings regarding their demography. Our work confirms the findings of previous studies, e.g., Lentzsch et al. [18], and supplements their results with analysis on the data up to May 2021.
- **Advancement of the ecosystem.** Our work provides new perspectives for third-party developers and promotes high-quality skills, contributing to the healthy development of the ecosystem.

2   Background and Related Work

2.1   Background

Amazon Alexa is the most popular VPA service at present. It allows third-party developers to create applications named skills. The interaction flow with a skill is shown in Fig. 1. When there is a voice input from the user, the Alexa Echo device converts it to an audio stream, which is then sent to the Alexa Cloud. The cloud recognizes texts from the audio stream and delivers them to the server of the corresponding skill [11]. All voice recognition and conversion are processed by Alexa Cloud [3] and the skills can only access the processed texts given by Alexa Cloud.

Amazon enforces a vetting process on the skills before they are put onto the skill store. The developer has to test and ensure the usability and ethical policy for their skill to be approved. Amazon Alexa has thousands of skills available on the skill store. However, since they are designated for personal use, security and privacy concerns can be raised. Some studies have reported that several issues exist with Alexa skill vetting process. For example, a dishonest or malicious developer can change the code of the skill server after the skill has been approved by Amazon, which opens the door for malicious activities [18]. Therefore, in this work, we also include the availability of developer privacy policy and terms of use into our dataset, and show how our dataset can facilitate the research on security and privacy of skills.

2.2   Related Work

Alexa-related Datasets. Lentzsch et al. [18] propose a large-scale data analysis of Amazon Alexa. They collect information from skill store in seven different countries, and their dataset is mainly used to analyze Alexa's security and privacy issues. Compared with it, our dataset includes updates in 2021, and contains more attributes including application icon, in-skill purchase, supported language and other related information to make the datasets more complete. It also enables some new researches, such as analyzing the relationship between the skills' popularity and other attributes like names and icons.

Another related dataset is from Gao et al. [14]. It collects 55,502 user reviews of Amazon Echo from 2015 to 2017. These reviews can reflect the attitudes of Alexa's users about Amazon's speech recognition capability, but they are not reviews about Alexa skills. In contrast, ours contains the rating of skills, which can be used to analyze the popularity and users' attitude about the skills.

Virtual Personal Assistants. Gokhan et al. [25] focus on how a VPA can understand the natural languages and distinguish the "target" of voice inputs. They use numerous random web search queries and VPA utterance datasets to train a binary SVM classifier. This study indicates that many VPA-related areas require relevant datasets to support research and train artificial intelligence. This is one of our motivation to build this dataset, which will facilitate more research in this area.

Privacy Concerns on Alexa Platform. Chung et al. [13] point out if the cloud native data of intelligent virtual assistant (IVA) was leaked, malicious attackers can not only obtain the detailed usage history of IVA services, but also reveal more information about users through data analysis. They collect data covering three months from Alexa cloud, and show that user's personal information such as interests, and sleeping and wake-up patterns can be identified by analyzing this dataset. This work also shows that the data collection process may contain potential user identity and private information. To avoid collecting any user private information, we only scrape the information that is publicly available and not related to users' identity.

In addition to the data collection process, some recent studies also show that privacy weakness may arise from other surfaces such as the enforcement of privacy policy [18], the integration of multi-party IoT platforms [21,26], and the data analysis pipeline [30,31]. For example, a large-scale analysis report of Alexa skill [18] finds that only 28.5% of skills in the US Amazon store provides a privacy policy. Our work confirms the findings and supplements their results with analysis on the data up to May 2021.

In a study in 2017 [9], researchers have deeply looked into those skills that provided privacy policy links, and find that 9.4% of them cannot be retrieved due to 404 errors or access denied errors. Additionally, some policy links direct to the developer's website instead of a specific privacy policy page, which showed the sloppy attitude of some developers. In addition, the relationship between privacy policy statistics and skill's star rating has also been analyzed. Surprisingly, they find that the skills with the lowest rating have the highest rate of inclusion of a privacy policy (26%). This research gives some inspirations in our data analysis process. We try to visit the privacy policy link and the terms of use link, and find that some links cannot be accessed or are redirected to a wrong page.

When dealing with privacy concerns, there is a study on how to improve user trust for Alexa System [12]. In this work, researchers design a skill application on Alexa platform and conduct a user study. The results show that when users can customize both content and privacy settings, user trust is highest, but may cause reluctance among sophisticated users. In our research, we are inspired from these aspects when collecting and analyzing the data of Amazon Alexa skills. We believe these findings can also have implications for designing more privacy-sensitive and trustworthy VPA apps.

3   The UQ-AAS21 Dataset

The UQ-AAS21 Dataset consists of two datasets, UQ-AAS21-I and UQ-AAS21-II, include rigorous information of Amazon Alexa skills. UQ-AAS21-I provides basic information about skills and UQ-AAS21-II summarizes attributes related to privacy issues. Our work on the UQ-AAS21 dataset includes three phases: data scraping, data processing and data analysis. We discuss on the data scraping and data processing in this section, and defer the data analysis to Sect. 4. In the data scraping phase, we scrape the web pages of 65,195 Alexa skills, strictly following the ethics of scraping. In the data processing phase, we extract and format the key information.

3.1   Data Scraping

We build a crawler with Python 3.6 to scrape data from Amazon skill store. Before we start crawling, we analyze the target web pages' source and the architecture of the skill store website, to make sure we cover all the essential information in our crawling. We find that the skills are arranged in 23 categories, such as "Business & Finance" and "Home Services". The skills are unevenly distributed in these categories. For those categories with more skills, we assign more threads from the maintained threat pool for crawling.

During the crawling process, we use the Requests library [7] to send HTTP requests to the server. To pass the anti-robot checking of Amazon, we register a testing account, and reuse its HTTP headers and session cookies. Our crawler downloads the pages of each category in which the skills are catalogued, and uses Beautiful Soup [2] library to extract the URLs of skills from the pages. The crawler then requests for the skills' web pages through the URLs, and stores the HTML files.

During our crawling process, sometimes the attempts may trigger Amazon's anti-crawler mechanisms. Four types of mechanisms may be triggered: (1) The crawler is redirected to the "Robot Check" pages. If it fails to pass the anti-robot checking, the connection will be terminated. (2) When the crawler visits Amazon's websites too frequently, Amazon might reject the next request, and the crawler exits with an error message of "Connection Reject by Peers". (3) After the crawler has accessed the website with the same IP address for multiple times, Amazon blocks that IP address for a period ranging from a few hours to a day. (4) After scraping 500–800 web pages, Amazon sends a status code 403 such that the correct information page cannot be visited. To prevent these mechanisms from being triggered frequently, we add a longer random waiting time to each visit interval ranged from 5–10 s, and also distribute our crawler across multiple virtual machines in our server which has multiple IP addresses.

Ethical Considerations. To avoid introducing negative influence to the Amazon website and its users, we strictly follow the ethics of scraping. We comply with Amazon's terms of use policy before attempting website crawling, and also honour the "Robot.txt" to avoid scraping sensitive user information. All crawled data is public available and used for legitimate purposes, without any user private information or secret information of Amazon. In addition, as mentioned above, we control the frequency of scraping and make the program run at a low speed to ensure that the availability of Amazon servers would not be affected.

3.2 Data Processing

After scraping the web pages of skills, we start our data processing to extract crucial information from them. Meanwhile, we also organize the information to make our dataset easy to use. First, we analyze the page structure of the down-loaded HTML file. we use Beautiful Soup library to extract critical information from the HTML files, including skill name, developer invocation name, number of rating, etc. After that, we store the information of each skill in a row of a table. Skills from the same category are stored in the same table.

In the next step, we fix the error data. We mainly handle the wrong pages or the 404 error pages in this step. Wrong pages are extracted because we scrape Amazon's advertisement pages unexpectedly. The 404 error pages or Amazon's robot check pages exist since the Amazon's anti-scraping mechanisms may be triggered sometimes. When this happens, the corresponding skill page information is lost. To make the checking efficient, we check the size of the files, as the size of normal skill pages ranges from 200–400 kb, and the size of error pages and 404 pages are less than 100 kb. If any of such pages are found, we re-scrape it.

The Beautiful Soup library is used to parse the structure of the HTML. The data extraction is also carried out per categories. We create an Excel file for each of the 23 categories and write information into the corresponding columns. In this way, the data can be easily converted into data frames, e.g., using the Pandas library, to fit into the desired input of various statistical operations.

Table 1. Skill feature overview for UQ-AAS21-I dataset

#	Attributes	Description	Example	Note
1	Skill name	The Alexa skill name	"Deadpool"	
2	Path	The path to the corresponding skill web page	"https://www. amazon.com/Austin-Koontz-Deadpool/dp/ B0754VRGVX"	
3	Developer	The developer of this skill	"by Austin Koontz"	The developer could be both Amazon and third-party developers
4	Supported languages	Different languages that this skill can support	"English (US) English (CA)"	Alexa skills can support 8 different languages[a]
5	Average rating	The average rating score of this skill (out of 5)	"2.9 out of 5"	
6	Number of rating	The number of ratings that this skill receives	"340"	
7	Price	The purchase price of this skill	"Free to Enable"	Label "Free to enable" if the skill is free
8	In-skill purchase	The price of in-skill purchase of this skill	"Premium $9.99/month"	Empty if the skill doesn't have in-skill purchase
9	Wake-up words	The corresponding words that can wake up Amazon echo and open this skill by voice	"Alexa, open deadpool"	Each skill has 1 to 3 wake-up words
10	Icon	The icon of this skill	"https://images-na. ssl-images-amazon. com/images/I/ 717ACt+384L.png"	Store as a link to a picture
11	Category	The corresponding category that this skill belongs to	"Movies & TV"	The Amazon Alexa skills system has overall 23 categories

[a] The supported languages include English, German, Italian, Spanish, Portuguese, Japanese, French, Hindi, where each language can also correspond to different country codes.

3.3 Dataset Features

After the data processing phase, UQ-AAS21 dataset is generated and divided into two parts. UQ-AAS21-I dataset includes 11 attributes, while UQ-AAS21-II dataset include 6 attributes, which covers all 16 attributes of the skill (the skill name appears in both datasets). These attributes together describe the feature of a skill. The specific attributes are listed and explained in Table 1 and 2. We separate some attributes into UQ-AAS21-II dataset because after comparing the related researches about Amazon Alexa field, we find that the privacy issues of Amazon Alexa platform is important. Therefore, we decide to put the privacy-related attributes into a single dataset.

Some attributes in UQ-AAS21-I and UQ-AAS21-II datasets have multiple possible values. For example, the "Supported Languages" attribute in UQ-AAS21-II dataset indicates the languages supported by the skill. As shown in

Table 2. Skill feature overview for UQ-AAS21-II dataset

#	Attributes	Description	Example	Note
1	Skill path	The link to skill application	See in Table 1	
2	Access	The permissions type that this skill request	"Email address, Reminders"	Label "No permission needed" if the skill requests no permission; The permission information has 12 subtypes[a]
3	Invocation name	The unique invocation name of this skill	"money exchange"	Label "Not exists" if the skill has no invocation name
4	Description	The description of the skill (aims, usage, related information, etc.)	"This is your local flash briefing ..."[b]	
5	Developer privacy policy	The developer privacy policy of this skill	"https://www.nbcuniversal.com/privacy"	Label "Not Exists" if the skill has no developer privacy policy
6	Developer terms of use document	The developer terms of use document of this skill	"https://www.cnbc.com/cnbc-amazon-alexa-skills-terms-of-use/"	Label "Not Exists" if the skill has no developer terms of use

[a] The subtypes of Access: Device Address, Device Country and Postal Code, Email Address, Alexa Notifications, Location Services, Mobile Number, Reminders, Lists Read Access, Lists Write Access, First Name, Full Name, Amazon Pay.
[b] Full Text: "This is your local Flash Briefing to help you sell, buy, and rent Southlake real estate with your Southlake real estate agent SONYA KENNEDY."

Table 1, Alexa skills can support 8 different languages at most, where each language can also correspond to a different country code. The "Access" attribute in UQ-AAS21-II dataset contains what user information is accessed by the skill. The skill needs users' permission to access the listed information in this field. It can be categorized into 12 types of Alexa skill permissions (listed in Table 2). We also include the "application icon" attribute to facilitate the research that may involve images. For example, the graphics and colors of the Alexa skill applications' icons can be analyzed to find out whether they are related to the popularity of the applications, so as to provide insights for Amazon Alexa developers in designing their icons.

4 Preliminary Studies Based on UQ-AAS21 Datasets

We conduct two studies based on the UQ-AAS21 dataset to explore its usability.

4.1 Demographic Study

In the demographic study, we examine the basic information about the collected skills and their developers.

Table 3. The number of skills in each category

Categories	Number of skills	Categories	Number of skills
Business & Finance	3,824	Movies & TV	949
Communication	567	Music & Audio	6,396
Weather	846	News	6,396
Connected car	172	Novelty & Humor	3,472
Education & Reference	6,414	Productivity	5,206
Food & Drink	1,336	Smart Home	2,817
Games & Trivia	6,383	Shopping	408
Health & Fitness	2,214	Social	1,881
Home services	343	Sports	1,733
Kids	3,759	Travel & Transportation	1,197
Lifestyle	6,204	Utilities	1,432
Local	1,246	**Total**	65,195

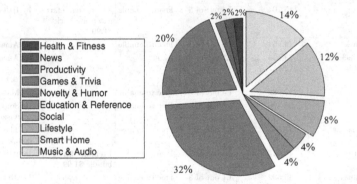

Fig. 2. Category distribution of top 50 popular skills

4.1.1 Skills Analysis

We reuse the 23 categories of Alexa skill store to organize the collected 65,195 skills. Their distribution among the categories is listed in Table 3. The smallest category is "connected car", which take up 0.26% of total skills, while the largest is "education and reference", which occupied 9.84% of total skills.

Popular Skills. We first analyze the top 50 popular skills[1]. Figure 2 shows their distribution among the categories. Most of them (32%) fall into the "Novelty & Humor" category, while the second popular category is "Games & Trivia", with 20% of the top 50 skills. The "Smart Home" and "Music & Audio" categories have the similar popularity, which has 12% and 14% of the skills respectively. The "Health & Fitness", "News" and "Productivity" have the least skills, which is 2% of the total.

---

[1] The popularity of a skill is measured based on the number of ratings it receives.

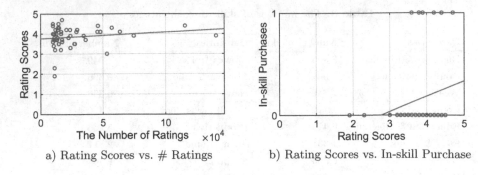

a) Rating Scores vs. # Ratings   b) Rating Scores vs. In-skill Purchase

Fig. 3. Analysis of top 50 popular skills

Table 4. Top ten popular skills

#	Top ten skills with the most of rating	The number of ratings	Average score	Price	In-skill purchase	Developer
1	4AFart	140,832	3.9 out of 5	Free to enable		by Bloatware
2	Big Fart	115,704	4.4 out of 5	Free to enable	The extreme farts extension pack $1.99	by HUGO.FM
3	Jurassic bark	74,554	3.9 out of 5	Free to enable		by Amaury gallais
4	Samuel L.Jackson - celebrity voice for Alexa	73,455	4.1 out of 5	$4.99		by Amazon
5	Find my phone	57,082	4.4 out of 5	Free to enable		by Matchbox.io Inc
6	Jeopardy!	53,326	3.3 out of 5	Free to enable		by Sony pictures television
7	Pikachu talk	47,865	4.1 out of 5	Free to enable		by The Pokemon company
8	Happy birthday	45,941	4.4 out of 5	Free to enable	Premium birthday bundle $1.99	by HUGO.FM
9	iRobot Home	45,532	4.1 out of 5	Free to enable		by iRobot
10	Repeat after me	36,191	3.7 out of 5	Free to enable		by Spraypaint

In Fig. 3, we demonstrate two observations on the rating scores of top 50 popular skills. (1) *Rating scores vs. the number of ratings*. As shown in Fig. 3a, the rating score of an app slightly increases with the number of ratings it receives, indicating a positive correlation between a skill's popularity and quality. (2) *Rating scores vs. in-skill purchase*. The skills with in-skill purchase achieves slightly higher ratings scores than those without (Fig. 3b). This may be attributed to its positive affect on users' engagement and retention rates. For example, the users are more likely to make an in-app purchase after playing the game for a while.

In Table 4, we list the top 10 popular skills in detail. As expected, the majority of popular skills are free to enable. Also, skills provided by reputable companies, such as Microsoft and Amazon, usually achieve high popularity as well as high rating scores.

Semantic Analysis. We conduct a preliminary semantic analysis of user reviews. Figure 4 show the keyword extracted from the reviews of two skills from

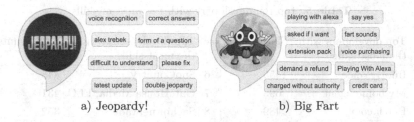

a) Jeopardy!   b) Big Fart

Fig. 4. Keywords extract from skills' reviews

the top ten list, namely "Jeopardy!" and "Big Fart". For "Jeopardy!", users' opinions tend to be negative, as shown in Fig. 4a the extracted keywords such as "difficult to understand" and "please fix". This is also reflected in the app's user rating score (3.3/5), which is the lowest of the 10 most popular skills. For "Big Fart", although it achieves high rating (4.4/5), our semantic analysis shows that users have negative opinions on its in-skill purchase (Fig. 4b).

4.1.2 Developer Analysis

We also analyze the top developers who have provided the most skills. In Table 5, we list the top ten developers. We find that high productivity may not imply high quality. For example, in the skills provided by the developer "My Home Agent" (the second productive developer), it contains a link which even directs to a 404-error page. In addition, the utilization rate of some skills provided by top developers is relatively low. Taking the top one productive developer as an example, among the 1,445 skills, only 15 skills (1.03%) have user rating.

Notably, some skills provided by extraordinarily productive developers may be susceptible to malicious injection. For example, the top developer "InfoByVoice" (who has provided 1,455 skills) put in an advertisement link in their skills' description page, which directs to a website that provides skill application templates and allows anyone to create skills. This makes it possible for a malicious user to publish a skill under the company name, and such process may raise security concerns.

4.2 Analysis of Privacy Policy and Term of Use Document

We find that the coverage of the developer privacy policy (DPP) and the developer terms of use (DTOU) for Alexa skills is low. Among the 65,195 skills, the number of skills that fail to provide a DPP is higher than two-thirds of the total number (67.7%), and the number of skills that fail to provide a DTOU is even higher (77.7%). Table 6 shows the ratios of skills without DPP or DTOU over all skills in the 23 categories. The "Smart Home" category performs the best, with only 6% of skills that do not provide a DPP, while the "Kids" category has the highest percentage of missing DPP of 87.6%.

Table 5. Top ten developers with the most of skills

#	Top developers with the most skills	Skill counts	#	Top developers with the most skills	Skill counts
1	InfoByVoice	1455	6	SnoCountry	445
2	My home agent	693	7	GateHouse Media, LLC	431
3	Patch.com	489	8	Sachin nelwade	352
4	Online radio	474	9	Amazon	340
5	GoVocal.AI	449	10	VoiceSkillsInc	320

5 Potential Usage of UQ-AAS21

In this section, we outline a few potential usages of the UQ-AAS21 dataset, surrounding the healthy development of the skill ecosystem.

Security Issue Identification. We see the opportunities of UQ-AAS21 dataset contributing to the research area in identifying security issues [26]. The rigorous information (such as links, invocation words, access permission) provided by the dataset can be used to identify potential flaws, which may include loopholes that can be exploited by a malicious actor to publish fictitious skills, adversarial examples that can trick voice-based interfaces, and various sophisticated attacks against VPA such as voice-squatting attacks and hidden voice attacks [17,19,27].

Kumar et al. [17] conduct a Speech-to-Text test on Alexa. They create a skill and use Alexa as a transcription service. In the testing, they record the voice inputs, text outputs and recognized query commands. Then, they present a skill squatting attacks that aim to construct a malicious skill and route users to it by a systematic error in the interpretation of the input. The "Wake-Up Words" attributes in our dataset (see Table 1) can help researchers to understand the common structure of skills' voice commands and also can be used to compare to the swapped "malicious" wake-up words.

Privacy Policy Compliance. Alexa mandates a privacy policy link for skills that request certain permission APIs. The DPP and DTOU information provided by the UQ-AAS21 dataset can be used to investigate privacy issues of IoT ecosystems [21] from the perspectives of (1) *the effectiveness of the privacy policy*, e.g., whether privacy policy links actually serve their purpose of informing users of their data practices; (2) *the compliance of the privacy policy*, i.e., whether the privacy violations (such as access policy breaches, unintended flows, over-privilege access) may arise throughout the lifecycle of the interaction flow.

For example, the attribute "Access" in UQ-AAS21 dataset can be used in privacy compliance analysis. The skills can be configured to request permission to access user's personal information (there are 12 subtypes of permissions in total, see Table 2). Lentzsch et al. [18] report instances where skills bypass the permission APIs and directly request information from users. In this case, user's privacy information is collected and used without authorization. To identify such

Table 6. Ratios of skills without developer privacy policy (DPP) or developer terms of use (DTOU)

Categories	Ratio without DPP	Ratio without DTOU	Categories	Ratio without DPP	Ratio without DTOU
Business & Finance	2280/3824 (59.6%)	2691/3824 (70.4%)	Movies & TV	780/949 (82.1%)	827/949 (87.1%)
Communication	218/567 (38.4%)	267/567 (47.0%)	Music & Audio	3316/6396 (51.8%)	3776/6396 (59.0%)
Weather	693/846 (81.8%)	762/846 (90.0%)	News	3942/6396 (61.6%)	4930/6396 (77.1%)
Connected car	42/172 (24.3%)	109/172 (63.0%)	Novelty & Humor	3021/3472 (87.0%)	3252/3472 (93.6%)
Education & Reference	4993/6414 (77.8%)	5322/6414 (83.0%)	Productivity	3597/5206 (69.1%)	4200/5206 (80.7%)
Food & Drink	992/1336 (74.2%)	1121/1336 (83.8%)	Smart Home	170/2817 (6.0%)	1620/2817 (57.5%)
Games & Trivia	4931/6383 (77.2%)	5200/6383 (81.5%)	Shopping	142/408 (34.7%)	203/408 (49.6%)
Health & Fitness	1263/2214 (57.0%)	1572/2214 (71.0%)	Social	1335/1881 (70.9%)	1471/1881 (78.2%)
Home services	142/343 (41.3%)	205/343 (59.6%)	Sports	1340/1733 (77.3%)	1463/1733 (84.4%)
Kids	3293/3759 (87.6%)	3408/3759 (90.6%)	Travel & Transportation	973/1197 (81.2%)	1082/1197 (90.3%)
Lifestyle	4513/6204 (72.7%)	4854/6204 (78.2%)	Utilities	1222/1432 (85.3%)	1283/1432 (89.5%)
Local	933/1246 (74.8%)	1049/1246 (84.1%)	**Total**	**44131/65195 (67.7%)**	**50667/65195 (77.7%)**

cases, researchers can record the personal information acquired by the skills and compare them with their declared permissions in our dataset.

Skill Quality Improvement. The user reviews provided by the UQ-AAS21 dataset can guide third-party developers with new perspectives and promote high-quality skills. It can facilitate the relevant research areas such as semantic analysis of VPA ecosystem, user profiling, and recommender systems. In addition, the UQ-AAS21 dataset can also contribute to the study of multiple levels of linguistic and paralinguistic features [28] and facilitate the research in the voice recognition area.

6   Conclusion

In this work, we build a comprehensive dataset of Amazon Alexa skills for research use. It contains 65,195 skill applications and their rigorous information including the privacy policy, user reviews, among over all 16 attributes. We also demonstrate the comprehensiveness and usability of our dataset with two preliminary studies. In the demographic study, we reveal the positive correlation between a skill's popularity and its quality. Our semantic analysis of user reviews shows users' negative attitude towards the in-skill purchase. Our statistical analysis of the developers shows that high productivity may not imply high quality, and we also identify potential security issues in a developer's development model. In the privacy analysis, we review the coverage of developer privacy policy and developer terms of use of Alexa skills is low. We hope our dataset will facilitate the future research in the health of various VPA ecosystems.

References

1. Amazon Alexa voice AI, Alexa developer official site (2021). https://developer.amazon.com/en-US/alexa
2. Beautiful soup documentation - beautiful soup 4.9.0 documentation (2021). https://www.crummy.com/software/BeautifulSoup/bs4/doc/
3. Create alexa skills kit, custom voice model skills (2021). https://developer.amazon.com/en-US/docs/alexa/custom-skills/understanding-how-users-invoke-custom-skills.html
4. Facts and statistics about virtual assistants (2021). https://www.statista.com/topics/5572/virtual-assistants/
5. General data protection regulation (2021). https://gdpr-info.eu
6. Google play store (2021). https://play.google.com/store?hl=en&gl=US
7. Requests: Http for humans^{TM} - requests 2.26.0 documentation (2021). https://docs.python-requests.org/en/master/
8. Total number of amazon Alexa skills from January 2016 to September 2019 (2021). https://www.statista.com/statistics/912856/amazon-alexa-skills-growth/
9. Alhadlaq, A., Tang, J., Almaymoni, M., Korolova, A.: Privacy in the amazon Alexa skills ecosystem. Star **217**(11) (1902)
10. Ammari, T., Kaye, J., Tsai, J.Y., Bentley, F.: Music, search, and IoT: how people (really) use voice assistants. ACM Trans. Comput. Hum. Interact. **26**(3), 1–17 (2019)
11. Bhargava, M., Safari, A.O.M.C.: Alexa skills projects : build exciting projects with Amazon Alexa and integrate it with Internet of Things. Birmingham, England; Mumbai : Packt, 1st edition edn. (2018). https://ebookcentral.proquest.com/lib/canterbury/detail.action?docID=5446037, electronic reproduction. Boston, MA : Safari. Available via World Wide Web., 2018
12. Cho, E., Sundar, S.S., Abdullah, S., Motalebi, N.: Will deleting history make Alexa more trustworthy? effects of privacy and content customization on user experience of smart speakers. In: Proceedings of the 2020 CHI Conference on Human Factors in Computing Systems, pp. 1–13 (2020)
13. Chung, H., Lee, S.: Intelligent virtual assistant knows your life. arXiv preprint arXiv:1803.00466 (2018)
14. Gao, Y., Pan, Z., Wang, H., Chen, G.: Alexa, my love: analyzing reviews of amazon echo. In: 2018 IEEE SmartWorld, Ubiquitous Intelligence Computing, Advanced Trusted Computing, Scalable Computing Communications, Cloud Big Data Computing, Internet of People and Smart City Innovation (SmartWorld/SCALCOM/UIC/ATC/CBDCom/IOP/SCI), pp. 372–380 (2018). https://doi.org/10.1109/SmartWorld.2018.00094

15. Guo, Z., Lin, Z., Li, P., Chen, K.: Skillexplorer: understanding the behavior of skills in large scale. In: 29th {USENIX} Security Symposium ({USENIX} Security 20), pp. 2649–2666 (2020)
16. Kinsella, B.: Google assistant actions total 4,253 in January 2019, up 2.5 x in past year but 7.5% the total number Alexa skills in us. Voicebot. AI, February 15 (2019)
17. Kumar, D., et al.: Skill squatting attacks on amazon Alexa. In: 27th {USENIX} Security Symposium ({USENIX} Security 18), pp. 33–47 (2018)
18. Lentzsch, C., Shah, S.J., Andow, B., Degeling, M., Das, A., Enck, W.: Hey Alexa, is this skill safe?: Taking a closer look at the Alexa skill ecosystem. In: 28th Annual Network and Distributed System Security Symposium (NDSS 2021), The Internet Society (2021)
19. Lit, Y., Kim, S., Sy, E.: A survey on amazon Alexa attack surfaces. In: 2021 IEEE 18th Annual Consumer Communications Networking Conference (CCNC), pp. 1–7 (2021). https://doi.org/10.1109/CCNC49032.2021.9369553
20. Lopatovska, I., et al.: Talk to me: exploring user interactions with the amazon Alexa. J. Librarianship Inf. Sci. **51**(4), 984–997 (2019)
21. Mahadewa, K., et al.: Identifying privacy weaknesses from multi-party trigger-action integration platforms. In: Proceedings of the 30th ACM SIGSOFT International Symposium on Software Testing and Analysis, pp. 2–15 (2021)
22. Malkin, N., Deatrick, J., Tong, A., Wijesekera, P., Egelman, S., Wagner, D.: Privacy attitudes of smart speaker users. Proc. Priv. Enhancing Technol. **2019**(4) (2019)
23. Schönherr, L., Kohls, K., Zeiler, S., Holz, T., Kolossa, D.: Adversarial attacks against automatic speech recognition systems via psychoacoustic hiding. arXiv preprint arXiv:1808.05665 (2018)
24. Sciuto, A., Saini, A., Forlizzi, J., Hong, J.I.: "Hey Alexa, what's up?" a mixed-methods studies of in-home conversational agent usage. In: Proceedings of the 2018 Designing Interactive Systems Conference, pp. 857–868 (2018)
25. Tur, G., Deoras, A., Hakkani-Tür, D.: Detecting out-of-domain utterances addressed to a virtual personal assistant. In: Fifteenth Annual Conference of the International Speech Communication Association (2014)
26. Wang, K., Zhang, J., Bai, G., Ko, R., Dong, J.S.: It's not just the site, it's the contents: intra-domain fingerprinting social media websites through CDN bursts. In: Proceedings of the Web Conference 2021, pp. 2142–2153 (2021)
27. Yuan, X., et al.: All your Alexa are belong to us: a remote voice control attack against echo. In: 2018 IEEE Global Communications Conference (GLOBECOM), pp. 1–6 (2018). https://doi.org/10.1109/GLOCOM.2018.8647762
28. Zarate, J.M., Tian, X., Woods, K.J., Poeppel, D.: Multiple levels of linguistic and paralinguistic features contribute to voice recognition. Sci. Rep. **5**(1), 1–9 (2015)
29. Zhang, N., Mi, X., Feng, X., Wang, X., Tian, Y., Qian, F.: Dangerous skills: understanding and mitigating security risks of voice-controlled third-party functions on virtual personal assistant systems. In: 2019 IEEE Symposium on Security and Privacy (SP), pp. 1381–1396. IEEE (2019)
30. Zhang, Yanjun, Bai, Guangdong, Li, Xue, Curtis, Caitlin, Chen, Chen, Ko, Ryan K. L..: PrivColl: practical privacy-preserving collaborative machine learning. In: Chen, Liqun, Li, Ninghui, Liang, Kaitai, Schneider, Steve (eds.) ESORICS 2020. LNCS, vol. 12308, pp. 399–418. Springer, Cham (2020). https://doi.org/10.1007/978-3-030-58951-6_20
31. Zhang, Y., Bai, G., Zhong, M., Li, X., Ko, R.: Differentially private collaborative coupling learning for recommender systems. IEEE Intell. Syst. **36**(1), 16–24 (2020)

Are Rumors Always False?: Understanding Rumors Across Domains, Queries, and Ratings

Xuan Truong Du Chau, Thanh Tam Nguyen$^{(\boxtimes)}$, Jun Jo,
and Quoc Viet Hung Nguyen

Griffith University, Gold Coast, Australia
`t.nguyen19@griffith.edu.au`

Abstract. Rumors are increasingly becoming a critical issue on the Web threatening democracy, economics, and society on a global scale. With the advance of social media networks, people are sharing content in an unprecedented scale. This makes social platforms such as microblogs an ideal place for spreading rumors. Although rumors may have a severe impact in the real world, there is not enough large-scale study regarding the characteristics of rumors. In this paper, by studying more than 1000 rumors with over 4 million tweets from about 3 million users, we aim to provide several insights in order to understand the distribution, correlation, and propagation of rumors, especially user behaviors, spatial and temporal characteristics. All the rumor data are publicly available.

Keywords: Rumor understanding · Social media analysis · Web mining

1 Introduction

Social platforms became widely popular as a means for users to share user-generated content and interact with other people [13,18]. Due to the distributed and decentralised nature of social platforms, respective content is propagated without any type of moderation and may therefore contain incorrect information. Wide and rapid propagation of such incorrect information quickly leads to *rumours* that may have a profound real-world impact. For the past few years, there has been a rapid rise in the use of different forms of rumors such as fake news, conspiracy theories, fauxtography, fraud and scams. For instance, in April 2013, there was rumour about two explosions in the White House, injuring also Barrack Obama [30]. The rumour was fuelled by content posted using a hacked Twitter account associated with a major newspaper. The resulting panic had major economic consequences, such as a loss of $136.5 billion at the stock market. The Digital News 2018 Australian report shows that three quarters of online news consumers say they encounter one or more instances of rumors every day. Journalism and politics have been impacted by rumors on a global scale, with

© Springer Nature Switzerland AG 2022
B. Li et al. (Eds.): ADMA 2021, LNAI 13087, pp. 174–189, 2022.
https://doi.org/10.1007/978-3-030-95405-5_13

weakened public trust in governments seen during the Brexit referendum and viral fake election stories outperforming genuine news on social media during the U.S. presidential election campaign.

Existing techniques for detecting rumors on the Web are focused on building fully autonomous algorithmic models [4]. However, such models become obsolete with the new generation of AI-driven attacks. Fabricated videos using AI to mimic real people such as Barack Obama as well as social media bots and clickbaits disguised to appear real can go by unnoticed with existing techniques [1]. Detecting this new generation of rumors requires a deep understanding of social contexts, which often exceeds the limits of autonomous algorithms. Though increasingly popular as surveyed in [32], detection techniques do not necessarily help to understand the characteristics of rumors in depth. There is a need to investigate rumors from a variety of different perspectives.

Although rumours can have severe impacts on the real world, to the best of our knowledge, there is little work that studies characteristics of rumors in depth. In this paper, by analysing over 4 million tweets from more than 3 million users about 1022 rumors, we aim to understand several aspects of rumors such as the effects of rumor truth values and categories on their propagation or whether there is a specific group of users that post rumors.

Results Overview. We observe and quantify a number of interesting patterns, including:

- Rumors about politics are highly popular as they constitute the most number of rumors and easily spark post sharings among users.
- Some rumors propagate faster than the others. For example, rumors related to politics and religion receive thousands of retweets only in the 1st hour.
- False rumors are not necessarily spread faster than true rumors. Rather, rumors with mixed information spread the fastest as they can attract both sides of users.
- Users who post scams have a very distinct profile (lowest numbers of friends, followers, lists, favorites) but there seems to be no correlation between the number of friends, followers a user has and their tendency to post true or false rumors. Similar observation is obtained for rumor category. This implies that rumors cannot be detected by looking at user profiles alone.
- The debunking of rumors might be too late as rumors can reach nearly ten thousands of users in half of a day and the speed is faster than linear.
- Rumors are always fake, but only for some domains. This could help to raise public awareness of sensitive domains in advance.

The rest of the paper is organized as follows. Section 2 discusses background and related work. Section 3 formulates and explains the research queries we are going to answer. Section 4 describes our method to collect, analyze, and understand rumors. Section 5 provides our analyses and findings on rumor characteristics in terms of distribution, correlation, and propagation. We discuss the findings, implications, and limitations in Sect. 6 and conclude the paper in Sect. 7.

2   Background

2.1   Detecting Rumors on the Web

Rumors are increasingly becoming a critical issue on the Web threatening democracy, economics, and society at a global scale. For the past few years, there has been a rapid rise in the use of different forms of rumors such as fake news, conspiracy theories, fauxtography, fraud and scams. While the emergence of rumors has quickly evolved into a worldwide phenomenon, there are a vast amount of efforts under way attempting to better comprehend this phenomenon. However, most of these efforts have only focused on reducing the problem to a detection task. Most works leverage microposts such as tweets or users to detect rumours [8, 11, 16, 30]. These techniques can be classified into those using hand-crafted features or deep features. Techniques based on hand-crafted features [8, 29, 30] are grounded in an ad-hoc definition of features, which are expected to be strong indicators of rumours. Zhao et al. [30] proposed a technique to identify rumours on Twitter using enquiry tweets, while Castillo et al. [8] leveraged different statistics of the tweets to define features. Recently, deep features to detect rumours based on the tweets and their temporal dependencies have been proposed [16, 19, 25]. While this technique achieves high detection accuracy, it first requires the detection of an explicit event and thus depends on the accuracy of this event detection step. There are further approaches [28] that take into account how rumours propagate.

2.2   Actions Against Detected Rumors

A nature reaction against rumors after they are detected is to prevent them from spreading and affecting innocent users. A leading company in this mission is Facebook, who has been criticized as a platform for spreading rumors during 2016 US election and manipulative campaigns [14]. Some counter-measures include a warning below the disputed posts, the reduction of the content's length, the listing of validation articles related to the rumors, the decrease of rumors' ranking in the news feed, some rumor identification tools such as user voting and rating.

While some research showed that counter-measures against rumors mitigate their perceived impacts [10, 15, 32], others proved that they might also backfire [7, 9, 17]. For example, Garrett et al. [10] found that confronting users with corrections of rumors too soon might make them believe in the rumors more. This is due to the confirmation bias: if the rumors confirm users' opinions and attitudes, they tend to accept rumors even after seeing factual evidences. However, Wood et a. [27] showed that users still pay much attention to factual evidences, even if they go against their conceptual priors.

In sum, research in this area is still in its infancy and demonstrates that preventing the spread of rumors is a formidable challenge. This is due to several reasons. First, the open nature of social platforms such as Facebook and Twitter allows users to freely produce and propagate any content without authentication, and this has been exploited to spread hundreds of thousands of fake news at a rate of more than three million social posts per minute [5]. Second, those responsible for the spread of fake news harvest the power of AI attacking models to mix and disguise falsehoods with common news. Methods of camouflage are used to cover digital footprints through synthesising millions of fake accounts and appearing to participate in normal social interactions with other users [12]. Third, innocent users, without proper alerts from algorithmic models, can accidentally spread fake news in an exponential wave of shares, posts and articles. The fake news wave is often only detected when already beyond control and consequently can cause large-scale effects in a very short time.

2.3 Research Gap

Though increasingly popular as surveyed in [32], detection techniques do not necessarily help to understand the characteristics of rumors in depth. There is a need to investigate rumors from a variety of different perspectives. In this paper, we present an analysis to understand rumors across domains, queries, and ratings that provides implications for mitigating rumors. To the best of our knowledge, there is little large-scale study of the characteristics of rumors. This is due to the difficulty in obtaining large a amount of data from social media such as Twitter. We have collected a large amount of rumor-related tweets and provide an in-depth analysis of different characteristics of the rumors. In order to facilitate further research, we also make the rumor dataset available online [2].

Similar to our work, a recent study compares fake news and true news on Twitter [26]. However, they focus only on the propagation patterns of rumors, which confirms that fake news spreads faster, farther, more widely, and more viral than true news. While such findings lay the foundation for many works on fake news early detection [23], it does not explain the underlying characteristics of rumors such as user profiles, content distribution, etc. Moreover, unlike our work, it does not distinguish fake news from other similar abnormal propagation of information on social platforms such as hypes and viral events [23].

3   Research Questions

This paper aims to understand how rumors are spread and how people react to rumors. Our research questions are about the distribution, the correlation, and the propagation of rumors on the Web regarding their perceived impacts on innocent users and beyond. Specifically, we posed the following five research queries:

RQ1: What are the rumors about? Rumors come from different domains. We would like to see if there are differences in the behavior of users coming from or reacting to different domains.

RQ2: Where do the rumors come from? Geographic information plays an important role in understanding rumors as it reflects such phenomena in different countries and cultures.

RQ3: Who contribute to rumors? It is interesting to investigate the profiles of users who spread rumors.

RQ4: When are the rumors reported? Whether the rumors can be detected early or not would decide the research directions in the next few years.

RQ5: How do rumors propagate? It was a common ground that false rumors spread faster, wider, and further than true rumors [26]. But it does no harm to test this hypothesis again.

We explore the above research queries through statistic data analyses on a large-scale dataset we collected, which are describe below.

4   Methodology

4.1   Data Collection

We begin with the description of the datasets we assemble for this study. For this, we first explain how we collected rumors from Snopes which is a leading rumor-rebunking services. Then, we describe how we collected posts that are related to these rumors on a popular social media platform, Twitter.

While our evaluation covers only one social media platform, Twitter is a large source of publicly available social media data, recognized as promising for many domains such as politics, healthcare, and entertainment. Twitter is also frequently used by users to express their opinions by retweeting others, which, along with their timestamps, may provide insights into how rumors propagate. This characteristic makes it suitable for our purpose.

Rumor Collection. Snopes is a world-leading rumour-debunking service. Unlike other organizations such as Politifact and Urbanlegends, it is considered to be objective when evaluating the veracity of rumours [6,20,24]. Snopes editors investigate each rumour along different dimensions and provide an argumentative report as shown in Table 1. Rumors on Snopes are organized by publishing date which allows us to collect all rumors starting from 08/04/2003. However, for the purpose of this study, we only consider the rumors from 01/05/2017 to 01/11/2017. This period is chosen as rumors are only considered as important recently and this period contains several rumor-related incidents such as the Las Vegas shooting and much fake news. In this time period, we are able to collect 1022 rumors. For each rumor, we collected all information available in the article describing the rumors. The list of information is shown in Table 1. Two important pieces of information are the claim and the rating of the rumor. While the claim describes the rumor succinctly, the rating represents the truth value of the rumor according to the fact-checker. We consider the rating to be the ground truth. This is reasonable as according to a study [6], Snopes is considered to be objective when it comes to rumors.

Table 1. Information about a rumor

Description	Examples
Id of the rumor	Trump-aid-puerto-rico
Date of the rumor	28 September 2017
Category of the rumor	Politics, Fake news, Fauxtography
Claim of the rumor	President Trump has dispatched [..]
Date the rumor is reported on Snopes	2 October 2017
Author of the reporting article	Dan Evon, David Emery
Date of the latest update	2 October 2017
Rating of the rumor	MIXTURE [3]
Content of the reporting article	In the wake of public criticism of the Trump administration [..]
Sources of information	Davis, Aaron, Lamothe, Dan and O'Keefe, Ed.

Table 2 and Table 3 describe the categories of collected rumors and the ratings provided Snopes, respectively.

Tweet Collection. Twitter is a large social platform with tweets covering various domains such as politics and crime. It is frequently used by users to express their opinions in a timely manner, e.g., by retweeting others, which provides insights into how rumours propagate. These characteristics make Twitter data particularly suitable for evaluating rumour detection methods.

We followed the dataset construction process described in [15]. For each rumor, we aim to identify its fingerprint which is a set of keywords that can specify this rumor. Then, we use these keywords to search for tweets that are related to this rumor using Spinnr[1] which is a data collection service. For each rumor, we take the ID of its Snopes article to be the starting point to create its fingerprint. There are cases that the IDs are not unique or too general which requires us to manual select keywords from the claims of the rumors to create its fingerprint. Then, using the fingerprints, we search for tweets that contain these keywords in the time period of 01/05/2017 to 01/11/2017. We also the collect the number of retweets each tweet has and also the user and posting time of these retweets. The rumour data is publicly available at[2] (due to Twitter policies, we cannot share Twitter contents).

---

[1] http://docs.spinn3r.com/.

[2] http://tiny.cc/p1s2qy.

Table 2. Description of important rumor categories

Category	Description
Politics	Rumors related to all political issues
Fauxtography	Rumors related to images or videos circulating on the web
Critter country	Rumors that are related to animals or pets
Fauxtography	Rumors related to images or videos circulating on the internet
Inboxer rebellion	Rumors from emails/messages that plead to find a missing kid or help a sick child [..]
Questionable quotes	Rumors containing seemingly-interesting/motivating quotes
Crime	Rumors related to criminology and incidents
Science & Technology	Rumors related to scientific myths and exaggerated technological inventions
Fraud & Scams	Rumors related to online hoax/scams under the false premise of a greater good

5   Empirical Analyses and Findings

5.1   What Are the Rumors About?

Content Distribution. In order to analyze the content of the rumors, we take into account rumor categories defined by Snopes. The list of categories and their description is shown in Table 2. The outer circle in Fig. 1a represents the number of rumors aggregated by its category while the inner circle displays the number

Table 3. Description of rumor ratings

Rating	Description
True	The primary elements of a claim are demonstrably true
Mostly true	Some of the ancillary details may be inaccurate
Mixture	Mixture rumors contain both correct and incorrect information
Mostly false	Some of the ancillary details surrounding the claim may be accurate
False	The primary elements of a claim are demonstrably false
Correct attribution	Rumors related to quotes/messages that actual come from the alleged author
Misattributed	Rumors related to quotes/messages that do not come from the alleged author
Miscaptioned	Rumors related to images/videos that are real but the captions are incorrect
Research in progress	Snopes is still researching the truth values of the rumors
Undetermined	The correctness of the rumors can not be determined
Unproven	There is not enough evidence to support these rumors
Outdated	Rumors about real events but with incorrect date

of tweets in each category. The top-3 categories with the most number of rumors are Fake News, Fauxtography and Politics. In total, they comprise over 60% of number of rumors.

We also observe strong discrepancies between the number of rumors and the number of tweets in each category. Although the majority of tweets is in the Politics category, the number of rumors belonging in this category is only the third highest. As political rumors are controversial, they tend to get more views and more shares which makes this category have the highest amount of tweets. On the other hand, although 22.5% of rumors are Fauxtography, only 8% of the tweets belong to this category. This is understandable as fauxtography rumors are easy to fabricate which explains the high number of them.

On the other hand, regarding rumor rating, we do not observe the discrepancy between number of tweets and number of rumors (Fig. 1b) as the top-3 ratings are the same (False, True and Mixture). While the majority of reported rumors are false, 51% of the tweets are also about false rumors. The fact that the majority of rumors are false can be explained by the aim of Snopes to debunk false rumors.

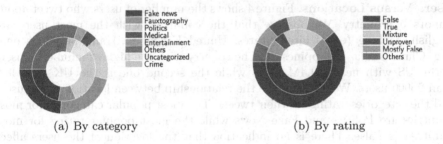

(a) By category   (b) By rating

Fig. 1. Rumor and tweet distribution

Rating Distribution. Figure 2 and Fig. 3 illustrate the relationship between categories and ratings with respect to the number of tweets. There are some interesting observations. As its name suggests, most of the tweets in the Fake News category are about false rumors. Tweets in the *Politics* category are interesting as the number of *true, false, mostly true* and *mostly false* tweets are nearly identical. This shows political rumors are contagious as it attracts sharing despite the truth values of the rumors.

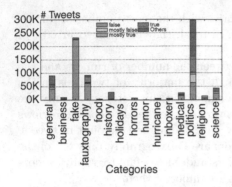

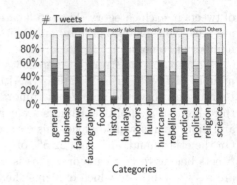

Fig. 2. Tweet distribution across categories and ratings

Fig. 3. Tweet distribution across categories and ratings

5.2 Where Do the Rumors Come From?

Users Versus Locations. Figure 4 shows the number of users who tweet about rumors by country. We observe that the countries with the most users are English-speaking (e.g. United States, United Kingdom...) and populous ones (e.g. China, India, Philippines...). The country with the highest number of users is the US with nearly 0.4M users while the second one is the UK with less than 25000 users. We also analyze the relationship between location of the users and the categories/ratings of their tweets. The most popular categories for most countries are Politics and Fake News while the most popular rating for most countries is False. There is no indication that the location of the users affect their postings as the most popular ratings and categories by country are similar to the most popular categories and rating overall.

Locations Versus Domains. Figure 5 analyses whether there is an indication that the location of the users affects the domain of their tweets. The top popular domains for most countries are *Politics*, *Fraud*, and *Faux*, which is similar to the

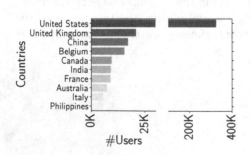

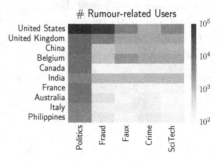

Fig. 4. Users by countries

Fig. 5. Locations versus domains

top domains in overall. Most of rumors in US are about Politics and Fraud. This fits with the data collection period after the 2016 US presidential election.

5.3   Who Contribute to Rumors?

In this part, we analyze characteristics of the users who tweet about rumors. We consider their location, number of friends, follows, favorites and lists as these information are available on the profiles of the users. It is worth noting that there are users who do not disclose these information. The analysis is based on users who have these information public.

Users vs. Rumor Truth Values. Figure 6 displays boxplots showing the relationship between the number of friends, followers, lists and favorites a user has and the truth values of the rumors they tweet. Although we expect users who has more friends and followers to post false rumors since they want to propagate false information as much as possible, this is not the case as shown in Fig. 6. The ranges of the number of friends and followers a user has are similar across rumor truth values. We observe the same phenomena with respect to the number of lists and favorites a user has.

User Versus Rumor Categories. Similarly, we also consider the categories of the rumors with respect to the users as shown in Fig. 7. An interesting observation is that users who post entertainment news tend to have higher number of followers in average in comparison with other categories. We also observe that users who post rumors related to entertainment news, racial and sports are more likely to have higher number of friends in average.

Correlation Between Users and Rumors. In Fig. 8, we display the histogram showing the number of users who post tweets related to different rumors. The histogram follows a long-tail distribution in which most users tweet about 1–2 rumors. There are users who tweet about more than 100 rumors. However, this number is extremely small. By analyzing the users who post more than 100 rumors, we identify several interesting characteristics. The accounts who post about most rumors are extremely similar. We suspect that they are bots or part of a network of "fraud" accounts. Another interesting characteristic is that the accounts who post about many rumors are spreading hate messages. Given space limitations, however, we refer to [26] for a further analysis of user accounts.

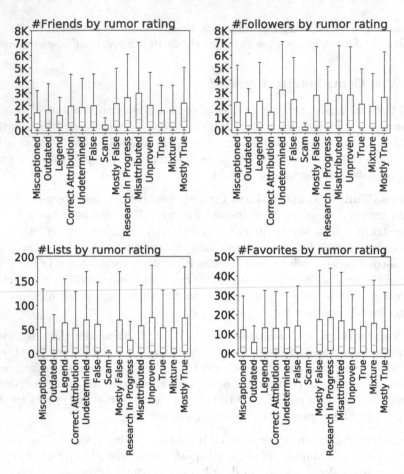

Fig. 6. Relationship between user behaviors and rumor ratings

5.4   When Are the Rumors Reported?

We measure the difference in time between detection time and origin time which is called lag time to detection. Origin time is the first time that a tweet about a rumor happens while detection time is the time the rumor is fact-checked. For each rumor, we measure the detection time as the publish date of the Snopes article about the rumor. Figure 9 illustrates the result. We observe that the difference in time varies by rumors and rumor ratings. While the average lag time to detection of all rumors is more than 1000 d, the average lag time for rumors with the 'false' rating is less than 100 d. This shows that Snopes do a good job in checking and detecting rumors early.

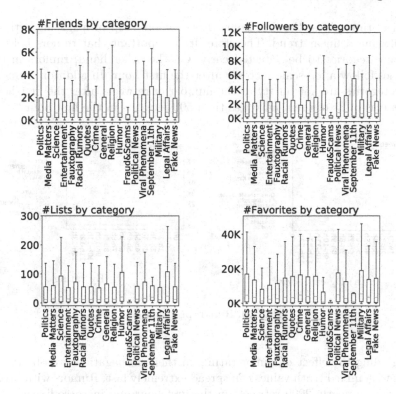

Fig. 7. Relationship between user behaviors and rumor domains

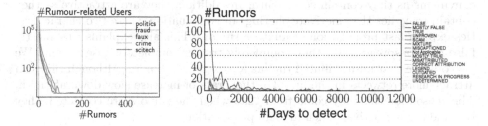

Fig. 8. Users who tweet/retweet rumors

Fig. 9. Lag time to detection

5.5 How Do Rumors Propagate?

To measure how rumors propagate, we collect the number of retweets each tweet in our dataset has. The more number of retweets a tweet has, the more influencing the tweet is. Figure 10 shows the number of retweets a rumor in different category/rating has in the first 13 h. Regarding the effect of rumor category, we observe that media, political, religious rumors are extremely bursty. In the first hour, the average number of retweets these rumors received is over 1000. This shows that these rumors are highly contagious as they can spread in a short amount of time. After the first hour, these rumors keep propagating extremely fast following a linear trend. Therefore, it is important that rumors belonging to these categories to be detected early. On the other hand, rumors in other categories follow a log-scale increase after the first hour. In addition, rumors in these categories are not bursty as the number of retweets after the first hour is moderate as most of them have less than 500 retweets in the first hour.

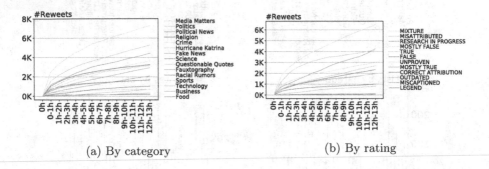

(a) By category   (b) By rating

Fig. 10. Rumor propagation

Regarding the effect of rumor rating on their propagation, we observe that rumors with mixed truth values can spread extremely fast. Rumors with Mixture rating receive nearly 2000 retweets in the first hour and increase linearly afterwards. As the best lies always contain a grain of truth, these rumors are pretty convincing as they contain some truth. In addition, they are attractive as they contain some lies that motivate sharing. In combination, these two characteristics explain fast propagation of mixture rumors. This also explains why mostly false rumors spread faster than completely true or completely false rumors. We also observe that misattributed rumors are extremely bursty. Although they can attract more retweets in the first 4 h, their rate of increase slow down after 5 h. The reason for this may come from that when the rumors are corrected, they become less attractive, which hinders propagation.

6   Discussion

6.1   Key Findings

We come up with the following key findings:

- *Rumors are always fake:* for some domains, such as holidays and horrors. This could be explained by the fact people do not discuss these topics publicly on social media just to say facts. Surprisingly, rumors about politics are not always false as many people think, but they are not completely true either. More than often, rumors originates from true news with some misleading presentations to serve some propaganda purposes (see Fig. 3).

- *False rumors do not necessarily spread fastest:* in fact, the fastest ones are mixture of correct and incorrect information (see Fig. 10). This could explained by the fact that having two sides of information attracts both users of different opinions. Moreover, true rumors even spread faster than false rumors in the long run because of many fact-checking services.
- *Detection of rumors might be too late:* while fact-checking services like Snopes do a good job of checking and detecting rumors early, rumors turn out to already affect many users just within a few hours. This suggests that early detection is an inherently unbound problem, where rumors can only be reliably detected with sufficient information of social network activities.

6.2 Implications for Public Trust and Explainable Rumor Detection

Discovering the characteristics of rumors in terms of distribution, correlation, and propagation is highly encouraged to distinguish them from other social events from different domains and languages. Such findings can deepen the public understanding of rumors and restore the public trust. Our analytic pipeline can provide data-journalism reports that help to raise public awareness against falsehood contents and educate a generation of Web users to be well versed in media literacy.

Moreover, our analyses of rumor characteristics also enhance the explainability of rumors detection by breaking down and focusing on the underlying features that help decision makers to understand and mitigate rumors more accurately. By not focusing on detection models, our analyses also facilitate interdisciplinary research to enhance the explainability of rumor investigation results to the broader public. The key findings also suggest that further research should focus on rumor prevention rather than detection, such as raising public awareness, increasing penalty of posting rumors, and introducing a lag control between consecutive posts.

6.3 Limitations and Future Work

While we could provide valuable findings to the research field on understanding rumors, our work comes with some limitations.

- We do not report the analyses on the content of social posts. This is because we did some preliminary studies on the textual analyses and they confirm similar findings of previous works that textual features are not strongly discriminative due to the character limitation of Twitter [31]. In future work, we plan to mine further textual data such as expert validation on fact-checking websites and user reviews/comments on the social posts [22].
- We do not include user surveys on their perspectives on rumors. This is because for large-scale datasets such as Twitter, the survey method is not suitable due to the long waiting time for user responses as well as the overwhelming amount of data to check compared to user cognitive load. In future work, we plan to employ some scalable user validation platforms such as crowdsourcing [21].

– Our analysis is limited one dataset due to the non-openness of data/APIs of social platforms such as Twitter, Weibo, and Facebook. This can be mitigated by using streaming APIs to store data gradually, but this will take time and a lot of storage.

7   Conclusion

In this paper, we provide a large-scale in-depth analysis of different characteristics of rumors. Our analysis shows the need for the early detection of rumors especially rumors in the media or politics category, but it might be too late compared to the number of affected users. We also observe no correlation between the category and rating of the rumors and characteristics of users who share these rumors. The findings suggest that we should focus more on rumor prevention mechanisms rather than only on rumor detection, as the former can be done in advance and has long-lasting effects for the next generations. In future work, we aim to study further rumor analyses such as review data and crowdsourcing.

Acknowledgments. This work was supported by ARC Discovery Early Career Researcher Award (Grant No. DE200101465).

References

1. https://www.cfr.org/report/deep-fake-disinformation-steroids
2. http://tiny.cc/p1s2qy
3. Is this viral list of U.S. government emergency aid sent to puerto rico accurate? (2021). https://www.snopes.com/fact-check/trump-aid-puerto-rico/
4. Zhou, X et al.: Fake news: a survey of research, detection methods, and opportunities. arXiv:1812.00315 (2018)
5. Allen, R.: What happens online in 60 seconds? http://tiny.cc/m1my2y (2017)
6. Aspray, W., Cortada, J.W.: From debunking urban legends to political fact-checking. In: From Urban Legends to Political Fact-Checking. HC, pp. 9–39. Springer, Cham (2019). https://doi.org/10.1007/978-3-030-22952-8_2
7. Berinsky, A.J.: Rumors and health care reform: experiments in political misinformation. Br. J. Polit. Sci. **47**(2), 241–262 (2017)
8. Castillo, C., Mendoza, M., Poblete, B.: Information credibility on twitter. In: WWW, pp. 675–684 (2011)
9. Garrett, R.K., Poulsen, S.: Flagging Facebook falsehoods: self-identified humor warnings outperform fact checker and peer warnings. J. Comput.-Mediated Commun. **24**(5), 240–258 (2019)
10. Garrett, R.K., Weeks, B.E.: The promise and peril of real-time corrections to political misperceptions. In: CSCW, pp. 1047–1058 (2013)
11. Gupta, A., Kumaraguru, P., Castillo, C., Meier, P.: Tweetcred: real-time credibility assessment of content on twitter. In: ICSI, pp. 228–243 (2014)
12. Hooi, B., Song, H.A., Beutel, A., Shah, N., Shin, K., Faloutsos, C.: Fraudar: bounding graph fraud in the face of camouflage. In: KDD, pp. 895–904 (2016)
13. Hung, N.Q.V., Tam, N.T., Tran, L.N., Aberer, K.: An evaluation of aggregation techniques in crowdsourcing. In: WISE, pp. 1–15 (2013)

14. Kirchner, J., Reuter, C.: Countering fake news: a comparison of possible solutions regarding user acceptance and effectiveness. In: CSCW, vol. 4, pp. 1–27 (2020)
15. Kwon, S., Cha, M., Jung, K.: Rumor detection over varying time windows. PLoS ONE **12**(1), e0168344 (2017)
16. Ma, J., et al.: Detecting rumors from microblogs with recurrent neural networks. In: IJCAI (2016)
17. Mena, P.: Cleaning up social media: the effect of warning labels on likelihood of sharing false news on Facebook. Policy Internet **12**(2), 165–183 (2020)
18. Nguyen, Q.V.H., Nguyen, T.T., Miklós, Z., Aberer, K., Gal, A., Weidlich, M.: Pay-as-you-go reconciliation in schema matching networks. In: ICDE, pp. 220–231 (2014)
19. Nguyen, T.T., et al.: Monitoring agriculture areas with satellite images and deep learning. Appl. Soft Comput. **95**, 106565 (2020)
20. Nguyen, T.T., Phan, T.C., Nguyen, Q.V.H., Aberer, K., Stantic, B.: Maximal fusion of facts on the web with credibility guarantee. Inf. Fusion **48**, 55–66 (2019)
21. Sethi, R.J.: Crowdsourcing the verification of fake news and alternative facts. In: HT, pp. 315–316 (2017)
22. Shu, K., Wang, S., Liu, H.: Beyond news contents: the role of social context for fake news detection. In: WSDM, pp. 312–320 (2019)
23. Tam, N.T., Weidlich, M., Zheng, B., Yin, H., Hung, N.Q.V., Stantic, B.: From anomaly detection to rumour detection using data streams of social platforms. PVLDB **12**(9), 1016–1029 (2019)
24. Thanh Tam, N., Weidlich, M., Yin, H., Zheng, B., Quoc Viet Hung, N., Stantic, B.: User guidance for efficient fact checking. PVLDB **12**(8), 850–863 (2019)
25. Trung, H.T., Van Vinh, T., Tam, N.T., Yin, H., Weidlich, M., Hung, N.Q.V.: Adaptive network alignment with unsupervised and multi-order convolutional networks. In: ICDE, pp. 85–96 (2020)
26. Vosoughi, S., Roy, D., Aral, S.: The spread of true and false news online. Science **359**(6380), 1146–1151 (2018)
27. Wood, T., Porter, E.: The elusive backfire effect: mass attitudes steadfast factual adherence. Polit. Behav. **41**(1), 135–163 (2019)
28. Wu, K., Yang, S., Zhu, K.Q.: False rumors detection on Sina Weibo by propagation structures. In: ICDE, pp. 651–662 (2015)
29. Yang, F., Liu, Y., Yu, X., Yang, M.: Automatic detection of rumor on Sina Weibo. In: MDS, p. 13 (2012)
30. Zhao, Z., Resnick, P., Mei, Q.: Enquiring minds: early detection of rumors in social media from enquiry posts. In: WWW, pp. 1395–1405 (2015)
31. Zhou, X., Zafarani, R.: A survey of fake news: fundamental theories, detection methods, and opportunities. CSUR **53**(5), 1–40 (2020)
32. Zubiaga, A., Aker, A., Bontcheva, K., Liakata, M., Procter, R.: Detection and resolution of rumours in social media: a survey. arXiv:1704.00656 (2017)

A Green Pipeline for Out-of-Domain Public Sentiment Analysis

Ming Xie[1], Jing Jiang[1(✉)], Tao Shen[1], Yang Wang[1,2], Leah Gerrard[1,2], and Allison Clarke[2]

[1] Australian Artificial Intelligence Institute, Faculty of Engineering and IT, University of Technology Sydney, Ultimo, Australia
Jing.Jiang@uts.edu.au
[2] Data and Analytics Branch, Health Economics and Research Division, Australian Department of Health, Phillip, Australia

Abstract. In the changing social and economic environment, organisations are keen to act promptly and appropriately to changes. Sentiment analysis can be applied to social media data to capture timely information of new events and the corresponding public opinions. However, currently both the social topics and trending words are changing just as rapidly as the target topics and domains that organisations are interested in investigating. Therefore, there is a need for a well-trained sentiment analysis model able to handle out-of-domain input. Current solutions mainly focus on using domain adaptation techniques, but these solutions require domain-specific data and inevitably introduce extra overheads. To tackle this challenge, we propose a green Artificial Intelligence (AI) solution for a sentiment analysis pipeline (GreenSAP) to gain a better understanding of the changing public opinions on social media. Specifically, we propose to leverage the expressively powerful capability of the pre-trained Transformer encoder, and make use of several publicly-available sentiment analysis datasets from various domains and scenarios to develop a pipeline model. A sarcasm detection model is also included to eliminate false positive predictions. In experiments, this model significantly outperforms its competitors on three public benchmark datasets and on two of our labelled out-of-domain datasets for real-world applications.

Keywords: Sentiment analysis · Green AI · Social media

1 Introduction

Sentiment analysis [20] is a popular research field in natural language processing (NLP), aiming to analyse people's opinions and the attitudes from text such as tweets and reviews. It is applied in most business and social domains since sentiments are pivotal to almost all human activities, and they significantly affect people's behaviours. For example, sentiment analysis has been widely used by

© Springer Nature Switzerland AG 2022
B. Li et al. (Eds.): ADMA 2021, LNAI 13087, pp. 190–202, 2022.
https://doi.org/10.1007/978-3-030-95405-5_14

many organisations to actively acquire public opinions of new topics and ideas. In contrast to a business-oriented survey, public sentiment analysis of social media can cover broader topics and a larger population at low cost.

As people utilise social media more in everyday life, there is an increasing number of changing topics and language habits. Organisations cannot provide timely and effective training data to learn a domain-specific machine learning model, especially a deep learning model. Looking for auxiliary data is a straight-forward solution to this low-resource scenario. However, the publicly available sentiment analysis datasets only focus on a few narrow domains, e.g. the Stanford Sentiment Treebank (SST) [4] for movie reviews, Restaurant [16] for restaurant reviews, etc. Hence, the building of a generic sentiment analysis system is urgently needed for a broad spectrum of practical applications. Usually, a common and straightforward way is to build a Bayesian model based on a dictionary of sentiment words (e.g., '*happy*' for positive attitude and '*sad*' for negative attitude), but this model completely ignores context of texts and thus cannot match the industrial requirements in terms of accuracy.

Recently, fine-tuning a pre-trained Transformer [22] encoder (e.g. BERT [4] and RoBERTa [14]) on task-specific data demonstrated capability to achieve a state-of-the-art (SOTA) performance on a variety of NLP tasks, such as text classification, natural language inference, and question answering. The Transformer encoder, mainly pre-trained by a self-supervised masked language modelling [4,14] task on large-scale unlabelled text corpora, produces more generic contextualised text representations to benefit various domains in downstream tasks. However, while utilising a pre-trained Transformer reduces sample complexity on a specific domain; the model is still data-driven. To implement a Green AI solution [19], a plausible approach [18] would be to use the domain-specific text corpora to continually pre-train a Transformer encoder by masked language modelling before fine-tuning the sentiment analysis in that domain. This, however, causes two problems: first, the large-scale domain-specific text corpus is not always handy in real-world applications with countless domains/topics. Second, continual pre-training on a large-scale domain-specific corpus introduces extra computational overheads. Consequently, this kind of domain adaptation method requires both costly pre-training and expensive domain-specific fine-tuning procedures, which inevitably leads to a consumption of energy and an inefficient use of human resources, respectively.

In this work, we propose a novel and versatile Green Sentiment Analysis Pipeline (GreenSAP) to understand the out-of-domain social topics for which there is neither a domain-specific corpus nor human-annotated training data. The advantages of the proposed method are four-fold. First, the model is built upon a pre-trained Transformer encoder (e.g. BERT) to inherit the generalisability and improve the performance during the out-of-domain evaluation. Second, the model consists of two kinds of sentiment analysis sub-models (i.e. sentence-level sentiment analysis [12] and aspect-based sentiment analysis [10,15]) trained on the corresponding datasets, which promotes cross-domain sharing and enables the model to handle various real-world application scenarios. Third, the model also introduces sarcasm detection to identify irony in text that is ubiquitous nowadays on social media, which substantially affects the sentiment analysis system. Lastly, the model can be directly applied to the data from a new domain without any labelled or unlabelled domain-specific data, resulting in saved labour and computation cost and hence why the approach is considered '*green*'. During inference, given texts presented in a new domain without any domain-specific corpus or training data, we expect the proposed model can still perform well.

By comparison, similar work [8] proposes to use Sentence-level sentiment analysis (SLSA) data to improve an aspect-based sentiment analysis (ABSA) model by either multi-task learning or transfer learning. But, the model only targets on ABSA datasets, and we empirically find that the performance gain is marginal when applied to pre-trained Transformer encoder-based models.

We evaluate our model on five datasets, including three aspect-based sentiment analysis benchmarks and two of our labelled twitter datasets relevant to COVID-19 (will be public). Our labelled data, only composed of test sets, is viewed as an out-of-domain evaluation resource. The empirical results show that the proposed model achieves a state-of-the-art performance, and outperforms its baselines and previous models specially designed for aspect-based sentiment analysis.

2   Related Work

Pre-trained Transformer Encoder. Attention mechanisms [2] were proposed to attend a sequence for a target entity in an RNN-based sequence-to-sequence encoder-decoder network. It has evolved into a stacked multi-head attention mechanism [22], i.e. Transformer, which focuses on capturing dependencies of the tokens within the same sequence. BERT [4] is built upon the Transformer encoder by expanding unidirectional language model to a bidirectional one. Liu et al. [14] propose RoBERTa for a robustly optimised BERT pre-training approach.

Sentence-Level Sentiment Analysis. (SLSA) determines the sentiment polarity of sentences [12]. Traditionally, it was closely related to the subjective classification task [25], which distinguishes subjective and objective sentences. With the rise of online product reviews [6] and social media [1], sentiment analysis has focused on how to extract people's opinions and emotions rather than identifying subjective sentences. Regarding the rule-based solution of sentiment analysis, the machine learning-based solution used to be a pipeline, including feature extraction and classification [13]. In the era of deep learning, the feature extraction component is changed to an encoder for representation learning, and the classification is to be a fully connected layer for a sentiment decision [26]. The recently developed BERT [4] has also demonstrated the SOTA performance on the Stanford Sentiment Treebank [20] benchmark dataset.

Aspect-Based Sentiment Analysis. (ABSA) [10,15] analyses text to identify the sentiments of fine-grained aspects, i.e. attributes or components of a product or service. In contrast to SLSA, the ABSA identifies various aspects of each text and determines the corresponding sentiment for each aspect. Recently, Sun et al. [21] proposed applying BERT for ABSA task.

Sarcasm Detection is an essential part of sentiment analysis, considering the prevalence of sarcasm text in social media [24]. It is challenging to judge the true opinion or sentiment of a text containing sarcasm. In this challenging scenario, a positive word could be used for expressing a negative meaning. Besides the general supervised setting, it could be solved by involving multi-modal analysis [3]. There are some publicly available benchmark datasets for sarcasm detection tasks [7].

3   Methodology

This section begins with a formal definition of sentiment analysis, including sentence-level and aspect-based analysis. We then introduce a Transformer encoder pre-trained via a masked language modeling objective. Lastly, we elaborate on our proposed model based on the pre-trained Transformer encoders.

3.1   Problem Definition

Typically, given the natural language sentence s, sentiment analysis predicts the expressed sentiment category $\hat{y}$ which can be *positive, neutral* or *negative*. This paper involves two kinds of sentiment analysis according to the different granularity of the inputted text. On one hand, *sentence-level sentiment analysis* (SLSA) analyses the sentiment label in light of the entire inputted sentence. On the other hand, *aspect-based sentiment analysis* (ABSA) is aimed at fine-grained sentiment analysis, and determines the sentiment polarities towards a specific aspect term, t, in a sentence. An example of ABSA is that, given the sentence *"the restaurant provided great food, but the service was dreadful"*, the sentiment polarity towards *"food"* is positive, while the polarity towards *"service"* is negative. In this work, a sentiment analysis model can be formally denoted as

$$p = P(\hat{y}|s, t; \theta), \tag{1}$$

where $p \in \mathbb{R}^3$ stands for the resulting categorical distribution, θ denotes learnable parameters of the model, s denotes the inputted sentence, and t denotes the aspect term. Note, $t = $ Null in SLSA while $t \in s$ in ABSA[1].

---

[1] In this work, we focus on the "aspect-term" setting where $t \in s$ rather than the "aspect-category" setting with pre-set aspect categories.

3.2   Pre-trained Transformer Encoder

We utilise a Transformer encoder [22] to project the inputted texts into a semantic space. To produce a generic contextualised representation, the Transformer encoder is initialised by a self-supervised learning task on large-scale corpora [4,14].

The most popular self-supervised learning task is masked language modelling (MLM) [4]. More specifically, given a piece of text s, a tokenising algorithm is invoked to obtain a sequence of tokens, i.e. $s = [x_1, x_2, \ldots, x_N]$. Based on this, the MLM self-learning method randomly masks 15% of the total tokens. The masked sequence is then passed into a Transformer encoder [22] to produce contextualised representations for each token, which is written as

$$H = \text{Transformer-Encoder}([\hat{x}_1, \hat{x}_2, \ldots, \hat{x}_N]) \in \mathbb{R}^{d \times N}, \tag{2}$$

where $H = [h_1, h_2, \ldots, h_N]$ is the sequence of the resulting contextualised representations. Last, the training loss of MLM is

$$\mathcal{L}^{(MLM)} = - \sum_{i \in \mathcal{M}} \log P(x_i | h_i) := \text{softmax}(\text{MLP}(h_i; \theta^{(mlm)})), \tag{3}$$

where $\mathcal{M}$ denotes the masked indices. Compared to the casual language model that auto-regressively predicts the next token, such as a masked language model, the Transformer considers both sides of the contexts to predict the masked token. After pre-training, the Transformer encoder [22] can be adapted by adding a task-specific neural module/classifier to tackle most of the natural language processing tasks, including sentiment analysis [18,21,23] and sarcasm detection [17]. In experiments, we initialise the Transformer encoder with either BERT [4] or RoBERTa [14].

3.3   Pipeline Sentiment Analysis Model

In this section, we elaborate on our proposed pipeline model for the out-of-domain public sentiment analysis of social media data. More specifically, the proposed model aims to provide accurate sentiment analysis and compatibility with various domains (in-domain or out-of-domain) and scenarios (sentence-level and aspect-based). To achieve this, in addition to employing the pre-trained Transformer encoder, we propose to (1) use two models to handle the different granularities of the input sentences and (2) introduce a sarcasm detection mechanism to further boost sentiment accuracy, both of which are detailed in the following (Fig. 1).

We first detail the two sentiment analysis models, i.e. the SLSA and ABSA models, respectively. Note that all the models are implemented using the simplest method based on the Transformer encoder, as the settings suggested by Devlin et al. [4]. This is because we mainly focus on pipeline development rather than tuning the model structure and avoiding model over-fitting/-adapting to certain datasets. Notably, for the SLSA model whose input is a piece of text and output

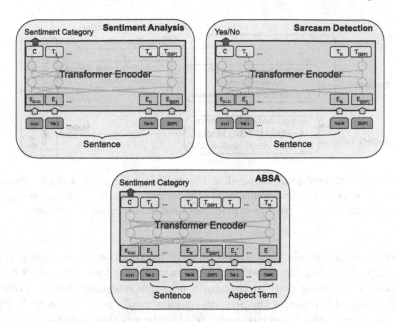

Fig. 1. The sentence-level sentiment analysis (upper left), the sarcasm detection (upper right) and the aspect-based sentiment analysis (bottom) models.

is a category, we simply pass the text into a Transformer encoder to obtain a contextualised representation for each token, i.e.

$$H^{(s)} = \text{Transformer-Encoder}(\texttt{[CLS]} + s + \texttt{[SEP]}; \theta^{(enc1)}), \qquad (4)$$

where "+" denotes string concatenation, and [CLS]/[SEP] is a special token [4]. Then, a pooling is applied to the sequence of representations for a single vector representation for the entire text, and lastly, the pooled representation is fed into a neural classifier to derive a categorical distribution. These are written as

$$p^{(s)} = \text{softmax}(\text{MLP}(\text{Pool}(H^{(s)}); \theta^{(cls1)})) \in \mathbb{R}^3. \qquad (5)$$

Differing from max-/mean-pooling, the Pool($\cdot$) is referred to as using the contextualised representation of the special token [CLS] to represent the sequence [4]. In contrast, for an ABSA model whose input is a pair of texts (sentence and aspect term), we directly concatenate them with a special token [SEP].

$$H^{(a)} = \text{Transformer-Encoder}(\texttt{[CLS]} + s + \texttt{[SEP]} + t + \texttt{[SEP]}; \theta^{(enc2)}), \qquad (6)$$

$$p^{(a)} = \text{softmax}(\text{MLP}(\text{Pool}(H^{(a)}); \theta^{(cls2)})) \in \mathbb{R}^3. \qquad (7)$$

Note, the two models are trained independently and are thus parameter-untied.

In addition, we also propose to employ a sarcasm detection [11] model to boost the accuracy of the sentiment analysis. Sarcasm is the use of language that normally signifies the opposite in order to mock or convey contempt. In

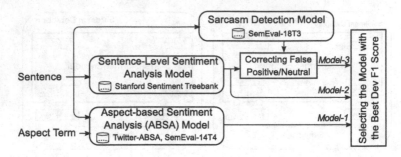

Fig. 2. Green sentiment analysis pipeline (GreenSAP) composed of three sub-models for various scenarios. The text following a cylinder indicates the training dataset(s) for the corresponding model. We will explore more ensembles in our experiments.

other words, some people tend to use positive words in order to convey a negative message. For example, a tweet *"My favourite thing to do at 4am is to go to the airport. How about you?"* expresses a negative sentiment but can often be wrongly classified because of the positive-opinion words, e.g., *"favourite"*. Therefore, we use a sarcasm detection model to identify whether a sentence expresses irony and forces the sentiment prediction to be negative. More specifically, we implement sarcasm detection with the same model architecture as sentence-level sentiment analysis, except the number of output ways is reduced to two, i.e. if a sarcastic attitude expressed. The model is written as

$$\boldsymbol{H}^{(d)} = \text{Transformer-Encoder}([\texttt{CLS}] + s + [\texttt{SEP}]; \theta^{(enc3)}), \tag{8}$$

$$\boldsymbol{p}^{(d)} = \text{softmax}(\text{MLP}(\text{Pool}(\boldsymbol{H}^{(d)}); \theta^{(cls3)})) \in \mathbb{R}^2. \tag{9}$$

Although the implemented model achieves satisfactory binary classification performance on sarcasm detection (about 80% F1 score in our experiments), applying this model inevitably results in error propagation of the sentiment analysis. Hence, we choose to lift the threshold to a relatively high level and push the precision value to be close to 90%. Although this hurts both the overall F1 score and the accuracy, the error propagation problem can be well-alleviated. As for training objective of the three models aforementioned models, we minimise the cross-entropy losses to individually fine-tune the models on task-specific datasets.

Finally, we illustrate our proposed pipeline model in Fig. 2, which is composed of the three well-trained models detailed above. It shows that our proposed model can handle both sentence-level and aspect-based sentiment analysis scenarios, and leverages the sarcasm detection model to boost the performance for SLSA by correcting false positive/neutral predictions.

4 Experiments

4.1 Experimental Setups

Dataset. We introduce datasets to train the three components of our pipeline model. To train the SLSA model, we use Stanford Sentiment Treebank (SST) dataset. In SST, the sentiment polarity of each sentence is labelled as a real number in $[0, 1]$ to express the negative to the positive. We discretise the continuous label into three categories: < 0.4 set to negative, greater than > 0.6 set to positive, and otherwise neutral. To train the ABSA model, we combine the training set from three benchmark datasets, i.e. Restaurant/Laptop from SemEval-2014 Task4 [16] and Twitter [5]. To train the sarcasm detection (SD) model, we use the dataset of SemEval-2018 Task3 [9]. As for the evaluation set, we evaluate on the standard test sets of the ABSA tasks, to facilitate a comparison with the previous SOTA approaches. Moreover, we also annotate two small Twitter evaluation datasets whose topics are related to the COVID-19 pandemic. When applying the ABSA model to our datasets, we use the query of twitter crawler API as aspect term. The statistics of these datasets are summarised in Table 1.

Table 1. Statistics of the datasets involved in this work.

Dataset	Positive		Neutral		Negative	
	Train	Test	Train	Test	Train	Test
SST	3,166	903	1,625	394	3,308	913
Laptop14	994	341	870	128	464	169
Restaurant	2,164	728	807	196	637	196
Twitter	1,561	173	3,127	346	1,560	173
COVID-19-Twitter-1	–	43	–	108	–	103
COVID-19-Twitter-2	–	60	–	35	–	95

Evaluation Metrics. We use standard metrics for a three-category problem, i.e. the accuracy (Accu) and macro F1 score (Ma-F1), where the latter one aims to correctly evaluate a sentiment analysis model, given the imbalanced datasets.

Hyperparameter. We use a mini-batch Stochastic Gradient Descent (SGD) to minimise the loss function of each model. And we use the Adam optimiser with a warmup and a linear decay of the learning rate. For the initialisation of Transformer encoder, we alternate between the BERT-large-uncased [4] and the RoBERTa-large [14]. For each model's hyperparameters, we conduct grid searches for the batch size, the number of training epochs and the learning rate. More specifically, the batch sizes $\in \{16, 32, 48\}$ and the number of training epochs $\in \{3, 5, 7\}$; and the learning rate $\in \{2 \times 10^{-5}, 5 \times 10^{-5}, 7 \times 10^{-5}\}$ for BERT and $\in \{7 \times 10^{-6}, 1 \times 10^{-5}, 1.3 \times 10^{-5}\}$ for RoBERTa. Moreover, the max sequence length is set to 64, and the learning rate warmup proportion is fixed at 10%.

4.2   Sentiment Analysis Evaluation

We first evaluate our proposed model on the three ABSA benchmark datasets. As shown in Table 2, the model consistently outperforms the previous competitive approaches and sets new state-of-the-art results. More specifically, our proposed model, which falls into the "Attention" genre, is significantly better than its baselines, and compared to the "Syntactic" methods that use a sentence dependency parsing tree from an external parser, our proposed model, without any extra inputs and toolkits, still surpasses these syntactic methods by a large-margin. Furthermore, it is observed that the SLSA model only obtains inferior results. One reason for this is that the sentences in the ABSA test data (e.g., Restaurant) usually involve more than one aspect, which is challenging to the SLSA model. Moreover, since these benchmark datasets barely include sarcastic sentences, applying the sarcasm detection model simply introduces a severe error propagation problem, and thus hurts the performance.

Table 2. Performance of methods on three ABSA datasets. The baseline results are copied from [23], please refer to that paper for model details. "SD": sarcasm detection.

Genre	Method	Restaurant		Laptop		Twitter	
		Accu	Ma-F1	Accu	Ma-F1	Accu	Ma-F1
Syn.	ASGCN	80.77	72.02	75.55	71.05	72.15	70.40
	CDT	82.30	74.02	77.19	72.99	74.66	73.66
	GAT	78.21	67.17	73.04	68.11	71.67	70.13
	TD-GAT	80.35	76.13	74.13	72.01	72.68	71.15
	R-GAT	83.30	76.08	77.42	73.76	75.57	73.82
	R-GAT+BERT	86.60	81.35	78.21	74.07	76.15	74.88
Att.	ATAE-LSTM	77.20	–	68.70	–	–	–
	IAN	78.60	–	72.10	–	–	–
	RAM	80.23	70.80	74.49	71.35	69.36	67.30
	MGAN	81.25	71.94	75.39	72.47	72.54	70.81
	LSTM	79.10	69.00	71.22	65.75	69.51	67.98
Ours BERT	SLSA	76.79	67.48	73.82	70.67	58.38	57.69
	SLSA+SD	59.38	54.36	54.86	54.27	48.55	47.39
	ABSA	87.68	80.93	82.76	79.14	76.59	75.89
Ours RoBERTa	SLSA	78.03	76.94	78.06	74.25	78.06	74.25
	SLSA+SD	78.30	66.99	73.98	70.70	56.50	56.33
	ABSA	89.91	84.60	84.95	82.22	78.03	76.94

Next, we further evaluate the proposed model in the two of our labelled datasets. They are related to the topic of the COVID-19 pandemic and viewed as out-of-domain data, which is used to verify if our proposed model can handle out-of-domain scenarios. We use these datasets merely as test sets to show the evaluation metrics. In Table 3, we also explore more combinations/ensembles. It is observed: (1) applying sarcasm detection to SLSA can promote the performance; (2) the ensemble of ABSA and SLSA models mutually benefit each other and thus improve the model's effectiveness; and (3) combining all three models can consistently achieve state-of-the-art performance. These results verify that each part of our proposed pipeline model is non-trivial and useful, especially for out-of-domain datasets.

Table 3. Performance on two our labelled evaluation sets. Note, "ABSA + SLSA" denotes using the most-confident polarity as the final output, i.e. $\arg\max([p^{(s)}; p^{(a)}])$

	Method	Covid19-Twitter-1		Covid19-Twitter-2	
		Accuracy	Macro-F1	Accuracy	Macro-F1
Ours BERT	SLSA	61.81	61.31	56.84	50.81
	SLSA+SD	60.23	58.67	58.42	50.45
	ABSA	60.23	59.31	55.78	52.87
	ABSA + SLSA	64.17	63.13	58.95	54.59
Ours RoBERTa	SLSA	72.44	71.31	62.63	57.69
	SLSA+SD	73.22	71.48	64.21	58.79
	ABSA	68.11	66.56	61.57	58.04
	ABSA + SLSA	73.62	71.60	64.21	59.09
	ABSA + SLSA + SD	74.40	72.18	66.31	61.72

Table 4. Performance comparison on ABSA datasets with different training settings. "Combined" denotes that all training sets are combined to learn one model and "Separated" denotes that each dataset is used to train and test separately.

Category	Method	Restaurant		Laptop		Twitter	
		Accu	Ma-F1	Accu	Ma-F1	Accu	Ma-F1
Ours BERT	ABSA (Combined)	87.68	80.93	82.76	79.14	76.59	75.89
	ABSA (Separated)	88.12	82.76	81.34	78.04	77.60	76.89
Ours RoBERTa	ABSA (Combined)	89.91	84.60	84.95	82.22	78.03	76.94
	ABSA (Separated)	89.10	83.09	83.69	80.01	77.74	77.12

4.3 Performance of Sub-models

To measure the effectiveness of each sub-model, we conduct a series of experiments. First, as for the ABSA model, since it is trained on a combination of Restaurant, Laptop and Twitter datasets, we desire to investigate the performance gap between cross-domain learning and single-domain learning. As shown in Table 4, the model trained on the combined training set performs well in terms of having the most metrics on most test sets. This verifies that a domain-specific example benefits from out-of-domain knowledge via a pre-trained Transformer encoder. Second, as for the SLSA model, it leads to 78.96% accuracy and a 72.36% macro F1 score on this three-category classification problem. To compare with previous SOTA models, we also train and evaluate a SST-binary [20] on the same neural architecture. The results are a 90% accuracy, which is competitive with previous works. Third, as for sarcasm detection, we show a PR curve in Fig. 3.

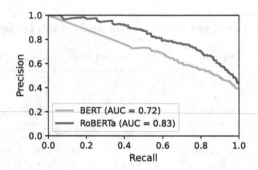

Fig. 3. Precision-recall (PR) curves for the implemented sarcasm detection models.

Table 5. Case study. "−1/ 0 /+1" stands for the negative, neutral and positive polarities, respectively. The values in the right part denote the predicted categorical distributions from both SLSA and ABSA; and underlined text denotes the aspect term.

No.	Sentence with aspect term	Label	SLSA	ABSA
			−1/ 0 /+1	0 / 0 /+1
1	It was good, but none of the <u>flavors</u> WOW	0	0/97/3%	50/48/2%
2	Its size is ideal and, <u>weight</u> is acceptable	0	4/31/65%	72/4/24%
3	I'm bored so I'm playing animal crossings city folk on the <u>Wii</u>. I love this game lol	+1	3/52/45%	0/1/99%
4	I would kill for a 1 h sit down interview with <u>Britney</u>	+1	2/98/0%	27/1/72%
5	The new <u>Britney Spears</u> song is proving she knows how to count to 3. well done?	−1	1/35/64%	**SD**: 96%

4.4   Analysis and Case Study

Applying SLSA Model to ABSA Example. As shown in Table 5 (1-st line), when only one aspect exists in a sentence, the ABSA model may outperform the SLSA model and produce accurate predictions. But, when one sentence involves multiple aspects, this introduces errors and impacts performance of the SLSA model (Table 5 (2-nd line)).

Ensemble of SLSA and ABSA Models. In Table 5 (3-rd line), the SLSA model fails to predict the polarity towards *"wii"*, but ABSA gives a high-confident correct answer. In Table 5 (4-th line), the SLSA model successfully captures the subtle attitude with high confidence, but the ABSA model fails. Hence, combining the models can improve the performance on sentiment analysis tasks.

Sarcasm Detection. To demonstrate how sarcasm detection promotes the pipeline, we show a case in the last line of Table 5. It is observed that, the sentence superficially expresses a positive opinion but entails ironic meanings, and thus the sarcasm detection model forcibly changes the prediction into a negative polarity regardless of the SLSA model's false positive results.

5   Conclusion

In this work, we present a new green sentiment analysis pipeline (GreenSAP) for out-of-domain public sentiment analysis to handle rapidly changing topics on social media. We make the best of the handy benchmark datasets related to either sentence-level or aspect-based sentiment analysis, and develop a pipeline model upon the pre-trained Transformer encoder. Moreover, a sarcasm detection model is also employed to correct false positive predictions. In the experiments, GreenSAP achieves state-of-the-art performance by cross-domain knowledge sharing and outperforms previous approaches. Evaluating GreenSAP on our labelled datasets also verifies the effectiveness. The case studies further provide comprehensive explanations of the improvements on sentiment analysis.

References

1. Agarwal, A., Xie, B., Vovsha, I., Rambow, O., Passonneau, R.J.: Sentiment analysis of Twitter data. In: LSM, pp. 30–38 (2011)
2. Bahdanau, D., Cho, K., Bengio, Y.: Neural machine translation by jointly learning to align and translate. In: ICLR, pp. 1–15 (2015)
3. Castro, S., Hazarika, D., Pérez-Rosas, V., Zimmermann, R., Mihalcea, R., Poria, S.: Towards multimodal sarcasm detection (an _obviously_ perfect paper). arXiv preprint arXiv:1906.01815 (2019)
4. Devlin, J., Chang, M.W., Lee, K., Toutanova, K.: BERT: pre-training of deep bidirectional transformers for language understanding. In: NAACL-HLT (2019)
5. Dong, L., Wei, F., Tan, C., Tang, D., Zhou, M., Xu, K.: Adaptive recursive neural network for target-dependent Twitter sentiment classification. In: ACL (2014)

6. Fang, X., Zhan, J.: Sentiment analysis using product review data. J. Big Data **2**(1), 1–14 (2015). https://doi.org/10.1186/s40537-015-0015-2
7. Ghosh, D., Vajpayee, A., Muresan, S.: A report on the 2020 sarcasm detection shared task. arXiv preprint arXiv:2005.05814 (2020)
8. He, R., Lee, W.S., Ng, H.T., Dahlmeier, D.: Exploiting document knowledge for aspect-level sentiment classification. In: ACL, pp. 579–585 (2018)
9. Hee, C.V., Lefever, E., Hoste, V.: SemEval-2018 task 3: irony detection in English tweets. In: SemEval@NAACL-HLT, pp. 39–50 (2018)
10. Jo, Y., Oh, A.H.: Aspect and sentiment unification model for online review analysis. In: WSDM, pp. 815–824 (2011)
11. Joshi, A., Bhattacharyya, P., Carman, M.J.: Automatic sarcasm detection: a survey. CSUR **50**(5), 1–22 (2017)
12. Liu, B.: Sentiment analysis and opinion mining. Synth. Lect. Hum. Lang. Technol. **5**(1), 1–167 (2012)
13. Liu, B.: Sentiment Analysis - Mining Opinions, Sentiments, and Emotions. Cambridge University Press, Cambridge (2015)
14. Liu, Y., et al.: RoBERTa: a robustly optimized BERT pretraining approach. arXiv preprint arXiv:1907.11692 (2019)
15. Pontiki, M., et al.: SemEval-2016 task 5: aspect based sentiment analysis. In: 1SemEval 2016 (2016)
16. Pontiki, M., Galanis, D., Pavlopoulos, J., Papageorgiou, H., Androutsopoulos, I., Manandhar, S.: SemEval-2014 task 4: aspect based sentiment analysis. In: SemEval 2014, August 2014
17. Potamias, R.A., Siolas, G., Stafylopatis, A.G.: A transformer-based approach to irony and sarcasm detection. Neural Comput. Appl. **32**(23), 17309–17320 (2020). https://doi.org/10.1007/s00521-020-05102-3
18. Rietzler, A., Stabinger, S., Opitz, P., Engl, S.: Adapt or get left behind: domain adaptation through BERT language model finetuning for aspect-target sentiment classification. In: LREC, pp. 4933–4941 (2020)
19. Schwartz, R., Dodge, J., Smith, N.A., Etzioni, O.: Green AI. arXiv preprint arXiv:1907.10597 (2019)
20. Socher, R., et al.: Recursive deep models for semantic compositionality over a sentiment treebank. In: EMNLP, pp. 1631–1642 (2013)
21. Sun, C., Huang, L., Qiu, X.: Utilizing BERT for aspect-based sentiment analysis via constructing auxiliary sentence. In: NAACL-HLT, pp. 380–385 (2019)
22. Vaswani, A., et al.: Attention is all you need. In: NeurIPS, pp. 5998–6008 (2017)
23. Wang, K., Shen, W., Yang, Y., Quan, X., Wang, R.: Relational graph attention network for aspect-based sentiment analysis. In: ACL, pp. 3229–3238 (2020)
24. Wang, Z., Wu, Z., Wang, R., Ren, Y.: Twitter sarcasm detection exploiting a context-based model. In: Wang, J., et al. (eds.) WISE 2015. LNCS, vol. 9418, pp. 77–91. Springer, Cham (2015). https://doi.org/10.1007/978-3-319-26190-4_6
25. Wiebe, J., Bruce, R., O'Hara, T.P.: Development and use of a gold-standard data set for subjectivity classifications. In: ACL, pp. 246–253 (1999)
26. Zhang, L., Wang, S., Liu, B.: Deep learning for sentiment analysis: a survey. Wiley Interdiscip. Rev. Data Min. Knowl. Discov. **8**(4), e1253 (2018)

Profiling Fake News: Learning the Semantics and Characterisation of Misinformation

Swati Agarwal$^{(\boxtimes)}$ ⓘ and Adithya Samavedhi

BITS Pilani, Goa Campus, Goa, India
agrswati@ieee.org, f20170071@goa.bits-pilani.ac.in

Abstract. Research shows that recent information spreading on social media is dubious and untrue, intended to mislead audiences. In the last few years, the fake news spreading community has emerged on a large scale, which intentionally promotes incorrect information, becoming challenging to detect even with human annotation. This paper aims to profile fake news and investigate the characteristics that make the news untrue and fake. We validate our features set on four open-source datasets popularly used in the community. We employ various machine learning, artificial, and recurrent neural network models to evaluate the proposed features set's performance and importance. Our results show that proposed features are generalized and not specific to a domain. Our findings reveal that the model outperforms raw content-based datasets (ISOT and Fake News Master) than interpretation-based datasets (Liar-Liar and Kaggle Emergent).

Keywords: Misinformation · Features extraction · Supervised learning · Context analysis · Applied computational linguistics

1 Introduction

The worldwide web (WWW) comes with a plethora of features that facilitate real-time information dissemination to a wide range of audiences worldwide. Due to the simplicity of navigation, low-cost publication, and wide reachability, online social media (OSM) has become a powerful platform for social interactions and information diffusion [17]. Recently, WWW, specially OSM has become an ideal platform for spreading fake news than mainstream or print media. Nowadays, phoney articles also tend to be obtrusive and diverse, including fake reviews, advertisements, misleading and targeted content, rumour, satire, political sentiments, counterfeit opinions. [22] describes fake news as *all kinds of false stories or information that are mainly published and distributed on the Internet, to purposely mislead, befool or lure readers for financial, political or other gains.* The issue of fake news gained researchers and practitioners' attention after 2016 U.S.A. presidential elections being accused of misleading political polarisation, conflicts, and influencing voters by making false claims [3,15].

© Springer Nature Switzerland AG 2022
B. Li et al. (Eds.): ADMA 2021, LNAI 13087, pp. 203–216, 2022.
https://doi.org/10.1007/978-3-030-95405-5_15

Research shows that over the past few years, fake news has been sprawling over the Internet, further leading to a harmful and overpowering impact on individuals, internet communities, and society [13]. Due to the exponential growth in fake news content, various online fact-checking systems and organisations identify and verify fake news. Majority of these systems (FactCheck, Hoax-Slayer, PolitiFact, Snopes, and TruthOrFiction) use manual detection approaches by experts and fact-checkers while Haoxy uses other fact-checker websites for verification. Furthermore, these systems are specific to political news and not applicable to a wide range of fake news [22]. The manual identification of fake news is overwhelmingly impractical due to large volume, real-time velocity, and uncertainty in fake news topics, eventually delaying the annotation process [1]. Due to online media's dynamic and heterogeneous nature, detecting credible news and mitigating misinformation is technically challenging. Classify and Factmata systems use artificial intelligence (AI)-based approaches for identifying misinformation posts. However, the lack of high-quality data on fake news is an additional challenge for developing automated models [16]. References [2] and [5] show that n-gram and bag-of-words are the most commonly used models. Recently, with the advancement of deep learning in natural language processing (NLP), deep syntax analysis, word2vec, LSTM (long short-term memory) neural network, sequence-2-sequence based deep neural network architectures are heavily used models [14,19]. [5] and [7] describe that semantic level attributes of documents can reveal the writing patterns and creators' intent and background to validate the credibility of the news. [17] discovers that while AI and knowledge-based analysis approaches are useful for fake news detection, they still require human intervention to validate a large size of inputs.

Due to large-scale vocabulary, diverse writing patterns and purposes, maintaining high classification accuracy is challenging for AI-based models as they need to depend on human knowledge. Furthermore, these models require a high-quality annotated dataset for learning, one of the primary technical challenges in the fake news detection research community. Additionally, existing datasets are incomplete, unstructured, and noisy posing challenges in automatic detector tools or applications. Recent studies analyse the content creators' network to capture anomalous information using social context analysis. Graph analysis based methods such as the user network analysis and distribution pattern analysis allow researchers to identify like-minded people [14] and capture the epidemic of misinformation spread across social networking websites. Among various different relations on social networking portals, *like*, *share*, *flag*, and *comment* are the most commonly used features in identifying the credibility of the user [10]. [8] proposed vector-based language models which use a deep, bidirectional LSTM architecture to identify fake news from genuine ones. On a different note, [18] proposes to use a multimodal approach combining text and visual content for fake news classification. They also reveal the visual features that are discriminatory between fake and real news articles.

Prior literature reveals that despite the existing models and systems for fake news identification, the problem persists. The linguistic, interaction or contextual metadata-based features are not sufficient for the classification since they are dependent on the platform. This paper aims to profile fake news to investigate their underlying patterns and identify features that are strong indicators of misinformation independent of the carrier platform. We aim to employ these features across various classification models and evaluate their performance to check the validity of proposed features.

2   Experimental Dataset

We conduct our experiments on various public datasets downloaded from different sources (existing literature, data challenges, and public repositories). We select these datasets as they are popularly used in the research community [15] and hence used for comparing and benchmarking our results. We downloaded four open-source datasets; Liar-Liar, Kaggle Emergent, ISOT, and Fake News Master. Unlike many other popular datasets, which are originally labelled as a rumour or satire, these datasets contain Fake, Real, and Unverified instances. Liar-Liar dataset is a benchmarking dataset on fake news published by [21]. It contains 11,552 short statements (10,269 training and 1283 testing) manually labelled into six categories: barely true, false, half true, mostly true, true, and pants on fire. The professional editor from PolitiFact label these statements. ISOT fake news dataset was published by Information Security and Object Technology Lab at University of Victoria [2]. The dataset contains links to 21,417 real news collected from Reuters News Agency and 23,481 fake news flagged by PolitiFact and Wikipedia. Similarly, the Fake News Master (FNM) dataset contains four dataset files consisting of hyperlinks to real and fake articles from Gossip Cop and PolitiFact records [16,17]. Gossip Cop data files contain links to 5324 fake and 16,817 real articles, whereas PolitiFact data files contain 434 fake and 655 real articles' links. Due to data size and labelling consistency, we merged Gossip-Cop and PolitiFact data and referred it to as Fake News Master (FNM) dataset. For both ISOT and FNM, we used *Newspaper3k* API to fetch the article content from URLs. We download Kaggle Emergent (KE) dataset from the Kaggle website. KE is a collection of all web pages cited in Emergent.info, an online real-time rumour tracker. KE contains 2146 claims reported on different news media sources, and the tracker identifies them as false, true, or unverified.

2.1   Data Pre-processing

We collect our experimental datasets from heterogeneous sources; therefore, we perform pre-processing to remove any possible biases from the datasets. We first remove all duplicate records from the dataset to avoid overfitting in our model. After removing duplicates in the Liar-Liar dataset, we had 8178 training and 2045 testing records. Similarly, in both ISOT and FNM datasets, we found several duplicate articles and URLs that were deleted and returned empty news articles at the time of data collection. In ISOT, we had 38,514 unique articles, whereas the final FNM dataset consisted of 833 fake and 2754 authentic news articles. As discussed above, the Liar-Liar dataset contains six classes identified in manual annotation by experts. We merge these classes into two groups: fake (barely true, false, and pants on fire) and real (half true, mostly true, and true) based on their intensity towards the truth of news to reduce the class imbalance for minority classes. During pre-processing, we observe a major limitation in the Kaggle Emergent dataset. Out of 2146 records, only 107 were unique, while the rest had the same link and the content.

Furthermore, both KE and Liar-Liar datasets contain claims reported online about fake and real news. Therefore, these datasets do not include the original news/article but their interpretation reported by different users. We further removed the instances with blank text (due to formatting or unavailability of the record). We used English as a base language for our experiments. Therefore, as a part of additional pre-processing, all non-English texts (partial or complete text) were translated into the English language using Yandex Translation API.

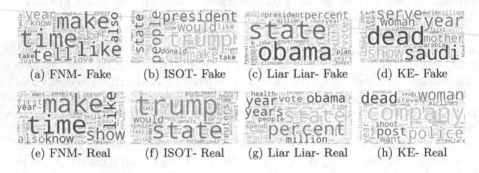

(a) FNM- Fake   (b) ISOT- Fake   (c) Liar Liar- Fake   (d) KE- Fake

(e) FNM- Real   (f) ISOT- Real   (g) Liar Liar- Real   (h) KE- Real

Fig. 1. Word cloud of terms present in fake and real news in each dataset

We removed English stopwords and converted the sentences into lowercase to ensure uniformity and reduce the sparsity in the term-document matrix. Figure 1 shows the word clouds of the terms present in fake (top) and real (bottom) news in each dataset. These word clouds reveal that there are several overlapping terms not only across different datasets but fake and real news within a dataset as well. The overlapping words and similar frequency pose challenges in learning the underlying patterns, extracting distinct features, or relying on keyword-based lookup approaches. Table 1 shows a summary of our experimental datasets.

Table 1. Summary of the experimental datasets. Dup = Duplicate, Size = Number of original instances, Final = Number of instances after pre-processing.

Source	Data	Public	Type	Dup	URL	Size	Final
Kaggle	Kaggle emergent (KE)	✓	Claim	✓	✓	2146	107
SotA	Fake news master (FNM)	✓	Article	✓	✗	23230	3587
SotA	Liar-Liar (Liar)	✓	Claim	✓	✓	11552	10223
SotA	ISOT	✓	Article	✓	✓	44898	38514

3 Proposed Solution Approach

In this section, we discuss the proposed methodology for the automated classification of fake news. We identified specific underlying characteristics of misinformation, which are crucial to differentiate them from genuine and authentic articles. The aim is to identify features independent of a data corpus and are reliable indicators of fake news. We use several natural language processing (NLP) models to extract these features and validate them on different datasets by employing machine learning and deep learning models. The extracted features are not limited by the training data, unlike the Bag-of-words models. The aim is to use features that extract linguistic and semantic attributes from the text. For example, out-of-context terms make use of proximity information of token sequences in the text. In contrast, unigram, bi-gram term frequencies make use of the linguistic metadata of the document. The frequent occurrences of particular n-grams in an instance (input article) can also indicate or characterise fake news. We also aim to look for both prevalent and unusual patterns in a news article but varying in real and fake news to identify low-level features for classification.

3.1 Features Extraction and Selection

While existing studies prioritise contextual metadata, we extract features based on fake news's linguistic and semantic characteristics. For example, the number of likes, shares, and reports/flags are subjective and vary based on the platform. Instead, the proposed features are based on the content and context of the news and not only their contextual metadata. Table 2 shows the list of all features. Based on their nature, the proposed features are grouped into eight broad categories; i.e., F1: statistical, F2: syntactic, F3: semantic, F4: temporal (time instance), F5: writing cues, F6: emotion, F7: topical and context, and finally F8: named entities. The pre-processed text is void of stop-words and case-insensitive. While pre-processing, we store the number of stop-words in every instance; this makes up the number of Stop-words features. We use the sklearn CountVectorizer module to extract n-gram term frequencies, i.e. uni and bigrams. While extracting term frequencies, we store the average normalised scores of every instance (news post) using $\hat{X} = \frac{1+\log_{10} X_i}{1+\log_{10} \sum_{i \in I} (X_i)}$ where X_i represents the term frequency of ith n-gram. The unigram and bi-gram term frequency feature indicates the number of unigram and bi-grams in an instance with a normalised score greater than a threshold (median of the normalised scores of every input sample). This feature captures the unigrams and bi-grams that appear more often than usual. We use LIWC (Linguistic Inquiry Word Count) API to identify features that reveal that pattern of the writing style of fake news publishers or sources. These features primarily include syntactic properties of text, writing cues (mention of social, cognitive, and perceptual attributes), emotional range, and time instance (past, present, and future) mention. These features are essential to explore and investigate as they further reveal the intention and similarities in the agenda of fake news [12]. We also identify the pragmatic features of the text in faux and genuine articles. The out-of-context terms feature captures the number of semantically unfitted token pairs in the text frequently present in fake news targeting clickbait, misinformation spread, or manipulation. We use WordNet as a knowledge graph to compute the distance (path length) between every token (non-stop word) pair in the input text. In our experimental dataset D, given

Table 2. The list of features set used for classification

Code	Type	Feature		Description
F1	Statistical	F1.1	Unigram TF	Term frequency of unigram
		F1.2	Bi-gram TF	Term frequency of bigram
		F1.3	#Stopwords	#Common words
		F1.4	Sixltr	Words $> =$ six letters
F2	Syntactic	F2.1	Conjunction	Syntax and structure
		F2.2	Interrogation	
		F2.3	Number	
F3	Semantic	F3.1	Out-of-context	Keywords in context (KWICs)
F4	Temporal	F4.1	Focuspast	Time-based features
		F4.2	Focuspresent	
		F4.3	Timestamp	
F5	Writing cues	F5.1	Social	Societal mention
		F5.2	Certain	Cognitive
		F5.3	Perceptual	See, hear, feel
F6	Emotion	F6.1	Negative emotion	Psychological
F7	Topical and context	F7.1	Arts and entertainment	Topics and taxonomy
		F7.2	Conspiracy	
		F7.3	Business and industrial	
		F7.4	Economy and finance	
		F7.5	Law, govt & politics	
		F7.6	Science	
		F7.7	Religion and belief	
		F7.8	Education	
		F7.9	IT and technology	
F8	Named entities	F8.1	PERSON	An individual or group
		F8.2	ORG	Organization
		F8.3	GPE	Geo political entity
		F8.4	TIME	Time as an entity

three terms t_1, t_2, and t_3, if $d(t_1,t_2) \ggg d(t_2,t_3)$ then $\{t_1,t_2\}$ are less likely to semantically occur together than $\{t_2,t_3\}$. We compute the average path length l_D of all unique pairs in the experimental dataset and use l_D as a threshold value to identify out-of-context terms in each text instance. A token t_i with path length $d(t_i,t_j) > l_D \mid t_i, t_j \in D, t_j \neq t_i$ is marked as out-of-context term. We tokenise the clean text at two granularity levels: sentence and token. We compare the token pairs' path similarity in the same sentence using the wordnet module from the NLTK library. We use the median of average path similarities of all instances as the threshold. The word pairs in an instance with lesser path similarity than the threshold are considered to be out-of-context. [9] reveals that fake news uses more past tense compared to the present tense. They significantly use past news to support their claims. Therefore, we extract an additional feature "temporal" to identify past, present, and timestamps mentioned from the input text. Fake news may target individuals, groups of people, and organisations; therefore, inspired by these studies, we extract named entities present in the text posts. We use Spacy library to extract `person`, `organization`, `time`, and `geo political entity`.

[4] and [20] found that fake news may also be created for target audiences (focusing on a specific topic) and could be sensitive as well as trending. We perform topic modelling on our experimental dataset to identify each news's unique topics. We use TextRazor API to extract the list of categories and topics along with their confidence score in each topic. The median of the average confidence scores of categories and topics are selected as a threshold. Finally, the topics and categories with confidence scores greater than the threshold are selected; this procedure reduces the features set's dimensionality. The category tagging feature of TextRazor provides fixed standardised taxonomies of categories, whereas the topic tagging feature identifies topics at different levels of abstraction. The primary source for topic modelling is from the TextRazor categories. In the absence of categories for a given small size instance, we select topics identified by TextRazor. We group these categories and topics into generic groups based on the taxonomy defined by IBM Watson Natural Language Classifier Taxonomy. F7 feature set in Table 2 shows nine classes of taxonomies. The generalisation of these topics or categories curbs the dimensionality of the feature set. The category and topic confidence scores are then placed into respective taxonomy for topic modelling. Table 2 shows the list of topics and categories grouped into high-level features. [6] reveals that keywords in context (KWICs) are important features of linguistics since they reveal the structure and language of the text. We use GrammarBot API to identify the grammatical errors, which further compliments the out-of-context terms in the news.

3.2   Classification Models

The steps discussed in Sect. 2.1 reveal that the removal of duplicate and empty records affects the class imbalance in the training and testing dataset. Therefore, we merge the initial training and testing dataset respective to each source. To avoid any biases and class imbalance, we applied stratified sampling [11] on each dataset and divided the dataset into distinct groups called strata/stratum. The groups are equal to the number of classes adequately represented within the whole dataset, making it mutually exclusive and collectively exhaustive. Later, a simple random sample (or probability sample) is drawn from each stratum to create a test dataset with balanced classes. All datasets were split into 20% testing and 80% training and standardised using the StandardScalar module from *sklearn.preprocessing*. We employ several classification models covering a wide range of simple machine learning (ML) algorithms, artificial neural networks (ANNs), and context-based deep learning algorithms. In the case of ML models, we employ Gaussian Naive Bayes (GNB), Random Forest (RF), Decision Tree (DT), K-Nearest Neighbour (KNN), XGBoost (XGB), and Support Vector Machine (SVM) algorithms on each dataset. The ANN models employed varied between 2 to three hidden layers. For the FNM, Liar, ISOT datasets, the output layer of the ANNs consists of one neuron, and the models are optimised using binary cross-entropy loss. The models trained on the KE dataset employ categorical cross-entropy loss. Table 3 shows the detailed configuration of ANN models used for the experiments. We employed variants of RNNs such as Simple RNN, long short-term memory (LSTM), gated recurrent unit (GRU), Bi-directional LSTM to classify fake news. We designed a fixed architecture involving an embedding layer followed by an RNN layer. The GRU, LSTM, RNN models differ by the type of cell used in the RNN layer; GRU, LSTM, RNN cells, respectively, make up this layer. These four model architectures are employed on all datasets while varying the optimiser. We experimented with RMSprop (Root Mean Square Propagation), Adam, and SGD optimisers, giving us three variants in each architecture referred to as LSTM-1, LSTM-2, LSTM-3 RNN-1 and so on. The optimisers are used with their default parameters to carry out the experiments. The batch sizes are updated based on the average length of the document in each dataset. The batch size used for ISOT, FNM, Liar-Liar, and KE is 64, 64, 32, and 8, respectively, each with 10 epochs, early stopping on validation loss.

Table 3. ANN models variants. Learning rate = 0.005, Dropout probability = 0.4

Model	ANN-1	ANN-2	ANN-3	ANN-4
Hidden layers	(32: 32:8)	(32:8)	(32: 32:8)	(32:8)
Activation	ReLU	TanH	ReLU	TanH
Optimiser	Adam	Adam	SGD	SGD

4 Experimental Results

This section discusses the performance evaluation metrics carried out to test and validate our proposed features and models. We evaluate our models using standard binary and multiclass classifier accuracy, macro precision, macro recall, and area under the curve (AUC) of ROC. Additionally, we employ each ML model with 10-fold cross-validation to address any possible overfitting in the results. Table 4 shows the results grouped into ML, ANN, and context-based RNN models. The highlighted results demonstrate the variants of models that perform significantly better than other variants employed on the same dataset.

Table 4. Performance results of classifiers employed on all experimental datasets. P = Precision, R = Recall, and A= Accuracy

	FN Master			ISOT			Liar-Liar			KE		
	P	R	A	P	R	A	P	R	A	P	R	A
GNB	0.78	0.87	0.83	0.75	0.59	0.63	0.49	0.50	0.54	0.67	0.48	0.55
RF	0.98	0.96	0.98	0.92	0.92	0.92	0.56	0.56	0.58	0.63	0.49	0.50
DT	0.95	0.95	0.96	0.85	0.85	0.86	0.52	0.52	0.53	0.52	0.51	0.50
KNN	0.90	0.88	0.92	0.89	0.88	0.88	0.55	0.54	0.57	0.61	0.56	0.59
XGB	0.97	0.96	0.98	0.92	0.92	0.92	0.56	0.55	0.58	0.57	0.55	0.55
SVM	0.94	0.93	0.96	0.93	0.93	0.93	0.56	0.54	0.57	0.52	0.50	0.50
ANN-1	0.94	0.92	0.95	0.92	0.91	0.92	0.28	0.50	0.56	0.36	0.40	0.45
ANN-2	0.95	0.91	0.95	0.92	0.92	0.92	0.56	0.53	0.57	0.58	0.52	0.55
ANN-3	0.90	0.92	0.94	0.89	0.88	0.89	0.57	0.52	0.56	0.20	0.33	0.27
ANN-4	0.93	0.94	0.95	0.90	0.89	0.89	0.57	0.51	0.56	0.25	0.29	0.32
LSTM-1	0.56	0.52	0.74	0.96	0.96	0.96	0.59	0.57	0.60	0.23	0.28	0.32
LSTM-2	0.55	0.52	0.75	0.96	0.96	0.96	0.58	0.58	0.57	0.14	0.33	0.41
LSTM-3	0.38	0.50	0.77	0.27	0.50	0.55	0.29	0.50	0.57	0.28	0.33	0.36
RNN-1	0.38	0.50	0.77	0.47	0.48	0.51	0.55	0.55	0.57	0.20	0.25	0.27
RNN-2	0.59	0.50	0.77	0.75	0.57	0.61	0.54	0.54	0.56	0.23	0.31	0.36
RNN-3	0.38	0.50	0.77	0.27	0.50	0.55	0.54	0.53	0.57	0.32	0.42	0.50
GRU-1	0.54	0.52	0.74	0.94	0.93	0.93	0.57	0.57	0.54	0.14	0.33	0.41
GRU-2	0.54	0.51	0.75	0.94	0.93	0.93	0.58	0.50	0.57	0.14	0.33	0.41
GRU-3	0.38	0.50	0.77	0.27	0.50	0.55	0.29	0.50	0.57	0.28	0.33	0.36
BiLSTM-1	0.85	0.71	0.85	0.99	0.99	0.99	0.57	0.57	0.58	0.12	0.33	0.36
BiLSTM-2	0.67	0.72	0.73	0.99	0.99	0.99	0.59	0.59	0.60	0.30	0.34	0.41
BiLSTM-3	0.38	0.50	0.77	0.80	0.60	0.64	0.29	0.50	0.57	0.48	0.38	0.45

Table 4 shows that the instances FNM and ISOT datasets got classified with very high accuracy (mostly >90%). Whereas KE and Liar datasets got abysmal accuracy and sometimes even lower than the baseline. Furthermore, our results reveal that among all models, tree-based models (random forest and decision trees), XGBoost, and support vector machines outperform other models. Interestingly, while ANN gives significantly higher performance for ISOT and FNM, including all its variants, it does poorly on Liar and KE datasets. The best performance of ANN in these datasets is still <60%. Table 4 shows that almost all ML models and ANN variants gave above 92% accuracy on the FNM dataset except GNB, which provides 84% accuracy. Based on our manual inspection, we find that experts and journalists created KE and Liar datasets. The original news is interpreted and explained in these datasets and hence loses the linguistic and deep semantic features of fake news. Therefore, the model cannot find features in these datasets which results in poor accuracy.

On the contrary, ISOT and FNM datasets contain original news articles acquired from various sources. Hence they vary in writing style, topics, and other aspects. Across the classification model, the statistics in Table 4 unveil that either random forest, decision trees, XGBoost, support vectors or ANN can be used with the identified set of features. Table 4 further reveals that within the text-based RNN variants, the Bidirectional LSTM model performs better than the other RNN models in all datasets. The Bidirectional LSTM model with RMSProp optimiser outperforms both ISOT and FNM with an accuracy of 85% and 99%. Especially for the ISOT dataset, the model extracts more value from the text; hence, the LSTM with Adam optimiser and Bi-LSTM with RMSProp models show higher performance than the models trained on our extracted features. Across other datasets, the models trained on extracted features perform better than the benchmark RNN models. Due to the lack of sizable text, Liar and KE datasets, the performance declines significantly, affecting the macro precision for the KE dataset.

Table 5. Confusion matrix for outperforming ML, ANN, and RNN models employed on ISOT, FNM, and Liar data. Each field represents a quadruple [TP, FN, FP, TN]. TP= True Positive, FP= False positive, FN= False negative, TN= True negative.

Model	ISOT	FNM	Liar
GNB	[676, 2789, 80, 4158]	[797, 36, 577, 2177]	[117, 779, 157, 992]
RF	[3084, 381, 244, 3994]	[770, 63, 20, 2734]	[338, 558, 303, 846]
DT	[2898, 567, 542, 3696]	[772, 61, 65, 2689]	[417, 479, 489, 660]
KNN	[2807, 658, 242, 3996]	[671, 162, 115, 2639]	[251, 645, 230, 919]
XGB	[3070, 395, 220, 4018]	[775, 58, 30, 2724]	[290, 606, 263, 886]
SVM	[3136, 329, 217, 4021]	[740, 93, 65, 2689]	[274, 622, 252, 897]
ANN	[3071, 400, 225, 4007]	[739, 79, 89, 2680]	[139, 769, 116, 1021]
LSTM	[3250, 249, 49, 4155]	[78, 755, 158, 2596]	[262, 615, 193, 975]
RNN	[502, 2997, 40, 4164]	[8, 825, 11, 2743]	[332, 545, 332, 836]
GRU	[3154, 345, 168, 4036]	[66, 767, 143, 2611]	[639, 238, 693, 475]
BiLSTM	[3492, 7, 10, 4194]	[378, 455, 66, 2688]	[490, 387, 441, 727]

Table 5 shows the detailed result on classification using a confusion matrix where positive and negative classes correspond to fake and real news categories, respectively. Since the KE dataset has the worst performance across all datasets, we only report the confusion matrix of other datasets with all models with their outperforming variants. Table 5 reveals that GNB trained model on only one class and learnt very little about the second class, hence a large number of FNs. Results show that random forest increases the number of TPs by a significant margin compared to GNB and reduces the false alarms. The table also reveals that the number of TNs does not change significantly in GNB, while other models learn on positive class and hence increases the number of TPs by reducing FNs.

While ANN increases TPs by a considerable percentage, XGBoost increases TNs without compromising the TP rate, unlike GNB. The confusion matrix statistics of Liar data reveal that neither of the models can effectively segregate fake news from real. If XGBoost classifies real news well, it decreases the recall of fake news (learns from negative class only). Another outperforming model, i.e., ANN, increases the recall of positive class (fake) but reduces the recall of negative class by a huge margin. This happens due to the lack of variation in real or fake news in the dataset as they are the interpretations and not the original news. Among context-aware models, both LSTM and Bi-LSTM learn well on both positive and negative classes, reducing the number of FNs and FPs. However, simple RNN and GRU do not learn the fake class well in the FNM dataset. Within the Liar dataset, all context-aware models do not learn enough from either of the classes and give poor TP and TN, resulting in poor accuracy.

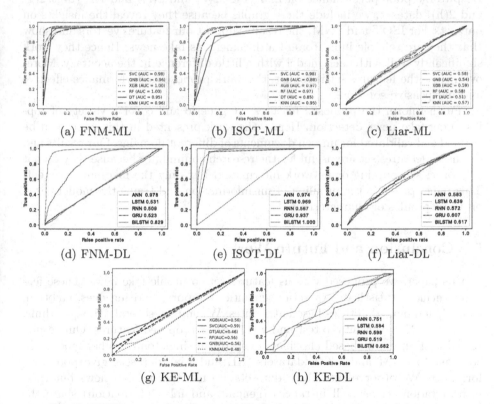

(a) FNM-ML (b) ISOT-ML (c) Liar-ML

(d) FNM-DL (e) ISOT-DL (f) Liar-DL

(g) KE-ML (h) KE-DL

Fig. 2. ROC curves of various models employed on experimental datasets

In addition to the accuracy metrics, we also plot the area under the ROC curve (AUC) for each model and dataset pair. Figures 2(a), 2(b), and 2(c) shows the AUC for all ML algorithms employed on FNM, ISOT, and Liar datasets. The graphs reveal that all models perform outstandingly on FNM and give a minimum AUC of 0.95, while XGB and RF give a perfect AUC. These statistics reveal that for any randomly selected input, XGB and RF will predict the classes correctly. Interestingly, all these models perform similarly on ISOT data as well. Since FNM is a more descriptive dataset and has many instances, we find a slightly better performance of the models in FNM compared to ISOT. Furthermore, for the ISOT dataset, SVM outperforms XGB and RF. In the KE and Liar dataset, we find that while the dataset's size is one of the primary issues of misclassification, the nature of the dataset (interpretation of actual news articles) is the major setback for the model. Figures 2(d) and 2(e) reveal that ANN gives high performance for both FNM and ISOT datasets. While, Bi-LSTM gives 100% AUC for ISOT, it gives a reasonably good performance for FNM data which aligns with our explanation of results from Tables 4 and 5. However, the simple RNN model does not do well for any of the datasets. Despite the poor performance on Liar (Figs. 2(c) and 2(f)) and KE (Figs. 2(g) and 2(h)) dataset, we include these graphs because they reveal the insights on datasets. For ISOT and FNM, the results support our features vectors and show that they are reliable indicators of a document as fake news. Hence they work significantly well with each model with a little difference in the accuracy. Moreover, since the features set is robust, this work proposes a performance-effective and inexpensive solution.

Furthermore, the proposed features are generic and cover a variety of topics under fake news detection. Hence, the work presented in this paper can be trained and validated for unseen documents of different domains. Our results and discussed features set are useful for the research community because they do not rely on crowdsourcing or network information but only the fake news content. This paper presents the profiling of misinformation and trains the model based on these profiles or characteristics.

5   Conclusion and Future Work

In this paper, we proposed various features set to profile fake news. These features include statistical, syntactic, semantic, temporal, writing cues, emotion, topical, and named entities based attributes. We employ several ML algorithms, ANN, and RNN variants to test and validate our proposed features. Our results reveal that ensemble-based classifiers outperform singleton classifier models. In contrast to FNM and ISOT datasets, KE and Liar datasets give poor performance. We observe that these datasets are not the original news but their interpretation. Hence, all instances (genuine and fake information) share the same writing style, grammar structure, and emotional range. We conclude that XGBoost, SVM, and tree-based algorithms give at least 90% accuracy in the classification with the proposed features set. Similar to ML models, ANN models and Bi-LSTM also outperform for ISOT and FNM datasets. Due to the small text and interpretation in KE and Liar datasets, Bi-LSTM does not learn more from the text and performs poorly than the models employed on extracted features. Future work includes mining the multimedia metadata associated with news articles. We also plan to have domain-specific concept extraction for specialised fake news detection. For example, fake news specific to the COVID-19 pandemic and health beliefs.

References

1. Ahmed, H., Traore, I., Saad, S.: Detection of online fake news using n-gram analysis and machine learning techniques. In: Traore, I., Woungang, I., Awad, A. (eds.) ISDDC 2017. LNCS, vol. 10618, pp. 127–138. Springer, Cham (2017). https://doi.org/10.1007/978-3-319-69155-8_9
2. Ahmed, H., Traore, I., Saad, S.: Detecting opinion spams and fake news using text classification. Secur. Priv. 1(1), e9 (2018)
3. Bovet, A., Makse, H.A.: Influence of fake news in twitter during the 2016 us presidential election. Nat. Commun. 10(1), 1–14 (2019)
4. Brennen, B.: Making sense of lies, deceptive propaganda, and fake news. J. Media Ethics 32(3), 179–181 (2017)
5. Conroy, N.K., Rubin, V.L., Chen, Y.: Automatic deception detection: methods for finding fake news. Proc. Assoc. Inf. Sci. Technol. 52(1), 1–4 (2015)
6. Cunha, E., Magno, G., Caetano, J., Teixeira, D., Almeida, V.: Fake news as we feel it: perception and conceptualization of the term "Fake News" in the Media. In: Staab, S., Koltsova, O., Ignatov, D.I. (eds.) SocInfo 2018. LNCS, vol. 11185, pp. 151–166. Springer, Cham (2018). https://doi.org/10.1007/978-3-030-01129-1_10
7. Feng, V.W., Hirst, G.: Detecting deceptive opinions with profile compatibility. In: 6th International Joint Conference on Natural Language Processing, pp. 338–346. Asian Federation of Natural Language Processing/ACL (2013)
8. Ghosh, S., Shah, C.: Towards automatic fake news classification. Proc. Assoc. Inf. Sci. Technol. 55(1), 805–807 (2018)
9. Horne, B.D., Adali, S.: This just. In: Fake news packs a lot in title, uses simpler, repetitive content in text body, more similar to satire than real news. In: 11th International AAAI Conference on Web and Social Media (2017)
10. Kumar, S., West, R., Leskovec, J.: Disinformation on the web: impact, characteristics, and detection of Wikipedia hoaxes. In: Proceedings of the 25th International Conference on World Wide Web, pp. 591–602 (2016)
11. Liberty, E., Lang, K., Shmakov, K.: Stratified sampling meets machine learning. In: International Conference on Machine Learning, pp. 2320–2329 (2016)
12. Potthast, M., Kiesel, J., Reinartz, K., Bevendorff, J., Stein, B.: A stylometric inquiry into hyperpartisan and fake news. In: Proceedings of the 56th Annual Meeting of the Association for Computational Linguistics, pp. 231–240 (2018)
13. Roets, A., et al.: 'fake news': incorrect, but hard to correct. the role of cognitive ability on the impact of false information on social impressions. Intelligence 65, 107–110 (2017)
14. Ruchansky, N., Seo, S., Liu, Y.: CSI: a hybrid deep model for fake news detection. In: Proceedings of the 2017 ACM on Conference on Information and Knowledge Management, pp. 797–806. ACM (2017)
15. Sharma, K., Qian, F., Jiang, H., Ruchansky, N., Zhang, M., Liu, Y.: Combating fake news: a survey on identification and mitigation techniques. ACM Trans. Intell. Syst. Technol. (TIST) 10(3), 1–42 (2019)
16. Shu, K., Mahudeswaran, D., Wang, S., Lee, D., Liu, H.: Fakenewsnet: a data repository with news content, social context, and spatiotemporal information for studying fake news on social media. Big Data 8(3), 171–188 (2020)

17. Shu, K., Sliva, A., Wang, S., Tang, J., Liu, H.: Fake news detection on social media: a data mining perspective. SIGKDD Explor. Newsl. **19**(1), 22–36 (2017)
18. Singh, V.K., Ghosh, I., Sonagara, D.: Detecting fake news stories via multimodal analysis. Assoc. Inf. Sci. Technol. **72**(1), 3–17 (2021)
19. Singhania, S., Fernandez, N., Rao, S.: 3han: a deep neural network for fake news detection. In: Liu D., Xie S., Li Y., Zhao D., El-Alfy ES. (eds.) Neural Information Processing, ICONIP 2017, Lecture Notes in Computer Science, vol. 10635, pp. 572–581. Springer, Cham (2017). https://doi.org/10.1007/978-3-319-70096-0_59
20. Tandoc, E.C., Jr., Lim, Z.W., Ling, R.: Defining "fake news" a typology of scholarly definitions. Digital Journalism **6**(2), 137–153 (2018)
21. Wang, W.Y.: "Liar, liar pants on fire": a new benchmark dataset for fake news detection. In: Association for Computational Linguistics, pp. 422–426. ACL (2017)
22. Zhang, X., Ghorbani, A.A.: An overview of online fake news: characterization, detection, and discussion. Inf. Process. Manage. **57**(2), 102025 (2020)

Mining Social Networks for Dissemination of Fake News Using Continuous Opinion-Based Hybrid Model

Maneet Singh[1], S. R. S. Iyengar[1], and Rishemjit Kaur[2,3](✉)

[1] Indian Institute of Technology Ropar, Rupnagar, India
{2018csz0008,sudarshan}@iitrpr.ac.in
[2] CSIR-Central Scientific Instruments Organization, Chandigarh, India
rishemjit.kaur@csio.res.in
[3] Academy of Scientific and Innovative Research, Ghaziabad, India

Abstract. The entire world is confronting the challenge of fake news disseminated online, as its consequences could be exceptionally catastrophic. In this paper, we have proposed a hybrid model that integrates the opinion evolution process with the propagation of fake news. The level of extremity in opinions, the amount of support from social connections and the social influence were used as the major design considerations in modeling the spread of fake news. As polarized opinions on social media often lead to polarized networks, the proposed model was utilized to study the effect of evolving opinion on the spread of fake news on polarized networks of varying degrees. Our findings suggested that there are more users involved in sharing fake news in the presence of a highly polarized network. Moreover, the tendency of a user to adapt the opposing opinion seems to be correlated with the exposure of fake news. Besides this, we also assessed the consequences of the spread of fake news on the user's opinion and found that the users that are mainly influenced are the ones having an unclear stance towards a given issue. Overall, our proposed model highlights the interrelation between fake news and the opinion evolution on social networks.

Keywords: Spread of fake news · Agent based modeling · Opinion dynamics · Network polarization

1 Introduction

Social networking sites like Twitter, Facebook and WhatsApp have gained enormous attraction among people across the globe. This popularity has come at a cost, i.e., these platforms are being used for sharing fake news [17]. Although, several measures have been taken by the social networking sites and the administration of different nations [1,17] to ensure the integrity of the content shared online. Despite these efforts, the problem of using the online medium to spread fake news persists [21].

© Springer Nature Switzerland AG 2022
B. Li et al. (Eds.): ADMA 2021, LNAI 13087, pp. 217–228, 2022.
https://doi.org/10.1007/978-3-030-95405-5_16

Several researchers have analyzed the dissemination of fake news based on different aspects such as the content of the news [19], the profile of the users engaged in spreading the news [15] or engagement of bots [14]. Besides these approaches, there is another area of research that aims to model the diffusion process of fake news. The process of modeling has been studied using different methods including the concepts of physics [8], natural phenomenons [9] and epidemiology [3]. The epidemiology-based modeling is considered to be an adequate method as the diffusion process of both infectious disease and fake news are quite similar in nature [10].

The spread of fake news on online platforms has often been linked with the polarized opinion of the users [4,18]. Furthermore, it has been found that users with similar opinions like to connect with each other and thus results in the formation of polarized communities within the network (or simply polarized network) [4]. These polarized communities then act as a deciding factor for the virality of the fake news on social media platforms [4]. Tornberg and Petter [18] also observed that the spread of misinformation is boosted by the existence of echo chambers within a social network. Here an echo-chamber corresponds to a closed environment where people perceive and amplifies opinion of their own. The existence of polarized opinions accompanied by fake news could even disregard social welfare activities such as vaccination [13].

As seen above, the majority of work studying polarization and fake news assumes opinion to be a static entity and hence does not incorporate the dynamics of opinion formation with the propagation of fake news. Although, recently Zeng et al. [22] studied the change in the state of emotion under the influence of the rumour refutation process. The refutation process was successful in transforming the state of emotions from negative to a positive or an immune state. Thus in their study opinion is represented through emotions, which could be either positive, negative or neutral, whereas our focus is on the continuous opinion and their evolution with the spread of fake news.

In this study, we have proposed a hybrid model to analyze the propagation of a post containing fake news, based on evolving opinions. The term "hybrid" is used for the model, as it combines the diffusion of opinion with the diffusion of fake news. The model uses the epidemic-based nature-inspired approach for modeling the spread and a bounded-confidence method for modeling the dynamics of opinion formation. The level of extremity in the opinions is considered to one of the key players, in the spread of fake news, during the design of the model [7]. The proposed model is used to establish a relationship between the polarized opinions and the spread of fake news, for networks representing a varying level of heterogeneity among users of different opinions.

Based on our knowledge, modeling continuous opinion with the diffusion of fake news for analyzing the effect of polarized opinion on the spread of fake news has not been done previously. The paper is organized as follows. The proposed model is discussed in Sect. 2. The findings related to the implementation of the proposed model on networks with varying degree of polarization are reported and discussed in Sect. 3. Finally, the overall conclusion of our study is provided in Sect. 4.

2   Proposed Model

In this section, we have discussed the design of an agent-based model[1] to identify the association between the spread of fake news and polarized opinions. As
discussed previously, the opinion of an individual is an essential factor that facilitates in spreading of fake news on social media. Hence, we propose a hybrid
model that collectively analyses the dynamics of opinion formation and the diffusion of fake news on social networks. For analyzing the dissemination of fake
news, we have used the SEIR model [11], designed for assessing the spread of
infection-based disease. Every agent in the hybrid model is considered to be in
one of the following four states.

- **Susceptible (S)**: The state corresponds to those individuals that have not
  yet consumed the fake news.
- **Exposed (E)**: An agent which has consumed fake news but hasn't shared
  with others yet, is said to be in an "Exposed" state.
- **Infected (I)**: As the name suggests, those agents which have consumed as
  well as shared the fake news with their neighbours, are considered to be in
  an "Infected" state.
- **Recovered (R)**: The agents in this state can be considered to be those that
  have explicitly realized that the given news is fake by deleting the shared
  news.

For studying the propagation of fake news in combination with opinion
dynamics, the hybrid model takes inspiration from a bounded confidence-based
model [20]. In a bounded confidence based model, the opinion of an agent is
considered to be influenced by the opinion of its neighbours, where only those
neighbouring agents are considered that are similar in opinion within a certain
threshold. In our proposed model, the opinion of every agent is updated on being
exposed to the post containing fake news and the change in opinion of the agent
is done following the principles of opinion similarity between an agent and its
neighbours. The steps involved in the proposed model is explained in detail as
follows:-

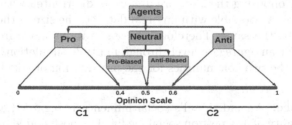

Fig. 1. Initialization of opinion of the agents.

---

[1] Code for the model is available at https://github.com/maneetsingh88/fakenews
Modeling

2.1   Initialization

Opinion: The opinion O_i of an agent i is considered to be a continuous quantity i.e. $O_i \in [0,1]$. The initialization process of opinion is divided into following two phase:-

Categorization: For a given issue, we have assumed, three categories of agents as shown in Fig. 1. The pro group corresponds to the set of agents supporting the issue with varying degrees (i.e. opinion from 0 to 0.4), on the other hand, the anti group corresponds to the set of agents opposing the issue (i.e. opinion from 0.6 to 1). The remaining agents belong to the neutral group. They are further divided into two subgroups- *pro-biased* and *anti-biased.* The agents with opinion from 0.4 to 0.5 are considered to have an unclear stance with relatively more social connections on the platform with the ones supporting the issue than those opposing it. We referred to these agents as pro-biased neutral agents. Similarly, agents with an unclear stance towards the given issue (i.e. opinion from 0 .5 to 0.6) and relatively greater connections with the anti group agents, were referred to as anti-biased neutral agents.

Assignment: For assigning the opinions to the agents, the given network was divided into two communities, say C_1 and C_2, using a community detection algorithm [2]. The two-community structure of a network has been observed for both controversial as well as non-controversial topic based social network [6]. Thus, the community C_1 would comprise of agents from pro and pro-biased neutral groups and similarly the community C_2 contains agents from anti and anti-biased neutral groups. Therefore, the opinion of an agent is assigned as follows:-

$$O_i = \begin{cases} rand(0,0.5), & \text{if } i \in C_1 \\ rand(0.5,1), & \text{otherwise} \end{cases} \tag{1}$$

where rand is the function that provide a random number within the given range from a uniform distribution.

This method of opinion initialization ensures that people with varying degrees of supporting or opposing the issue are uniformly distributed within the respective communities. As possible with any real dataset, the size of the two communities may not be the same. Therefore any observations made from the model should be done at an aggregate level through multiple simulations, with equally selecting one of the two communities for the propagation of fake news.

Social Influence: An individual's social influence is regarded as an essential factor in the virality of any post on social media. The post shared on social media by highly influential nodes (i.e. those having large number of followers) has a far reach among the users of the platform. Thus, the degree D_i of an agent i in the given network is used to compute the social influence as per the following equation:-

$$S_i = \text{norm}(D_i) \tag{2}$$

where norm is a scaling function applied to ensure $S_i \in [0, 1]$, without affecting the degree distribution of the network.

Extremeness: The extremeness attribute of an agent is derived from its opinion. It measures the closeness of any agent towards one of the ends of the opinion spectrum. The extremeness E_i of an agent i is computed using the following equation:-

$$E_i = abs(2 * O_i - 1) \tag{3}$$

where abs is a function used to find the absolute value of the given number.

Group Support: The level of support an individual possess from its social connections could greatly influence the decision to express an opinion publicly. Here expressing an opinion is associated with sharing a post on social media platforms. The group support G_i for an agent i is computed as follows:-

$$G_i = \begin{cases} |P|/D_i, & \text{if } O_i \leq 0.4 \\ |A|/D_i, & \text{if } O_i \geq 0.6 \\ |N|/D_i, & \text{otherwise} \end{cases} \tag{4}$$

where

$$P = \{i \mid O_i \leq 0.4\} \quad \forall i \in Ag$$
$$A = \{i \mid O_i \geq 0.6\} \quad \forall i \in Ag$$
$$N = \{i \mid O_i > 0.4 \text{ and } O_i < 0.6\}$$

In the above equation, P, A and N represents set of agents belonging to "pro","anti" and "neutral" group respectively, whereas Ag denotes the set of all agents.

State: Initially every agent is assumed to be in a "susceptible" state, i.e. they are unaware of the fake news.

2.2 Propagation

The actual spread of the post containing the fake news, into the network, takes place in this phase. First, one of the agents is selected as an initiator of the fake news. The state of the selected agent is changed from "susceptible" to "infected". At each step k of propagation of fake news, an agent's opinion as well as state is updated as follows:-

– If an agent i is in a "susceptible" state and one of its neighbour j is infected, the opinion of an agent i is updated on seeing the post from its neighbour j, based on the following equation:-

$$O_i^{(k+1)} = \begin{cases} O_i^{(k)} + 0.2 * M_i * \Delta O & \text{if } \Delta O \leq \epsilon \\ O_i^{(k)} & \text{otherwise} \end{cases} \tag{5}$$

where $M_i = 1 - E_i$ represents the degree of moderation of an agent i and $\Delta O = O_j - O_i$. Thus, the opinion of an agent i will be influenced by its neighbors' self opinion (O_j), only if O_j is similar to its own opinion (O_i) within the given threshold (ϵ). Apart from updating the opinion, the given agent will enter the "infected" state based on the probability α, given as:-

$$\alpha = \begin{cases} (S_j + E_i + G_i)/3 & \text{if } \Delta O \leq \epsilon \\ 0 & \text{otherwise} \end{cases} \tag{6}$$

In case of state transition from "susceptible" to "infected", the opinion of the neighbour posting the fake news needs to be similar to an agent's self-opinion. The value of the state transition probability i.e. α for agent i is computed with the assumption that the extremeness of opinion(E_i), social influence (S_j) of the neighbour j and the tendency to incline towards self-belief (G_i) are the major drivers of dissemination of fake news online [7,21]. We have computed and assessed the state transition probability for every infected neighbour j separately and thus an agent with a large number of infected neighbours, has larger chances of getting infected [18]. In case an agent does not move to an infected state in the current step even after having at least one infected neighbour, then it is automatically moved to an "exposed" state.

- If an agent i is in an "exposed" state and one of its neighbours is "infected" then the agent will update its opinion and stochastically its state, based on the procedure discussed above.
- If an agent i is in an "infected" state then it will move to a "recovered" state based on a probability β. This transition could be considered as the case where an agent deletes its post and hence will no longer infect or spread the news to its neighbours.

The propagation phase of the model is repeatedly executed until equilibrium, i.e. when there is no change in the opinion as well as the state of each agent. The value of both ϵ and β was experimentally kept fixed at 0.2. The purpose of keeping the value of ϵ low is quite intuitive, as higher values would have eradicated the issue of polarized opinions [18,20]. Similarly, for β, there has been a previous study [5], which found the probability of deleting the post not more than 0.2. Although in the upcoming section, we have also analysed and reported our findings on varying the values of these parameters. The overall workflow of the model can also be seen in Fig. 2.

3   Results and Discussions

In this section, we analyzed the role played by the polarized opinion of users in the spread of fake news. Therefore, the proposed model was simulated on three different networks (Fig. 3) to compare the spreading behaviour of fake news on different levels of network polarization. The first network is the follower's network of users engaged in discussing Article 370 on Twitter, obtained from our previous study [16]. We will be referring to this network as a "Real" network

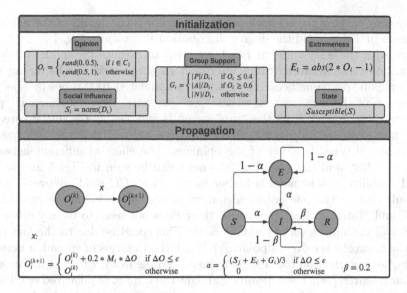

Fig. 2. Opinion-based hybrid model for propagation of fake news on social networks.

in our future discussions. The "Real" network was then used to construct the other two networks. In this regard, we first divided the "Real" network into two communities say C_1 and C_2 [2]. Subsequently, the second network was constructed by adding 1000 edges (around 20%) within both the communities (i.e. 500 edges to communities C_1 and C_2 separately). In order to construct our third network, we added a similar number of edges (i.e. 1000) between the community C_1 and C_2 in the "Real" network. As both the networks were obtained by adding either intra-community connections or intra-community connections within our "Real" network, we will refer to them as "IntraCC Real" network and "InterCC Real" network respectively in our future discussions. The reason for adding intra-community edges is straightforward, more connections among users belonging to similar communities, more chances of communication between them and similarly more chances of polarization. The purpose of adding connections between two communities is just the opposite, where these connections might facilitate more communication among nodes of different communities and thereby might reduce polarization. To verify that the network polarization of "Real" network is increased by "IntraCC Real" network and decreased by "InterCC Real" network, we computed the heterogeneity scores for both the network [12], which comes out to be 0.09 and 0.78 respectively. The very low heterogeneity score for "IntraCC Real" network indicates that the network is extremely polarized and very high heterogeneity score for "InterCC Real" network shows that it is "non-polarized". The reason for synthetically generating the networks using the "Real" network is two-fold. First, we will have a similar set of nodes to assess and second, by doing this, we could easily quantify the difference in the spread of fake news by varying the network polarization. The basic details of the networks are shown in Table 1 and the degree distribution is shown in Fig. 4.

Now with these networks at hand, we want to execute the model proposed in Sect. 2 on these networks. Since the originating fake news can lie on any side of the opinion spectrum, hence the model was simulated 1000 times by selecting the opinion of the fake news as either "pro" or "anti" in equal share. If "pro" is selected then a node from the "pro" group is assigned as the initial spreader of the fake news and vice-versa. This approach ensures that the final results are not biased towards either of the opinions. The effect of different networks on the visibility and the spread of fake news can be seen in Figs. 5 and 6. The overall visibility of fake news is higher for the "InterCC Real" network, which is mainly due to the non-polarized nature of the network. In the case of the "Real" and "IntraCC Real" networks, there does not seem to be any difference in the final visibility level of the fake news. This could be due to the fact that, both the networks are overall polarized. Similarly, in terms of spread, a network with higher polarization has a higher spread of fake news, which is in line with previous research [18]. These results highlight the impact of polarized opinion on the diffusion process of fake news in networks with varying levels of polarization.

The effect of the initial opinion of the initiator of fake news on the overall spread is also studied and results are shown in Fig. 7. It can be observed that our previous results hold irrespective of the initial opinion of the first spreader. The visibility of fake news is higher for a non-polarized network and is independent of the initial opinion of the originator of fake news. In the case of the spreading pattern, "IntraCC Real" network has the highest number of posts shared, followed by "Real" network. Thus, it seems that users like to spread fake news that aligns with their stance irrespective of the degree of extremeness in the opinion of the initiator.

Table 1. Basic properties of "IntraCC Real", "Real" and "InterCC Real" Networks (Deg stands for degree, CC stands for clustering coefficient and het stands for heterogeneity).

Network	#Nodes	#Edges	avgDeg	avgCC	hetScore
IntraCC real	1606	6934	8.63	0.20	0.09
Real	1606	5934	7.40	0.23	0.17
InterCC real	1606	6934	8.63	0.15	0.78

The effect of the conformity bias (ϵ) and the likelihood of explicit recovery (β) on the overall visibility and the number of users sharing the fake news are also evaluated (Figs. 8 and 9). The level of conformity bias seems to be associated with the visibility of fake news. As we increase the value of the ϵ, the level of exposure and the number of spreaders both increases. In the case of the parameter β, the explicit deletion of the shared post, do not make major changes to the exposure of the fake news within the social network and hence we can say that the damage was already being done.

Fig. 3. Visualization of (a) "IntraCC Real", (b) "Real" and (c) "InterCC Real" networks.

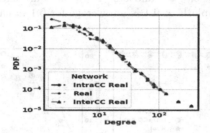

Fig. 4. Degree distribution of "IntraCC Real","Real" and "InterCC Real" networks.

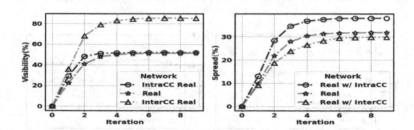

Fig. 5. Cumulative proportion of visibility and spread of fake news with time.

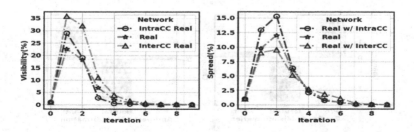

Fig. 6. Step-wise proportion of visibility and spread of fake news with time.

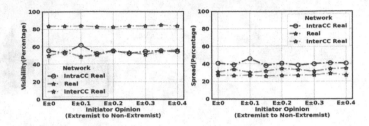

Fig. 7. Proportion of visibility and spread on varying the opinion of the "initiator" node from both sides of the spectrum. Here E represents Extremism either for "pro" or "anti". In case of "pro" it should be read as 0, 0.1, 0.2, 0.3 and 0.4. For "anti", it should be read as 1, 0.9, 0.8, 0.7 and 0.6. The results are aggregated for "pro" and "anti" opinion, for example E ± 0.1 is an average for 0.1 in case of "pro" and 0.9 in case of "anti".

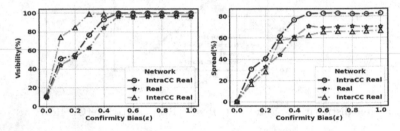

Fig. 8. Effect of varying conformity bias on the visibility(V) and the spread(S) of fake news

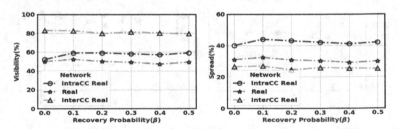

Fig. 9. Effect of varying recovery probability on the visibility(V) and the spread(S) of fake news

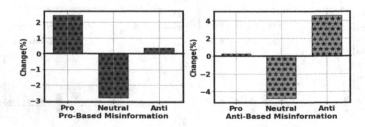

Fig. 10. The share of users belonging to "pro","neutral" and "anti" group before and after the diffusion of "pro-based" and "anti-based" fake news.

Next, we aim to study the effect of fake news on opinions at a macroscopic level. It has been reported that fake news campaigns can play a vital role in manipulating the voter's decision during the elections [7]. We want to verify whether our model can identify such associations between the change in opinions and the spread of fake news. Therefore, the proposed model was executed on the "Real" network. For the sake of simplicity, the change in opinion is analysed categorically using "pro", "anti" and "neutral" users (Fig. 10) for both kinds of fake news, i.e. supporting and opposing the given issue. The results indicate that there are more number of users in the "anti"("pro") group after the spread of fake news depicting "anti"("pro") opinion. This change seems to be mainly due to the shifting of users with a neutral opinion towards the opinion side depicted by the post containing fake news. Thus, users with an unclear stance seem to be more vulnerable to be influenced by fake news.

4 Conclusion

In this paper, we have analyzed the spread of fake news on social networks, by introducing a hybrid model for assessing opinion evolution with the spread of fake news. Specifically, we examined the effect of varying degrees of network polarization on the spread of fake news, when opinion is considered to be a dynamic as well as a continuous entity. The higher level of polarization in the network causes more users to share fake news. The conformity bias seems to be directly correlated with the spread of fake news. The efforts by spreaders to repudiate by deleting the shared post do not significantly affect the exposure of the post containing fake news. We have also observed the impact of fake news on the opinion of the users in a social network. In this study, we have focused on fake news that our polarized in nature, but in the future, we would like to extend the model to incorporate generic fake news on a large network of users on social media to make it more robust and practical. Overall, the findings of our study highlight the dynamic nature of opinion and its role in the spread of fake news on social networks. Hence, any model for analysing the spread of fake news must integrate the process of opinion evolution.

References

1. Arafa, M.: The archeology of freedom of information laws: Egypt and fake-news laws. Fla. Coastal L. Rev. **20**, 73 (2020)
2. Blondel, V.D., Guillaume, J.L., Lambiotte, R., Lefebvre, E.: Fast unfolding of communities in large networks. J. Stat. Mech: Theory Exp. **2008**(10), P10008 (2008)
3. Chen, J., Song, Q., Zhou, Z.: Agent-based simulation of rumor propagation on social network based on active immune mechanism. J. Syst. Sci. Inf. **5**(6), 571–584 (2017)
4. Del Vicario, M., Bessi, A., Zollo, F., Petroni, F., Scala, A., Caldarelli, G., Stanley, H.E., Quattrociocchi, W.: The spreading of misinformation online. Proc. Natl. Acad. Sci. **113**(3), 554–559 (2016)

5. Friggeri, A., Adamic, L., Eckles, D., Cheng, J.: Rumor cascades. In: Proceedings of the International AAAI Conference on Web and Social Media, vol. 8 (2014)
6. Garimella, K., Morales, G.D.F., Gionis, A., Mathioudakis, M.: Quantifying controversy on social media. ACM Trans. Soc. Comput. 1(1), 1–27 (2018)
7. Grinberg, N., Joseph, K., Friedland, L., Swire-Thompson, B., Lazer, D.: Fake news on twitter during the 2016 us presidential election. Science 363(6425), 374–378 (2019)
8. Han, S., Zhuang, F., He, Q., Shi, Z., Ao, X.: Energy model for rumor propagation on social networks. Physica A 394, 99–109 (2014)
9. Indu, V., Thampi, S.M.: A nature-inspired approach based on forest fire model for modeling rumor propagation in social networks. J. Netw. Comput. Appl. 125, 28–41 (2019)
10. Kucharski, A.: Study epidemiology of fake news. Nature 540(7634), 525–525 (2016)
11. Li, M.Y., Muldowney, J.S.: Global stability for the seir model in epidemiology. Math. Biosci. 125(2), 155–164 (1995)
12. Lužar, B., Levnajić, Z., Povh, J., Perc, M.: Community structure and the evolution of interdisciplinarity in slovenia's scientific collaboration network. PLoS ONE 9(4), e94429 (2014)
13. Schmidt, A.L., Zollo, F., Scala, A., Betsch, C., Quattrociocchi, W.: Polarization of the vaccination debate on facebook. Vaccine 36(25), 3606–3612 (2018)
14. Shao, C., Ciampaglia, G.L., Varol, O., Yang, K.C., Flammini, A., Menczer, F.: The spread of low-credibility content by social bots. Nat. Commun. 9(1), 1–9 (2018)
15. Shu, K., Wang, S., Liu, H.: Understanding user profiles on social media for fake news detection. In: 2018 IEEE Conference on Multimedia Information Processing and Retrieval (MIPR), pp. 430–435. IEEE (2018)
16. Singh, M., Kaur, R., Iyengar, S.R.S.: Multidimensional analysis of fake news spreaders on Twitter. In: Chellappan, S., Choo, K.-K.R., Phan, N.H. (eds.) CSoNet 2020. LNCS, vol. 12575, pp. 354–365. Springer, Cham (2020). https://doi.org/10.1007/978-3-030-66046-8_29
17. Smith-Roberts, A.: Facebook, fake news, and the first amendment. In: Denver Law Review Forum, vol. 95, p. 21 (2018)
18. Törnberg, P.: Echo chambers and viral misinformation: modeling fake news as complex contagion. PLoS ONE 13(9), e0203958 (2018)
19. Vosoughi, S., Roy, D., Aral, S.: The spread of true and false news online. Science 359(6380), 1146–1151 (2018)
20. Weisbuch, G.: Bounded confidence and social networks. Eur. Phys. J. B 38(2), 339–343 (2004). https://doi.org/10.1140/epjb/e2004-00126-9
21. Yang, K.C., Pierri, F., Hui, P.M., Axelrod, D., Torres-Lugo, C., Bryden, J., Menczer, F.: The covid-19 infodemic: Twitter versus facebook. Big Data Soc. 8(1), 20539517211013860 (2021)
22. Zeng, R., Zhu, D.: A model and simulation of the emotional contagion of netizens in the process of rumor refutation. Sci. Rep. 9(1), 1–15 (2019)

Predicting Network Threat Events Using HMM Ensembles

Akshay Peshave[✉], Ashwinkumar Ganesan, and Tim Oates

University of Maryland, Baltimore County, Baltimore, MD 21250, USA
{peshave1,gashwin1,oates}@umbc.edu

Abstract. Network traffic analysis, with the objective of identifying and preempting malicious campaigns, is an active area of research. An effective model that predicts future malicious network events based on observed malicious event sequences can aid with preemptive action that includes intervention by a security analyst. Predicting threat events that are part of a cybersecurity threat campaign that spans a long duration of time remains a challenge as the time lag between various steps in a campaign is unbounded. In this paper, we describe an approach to create an ensemble of Hidden Markov Models trained on sequences of malicious network events. The ensemble is used to predict the next expected malicious event given an already observed malicious traffic sequence at any network host. Ensembles of different sizes in combination with two prediction strategies are evaluated using prediction accuracy relative to two baselines predictors.

Keywords: Network threat prediction · Malicious traffic sequence analysis · Hidden Markov Model ensemble

1 Introduction

Network traffic analysis with the objective of identifying malicious campaigns is an active area of research. Network threats escalate as the severity of malicious or adverse events increases based on threat or severity levels defined by network monitoring tools. The ability to preempt network threat escalations and proactively address the situation is a current need. Several network monitoring tools [9,10] are available for monitoring network traffic at different granularities. These sensors utilize large and diverse rule sets to identify malicious network events, and in some cases long, persistent patterns of malicious network traffic. As organization networks have grown in size and complexity, the available attack surfaces (i.e. potential vulnerabilities in network security setups and available avenues to compromise a network) have increased. This coupled with sophisticated and persistent network threat campaigns has led to increasingly complex network traffic monitoring that generates enormous amounts of data.

This research was conducted in the UMBC Accelerated Cognitive Computing Lab (ACCL), supported in part by a gift from IBM.
Ashwinkumar Ganesan—Research completed prior to joining Amazon.

© Springer Nature Switzerland AG 2022
B. Li et al. (Eds.): ADMA 2021, LNAI 13087, pp. 229–240, 2022.
https://doi.org/10.1007/978-3-030-95405-5_17

Analyzing such large amounts of raw information to generate actionable insights has become increasingly difficult for human analysts. Human-in-the-loop paradigms for such analyses that are facilitated by machine learning-based systems have been evolving over time. These machine learning based systems employ sophisticated pattern analysis and anomaly detection methods to provide actionable insights to human analysts.

We propose an approach to train an ensemble of Hidden Markov Models (HMMs) to predict future malicious network events based on observed malicious event sequences. We evaluate two prediction strategies using the trained HMM ensemble and compare their prediction accuracy to two baseline predictors, namely the uniform random predictor and the most frequent event predictor.

The rest of the paper is organized as follows: Sect. 2 discusses the background and related research work. Section 3 describes the proposed HMM ensemble, its training and the prediction strategies employed by the ensemble. Section 4 describes the data set used to evaluate our method followed by Sect. 5 that discusses the performance of our approach relative to the baselines. Section 6 concludes this work.

2   Background and Related Work

Machine learning applications in cybersecurity event analysis for intrusion pattern characterization and malicious traffic prediction is an active area of research [3,7]. HMMs have been shown to be effective for cybersecurity sequence analysis tasks. HMMs have been utilized in a competitive ensemble setting for detecting specific intrusion methods such as SQL-injection [2]. Pre-configured HMMs used for intrusion detection [11] are highly sensitive to the selected feature set.

An anomaly detection approach for detecting cyber-attacks [13] trains a Markov chain model using past observed data in normal operating conditions at a host or on the network as a whole. The model assesses the generation probability of data sequences in live conditions to detect anomalies when the generation probability is lower than expected. This model is sensitive to noise in the training data. Further, novel benign traffic patterns in live conditions may be detected as anomalies.

A stochastic prediction model that learns absorbing Markov chains from simulated attack graphs [1] is another approach for network threat prediction. It is based on a cyber-situational awareness model that describes four levels of increasing awareness in a cybersecurity ecosystem - perception, comprehension, mitigation and forecasting. Forecasting requires effective perception and comprehension of network traffic to identify malicious sequences that need mitigation.

Intrusion Detection Systems (IDS) and network sensor alerts are typically fine-grained and only a very small subset of alerts may constitute absorbing states in the context of a complete attack campaign. Further, threat escalation prediction implies the ability to preempt escalation from sequences of varied lengths available in the training (or observed) traffic data. These sequences may or may not contain the predefined absorbing states required by the absorbing Markov chains described in [1].

Our proposed approach trains an HMM ensemble using observed malicious event sequences of varied lengths without explicitly specifying absorbing states. Further, benign network traffic is not utilized. This ensures that our method is not sensitive to evolving patterns of benign traffic and relies solely on malicious events described in, and consequently detected by, IDS and network monitoring tools.

3   Ensemble of Hidden Markov Models

The goal of this work is to build a model to predict the next malicious network event given a sequence of observed malicious network events. The set of malicious events are predefined events in the network monitoring tools deployed on the network (e.g. [10]) that are considered as sensors. The model is trained using malicious event sequences observed at each network host as detected by the network sensors. The working assumption is that a network monitoring tool will assign a single class or category to each malicious network traffic event it detects, i.e. the tool does not provide a probabilistic set of malicious event classes or categories.

Section 3.1 discusses preliminaries about ergodic Hidden Markov Models and describes the structure of HMMs used for our proposed method along with related nuances. Section 3.2 describes the clustering of malicious event sequences using HMM clustering. Lastly, Sect. 3.3 describes the creation of the HMM ensemble using clustered sequences and two malicious network event prediction strategies using the ensemble that will be evaluated in this work.

3.1   Hidden Markov Model Structure

HMM Preliminaries: HMMs learn patterns from a set of observed sequences and model them as a set of latent/hidden states, inducing probabilities of transitioning between the states and probability distributions over possible emission symbols at each state. An HMM trained on a set of sequences models the state transitions and per-state emission probability distributions that are most likely to generate those sequences. An HMM can be formalized using the following properties:

N = number of states

T = number of emission symbols

s_i = hidden state, $1 \leq i \leq N$

y_j = emission symbol, $1 \leq j \leq T$

φ = NxN matrix, where $\varphi_{i,j}$ is the transition probability $P(s_j|s_i)$

θ = NxT matrix, where $\theta_{n,t}$ is the emission probability $P(y_t|s_n)$

Figure 1 shows the general structure of an ergodic HMM using the symbols described above. An ergodic HMM is one in which every hidden state can transition to all the HMM hidden states including itself.

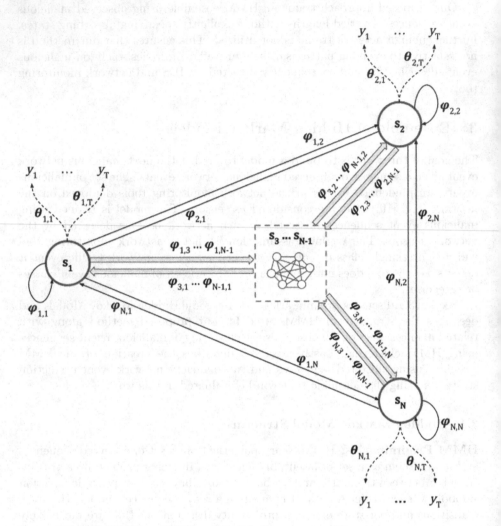

Fig. 1. Ergodic Hidden Markov Model Structure. All states can transition to any of the other states including itself. Additionally, each hidden state may emit all of the emission symbols.

HMM Structure for the Proposed Method: The threat pyramid for advanced persistent network threats [4] consists of 7 categories of malicious network traffic or events. These 7 categories can be further abstracted into 3 threat levels: reconnaissance, infiltration and exfiltration. Reconnaissance activities encompass attempt to understand the network structure and identify potential network vulnerabilities. Infiltration network activities focus on exploiting discovered vulnerabilities to gain access to network hosts and/or organization data. Exfiltration refers to network activities aimed at exfiltrating accessed data from the organisation's network and is possible once the attacker successfully infiltrates the network.

The proposed method uses ergodic Hidden Markov Models with $N = 3$, in which each state may emit any of the emission symbols that correspond to the dictionary of malicious events provided by the network sensors. The choice of $N = 3$ is based on the 3 abstract network threat levels of reconnaissance, infiltration and exfiltration discussed above.

HMMs trained on malicious event sequences that contain events belonging to all three threat levels will induce a model that generates macro-patterns of malicious event sequences that result in ex-filtration activities. On the other hand, HMMs trained on sequences that do not contain events belonging to all three threat levels will induce a model that generates micro-patterns of malicious event sequences belonging to ≤ 2 threat levels.

Discount Smoothing Applied to HMMs. It is expected that every malicious event sequence will not contain all the emission symbols from the event dictionary. Further, some emission symbols may occur with higher frequency than others in a sequence. This is due to two reasons:

1. Most network intrusion campaigns may go through prolonged periods of reconnaissance before they find exploitable vulnerabilities that allow them to infiltrate the network and exfiltrate data [1]. Consequently, frequencies of observed malicious events are unbalanced and often heavily skewed towards reconnaissance events.
2. Sequences that go through one or two threat levels may have a skew in frequencies of events belonging to each threat level as well as a skew in frequencies of events belonging to the same threat level.

Thus, a large portion of emission symbols may have zero emission probabilities at one or more states in an HMM. Smoothing of the emission probabilities for each hidden state in the HMM helps eliminate the zero emission probabilities of some state emission symbols by assigning tiny emission probabilities to them. We use a variation of discount smoothing that adds a tiny probability mass to near-zero ($\leq 10^{-4}$) emission probabilities of a state. This probability mass is obtained by discounting it from the other emission probabilities at that state.

Let, $A = \{a \in [1, T]\}$ be indices of emission symbols at state s_i such that $\forall a \in A, \theta_{i,a} \leq 10^{-4}$. Let, $B = \{b \in [1, T]\}$ be indices of emission symbols at state s_i such that $\forall b \in B, \theta_{i,b} > 10^{-4}$. The discount d_i at state s_i is computed as follows:

$$d_i = \sum^{b \in B} 10^{-3} * \theta_{i,b} \tag{1}$$

This discount is evenly distributed among the emission probabilities of emission symbols with indices in A while subtracting the probability mass contributed by each emission symbol in B from their respective emission probabilities. The resultant emission probabilities at state s_i after discount smoothing are as follows:

$$\forall a \in A, \quad \theta_{i,a} = \theta_{i,a} + \frac{d_i}{|A|} \tag{2}$$

$$\forall b \in B, \quad \theta_{i,b} = \theta_{i,b} - 10^{-3} * \theta_{i,b} \tag{3}$$

3.2   Event Sequence Clustering

Clustering of sequences is a hard problem. Traditional methods to cluster categorical data such as k-modes [5,6] can be employed by treating event sequences as event itemsets. But, this approach disregards temporal ordering of the events in the sequence. In the case of malicious network event sequences, both the events occurring in the sequence as well as their order of occurrence is important. We need a clustering method which takes both these into account.

An approach to cluster sequences trains one HMM per sequence [12]. This work shows that clustering per-sequence HMMs using pairwise KL-divergence is equivalent to clustering of the individual sequences that the HMMs are trained on. [12] explain that this clustering approach is computationally expensive and clustering over a representative sample of sequences is a recommended practice.

In our method, per-sequence HMMs are clustered using symmetric KL–divergence over sub-sequence generation probabilities of the HMMs as the distance metric for hierarchical, agglomerative clustering [8]. The linkages between clusters are evaluated in order to merge clusters hierarchically. The flattened clusters of HMMs are obtained by applying a threshold on the cophenetic distances between training sub-sequences. We utilize this sub-sequence clustering approach in the first stage of our method.

3.3   Ensemble Creation and Prediction Methods

The ensemble of HMMs consists of a set of one cluster-HMM per sub-sequence cluster obtained above. These HMMs have the same structure as described in Sect. 3.1. The intuition is that cluster-HMMs will enable good prediction performance and generalization over a wide range of sub-sequence variations using a small sized ensemble. The prediction from each cluster-HMM is the most probable emission from the most probable next state in the HMM having observed the input sequence of malicious events. The Viterbi process is used to reach the current state in the HMM by observing the input sequence. The most probable next malicious event can be obtained from the emission probability distribution of the current state.

Each cluster-HMM can provide a malicious event prediction given an observed event sequence. Two methodologies are assessed in this work for the HMM ensemble to collectively predict the next malicious event:

1. **Majority Vote Prediction**: This strategy generates next-step emissions as predictions from all HMMs in the ensemble given an input subsequence. Each prediction is given a uniform weight of 1. The final prediction by the ensemble is the prediction with the most cumulative weight i.e. the most number of votes.
2. **Maximum Generation Likelihood Prediction**: This prediction strategy chooses the HMM from the ensemble that has the maximum generation likelihood for the input subsequence and uses this HMMs next-step emission prediction as the final prediction by the ensemble.

4 Data Set

The dataset used for the evaluation of our approach is Snort logs generated for the U.S. National CyberWatch Mid-Atlantic Collegiate Cyber Defense Competition (MACCDC)[1] 2012 capture files. These logs were obtained from the SecRepo[2] website. The MACCDC competition has two competing teams and consists of two rounds. Each competing team gets an opportunity to be the attacking team while the other team defends the network setup for the competition. In the first round, team A attacks the network while team B defends it. In the second round, team B attacks the network while team A defends it. Each team employs their own campaigns to attack the network and circumvent preemptive and protective strategies implemented by the defending team.

The network staged for the competition consists of 4,757 hosts of which 4,739 face some incoming malicious network traffic events during the entire competition, as evidenced from the dataset. The malicious traffic generates 2,677,375 snort alerts distributed over 25 snort classes over the entire course of the competition as shown in Table 1. The 4,739 malicious network event trajectories, one per sink host on the network, are used to generate sub-sequences of length 10 using a sliding event index window. This results in 658,343 sub-sequences of which 51,606 are unique. The evaluation in Sect. 5 samples these sub-sequences to train and test the HMM ensemble for malicious event prediction using our approach.

5 Evaluation

The evaluation of the HMM ensemble prediction performance needs us to sample the 51,606 unique sub-sequences generated as described in Sect. 4. We train the HMM ensemble using three random samples of sizes 100, 1,000 and 5,000. The cophenetic distance threshold for agglomerative clustering is specified as a percentile of all the pairwise cophenetic distances between the HMMs trained on the sub-sequence samples. As the sample size grows the separation of HMMs into multiple clusters is achieved at a lower percentile. This can be seen in Table 2.

---

[1] http://www.maccdc.org.
[2] http://www.secrepo.com.

Table 1. Dataset Description. The table shows the distribution of observed malicious activity alerts over different Snort alert classes. As seen in the table, the dataset is skewed wherein Snort classes such as *"Attempt to Login By a Default Username and Password"* and *"Detection of a Network Scan"* are observed less than 100 times whereas *"Web Application Attack"* is observed 1, 348, 695 times.

ID	SNORT alert class	Total	Team A	Team B
1	A Network Trojan was Detected	3272	2471	801
2	A Suspicious Filename was Detected	7	7	0
3	A Suspicious String was Detected	192	182	10
4	Access to a Potentially Vulnerable Web Application	31376	25895	5481
5	Attempt to Login By a Default Username and Password	55	55	0
6	Attempted Administrator Privilege Gain	10014	9777	237
7	Attempted Denial of Service	469	218	251
8	Attempted Information Leak	421782	244177	177605
9	Attempted User Privilege Gain	2835	2675	160
10	Decode of an RPC Query	674	396	278
11	Detection of a Denial of Service Attack	264	250	14
12	Detection of a Network Scan	34	24	10
13	Detection of a Non-Standard Protocol or Event	207	199	8
14	Executable Code was Detected	9301	5139	4162
15	Generic Protocol Command Decode	27259	25566	1693
16	Information Leak	8672	4674	3998
17	Misc activity	588532	225353	363179
18	Misc Attack	19649	11269	8380
19	Potential Corporate Privacy Violation	148860	141401	7459
20	Potentially Bad Traffic	36995	23752	13243
21	Successful Administrator Privilege Gain	38	11	27
22	Successful User Privilege Gain	7003	35	6968
23	Unknown Traffic	39	16	23
24	Unsuccessful User Privilege Gain	11151	11121	30
25	Web Application Attack	1348695	1337473	11222
Total		2677375	2072136	605239

Further, the number of clusters formed does not vary as we continue decreasing the cophenetic distance threshold after the initial breakup into multiple clusters is achieved. This is indicative of optimal discrimination achieved between the generative process of the sub-sequence HMMs at the cophenetic distance threshold at which the first split into multiple clusters occurs.

Table 2. Size of HMM Ensembles defined by Cophenetic Distance Linkages for differing thresholds and training sample size.

Linkage	Number of clusters per		
Threshold %ile	Training sample size		
	100	1,000	5,000
0.010	7	528	2,559
0.015	7	528	2,559
0.020	7	528	1
0.025	7	528	1
0.050	7	528	1
0.075	7	528	1
0.080	7	528	1
0.090	7	528	1
0.100	7	528	1
0.200	7	1	1
0.300	7	1	1
0.400	7	1	1
0.500	7	1	1
1.000	7	1	1
2.000	1	1	1
3.000	1	1	1
4.000	1	1	1
5.000	1	1	1

We use two baselines for comparison of prediction accuracy by the HMM ensemble. The first baseline is the uniform random predictor accuracy. This is the accuracy of a predictor that randomly predicts one of the 25 snort alert class with uniform probability. The random predictor accuracy is $\frac{1}{25}$ or 4%. The second baseline is the most frequent class predictor accuracy. This is the accuracy of a predictor that always predicts the most frequently observed snort alert class in the dataset. This most frequent class predictor accuracy is 21.98%.

Table 3. Accuracy of prediction strategies for 25% random sample of MACCDC 2012 subsequences as test set.

Training sample	Prediction strategy	
	Majority vote	Generation likelihood
100	58.63	7.62
1,000	55.25	51.12
5,000	55.22	51.20

The evaluation is done using two test sets and prediction accuracy is measured for both the prediction strategies described in Sect. 3. The first test set is a random sample of 25% of the unique sub-sequences from the dataset. The second test set is the complete set of unique sub-sequences from the dataset inclusive of the training sample. Inclusion of the training random sample does not bias the test set accuracy in the latter case since the training set is at most 5,000 sub-sequences which is less than 10% of the complete dataset of unique sub-sequences.

The prediction accuracy of both prediction strategies of the HMM ensemble for the 25% random sample test set is shown in Table 3. Prediction accuracy for the majority vote prediction strategy for all three samples is similar and outperforms both the baseline predictors. The maximum generation likelihood prediction strategy under-performs both the baseline predictors when trained using 100 samples while outperforming both the baselines when trained using 1,000 and 5,000 samples.

Table 4. Accuracy of prediction strategies for All MACCDC 2012 subsequences as test set.

Training sample	Prediction strategy	
	Majority vote	Generation likelihood
100	47.42%	2.10%
1000	54.82%	14.91%
5000	54.78%	14.95%

The prediction accuracy of both prediction strategies of the HMM ensemble for the complete dataset as the test set is shown in Table 4. Prediction accuracy for the majority vote prediction strategy when trained using 1,000 and 5,000 samples is similar while it's slightly lower when trained using 100 samples. This strategy outperforms the two baselines for all three training sample sizes. Training using the larger sample sizes generalizes to the complete dataset better than training using the smaller sample size.

Prediction accuracy for the maximum generation likelihood prediction strategy using the complete dataset as the test set is lower than its accuracy for the 25% random sample test set. This strategy under-performs the most frequent class predictor contrary to its performance for the 25% random sample test set. This is suggestive of the lack of generalization of the maximum generation likelihood prediction strategy. This is not the case with the majority vote prediction strategy when trained using 1,000 and 5,000 random samples. The prediction accuracy for both these random sample sizes for this strategy does not vary much between the two test sets. The under-performance and lack of generalization of the maximum generation likelihood prediction strategy also indicate that it is uncommon to find an HMM in the ensemble that can predict the next malicious network event by itself. Hence, an ensemble of HMMs serves our prediction task better.

6   Conclusion

An ensemble of Hidden Markov Models trained using clustered malicious network event sequences performs significantly better than the two baseline predictors - uniform probability random predictor and most frequent label predictor. The majority vote ensemble prediction strategy outperforms the maximum generation likelihood prediction strategy for all three training sample sizes used to train the HMM ensemble. The majority vote HMM ensemble prediction strategy generalizes better than the latter for prediction over the entire dataset using training sample sets that are approximately 2% and 10% of the dataset.

References

1. Abraham, S., Nair, S.: Cyber security analytics: a stochastic model for security quantification using absorbing Markov chains. J. Commun. **9**, 899–907 (2014)
2. Ariu, D., Tronci, R., Giacinto, G.: Hmmpayl: an intrusion detection system based on hidden markov models. Comput. Secur. **30**(4), 221–241 (2011). https://doi.org/10.1016/j.cose.2010.12.004. http://www.sciencedirect.com/science/article/pii/S0167404811000022
3. Buczak, A.L., Guven, E.: A survey of data mining and machine learning methods for cyber security intrusion detection. IEEE Commun. Surv. Tutorials **18**(2), 1153–1176 (Secondquarter 2016). https://doi.org/10.1109/COMST.2015.2494502
4. Giura, P., Wang, W.: A context-based detection framework for advanced persistent threats. In: 2012 International Conference on Cyber Security, pp. 69–74 (2012). https://doi.org/10.1109/CyberSecurity.2012.16
5. Huang, Z.: Clustering large data sets with mixed numeric and categorical values. In: The First Pacific-Asia Conference on Knowledge Discovery and Data Mining, pp. 21–34 (1997)
6. Huang, Z.: Extensions to the k-means algorithm for clustering large data sets with categorical values. In: Data Mining and Knowledge Discovery, vol. 2(3), pp. 283–304 (1998)
7. Husák, M., Komárková, J., Bou-Harb, E., Čeleda, P.: Survey of attack projection, prediction, and forecasting in cyber security. IEEE Commun. Surv. Tutorials **21**(1), 640–660 (2019). https://doi.org/10.1109/COMST.2018.2871866
8. Müllner, D.: Modern hierarchical, agglomerative clustering algorithms. arXiv e-prints arXiv:1109.2378, September 2011
9. Paxson, V.: Bro: a system for detecting network intruders in real-time. In: Proceedings of the 7th Conference on USENIX Security Symposium - Volume 7, SSYM'98, p. 3. USENIX Association, USA (1998)
10. Roesch, M.: Snort - lightweight intrusion detection for networks. In: Proceedings of the 13th USENIX Conference on System Administration, LISA 1999, pp. 229–238. USENIX Association, USA (1999)
11. S. Joshi, S., Phoha, V.: Investigating hidden Markov models capabilities in anomaly detection. In: Proceedings of the Annual Southeast Conference, vol. 1, pp. 98–103, January 2005

12. Tamang, S., Parsons, S.: Using semi-parametric clustering applied to electronic health record time series data. In: Proceedings of the 2011 Workshop on Data Mining for Medicine and Healthcare, DMMH 2011, pp. 72–75. ACM, New York (2011). https://doi.org/10.1145/2023582.2023596, https://doi.org/10.1145/2023582.2023596
13. Ye, N., Zhang, Y., Borror, C.M.: Robustness of the Markov-chain model for cyber-attack detection. IEEE Trans. Reliab. **53**(1), 116–123 (2004). https://doi.org/10.1109/TR.2004.823851

On-device Application

Group Trip Planning Queries on Road Networks Using Geo-Tagged Textual Information

Mayank Singhal and Suman Banerjee[✉]

Department of Computer Science and Engineering, Indian Institute of Technology
Jammu, Jammu and Kashmir 181221, India
2018ucs0064@iitjammu.ac.in, suman.banerjee@iitjammu.ac.in

Abstract. Due to the advancement of wireless internet and
location-enabled mobile devices, *Location Based Services (LBS)* have
become very popular. The primary goal of such services is based on
the searched keywords, it can recommend hotels, restaurants, cafeterias,
parks, etc. These kinds of services are quite useful for trip planning. In
this paper, we study the group trip planning query problem on road networks, where the vertices represent point of interests (hotels, restaurants,
cafeterias, parks, movie theater, etc., henceforth POI) and edges represent the road segment joining the POIs, and also each POI is marked
with some textual information (e.g., restaurant reviews in the form of
hashtags). A group of friends with different sources and destination locations within the city wants to plan a trip for visiting a number POIs of
different types in between. The job of the LBS Provider is to recommend one POI from each category of POIs as queried by the group of
friends such that the aggregated travel distance is minimized. For this
problem, we propose three solution approaches with detailed analysis.
Proposed methodologies have been implemented with three real-world
road network datasets and several experiments have been conducted to
show their effectiveness and efficiency. In particular, the $\mathcal{R}$-tree approach
can process a road network with million edges within a feasible computational time.

Keywords: Group Nearest Neighbor Queries (GNN) · $\mathcal{R}$-Tree · Point
of Interest (POI)

1 Introduction

The past two decades have witnessed a significant development in wireless internet and location enables hand holding devices. Due to this, capturing location
information of moving objects become very easy, and hence, lots of trajectory

The work of Dr. Suman Banerjee is supported by the Start Up Grant provided by
the Indian Institute of Technology Jammu, India. Both the authors have contributed
equally in this study and they are joint first authors.

© Springer Nature Switzerland AG 2022
B. Li et al. (Eds.): ADMA 2021, LNAI 13087, pp. 243–257, 2022.
https://doi.org/10.1007/978-3-030-95405-5_18

data is publicly available [21,24]. These kinds of data are heavily used for route recommendation [8], POI recommendation [11], location prediction [23], mobility prediction [20], providing location-based services [7], and so on. A *Location-Based Service Provider (LBSP)* is an online service whose job is to recommend POIs based on the searched keywords of the users. It is expected that the annual market for LBSs is expected to reach USD 77.84 Billion by the end of 2021[1]. Now-a-days, several online giants including Google and Alibaba are in the business of providing location-based service. These kinds of services are quite useful for planning travel trips for getting proper recommendations for hotels, restaurants, etc.

In recent times, trip planning quires have been studied extensively by the researchers of the data management community [2,13,14] (and references therein). This problem is posed as follows: Given a set of POIs, where each one of them belongs to some category, a start and destination location, the trip planning query returns a trip starting at the start location going through one POI of each category and ends at the destination point such that some specific objective id fulfilled (e.g., minimization of travel time or travel cost, etc.). As the problem is quite practical, this is well studied and a number of solution methodologies are available [4,18,22]. Also, recently the notion of trip planning query problem has been extended even for a group and named it as Group Trip Planning Query Problem [1,10,15,19]. Here, instead of one person, there is a group of people and the goal of the LBSP is to recommend one POI for each category such that the aggregated distance is minimized.

To the best of our knowledge most of the studies on group trip planning queries, it is assumed that the source, destination location, and also location of the POIs are marked with their corresponding X and Y coordinates and the people are moving in the Euclidean Plane. However, in the real world, it is quite natural that people will be moving on the road networks. Therefore, in this paper, we study the Group Trip Planning Query Problem on Road Networks, and in particular, we make the following contributions in this paper.

- We study the problem of Group Trip Planning Queries on road networks where the objective is to minimize the aggregated travel distance.
- We propose two different solution methodologies for these problems with detailed mathematical analysis and examples.
- Proposed methodologies have been implemented with three real-world trajectory data sets and a number of experiments are conducted to show the efficiency of the proposed methodologies.

The rest of the paper is organized as follows: Sect. 2 describes some preliminary concepts and defines our problem formally. The proposed solution methodologies have been described in Sect. 3. Section 4 contains the detailed experimental evaluations of the proposed methodologies. Finally, Sect. 5 concludes our study and gives future research directions.

---

[1] https://www.marketsandmarkets.com/Market-Reports/nanophotonics-advanced-technologies-and-global-market-125.html.

2   Background and Problem Definition

In this section, we describe the preliminary concepts required in this study and subsequently define our problem formally. Initially, we start by defining Road Network.

Definition 1 (Road Network). *We define the road network of a city as a weighted graph as a simple, undirected, weighted graph $G(V, E, W)$, where*

- *the vertex set $V(G) = \{v_1, v_2, \ldots, v_n\}$ is the set of all Point of Interests (POIs) of the city,*
- *the edge set $E(G) = \{e_1, e_2, \ldots, e_m\} \subseteq V(G) \times V(G)$ is the road segments joining the POIs,*
- *W is the edge weight function that assigns the each edge to its corresponding distance; i.e.; $W : E(G) \longrightarrow \mathbb{R}^+$.*

As in this study, we consider that the vertices represent the POIs, hence, we use the terms POI and vertex interchangeably. The number of vertices and edges of G are denoted by n and m, respectively. For a particular edge $e = (uv) \in E(G)$, $W(e)$ denotes the distance from the POI u to v. Next, we state the path in a road network in Definition 2.

Definition 2 (Path in a Road Network). *A path $\mathcal{P}$ in a road network is defined as a sequence of vertices $< v_1, v_2, \ldots, v_p >$ such that for every $1 \leq r < p$, (v_r, v_{r+1}) is an edge in the road network. For a path $\mathcal{P}$, let $E(\mathcal{P})$ denotes the set of edges that constitute the path. The weight of a path is defined as the sum of the weights of the edges that constitute the path. Hence, $W(\mathcal{P}) = \sum\limits_{e \in E(\mathcal{P})} W(e)$.*

It is quite natural that after visiting a hotel, restaurant, cafeteria etc. we provide feedback in terms of hashtags in different online platforms like `google reviews`, `zonkafeedback.com`, `ezeeabsolute.com`, and many more. We formally call these information as geo tagged textual information which is stated in Definition 3.

Definition 3 (Geo Tagged Textual Information). *Let $\mathcal{X}$ denotes the set of all the hashtags associated with the POIs considered in the road network. In the context of road network, the geo tagged textual information is defined as a mapping Φ from the set of vertices (i.e., POIs) to the all possible subsets of the hashtags, i.e., $\Phi : V(G) \longrightarrow 2^{\mathcal{X}}$.*

For any vertex $v \in V(G)$, let $\Phi(v)$ denote the set of hashtags associated with the POI v. Naturally, $\mathcal{X} = \bigcup\limits_{v \in V(G)} \Phi(v)$. We assume that the POIs are classified into d many categories $\mathcal{C} = \{\mathcal{C}_1, \mathcal{C}_2, \ldots, \mathcal{C}_k\}$ (e.g., $\mathcal{C}_1 \equiv$ Cafteria, $\mathcal{C}_2 \equiv$ Hotel, etc). For any positive integer x, $[x]$ denote the set $\{1, 2, \ldots, x\}$. Now, assume that a group of friends $\mathcal{U} = \{u_1, u_2, \ldots, u_b\}$ wants to plan a trip. For any $i \in [b]$ starting and destination of the user u_i is denoted as u_i^s and u_i^d, respectively. Now, the group of friends makes a query to a LBS provider $\mathcal{L}$ with c distinct hashtags $\{h_1, h_2, \ldots, h_k\}$. Suppose in the considered road network, there are n_1 many POIs corresponding to the hashtag h_1, n_2 many POIs corresponding to the hashtag h_2 and so on. Now, the job of the LBS Provider is to recommend one POI out of many in each category such that the aggregated distance traveled by the group is minimized. Now the aggregated distance is stated in Definition 4 and the query model of the LBS is shown in the subsequent text box.

Definition 4 (Aggregated Distance). *Given a road network $G(V, E, W)$, a group of friends $\mathcal{U} = \{u_1, u_2, \ldots, u_b\}$ with their source and destination locations $\{u_1^s, u_2^s, \ldots, u_b^s\}$ and $\{u_1^d, u_2^d, \ldots, u_b^d\}$, respectively, and k many distinct intermediate POIs $v_1, v_2, \ldots, v_k$, the aggregated distance traveled by all the friends is denoted by $\mathcal{D}_\mathcal{U}$ and defined as*

$$\mathcal{D}_\mathcal{U} = \sum_{i \in [b]} dist(u_i^s, v_1) + b \sum_{i \in [k-1]} dist(v_i, v_{i+1}) + \sum_{i \in [b]} dist(v_k, u_i^d) \qquad (1)$$

Here, $dist(u, v)$ denotes the shortest path distance from u to v.

QUERY AND RESPONSE OF THE LBS PROVIDER

Information of LBS Provider: Set of b friends $\mathcal{U} = \{u_1, u_2, \ldots, u_b\}$; Their source and destination locations $\{u_1^s, u_2^s, \ldots, u_b^s\}$ and $\{u_1^d, u_2^d, \ldots, u_b^d\}$, respectively; Road Network $G(V, E, W)$, The hashtag set $\mathcal{X}$ and $\Phi(v)$ for all $v \in V(G)$.

Query: The query format to the LBS Provider is as follows:
$$Q = < \{u_1^s, u_2^s, \ldots, u_b^s\}; h_1, h_2, \ldots, h_k; \{u_1^d, u_2^d, \ldots, u_b^d\} >$$

Response: The response of LBS Provider will be as follows:

$$< v_1^*, v_2^*, \ldots, v_k^* >$$

where $h_1 \in \Phi(v_1^*)$, $h_2 \in \Phi(v_2^*)$, so on and also the total aggregated distance is minimized.

From the searched hashtags, we can easily classify the POIs into different categories. Let, for any $i \in [k]$ V_{h_i} denotes the set of POIs corresponding to the hashtag h_i. It is important to observe that the aggregated distance function mentioned in Eq. 1 is the sum of three different components: (i) Total distance traveled by the friends starting from their initial location to the first POI, (ii) Total distance traveled by the friends from the first POI to the last one through the intermediate POIs, and (iii) Total distance traveled by the friends from the last POI to their respective destinations. Now, it is easy to follow that among these three the second one is equal for all the friends. Now, we formally state the Problem of GROUP TRIP PLANNING QUERIES WITH AGGREGATED DISTANCE in Definition 5.

Definition 5 (Group Trip Planning Queries with Aggregated Distance). *Given a road network $G(V, E, W)$, where each POI is tagged with textual information (in the form of hashtags), a group of friends along with their respective source and destination address, and a set of categories of hashtags to a LBS Provider, its job is to recommend to one POI for each category such that the aggregated travel distance is minimized. Mathematically, this problems can be posed in Eq. 2.*

$$(v_1^*, v_2^*, \ldots, v_k^*) = \underset{(v_1, v_2, \ldots, v_k): v_1 \subseteq V_{h_1}, v_2 \subseteq V_{h_2}, \ldots, v_k \subseteq V_{h_k}}{argmin} \mathcal{D}_{\mathcal{U}} \qquad (2)$$

3 Proposed Solution Methodologies

In this section, we describe the proposed solution methodologies for our problem. Initially, we start with the Brute Force Approach with Precomputed Distance.

3.1 Brute Force Approach with Precomputed Distance

Let, $\mathcal{V_S}$ and $\mathcal{V_D}$ denote the set of initial and destination locations of the group members. Now, Fig. 1 shows a layered view of the network. The brute Force solution approach works as follows: For all $v_1 \in V_{\mathcal{C}_1}$, $v_2 \in V_{\mathcal{C}_2}$, ..., $v_k \in V_{\mathcal{C}_k}$ the LBSP computes all possible trips and finally recommends the POIs corresponding to the path that leads to the minimum aggregated distance. Due to both simplicity and page restriction, we are not able to provide the pseudo code.

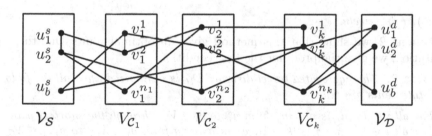

Fig. 1. Layered view of the road network

It is easy to observe that the running time of this algorithm depends on the number of times the shortest path is computed. It is easy to observe that the possible recommendations corresponding to the first category is n_1, second category is n_2, and so on. Therefore, the number of shortest path computations for the POIs recommendation $\mathcal{O}(\prod_{i \in [k]} n_i)$, and the shortest path computations for moving from starting locations to the first POI and from the last POI to their destinations is of $\mathcal{O}(b(n_1 + n_k))$. So, the total number of shortest path computations are $\mathcal{O}(\prod_{i \in [k]} n_i + b(n_1 + n_k))$. Now, for the worst case analysis we have to find out when the number of shortest path computations are maximum. This can be obtained by solving the following optimization problem: maximization of the function $f(n_1, n_2, \ldots, n_k) = \prod_{i \in [k]} n_i$ subject to the constraint $\sum_{i \in [k]} n_i = n$. The constraint here signifies that the sum of the POIs of all the categories can be maximum n. Lemma 1 tells the condition for the maximum value of the function [3].

Lemma 1. *Let, $f : \mathbb{R}^k \longrightarrow \mathbb{R}$ is a real valued function and $f(x_1, x_2, \ldots, x_k) = \prod_{i \in [k]} x_i$ and $\sum_{i \in [k]} x_i = n$. The maximum value of f attains at $x_1 = x_2 = \ldots = x_c = \frac{n}{k}$.*

It is easy to observe that in the worst case the number of shortest path computations will be of order $\mathcal{O}(n^k)$. Using Dijestra's All Pair Shortest Path Algorithm, we can compute an $n \times n$ matrix whose (i,j)-th entry stores the shortest path between the POI v_i and v_j and this requires $\mathcal{O}(n^3)$ time [17]. However, as the POIs of a city does not change frequently, we can compute the distance between every pair of POIs and store them in a matrix such that they can be used as and when required. In this study, we do not consider the cost of offline computation. Let, h^{max} denotes the maximum number of hashtags associated with any POI; i.e.; $h^{max} = \max_{v \in V(G)} |\Phi(v)|$. Now, it is easy to observe that classifying the POIs into different categories requires $\mathcal{O}(k \cdot n \cdot h^{max})$ time. The running time and space requirement of this approach is stated in Theorem 1.

Theorem 1. *The running time and space requirement of the Brute Force Approach with Precomputed Distance is of $\mathcal{O}(k \cdot n \cdot h^{max} + \prod_{i \in [k]} n_i + b(n_1 + n_k))$ and $\mathcal{O}(n^2)$, respectively.*

In Lemma 2, we show that this method gives an optimal route. Due to page limitation, we give the proof for the first condition.

Lemma 2. *The aggregated travel distance $\mathcal{D}_{\mathcal{U}}$ is minimized when all the following statements are true:*

1. *For all $i \in [b]$, u_i is moving from u_i^s to $v_1 \in V_{C_1}$ through the shortest path.*
2. *For all $i \in [b]$ and $j \in [k-1]$, u_i is moving from $v_j \in V_{C_j}$ to $v_{j+1} \in V_{C_{j+1}}$ through the shortest path.*
3. *For all $i \in [b]$, u_i is moving from $v_k \in V_{C_k}$ to u_i^d through the shortest path.*

Proof. **Proof of Statement 1:** Assume that in the optimal solution there exist a group member $p \in [b]$ such that u_p is moving from u_p^s to $v_1 \in V_{C_1}$ not through the shortest path. We denote the set of shortest paths form u_p^s to $v_1 \in V_{C_1}$ as $\mathcal{SP}(u_p^s, v_1)$. As per our assumption, u_p has not used any path from $\mathcal{SP}(u_p^s, v_1)$. If it is true then the claim that $\mathcal{D}_{\mathcal{U}}$ is minimum is false. The reason is that we can replace the current non-shortest path with any shortest path from $\mathcal{SP}(u_p^s, v_1)$ and this certainly leads to lesser value of $\mathcal{D}_{\mathcal{U}}$. This means that our initial assumption "there exist a group member $p \in [b]$ such that u_p is moving from u_p^s to $v_1 \in V_{C_1}$ not through the shortest path" is false. This implies the Statement 1 is correct. In the similar way, we can prove the other two statements.

3.2   Group Nearest Neighbor (GNN) to Compute GTP Queries

It is important to observe that though the previous approach is easy to understand, simple to implement, and it produces the optimal route still due to its huge computational burden so that we can not use it for solving the GTPQ Problem on large scale road networks. One possible way to reduce the computational burden is as follows. For moving from one category of POI to the next category, instead of exploring all possible options we can explore which are closer to the location of previous POI. This concept is formalized as the *Group Nearest Neighbor Queries*, which is stated in Definition 6 in the context of a road network [16].

Definition 6 (Group Nearest Neighbor Queries). *Given a road network* $G(V, E, W)$, *and a set of* k *query objects placed at* $\mathcal{Q} = \{q_1, q_2, \ldots, q_k\} \subset V(G)$ *vertices, the Group Nearest Neighbor Query Problem asks to return one of the remaining vertices (i.e., from* $V(G) \setminus \mathcal{Q}$) *such that the aggregated distance from all the query vertices to the solution vertex is minimized.*

Now, we describe the working principle of our proposed methodology. First, for every POI $v \in V(G)$, given the associated hashtags (i.e., $\Phi(v)$), we classify the POIs into categories $\mathcal{C} = \{\mathcal{C}_1, \mathcal{C}_2, \ldots, \mathcal{C}_k\}$. In this study, for any two POIs belongs to two different categories their hashtags are also different, i.e., for all v_i and v_j if $v_i \in \mathcal{C}_i$, $v_j \in \mathcal{C}_j$, and $\mathcal{C}_i \neq \mathcal{C}_j$ then $\Phi(v_i) \cap \Phi(v_j) = \emptyset$. After performing this step, at the conceptual level we can view the road network in a layered form as show in Fig. 1. Next, our job is to recommend the POI for the first category. Without loss of generality assume that $\{v_1, v_2, \ldots, v_s\}$ are the set of POIs belongs to the first category, and let $\{u_1^s, u_2^s, \ldots, u_b^s\}$ are the set of initial location of the group members. Now, for recommending the POI of the first category, the LBSP will make a GNN Query $\mathcal{Q} = < \{u_1^s, u_2^s, \ldots, u_b^s\}, \{v_1, v_2, \ldots, v_k\} >$ and it will return one of the s many POIs such that the aggregated distance so far is minimized. If LBS returns v_i as the solution of the GNN Query, mathematically, this can be written as Eq. 3.

$$v_i = \underset{v \in \{v_1, v_2, \ldots, v_k\}}{argmin} \sum_{i \in [b]} dist(u_i^s, v) \tag{3}$$

Now, for finding the POI of the 2nd category the LBSP will invoke a Nearest Neighbor Query $\mathcal{Q} = < v_i, V_{\mathcal{C}_2} >$, where $V_{\mathcal{C}_2}$ denotes the set of POIs of 2nd category. This will return a POI from the set $V_{\mathcal{C}_2}$ such that the distance from that vertex to v_i is minimized compared to any other vertex of $V_{\mathcal{C}_2}$. In general for recommending a POI for category $\mathcal{C}_j$ for any $2 \leq j \leq k - 1$, the LBSP will make a Nearest Neighbor Query $\mathcal{Q} = < v_{j-1}, V_{\mathcal{C}_j} >$, where v_{j-1} is the POI returned by the LBS for the $(j - 1)$-th category and $V_{\mathcal{C}_j}$ is the set of POIs of j-th Category. In this case, if the LBS returns POI v_j as a reply, then mathematically this can be expressed by Eq. 4.

$$v_j = \underset{v \in V_{\mathcal{C}_j}}{argmin} \, dist(v_{j-1}, v) \tag{4}$$

Now, only job left for the LBS to recommend a POI of k-th category. For this the LBSP make a GNN Query $Q =< \{u_1^d, u_2^d, \ldots, u_b^d\}, V_{C_k} >$, and it will return a POI from V_{C_k} such that the aggregated distance from this POI to their respective destination is minimized. If the reply of the LBSP in this case is v_q, then Eq. 5 holds.

$$v_q = \underset{v \in V_{C_k}}{argmin} \sum_{i \in [b]} dist(v, u_i^d) \tag{5}$$

The entire procedure is described in the form of pseudo code in Algorithm 1. Before analyzing the algorithm to understand its time and space requirement, we prove few important lemmas that will be helpful in this regard.

Algorithm 1: Algorithm to find GTP query response using GNN queries for $|\mathcal{H}| = c$

Input: Road Network $G(V, E, W, \Omega)$, $\Phi(v)$ for all $v \in V(G)$, Set of friends $\mathcal{U} = \{u_1, u_2, \ldots, u_b\}$, The query to LBS $\mathcal{L}$
$Q =< \{u_1^s, u_2^s, \ldots, u_b^s\}; \{h_1, h_2, \ldots, h_k\}; \{u_1^d, u_2^d, \ldots, u_b^d\} >$

Output: Recommendation of a POI of Each Type $(v_1^*, v_2^*, \ldots, v_k^*)$ such that $\mathcal{D}_\mathcal{U}$ is minimized

1 $\mathbb{D} \leftarrow$ All Pair Shortest Path Algorithm on Road Network $G(V, E, W)$
2 Classify the POIs based on the Categories
3 $v_1 \leftarrow FindGNN(\{u_1^s, u_2^s, \ldots, u_b^s\}, V_{C_1})$
4 **for** *All* $i \in \{2, 3, \ldots, k-1\}$ **do**
5 $\quad | \quad v_i \leftarrow FindNN(v_{i-1}, h_i)$
6 **end**
7 $P_c \leftarrow FindGNN(\{\{u_1^d, u_2^d, \ldots, u_b^d\}\}, h_c)$
8 $Sum\_1 \leftarrow 0$
9 **for** *All* $i \in \{1, 2, \ldots, b\}$ **do**
10 $\quad | \quad Sum\_1 \leftarrow Sum\_1 + \mathbb{D}[u_i^s][v_1]$
11 **end**
12 $Sum\_2 \leftarrow 0$
13 **for** *All* $i \in \{1, 2, \ldots, k-1\}$ **do**
14 $\quad | \quad Sum\_2 \leftarrow Sum\_2 + \mathbb{D}[v_i][v_{i+1}]$
15 **end**
16 $Sum\_3 \leftarrow 0$
17 **for** *All* $i \in \{1, 2, \ldots, b\}$ **do**
18 $\quad | \quad Sum\_3 \leftarrow Sum\_3 + \mathbb{D}[v_k][u_i^d]$
19 **end**
20 $Total\_Path\_Cost \leftarrow Sum\_1 + b \times Sum\_2 + Sum\_3$
21 Return the path and its cost

Lemma 3. *Algorithm 1 will invoke 2 GNN Queries and $(k-2)$ many NN Queries, where c is the number of categories.*

Proof. From the description of Algorithm 1 it is clear that the GNN Query is invoked for recommending the first and k-th category POI. From 2nd on-wards till $(k-1)$-th as all the group members are on a single POI, and hence NN Query is sufficient and this number is $(k-2)$.

Lemma 4. *The number of shortest path computations by Algorithm 1 is upper bounded by $\mathcal{O}(b(n_1 + n_k) + \sum_{i \in \{2,3,\ldots,k-1\}} n_i)$.*

Proof. In Lemma 3, we have already shown that there will be 2 GNN Queries and $(k-2)$ many GNN Queries. Among the 2 GNN Queries, the first one is to recommend the POI from the first category and the other one is to recommend POI of the k-th Category. It is easy to observe that for recommending the POI of the first and k-th category it require $\mathcal{O}(b.n_1)$ and $\mathcal{O}(b.n_k)$ many shortest path computations, respectively. For recommending the POI of the second category, for all $v \in V_{\mathcal{C}_2}$, $dist(v_1, v)$ is computed. In this case the number of shortest path computations are of $\mathcal{O}(n_2)$. It is easy to observe that for any $i \in \{2, 3, \ldots, k-1\}$ for recommending POIs of the LBSP requires $\mathcal{O}(n_i)$, where n_i denotes the number of POIs of i-th category. Hence, the total time requirement for recommending POIs from 2-nd to $(k-1)$-th category is of $\mathcal{O}(\sum_{i \in \{2,3,\ldots,k-1\}} n_i)$. Now, including the first and k-th category POI recommendation, total number of shortest path computations will be of $\mathcal{O}(b(n_1 + n_k) + \sum_{i \in \{2,3,\ldots,k-1\}} n_i)$.

Lemma 5. *Algorithm 1 may not produces an optimal route.*

Proof. The working approach of Algorithm 1 is 'Greedy' which picks a locally optimal solution, and in this case it does not lead to the global optimal solution. Assume that Algorithm 1 always returns an optimal route. Now, for any $2 \leq i \leq k-1$, consider $(i-1)$-th, i-th, and $(i+1)$-th category of POIs. Let, v_{i-1}, v_i, v_{i+1} are the POIs recommended by the LBSP. Assume that the shortest path distance between v_{i-1} to v_i is x and v_i to v_{i+1} is y. As per the working principle of Algorithm 1 v_i is nearest from v_{i-1} and v_{i+1} is nearest from v_i. However, there may be two other POIs $v_i' \in V_{\mathcal{C}_k}$ and $v_{i+1}' \in V_{\mathcal{C}_{i+1}}$ with distance from v_{i-1} to v_i' and v_i' to v_{i+1}' are x' and y', respectively such that $x' + y' < x + y$. In that case, we can replace v_i by v_i' and v_{i+1} by v_{i+1}' and this will certainly give a route with less aggregated distance. So, our assumption that Algorithm 1 will always returns optimal route is not true. This proves the lemma statement.

Now, we analyze the time and space requirement of Algorithm 1. As mentioned previously computing the distance matrix requires $\mathcal{O}(n^3)$ time. However, in this study, we do not consider the cost of the offline computations. Also, we have seen in Sect. 3.1 that classifying the POIs based on the categories requires $\mathcal{O}(c \cdot n \cdot h^{max})$ time. Now, in the remaining part of Algorithm 1, the computational time requirement is due to shortest path computations. However, as we have already computed the distance matrix in the beginning, we can access it as per the requirement. As shown in Lemma 4, the number of such accesses are upper bounded by $\mathcal{O}(b(n_1 + n_k) + \sum_{i \in \{2,3,\ldots,k-1\}} n_i)$. Also, there are very simple arithmetic and comparison operations that take $\mathcal{O}(1)$ time. Only space requirement is to store the distance matrix which is of $\mathcal{O}(n^2)$.

Theorem 2. *The running time and space requirement of GNN Query approach is of $\mathcal{O}(k \cdot n \cdot h^{max} + b(n_1 + n_k) + \sum\limits_{i \in \{2,3,...,k-1\}} n_i)$ and $\mathcal{O}(n^2)$, respectively.*

3.3   Using $\mathcal{R}$-trees to Compute GTP Queries

In our experiments (in Sect. 4), we can observe that the proposed GNN Query-based approach improves the efficiency of the 'Brute Force Approach with Pre-computed Distance Matrix to a great extent. However, for handling large-scale road networks, we need even faster methods for computing the GTP Queries. This is possible if we can index the input road network (spatial database). In our study, we use $\mathcal{R}$-Tree data structure for indexing the road network [9]. In the literature, several problems on spatial databases have been solved using $\mathcal{R}$-Tree data structure [5,12]. In this study, we construct one $\mathcal{R}$-Tree for each category. The basic idea of this algorithm is to exploit the hierarchical properties of $\mathcal{R}$-trees and use a modified best first search (BFS) on $\mathcal{R}_1, \mathcal{R}_2, \mathcal{R}_3,..., \mathcal{R}_k$ to find set of data points that minimize the total travel distances for the group trip.

The working principle of this approach is the same as the GNN Query-Based Approach other than the use of $\mathcal{R}$-tree for executing the GNN and NN Queries. Hence, instead of describing the whole algorithm, we only state the required changes in Algorithm 1. Likewise GNN Query Approach, this approach also starts with classifying the POIs into categories. Now, instead of searching POI from the first category, this method builds the $\mathcal{R}$-Trees. While constructing the $\mathcal{R}$-Tree, corresponding to each POI (say v_i) it stores a quadruple r_{v_i} ($v_i - $left$, v_i - $right$, v_i - top, v_i - $bottom$)$. Now, the rest of the algorithm is by and large same as Algorithm 1 with a small difference that the execution of GNN and NN Queries will be executed on the constructed $\mathcal{R}$-Tree.

Now, we analyze the time and space requirement of our $\mathcal{R}$-Tree Based Approach. The time requirement for constructing an $\mathcal{R}$-Tree will depend on many factors such as: (i) The number of spatial objects a node can hold, (ii) the height of the tree, and so on. However, as we do not consider the cost of offline computation, it does not matter much. So, the only cost is to execute the NN and GNN Queries using $\mathcal{R}$-Tree. The concept of $\mathcal{R}$-Tree is based on the *minimum bounding rectangle* (MBR). Suppose, $\mathcal{M}$ be a minimum bounding rectangle for the data points $\mathcal{D} = \{d_1, d_2, \ldots, d_k\}$ and q is the query point. Now, to compute the minimum distance and the minimum among the maximum distances from the query point to the MBR, we need to do four distance computations [6]. Now, assume that there are p many different MBRs. For all $i \in \{1, 2, \ldots, p\}$, let md_i and mmd_i denotes the minimum distance and the minimum among the maximum distances for the i-th MBR to the query POI q. Suppose for all $i \in \{1, 2, \ldots, p\} \setminus \{j\}$, $mmd_i > md_j$. This means minimum distance of any POI within the MBRs other than the j-th one from the query POI q is more than that of the j-th one. Hence, it is guaranteed that the nearest neighbor of q will only lie in the j-th MBR. Now, we can compute the distances between each POI within the j-th MBR and q. The POI corresponding to the minimum distance is returned as the nearest neighbor. With a minor modification of this approach, GNN Queries can also be executed in $\mathcal{R}$-Trees. Finally, we can observe that in the worst case the time requirement of this approach can be as much as the GNN Query-Based Approach. However, in practice, it is much faster as we will see in our experiments. Next, we proceed to describe our experiments.

4   Experimental Evaluation

In this section, we present the experimental evaluation of the proposed methodologies. Initially, we present the description of the datasets.

Datasets Used. We use three road network datasets, namely, **City of Oldenburg Road Network** (Dataset 1), **City of San Joaquin Road Network** (Dataset 2), and **Road Networks of North America** (Dataset 3). See Table 1 for the basic statistics of the datasets. All of them has been downloaded from https://www.cs.utah.edu/~lifeifei/SpatialDataset.htm. This datasets have been previously used by many existing studies on spatial databases.

Table 1. Basic statistics of the datasets

Dataset name	n	m	Density	Avg. degree
City of Oldenburg	6104	7034	0.000377	2.302
City of San Joaquin	18262	23873	0.000143	2.606
North America	175812	179178	0.000011	2.037

Experimental Setup. These road network datasets contain POI information (along with the coordinates) but do not contain the tag information. Hence, we create this information in the following way. First, we have chosen 32 random categories like Hotels, Cinema Halls, Airport, Industries, and so on. Next, we assign 8 random tags to each category of POIs. For example, in case of Hotels, we assigned the following tags: rooms, terrace area, festive food, Business Suite, meeting hall, etc. Finally, we assigned 2 random tags to each POI from the set of eight tags corresponding to that category. The same process is carried out for all three datasets. Now, for performing our experiments, we consider three different sizes of groups 4, 8, and 12. Also, we vary the number of categories of POIs 2, 3, and 4. To evaluate the performance of any method, we define the metric as the ratio between the aggregated distance due to that algorithm to the optimal algorithm (i.e., brute force approach). Naturally, the lesser the value of the metric, the better the algorithm is.

Baseline Methods. We compare the performance of the proposed solution approaches with the following baseline approaches. The first one is the **Random**. In this case, the LBS randomly chooses one of the POIs from each category and returns them as a solution. The second one is the **Maximum Degree (MAX_DEG)**. In this case, the LBSP will recommend the highest degree POI from each category. Ties can be broken arbitrarily. The third one is the **Maximum Balanced Degree (MAX_B_DEG)** which is a modified version of the MAX_DEG. In this case instead of choosing the highest degree nodes, here LBSP will recommend one POI from each category whose number of neighbors in its previous and next category is balanced.

Experimental Results with Discussion. Now, we explain the obtained results with detailed discussions. Figure 2 shows the (Number of People in the Group, Number of Kinds of POIs) Vs. Total Distance Traveled for recommended POIs by different algorithms for three datasets.

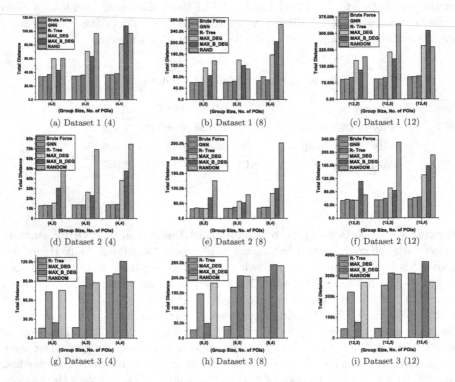

(a) Dataset 1 (4)   (b) Dataset 1 (8)   (c) Dataset 1 (12)

(d) Dataset 2 (4)   (e) Dataset 2 (8)   (f) Dataset 2 (12)

(g) Dataset 3 (4)   (h) Dataset 3 (8)   (i) Dataset 3 (12)

Fig. 2. (Group Size, No. of POIs) Vs. Aggregated Distance Traveled for all the methods on three datasets

From the results, we can immediately observe that the POIs recommended by the proposed methodologies lead to much lesser distance compared to the baseline methods. Here, we explain the results with examples. For the City of Old-enburg dataset, when the group size is 4 and the number of categories is also 4, the POIs recommended by the brute force approach with precomputed distance lead to the total distance of 36219.54 Units. In the same setting, the total distance due to the GNN Query-Based method and $\mathcal{R}$-Tree method is 40925.71 and 37936.75, respectively. According to our performance measure, the ratio for these two methods is 1.12 and 1.04, respectively. However, the total distance returned by the baseline methods is much more compared to the proposed approaches. Under the same setting, the recommended POIs by RANDOM, MAX_DEG, and MAX_B_DEG lead to the total distance of 96505.31, 81409.25, and 107515.94 units, respectively. The ratio for these methods is 2.66, 2.23, and 2.96, respectively. This observation is consistent even when we increase the number of group members. As an example, when the group size is increased to 12 and the number of categories is 4, between the GNN Query-Based Approach and $\mathcal{R}$-Tree Approach the best quality solution is produced by GNN Query-Based Approach and leads to the total distance of 101510.91 and the ratio for this is 1.008. However, in the same setting, the POIs recommended by RANDOM, MAX_DEG, and MAX_B_DEG lead to the total distance of 237620.82, 242173.44, and 312133.01. The ratio for these methodologies is 2.36, 2.40, and 3.10, respectively.

Now, we focus on the results for the other two datasets. In these two cases also, we observe that the POIs recommended by the proposed solution approaches lead to less aggregated distance compared to the baseline methods. Here, we point out that the size of the North America Road Network Dataset is large. Both the Brute Force Approach with Precomputed Distance and GNN Query-Based Approach take computational time which is not affordable. As an example, when the group size is 4 and the number of categories is 2, the execution time for GNN Query-Based approach is 467.71 s. On the other hand, under the same setting, the computational time for the $\mathcal{R}$-Tree approach is 1.1430 s. Hence, we decide to execute only $\mathcal{R}$-Tree method on the North America Road Network Dataset. The aggregated distance returned by the $\mathcal{R}$-Tree under this setting is 15859.47 units. Under the same setting, the total distance due to the RANDOM, MAX_DEG, and MAX_B_DEG lead to the total distance of 75402.24, 73116.63, and 24340.07, respectively. These are 3.75, 3.61, and 0.53 times more than the distance due to the $\mathcal{R}$-Tree method. Similarly, for the City of San Joaquin Road Network Dataset also, we observe that the performance of the proposed solution approaches is much better than the baseline methods. As an example, when the group size is 12 and the number of categories is 4, the distance due to the Brute Force Approach with Precomputed Distance, GNN Query-Based Approach, and $\mathcal{R}$-Tree Method is 56962.41, 61052.88, and 63009.08 units, respectively. Under the same setting, the distance due to the RANDOM, MAX_DEG, and MAX_B_DEG methods are 190966.07, 129855.36, and 157469.04, respectively.

5   Conclusion and Future Direction

In this paper, we have studied the problem of Group Trip Planning Queries on Road Network and proposed three different solution approaches for this problem. Detailed analysis of all the algorithms has been done. Extensive experiments with real-world road-network datasets show that the proposed $\mathcal{R}$-Tree based approach can process the GTP Queries on million-sized networks within feasible computational time. Our future study on this problem will be concentrated on developing more scalable algorithms for this problem using different spatial data structures.

References

1. Ahmadi, E., Nascimento, M.A.: A mixed breadth-depth first search strategy for sequenced group trip planning queries. In: 2015 16th IEEE International Conference on Mobile Data Management, vol. 1, pp. 24–33. IEEE (2015)
2. Barua, S., Jahan, R., Ahmed, T.: Weighted optimal sequenced group trip planning queries. In: 2017 18th IEEE International Conference on Mobile Data Management (MDM), pp. 222–227. IEEE (2017)
3. Bullen, P.S., Mitrinovic, D.S., Vasic, M.: Means and their inequalities, vol. 31. Springer Science & Business Media (2013)
4. Chen, H., Ku, W.S., Sun, M.T., Zimmermann, R.: The multi-rule partial sequenced route query. In: Proceedings of the 16th ACM SIGSPATIAL International Conference on Advances in Geographic Information Systems, pp. 1–10 (2008)
5. Chen, X., et al.: S 2 r-tree: a pivot-based indexing structure for semantic-aware spatial keyword search. GeoInformatica **24**(1), 3–25 (2020)
6. Cheung, K.L., Fu, A.W.C.: Enhanced nearest neighbour search on the r-tree. ACM SIGMOD Rec. **27**(3), 16–21 (1998)
7. Chow, C.Y., Mokbel, M.F.: Trajectory privacy in location-based services and data publication. ACM SIGKDD Explorations Newsl. **13**(1), 19–29 (2011)
8. Dai, J., Yang, B., Guo, C., Ding, Z.: Personalized route recommendation using big trajectory data. In: 2015 IEEE 31st International Conference on Data Engineering, pp. 543–554. IEEE (2015)
9. Guttman, A.: R-trees: a dynamic index structure for spatial searching. In: Proceedings of the 1984 ACM SIGMOD International Conference on Management of Data, pp. 47–57 (1984)
10. Hashem, T., Hashem, T., Ali, M.E., Kulik, L.: Group trip planning queries in spatial databases. In: Nascimento, M.A., Sellis, T., Cheng, R., Sander, J., Zheng, Yu., Kriegel, H.-P., Renz, M., Sengstock, C. (eds.) SSTD 2013. LNCS, vol. 8098, pp. 259–276. Springer, Heidelberg (2013). https://doi.org/10.1007/978-3-642-40235-7_15
11. Huang, H., Gartner, G.: Using trajectories for collaborative filtering-based poi recommendation. Int. J. Data Mining Modell. Manage. **6**(4), 333–346 (2014)
12. Kothuri, R.K.V., Ravada, S., Abugov, D.: Quadtree and r-tree indexes in oracle spatial: a comparison using gis data. In: Proceedings of the 2002 ACM SIGMOD International Conference on Management of Data, pp. 546–557 (2002)
13. Li, F., Cheng, D., Hadjieleftheriou, M., Kollios, G., Teng, S.-H.: On trip planning queries in spatial databases. In: Bauzer Medeiros, C., Egenhofer, M.J., Bertino, E. (eds.) SSTD 2005. LNCS, vol. 3633, pp. 273–290. Springer, Heidelberg (2005). https://doi.org/10.1007/11535331_16

14. Ohsawa, Y., Htoo, H., Win, T.N.: Continuous trip route planning queries. In: Pokorný, J., Ivanović, M., Thalheim, B., Šaloun, P. (eds.) ADBIS 2016. LNCS, vol. 9809, pp. 198–211. Springer, Cham (2016). https://doi.org/10.1007/978-3-319-44039-2_14

15. Osborn, W., Shaik, S.: Strategies for alternate group trip planning queries in location-based services. In: Barolli, L., Li, K.F., Enokido, T., Takizawa, M. (eds.) NBiS 2020. AISC, vol. 1264, pp. 64–76. Springer, Cham (2021). https://doi.org/10.1007/978-3-030-57811-4_7

16. Safar, M.: Group k-nearest neighbors queries in spatial network databases. J. Geogr. Syst. **10**(4), 407–416 (2008)

17. Skiena, S.S.: The algorithm design manual. Springer International Publishing (2020)

18. Soma, S.C., Hashem, T., Cheema, M.A., Samrose, S.: Trip planning queries with location privacy in spatial databases. World Wide Web **20**(2), 205–236 (2016). https://doi.org/10.1007/s11280-016-0384-2

19. Tabassum, A., Barua, S., Hashem, T., Chowdhury, T.: Dynamic group trip planning queries in spatial databases. In: Proceedings of the 29th International Conference on Scientific and Statistical Database Management, pp. 1–6 (2017)

20. Wang, H., Zeng, S., Li, Y., Zhang, P., Jin, D.: Human mobility prediction using sparse trajectory data. IEEE Trans. Veh. Technol. **69**(9), 10155–10166 (2020)

21. Wang, S., Bao, Z., Culpepper, J.S., Cong, G.: A survey on trajectory data management, analytics, and learning. arXiv preprint arXiv:2003.11547 (2020)

22. Xu, J., Chen, J., Zhou, R., Fang, J., Liu, C.: On workflow aware location-based service composition for personal trip planning. Futur. Gener. Comput. Syst. **98**, 274–285 (2019)

23. Yao, D., Zhang, C., Huang, J., Bi, J.: Serm: a recurrent model for next location prediction in semantic trajectories. In: Proceedings of the 2017 ACM on Conference on Information and Knowledge Management, pp. 2411–2414 (2017)

24. Zheng, Y.: Trajectory data mining: an overview. ACM Trans. Intell. Syst. Technol. (TIST) **6**(3), 1–41 (2015)

Deep Reinforcement Learning Based Iterative Participant Selection Method for Industrial IoT Big Data Mobile Crowdsourcing

Yan Wang[1], Yun Tian[2], Xuyun Zhang[3(✉)], Xiaonan He[4], Shu Li[5], and Jia Zhu[6]

[1] Tencent, Shenzhen, China
[2] Shanghaitech University, Shanghai, China
tianyun@shanghaitech.edu.cn
[3] Macquarie University, Sydney, Australia
xuyun.zhang@mq.edu.au
[4] Baidu, Beijing, China
[5] Nanjing University, Nanjing, China
shuli@smail.nju.edu.cn
[6] Tongji University, Shanghai, China
zhujia@tongji.edu.cn

Abstract. With the massive deployment of mobile devices, crowdsourcing has become a new service paradigm in which a task requester can proactively recruit a batch of participants with a mobile IoT device from our system for quick and accurate results. In a mobile industrial crowdsourcing platform, a large amount of data is collected, extracted information, and distributed to requesters. In an entire task process, the system receives a task, allocates some suitable participants to complete it, and collects feedback from the requesters. We present a participant selection method, which adopts an end-to-end deep neural network to iteratively update the participant selection policy. The neural network consists of three main parts: (1) task and participant ability prediction part which adopts a bag of words method to extract the semantic information of a query, (2) feature transformation part which adopts a series of linear and nonlinear transformations and (3) evaluation part which uses requesters' feedback to update the network. In addition, the policy gradient method which is proved effective in the deep reinforcement learning field is adopted to update our participant selection method with the help of requesters' feedback. Finally, we conduct an extensive performance evaluation based on the combination of real traces and a real question and answer dataset and numerical results demonstrate that our method can achieve superior performance and improve more than 150% performance gain over a baseline method.

Keywords: Reinforcement learning · Mobile crowdsourcing

Y. Wang and Y. Tian—Contribute equally to this work.

© Springer Nature Switzerland AG 2022
B. Li et al. (Eds.): ADMA 2021, LNAI 13087, pp. 258–272, 2022.
https://doi.org/10.1007/978-3-030-95405-5_19

1 Introduction

In recent years, mobile crowdsourcing has become a new service paradigm in which organizations use contributions from mobile users to obtain needed services, including web research of product offers, categorization for the sports video, and so on [1–4]. Today, it has deployed mainly to the cloud, which provides a particularly good venue for mobile crowdsourcing since individuals equipped with mobile devices enjoy high bandwidth services. In a mobile industrial crowdsourcing platform, a large amount of data is generated from many real-time tasks, collected from many IoT devices, extracted information on the cloud, and distributed to the requesters. Accordingly, distributed technology, data mining, and game theory are merged to improve the effectiveness of mobile crowdsourcing.

There are two main roles in a typical mobile crowdsourcing system, recruiters and participants. The recruiters are those who outsource their work or tasks to the crowd. The participants are those willing to help complete the task. Accordingly, The undertaking of the task; of variable complexity and modularity, in which the crowd should participate, bringing their work, money, knowledge, and experience, always entails mutual benefit [5,6]. The recruiter will receive the satisfaction of a given type of need, be economic, social recognition, self-esteem, or the development of individual skills, while the participant will obtain and use their advantage which the recruiter has brought to the venture, whose form (monetary or non-monetary incentives) will depend on the type of activity undertaken.

Accordingly, how to select suitable participants to complete a task for the recruiter is a crucial point that many researchers focus on [7–10]. The effectiveness of participant selection procedure in a mobile crowdsourcing task is affected by the participant mobility and preference pattern. Accordingly, the participant selection method in previous work is always based on the pattern prediction of those participants. Given a closed environment where the number and pattern of participants are changeless, this participant selection method is effective.

However, the mobile crowdsourcing tasks are always exposed to an open environment just like a motivation example showed in Fig. 1. In time slot 0, the relevance between a task and the participant preference around it has been predicted in the right table. With a simple participant selection method (the system just selects two participants with the highest relevance), participants $V1$ and $V2$ are selected to complete it. After an interval, the preference of participants is changed in a time slot 1. Given the same task and prediction of participant preference, the $V1$ and $V2$ would be selected rather than $V2$ and $V4$ who have a higher preference on the task. Moreover, a new participant $V5$ arrives in our system in time slot $T2$ and there is nothing about his/her preference. When the arrival of the same task, the participant $V5$ would not be selected. Finally, the prediction of the participant preference has been completely ineffective due to the change in the environment. In this paper, we address the fundamental research issue: how to select participants to complete a task for satisfying the recruiter under an open environment? In previous research [10], it always needs to accumulate the personal information of the participants to predict their preference pattern. However, it is unrealistic to obtain full information about a participant. In addition, the accumulation of participants' information is a time-consuming labor-intensive side process. Based above-mentioned problems, several open challenges remain to be solved. First, the limited information about the participants affects the precision of our prediction about participants' behaviors. Therefore, an effective prediction model based on limited information about participants is needed. Second, the changing of the participant preference influences our participant selection strategy. The system is required to update the participant selection strategy timely based on the changing of participant preference. Finally, an effective prediction method is required without the process of participants' information accumulation.

In response to the challenges mentioned above, an iterative participant selection method using Deep Reinforcement Learning [11,12] was introduced in our system framework. There are two critical reasons why a participant selection problem is formulated as a reinforcement learning problem in our paper: 1) In a reinforcement learning problem, the reward is the only information needed to be obtained from the environment. 2) It not only formulate the environment (participants preference pattern and mobility pattern) but also the interactions between the action (the participant's selection strategy) and the environment. In addition, there are also two critical reasons why a policy gradient method with a deep neural network is adopted to solve this reinforcement learning problem: 1) the generalization ability is powerful in deep neural networks. Therefore, a new participant preference could be learned with a few tasks. 2) Policy gradient method has been proved to be an effective method in reinforcement learning. 3) The participant selection strategy and the participant preference prediction process are combined in an end-to-end neural network that is easily optimized overall. Finally, Deep Reinforcement Learning is also a model-free learning method that has been successfully applied to a range of challenging problems. The goal of this deep network adopted by our framework is to learn participant selection policy for sequential decision problems, by optimizing a cumulative future reward signal.

To the best of our knowledge, this is the first paper that proposes an iterative participant selection method using Deep reinforcement learning. Specifically, the main contributions of our work are summarized as follows:

- We propose a system model which contains a task model, participant ability model, and user satisfaction model to formulate a participant selection problem in mobile crowdsourcing.
- We design an iterative participant selection system framework in which a Deep neural network is adopted. This framework consists of Input, Bag-of-words, Concat, Policy, and Loss part.
- We reduce a prediction and participant selection problem to a reinforcement learning problem.

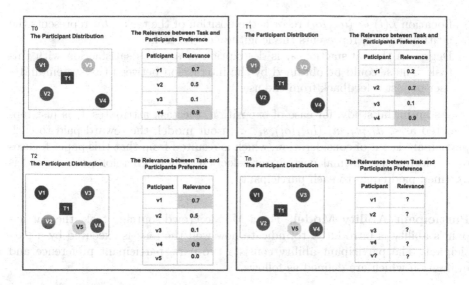

Fig. 1. A motivation example

2 System Model and Deep Neural Network

In this section, we introduce the system model of Mobile Crowdsourcing and then discuss the sequential participant selection problem.

2.1 System Model

A Mobile Crowdsourcing user u can submit a task T_i to the platform. Then, the platform selects some participants $\mathbf{P}*i$ and publishes the task to them. Within the permitted time pt_i, the task answer a_i submitted by the selected participants could be accepted by the platform. At last, the platform would transfer these answers to u and get the users' degree of satisfaction s with this task. In addition, a task model, a participant ability model, and a user satisfaction model are proposed as following.

Task Model. In our platform, a task i is described by a set of attributes T_i:

- Description is the text description of the task i. In our model, a words vector d_i is used to represent this text description. For instances, a description could be "what is the nearest toilet around me" and the words vector is $< w_i, w_j, ... >$ where w_i represents the position of the word "what" in the vocabulary.
- Permitted Time pt_i represents the maximum allowed execution time within which a participant is required to return the result.
- Amount of participants m_i is the number of participants the system select to complete the task.

- Location $L(i) \leftarrow (la_i, lo_i)$ records the position of the task i. la_i represents the latitude and lo_i represents the longitude of the task.
- Degree of the satisfaction s_i is description of a user's satisfaction with this task. The s_i could be obtained by the interaction between the system and a user or just a feedback from the user.

As an initial study, for ease of exposition, the task attributes T_i is just represented as $< d_i, pt_i, m_i, (la_i, lo_i), s_i >$. In our model, the reward paid to each participant is out of consideration, which is resulted from that this paper focuses on exploring the optimal participant selection policy. Therefore, the reward is assumed paid equal to each participant.

Participant Ability Model. For a Mobile crowd-sourcing task, the participant's ability is introduced to indicate how well the task is executed by a participant. The participant ability consists two-part, participant preference and evaluation which are defined as follows.

Definition 1 (Participant Preference). *The participant preference o_j^K is a description vector of a participant j's preference to K categories. Therefore, the Participants preference of participant set P could be represented as Matrix $O^{P \times K}$, where $|P| = P$ and K is the number of categories.*

Definition 2 (Participant Evaluation). *The participant evaluation $e * j^K$ is an evaluation vector to evaluate the performance on the K categories.*

Based on these two definitions, the ability of a Participant j with respect to the k-th category could be represented as follows:

$$q * j, k = o * j, k * e_{j,k} \tag{1}$$

Therefore, the ability matrix $Q^{P \times K}$ of a set participant P could be calculated as $O^{P \times K} * E^{P \times K}$.

User Satisfaction Model. In a Mobile Crowdsourcing task, a user publishes his/her request on the platform and obtain the replies from it. The quality and amount of replies have a immediate impact on his/her satisfaction. Moreover, the quality of replies depends on the participants which the system select to complete this task. Specifically, it is related to the ability of the selected participants **S** with respect to task i and their locations.

Accordingly, there are four main elements assumed to have a impact on the user's satisfaction with a task i: task description, participants' ability, participants' locations and the amount of selected participants. It could be represented as $< d_i, Q_i, L_i, m >$, where L_i is location matrix of selected participants.

2.2 Participant Selection Problem

Due to user mobility, a task requester needs to decide whether to recruit an arrived participant in permitted time. In general, a participant selection policy is needed to decide whether a participant should be selected to complete a specific task i with its environment. Before the statement of the problem, we first define the concept of the task environment.

Definition 3 (Task Environment). *The environment of task i is composed of the attributes of i and the participants around it. Specifically, the attributes of a task environment V_i contains the attributes of task T_i, the ability Q_i of participants around it and their locations L_i. Accordingly, V_i can be represented as $< T_i, Q_i, L_i >$.*

Instead of many previous research on participant selection problem, The goal of this research is to satisfy the users or improve the users' satisfaction. Accordingly, given a task environment V_i, we need to obtain a participant selection policy to minimize the users' satisfaction, which could be represented as follows.

$$\arg\max_{\mathbf{S}_i} \sum_i s_i, \ s.t. \ \mathbf{S}_i \subset \mathbf{P}_i \tag{2}$$

In the following section, we would design a framework to select a set of participants $\mathbf{P}_i$ around task i and utilize a Deep Q-Network to train a participant selection policy to select $\mathbf{S}_i$ from $\mathbf{P}_i$.

3 System Framework and Deep Q-Network

3.1 System Framework

For a specified Mobile Crowdsourcing task i, the system should first select its environment V_i which is composed of task attributes T_i and participants attribute Q_i and L_i. Accordingly, the scope of the participants $\mathbf{P}_i$ should be determined. Then it is transferred to a Deep Q-Network to select m_i participants to complete the task i. Finally, the score of this task s_i would be feedback to this Deep Q-Network, which is the main component of our evaluation. The steps in the system framework would be specified as follows.

Select the Scope of Participants. In this step, the scope of participants would be selected from the system based on the location of a task i. In our framework, the participants near the task i are possible to complete it. Accordingly, the rule we select the scope of participants $\mathbf{P}_i$ could be represented as

$$\mathbf{P}_i = \{p \mid dis(L(p), L(i) < d\} \tag{3}$$

where $dis(x, y)$ is a distance between x and y (it could be "Hamilton Distance" or "Euclidean distance").

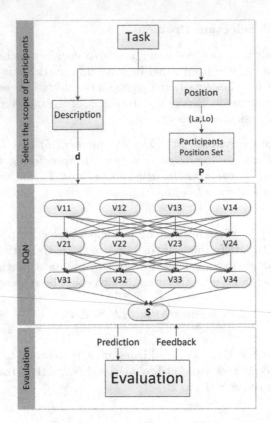

Fig. 2. Iterative participant selection system framework for mobile crowdsourcing

Deep Q-Network. The Deep Q-Network receives the attributes of the task i and the scope of participants P_i. Then it transfers them into an input layer. After the transformation of n neural networks, it select the appropriate m_i participants $\mathbf{S}_i$.

Evaluation. After the completion of the task i, the user who requests it would evaluate this task. This evaluation would later be feedback to our Deep Q-Network, which takes advantage of the backpropagation algorithm to train our DQN. Accordingly, the model is iterative updated.

3.2 Deep Q-Network

The main novel part of this paper is designing a Deep Q-Network to train a participant selection policy. The DQN we designed is specified in Fig. 3. It consists of five main parts: input, bag-of-words, concat, policy, and loss.

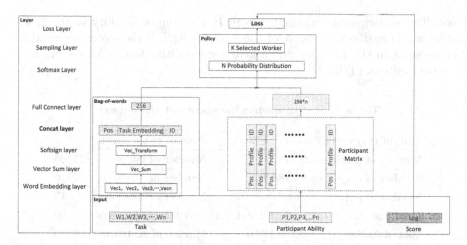

Fig. 3. The Deep Q-Network in the system framework which consists of input, bag-of-words, concat, policy, and loss.

Input. The input layer of DQN has received the input vector, which contains task attributes T_i, participants ability matrix Q_i and location matrix L_i. In the input layer, the Q_i comes from the previous prediction or just a randomized matrix.

Bag-of-Words. To do with the description vector of the task d_i, the bag-of-words part is designed to transfer it into a 256-dimensional vector, which has been proved to be successful in many machine learning tasks. The word-embedding layer first transfer each words in d_i into a 256-dimensional vector x_1. Then it is transformed to vector sum layer which sums each word-embeddings into a vector x_2. After soft sign transformation, it is sent to a full connected layer in which the x_2 is linearly transformed as x_3. Accordingly, the x_3 could be represented as:

$$x_3 = W_{fc} \cdot \sum_j W_{emb} \cdot d_i \tag{4}$$

where $\sum *j$ represents the sum of the elements in each column of a matrix.

Concat. The concat layer concats the x_3 and location vector $L(i)$ to a vector x_4 and concats each participant ability vector q_p and location $L(p)$ to a vector y_p.

Policy. The policy part of the Deep Q-network first receives the vector x_4 and y_p. Then it would calculate the cos value between x_4 and each y_p, for $0 \leq p \leq |P_i|$. Finally, it concats each cos value into a vector $z^{|P_i| \times 1}$. Through the Softmax transformation, each participant p has a probability to be selected corresponding to each row of the z.

Loss. The participants are sampled from P_i with the probability vector z. The system would feedback the score of this task to DQN. If the score is beyond the average score in the past, we would give some positive feedback and else some negative feedback (Table 1).

Table 1. The parameters in experiment and dataset

Scale of trajectory data set		Scale of QA dataset	
Number of participants	182	Number of queries	25186
Number of trajectory	18670	Number of words	7530
Number of points	24, 876, 978	Number of categories	17
Total distance	1, 292, 951 km	Max len of sentences	50
Total duration	50,176 h	Min len of sentences	3

4   Evaluation

The performance of our algorithms are evaluated by a simulate experiment based on the data generated from a real-life data traces and a real question and answer dataset. In our evaluation, The real-life datasets and experiment settings are specified. Secondly, a baseline algorithm is introduced in detailed.

4.1   Dataset and Experiment Setups

The dataset we used in evaluation is the GeoLife GPS Trajectory dataset [13–15], which was collected in (Microsoft Research Asia) Geolife project by 182 users in a period of over three years (from April 2007 to August 2012). In this dataset, each users' outdoor movements, including not only life routines like go home and go to work but also some entertainments and sports activities are recorded. In our study, we design experiments based on two periods. The trajectory in first two years were used for participant selection, and we test our algorithm in the last year.

The score algorithm plays a key role in our score generator. The evaluation of users' satisfaction has been proved to be a complex problem, which is a kind of Quality of Service problem in Service computing. The data mining method is adopted to this problem and lead to a remarkable improvement. However, the users in our data is so inadequate that a fixed algorithm is adopted to generate users' satisfaction in our experiment. The score is calculated as

$$score = \frac{1.0}{\min_{T \in Q_i} dis(g_t, g_i)} \tag{5}$$

where Q_i is set of queries which a participant i could answer and g_t and g_i is task gps information and participant gps information respectively.

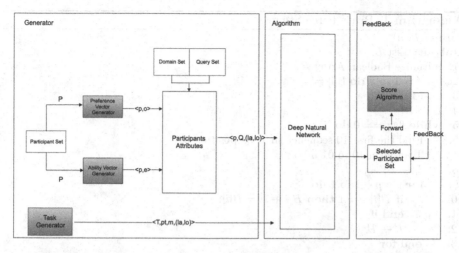

Fig. 4. The experiment design (There are four generators in our simulate experiment, which are used to combine two real dataset to stimulate the participant selection process and users' feedback. The Preference Vector Generator and Ability Vector Generator are used to allocate the QA pairs to each participants. The Task Generator randomly select a query and a gps point as a task. The Score Generator execute our score algorithm which stimulates the evaluation of different users.)

In a DQN method, some tricks are adopted to reduce the variance of algorithm and accelerate the speed of convergence. In a episode, the batch size is set 32 and $b_t(s_t)$ is estimated as the mean of the score. In addition, the standard deviation of the mean score is divided from the scores. Hence, the score that is transferred to neural network is

$$\hat{s} = \frac{s - \text{mean}(s)}{\text{std}(s)} \tag{6}$$

Additionally, the size of the candidate participants set is set as num in our experiment, which help us reduce the search space of the algorithm (Fig. 4).

4.2 BaseLine Method

The baseline method is derived from [10]. In this paper, task, worker arrival and worker ability models are defined to maximize the expected sum of service quality with an online algorithm. Because the task in our system is a kind of instant task. The exponential decaying function is omitted in our baseline method. In addition, some details in original methods are modified to adapt our system.

First, a linear classification method is adopted to predict the task (T) and worker (A) ability models. Then, worker (G) arrival pattern is predicted by a Poisson distribution based on the historical data of participants. Based on these models, a greedy algorithm (Algorithm 1) is adopted to solve this participant selection problem. In this algorithm, the input consists of a task t_i, the number of

---

Algorithm 1. Brute Force Stage

Input: k, n
Output: List L
 1: Initialize Boolean Array B
 2: **for** $i = 1$ to k **do** B[i] = 1;
 3: **end for**
 4: $L \leftarrow B$;
 5: **while** flag $== 0$ **do**
 6:     Find the first 10 sequence in B as position p;
 7:     Transform 10 to 01 in B;
 8:     $L \leftarrow B$;
 9:     **for** $i = p - 1$ to 1 **do**
10:         **if** $B[i] == 1$ **then** $B[i + 1] = B[i]$;
11:         **end if**
12:         $L \leftarrow B$;
13:     **end for**
14:     flag $= 1$;
15:     **for** $i = n - k + 1$ to n **do**
16:         **if** $B[i] \; != 0$ **then** flag $= 0$;
17:         **end if**
18:     **end for**
19: **end while**

---

participant need to be selected sel/num, a participants set P and three models: task model $T(t_i) = v$, worker ability model $A(p_i) = w$ and worker arrival model $G(p_i) = [la_i, lo_i]$. The output L is a set of suitable participants to complete the task.

4.3   The Performance Evaluation and Comparison

Figure 5 specifies the performance comparison between the DQN method and baseline method with different parameters. The mean score in baseline method is almost unchanged with the increasing episode. While, the mean score continues changes in DQN method. It is because that DQN method is a iterative method which takes advantage of requesters' feedback to update the parameters. In Fig. 6, it could find that the DQN method curves fluctuates in early episodes, grows steadily in mediate episodes and stay stable in last episodes. Additionally, the standard deviation of DQN method in Fig. 6 also reflects this fact. The standard deviation of 1000 and 5000 episodes is always greater than those in 10000 episode, which applies a traditional deep reinforcement learning process.

In addition, the red solid curves of (a), (b), (d) subfigures in Fig. 6 are similar, which has a little fluctuation in early episodes. However, the red solid curves of (c), (e), (f) fluctuates largely in early episodes. In (a), (b), (d), the search space of actions is 10,45 and 50 respectively. While, the search space in (c), (e), (f) is at least 1225. This fact demonstrates that the learning or convergence speed would decrease with the growth of the search space.

The mean score of baseline method (the blue dotted line) in Fig. 6 is almost the same or even exceed the DQN method in episode 0. When $num = 10$ and $sel_num = 10$, the base line method is superior to DQN method in episode 10000. This fact shows that the DQN training process is not always stable which is affected by the initial state of deep neural network and the tasks that it encounters in early episodes. How to use a stable baseline method to help us train DQN method would be our future work.

(a) $num = 10$, $sel\_num = 1$

	mean score	mean std
BSL/DQN (episode 1000)	0.2/6.3	0.4/4.7
BSL/DQN (episode 5000)	0.3/5.7	0.5/8.4
BSL/DQN (episode 10000)	0.2/7.3	0.4/7.3

(b) $num = 10$, $sel\_num = 2$

	mean score	mean std
BSL/DQN (episode 1000)	3.2/4.7	5.3/5.7
BSL/DQN (episode 5000)	3.0/4.9	5.9/3.2
BSL/DQN (episode 10000)	3.0/4.7	10.5/2.9

(c) $num = 10$, $sel\_num = 5$

	mean score	mean std
BSL/DQN (episode 1000)	5.2/8.2	9.4/12.2
BSL/DQN (episode 5000)	5.2/7.4	10.9/9.3
BSL/DQN (episode 10000)	5.2/6.8	5.3/5.6

(d) $num = 50$, $sel\_num = 1$

	mean score	mean std
BSL/DQN (episode 1000)	0.3/5.1	0.5/4.9
BSL/DQN (episode 5000)	0.3/6.6	0.4/4.2
BSL/DQN (episode 10000)	0.3/7.8	0.5/ 4.6

(e) $num = 50$, $sel\_num = 2$

	mean score	mean std
BSL/DQN (episode 1000)	3.1/0.8	4.9/0.5
BSL/DQN (episode 5000)	3.1/0.9	9.0/7.9
BSL/DQN (episode 10000)	3.1/2.3	2.4/4.5

(f) $num = 50$, $sel\_num = 5$

	mean score	mean std
BSL/DQN (episode 1000)	4.8/10.5	7.8/7.5
BSL/DQN (episode 5000)	5.0/11.6	6.7/8.2
BSL/DQN (episode 10000)	5.0/10.4	9.3/3.2

Fig. 5. The performance comparison between the DQN method and the baseline method

5 Related Work

Our study of Participant Selection Problem in mobile crowdsourcing touches upon a number of active areas of interest. In what follows, we describe the most salient related work in two key areas while also highlighting the novel contributions being made by mobile crowd sourcing [5].

Participant Selection Problem in Mobile Crowdsourcing: due to the dynamic and comprehensive environment, how to select a suitable crowd to complete a task is a key problem in mobile crowdsourcing [17]. It has been a NP-hard problem by [18] and many researchers design approximate algorithm to solve it. In addition, the researchers use the greedy algorithm and genetic algorithm respectively to solve the offline and online participant selection problem in mobile crowdsourcing [19]. Besides, a amount of utility functions in greedy algorithm have been designed for mobile crowdsorucing with respect to different objection, such as energy-efficient or fairness.

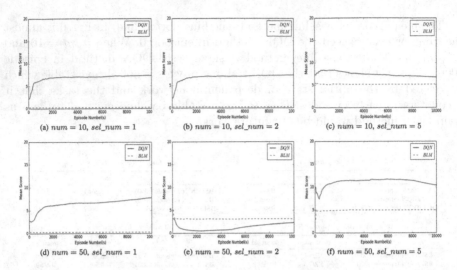

Fig. 6. The mean score (requesters' feedback) of DQN method and baseline method with training episodes (Color figure online)

Information Extraction and Preservation in Mobile Crowdsourcing: a large scale of data in crowdsourcing platform is collected from many participants with distinct attributes, for example, ages, position, technical knowledge and so on. Accordingly, we need to take advantage of these private information to help us wash the data and meanwhile preserve the privacy of the participants [20]. In [21], the authors introduce and compare approaches to handle both types of crowdsourced data ("passive data" and "active data") for the tasks including data aggregation, budget allocation, etc. However, Agadakos et al. focus on the privacy preservation of participants' GPS information while using them [3].

6   Conclusion

A MCS system intend to monitor air quality for citizens. It divides the urban area into multiple parts. For simplicity, we only need to complete a sensing task in 6 divided areas during a time slot in our example. In a hexagon, if a participant uploads the air information in a time slot, we call it is covered. Meanwhile, we define the coverage rate as the number of covered area divide the amount of the divided areas.

In Fig. 2, there are five participants willing to complete the task. In addition, we accumulate the information of their trajectories and select the minimum people to complete this task while the coverage rate is to be 100%. The trajectories information of five participants is accumulated in Fig. 2. For example, the participant 1 would pass region 1, 2 and 3. Accordingly, the participant A and C are selected to cover the entire region.

However, the assumption that each participant would upload their information to the server is too desirable. Some exceptions would come out to break it, such as the power-off of the telephone or the error of our sensor. Accordingly, some evaluations should be proposed to evaluate the participants' ability. In the Fig. 1 (T2 part), the probability or ability of participants are specified. In this table, the participant A has just 30% probability to complete the task in each hexagon. Then, the task would fail.

Accordingly, a participant selection method should be designed to solve this problem considering the participants' ability. In this example, the participant B, C, D should be selected instead of participant A and B. The evaluation of participant ability is a key factor of our algorithm, which should be specified in next section besides the system model for our mobile crowdsourcing.

Acknowledgment. Dr Xuyun Zhang is the recipient of an ARC DECRA (project No. DE210101458) funded by the Australian Government.

References

1. Wu, Y., Wang, Y., Cao, G.: Photo crowdsourcing for area coverage in resource constrained environments. In: Proceeding of IEEE Conference on Computer Communications, pp. 1–9 (2017)
2. Fan, J., Zhang, M., Kok, S., Lu, M., Ooi, B.C.: CrowdOp: query optimization for declarative crowdsourcing systems. In: Proceeding of Conference on Empirical Methods in Natural Language Processing, pp. 1546–1547 (2016)
3. Agadakos, I., Polakis, J., Portokalidis, G.: Techu: open and privacy-preserving crowdsourced GPS for the masses. In: Proceeding of International Conference on Mobile Systems, Applications, and Services, pp. 475–487 (2017)
4. Wang, X., Zheng, X., Zhang, Q., Wang, T., Shen, D.: Crowdsourcing in its: the state of the work and the networking. IEEE Trans. Intell. Transp. Syst. **17**(6), 1596–1605 (2016)
5. Mao, K., Capra, L., Harman, M., Jia, Y.: A survey of the use of crowdsourcing in software engineering. J. Syst. Softw. **126**(22), 15–27 (2016)
6. To, H., Ghinita, G., Fan, L., Shahabi, C.: Differentially private location protection for worker datasets in spatial crowdsourcing. IEEE Trans. Mob. Comput. **16**, 934–949 (2017)
7. Tong, Y., She, J., Ding, B., Wang, L., Chen, L.: Online mobile micro-task allocation in spatial crowdsourcing. In: Proceeding of IEEE International Conference on Data Engineering, pp. 49–60 (2016)
8. Pan, Z., Yu, H., Miao, C., Leung, C.: Efficient collaborative crowd-sourcing. In: Proceeding of the National Conference on Artificial Intelligence, pp. 4248–4249 (2016)
9. Qiu, C., Carminati, B., Carminati, B., Caverlee, J., Khare, D.R.: CrowdSelect: increasing accuracy of crowdsourcing tasks through behavior prediction and user selection. In: Proceedings of International on Conference on Information and Knowledge Management, pp. 539–548 (2016)
10. Pu, L., Chen, X., Xu, J., Fu, X.: Crowdlet: optimal worker recruitment for self-organized mobile crowdsourcing. In: Proceedings of International Conference on Computer Communications, pp. 1–9 (2016)
11. Duan, Y., Chen, X., Houthooft, R., Schulman, J., Abbeel, P.: Benchmarking deep reinforcement learning for continuous control. In: Proceedings of International Conference on International Conference on Machine Learning, pp. 1329–1338 (2016)

12. Narasimhan, K., Yala, A., Barzilay, R.: Improving information extraction by acquiring external evidence with reinforcement learning. In: Proceeding of International Conference on Data Engineering, pp. 2355–2365 (2016)
13. Zheng, Y., Li, Q., Chen, Y., Xie, X., Ma, W.Y.: Understanding mobility based on GPS data. In: Proceedings of International Conference on Ubiquitous Computing, pp. 312–321 (2008)
14. Zheng, Y., Zhang, L., Xie, X., Ma, W.-Y.: Mining interesting locations and travel sequences from GPS trajectories. In: Proceedings of International Conference on World Wide Web, pp. 791–800 (2009)
15. Zheng, Y., Xie, X., Ma, W.Y.: GeoLife: a collaborative social networking service among user, location and trajectory. Trans. Bull. Tech. Committee Data Eng. **33**(2), 32–39 (2010)
16. Cheng, P., Lian, X., Chen, L., Han, J., Zhao, J.: Task assignment on multi-skill oriented spatial crowdsourcing. IEEE Trans. Knowl. Data Eng. **28**(8), 2201–2215 (2015)
17. Cui, L., Zhao, X., Liu, L., Yu, H., Miao, Y.: Learning complex crowdsourcing task allocation strategies from humans. In: Proceedings of International Conference on Crowd Science and Engineering, pp. 33–37 (2017)
18. Zhang, D., Xiong, H., Wang, L., Chen, G.: CrowdRecruiter: selecting participants for piggyback crowdsensing under probabilistic coverage constraint. In: Proceedings of International Joint Conference on Pervasive and Ubiquitous Computing, pp. 703–714 (2014)
19. Li, H., Li, T., Wang, Y.: Dynamic participant recruitment of mobile crowd sensing for heterogeneous sensing tasks. In: Proceeding of International Conference on Mobile Ad Hoc and Sensor Systems, pp. 136–144 (2015)
20. Jung, S.H., Moon, B.C., Han, D.: Unsupervised learning for crowd-sourced indoor localization in wireless networks. IEEE Trans. Mob. Comput. **15**(11), 2892–2906 (2016)
21. Gao, J., Li, Q., Zhao, B., Fan, W., Han, J.: Mining reliable information from passively and actively crowdsourced data. In: Proceedings of International Conference on Knowledge Discovery and Data Mining, pp. 2121–2122 (2016)
22. Kulkarni, T.D., Narasimhan, K., Saeedi, A., Tenenbaum, J.: Hierarchical deep reinforcement learning: integrating temporal abstraction and intrinsic motivation. In: Proceedings of Annual Conference on Neural Information Processing Systems, pp. 3675–3683 (2016)

Know Your Limits: Machine Learning with Rejection for Vehicle Engineering

Kilian Hendrickx[1,2]([⊠])(iD), Wannes Meert[2](iD), Bram Cornelis[1],
and Jesse Davis[2](iD)

[1] Siemens Digital Industries Software, Interleuvenlaan 68, 3001 Leuven, Belgium
{kilian.hendrickx,bram.cornelis}@siemens.com
[2] KU Leuven, Department of Computer Science, Celestijnenlaan 200A, Box 2402,
3001 Leuven, Belgium
{kilian.hendrickx,wannes.meert,jesse.davis}@cs.kuleuven.be

Abstract. New vehicle designs need to be tested in representative driving scenarios to evaluate their durability. Because these tests are costly, only a limited number of them can be performed. These have traditionally been selected using rules of thumb, which are not always applicable to modern vehicles. Hence, there is a need to ensure that vehicle tests are aligned with their real-world usage. One possibility for obtaining a broad real-world usage overview is to exploit the data collected by sensors embedded in production vehicles. But these do not produce the detailed data needed to derive the metrics computed using expensive sensors during testing. Therefore it is necessary to correlate the low-end sensor measurements available in production vehicles with the relevant metrics acquired using high-end sensors during testing. Machine learning is a promising avenue for doing this. The key challenge is that vehicles will be used "in the wild" in many scenarios that were not encountered in the controlled testing environment, and it is unlikely that learned models will perform reliably in these previously unseen environments. We overcome this challenge by allowing learned models to abstain from making a prediction when unexpected vehicle usage is identified. We propose a general framework that combines standard machine learning with novelty detection to identify previously unseen situations. We illustrate our framework's potential on data we collected from a large-scale road-roughness analysis use case. Empirically, our approach can identify novel road types in the wild and by doing so it yields better performance.

Keywords: Vehicle engineering · Machine learning with rejection · Novelty detection

1 Introduction

When working on new car designs, manufacturers validate that their vehicle meets safety requirements and ensure that its components will be sufficiently

© Springer Nature Switzerland AG 2022
B. Li et al. (Eds.): ADMA 2021, LNAI 13087, pp. 273–288, 2022.
https://doi.org/10.1007/978-3-030-95405-5_20

durable. These evaluations involve operating the vehicle in a number of development tests, measuring several Key Performance Indicators (KPI) with high-end sensors. However, these tests are time-consuming and very costly to carry out as some sensors cost > \$100 000. This precludes carrying out an extensive number of tests and hence requires selecting a small but representative subset corresponding to typical vehicle usage. Traditionally, common real-world usage was deduced from polls and small-scale tests using high-end sensors [10, 34].

Recent developments in connected cars give manufacturers access to a rising amount of real-world vehicle usage data [14, 23, 31]. However, this data is of lower quality than the data from development tests. Unfortunately, it is impossible to directly compute many of the relevant KPIs from the data produced by the low-end sensors included in production vehicles. Traditionally, the relation between the low-end sensor data and high-end sensors KPIs is manually derived using extensive engineering insights and expertise, which is difficult and costly to scale [28, 30]. Machine learning has been proposed to overcome this challenge, by automatically inferring the relationship between the low and high-quality data [2, 22]. However, this poses a major challenge: learned models are only reliable in situations similar to their training data. In contrast, real-world vehicle usage is not limited to scenarios that arose in the restricted number of development tests. Hence, a model's prediction for a KPI should only be trusted if it derives from a situation that was encountered during the testing phase.

We tackle this challenge by pursuing the recently emerging machine learning paradigm of incorporating a novelty reject option into a model [17]. Such an option permits a model to abstain from making a prediction for samples that substantially differ from those present in the training set. For vehicle usage analysis, using a reject option provides two benefits. First, it enables analyzing real-world vehicle usage data without artifacts arising from unexpected vehicle usage. For example, manufacturers might be interested in the distributions of most common road types customers drive over. A model estimating these types might make incorrect predictions due to encountering unexpected road types. Second, a rejection indicates an unexpected vehicle usage event, which might be accounted for in future vehicle designs and vehicle development tests. For example, the rejects can indicate novel road types in the road analysis use case.

Motivated by vehicle usage analysis, we propose a framework that provides a learned model with a reject option by combining a standard predictive model with a novelty detector. Our approach is model-agnostic in that it works with any predictive model. We evaluate our approach on a novel data set we collected by monitoring a vehicle that was driven over 20 000 kilometers over the course of nearly two years. Concretely, we show how incorporating a reject option substantially improves predictive performance when estimating road roughness in the wild. To summarize, we make the following contributions:

1. Highlight the data science challenges that arise when analyzing real-world vehicle usage to inform design engineering;
2. Propose a model-agnostic machine learning with rejection framework that helps overcome some of the aforementioned challenges for this task;

3. Demonstrate the efficacy of our framework on a large-scale road-roughness analysis use-case.

2   Background

2.1   Vehicle Engineering: The Need for Usage Profiling

Manufacturers need to constantly trade off performance attributes. For example, lightweight designs lead to better fuel efficiency [21], but this needs to be balanced against durability and safety aspects [15]. Instead of relying on rules of thumb for design decisions as was done in the past, pursuing environmentally friendly designs requires aligning performance attributes with real-world usage.

Nowadays, both the design and its requirements can be optimized by better insights into real-world vehicle usage. Firstly, these insights help engineers to better tailor vehicle designs to the targeted customer market. For example, one could adapt vehicles for different geographical markets based on the quality of the roads within each region [11]. Secondly, validating the requirements in development tests is an expensive development phase, as it involves high-end sensors, specialized proving grounds, and skilled drivers [8]. Consequently, insights in real-world usage help to minimize testing time by selecting the most representative scenarios [13, 24].

2.2   Related Work on Machine Learning with a Reject Option

Machine learned models have difficulty extrapolating from the data they were trained on. Hence, if a model encounters a sample that is novel or different from what was seen in the training data, it is more prone to making an incorrect prediction [4]. In applications where such mistakes are costly, it might be better to abstain from making a prediction [17]. This option to reject can improve the model's reliability by providing more robustness and better overall performance [27], which ultimately increases the trustworthiness of its predictions [32].

Formally, we can define a machine learning model with a reject option as a function pair: a predictor h and a rejector r [6]. The predictor models the relation $h : X \rightarrow Y$ for the input space X and output space Y. The rejector $r : X \rightarrow \{accept, reject\}$ assesses whether or not h is likely to produce an incorrect prediction (reject) or not (accept) for a given sample. This work focuses on *novelty* rejection, where the goal is to abstain from making a prediction if a test sample is too dissimilar to the training data. This setting is fundamentally different than *ambiguity* rejection, for example, studied in [7], which aims to abstain from making a prediction for samples that fall in a region of the instance-space where h was unable to find a deterministic relation between the input variables and the target.

Ideally, the rejector would decide to abstain from making a prediction based on the predictor's epistemic uncertainty, indicating its lack of knowledge [19]. When a prediction for a sample has high epistemic uncertainty, this indicates that the prediction is likely incorrect. However, truly quantifying this uncertainty is hard. Instead, most rejection approaches either evaluate the predictor's output or directly embed the rejector into the predictor. The former uses soft-predictions, for example, provided by a Neural Network's activation layer [5], or exploits specific model properties such as a sample's distance to a point of interest [9,35]. Both are assumed to monotonically map the uncertainty. The latter embeds the rejector into the predictor to combine both tasks into a single model, for example by considering multiple one-class models [16] or designing a Neural Network with two output layers [33]. However, this requires h to simultaneously solve its primary task of inferring $X \to Y$ as well as to faithfully modeling the training data.

Both approaches have rejectors tied to a specific class of models, conflicting with our aim of developing a general framework, applicable for various classification and regression tasks. Instead, we simply assume that the predictor is likely to be inaccurate on data points that are highly dissimilar to those samples in the training data. This yields a model-agnostic approach where r models the training data using, for example, a one-class model such as a Gaussian-mixture [20] or a One-Class Support Vector Machine (OCSVM) [3,18]. During deployment, r only passes samples to h that are similar to those found in the training data.

Regression with a novelty reject option is extremely rare [7,17]. Our machine learning contribution is that we study a model-agnostic reject option for regression problems.

3   Usage Profiling: Data Science Challenge

The vehicle usage profiling task involves deriving insights into the real-world usage of production vehicles by the customers that bought the vehicle. The goal is to improve the vehicle's design by better aligning its requirements to how the vehicle will be used in practice. Performing a proper analysis requires taking the following challenges into account:

1. **Automatization.** The same framework should be generic enough that it can be applied to analyze a large number of different usage parameters with minimal modifications. That is, given a new KPI, the time needed to derive a relation between this KPI and the low-end sensors should be minimized.
2. **Small data.** High-end vehicle measurement data is often limited, as it is expensive to collect. The selected machine learning techniques must be able to cope with a limited amount of training data.
3. **Incomplete training data.** Due to cost and time restrictions associated with testing, manufacturers can only collect ground truth data with high-end sensors for a limited number of real-life usage scenarios. The methodology should be robust to data arising from previously unseen scenarios.
4. **Identify unexpected usage.** Vehicles operated in real life are used in unexpected or novel ways. It is important to automatically identify these scenarios as doing so can yield insights that can improve the designs of future vehicles.

5. **Model-agnostic architecture.** Users need to fully trust the model before using it to make impactful decisions. In addition to the required robustness, users might favor white-box techniques or want to reuse established models. To support any such model, the rejection architecture should not pose any constraints on the predictor.

4   Our Approach for Vehicle Usage Profiling

Our goal is to investigate how to automatically detect vehicle usage in the real world that differs from scenarios seen during the development tests in order to minimize errors arising from predictions made during unexpected usage. Formally, this translates to the following data science problem:

Given: Training set X_{train} with target Y_{train} collected in a controlled setting.
Do: Learn a model h' that 1) predicts Y for samples similar to X_{train} and 2) abstains from making a prediction for samples highly dissimilar to X_{train}.

The overall goal can be divided into three subtasks: (i) learning a predictive model capturing the relationship between the features and the target variable, (ii) learning a rejector modeling X_{train} in order to assess how novel a test sample is, and (iii) integrating the rejector's output in order to decide if a prediction should be made for a sample. Next, we describe each component in detail.

4.1   Predictor h

The predictor models the relationship between the low-end sensors and the desired KPI. This corresponds to the standard machine learning setting, with the model learned from the vehicle development test data X_{train}. As our architecture is model-agnostic, it does not pose any constraints on the considered model class. Moreover, it does not require altering the underlying learning algorithm.

4.2   Rejector r

The rejector uses a novelty detector to model X_{train}, assessing whether a sample is an outlier to the samples in X_{train} [26]. We generalize prior work on model-agnostic rejection approaches in the context of classification [18,20], to define four criteria that a novelty detector must satisfy to be useful in the context of vehicle usage:

1. KPIs in vehicle engineering can be discrete or continuous, so the architecture must be applicable to both classification as regression problems. For regression, estimating parameters of novelty detectors such as the expected number of classes or clusters is challenging. Therefore, the novelty detector should require little apriori knowledge about the data distributions.
2. The detector should return a novelty score instead of a hard prediction. This allows a user to control how sensitive the rejector is to novel data points. For example, this allows us to still make predictions for samples that fall just outside a OCSVM's minimal sphere.

3. Novelty scores should be representative of how similar a sample is to the training data. That is, the further a point is from the training set, the higher its novelty. If this were not the case, it would not be possible to tune the rejector's sensitivity by varying its threshold.
4. The model should be able to return scores falling outside the range of scores assigned to samples in the training set. If this were not the case, a novel sample cannot be distinguished from the training data.

Two models satisfying these criteria for novel samples are k-Nearest Neighbors outlier detector (kNNO) and the OCSVM. kNNO considers test samples that fall in low data density regions to be novel, which is a valid indicator of novelty. OCSVM has been extensively used, and it models the data by finding a hypersphere enclosing the training data.

Novelty detection typically identifies samples that are novel due to differences in the observed value of *any* feature. However, for this application, we mostly care about differences in features that are most important for the predictor. That is, we do not care if a sample is novel because it arises due to the car being driven on an unusually hot or cold day. Therefore, we restrict the novelty detectors to only use the predictor's most informative features. Moreover, this is beneficial as kNNO struggles with irrelevant features and high-dimensional spaces.

4.3   Combined Model h'

Given a test sample x, it is necessary to integrate the rejector and predictor to arrive at a final model. Our approach uses the following rule to determine whether to make a prediction for x:

$$h'(x) = \begin{cases} \emptyset & \text{if } r(x|X_{train}) > thr \\ h(x) & \text{otherwise} \end{cases} \tag{1}$$

That is, it first applies the rejector to obtain the novelty score $r(x)$. If $r(x)$ is greater than a user-defined threshold thr, then h' abstains from making a prediction. Otherwise, it applies the predictor h to x and returns its prediction. The key parameter is thr which determines h''s coverage $(N_{accepted}/N)$, which is the fraction of test samples for which a prediction is made $(N_{accepted})$ over the total number of samples tested (N). The value of thr controls the trade-off between h''s predictive performance and its coverage. Lower values of thr mean that h' is very conservative and will only make predictions for samples that are very similar to the training data. Hence, one would expect a higher accuracy on those samples where a prediction was made, but at the cost of abstaining from making a prediction for many test samples. In contrast, picking a larger value for thr means h' will be making predictions for a greater percentage of the test samples, but it comes with an increased risk of making a larger mistake for those samples that differ from the training data.

5   Use-Case: Road-Roughness Analysis

We will evaluate our rejection-based machine learning methodology by analyzing real-world car usage data that we collected. Specifically, we will focus on assessing road roughness based on the inexpensive sensors that are present in most modern cars. Understanding road conditions is crucial for design as a road's roughness is one of the primary sources of vibrations, which have a large impact in terms of degrading the components in a car. Because geographic differences exist, obtaining large-scale insights into the prevalence of different road types and their quality would enable a manufacturer to tailor a new vehicle to the expected conditions in its target market. The gold standard for assessing road roughness is the International Roughness Index (IRI) [29]. Unfortunately, the IRI must be computed using high-end laser sensors [29] which are impossible to include in production vehicles because they are too fragile and expensive. However, validating our methodology requires estimating the road-roughness for the real-world usage data. Since a laser system cannot be used for long-term measurements, we opt for a road roughness KPI derived from a temporarily installed high-end accelerometer [1]. Typically, it is only feasible to use such a sensor in development tests or a low-end end variant of luxury cars with active suspension systems. For the majority of the cars, this is not the case.

We hypothesize that:

1. using the low-end sensors typically included in production vehicles will permit accurately assessing the road roughness;
2. incorporating a rejector will result in better performance than just using a predictor while still maintaining acceptable coverage; and
3. analyzing the rejected segments will give insights into novel road types encountered during daily vehicle usage.

5.1   Data Collection and Preprocessing

We collected two datasets using the same vehicle, a controlled data set and a real-world data set. The former contains ground truth data obtained by driving at predefined speeds over Belgium's three most common road types: smooth asphalt, rough asphalt, and concrete slabs. Additionally, we also measured the car while it was idling. Table 1 shows the details about the controlled data along with the observed road roughness for each road type. The real-world data set contains data arising from natural driving behavior collected over a period of 23 months. During this period, the vehicle was used for daily travel by 39 volunteer drivers for over 20 000 kilometers, mainly on Belgian roads. To anonymize the data, we did not save driver names and removed data points within a radius of 400m $+rand(100m, 200m)$ of each trip's start and end locations.

In both settings, the same data was measured. First, a high-end DC accelerometer[1] was mounted on the front wheel hub (Fig. 1) and sampled 2048 Hz to derive the true road-roughness. To remove the low-frequent sensor drift due to the data acquisition system, we used a high-pass filter 1 Hz. Second, 16 low-end sensors were measured through the vehicle's Controller Area Network (CAN) bus with a sample-and-hold approach 200 Hz. Table 2 provides a full overview of the sensors and their quantities. Finally, we acquired the vehicle's location through a GPS antenna for documentation purposes.

We process the high-end accelerometer data and low-end control system data in consecutive, non-overlapping, 1-second windows. In each window, we derive the true road-roughness from the high-end accelerometer and extract the 21 statistical features listed in Table 3 for each of the 15 low-end sensors, which yields 315 features. Each feature is normalized using an outlier-robust scaler $(X - P_{50\%}(X_{train})/P_{75\%}(X_{train}) - P_{25\%}(X_{train}))$, where P_X corresponds to the X'th percentile.

Fig. 1. We instrumented the front wheel hub with a high-end accelerometer in order to derive the true road-roughness.

Table 1. The predefined speeds and road types the controlled data set was collected on. For each category, we indicate its size by total measurement time and indicate its 95-th percentile ($P_{95\%}$) of the true road roughness.

Scenario	Vehicle speeds (km/h)	Time (s)	$P_{95\%}$ (Road roughness)
Smooth asphalt	30, 40, ..., 100	467	0.047
Rough asphalt	30, 40, ..., 100	386	0.190
Concrete	30, 40, 50	272	0.334
Car idle	0	415	0.002

---

[1] PCB 3713B11200G.

Table 2. The 15 low-end sensors used to estimate the road-roughness

Sensor	Unit	Sensor	Unit
Vehicle speed	Km/h	Total vehicle acceleration	m/s^2
Yaw	Rpm	Low-end accelerometer	*Unknown*
Wheel propulsion torque	Nm	Gear indicator	Gear
Angle steering wheel	Degrees	Rotational speed front right wheel	Rpm
Tortion bar torque	Nm	Rotational speed front left wheel	Rpm
Speed limit	*Unknown*	Rotational speed rear right wheel	Rpm
Lateral accelerations	m/s^2	Rotational speed rear left wheel	Rpm
Longitudinal accelerations	m/s^2		

Table 3. The 21 statistical features extracted from each of the low-end sensors

Feature	Formula	Feature	Formula
Amplitude	$max(X) - min(X)$	Maximum	$max(X)$
Crest factor	$\frac{max(|X-\overline{X}|)}{rms(X)}$	Extremum	$max(|X|)$
Extreme deviation	$max(\frac{max(X)-\overline{X}}{std(X)}, \frac{X-min(X)}{std(X)})$	Median	$\tilde{X}$
Integration	$\sum_{i=1}^{n} \frac{f(x_{i-1})+f(x_i)}{2} \Delta x_i$ with $\Delta x_i = 1$	Minimum	$min(X)$
Kurtosis	$\frac{(X-\overline{X})^4}{std(X)^4}$	Percentile 10	$P_{10\%}(X)$
Markov regression	$\frac{R(1)}{R(0)}$ with $R(0) = \sum_{i=0}^{n-1} x_i^2$ and $R(1) = \sum_{i=0}^{n-2}(x_i x_{i+1}) + x_0 x_{n-1}$	Percentile 25	$P_{25\%}(X)$
Mean	$\overline{X} = \frac{1}{n}\sum_{i=1}^{n} x_1$	Percentile 75	$P_{75\%}(X)$
Skewness	$\frac{m_3}{m_2^{\frac{3}{2}}}$ with $m_j = (X-\overline{X})^j$	Percentile 90	$P_{90\%}(X)$
Standard deviation	$\sqrt{variance(X)}$	RMS	$\sqrt{\overline{X^2}}$
Sum	$\sum_{i=1}^{n} x_i$	Avg. abs. deviation	$\overline{|X-\overline{X}|}$
Variance	$|X-\overline{X}|^2$		

5.2   Experimental Methodology

The predictor is a regressor for road-roughness estimation. The rejector is a novelty detector that indicates when to abstain from predicting the roughness. Both algorithms are trained on the data collected in the controlled setting. We evaluate performance on the controlled data using ten-fold cross-validation.

Predictor. On the controlled data set we evaluated six different regression models as shown in Table 4. Since this work's main focus is on the rejection component, we opt for the predictor's default parameters as selected in Scikit Learn [25] shows. For the real-world analysis, we focus on the two best performing models: Random Forest (RF) and XGBoost.

Rejector. We study two types of novelty detectors that require limited a-priori knowledge about the data distributions:

1. OCSVM, which is a domain-based method that attempts to model the training data's boundary. We use a RBF kernel with $\nu = 0.005$ and $\gamma = 0.1$.
2. kNNO, which is a distance-based method that attempts to capture the training set's density. We set $k = 10$ and use the Euclidean distance.

To limit the dimensionality of data, the rejector only considers the chosen predictor's 10 top-ranked features. These were determined using the Gini importance metric for RF and the average gain across all splits the feature for XGBoost.

5.3   Results

Figure 2 shows how the Mean Absolute Error (MAE) varies as a function of coverage on the real-world data. We compare each predictor/rejector model with a standard learned model that makes a prediction for every sample. Additionally, for the predictor/rejector model, we show the MAE on the rejected samples to provide insights into the relationship between novelty scores and prediction errors.

Table 4. The performance of six different regression models on the controlled data set as determined by ten fold cross validation.

Predictor	R^2	Mean absolute error	Mean squared error
Random Forest	0.5627	0.0258	0.0028
XGBoost	0.5435	0.0304	0.0029
Regression Tree	0.2800	0.0338	0.0046
k-Nearest Neighbors Regressor	−0.0203	0.0506	0.0065
Linear Regression	−0.1287	0.0612	0.0072
Support Vector Regressor	−0.2429	0.0717	0.0079

Hypothesis 1: Low-end sensors permit accessing the road roughness.
The standard model that always makes a prediction obtains a MAE of around 0.05 for both XGBoost and RF. Given that the road roughness scores lie between 0 and 0.334 in the controlled data, this performance is sufficient to distinguish among the most common road types as well as capture variation within a single road type.

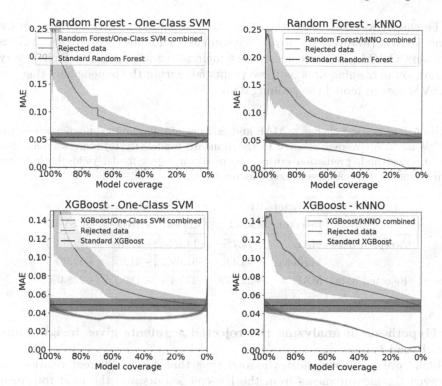

Fig. 2. Each plot shows the MAE (solid line) and error variance (band around MAE) of a standard model that always makes a prediction (black) and a specific predictor/rejector combination (blue) as a function of coverage. The combined predictor/rejector model always outperforms the standard model. Evaluating the MAE of rejected samples (red) shows that the model makes bigger mistakes on the most novel samples, implying a relationship between the rejector's novelty score and the magnitude of the error in a prediction. (Color figure online)

Hypothesis 2: Incorporating a rejector results in better performance, while maintaining an acceptable coverage.

The results show that our proposed predictor/rejector combinations outperform the standard learned model that always makes a prediction. This holds even when they only abstain from making a prediction for a relatively small fraction of the data. In aggregate, (much) larger errors are made on the rejected samples. For example, without making claims about the model's optimal coverage which is application dependent, Table 5 shows that abstaining from making a prediction on the top 5% most novel samples reduces the model's MAE by between 10% and 15%. The MAE on the rejected samples is up to 275% higher than the MAE on the standard learned model. Our approach is also more robust as it yields lower variances on the prediction errors. Compared to the standard model, this reduces the variance by up to 53%. The improved performance and robustness will increase users' trust and confidence in the model.

For high coverages, using the OCSVM as the novelty detector outperforms using kNNO. However, its advantage diminishes for lower coverages. This is because OCSVM novelty scores are not informative when a test sample is very similar to the training data as these points fall within the hypersphere that the OCSVM uses to model the training data.

Table 5. The percent change in MAE and variance of the combined predictor/rejector models for 95% coverage relative to the standard model. By rejecting samples that tend to yield high prediction errors, the predictor/reject model yields both better performance and robustness, thereby increasing trust.

	Predictor	RF		XGBoost	
	Rejector	kNNO	OCSVM	kNNO	OCSVM
Accepted data	MAE	−11.7%	−14.5%	−9.9%	−12.0%
	Variance	−43.4%	−52.6%	−31.2%	−52.0%
Rejected data	MAE	+221.7%	+275.4%	+180.7%	+228.0%

Hypothesis 3: analyzing the rejected segments gives insights into novel road types.

A high novelty score indicates a road type that has a different relationship between the measurements from the low-end sensors and the road roughness than was observed in the training data. Indeed, inspecting the road types that receive high novelty scores reveals that these differ substantially from the road types included in the controlled data test. For example, within the top 1% most novel samples, we observe several novel road types such as those shown in Fig. 3.

The MAE on the rejected samples shows that there is a correlation between the magnitude of the predictor's errors and the novelty scores. Larger errors are made on those samples with the highest novelty scores. Lowering the model's coverage monotonically decreases the MAE on the rejected samples. Note that there is high variability in the MAE for coverages close to 100% as only very few samples are rejected in this region.

Fig. 3. Analyzing the samples identified as being most novel shows that our methodology finds novel road types. Our results highlight road types such as cobblestones (left [12]), gravel roads (middle [12]), and road gutters (right [12]).

5.4   Discussion and Lessons Learned

Our approach offers the capability to abstain from estimating the roughness in novel road conditions, which has three benefits to such analysis. First, automatically detecting and declining to make predictions on samples that deviate from the controlled data yields a more robust and better-performing machine learning model. Consequently, this leads to better insights about expected vehicle usage. If such insights are more accurate and reliable, this results in better vehicle designs and development tests. Second, analyzing the rejected samples offers additional insights, such as identifying road types that are not currently considered in vehicle tests. If a novel road type is frequently encountered in the real-world scenario, this indicates it could be useful to include it in future testing protocols. As we find novelty scores are correlated with the estimation errors, it is easy to prioritize analyzing novel road types based on their prevalence.

More generally, we highlight the lessons learned from this use case:

- **Do not underestimate the challenges of collecting real data.** First, even for a vehicle shared by multiple drivers, the data set needs to be adequately anonymized such that it does not include any personal information. Second, a long-term measurement setup requires regular maintenance and data integrity checks. For example, these checks allowed us to quickly identify issues such as cables being bit by a marten. Interestingly, our methodology assigned high novelty scores to samples where the vehicle's control system produced incorrect measurements, which allowed us to identify the issue and clean the data set.
- **Domain knowledge is crucial.** While it is appealing to design a fully automated analysis pipeline with machine learning, we found that is generally better to combine automation with engineering insights. First, automated feature selection identified the fuel level indicator sensor as being highly predictive of the road-roughness estimate. Human reasoning helped to identify this as a quirk of the data collection process. The controlled data was collected sequentially per road type without refueling. Second, understanding the sensors allowed us to identify and optimally remove the drift in the measurements of the high-end accelerometer without losing informative data.
- **Models with a reject option have significant potential for use-cases where trust is important.** Rejection provides more context and transparency about how the learned model will behave as the user will know that the model will abstain from making predictions in novel scenarios. For example, this technology can aid autonomous driving systems by allowing them to return control to the driver by recognizing atypical or previously unencountered scenarios.

6   Conclusion

Machine learning with rejection helps to overcome several challenges in vehicle engineering. Enabling machine learning usage to estimate KPIs facilitates scalable usage profiling setups, requiring less or no high-end sensors, and scalable usage profiling analysis, requiring less engineering effort. Additionally, our methodology is more robust to novel vehicle usage, which can enhance the users' trust in the data-driven decision-making process. Finally, its capability to identify novel vehicle usage helps to better align production vehicles with the customer's expectations and actual usage: insights derived from this identification can result in new vehicle requirements or design changes. To summarize, these benefits give better insights into vehicle usage, which helps a manufacturer to optimally design and validate new vehicle models.

We validated our methodology in a road-roughness analysis study. Our results show that this approach returns more robust and accurate estimates of the road-roughness KPI. Interestingly, rejecting only a small fraction of the data already results in drastic improvements, we find a clear relationship between the rejector's novelty score and the roughness estimation error.

Acknowledgments. KH is funded by VLAIO (Flemish Innovation & Entrepreneurship) through the Baekeland Ph.D. mandate [nr. HBC.2017.0226]. JD is partially supported by the KU Leuven research funds [C14/17/070]. JD and WM received funding from the Flemish Government under the "Onderzoeksprogramma Artificiële Intelligentie (AI) Vlaanderen" programme. The authors have no conflict of interest to declare.

References

1. Alessandroni, G., et al.: SmartRoadSense: collaborative road surface condition monitoring. In: UBICOMM 2014, pp. 210–215. Rome, Italy (2014)
2. Balakrishnan, S., Anoop, P.P., Kharul, R.V., Sasun, C.: Accurate estimation of time histories for improved durability prediction using artificial neural networks. In: SAE Technical Paper, April 2012
3. Coenen, L., Abdullah, A.K., Guns, T.: Probability of default estimation, with a reject option. In: 7th International Conference on Data Science and Advanced Analytics (DSAA), pp. 439–448, October 2020
4. Cordella, L.P., De Stefano, C., Sansone, C., Vento, M.: An adaptive reject option for LVQ classifiers. In: Braccini, C., DeFloriani, L., Vernazza, G. (eds.) ICIAP 1995. LNCS, vol. 974, pp. 68–73. Springer, Heidelberg (1995). https://doi.org/10.1007/3-540-60298-4_238
5. Cordella, L., De Stefano, C., Tortorella, F., Vento, M.: A method for improving classification reliability of multilayer perceptrons. IEEE Trans. Neural Networks **6**(5), 1140–1147 (1995)
6. Cortes, C., DeSalvo, G., Mohri, M.: Learning with rejection. In: 27th International Conference on Algorithmic Learning Theory (ALT), Bari, Italy (2016)
7. Denis, C., Hebiri, M., Zaoui, A.: Regression with reject option and application to kNN. In: Advances in Neural Information Processing Systems (2020)
8. Dodds Colin, J.: Structural testing of complete vehicles, aggregates and components in the laboratory, The Test Engineer's Handbook, 2 edn. (2012)
9. Dübuisson, B., Usai, M., Malvache, P.: Computer aided system diagnostic with an incomplete learning set. Progress Nuclear Energy **15**(C), 875–880 (1985)

10. G. Willén, R., Großkopf, M., Streicher, S., Allouch, R., Heim, T.M.: Fokus Internationalisierung: Herausforderungen in der Definition der Lastdaten für Nutzfahrzeuge. In: Tagung des DVM-Arbeitskreises Betriebsfestigkeit, Ingolstadt, Germany (2014)
11. Gnamm, J., Lundgren, J., Stricker, K., Nilvall, M.: Winning in Europe: truck strategies for the next decade, September 2012
12. Google Street View
13. Halfpenny, A.: Methods for accelerating dynamic durability tests. In: 9th International Conference on Recent Advances in Structural Dynamics, Southampton, UK (2006)
14. Hamid, A.F.A., et al.: Connected car: Engines diagnostic via Internet of Things (IoT). J. Phys. Conf. Series **908**(1), October 2017
15. Hammer, B., Klem, A.: Fahrzeugauslegung als Spagat zwischen Leichtbau und Produkthaftung. In: Tagung des DVM-Arbeitskreises Betriebsfestigkeit, Ingolstadt, Germany (2014)
16. Hanczar, B., Sebag, M.: Combination of one-class support vector machines for classification with reject option. In: Calders, T., Esposito, F., Hüllermeier, E., Meo, R. (eds.) ECML PKDD 2014. LNCS (LNAI), vol. 8724, pp. 547–562. Springer, Heidelberg (2014). https://doi.org/10.1007/978-3-662-44848-9_35
17. Hendrickx, K., Perini, L., Van der Plas, D., Meert, W., Davis, J.: Machine learning with a reject option: a survey (2021). http://arxiv.org/abs/2107.11277
18. Homenda, W., Luckner, M., Pedrycz, W.: Classification with rejection based on various SVM techniques. In: International Joint Conference on Neural Networks (IJCNN), pp. 3480–3487, July 2014
19. Hüllermeier, E., Waegeman, W.: Aleatoric and epistemic uncertainty in machine learning: an introduction to concepts and methods. Mach. Learn. **110**(3), 457–506 (2021). https://doi.org/10.1007/s10994-021-05946-3
20. Landgrebe, T.C., Tax, D.M., Paclík, P., Duin, R.P., Andrew, C.: A combining strategy for ill-defined problems. In: 15th Annual Symposium of the Pattern Recognition Association of South Africa, pp. 57–62 (2004)
21. Ludanek, H., Bremer, G.: Herausforderungen an die Betriebsfestigkeit zukünftiger Automobilentwicklungen. In: Tagung des DVM-Arbeitskreises Betriebsfestigkeit, Wolfsburg, Germany (2007)
22. Luo, H., Huang, M., Xiong, W.: Application of a recurrent neural network and simplified semianalytical method for continuous strain histories estimation. Shock. Vib. **2019**, 7289314 (2019)
23. Markets and Markets: Connected Car Market by Service - Global Forecast to 2025. Technical report, Markets and Markets (2020)
24. P, P.K., J, P., Palanisamy, K.: Optimization of Proving Ground Durability Test Sequence Based on Relative Damage Spectrum. In: SAE Technical Paper (2018)
25. Pedregosa, F., et al.: Scikit-learn: machine learning in python. J. Mach. Learn. Res. **12**(85), 2825–2830 (2011)
26. Pimentel, M.A.F., Clifton, D.A., Clifton, L., Tarassenko, L.: A review of novelty detection. Signal Process. **99**, 215–249 (2014)
27. Pudil, P., Novovičova, J., Bláha, S., Kittler, J.: Multistage pattern recognition with reject option. In: Conference on Pattern Recognition, vol. 2, pp. 92–95 (1992)
28. Rupp, A., Masieri, A., Dornbusch, T.: Durability transfer concept for the monitoring of the load and stress conditions on vehicles. In: Innovative Automotive Technology IAT, pp. 31–39, Bled, Slovenia (2005)
29. Sayers, M.W., Karamihas, S.M.: The little book of profiling. Michigan (1998)

30. Städele, M., Rupp, A., Willén, G., Romann, P., Streicher, M.: Ableitung der Beanspruchungs- und Lastzeitfolgen aus Referenzgrößen bei Langzeitmessungen an Nutzfahrzeugen. In: 41. Tagung des DVM-Arbeitskreises Betriebsfestigkeit, Ingolstadt, Germany (2014)
31. Stricker, K., Wegener, R., Anding, M.: Big Data revolutioniert die Automobilindustrie (2014)
32. Varshney, K.R.: On Mismatched Detection and Safe, Trustworthy Machine Learning. In: 54th Annual Conference on Information Sciences and Systems (CISS), pp. 2019–2022, Princeton, NJ, USA (2020)
33. Vasconcelos, G., Fairhurst, M., Bisset, D.: Enhanced reliability of multilayer perceptron networks through controlled pattern rejection. Electron. Lett. **29**(3), 261 (1993)
34. Winterling, H., Teutsch, R., R. Müller, C.W.: Ableitung Einsatzspezifischer Fahrprogramme für die Betriebsfestigkeitserprobung schwerer Nutzfahrzeuge - Beispiel Baustellensegment. In: 41. Tagung des DVM- Arbeitskreises Betriebsfestigkeit. Ingolstadt, Germany (2014)
35. Zou, C., Zheng, E.h., Xu, H.w., Chen, L.: Cost-sensitive Multi-class SVM with reject option: a method for steam turbine generator fault diagnosis. Int. J. Comput. Theory Eng. **3**(1), 77–83 (2011)

Towards Generalizable Machinery Prognostics

Cahit Bağdelen[1,3]([✉]), Heiko Paulheim[1], Markus Döhring[2],
and Atreju Florian Tauschinsky[3]

[1] University of Mannheim, Mannheim, Germany
{cahit,heiko}@informatik.uni-mannheim.de
[2] Darmstadt University of Applied Sciences, Darmstadt, Germany
markus.doehring@h-da.de
[3] SAP SE, Walldorf, Germany
{cahit.bagdelen,atreju.florian.tauschinsky}@sap.com

Abstract. In recent scientific work, a classification-based approach to
the machinery prognostics problem has been elaborated as an alternative to the Remaining Useful Life approaches. The classification-based
approaches rely on a *prediction horizon* parameter, to which the model
quality is sensitive. However, existing studies do not provide any means of
determining this critical parameter. Instead, they rely on assumptions.
We argue that the *prediction horizon* should be learned from data in
order to overcome the challenges of its uncertainty. We propose a heuristic algorithm to learn the *prediction horizon* from data, as the first of its
kind in the literature. We test its effectiveness with an ablation study
based on a rich set of data. The results indicate a statistically significant improvement in model quality. This in turn increases the usability
and generalizability of classification-based failure prediction approaches
in the industry.

Keywords: Data-driven prognostics · Prediction horizon ·
Multivariate time series · Binary classification · Semi-supervised
anomaly detection

1 Introduction

Predicting faults or failures in advance is a central aspect of *condition-based
maintenance* programs. Such predictive capabilities are highly desired by the
operators of mission critical machinery to avoid unnecessary maintenance, while
ensuring reliability [12].

As an emerging type of such predictions, researchers and practitioners
recently tried to associate patterns in *condition monitoring (CM)* data with the
precursors of the failure events using classification-based approaches [10,14,15,

Supported by SAP SE, Walldorf, Germany.

© Springer Nature Switzerland AG 2022
B. Li et al. (Eds.): ADMA 2021, LNAI 13087, pp. 289–306, 2022.
https://doi.org/10.1007/978-3-030-95405-5_21

21,23]. Such approaches to the problem, which we call *Incipient Failure Prediction (IFP)*, are also being used in the industry as part of *predictive maintenance (PdM)* solutions [15,16].

A generalizable IFP approach, which does not depend on domain or machine specific knowledge, needs to consider two important parameters, namely the *warning time (wt)* and the *prediction horizon (ph)*, as explained in the next sections. Existing approaches are lacking any detailed discussion about these parameters and their implications. They rely on a *ph* which is assumed to be known [4,10,15,16,20,23].

In fact, selecting a suitable *ph* is a difficult decision for machine operators, since the value of *ph* also determines the positively labelled instances, i.e. positive windows, which need to include the patterns associated with the precursors of failures, and exclude every other instance, as much as possible. Hence, *ph* is primarily a property of data. Although machine operators can set some upper bounds for *ph*, it cannot be known by operational requirements.

The uncertainty of *ph* results in several problems: Firstly, any biased *ph* causes label noise. Secondly, evaluation and comparison of models, based on different *ph* values, becomes cumbersome, due to missing consensus on the ground truth. Lastly, an unknown *ph* avoids generalizability, as *ph* is a property of data, and a generalizable approach needs to provide a way of learning *ph* from data.

The contributions of this study are as follows:

1. We propose a generalizable approach to the IFP problem in Sect. 3. The Sect. 2 on the related work further contrasts this aspect and also provides a unique discussion of the place of IFP approaches in the big picture of data-driven machinery prognostics.
2. To avoid the dependency on machine-specific knowledge, we propose a heuristic algorithm for *ph* determination, as one component of our approach in Sect. 4.
3. The richness of the set of data sets is also unique in the related literature. The experimental method including data sets is described in Sect. 5.

We tested our approach with and without the *ph* determination component. The improvement in model quality, provided by the *ph* determination algorithm is statistically significant (Sect. 6). These results and the richness of the data sets provide stronger evidence for generalizability of the approach, compared to any existing study with generalizability concerns (Sect. 7).

2 Background and Related Work

Machinery prognostics aims at predicting faults or failures in advance. It includes predicting future conditions, the remaining operational (useful) life, probability of reliable operation of an equipment until some future time, and risk for one or more incipient failure modes [1,7,11,12].

In their remarkable review on diagnostics and prognostics, Jardine et al. consider two main types of predictions in machinery prognostic. Besides the most widely used Remaining Useful Life (RUL) prediction, they mention that: *In some situations, ..., it would be more desirable to predict the chance that a machine operates without a fault or a failure up to some future time (e.g., next inspection interval) given the current machine condition and past operation profile. Actually, in any situation, the probability that a machine operates without a fault until next inspection (or condition monitoring) interval could be a good reference for maintenance personnel to determine whether the inspection interval is appropriate or not* [12]. As one form of this second type of prediction, recent conference workshops have considered the question whether or not a failure is expected until a certain future time [15, 23]. Those models can also involve a notion of risk, if the evaluation and the objective (loss) function of the learning algorithm is based on cost measures, considering costs due to unexpected break downs, as well as costs due to unnecessary over maintenance and interference. Researchers predominantly reduce the prognosis problem to Remaining Useful Life (RUL) i.e. Estimated Time To Failure (ETTF) [18]. Studies considering alternative prediction types, are extremely few [10, 12, 14, 15, 20, 21, 23].

Irrespective of prediction types and problem formulations there are several different approaches to prognostics in the literature. Unlike model-based approaches, data-driven methods do not rely on any known mathematical model of the degradation process, instead, an implicit degradation model of the faulty system is learned from data. Data-driven methods typically depend on one or few degradation signals, known through domain experts. A *degradation signal* is defined to be a quantity, calculated based on condition monitoring (CM) data which *captures the current state of the device and provides information on how that condition is likely to evolve in the future* [9].

According to the type of this dependence, Si et al. further group data-driven methods into two subcategories: (1) Methods based on direct degradation signals, versus (2) Methods based on indirect degradation signals. Examples of the former are wear and crack sizes, when they are observable. And prognosis is nothing but predicting the remaining time until this degradation signal jumps over the predefined (failure) threshold which is machine-specific. In the latter case, CM data such as vibration data, oil conditions or other sensor readings indicate the underlying state indirectly [19].

There are studies which could be considered as a third subcategory, where (3) the degradation information is implicitly inherent in CM data, but there exist no known direct or indirect degradation signals. In such cases, especially for multi-component systems, for which possibly hundreds of different sensor readings are recorded, the CM data can still potentially and implicitly bear prognostics relevant information. For such systems, researchers and practitioners recently tried to associate patterns in CM data with the precursors of the failures, by utilizing historical failure event data, besides the CM data [4, 6, 10, 15, 20, 23, 25].

These approaches do not try to learn the degradation process up to the failure time based on an explicit degradation signal, but they either predict the RUL without identifying degradation signals [6, 25], or they predict whether or not a failure (mode) is expected within a given *ph* using classification-based approaches [4, 10, 15, 20, 23].

This type of prediction needs alternative handling during the post-prognostic decision steps [2]. Complementary studies exist addressing the question how to best utilize classification-based predictions, during the post prognostic decision steps. For instance, Susto et al. proposed an appropriate maintenance strategy based on a *multiple classifier approach*, in *condition-based maintenance* context. They train multiple classifiers based on different *ph* values [21].

To the best of our knowledge, none of the studies provide a means of determining *ph*, instead, they either assume a specific *ph* value to be known [4, 10, 15, 20, 23] or they train multiple classification models based on multiple *ph* values, and try to combine those [10, 21].

On the one hand, *ph* and *wt* determine labeling, where a $|wt|$ time period is excluded from training data; on the other hand, they affect interpretation of the prediction, as described in Sect. 3. Weiss and Hirsh have discussed *warning time* only for the interpretation of the predictions, but in a different context [24]. Wang briefly mentioned ignoring (excluding) a certain time window before the failure from training data, without naming it [23]. Existing IFP approaches are lacking a detailed discussion of these parameters and their implications in the learning task as well as in the usability of the learned models in practice. This can be due to the machine specific contexts of existing IFP approaches.

Also RUL approaches have been developed in machine-specific contexts [12, 18]. As an exception Zhou et al. considered generalizability of their RUL approach in [25], but they tested insufficiently on only two different machine data. Therefore, the extensively tested generalizability aspect is unique in the overall literature of data-driven machinery prognostics, to the best of our knowledge.

3   A Generic Approach to Incipient Failure Prediction

The IFP problem is about learning patterns or anomalies associated with the precursors of known historical failures, and inferring incipient failures within a specified time span. The problem can be modeled as a binary classification, where the classifier learns a model for a specific *prediction horizon* (*ph*). A positive prediction implies that an incipient failure is expected during the span of the *ph* (Fig. 1).

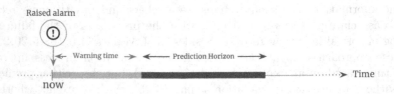

Fig. 1. Inference with respect to $|wt|$ and $|ph|$

When a predictive maintenance solution raises an alert [16] machine operators need to react with a maintenance operation, for which they need a *warning time* (*wt*). For instance, for $wt = 2\ days$ and $ph = 13\ days$ a raised alarm would be interpreted as *an increased probability of failure within 2 to 15 days* (Fig. 1).

Making a prediction just before a failure event may be accurate, but unusable, since a *wt* is required for a proper action [24]. In PdM context a proper action could be an inspection, necessary operational measures, planning maintenance or in some cases procurement of spare parts. Accordingly, when training and validating an algorithm on different subsets of historical data, we exclude a certain time period of length $|wt|$. This prevents the algorithm from learning from possibly quite strong signals shortly before the failure, and imposes learning to be based on earlier precursors.

The value of *wt* depends on the operational requirements and preferences of the PdM, and can be specified by the machine operators by answering the following question: *How much time do we need in order to react to a true positive failure prediction?*

Note that, besides the time point of the alert, the *length of the warning time* ($|wt|$) is enough to determine the beginning of the critical period. As far as inference time is considered, the maintenance operations management is primarily interested in the extent of *wt*, and not in that of *ph*. In other words, the beginning of the *ph* is primarily important for operations, as they should react before the beginning of *ph*. As long as the *ph* ends before the next planned maintenance the *length of the prediction horizon* ($|ph|$) is not critical for the maintenance operations.

However, *ph* is a very significant parameter for the learning task, since it also affects the labeling. In Fig. 2 we now look at the historical data. In this case the time window marked in red is in the past, and we name it *positive window* (*pw*), nevertheless $|pw| = |ph|$.

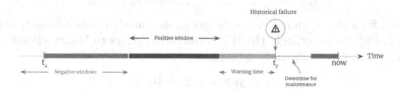

Fig. 2. Labeling with respect to $|wt|$ and $|ph|$ (Color figure online)

The time period $[t_0,\ t_F)$ in Fig. 2 is called a *run to failure* (RTF) sequence. At time stamp t_0 the machine is in a healthy state. Later in the RTF sequence a faulty state starts, (which may be unobservable without an intrusive inspection). And eventually the faulty state evolves into a failure event at time stamp t_F [12].

For each RTF sequence in the historical data, we perform the labeling based on *ph* and *wt* as follows:

$$x_t \mapsto \begin{cases} 0, & \text{if } t \in [t_0,\ t_F - |wt| - |ph|) \\ 1, & \text{if } t \in [t_F - wt - ph,\ t_F - wt) \end{cases} \tag{1}$$

Unlike wt, selection of a suitable ph is a difficult decision for operations management, although certain constraints can be specified based on maintenance operational requirements. The time until the next relevant planned maintenance can provide a good upper bound for the ph. The other way around, the given (or learned) ph can also help the operations to align regular inspection intervals according to $|ph|$, as suggested by Jardine et al. [12]. In PdM, regular inspections are performed in addition to inspections triggered by failure predictions.

As for most data-driven machinery prognostics problem formulations, the main input to IFP is the condition monitoring data which in general consists of time series of sensor readings, as well as other categorical variables such as operation mode. The prediction target is implicitly determined by the failure event data [12,19]. We will consider the input as multivariate time series (MvTS) of numerical data, since the categorical variables can also be encoded as such.

For the simplicity of the notation, we assume equidistant time series, where the time stamps of different series are synchronized so that the time stamp does not need to be noted explicitly as an additional variable, but it implicitly determines the order of the values within series as well as synchronization of values across series. Nevertheless, the below discussed arguments can easily be generalized for non-equidistant time series data. Accordingly, the input consists of n series, i.e. it consists of $n \times T$ variables:

$$X = \{X^0, X^1, ..., X^{n-1}\} \ where \ X^j \in \mathbb{R}^T \tag{2}$$

Each series X^j corresponds to an equidistant time series from a different channel such as a specific sensor's readings, consisting of measurements at T time stamps, unless otherwise is explicitly stated:

$$X^j = \{x_0^j, x_1^j, ..., x_{T-1}^j\} \ where \ x_t^j \in \mathbb{R} \tag{3}$$

Considering a specific time point t the input is denoted as:

$$x_t = \{x_t^0, x_t^1, ..., x_t^{n-1}\} \ where \ x_t \in \mathbb{R}^n \tag{4}$$

When focusing on an individual failure mode, binary labels are used, as illustrated in Fig. 2. Accordingly the IFP formulation refers to binary classification or (semi-) supervised anomaly detection:

$$x_t \mapsto y_t \ where \ y_t \in \{0, 1\} \tag{5}$$

By default we use aggregated values for x_t^j over a history window Δh. The aggregated multivariate point at each time stamp constitutes an individual input instance for classification. Aggregation is used in order to represent or summarize some of the time series characteristics at instance level, and to let representation at time stamp instance level.

Note that, IFP is not about classifying whole time series, but classifying the state of the machine at given time stamp, considering a history window of Δh.

Although for simplicity we notate it with reference to time point t, each x_t^j is an aggregation of one or more raw sensor readings over the time window $(t - \Delta h, t]$. For instance using *mean* as the aggregation function, based on a raw series R^j:

$$x_t^j = \sum_{i=t-\Delta h+1}^{t} (r_i^j) \, / \, |\Delta h| \qquad (6)$$

In general, any aggregation function can be used, the aggregation can include one or more raw features, and the aggregation can use sliding windows as well as disjoint windows. If disjoint windowing is used with a history window of Δh, the dimensionality is also reduced from $n_0 \times T_0$ to approximately $n_0 \times (T_0/\Delta h)$ as a side effect of aggregation, where T_0 represents the number of measurements (sensor readings) during the complete time span of the series. Similarly, if m different aggregated features (e.g. mean, std.deviation, etc.) are calculated per raw feature, the eventual dimensionality would be $n \times T = (n_0 * m) \times (T_0/\Delta h)$.

If we include the aggregation preprocessing into the above mapping, in terms of raw features Eq. 5 can be rewritten as:

$$f(r_{t-\Delta h+1}, .., r_t) \mapsto y_t \text{ where } y_t \in \{0, 1\} \qquad (7)$$

We use xgboost implementation of gradient boosting to train the binary classification model. Besides its proven performance in recent competitions it is able to provide feature importance information [3]. This provides explainability and enables domain experts to interact with our generic approach. We use hyper-parameter tuning to tune the boosting parameters. In the basic version of our approach also the ph parameter is tuned.

4   Learning the Prediction Horizon

The ph should ideally not be handled like an ordinary hyper-parameter, due to discussed issues. From a practical point of view, the ph usually ranges from a few hours up to several weeks. The range is too large to try a brute-force search, as the training needs to be repeated for each possible ph value.

The sensitivity of model quality to ph value can be seen in Fig. 3, where we have used the *Kaggle water pump* data set to illustrate this point.

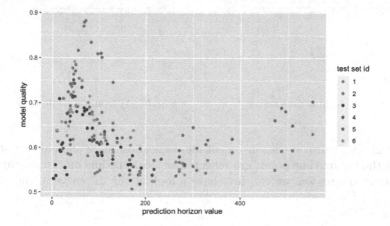

Fig. 3. Sensitivity of model quality to prediction horizon

The sample plot shows model quality (y axis) for different *ph* values (x axis) on different test sets (color-coded). For each test set 30 *ph* values are plotted, since training and testing for all possible *ph* values would take too long. Note that in some regions, for certain test sets small changes in the *ph* affect the resultant model's quality dramatically. Note also that different local maxima are observable.

With Algorithm 1 we propose a heuristic algorithm that iteratively searches for good *ph* candidates, based on two main pieces of information:

– *Set of important features* (S_j), learned by the model in a previous iteration,
– an *Array of distances* (Δ^j), for the features in S_j, as explained below.

We group each RTF sequence $[t_0, t_F)$ into 2 phases, separated at each possible cutoff value (c), illustrated with the blue vertical line in Fig. 4:

$$\{phase_{c,1}, phase_{c,2}\} = \{[t_0, c), [c, t_F)\} \tag{8}$$

Let $\delta_{f,c}$ be the Wasserstein distance between *relative frequency distributions (RFDs)* for the two phases of a single feature f and given c.

$$\delta_{f,c} \leftarrow |RFD_{f,c,1} - RFD_{f,c,2}| \tag{9}$$

$$\Delta^j_c \leftarrow \sum_{f \in S_j} (\delta_{f,c}) / n \tag{10}$$

For given c, the Δ^j_c gives the average of $\delta_{f,c}$ distances, considering all features of the given subset (S_j). And Δ^j represents the array of average distances for all possible cutoff (c) values.

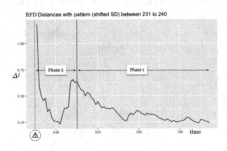 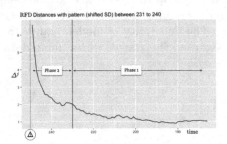

Fig. 4. δ_f from a time series   **Fig. 5.** Δj from multiple time series

The Δ^j curve provides a convenient representation, since anomalous patterns, close to the failure time point, are reflected as local maxima on the Δ^j curve. To understand the reason, we can first have a look at the Δ^j curve in the absence of such anomalous patterns in data. Without any anomalous subsequence, Δ^j is expected to decrease monotonically in the first half of the (reversed) time series, for decreasing time stamps, if we ignore the smaller increases due to noise. This is because a shorter $phase_2$ period leads to less diverse values during that period in terms of frequency distribution. A less diverse $phase_2$ is expected to be dissimilar to $phase_1$ in terms of RFDs. This in turn leads to greater distance between $RFD_{f,c,1}$ and $RFD_{f,c,2}$.

Instead, when we move the cutoff to the right, diversity of $phase_2$ increases, which in turn leads to increased similarity of their RFDs, and obviously the distance between RFDs of both phases decreases. Therefore, on the reversed time scale, as we move from left to right, the general trend of Δ^j should be decreasing, in case no anomalous pattern (subsequence) exists in the time series.

The reason why we consider only the first half of a (reversed) RTF sequence is simple. In the middle of the RTF sequence, both phases have identical length. If we move the cutoff further to the right, $phase_1$ gets incrementally less diverse in terms of its relative frequency distribution. So, as we move further to the right, the distance between both RFDs start to increase in a general increasing trend, which is analogous to Δ^j's trend in the first half of the sequence. Fortunately, we are not interested in the second half, as we know that critical machinery has long RTF periods and the failure happens in the second half of the RTF sequence, i.e. in the first half of the reversed sequences. For the synthetic examples given in Fig. 4 and 5 we only plot the first half of the RTF, hence the general decreasing trend is observable.

An opposite (increasing) trend, which leads to a local peak, implies the existence of a pattern which is included in phase 2, but not in phase 1. An example of such local maxima is visible at $time = 232$ in Fig. 4.

The key task of searching possible ph candidates is about identifying such peaks on Δ^j curves from left to right, and selecting the cutoff values after such peaks. For such special cutoff values, the ph candidates can be simply determined since $|phase_2| = |ph| + |wt|$. Note that wt is a given operational parameter. In case the $|wt|$ time period is already excluded from training data during data preparation: $|phase_2| = |ph|$.

Figure 4 illustrates the effect of an anomalous pattern, close to the end of a single time series, on the δ_f. For illustrative purposes we use here a synthetic time series, which contains an anomalous pattern in time range (230, 240]. The red vertical line denotes the time point of failure (t_F). The blue line, to the right of the highest local maxima, denotes a convenient ph value. With this ph the positive window, between red and blue lines, would include the pattern.

Figure 5 illustrates the averaged distances Δ^j, based on several normally distributed time series. One of these series is the one in Fig. 4, which includes an anomalous pattern. The rest of the series are normally distributed without any anomalous patterns. As illustrated, a Δ^j curve is typically smoother than δ_f

curves based on individual features (f) i.e. individual time series, as different kinds of noise from multiple series get balanced by each other. This helps distinguishing relevant peaks.

In case of seasonality, we assume that the RTF period includes at least two complete seasons, such that cutting the time series in the middle gives two phases, which have similar RFDs. Obviously, the amount of noise, cumulated from unimportant features, can dominate and make the interesting patterns invisible if too many unimportant features are included. Fortunately, in the course of iterations of the algorithm, the unimportant features are iteratively eliminated from consideration so that the relevant peaks gets distinguishable, for an effective ph selection.

Exploiting these observations, the algorithm utilizes the Δ^j curve (i.e. array) based on multiple possibly important features, finds points to the right of the local maxima to propose ph candidates. As the feature importance evolves during the iterations, it comes up with better ph candidates, which improve the overall model quality.

In Algorithm 1, variable S refers to the set of important features and is initialized as the set of all features (Line 1). In the first 5 lines a $\delta_{f,c}$ is calculated for every feature f in the data set and for each c in the range of possible cutoff values C, w.r.t. the equality $|phase_2| = t_F - c = |ph| + |wt|$; and subject to possible operational constraints $PH_{lower} \leq |ph| \leq PH_{upper}$.

Algorithm 1. Heuristic algorithm for PH determination

1: $S_0 \leftarrow features$
2: **for** $f \in S_0$ **do**
3:     **for** $c \in C$ **do**
4:         $(RFD_{f,c,1}, RFD_{f,c,2}) \leftarrow getRFDs(X, f, c)$
5:         $\delta_{f,c} \leftarrow wasserstein(RFD_{f,c,1}, RFD_{f,c,2})$
6: $j \leftarrow 0$
7: **while** $converged = 0$ **do**
8:     $n \leftarrow |S_j|$ ▷ number of features in S[j]
9:     $\Delta^j \leftarrow \sum_{f \in S_j}(\delta_f) / n$
10:    $ph_j \leftarrow selectPromisingPH(\Delta^j)$
11:    $Y \leftarrow doLabel(X, ph_j)$ ▷ redo labeling w.r.t. ph[j]
12:    $(model_j, S'_j) \leftarrow binClassifier(X, Y)$
13:    $consistency_j \leftarrow |S'_j \cap S_j| / |S'_j \cup S_j|$
14:    $j \leftarrow j + 1$
15:    $S_j \leftarrow S'_{j-1}$
16:    $converged \leftarrow checkConvergence(j,$
17:                    $maxIter, model, consistency)$
18: $b \leftarrow \operatorname{argmax}_j(model.quality_j)$
19: $PH \leftarrow ph_b$

As of line 7 the main iterations start. Within each iteration, Δ^j is calculated (Line 9); and c value to the right of most promising local peak is determined, which in turn gives the jth ph candidate i.e. ph_j (Line 10). Based on ph_j relabeling is done (Line 11). Then a model is learned, using a classification algorithm, capable of providing a ranked list of important features such as xgboost [3].

The list of features (S'_j), contributing a given large portion of the gain, is extracted, besides the learned model (Line 12). Then, model consistency is determined (Line 13), as one of the possible criteria for early stopping or convergence (Line 16). At the end of the loop the iteration b, with the best model quality is selected (Line 18); and finally the ph value of that iteration (ph_b) is proposed (Line 19).

Getting δ_f arrays for each c (w.r.t. range of ph) requires calculating one-dimensional Wasserstein distances (first 5 lines), which is computationally much simpler than training a different model for each possible ph. Once δ_f arrays are calculated, getting Δ^j in Line 9 is an efficient matrix operation.

5 Ablation Study

To the best of our knowledge, so far no reproducible study has been performed on the IFP problem in the literature. We name our overall method the *Generic approach to Incipient Failure Prediction (GIFP)*. The same method excluding the ph determination component, can be called the *basic approach (BASE)*. To measure the contribution of the proposed ph determination component (given in Algorithm 1) we compared the GIFP to the BASE approach. The Null hypothesis assumes no significant difference between them, and hence no improvement by the ph determination algorithm:

- *H0: There exists no significant difference between model qualities of BASE and GIFP.*
- *H1: The proposed ph algorithm significantly improves model quality.*

To compare the performances of GIFP and BASE classifiers, across multiple data sets, the *paired t-test* is not applicable as the classifier performances on different data sets may not be normally distributed. Following Demšar's guidance [5] we used the non-parametric Wilcoxon signed ranks test. Unlike paired t-test, it does not assume normal distribution of classifier performances. All the requirements of Wilcoxon signed ranks test are met. Each pair of measurements is based on completely different data, and hence independent. We account for variability within each data set using nested cross validation.

We applied $5 \times n$ cross validation, where n denotes the number of folds for the inner loop, and 5 is the number of folds for the outer loop of the *cross validation (CV)*. Independent of data set, we select n to be a value around 5, trying to put equal number of RTF cycles in each fold. Both classifiers, namely GIFP and BASE, are trained, validated and tested on identical RTF sequences throughout the CV iterations. Both classifiers utilize hyper-parameter tuning via grid search, in the nested CV setup. The BASE approach treats the ph as an ordinary hyper parameter, whereas GIFP uses the ph determination algorithm. For each outer loop of the nested CV, GIFP calls the algorithm for 15 iterations, which proposes

15 *ph* values, from which the *ph* value providing the best model within the inner CV runs, is used when testing on the unseen test fold of the outer CV run. Similarly BASE makes 15 random *ph* selections within the identical nested CV setup. Since the *ph* selection is the only difference, if both classifiers by chance use the identical *ph* value in any iteration, they end up with the identical result.

Data Sets: We used seven different data sets to evaluate the proposed algorithm's performance. Three of them are multi-component CM data of RTF cycles. The first one is the C-MAPSS data set for turbofan engine degradation data, provided by NASA. This well known prognostics benchmark data consists of 21 sensor readings during several hundreds of RTF runs [17]. The second data set is the *Kaggle production plant (Pr. Plant)* data containing 25 sensor readings during 8 run to failure periods [22]. As the third set, the *Kaggle water pump (W. Pump)* data contains 52 sensor readings during 7 run to failure periods [13]. We used four further data sets, based on time series of sensor readings of different human exercise anomaly detection data. These are variants of the data sets used by the PBAD Study, where real human activity sensor data is synthetically combined in different proportions to simulate an anomalous pattern within the multivariate time series [8]. Each of these PBAD data sets, namely *Lunges vs. Side-lunges (Lun. Sid.)*, *Squats vs. Side-lunges (Sqt. Sid.)*, *Lunges vs. Squats (Lun. Sqt)*, *Lunges and Side-lunges vs Squats (LSid. Sqt.)*, contains 75 sensor readings. In our construction, the activity which is considered as anomaly makes up the 1% of the whole time series, and follows a longer period of normal activities. This makes the problem more challenging and simulates the rare character of the precursors of a failure in CM data sets.

Identical Preparation Across Data Sets: In order to show the generalizability of our approach, we did not apply data set specific feature engineering of any kind. Each aggregated feature depends on a single raw feature; using conventional time domain functions, namely median, standard deviation, min and max; based on disjoint windows for all experiments across all data sets. Nevertheless, in presence of domain experts, any specific time or frequency domain function, known to be effective, could be used to further improve the results of GIFP. Data preparation on each data set has been performed identically, with one exception. We reduced dimensionality of PBAD data sets using PCA which is a common practice for such human activity data sets. We have done this to reduce run time for both approaches, nevertheless the algorithm gives comparable results also using raw data. The normalization, handling of missing values, the applied aggregate functions, etc. are all identical across 7 data sets. As aggregation period we used one hour for all machinery data where time stamps are available, and a fraction of median number of cycles otherwise, independent of data set. When splitting into train, validation and test folds, we put the complete sequence of an RTF period in one of these folds as a whole, to avoid any dependency between these folds.

Window-Based Evaluation: The time points of input instances are determined by the frequency of time series of sensor readings which can e.g. be one per minute or second. Although for each input instance a prediction can be output, such a prediction frequency would be too high for the takt of operations, and machine operators would not be able to take necessary actions. For instance, several alerts within a few minutes are equivalent to a single alert. From a practical usability point of view an alert de-duplication is necessary, such that positive predictions are not repeated in the course of an appropriate time window. Also, for a fair evaluation, an appropriate window size is needed to count only the useful predictions, and not the duplicates within short intervals. The maintenance operational consideration is about the expected time to react to a false alert (*false positive*), e.g. to perform an inspection to falsify the alert. We call this parameter the *negative window size*. We assume that an inspection can either reveal the state of the machine, or at least it can assess whether or not the machine can function normally during the next $ph + wt$ time period. The question to be answered by machine operators would be: *How much time do we need in order to react to a false positive failure prediction, i.e. in order to inspect and falsify a positive prediction?* This is very similar to the wt question, but it only includes an inspection, and does not involve any further maintenance preparation or execution, since we consider only the false alerts here. Depending on the situation, *negative window (nw)* could be simply a fraction of the wt. Independent of data sets, GIFP uses default value of $nw = 0.5 * wt$, in the absence of information about the inspection time, and this default has been used for all data sets in this study. Consequently, for the complete negatively labeled period, we consider subsequent *negative windows* of equal size. For each *negative window*, if all predictions are negative it is considered as one *true negative*. Similarly, if there are one or more positive predictions it is considered as one *false positive*. On the other hand, each positively labeled sequence corresponds to a positive window of size ph, as mentioned in the labeling discussion above. A single positive prediction is enough to raise an alert. Accordingly, if there exist one or more positive prediction within a positive window, it is considered as one True Positive. If all predictions are negative it is considered as one *false negative*.

Evaluation Metric: We report multiple F_β scores, which considers *Recall* to be β times more important than the *Precision*. The appropriate value for β is data set specific. It depends on the degree of imbalance and the costs of different errors for the machine. IFP is an imbalanced problem, where positive instances are significantly in minority. *False negative* errors lead to unexpected break downs, and *false positive* errors lead to unnecessary inspection, interference or maintenance. The cost of *false negatives* is typically much higher than the cost of *false positives*. However, the proportion of these costs are unknown for the data sets. We assume $\beta = 10$ to be an appropriate value, but report for $\beta = \{1, 2, 10, 20\}$, to check whether this decision has any effect in the relative results. We further report the *auc* scores indicating the ability of appropriately ranking negative and positive instances, as an additional metric independent of any binary classification threshold.

Reproducibility: Data and the code to reproduce all experimental results are located under https://github.com/cbagdel/GIFP.

6   Results and Discussion

The F_{10} score distributions, grouped by data set are shown below. The horizontal line within each box refers to the median of the scores on test folds of the nested cross validation. Color coding indicate different classifiers (Fig. 6).

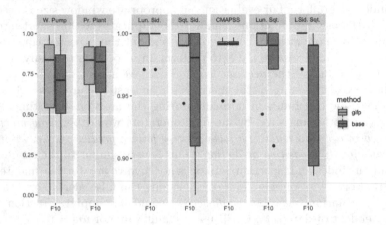

Fig. 6. F10 Scores: GIFP vs BASE

The *ph* determination algorithm improves the median F_{10} scores in five data sets out of seven, and there are two ties. These results correspond to the *p-value* = 0.02895 based on the non-parametric Wilcoxon signed ranks test. The improvement is statistically significant.

Also the absolute model qualities of GIFP are promising, given that data set specific treatments were avoided, and only simple and generic aggregation functions for the calculated features were utilized (Fig. 6).

The detailed results in multiple metrics including means and standard deviations are shown in Table 1. For alternative values of β the algorithm's relative performance, compared to BASE, does not get worse, and the statistical significance of the improvement is also not affected by the β decision. This increases the confidence in the results (Table 1).

In *Kaggle water pump* data set we observe one extreme test fold result where $F_{10} = 0$ (Fig. 6). The fact that *auc* scores are not affected by the problem (Table 1), points to a bias in the learned classification threshold. This can be due to small data size and very few positive instances in each test fold. It can also be due to noise in the data, e.g. different failure modes in train and test folds. For the two *Kaggle* data sets the failure modes are not given. If they were given, we would have trained separate models per failure mode. Nevertheless, the GIFP approach generates this kind of prediction failures only exceptionally in case of a too small data size. However, in practical situations, as more data is accumulated in the course of time, the models would gradually improve, and for such small number of RTFs these cases are not surprising.

Table 1. BASE vs GIFP (including *ph* Determination Algorithm)

Data set	Method	Mean F10	Sd F10	Mean AUC	Sd AUC	Med F1	Med F2	Med F10	Med F20
W. Pump	GIFP	0.6778	0.3821	0.8710	0.2605	0.1195	0.2444	0.8360	0.9510
W. Pump	BASE	0.6284	0.3631	0.9308	0.0841	0.0465	0.1087	0.7113	0.9072
Pr. Plant	GIFP	0.7657	0.2319	0.8706	0.0756	0.1113	0.2307	0.8355	0.9514
Pr. Plant	BASE	0.7295	0.2896	0.8196	0.1954	0.1070	0.2238	0.8242	0.9471
CMAPSS	GIFP	0.9836	0.0212	0.9967	0.0018	0.7407	0.8716	0.9917	0.9979
CMAPSS	BASE	0.9836	0.0212	0.9967	0.0018	0.7407	0.8716	0.9917	0.9979
Lun. Sqt.	GIFP	0.9851	0.0282	1.0000	0.0000	1.0000	1.0000	1.0000	1.0000
Lun. Sqt.	BASE	0.9743	0.0378	1.0000	0.0000	0.6667	0.8333	0.9902	0.9975
Lun. Sid.	GIFP	0.9923	0.0125	1.0000	0.0000	1.0000	1.0000	1.0000	1.0000
Lun. Sid.	BASE	0.9942	0.0129	1.0000	0.0000	1.0000	1.0000	1.0000	1.0000
Sqt. Sid.	GIFP	0.9849	0.0234	0.9997	0.0005	0.6667	0.8333	0.9902	0.9975
Sqt. Sid.	BASE	0.9522	0.0588	0.9963	0.0077	0.5000	0.7143	0.9806	0.9950
LSid. Sqt.	GIFP	0.9942	0.0129	0.9996	0.0009	1.0000	1.0000	1.0000	1.0000
LSid. Sqt.	BASE	0.9520	0.0569	1.0000	0.0000	0.6667	0.8333	0.9902	0.9975

To produce meaningful results the algorithm relies on the existence of peaks on Δ^j curves. This is because the precursors of failures are expected to produce local peaks on Δ^j, and the algorithm utilizes such peaks. In other words, it relies on non-monotonic Δ^j curves. For each type of data set, a Δ^j curve from one iteration of the algorithm is given in Fig. 7. For the first three types of data sets local maxima are available, hence the prerequisite is fulfilled. In contrast, for the C-MAPSS data set the Δ^j curve is monotonic, and hence the prerequisite is not fulfilled (Fig. 7).

If the prerequisite is also not fulfilled in the subsequent iterations based on new sets of important features (S_j), the eventual results of both approaches would be identical. Since this is the case for C-MAPSS data, the results with and without the *ph* determination algorithm are identical (Table 1).

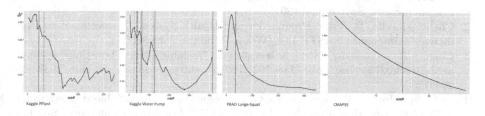

Fig. 7. Δ^j on different data sets

7   Conclusion

We introduced the IFP problem and presented a general approach to the problem. As one important component of the approach, we proposed a heuristic algorithm to learn a suitable *prediction horizon (ph)*. Based on the experiments performed on seven different data sets the proposed algorithm significantly improves the classification model quality. These results show the effectiveness of Wasserstein distances between relative frequency distributions within *run to failure* sequences of condition monitoring data.

Learning this critical *ph* parameter from data eliminates the ambiguity of supervision, and reduces the dependence to domain expertise. All other required parameters can easily be set according to the operational requirements of the users, without requiring machine specific knowledge. Unlike *remaining useful life* approaches, which have been developed in machine specific contexts by engineering communities for decades, and unlike any existing classification-based approaches, the proposed approach to data-driven machinery prognostics can be applied without availability of any domain experts, independent of machine or component. The approach still enables utilization of domain expert knowledge by means of feature engineering, for further improvements of model quality.

8   Future Work

For the rich set of data sets used in this study the distances between RFDs with respect to individual features was sufficient to learn *ph* values which improve model quality significantly. Should a correlation of two or more features be relevant for a failure pattern, Wasserstein distances between RFDs of a grid of two or three features can be examined as next steps.

References

1. ISO 13381-1:2015, Condition monitoring and diagnostics of machines—Prognostics—Part 1. Technical report, International Organization for Standardization, Geneva, Switzerland (2015)
2. Chebel-Morello, B.: From Prognostics and Health Systems Management to Predictive Maintenance 2. ISTE Ltd./Wiley, Hoboken, NJ (2017)
3. Chen, T., Guestrin, C.: XGBoost: a scalable tree boosting system. arXiv:1603.02754 [cs], pp. 785–794 (2016). https://doi.org/10.1145/2939672.2939785
4. de Pádua Moreira, R., Nascimento, C.L.: Prognostics of aircraft bleed valves using a SVM classification algorithm. In: 2012 IEEE Aerospace Conference, pp. 1–8 (March 2012). https://doi.org/10.1109/AERO.2012.6187377
5. Demšar, J.: Statistical comparisons of classifiers over multiple data sets. J. Mach. Learn. Res. **7**, 1–30 (2006)

6. Deutsch, J., He, D.: Using deep learning-based approach to predict remaining useful life of rotating components. IEEE Trans. Syst. Man Cybern. Syst. **48**(1), 11–20 (2018). https://doi.org/10.1109/TSMC.2017.2697842

7. Elasha, F., Shanbr, S., Li, X., Mba, D.: Prognosis of a wind turbine gearbox bearing using supervised machine learning. Sensors **19**(14), 3092 (2019). https://doi.org/10.3390/s19143092

8. Feremans, L., Vercruyssen, V., Cule, B., Meert, W., Goethals, B.: Pattern-based anomaly detection in mixed-type time series. In: Brefeld, U., Fromont, E., Hotho, A., Knobbe, A., Maathuis, M., Robardet, C. (eds.) ECML PKDD 2019. LNCS (LNAI), vol. 11906, pp. 240–256. Springer, Cham (2020). https://doi.org/10.1007/978-3-030-46150-8_15

9. Gebraeel, N.Z., Lawley, M.A., Li, R., Ryan, J.K.: Residual-life distributions from component degradation signals: a Bayesian approach. IIE Trans. **37**(6), 543–557 (2005). https://doi.org/10.1080/07408170590929018

10. Gutschi, C., Furian, N., Suschnigg, J., Neubacher, D., Voessner, S.: Log-based predictive maintenance in discrete parts manufacturing. Procedia CIRP **79**, 528–533 (2019). https://doi.org/10.1016/j.procir.2019.02.098

11. Heng, A., Zhang, S., Tan, A.C., Mathew, J.: Rotating machinery prognostics: state of the art, challenges and opportunities. Mech. Syst. Sig. Process. **23**(3), 724–739 (2009). https://doi.org/10.1016/j.ymssp.2008.06.009

12. Jardine, A.K.S., Lin, D., Banjevic, D.: A review on machinery diagnostics and prognostics implementing condition-based maintenance. Mech. Syst. Sig. Process. **20**(7), 1483–1510 (2006). https://doi.org/10.1016/j.ymssp.2005.09.012

13. Kaggle Inc.: Kaggle Pump Sensor Data for Predictive Maintenance Data Set, Version 1. San Francisco, United States (2018). https://kaggle.com

14. Lin, D., Makis, V.: Recursive filters for a partially observable system subject to random failure. Adv. Appl. Probab. **35**(1), 207–227 (2003)

15. Nowaczyk, S., Fink, O., Bulthe, J.: ECML PKDD Workshop and Tutorial: IoT Stream for Data Driven Predictive Maintenance (September 2020)

16. SAP SE: SAP Predictive Asset Insights Software, Version 2105. Walldorf, Germany (2021). https://help.sap.com

17. Saxena, A., Goebel, K.: Turbofan engine degradation simulation data set. NASA Ames Prognostics Data Repository, pp. 1551–3203 (2008)

18. Schwabacher, M.: A survey of artificial intelligence for prognostics. In: AAAI Fall Symposium: Artificial Intelligence for Prognostics, pp. 108–115 (2007)

19. Si, X.S., Wang, W., Hu, C.H., Zhou, D.H.: Remaining useful life estimation – a review on the statistical data driven approaches. Eur. J. Oper. Res. **213**(1), 1–14 (2011). https://doi.org/10.1016/j.ejor.2010.11.018

20. Sipos, R., Fradkin, D., Moerchen, F., Wang, Z.: Log-based predictive maintenance. In: Proceedings of the 20th ACM SIGKDD International Conference on Knowledge Discovery and Data Mining, KDD 2014, pp. 1867–1876. Association for Computing Machinery, New York (August 2014). https://doi.org/10.1145/2623330.2623340

21. Susto, G.A., Schirru, A., Pampuri, S., McLoone, S., Beghi, A.: Machine learning for predictive maintenance: a multiple classifier approach. IEEE Trans. Industr. Inf. **11**(3), 812–820 (2015). https://doi.org/10.1109/TII.2014.2349359

22. von Birgelen, A., Buratti, D., Mager, J., Niggemann, O.: Self-organizing maps for anomaly localization and predictive maintenance in cyber-physical production systems. Procedia CIRP **72**, 480–485 (2018). https://doi.org/10.1016/j.procir.2018.03.150

23. Wang, Z.: ECML PKDD Tutorial: Predictive Maintenance From a Machine Learning Perspective (September 2015)

24. Weiss, G., Hirsh, H.: Learning to predict rare events in event sequences. In: Proceedings of the 4th International Conference on Knowledge Discovery and Data Mining, pp. 359–363. AAAI Press (1998)
25. Zhou, Y., Gao, Y., Huang, Y., Hefenbrock, M., Riedel, T., Beigl, M.: Automatic remaining useful life estimation framework with embedded convolutional LSTM as the backbone. arXiv arXiv:2008.03961 [cs, stat] (August 2020)

A Trust Management-Based Route Planning Scheme in LBS Network

Xinyang Song, Bohan Li$^{(\boxtimes)}$, Tianlun Dai, and Jiaying Tian

Nanjing University of Aeronautics and Astronautics, Nanjing, China
{sx2016017,bhli,sx2016060}@nuaa.edu.cn

Abstract. Location-based Service (LBS) has attracted growing attention in the field of Internet of Vehicles (IoV), and a route planning scheme is a research hotspot. Research shows that one serious problem in the field of intelligent transportation is the waste of computing resources. In addition, the process blockage caused by malicious requests from vehicles is another overlooked issue needs to be considered. In this paper, a dual-tiered path index based parallel route planning model is proposed to accelerate the process of route planning. Then, based on the decentralization and security of the blockchain, we propose a trust management for identifying malicious vehicles, and the sensitive information is stored in the blockchain. Extensive experiment results show that our proposal is feasible and effective.

Keywords: Route planning · Blockchain · Trust management · LBS

1 Introduction

With the acceleration of urbanization, the requirements for intelligent transportation systems (ITSs) in all aspects are constantly improving. However, due to the continuous increase in the number of vehicles on the road, increasing cities are experiencing traffic congestion and even car accidents. In LBS network, each vehicle is equipped with an On-board Unit (OBU) to communicate with surrounding vehicles and infrastructure, which can broadcast and obtain information about nearby traffic conditions, as thus vehicle owners can have enough time to react to external conditions. However, there exist several issues including the large computation overhead of route planning algorithms [1,2,17,19,20], the actual problems of trust management [7,12,14,15,21,22] and resource constraints. These issues, as well as fail to take route query participation of malicious vehicles into account, result in considerable waste of computation and leakage of private information. In view of aforementioned problems, we firstly introduce a parallel route planning model, then present a trust management.

In order to improve the efficiency of route planning, we first introduce Dual-Tired Path (DTP) index over dynamic road network and parallelize it on Master-Worker cluster. The bottom layer of DTP is the subgraph layer, which divides the road network into subgraphs of equal size (with the same number of vertices).

© Springer Nature Switzerland AG 2022
B. Li et al. (Eds.): ADMA 2021, LNAI 13087, pp. 307–322, 2022.
https://doi.org/10.1007/978-3-030-95405-5_22

In the subgraph layer, if two vertices of a road are located in different subgraphs, they are called boundary vertices. For any two boundary vertices in a subgraph, the k shortest paths (ksp) between the two vertices are calculated to determine the weights on skeleton graph. The top layer of DTP is the skeleton graph of the global road network, which is composed of all the boundary vertices of each subgraph. The two boundary vertices of different subgraphs are directly connected by the original edges in the skeleton graph. For two boundary vertices in the same subgraph, if they are reachable, then build an edge in the skeleton graph, and the weight of the edge is determined by the ksp between the two vertices, which means that the smallest weight of ksp is regarded as the weight of this edge. For a given query, TORP algorithm first calculates the overall path p_o according to the skeleton graph G_s. Then follow the path p_o continuously optimize the planned path in the local area around the user location.

Trust management model can judge the rationality of the vehicle's behavior according to established standards. It can not only filter out useless information, but also identify malicious vehicles on the road. Currently, trust management can be divided into two categories: centralized and decentralized [22]. In centralized management, all data is stored in a central server which will bear huge computing pressure. On the other hand, if this server is unreliable, data leakage can easily occur. While in decentralized management, the calculation pressure will be distributed to the Roadside Unit (RSU) or the vehicles. Blockchain [18], as a distributed ledger, can well solve the problem of centralized servers [5]. Our main contributions are summarised below:

- A new method of judging whether a vehicle is malicious is proposed to reduce the waste of computing resources. At the same time, various information is stored in the blockchain to ensure data security.
- We introduce a dual-tiered path index based route planning algorithm TORP, which is conducive to decomposing complex tasks into multiple lightweight sub-tasks, and is easy to be implemented in a distributed way.
- Extensive experiments are conducted to evaluate the performance of our proposal that confirms the effectiveness and superiority in route planning and trust management.

2   Related Work

Trust Management. Trust management of vehicles in LBS network has always been a serious issue. Previous trust models were mostly based on centralization [6,8,16]. However, due to the high-speed movement of vehicles and the unreliability of central institutions, the centralized trust model is not suitable for the current transportation network and decentralized trust model came into being. Li et al. [9] proposed an Attack-resistant Trust management scheme (ART) to deal with malicious attack and judge the credibility of a node from two aspects. The emergence of blockchain has greatly increased the implementability of the decentralized trust model. Luo et al. [15] build an anonymous area by calculating the trust value between vehicles to protect the privacy of vehicle location, and records the trust value on the blockchain. In addition, a Blockchain-based Anonymous Reputation System (BARS) is proposed by Lu et al. to protect the privacy of vehicles. Three blockchains are used in their strategy [14], which are used for message proof, certificate proof and certificate revocation proof respectively.

Route Planning. The goal of route planning is to calculate the optimal paths for users. Dijkstra's algorithm [3] proposed in 1959, can be applied to solve the single-source shortest-path problem. A* algorithm is a common basic heuristic search algorithm [4]. The algorithm combines the advantages of Best-First Search and Dijkstra algorithm, where the algorithm can find the best path while performing heuristic search, so as to improve the efficiency of the algorithm. Later, increasing researchers start to focus on the issues of route planning. Xu et al. [20] propose a partial path planning algorithm. Several fixed intermediate destinations are selected between the source and the destination for reducing the re-calculation complexity. The segment route was monitored for vehicles' arrival speed and when necessary, a better route was re-calculated. Malviya et al. [17] argue that the frequent calculation of optimal routes in large-scale road networks would have considerable computational expense and propose two methods for calculating approximate optimal routes based on real-time road conditions. Tong et al. [19] propose a unified function for sharing mobility problems, solving the bottleneck problem of insert operation. Dai et al. [2] propose a continuous route planning algorithm, named LOM, based on a cascading pruning strategy, which adjusts the varying traffic condition in real-time. LOM can gain a better performance of routing with lower computation expense based on greedy principle. In addition, Li et al. [1] propose a multi-objective optimization algorithm DSP-Topk, which uses the visual region method based on the maximum angle difference to improve the efficiency of distance calculation, and improves the efficiency of operation through pruning strategy. However, the algorithm is based on a certain measure and is limited to indoor query.

3   Framework of System

In this section, the framework of our system is shown in Fig. 1, and we will introduce the function of each entity and blockchain.

3.1   Definition of Entities

Trusted Government (TG). TG is an authoritative entity which is used to verify and store the true information of the vehicle. When the vehicle's identity is successfully verified, TG provides a digital signature to authorize the CA to issue a certificate for the vehicle. It is worth noting that TG contains the corresponding relationship between the pseudonym of the vehicle and the real identity.

Certificate Authority (CA). As a certificate management center, CA needs to maintain the blockchain CerBC. At the same time, it receives commands from TG to manage the issuance, update and revocation of certificates.

Road Side Unit (RSU). RSUs can communicate with each other and with vehicles. On the one hand, RSUs are responsible for receiving the query request information of vehicles on the road and storing it in QueBC. On the other hand, RSUs evaluate the rationality of the query request of the vehicle and store the result in EvaBC.

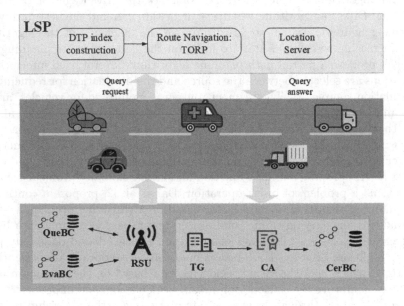

Fig. 1. The framework of our scheme

Vehicles. Vehicles refer to the various cars that issued the query request. When the vehicle enters the network for the first time, it generates a pair of public and private keys and sends the real information to TG for verification. If the verification succeeds, it will obtain a certificate issued by the CA. Each time a vehicle sends a query request, the RSU will evaluate the rationality of the request, and use the historical evaluation information recorded on EvaBC to determine whether the vehicle is malicious.

Location-Based Service Provider (LSP). In our scheme, LSP is responsible for using the route planning algorithm to process the query request sent by the vehicle and return the result to Request cars. The route planning algorithm will be introduced later.

3.2 Blockchain for System

Our model consists of three blockchains. EvaBC and QueBC are managed by RSU, and CerBC is managed by CA. Firstly, EvaBC stores the evaluation information of the RSU on the vehicle, and the RSU judges whether the vehicle is malicious based on the current vehicle behavior and the historical evaluation information. QueBC. The vehicle request information stored in QueBC can be used as the basis for vehicle behavior evaluation. Besides, the certificates of all vehicles are stored in CerBC, and all operations on the certificates are also transparent.

4 Trust Management

In this section, we extend the Public Key Infrastructure and will introduce the mechanism of certificate and malicious vehicle identification.

4.1 The Management of Certificate

Certificate Initialization and Revocation. When the vehicle first enters the network, it has to generate a pair of public and private keys and send its real information with public key to TG. The vehicle will get the certificate from CA if the information is verified successfully. Then the vehicle sends the query information with the public key as the pseudonym and only TG knows the real identity of the vehicle. Once the vehicle is judged by the system as a malicious vehicle or the certificate expires, the certificate will be withdrawn.

Certificate Update. For security, users can change the public key and private key from time to time to prevent privacy leakage, or change the certificate before it expires. These operations require the certificate to be updated. The certificate of the vehicle v is as follows:

$$Cer_v^n = \langle ID_V, PU_v^n, Sig_{TG}, Sig_{CA}, T_{update}, T_{expire} \rangle \tag{1}$$

ID_V is the certificate number, and it can uniquely identify a certificate. PU_v^n is the public key of the vehicle v, and in LBS network it can be used as a pseudonym for the vehicle. Sig_{TG} and Sig_{CA} are the digital signatures of TG and CA respectively. T_{update} and T_{expire} refer to the issuance time and expiration time of the certificate.

4.2 Malicious Node Identification

We will first evaluate the rationality of the vehicle's current request, and then combine the evaluation results in EvaBC to determine whether the vehicle is malicious.

Vehicle Current Behavior Evaluation. We will evaluate the current behavior of the vehicle from two aspects: space and frequency.

In terms of space, if the direction of the vehicle is different from the prescribed direction on the road, or the location provided by the vehicle is unreasonable, such as in a green belt or a pond, it can be directly determined that the vehicle is malicious. Otherwise, The vehicle may provide a reasonable false location. However, research [11] shows that it takes more time to generate false locations, so we can judge the rationality of the query based on the delay time. When the RSU receives the query request of the vehicle, it needs to immediately request the location of the vehicle, and judge the rationality based on the delay time. The spatial rationality R_s can be represented as follows:

$$R_s = \frac{\max T - (T_s - T_e)}{\max T_v} \tag{2}$$

where T_s and T_e refer to the time when the RSUs issue the request to obtain the location of the vehicle and receive the location information, and $\max T_v$ is the maximum time that RSU can wait.

In order to prevent the vehicle from repeatedly sending query requests resulting in a waste of computing resources, we will judge the rationality of the vehicle query request from the query frequency. Assuming that Int is the reasonable time interval between two queries, then we divide it into m time intervals $t_0, t_1, ..., t_m$ [7,13]. If the vehicle's two request time is greater than Int, then the request is reasonable. Otherwise, the frequency rationality R_f is calculated as follows:

$$R_f = \begin{cases} 1 - \rho^{m-i}, 0 \leq i < m \\ 1, i \geq m \end{cases} \tag{3}$$

where $\rho \in (0,1)$ is the time decay rate.

Based on the spatial rationality and frequency rationality calculated by RSU, we can get the rationality of the current vehicle query request if the vehicle is not defined as a malicious vehicle:

$$R_v = \lambda R_s + (1 - \lambda) R_f \tag{4}$$

where $\lambda \in [0,1]$ is to control the balance of R_s and R_f.

Comprehensive Evaluation of Vehicle Behavior. In this part, we will combine the vehicle's current behavior with the historical evaluation stored in EvaBC to judge the accuracy of a given evaluation.

In the actual road scenario, we can divide the behavior of the vehicle into k levels according to the Dirichlet probability distribution, and the levels are $l = (l_1, l_2, ..., l_k)$. It is worth noting that the value represented by each level is between 0 and 1, and when i increases, more reliable the l_i is. Also, EvaBC records the number of times the vehicle has obtained each level which is defined as $\vec{A_v^p} = (a_1^p, a_2^p, ..., a_k^p)$. a_i^p represents the total number of times that vehicle has obtained rank i until the p-th transaction. We combine the historical rating information recorded in EvaBC into the Dirichlet probability density function distribution to get the probability of obtaining each level, which is $p(l_i)$. Then we set Thr to measure the rationality of the current request. If $p(l_i) > Thr$, we think the current behavior of the vehicle is reasonable, and $a_i^p = a_i^p + i$ at the same time waiting for the next block update. Here we set the value of Thr is 0.15.

Blockchain Update and Malicious Node Identification. After the RSU has collected enough evaluation information, the leader RSU will pack the evaluation into a block with PBFT consensus algorithm. The specific process is as follows.

Assuming that before p+1 transactions, the number of times that vehicle v has obtained level l_i is b_i, and the update level of the blockchain during p+1 transactions is l_j, then we have:

$$j = \lfloor \frac{\sum_{i=1}^{k}(b_i * i)}{\sum_{i=1}^{k} b_i} \rfloor \tag{5}$$

$$a_j^{p+1} = a_j^p + k - j + 1 \tag{6}$$

Besides, if $j < \epsilon$, we think that v is malicious. In our experiment, we set the value of ϵ is 3.

5 Route Planning Scheme

5.1 Framework of DTP

The naive method to optimize the planned route is to repeatedly calculate the shortest path from the user's location to the destination on the dynamic graph G. However, the dynamic nature of the road network and a large number of concurrent queries make it infeasible to handle route queries in this way. In this section, we introduce the Dual-Tiered Path index.

5.2 Graph Partitioning

The construction of DTP index starts from graph partitioning. Firstly, we traverse graph $G(E, V)$ from any vertex, and use Breadth First Strategy to generate subgraphs, and the number of vertices in each subgraph is not more than z. We denote that the set of subgraphs as $S = \{SG_1, ..., SG_n\}$, where $V_1 \cup ... \cup V_n = V$ and $E_1 \cup ... \cup E_n = E$.

Definition 1 (Boundary vertex). *A vertex $v_x \in V$ is a boundary vertex if and only if $\exists v_y \in V$ such that 1) v_x and v_y on the same edge; 2) v_x and v_y are covered by SG_i and sg_j respectively ($x \neq y, i, j \in [1, n]$).*

In our strategy, boundary vertices help calculate overall path in skeleton graph and provide coarse-grained navigation direction. For each pair of boundary vertices in the same subgraph, we index their k shortest paths (ksp). In this paper, we utilize Yen algorithm [23] to calculate ksp from any pair of boundary vertices.

5.3   Distributed Deployment of DTP

To support the parallel processing of route planning query, we parallelize DTP in the cluster of Master Worker model. The model includes three roles: Master, SubgraphWorker and QueryWorker. In essence, each role is a virtual processor like a thread. The master is responsible for graph G and graph partitioning information. Each QueryWorker maintains a copy of the skeleton graph, and the subgraph is distributed on the SubgraphWorker.

5.4   Design Mentality of TORP

TORP needs to continuously optimize the planning route on the dynamic graph in a short response time. As it is unable to accurately predict the future traffic conditions, it is impossible to calculate the absolute optimal path for users on the dynamic graph. It is unnecessary to repeatedly calculate the shortest path from the user's current location to the destination with traffic conditions evolving, as this method only consumes a lot of computing resources, but it can not guarantee that the planned route is optimal. The framework is shown in Fig. 2. There also exists an important problem, that is, how to correctly evaluate the impact of traffic conditions in the area far from the user's location on the current planned path. If this effect is ignored, users may fall into the congested road along the planned path. On the contrary, if the influence is considered too much, the planned route may need to be adjusted frequently, which will bring huge

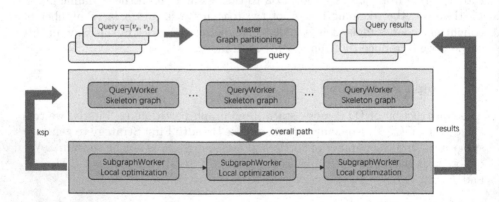

Fig. 2. Framework of TORP

computational cost. Moreover, the huge computational cost is bound to prolong the response time of the query, which can not avoid users entering the congested area in advance, resulting in the meaningless path optimization work.

Considering the above problems, TORP algorithm no longer calculates the exact shortest path in each optimization, but tends to calculate the approximate optimal path continuously at a faster speed. The reason is that the approximate optimal path can also meet the needs of users, and can greatly save the calculation cost. TORP algorithm first calculates the overall path p_o according to the skeleton graph G_s. Then follow the path p_o continuously optimize the planned path in the local area around the user location.

Overall Path. We firstly identify the overall path p_o on skeleton graph g_s, and the corresponding pseudocode is shown in Algorithm 1.

Algorithm 1. Calculation of overall path p_o

Require: G_s, $q(v_s, v_t)$, partitioned graphs;
Ensure: the overall path p_o from v_s to v_t;
 1: Identify SG_s and SG_t by qw_i;
 2: **if** v_s and v_t are not boundary vertices **then**
 3:    qw_i sends $q(v_s, v_t)$ to sw_s and sw_t;
 4:    sw_s and sw_t compute ksp from v_s and v_t to each boundary vertex;
 5:    sw_s and sw_t return path information to qw_i;
 6:    qw_i adds v_s and v_t into G_s;
 7: **end if**
 8: Search the shortest path from v_s to v_t on G_s as p_o;
 9: **return** p_o;

---

1. If v_s and v_t are boundary vertices, it goes to step 3 (line 8). Otherwise, QueryWorker identifies subgraphs covering v_s and v_t. The subgraphs where v_s and v_t are located are denoted as SG_s and SG_t (line 1). Then, the query q is sent to SubgraphWorker sw_i and sw_t (lines 2–3).
2. SubgraphWorker sw_i and sw_t in subgraph SG_s and SG_t calculate ksp from v_s and v_t to other boundary vertices in corresponding subgraph (lines 4–5). Then send the updated travel cost to qw_i. Add v_s and v_t to skeleton graph g_s (line 6).
3. QueryWorker qw_i calculates the shortest path from v_s to v_t based on skeleton graph g_s.(line 8).

Local Route Optimization. Firstly, we introduce the concept of slot. For a path p, we divide it into several segments by calculating the slot. Supposed that $V_{slot} = \{slot_1, slot_2, ..., slot_m\}$, where $slot_i$ is on path p ($i \in [1, m]$). In order to further prune the search space, we divide route planning path into multiple tasks, and the local route optimization is decomposed into the following $m + 1$ tasks:

route from s to $slot_1$, $slot_1$ to $slot_2$,..., $slot_m$ to t. This strategy is reasonable as the traffic condition in the remote area probably has only a little influence on the route planning for the user, so we adopt the greedy principle and just consider the area around the user to find a local optimal path.

Algorithm 2. Calculation of slot

Require: source node s, destination node t, benchmark path $p_{origial}$
Ensure: slot
  1: $i = 0, slot = t$
  2: **for** each edge e in p **do**
  3:     $i = i + 1$
  4:     $slot = (i + 1)^{th}$ node from p //After the congested node
  5:     $dist_0 += orginal\ weight\ w^{'}(e)$
  6:     $dist_1 += updated\ weight\ w(e)$
  7:     **if** $\dfrac{dist_1}{dist_0} > \gamma$ and Degree($slot$) > 1 **then**
  8:         **return** $slot$
  9:     **else if** i $== \eta$ **then**
 10:         **return** $slot$
 11:     **end if**
 12: **end for**

Then the travel cost function can be calculated as follows:

$$R(x) = \frac{C(v_s, v_d)}{C'(v_s, v_d)}, \qquad (7)$$

where $C(v_s, v_d)$ and $C'(v_s, v_d)$ denote the original and updated travel cost from v_s to v_d respectively. In order to find slot easily, we compute the shortest path from s to t in the subgraph as a benchmark path and we select the slot by calculating the R value of each vertex along the benchmark path within η steps. When $R(x)$ is greater than γ (the threshold of congestion) and the degree of x is greater than 1 (means more selections on route planning), we identify x as a slot. η and γ are both user specified parameters.

Algorithm 2 shows the identification of slot. We sequentially access the nodes and edges on the benchmark path and calculate the R value in turn (line 2 to 6). If the R of a node is greater than γ and its degree is greater than 1, then we get the proper slot (line 7 to 8). If we find no proper slot, then we select the ηth node on benchmark path as slot.

Then we demonstrate the strategy for route planning. Firstly, we compute the benchmark path. Then we obtain a slot and process a route planning from source to slot. Repeat above operations until it reaches destination. We remark that the travel cost is not guaranteed to be the best-possible (optimal or near optimal) because the TORP routes over subgraph rather than complete graph. Therefore it is approximately optimal.

6   Experiment

6.1   Experiments Settings and Datasets

As IBM's open source blockchain project, Hyperledger Fabric is extensible and flexible, and the CA, database, and consensus algorithm it provides are all pluggable. In our experiment, necessary deployment is done to fit our configuration. Specifically, we changed the data structure of the transaction bill to record past evaluation information, and adopt PBFT as the consensus algorithm. In addition, ECC-secp256k1 and ECDSA-secp256k1 are utilized as our encryption and decryption algorithms. The data samples used in the trust management are all from website[1]. The DTP index and the TORP model are implemented on a cluster of multiple threads that simulate the *Master-Worker* model. The system is deployed on a PC with 2.00 GHz 4-core Intel Core, Windows 10 operating system and 16 Gigabytes. We use the road network of San Francisco Bay Area (BAY), Northeast USA (NE) and LKS (Great Lakes), provided by DIMACS[2]. The sizes of these road networks are shown in the following Table 1. Each tuple in the dataset consists of two vertices and their distances. We use all tuples to build a directed graph. As the weight of the graph is static, we set the change rate to plus or minus 30%.

Table 1. Road networks datasets

Name	Region	#vertices	#edges
BAY	San Francisco Bay Area	321,270	800,172
NE	Northeast USA	1,524,453	3,897,636
LKS	Great Lakes	2,758,119	6,885,658

Baseline

- **Naive** is a method to frequently optimize the route from current location to the destination.
- **Liang** represents the scheme in [10]. It is worth noting that the method we compare is the evaluation of the trust level of request vehicles and detection of malicious vehicles.

Parameters. We summarize the parameters in Table 2.

---

[1] http://users.diag.uniroma1.it/challenge9.
[2] https://www.cse.ust.hk/scrg/.

Table 2. Summary of parameters

Parameter	Description
N_q	Number of concurrent queries
L_p	The number of vertices of route path
z	Size of subgraph

6.2   Trust Management Evaluation

Trust Level. Considering the specific behaviors of vehicles in reality, ordinary malicious vehicles will carry out malicious attacks after reaching a certain high trust level. We design the experiment based on this point. In the following experiments, the behaviors of vehicles are divided into 10 levels. We set the vehicle to maintain honest behavior in the first 20 rounds, then continue to make malicious behaviors in the 20–30 rounds, and finally switch to honest behavior in the last 20 rounds. As shown in Fig. 3, it is obvious that the trust level of Liang's scheme grows faster than our strategy when the vehicle exhibits honest behavior. However, our strategy shows that after the vehicle has malicious behavior, the trust level will increase relatively slowly if the vehicle again exhibits honest behavior. On the other hand, as long as there is malicious behavior, the trust level of the vehicle will drop faster in our scheme.

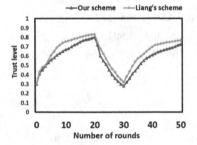

Fig. 3. Changes in trust level

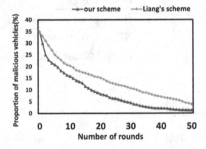

Fig. 4. Proportion of malicious vehicles

Inspection of Malicious Vehicles. In this part, we assume that the number of vehicles is 1000, and 35% of them are malicious. According to the criteria for judging malicious vehicles mentioned in Sect. 4, we can intuitively get the specific results of the two strategies from Fig. 4. In terms of process, our strategy can eliminate malicious vehicles more quickly. From the results, we can exclude a higher percentage of malicious vehicles.

6.3   TORP Evaluation

In this section, we evaluate the performance of TORP, and conduct the comparisons with baseline method in terms of response time and real time cost.

Response Time. We evaluate the response time of TORP and Naive in terms of increasing subgraph size z. The response time here refers to the average time consumed for each optimization, and the results are shown in Fig. 5. We firstly feed a batch of queries (i.e. $N_q = 100$), then measure the average response time for these queries. Then, we measure the response time with the methods combining Trust Management. The results demonstrate that the response time of TORP is obviously lower than that if Naive. With the increase of subgraph size z, the response time of TORP decreases slightly at first, and then increases gradually. This is because the size of subgraph is too small, routing planning query will suffer more local routing optimization. Then the cost of scheduling multiple threads will increase, and the average response time of each optimization will also increase. With subgraph size increasing, the number of local optimizations of queries decreases, and the thread scheduling overhead also decreases, resulting in lower response time. We can also observe that the methods with Trust Management cost more time for each optimization, as the process of Trust Management causes extra time cost.

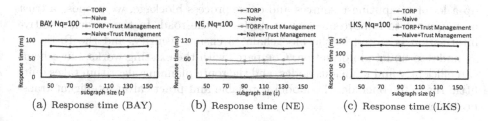

(a) Response time (BAY)   (b) Response time (NE)   (c) Response time (LKS)

Fig. 5. Response time w.r.t. z

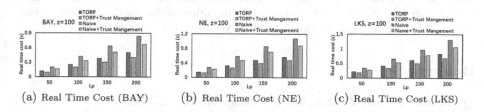

(a) Real Time Cost (BAY)   (b) Real Time Cost (NE)   (c) Real Time Cost (LKS)

Fig. 6. Real time cost w.r.t. L_p

Real Time Cost. We further examine the real time cost among these three road networks. Real time cost is the average time of processing time of non-malicious vehicles. We firstly feed a batch of queries (i.e. $N_q = 100$), then measure the Real Cost Time among these two methods. At the same time, we do the comparison with the methods combining Trust Management. As shown in Fig. 6, The results indicate that, as the path length increases, the real time cost grows rapidly while TORP has a much slower growth on the real time cost, as Naive has to frequently repeat calculating the shortest path on the entire graph. The larger of path length leads to the greater time cost. TORP, in turn, only adjusts a small segment of the planned path within a limited local scope in each optimization, which costs lower real time cost. We can observe that the real time cost of Trust Management enabled methods significantly lower than that of methods with non-Trust Management, as Trust Management can effectively detect the malicious vehicles which reduces the consumption of computing resources.

7   Conclusion

In order to improve the efficiency of route planning in LBS network, we first propose a new parallel route planning algorithm TORP. In TORP, we introduce DTP index over dynamic road network to decompose complex tasks into multiple lightweight sub-tasks which is quite efficient. In addition, considering the repeated or unreasonable query requests malicious vehicles send, which will take up a lot of computing resources and cause process blockage, we propose a trust management to remove malicious vehicles on the road. In the model, sensitive information is stored in the blockchain to ensure security, and the RSUs act as nodes to update information. Compared with the existing works, our scheme can efficiently find malicious nodes, and the route planning algorithm takes quite little time. To conclude, the model is reliable and practical in intelligent transportation.

Acknowledgements. This work was supported partly by National Natural Science Foundation of China (61728204, 62172351), CCF-Huawei Database System Innovation Research Plan under Grant CCF-HUAWEIDBIR2020001A, Key Laboratory of Safety Critical Software Ministry of Industry and Information Technology (NJ2018014), Fundamental Research Funds for the Central Universities (NS2019001).

References

1. Bohan, L., Chao, Z., Dongjing, L., Jianqiu, X., Bin, X., Xiaolin, Q.: A DSP-Topk query optimization algorithm supporting indoor obstacle space. J. Comput. Res. Develop. **54**(3), 557 (2017)
2. Dai, T., et al.: Continuous route planning over a dynamic graph in real-time. Procedia Comput. Sci. **174**, 111–114 (2020)
3. Dijkstra, E.W., et al.: A note on two problems in connexion with graphs. Numer. Math. **1**(1), 269–271 (1959)

4. Hart, P.E., Nilsson, N.J., Raphael, B.: A formal basis for the heuristic determination of minimum cost paths. IEEE Trans. Syst. Sci. Cybern. **4**(2), 100–107 (1968)
5. Ji, Y., Chai, Y., Zhou, X., Ren, L., Qin, Y.: Smart intra-query fault tolerance for massive parallel processing databases. Data Sci. Eng. **5**(1), 65–79 (2020)
6. Lai, C., Zhang, K., Cheng, N., Li, H., Shen, X.: SIRC: a secure incentive scheme for reliable cooperative downloading in highway VANETs. IEEE Trans. Intell. Transp. Syst. **18**(6), 1559–1574 (2016)
7. Li, B., Liang, R., Zhu, D., Chen, W., Lin, Q.: Blockchain-based trust management model for location privacy preserving in VANETs. IEEE Trans. Intell. Transp. Syst. **22**, 3765–3775 (2020)
8. Li, Q., Malip, A., Martin, K.M., Ng, S.L., Zhang, J.: A reputation-based announcement scheme for VANETs. IEEE Trans. Veh. Technol. **61**(9), 4095–4108 (2012)
9. Li, W., Song, H.: Art: an attack-resistant trust management scheme for securing vehicular ad hoc networks. IEEE Trans. Intell. Transp. Syst. **17**(4), 960–969 (2015)
10. Liang, R., Li, B., Song, X.: Blockchain-based privacy preserving trust management model in VANET. In: Yang, X., Wang, C.-D., Islam, M.S., Zhang, Z. (eds.) ADMA 2020. LNCS (LNAI), vol. 12447, pp. 465–479. Springer, Cham (2020). https://doi.org/10.1007/978-3-030-65390-3_36
11. Liu, H., Li, X., Li, H., Ma, J., Ma, X.: Spatiotemporal correlation-aware dummy-based privacy protection scheme for location-based services. In: IEEE Conference on Computer Communications, IEEE INFOCOM 2017, pp. 1–9. IEEE (2017)
12. Liu, X., Huang, H., Xiao, F., Ma, Z.: A blockchain-based trust management with conditional privacy-preserving announcement scheme for VANETs. IEEE Internet Things J. **7**, 4101–4112 (2020)
13. Liu, Y., Fang, X., Xiao, M., Mumtaz, S.: Decentralized beam pair selection in multi-beam millimeter-wave networks. IEEE Trans. Commun. **66**(6), 2722–2737 (2018)
14. Lu, Z., Liu, W., Wang, Q., Qu, G., Liu, Z.: A privacy-preserving trust model based on blockchain for VANETs. IEEE Access **6**, 45655–45664 (2018)
15. Luo, B., Li, X., Weng, J., Guo, J., Ma, J.: Blockchain enabled trust-based location privacy protection scheme in VANET. IEEE Trans. Veh. Technol. **69**(2), 2034–2048 (2019)
16. Mahmoud, M.E., Shen, X.: An integrated stimulation and punishment mechanism for thwarting packet dropping attack in multihop wireless networks. IEEE Trans. Veh. Technol. **60**(8), 3947–3962 (2011)
17. Malviya, N., Madden, S.R., Bhattacharya, A.: A continuous query system for dynamic route planning. In: 2011 IEEE 27th International Conference on Data Engineering, pp. 792–803 (2011)
18. Nakamoto, S.: Bitcoin: a peer-to-peer electronic cash system. Decentralized Business Review, p. 21260 (2008)
19. Tong, Y., Zeng, Y., Zhou, Z., Chen, L., Xu, K.: A unified approach to route planning for shared mobility. Proc. VLDB Endow. **11**(11), 1633–1646 (2018)
20. Xu, J., Guo, L., Ding, Z., Sun, X., Liu, C.: Traffic aware route planning in dynamic road networks. In: International Conference on Database Systems for Advanced Applications, pp. 576–591 (2012)
21. Yagitala, B.P., Prince Mary, S.: Traffic status update system with trust level management using blockchain. In: Bhoi, A.K., Mallick, P.K., Balas, V.E., Mishra, B.S.P. (eds.) Advances in Systems, Control and Automations. LNEE, vol. 708, pp. 471–478. Springer, Singapore (2021). https://doi.org/10.1007/978-981-15-8685-9_49

22. Yang, Z., Yang, K., Lei, L., Zheng, K., Leung, V.C.: Blockchain-based decentralized trust management in vehicular networks. IEEE Internet Things J. **6**(2), 1495–1505 (2018)
23. Yen, J.Y.: Finding the k shortest loopless paths in a network. Manage. Sci. **17**(11), 712–716 (1971)

FreeSee: A Parameter-Independent Pattern-Based Device-Free Human Behaviour Sensing System with Wireless Signals of IoT Devices

Hongyu Sun[1] , Xinyu Zhang[1], Yang Lu[1(✉)], Chin-Ling Chen[2,3(✉)],
and Xinyu Song[1]

[1] Department of Computer Science, Jilin Normal University, Siping 136000, China
hongyu@jlnu.edu.cn
[2] Information Engineering, Changchun Sci-Tech University,
Changchun 130600, Jilin, China
clc@mail.cyut.edu.tw
[3] Department of Computer Science and Information Engineering,
Chaoyang University of Technology, Taichung City, Taiwan

Abstract. Wireless signal-based device-free human behavior sensing is an innovative method for accurate sensing and understanding human behaviors, which is the core technology to enable high level human computer interaction via off-the-shelf IoT devices. Currently, tremendous on-site human behavior sensing methods with wireless signals collected from IoT devices were proposed to use for fall detection, daily behaviors sensing, finger gesture recognition and other potential applications. However, wireless signal-based human behavior sensing often occurs in different indoor environments with different structures, room sizes, and obstacles. Therefore, it is difficult to get the empirical parameters for accurate human behavior sensing in practical use, the history data presented in current works also could not fit all the scenarios. In order to resolve this issue, this paper proposes FreeSee, a parameter-independent pattern-based human behaviour sensing system, the main contributions include i) we added time-domain features to the training data to accurate sense human behaviours both by coarse-grained and fine-grained wireless signatures; ii) we extract the dominant parameters from each module as the decision variables; and iii) we propose to use a genetic algorithm (GA) to find the optimized parameters for accurate human behaviour sensing which could be adapted in the multiple scenarios. Experimental results show that FreeSee could optimize the parameters in decision variables according to different datasets with accepted converge time.

Supported by Science and Technology Project of Jilin Provincial Department of Education (JJKH20210457KJ), Undergraduate Training Programs for Innovation and Entrepreneurship Project of Jilin Province (2021JLSFDX-JSJ03) and Innovation capacity building Foundation of Jilin Provincial Development and Reform Commission, grant number 2021C038-7.

© Springer Nature Switzerland AG 2022
B. Li et al. (Eds.): ADMA 2021, LNAI 13087, pp. 323–337, 2022.
https://doi.org/10.1007/978-3-030-95405-5_23

Keywords: Wireless sensing · Parameter-independent · Human behaviour sensing

1   Introduction

Wireless signal-based device-free human behavior sensing is an innovative method for accurate sensing and understanding human behaviours, which is the core technology to fuse the physical and cyber world [35]. The device-free human behavior sensing technologies have great potentials in elder/infant monitoring, personal identification, health indicator monitoring, etc. applications [5]. This research is motivated by a desire to develop low-cost, ubiquitous solutions by leveraging propagation features caused by pervasive wireless signals which could be collected from off-the-shelf IoT devices. In contrast to traditional vision-based [21], infra-red-based [6], wearable-based method [31], wireless signature-based human behavior sensing could achieve low cost, none-line-of-sight (NLoS), sensorless sensing in indoor scenarios. Bahl, etc. first propose to use a wireless signal to sense a person's indoor locations which is the first time to use the wireless signal for sensing, with the development of the sensing technologies, fall detection [27,28], daily behaviors sensing [13,15], finger gesture recognition [12,20,26,40], gait identification [14], emotion-sensing [22], breath and heartbeat detection [8,9,11,16] emerged sequentially. The current related works could accurately sense human behaviors with a set of empirical parameters which learned from multiple round pieces of training with different datasets.

However, wireless signal-based human behaviour sensing often occurs in different indoor environments with different structures, room sizes, and obstacles. Besides, the current human behavior sensing method also uses various pattern-based or model-based technologies which have different settings of parameters [5]. Therefore, it is difficult to get the empirical parameters for accurate human behavior sensing in practical use, the history data presented in current works also could not fit all the scenarios. Enabling a parameter-independent device-free human behavior sensing algorithm that could be adapted in different scenarios is significant. However, enabling parameter-independent human behaviour sensing suffers from several challenges including i) how to enabling accurate human behavior sensing by both coarse-grained (e.g., Received Signal Strength, RSS) and fine-grained (e.g., Channel State Information) wireless signatures; ii) how to select the decision variables as the optimizing parameters are difficult, since there are tremendous parameters in the whole human behavior sensing process, for example, the window size, overlapping and sampling rate for feature extraction module, the initial value of machine-learning-based human behaviour classifiers, etc.; and iii) how to find a fast convergence optimization algorithm for optimized decision variables calculation is another challenge for parameter-independent human behaviour sensing scenarios.

This paper proposes FreeSee to resolve the challenges, firstly, we added time-domain features to the training data to accurate sense human behaviours both by coarse-grained and fine-grained wireless signatures; secondly, we choose a group of data processing method, feature extraction method, classification method which performs better in the state-of-the-art works, and we extract the dominant parameters from each module as the decision variables; thirdly, we propose to use a genetic algorithm (GA) to find the optimized parameters for accurate human behaviour sensing which could be adapted in the multiple scenarios. In summary, the main contributions of this paper are as follows:

- We propose to add time domain information to enhance the features of different human behaviors, FreeSee could sense the human behaviors both with coarse-grained and fine-grained wireless signatures. Therefore, FreeSee could achieve wireless signature independent human behaviors sensing.
- According to the results conducted by state-of-the-arts, we selected a group of data processing methods, and find a series of dominant parameters as the decision variables for the input of optimization algorithms.
- We propose to use a genetic algorithm to optimize the decision variables which summarize in contribution (2) and find the optimized parameters according to different training datasets.
- We conducted the experiments both in our collected dataset, experimental results show that FreeSee could optimize the parameters in decision variables with an accepted converge time.

The rest of this paper is organized as follows: Sect. 2.1 discusses the related works. Section 3 introduces the motivation of proposing a parameter-independent human behaviour sensing method. Section 4 introduces the design of FreeSee, followed by the evaluation in Sect. 5. Section 6 concludes the paper.

2   Related Works

2.1   Pattern-Based Approaches

The pattern-based method focuses to find the unique and consistent relations between certain human activity and wireless signal variation [5]. The key to design pattern-based approaches is to find patterns to math different human behaviors, the complexities of the human behaviors depend on the required granularity and the complexity of the recognition tasks [2,37,38]. Currently, the classical pattern-based sensing system could accurately sense human behaviors with different granularities, the classical pattern-based works and their accuracies are considerable. The accuracy of Aryokee [36] is 92% for the fall detection category, while the accuracy of WiPose [15] for daily behaviour sensing could achieve 96%, the accuracy of UltraGesture [19] is 97% for fine-grained finger gesture recognition domain, the accuracy of Mar [14] in gait detection category is 95%, the motion-sensing accuracy of EQ-Radio [23] is 87%, and the highest sensing accuracy of breath and heartbeat category could get 98.5%, the average accuracy of rRuler [10] could achieve 90%. Other state-of-the-art works such as [1,17,24,25,29,32,33] also conduct a accuracy higher than 90%. However, the accuracies of state-of-the-art works illustrate that the values in a certain scenario with a certain training dataset, and the parameters which could get these accuracies are empirical values tested by the authors in their scenarios and datasets

[39]. Therefore, it is hard to get the optimized parameters to increase the sensing accuracy in practical applications. In this paper, we propose FreeSee, which aims to get the optimized parameters automatically for different scenarios and datasets. Freese could be narrow down the experimental results and real-world deployments for the wireless-based human behaviour sensing applications.

2.2 Model-Based Approaches

Model-based model is to relate the signal space to the physical space including human and environment, and reveal the physical law and mathematical relationships between channel state information (CSI) and sensing targets [5]. The current model-based approaches include CSI-Speed model, Angle of Arrival (AoA) model and Fresnel Zone model. CARM [30] and Widar [18] are the classical work of CSI-Speed model, in which CARM [30] also uses pattern-based method to classifier the CSI-Speed features. Angle of arrival (AoA) measurement is a method of determining the direction of propagation of a radio frequency wave incident on an antenna array, and uses MUSIC algorithm to calculate the AoA between wireless devices and sensing targets, MaTrack [34] is the classical work for AoA model, the AoA model are mostly used in localization scenarios. The method proposed in article [7] is the classical work uses Fresnel Zone model. Other works with deep learning methods such as [3,4] are also conducted to evaluate human behaviors in medical use.

There is an assumption that the model-based approaches have to use the fine-grained wireless signatures which obtained by an antenna array, the wireless devices with signal antenna could not uses the model-based approaches. Therefore, FreeSee proposed in this paper focusing on the pattern-based approaches. How to realize the parameter-independent human behaviours sensing system with model-based approaches is not the research concern of this paper.

3 Motivation

State-of-the-art pattern-based human behaviour sensing systems have several parameters in each process showed in Fig. 1.

Figure 1 shows that the parameters are distributed in every process of the human behaviour sensing procedures. The value of each parameter could affect the final sensing accuracy of the pattern-based human behaviour sensing systems. We take our previous work rRuler [10] as an example, we find that the sensing accuracy has close correlations with the grained of the collected wireless signatures, the parameters of the feature extraction methods and classification algorithms.

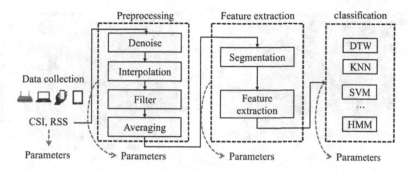

Fig. 1. The parameters distributed in the whole processes of the pattern-based human behaviour sensing systems.

3.1 Correlation Between Sensing Accuracy and the Grains of the Wireless Signatures

In order to evaluate the correlation between sensing accuracy and the grains of the wireless signals, we collected RSS and CSI data for the 7 gestures discussed in article [10], we fixed other parameters in the feature extraction and classification procedures. The sensing accuracy by RSS and CSI are different, the accuracy by using RSS is 93.75% and the accuracy by using CSI could achieve 99% in average. Therefore, sensing accuracy has close correlation with the grains of the collect signal signatures, how to narrow down the effects of the wireless signatures collected from the off-the-shelf devices is an essential issue to construct a parameter-independent pattern-based device-free human behaviour sensing system. FreeSee proposes to add a time domain features to enhance the feature contains in coarse-grained RSS, which will be introduced in design part.

3.2 Correlation Between Sensing Accuracy and Feature Extraction Parameters

In our previous work rRuler [10], we propose to use short-time Fourier transform and k-means algorithm to extract the feature for each gesture, the parameters of the short-time transform algorithm including the window size, overlap, frequency range and sampling rate and etc., the parameters of k-means are the cluster number. Figure 2 and Fig. 3 shows the impacts of the windows size and overlap on feature extraction results. It is obvious that the feature shows in Fig. 2 is not accurate as the features shows in Fig. 3, therefore, how to set the windows and overlap of the short-time Fourier transform method is a significant for increasing the sensing accuracy in practical sensing systems. The value of k-means also affects the final sensing accuracy of the sensing systems. The results showed in Fig. 4 illustrates this phenomenon.

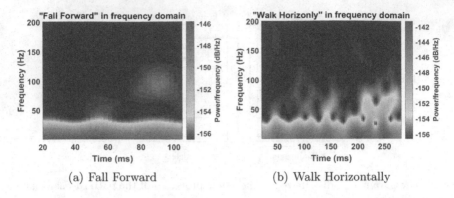

Fig. 2. Frequency domain features of 6 classical gestures collected by article [10] when window size = 128 and overlap = 120.

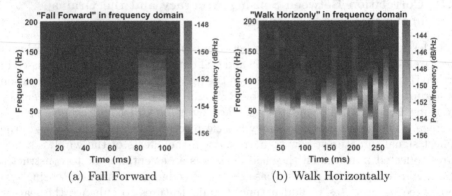

Fig. 3. Frequency domain features of 6 classical gestures collected by article [10] when window size = 64 and overlap = 32.

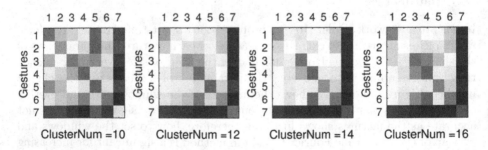

Fig. 4. The impact by the k-means values.

4   Design of FreeSee

According to the analysis in Sect. 3, this section design FreeSee from three aspects: i) achieving wireless signal independent sensing, ii) defining a set of decision variables for optimization to realize feature extraction and classifier parameter-independent design and iii) achieving a fast convergence optimization by using genetic algorithm. The design overview of FreeSee is showed in Fig. 5

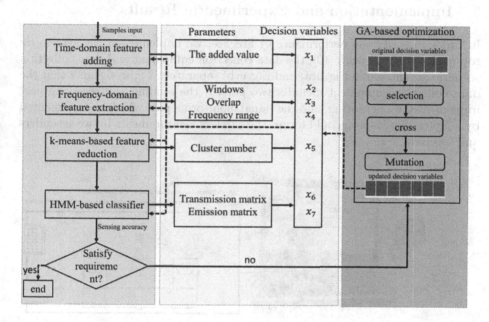

Fig. 5. The impact by the k-means values.

4.1   Correlation Between Sensing Accuracy and Classification Parameters

The main function of each module is summarized as follows:

– Human behavior sensing module; the main function of this module is showed in the green part in Fig. 5, in this module we added a time-domain feature adding subfunction to enhance the features for different human behaviors, then we do the frequency-domain feature extraction, k-means-based feature reduction, and SVM-based human gesture classification.

- Decision variables defining module; the main function of this module is defining the parameters which have dominant affects to the sensing accuracy, in this part, we summarized the dominant parameters which have been analysed in motivation part, and take the decision variables as the target optimizing parameters.
- GA-based optimization part; the main function of this module is to choose the decision variables for parameter-independent human behavior sensing.

5   Implementation and Experimental Results

In order to verify the performance of FreeSee, we implemented the system on top of our previous work [10], the data collection equipment and data collection scenario are showed in Fig. 6(a) and Fig. 6(b) separately. Figure 6 shows that the data collection equipment includes two part: i) the sending and receiving part implemented by Sensortag, and the signal monitoring part which is implemented by a laptop. The laptop could record the wireless measurements between senders and receivers.

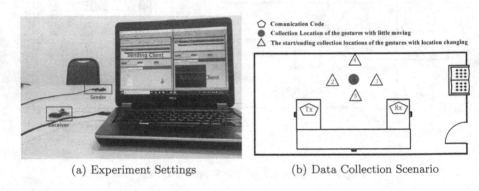

(a) Experiment Settings   (b) Data Collection Scenario

Fig. 6. Experiment settings and data collection scenarios

5.1   Performance Metrics

We take the sensing accuracy and coverage time of genetic algorithm as the performance metrics.

- **Sensing Accuracy:** We uses sensing accuracy to evaluate the performance of *FreeSee* system, which also could further verify the efficiency of *FreeSee*. Sensing accuracy is the ratio of the number of gestures which could be predicted correctly by *FreeSee* and those could not be.
- **Convergence time:** We uses the running time of our python-based simulator to evaluate the time to find the optimized parameters.

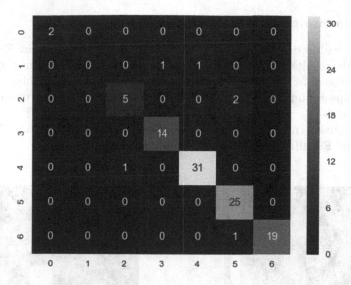

Fig. 7. Sensing accuracy of different gestures of *FreeSee*.

5.2   Performance of the Optimized Results

The optimized sensing accuracy of *FreeSee* proposed in this paper are showed in Fig. 7. The results in Fig. 7 shows that the sensing accuracy of gesture 3, 4, 5, 6 have a accuracy around 99%. While the results of gesture 0, 1, 2 has a lower accuracy since they do not have enough samples. The convergence time of genetic algorithm for searching the optimizing results is showed in Fig. 8.

Figure 8 shows that GA-based FreeSee could be converged in a accepted time.

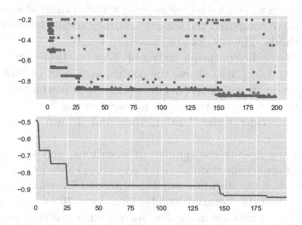

Fig. 8. The convergence time of *FreeSee*

5.3   Comparison with Other Algorithms

In order to evaluate the efficiency of time-domain feature added in *FreeSee*, we compared the results with two other feature added method: i) Cut method, which truncating the data according to the shortest sequence and ii) Interp Method, which use upsampling method to add points to the raw data. Our method called "add" in short.

The confusion matrix of Cut method and Interp Method are showed in Fig. 9(a) and Fig. 9(b) respectively.

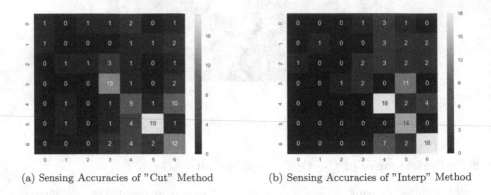

(a) Sensing Accuracies of "Cut" Method   (b) Sensing Accuracies of "Interp" Method

Fig. 9. Sensing accuracies of other algorithms

5.4   Comparison with the Algorithm Without GA

In order to evaluate whether *FreeSee* could get the optimized sensing accuracy of each gestures. We compared the sensing accuracy results between FreeSee and SVM-based methods. The results are showed in Fig. 9.

Figure 9(a) shows the confusion matrix of "Cut" method, with average accuracy of 43.14%, and Fig. 9(b) shows the confusion matrix of "Interp" method, with the average accuracy of 50.98%. The results of our method is 87.25% including the two gestures with littler samples (showed in Fig. 7).

The convergence time of the "Cut" method and "Interp" method are showed in Fig. 10,

The "x" axis represents the number of iterations, and the "y" axis represents the value of object function of GA. Figure 10(a) shows that "Cut" method would converge when the iteration number is around 55, while "Interp" method would converge when the iteration number is around 75 (showed in Fig. 10(b)). Compared with these two methods, *FreeSee* would converge when the iteration number is 25 (showed in Fig. 8).

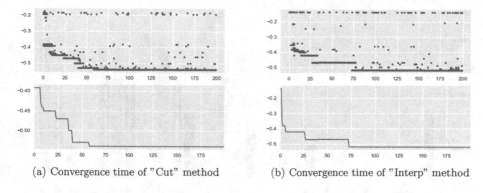

(a) Convergence time of "Cut" method   (b) Convergence time of "Interp" method

Fig. 10. Convergence time of other algorithms

5.5 Comparison with the Algorithm Without GA

In order to evaluate whether *FreeSee* could get the optimized sensing accuracy of each gestures. We compared the sensing accuracy results between FreeSee and SVM-based methods. The results are showed in Fig. 11.

Figure 11 shows the confusion matrix before and after using genetic algorithm. The results show that the average accuracy is increased to 91.30% compared with the results without genetic algorithm. The detailed accuracy of each gesture are showed in Fig. 12.

The results showed in Fig. 12 show that the accuracy of most of the gestures are increased after using genetic algorithm for parameters optimization.

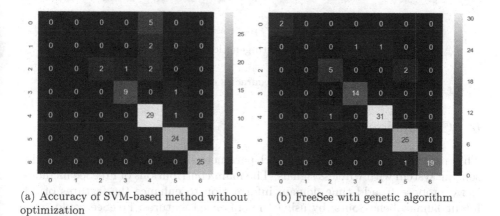

(a) Accuracy of SVM-based method without optimization   (b) FreeSee with genetic algorithm

Fig. 11. Accuracy comparison between SVM-based method and FreeSee with genetic algorithm

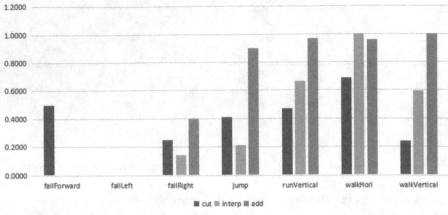

(a) Accuracy of SVM-based method without optimization

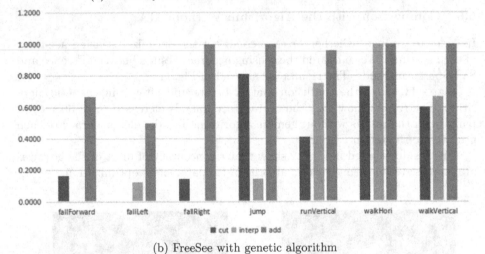

(b) FreeSee with genetic algorithm

Fig. 12. Detailed accuracies of each gestures

6   Conclusion

This paper proposes FreeSee, a novel parameter-independent human behavior sensing system with wireless signals. The main contributions of FreeSee includes: i) we propose to add time domain information to enhance the features of different human behaviours, by using the enhanced features, FreeSee could sense the human behaviours both with coarse-grained and fine-grained wireless signatures. Therefore, FreeSee could achieve wireless signature independent human behaviours sensing. ii) according to the results conducted by state-of-the-arts, we selected a group of data processing methods, and find a series of dominant parameters as the decision variables for the input of optimization algorithms. And iii) we propose to use genetic algorithm to optimize the decision variables which summarize in contribution (2), and find the optimized parameters according to different training datasets. Experimental results show that our method could optimized the decision variables automatically.

References

1. Wu, C., Zhang, F., Hu, Y., Liu, K.J.R.: GaitWay: monitoring and recognizing gait speed through the walls. IEEE Trans. Mob. Comput. **20**, 2186–2199 (2020)
2. Chen, W., Long, G., Yao, L., et al.: AMRNN: attended multi-task recurrent neural networks for dynamic illness severity prediction. World Wide Web **23**(5), 2753–2770 (2020)
3. Chen, W., Yue, L., Li, B., Wang, C., Sheng, Q.Z.: DAMTRNN: a delta attention-based multi-task RNN for intention recognition. In: Li, J., Wang, S., Qin, S., Li, X., Wang, S. (eds.) ADMA 2019. LNCS (LNAI), vol. 11888, pp. 373–388. Springer, Cham (2019). https://doi.org/10.1007/978-3-030-35231-8_27
4. Chen, W., Wang, S., Zhang, X., et al.: EEG-based motion intention recognition via multi-task RNNs. In: Proceedings of the 2018 SIAM International Conference on Data Mining. Society for Industrial and Applied Mathematics, pp. 279–287 (2018)
5. Wu, D., Zhang, D., Xu, C., Wang, H., Li, X.: Device-free WiFi human sensing: from pattern-based to model-based approaches. IEEE Commun. Mag. **55**(10), 91–97 (2017)
6. Decker, R., Shademan, A., Opfermann, J., Leonard, S., Kim, P., Krieger, A.: A biocompatible near-infrared 3D tracking system. IEEE Trans. Biomed. Eng. **64**(3), 549–556 (2017)
7. Zhang, D., Wang, H., Wu, D.: Toward centimeter-scale human activity sensing with Wi-Fi signals. IEEE Comput. **50**(1), 48–57 (2017)
8. Zhang, F., et al.: SMARS: sleep monitoring via ambient radio signals. IEEE Trans. Mob. Comput. **20**, 217–231 (2019)
9. Adib, F., Mao, H., Kabelac, Z., Katabi, D., Miller, R.C.: Smart homes that monitor breathing and heart rate. In: ACM Conference on Human Factors in Computing Systems (CHI) (2015)
10. Sun, H., Lu, Z., Chen, C., Cao, J., Tan, Z.: Accurate human gesture sensing with coarse-grained RF signatures. IEEE Access **7**, 81227–81245 (2019)
11. Abdelnasser, H., Harras, K.A., Youssef, M.: UbiBreathe: a ubiquitous non-invasive WiFi-based breathing estimator. In: ACM International Symposium on Mobile Ad Hoc Networking and Computing (MobiHoc) (2015)
12. Li, H., Yang, W., Wang, J., Xu, Y., Huang, L.: WiFinger: talk to your smart devices with finger-grained gesture. In: ACM International Joint Conference on Pervasive and Ubiquitous Computing (UbiComp) (2016)
13. Wang, H., Zhang, D., Wang, Y., Ma, J., Wang, Y., Li, S.: RT-Fall: a real-time and contactless fall detection system with commodity WiFi devices. IEEE Trans. Mob. Comput. **16**(2), 511–526 (2017)
14. Fei, H., Xiao, F., Han, J., Huang, H., Sun, L.: Multi-variations activity based gaits recognition using commodity WiFi. IEEE Trans. Veh. Technol. **69**(2), 2263–2273 (2020)
15. Jiang, W., et al.: Towards 3D human pose construction using WiFi. In: International Conference on Mobile Computing and Networking (MobiCom) (2020)
16. Chauhan, J., Hu, Y., Seneviratne, S., Misra, A., Seneviratne, A., Lee, Y.: BreathPrint: breathing acoustics-based user authentication. In: International Conference on Mobile Systems, Applications, and Services (MobiSys) (2017)

17. Niu, K., et al.: WiMorse: a contactless Morse code text input system using ambient WiFi signals. IEEE Internet Things J. **6**(6), 9993–10008 (2019)
18. Qian, K., et al.: Decimeter level passive tracking with WiFi. In: Proceedings of the ACM Workshop on Hot Topics in Wireless, pp. 44–48 (2016)
19. Ling, K., Dai, H., Liu, Y., Liu, A.X.: UltraGesture: fine-grained gesture sensing and recognition. In: IEEE International Conference on Sensing, Communication, and Networking (SECON) (2018)
20. Ali, K., Liu, A.X., Wang, W., Shahzad, M.: Keystroke recognition using WiFi signals. In: International Conference on Mobile Computing and Networking (MobiCom) (2015)
21. Li, T., An, C., Tian, Z., Campbell, A.T., Zhou, X.: Human sensing using visible light communication. In: Annual International Conference on Mobile Computing and Net-working (MobiCom), New York, NY, USA, pp. 331–344 (2015)
22. Raja, M., Sigg, S.: RFexpress! - exploiting the wireless network edge for RF-based emotion sensing. In: IEEE International Conference on Emerging Technologies and Factory Automation (ETFA) (2017)
23. Zhao, M., Adib, F., Katabi, D.: Emotion recognition using wireless signals. Commun. ACM **61**(9), 91–100 (2018)
24. Yu, N., Wang, W., Liu, A.X., Kong, L.: QGesture: quantifying gesture distance and direction with WiFi signals. ACM Interact. Mob. Wearable Ubiquit. Technol. Arch. **2**(1), 51:1-51:23 (2018)
25. Zhang, O., Srinivasan, K.: User-friendly fine-grained gesture recognition using WiFi signals. In: International on Conference on Emerging Networking Experiments and Technologies (CoNEXT) (2016)
26. Nguyen, P., Zhang, X., Halbower, A., Vu, T.: Continuous and fine-grained breathing volume monitoring from afar using wireless signals. In: IEEE Conference on Computer Communications (INFOCOM) (2016)
27. Pu, Q., Gupta, S., Gollakota, S., Patel, S.: Whole-home gesture recognition using wireless signals. In: International Conference on Mobile Computing and Networking (MobiCom) (2013)
28. Maheshwari, S., Tiwari, A.K.: Ubiquitous fall detection through wireless channel state in-formation. In: International Conference on Computing and Network Communications (Co-CoNet) (2015)
29. Shi, S., Xie, Y., Li, M., Liu, A.X., Zhao, J.: Synthesizing wider WiFi bandwidth for respiration rate monitoring in dynamic environments. In: Conference on Computer Communications (INFOCOM) (2019)
30. Wang, W., Liu, A.X., Shahzad, M., Ling, K., Lu, S.: Understanding and modeling of WiFi signal based human activity recognition. In: International Conference on Mobile Computing and Networking (MobiCom) (2015)
31. Chen, W., et al.: Taprint: secure text input for commodity smart wristbands. In: The 25th Annual International Conference on Mobile Computing and Networking (MobiCom), New York, NY, USA, pp. 1–16 (2019)
32. Wu, C., Zhang, F., Fan, Y., Ray Liu, K.J.: RF-based inertial measurement. In: Annual Conference of the ACM Special Interest Group on Data Communication (Sigcomm) (2019)
33. Ma, X., Zhao, Y., Zhang, L., Gao, Q., Pan, M., Wang, J.: Practical device-free gesture recognition using WiFi signals based on metalearning. IEEE Trans. Ind. Inf. **16**(1), 228–237 (2020)
34. Li, X., et al.: Dynamic-music: accurate device-free indoor localization. In: Proceedings of the ACM International Joint Conference on Pervasive and Ubiquitous Computing, pp. 196–207 (2016)

35. Lu, Y., Lv, S.H., Wang, X.D., Zhou, X.M.: A survey on WiFi based human behavior analysis technology. Chin. J. Comput. **41**(27), 1–23 (2018)
36. Tian, Y., Lee, G.-H., He, H., Hsu, C.-Y., Katabi, D.: RF-based fall monitoring using convolutional neural networks. Proc. ACM Interact. Mob. Wearable Ubiquit. Technol. **2**(3), 1371–13724 (2018)
37. Yue, L., Tian, D., Chen, W., et al.: Deep learning for heterogeneous medical data analysis. World Wide Web **23**(5), 2715–2737 (2020)
38. Yue, L., Shen, H., Wang, S., et al.: Exploring BCI control in smart environments: intention recognition via EEG representation enhancement learning. ACM Trans. Knowl. Disc. Data (TKDD) **15**(5), 1–20 (2021)
39. Yue, L., Tian, D., Jiang, J., Yao, L., Chen, W., Zhao, X.: Intention recognition from spatio-temporal representation of EEG signals. In: Qiao, M., Vossen, G., Wang, S., Li, L. (eds.) ADC 2021. LNCS, vol. 12610, pp. 1–12. Springer, Cham (2021). https://doi.org/10.1007/978-3-030-69377-0_1
40. Zeng, Y., Gu, T., Zhang, D.: FingerDraw: sub-wavelength level finger motion tracking with WiFi signals. Proc. ACM Interact. Mob. Wearable Ubiquit. Technol. **4**(1), 31–58 (2020)

Others

PS-QMix: A Parallel Learning Framework for Q-Mix Using Parameter Server

Xunyun Liu, Xiang Li[✉], Yuan Li, and Boren Xiao

Academy of Military Science, Beijing 100091, China
lixiang41@nudt.edu.cn

Abstract. With the development of deep reinforcement learning and multi-agent modeling, Multi-Agent Reinforcement Learning (MARL) has become a very active research topic recently. Q-Mix is a popular algorithm for solving MARL tasks where the individual agents are allowed to be trained in a centralized manner. As the scale and complexity of MARL tasks grow, there is an urging requirement for a more efficient training strategy. As a consequence, it is demanding to develop a Q-Mix training algorithm which can benefit from parallel computation. However, how classic distributed machine learning frameworks work with Q-Mix is a less studied problem. In this paper, we propose the PS-Qmix algorithm to apply the Parameter Server framework to training QMix agents in parallel. Our algorithm employs multiple distributed worker threads for data generation and model learning, where these two processes are decoupled and executed in alternation. To cater for different simulation speed of the environment, the proposed algorithm allows the user to tune the relative proportion of computation allocated to data generation and model learning. We evaluate the PS-Qmix algorithm on a StarCraft II micro-combat task. As we increase the number of worker threads, we observe significant speed-up in both data generation and model learning. The evaluation results indicate that our method is effective in utilizing distributed computation resources to train Q-Mix agents.

Keywords: Multi-agent system · Deep reinforcement learning · Distributed learning

1 Introduction

Reinforcement Learning (RL) [29] studies the problem of how an agent learns intelligent policy by interacting with the environment to maximize its cumulative reward. Different from supervised learning, RL learns from reward signals rather than direct instructions. With the marriage of reinforcement learning and deep neural networks, recent years have witnessed tremendous success of the Deep Reinforcement Learning approach in fields such as video game playing [18], Go [25,26], robot control [15], poker [19], Real-Time-Strategy games [33], to name a few.

© Springer Nature Switzerland AG 2022
B. Li et al. (Eds.): ADMA 2021, LNAI 13087, pp. 341–352, 2022.
https://doi.org/10.1007/978-3-030-95405-5_24

Many complex problems are essentially Multi-Agent Systems (MAS), where one requires multiple agents to act in an environment either cooperatively or competitively to accomplish certain tasks. Because of its generality, MAS modeling has been applied in problems such as autonomous vehicles [5], network packet delivery, distributed logistics [34] and robot cooperation [13]. In such cases, we may resort to a family of methods named Multi-Agent Reinforcement Learning (MARL). Because of many practical reasons such as computational complexity, communication constraint and/or private observability [9], each participant agent of MARL often has to use decentralized policy while learning towards a coordinated goal, such as to win a certain game. Meanwhile, the whole team is often allowed to learn in a centralized fashion, meaning that global observation information is available and no communication constraints are considered. The above paradigm is denoted as MARL with Centralized Training for Decentralized Execution (CTDE).

Among others, QMix [23] is one of the most widely used CTDE MARL algorithms. QMix models the joint action-value function using a monotonic mixing of each individual's utility function, which entails a rich representational capacity of learning the coordination of the participant agents. Specifically, this is achieved by adding a mixing network over the deep neural network that models the utility function of each agent. The mixing weights, which are produced by hypernetworks [11] from global state information, are restricted to be non-negative. In line with many modern Q-learning algorithms such as DQN, QMix also uses a replay buffer to store historical experiences and a periodically updated target network to achieve efficient learning.

However, as the underlying environment becomes more complex, training MARL algorithms require a huge amount of time for gathering agent experiences from environment interaction. In many scenarios such as physical simulation and complex RTS games, the time needed for data generation grows to be the bottleneck of the whole RL system. In these situations, one often needs to use parallel computation to design a more scalable training architecture. Recently, many distributed reinforcement learning frameworks such as IMPALA [8], APEX [12], GALA [1] and SEED [7] are proposed. However, no empirical evidence has shown that any of these architectures can accelerate the learning of QMix algorithm. In fact, most of the existing distributed RL architectures are designed for training single-agent algorithms. In this paper, we take a primary step to use parallelization in making QMix more scalable. Specifically, we borrow the Parameter Server distribution framework to design a new algorithm named PS-QMix which allows distributed training. By using a central Parameter Server, PS-QMix can launch multiple QMix learner instances (clients) simultaneously. During the training process, the Parameter Server maintains the latest QMix model weights, which are periodically broadcast to all the clients for decentralized execution. The clients are responsible for gathering experiences and perform gradient computation using their local experiences. Data sampling and learning are decoupled and implemented as separate functions in the worker thread. The server collects clients gradients in an asynchronous fashion and apply them to update the server model weights.

In this paper, we made the following contributions:

(1) We propose a novel algorithm PS-QMix which combines QMix with the parameter server framework. By doing so, we allow the QMix algorithms to be trained in a distributed fashion thus to accelerate data gathering and learning.
(2) Using the micro-combat tasks in the StarCraft II environment, we empirically verify that the PS-QMix algorithm can take advantage of parallel computation and achieves faster training.

The following sections are organized as follows. In Sect. 2, we review related works on MARL and parallel reinforcement learning. In Sect. 3, we describe the PS-QMix algorithm in detail. In Sect. 4, we present our experiments and results on the StarCraft II environment. In the final section, we conclude our paper.

2 Related Works

In this section, we will review related works in the field of multi-agent reinforcement learning and distributed reinforcement learning methods.

2.1 Multi-agent Reinforcement Learning

[27] have given the definition of Multi-Agent Systems and identified the open problems in the context of machine learning. The multi-agent Learning problem is essentially more complicated than single-agent learning, because agents would also interact with each other while acting in the environment [4]. [31] have proposed the independent or decentralized learner approach, where each agent treats other agents as part of the environment and learns its own policy. However, this algorithmic assumption is often violated in most Multi-Agent Systems. Specifically, the environment of a MAS is non-stationary from the perspective of each local agent. This makes the learning process unstable [31]. However, despite this theoretic flaw, the independent learner approach is often used in practice and achieves satisfactory results because of its efficiency.

[30] studied a simple MAS problem of two individual DQN agents playing the Pong game and the authors adapted the reward function for the agents. [3] have studied how 2 PPO (Proximal Policy Optimization) learners could be trained in a MAS setting using the MuJoCo simulator.

Meanwhile, many research works have studied the problem of training agents to cooperate in a MARL setting. For example, MADDPG [16] is an actor-critic approach where the critic is used to evaluate the actions selected by the actors. During the centralized learning process, the critic receives information from other agents, while the actors only see the local observations for decentralized execution. MD-MADDPG [22] extends MADDPG and achieves multi-agent communication by using a shared memory. [6] have identified that the multi-agent credit assignment problem is the key to encourage agent coordination, i.e., to correctly allocate the reward for each agent. COMA [9] is a policy gradient based approach which utilized a centralized critic and a counter-factual advantage function to solve the multi-agent credit assignment problem in a fully-decentralized setting. VDN [28] decomposes the team action-value function into additive components contributed from each agent. Q-Mix [23] further relaxes this additive assumption and proposes to combine local value functions using a non-linear mixing which is monotonic. Recently, Q-Mix has been widely in the literature and industry.

2.2   Distributed Reinforcement Learning

Distributed computation is the key to improve the efficiency of reinforcement learning. At an earlier time, [32] studied the convergence of Q-learning in the setting of asynchronous optimization. [10] proposed to use multiple separate actor-learners to accelerate the training of the SARSA algorithm. The actors and learners exchange weight updates in a peer-to-peer approach. [14] applied the Map Reduce framework to parallelize batch reinforcement learning methods with linear function approximation. Parallelism was used to speed up large matrix operations but not to parallelize the collection of experience or stabilize learning.

For deep reinforcement learning, most existing distributed computation methods rely on asynchronous SGD [7] with multiple workers. To parallelize Q-learning algorithms, the Gorilla architecture [21] proposes to use several distributed actors where each actor has its own environment. Meanwhile, it introduces multiple separated learners a central parameter server and an experience replay buffer. Both the learner and the actor has a replica of the network. The learner computes DQN network gradients and communicates with the server, while the actor network is periodically synchronized with the server. A-PEX [12] is a more advanced distributed Q-learning algorithm which uses prioritized replay memory to place more focus on important data samples.

For parallelizing policy-gradient methods, Distributed Asynchronous Advantage Actor-Critic (A3C) [17] proposes to execute multiple agents in parallel asynchronously on a single machine with multiple CPUs. GA3C [2] is the GPU version of A3C where the convergence speed is improved due to GPU's computational power. However, since the policy used on the actor could be outdated, learning becomes off-policy. The IMPALA architecture [8] introduces the v-trace algorithm to correct this off-policy discrepancy and it becomes a widely-adopted distributed reinforcement learning approach in recent days, including [7,33] However, none of the existing works are tailored for Q-Mix algorithm. We still do not know whether existing distributed reinforcement learning framework could accelerate the training of Q-Mix learners in practice.

3   The Parameter Server Q-Mix Algorithm

In this section, we present our customized parameter sever algorithm for training Q-Mix in parallel. As shown in Algorithms 1, 2, 3 and 4, the PS-Qmix algorithm consists of four subroutines. The main program is responsible to launch the parameter server and several workers. Each worker has its own data sampling and the model learning routines. All workers share one central parameter server. Next we introduce each component in detail.

3.1 The Worker

Each worker has its own environment, a copy of the Q-Mix policy network and a local buffer to store the local trajectory data. The environment is where the target agents can make certain observations and perform actions in an informed manner. In the context of Q-Mix, the policy network is a Multi-Agent Controller (MAC) which reads the current local observation of each agent and the global state of the environment to decide the next actions of each agent. The worker runs the data sampling and model learning subroutines in an alternative manner, which is coordinated by the main program to be described later. The advantage of such a design is to decouple data sampling from the model learning processes.

When executing the data sampling procedure, a worker initially pulls weights of the policy network from the server, and uses it to interact with the environment by generating actions based on the current observations and state of the environment. This process generates agent trajectory data which will be inserted to the local buffer of the worker. We repeat until N episodes of data are generated and stored. During this data sampling process, the worker does not pull new weights from the server.

After the data sampling stage, the worker will start the learning process which consists of B steps. To prepare the data and model weights for learning, it samples a mini-batch of data trajectories from the local buffer and pulls new weights of the policy network from the parameter server. Before computing the gradients, it periodically updates the target network as is done in most modern DQN methods [19]. Then, it computes and back-propagates the loss on the Q-Mix network to get the latest gradients. Finally, the weight gradients will be pushed to the parameter server for update.

Notice that the parameters N and B controls the number of iterations for data sampling and learning, respectively. These two parameters allow algorithm users to calibrate the speed of data sampling and learning, which is important in practice, since the underlying environment may have significantly different running speed.

All worker processes run in asynchronous mode, meaning that delayed gradients are theoretically possible. Specifically, it means that while one worker computes gradients using weight w_t, the weight on the server side may already have become $w_{t+\tau}$ due to gradient updates issued by some other worker. However, for a moderately complex environment, the worker thread would spend much more time in data sampling than that of model parameter learning, leading to less frequent gradient updates on the parameter server side. As a consequence, the delayed gradient phenomenon may not be significant, as we have observed in our experiments to be described later.

Algorithm 1. PS-QMix **Parameter Server**

1: $w_0 \leftarrow$ InitWeights()
2: **repeat**
3:    **if** receive g_t **then**
4:       $w_{t+1} \leftarrow w_t - \eta g_t$
5:    **end if**
6: **until** forever

Algorithm 2. PS-QMix **Worker.dataSampling()**

1: $w_t \leftarrow$ UpdateWeightsFromServer()
2: **for** $n = 1, \cdots, N$, generates N episodes of data **do**
3:    **repeat**
4:       $a_i \leftarrow \pi(s_i; w_{t-1})$
5:       $(r_{i+1}, o_{i+1}, s_{i+1}) \leftarrow$ ENV.step(a_i)
6:       LocalBuffer.add($(a_t, r_{t+1}, o_{t+1}, s_{t+1})$)
7:    **until** episodeEnds
8: **end for**

3.2   The Parameter Server

The parameter server is responsible for keeping and distributing the latest version of the Q-Mix network model parameters. It always waits for gradients sent from any of the M workers. After receiving gradients from any of the workers it immediately applies the gradients to update the weights. Upon request, it will send the latest model weights to the requester worker thread. This is implemented in the PullWeightsFromServer() routine.

3.3   Main Program and Its Ray Implementation

As can be seen in Algorithm 4, the main program is responsible for launching the parameter server and the workers while coordinating the data sampling and model learning subroutines using remote calls. To achieve distributed computation, we use the $ray.get(), ray.remote$ and $ray.wait()$ operators provided by the Ray distributed machine learning library [20].

At the worker side, both the *learning* and *dataSampling* procedures are implemented as @*ray.remote* functions which can be invoked from the main program. The main program first invokes the *dataSampling* remote call on all workers. It then waits for the first worker to finish data sampling and starts the learning remote call on that worker followed by another data sampling remote call. The function WaitForReadyWorker() is a blocking call implemented by the $ray.wait()$ operator that waits for at least one worker to finish *dataSampling* and returns the worker id. In this way, each outer iteration of the main program will complete one *dataSampling* process (N episodes of data) plus one *learning* process. The *stopCondition* can be set as needed, in our experiments, we use 10000 episodes of game runs as the *stopCondition*.

Algorithm 3. PS-QMix **Worker.learning()**

1: for $b = 1, \cdots, B$ do
2:     $\tau_b \leftarrow$ LocalBuffer.Sample()
3:     $w_t \leftarrow$ UpdateWeightsFromServer()
4:     if i%T then
5:        $w'_t \leftarrow$ UpdateTargetNetwork(w_t)
6:     end if
7:     $g_t \leftarrow$ ComputeGradient($\tau_t; w_t, w'_t$)
8:     PushGrad(g_t)
9: end for

Algorithm 4. PS-QMix **MainProgram**

1: start the Parameter Server
2: repeat
3:     for $i = 1, \cdots, M$ do
4:        worker$_i$.dataSampling()
5:     end for
6:     $j \leftarrow$ WaitForReadyWorker().
7:     worker$_j$.learning()
8:     worker$_j$.dataSampling()
9: until StopCondition
10: stop the Parameter Server PS

In the next section, we describe our experiments to evaluate the effectiveness of PS-QMix on StarCraft II micro-combat tasks.

4 Experiments

To verify that PS-QMix can accelerate training in practice, we use the StarCraft II micro-combat tasks [24]. Specifically, we choose the 3 m scenario where the MARL algorithm needs to command and control three marine units to fight against three enemy marines.

In this setting, each agent models one marine unit. Its action space include moveUp, moveDown, moveLeft, moveRight, attackEnemyId, stop and noOp, where noOp means no operation. Each marine can only attack when the target unit is within the shooting range. The observation space for each unit includes the relativeX, relativeY, health, shield and unitType of each allied and enemy marine unit. The global state used for centralized execution of Q-Mix include information of all units on the map plus their local observation vectors. Meanwhile, the last action taken by each agent is also recorded in the global state. In our experiment, we aim to train agents that maximize the probability of winning a battle, therefore, we use a sparse reward where +1 stands for winning and −1 for losing.

With the 3 m scenario, we run PS-QMix with a central parameter server and a varied number of distributed workers, starting from 1 to 10. The stop criterion is met whenever the worker has sampled and learned 10000 episodes of game data.

We chose the default neural network model used in the Q-Mix paper, where the agent network is a Deep-Recurrent-Q-Network with a GRU recurrent layer and two fully-connected layers before and after. The hidden size is set to 64.

During the training process, we run evaluation every 20 episodes of the main program, which consists of 100 independent game runs. We record the evaluation winning rate during the whole process. As can be seen in Fig. 1 and 2, we have the following observations:

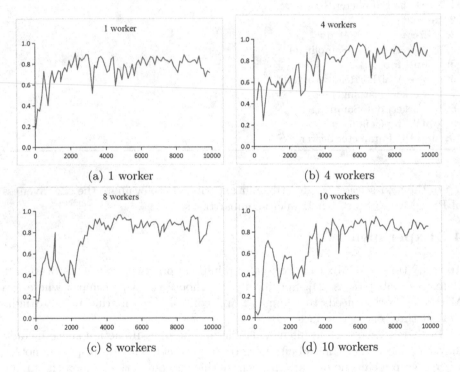

Fig. 1. Evaluation win-rate with respect to the number of game episodes collected by the rollout workers. It can be observed that using more rollout workers do not harm sample efficiency, which is the improved agent performance contributed from learning one data sample in average.

Observation 1. As we increase the number of workers, the evaluation winning rate consistently converges to around 0.8. This entails that the parameter server parallelism we use does not increase the complexity of the underlying reinforcement learning problem. As we use the parameter server to gather gradients and synchronize model parameters after each iteration of the worker thread, the worker is always able to use a (almost) latest version of the policy model to interact with the environment.

Observation 2. The number of training episodes needed to reach convergence does not vary with the number of workers used. In other words, using more workers does not harm sample efficiency which is the improved agent performance contributed from learning one data sample in average. This is understandable. On the one hand, using more workers only increases the speed of data collection, and does not change the number of learning updates needed for the QMix algorithm to converge. Specifically, each worker updates the policy network weights for B times whenever it finishes collecting N episodes of game data. No matter how many workers are used, the number of mini-batch updates performed during the whole training process is always $\frac{10000}{N} \cdot B$. On the other hand, this observation also entails that the delayed gradients phenomenon does not have significantly affect the convergence speed of the whole algorithm. Note that the delayed gradients phenomenon means that when one worker computes gradients the weight on the server side gets updated by some other worker. From Algorithm 2 and 3, we see that the worker thread is decomposed into two stages, i.e., data sampling and learning. In our case of running with the StarCraft II environment, the data sampling process is much more time consuming than model learning. As a consequence, it is less likely for delayed gradients to happen since while one worker pushes gradients other workers are more likely to be doing the data sampling task than updating and pushing gradients.

Observation 3. More workers reduce the needed training time to reach the converged winning rate value, this can be seen in the left subfigure of Fig. 2. This is also understandable since more workers imply that we could get more data samples for training within the same amount of time (see the right of Fig. 2). Meanwhile, the number of updates applied to the Q-Mix policy network also increases with the number of workers.

Overall, our experiments on the StarCraft II micro-combat task demonstrates that the PS-QMix algorithm is an effective distributed algorithm in terms of data sampling speed and convergence rate. It provides a useful paralleled implementation of Q-Mix to make better use of multi-core computation resources. Moreover, by changing the ratio of N and B, our distributed algorithm allows the user to tune the relative proportion of computation allocated for data generation and model learning. This is extremely useful since the algorithm needs to adapt to the speed of model learning as well as the speed of environment execution, which could be quite different for different scenarios.

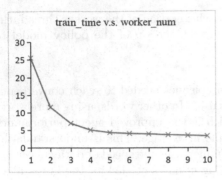
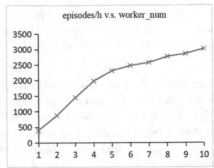

Fig. 2. Left: the training time spent (in hours) towards convergence. Right: The number of game episodes collected per hour w.r.t. the number of workers. Both curves demonstrate log-linear speed-up for using our PS-QMix algorithm.

5   Conclusion

Q-Mix is a popular multi-agent reinforcement learning algorithm for centralized learning and decentralized execution. However, like other reinforcement learning algorithms, the efficiency of Q-Mix greatly relies on the execution speed of the underlying simulation environment, which calls for parallelism for acceleration. In this paper, we propose PS-QMix, a parallel algorithm that uses distributed parameter server to accelerate the training process of Q-Mix. In our implementation, learning and acting are decoupled and called in an alternative manner. We evaluate the effectiveness of our algorithm using the StarCraft II micro-combat tasks. Experiment results on the datasets have shown log-linear speed-up for both environment data sampling and Q-Mix learning convergence.

Acknowledgement. This work is supported by the National Natural Science Foundation of China (61902425).

References

1. Assran, M., Romoff, J., Ballas, N., Pineau, J., Rabbat, M.: Gossip-based actor-learner architectures for deep reinforcement learning. In: Advances in Neural Information Processing Systems, vol. 32, pp. 13320–13330 (2019)
2. Babaeizadeh, M., Frosio, I., Tyree, S., Clemons, J., Kautz, J.: GA3C: GPU-based A3C for deep reinforcement learning (2016)
3. Bansal, T., Pachocki, J., Sidor, S., Sutskever, I., Mordatch, I.: Emergent complexity via multi-agent competition. In: International Conference on Learning Representations (2017)
4. Busoniu, L., Babuska, R., Schutter, B.D.: A comprehensive survey of multiagent reinforcement learning. Syst. Man Cybern. **38**(2), 156–172 (2008)
5. Cao, Y., Yu, W., Ren, W., Chen, G.: An overview of recent progress in the study of distributed multi-agent coordination. IEEE Trans. Industr. Inf. **9**(1), 427–438 (2013)

6. Chang, Y.H., Ho, T., Kaelbling, L.P.: All learning is local: multi-agent learning in global reward games. In: Advances in Neural Information Processing Systems 16, vol. 16, pp. 807–814 (2003)
7. Espeholt, L., Marinier, R., Stanczyk, P., Wang, K., Michalski, M.: SEED RL: scalable and efficient Deep-RL with accelerated central inference. In: ICLR 2020: Eighth International Conference on Learning Representations (2020)
8. Espeholt, L., et al.: IMPALA: scalable distributed Deep-RL with importance weighted actor-learner architectures. In: International Conference on Machine Learning, pp. 1406–1415 (2018)
9. Foerster, J.N., Farquhar, G., Afouras, T., Nardelli, N., Whiteson, S.: Counterfactual multi-agent policy gradients. In: AAAI, pp. 2974–2982 (2018)
10. Grounds, M., Kudenko, D.: Parallel reinforcement learning with linear function approximation. In: Proceedings of the 6th International Joint Conference on Autonomous Agents and Multiagent Systems, p. 45 (2007)
11. Ha, D., Dai, A., Le, Q.V.: Hypernetworks (2016)
12. Horgan, D., et al.: Distributed prioritized experience replay. In: International Conference on Learning Representations (2018)
13. Hüttenrauch, M., Sosic, A., Neumann, G.: Guided deep reinforcement learning for swarm systems. CoRR abs/1709.06011 (2017). http://arxiv.org/abs/1709.06011
14. Li, Y., Schuurmans, D.: MapReduce for parallel reinforcement learning. In: Sanner, S., Hutter, M. (eds.) EWRL 2011. LNCS (LNAI), vol. 7188, pp. 309–320. Springer, Heidelberg (2012). https://doi.org/10.1007/978-3-642-29946-9_30
15. Lillicrap, T.P., et al.: Continuous control with deep reinforcement learning. In: ICLR 2016: International Conference on Learning Representations 2016 (2016)
16. Lowe, R., Wu, Y., Tamar, A., Harb, J., Abbeel, O.P., Mordatch, I.: Multi-agent actor-critic for mixed cooperative-competitive environments. In: Advances in Neural Information Processing Systems, vol. 30, pp. 6379–6390 (2017)
17. Mnih, V., et al.: Asynchronous methods for deep reinforcement learning. In: ICML 2016 Proceedings of the 33rd International Conference on International Conference on Machine Learning - Volume 48, pp. 1928–1937 (2016)
18. Mnih, V., et al.: Human-level control through deep reinforcement learning. Nature 518(7540), 529–533 (2015)
19. Moravcík, M., et al.: DeepStack: expert-level artificial intelligence in no-limit poker. CoRR abs/1701.01724 (2017). http://arxiv.org/abs/1701.01724
20. Moritz, P., et al.: Ray: a distributed framework for emerging AI applications. In: OSDI 2018 Proceedings of the 12th USENIX Conference on Operating Systems Design and Implementation, pp. 561–577 (2018)
21. Nair, A., et al.: Massively parallel methods for deep reinforcement learning. arXiv preprint arXiv:1507.04296 (2015)
22. Pesce, E., Montana, G.: Improving coordination in multi-agent deep reinforcement learning through memory-driven communication (2019)
23. Rashid, T., Samvelyan, M., Schroeder, C., Farquhar, G., Foerster, J., Whiteson, S.: QMIX: monotonic value function factorisation for deep multi-agent reinforcement learning. In: International Conference on Machine Learning, pp. 4292–4301 (2018)
24. Samvelyan, M., et al.: The StarCraft multi-agent challenge. In: Proceedings of the 18th International Conference on Autonomous Agents and MultiAgent Systems, pp. 2186–2188 (2019)
25. Silver, D., et al.: Mastering the game of go with deep neural networks and tree search. Nature 529(7587), 484–489 (2016)
26. Silver, D., et al.: Mastering the game of go without human knowledge. Nature 550(7676), 354–359 (2017)

27. Stone, P., Veloso, M.: Multiagent systems: a survey from a machine learning perspective. Auton. Robot. **8**(3), 345–383 (2000)
28. Sunehag, P., et al.: Value-decomposition networks for cooperative multi-agent learning based on team reward. In: Proceedings of the 17th International Conference on Autonomous Agents and MultiAgent Systems, pp. 2085–2087 (2018)
29. Sutton, R., Barto, A.: Reinforcement Learning: An Introduction (1988)
30. Tampuu, A., et al.: Multiagent cooperation and competition with deep reinforcement learning. PLOS ONE **12**(4), e0172395 (2017)
31. Tan, M.: Multi-agent reinforcement learning: independent vs. cooperative agents. In: ICML 1993 Proceedings of the Tenth International Conference on International Conference on Machine Learning, pp. 487–494 (1997)
32. Tsitsiklis, J.N.: Asynchronous stochastic approximation and q-learning. Mach. Learn. **16**(3), 185–202 (1994)
33. Vinyals, O., et al.: Grandmaster level in StarCraft II using multi-agent reinforcement learning. Nature **575**(7782), 350–354 (2019)
34. Ying, W., Dayong, S.: Multi-agent framework for third party logistics in e-commerce. Expert Syst. Appl. **29**(2), 431–436 (2005)

A Comprehensive Feature Importance Evaluation for DDoS Attacks Detection

Lu Zhou[✉][iD], Ye Zhu[iD], and Yong Xiang[iD]

Deakin University, Melbourne 3125, Australia
{zhoulu,ye.zhu,yong.xiang}@deakin.edu.au

Abstract. DDoS attacks still be a critical threat to online services. To defend against attacks, many features are proposed to measure the difference between attack traffic and normal traffic in DDoS detection. However, the feature importance of the features has not been evaluated, and the distinctive features need to be selected for effective detection. In this paper, we propose a comprehensive feature importance evaluation for DDoS detection. We extract 22 features and use four feature selection methods to evaluate the importance in five DDoS attacks detection. We also evaluate and select the distinctive features in the specific, mixed types of attacks detection and attacks identification scenarios. The comprehensive experimental results show that the selected important features perform better than all extracted features using the six popular classifiers.

Keywords: DDoS attacks · Feature selection · Machine learning

1 Introduction

Distributed Denial of Service (DDoS) attacks have still been a great threat to online applications, services and infrastructure. A DDoS attack is a kind of cyber attack that an attacker deliberately sends massive malicious packets to a victim, aiming to exhaust the computational resources, such as CPU and memory, and thus disturb or deny benign users' requests. As the number of vulnerability devices (bots) increases, DDoS attacks' scale and size are significant and still keep increasing in recent years. For example, a recent report shows that the attack size reached 1.7 Tbps in 2019 [4]. Moreover, the complexity of the attack types makes it even more challenging to defend. A recent study shows that some DDoS botnets collaborate to launch multi-types of attacks, exploring the different vulnerabilities of the victim [23].

Detecting DDoS attacks is the foundation for a defense system, and many methods are proposed to distinguish attack traffic from benign traffic. Existing DDoS detection methods are mainly classified into two categories: statistical abnormal detection and machine learning detection. The statistical abnormal detection measures the deviation of the specific features that attack traffic

© Springer Nature Switzerland AG 2022
B. Li et al. (Eds.): ADMA 2021, LNAI 13087, pp. 353–367, 2022.
https://doi.org/10.1007/978-3-030-95405-5_25

present from benign traffic. For example, generalized entropy is applied to measure the probability difference between the low rate DDoS attack traffic and benign traffic [24]. Entropy rate is proposed to measure the difference of entropy changes between the spoofing attack traffic and normal traffic [28]. The abnormal increase in the number of SYN packets is used to detect the SYN flooding attack [26]. The machine learning methods measure distances or similarities in the feature space between benign traffic and attack traffic. For example, an improved KNN classifier is used to detect DDoS attacks in SDN [11]. A CNN deep learning model is proposed to detect DDoS attacks in IoT scenario [13].

Both statistical abnormal detection and machine learning detection methods propose distinctive features, and the detection performance heavily relies on the features. A good feature set can significantly distinguish attack traffic from benign traffic. Moreover, using the most relevant features can improve the classification accuracy and efficiency compared to all features used. Furthermore, the feature importance evaluation can also help us interpret how and why a method, especially a machine learning method, can achieve good results.

In this paper, we propose a comprehensive feature importance evaluation for DDoS attacks detection. We first extract 22 features are commonly used for the detection, and then apply four feature selection methods to evaluate the feature importance. Finally, we evaluate the selected features' detection performance when a victim is attacked by five types of attacks regardless of when the attack types are specific and mixed.

The rest of the paper is organized as follows. Section 2 reviews related work in DDoS attacks detection. We present four feature importance evaluation methods in Sect. 3. A large number of experiments are conducted in Sect. 4. We conclude the paper in Sect. 5.

2   Related Work

There are many features that have been widely studied in DDoS attack detection, such as entropy and the number of SYN packets. Yu et al. [25] used entropy and proposed an entropy variation mechanism to measure changes in the probability distribution to detect DDoS attacks. The detection mechanism focuses on the difference in the probability distribution between legitimate traffic and attack traffic; that is, the concentration degree of legitimate traffic is smaller than attack traffic. Therefore, the entropy value of attack traffic presents abnormal and significantly drops when a DDoS attack is ongoing. Xiang et al. [24] employed generalized entropy and presented an information distance metric to detect and traceback DDoS attacks. They argued that the probability distribution of the attack flows concentrated more than that of legitimate flows; the entropies of legitimate flows (including Shannon entropy and generalized entropy) were higher than those of attack flows. However, the false negative rate of entropy-based methods is high when the number of flows increases in the spoofing DDoS attack. Lu et al. improved the entropy-based methods by considering the number of flows and used the feature entropy rate to detect the low-rate and spoofing attacks [28]. Kumar et al. used the feature normalised entropy to detect and mitigate the SYN flooding attack in software-defined networking (SDN) [16].

Features that related to packet size are also studied in DDoS attack detection. The detection mechanism is that the attack traffic is prebuilt, and the packet size distribution of attack traffic presents abnormal compared to that of normal traffic. Based on this, the authors in [27] used the feature, expectation of packet size, to detect low-rate DDoS attack. They argued that the attack packets were distributed in small size, and the feature, which is the expectation of packet size, can effectively distinguish attack traffic from normal traffic. Oo et al. [19] used features like average packet size, packet-size variance to detect HTTP flooding attacks. An attack can be detected if the feature values exceed the thresholds.

Protocol-related features, such as the number of SYN packets, the number of ACK packets, are employed in DDoS attack detection. Attacks that targeted the protocol's vulnerability, such as SYN flooding, explore the vulnerability of TCP three-way-handshaking connection and send massive SYN packets to open half connection to exhaust TCP state resources. Based on the abnormal distribution in the feature number of SYN packets, Zheng et al. proposed a correlation-based detection method to detect SYN flooding attacks [26]. A feature, the ratio of the number of SYN packets to that of ACK packets, was applied, and they argued that the feature's value significantly increased in the SYN flooding attack traffic. Wang et al. also argued that the HTTP packets are the domain packets used for DDoS attacks [23]. Liu et al. applied features, such as the packet loss rate and the number of packets, to detect and mitigate DDoS attacks [18].

3   Feature Importance Evaluation

In this section, we present four methods to evaluate the feature importance in the DDoS attack detection, and they are AUC, decision tree (DT), random forest (RF) and mutual information (MI).

3.1   AUC

Since the attack duration is dynamic and determined by the attacker, the real DDoS attack may not last for a long term [23]. If we split the attack and benign traffic into the positive and negative sample using the same time interval, the positive sample is the minority class compared to negative samples and presents an imbalance distribution. Therefore, we use the area under the ROC (Receiver Operating Characteristics) curve (AUC) [7] to evaluate the feature importance since it considers the imbalanced data distribution [12].

Let $X \in R^{d \times n}$ be a feature set with n samples and d features, where $f_i \in R^{1 \times n}$ is the ith feature vector. Let Y be the class label and $Y = \{Y_i \in \{+1, -1\}\}$. For feature f, let $f^+ = \{x_i^+, Y_i = +1 | i \in [n_+]\}$ be the positive samples, where n_+ is the number of positive samples; let $f^- = \{x_i^-, Y_i = -1 | i \in [n_-]\}$ be the negative samples, where n_- is the number of negative samples. The AUC of feature f is defined as:

$$AUC(f) = \sum_{i=1}^{n_+} \sum_{j=1}^{n_-} \frac{\prod[f(\mathbf{x}_i^+) > f(\mathbf{x}_j^-)] + \frac{1}{2}\prod[f(\mathbf{x}_i^+) = f(\mathbf{x}_j^-)]}{n_+ n_-} \tag{1}$$

where $\prod[X]$ is the indicator function and we can have 1 when the case X satisfies and 0 otherwise, and we have $AUC \in [0,1]$. According to [9], the AUC score of a feature can be applied to measure the importance: the AUC score of an important feature is close to 0 or 1 as it is respectively relevant to the negative or positive class; while an irrelevant feature's AUC score is close to 0.5. For a fair comparison, we rescale the score by $AUC'(f) = 1 - AUC(f)$ for $AUC(f) < 0.5$ and thus $AUC' \in [0.5, 1]$. We use the AUC' as the final feature importance evaluation for this method, and an important feature can be identified if the AUC' exceeds the threshold α. For simplicity, we refer to AUC' as AUC in the rest of the paper.

3.2 DT and RF

Both DT [21] and RF [8] are tree-based classifiers such that each node on a tree represent a feature selected to make decision about how to split the data set into two separate subsets with similar responses within. Then it can calculate how much each feature decreases the weighted impurity in each node of a tree. Here we apply the Gini feature importance for measuring feature relevance.

For a set of N_τ samples with K classes at node τ, let p_k be the probability of samples labelled with class k, $k \in \{1, 2, ..., K\}$, N be the total samples, the Gini impurity $i(\tau)$ of node τ is calculated as:

$$i(\tau) = \sum_{k=1}^{K} p_k(1 - p_k) \tag{2}$$

In a binary tree, $K = 2$. The decrease of the impurity Δt that split the samples into left child τ_L and right child τ_R is:

$$\Delta i(\tau) = i(\tau) - w_L i(\tau_L) - w_R i(\tau_R) \tag{3}$$

where $w_L = \frac{N_{\tau L}}{N_\tau}$ and $w_R = \frac{N_{\tau R}}{N_\tau}$ are the weight of left and right child at node τ. For a feature i, the feature importance $I(i)$ on a decision tree is calculated as the sum of the weighted impurity decreases for all nodes τ:

$$I(i) = \sum_{\tau} w_\tau \Delta i(\tau) \tag{4}$$

where $w_\tau = \frac{N_\tau}{N}$ is the proportion of samples reaching τ. The normalized feature importance for a decision tree as follows:

$$I(i)' = \frac{I(i)}{\sum_{i=1}^{N_f} I(i)} \tag{5}$$

where $\sum_i I(i)' = 1$. If $I(i)'$ reaches or exceeds a threshold β, we identify feature i as an important feature using DT.

In a random forest, let N_T be the number of trees, the feature importance $I_R(i)$ is the average of $I(i)'$ over all trees:

$$I_R(i) = \frac{1}{N_T} \sum_{N_T} I(i)' \tag{6}$$

where $\sum_i I_R(i) = 1$. If $I_R(i)$ reaches or exceeds a threshold γ, we identify feature i as an important feature using RF.

3.3 Mutual Information

The MI measures the mutual dependency between two random variables, i.e., it quantifies how much knowing the response reduces uncertainty about the predictor [6], e.g., in our case, the feature and the class. In this section, we output the MI score as the importance weight for the feature.

Let (X, Y) be a pair of feature X and class label Y, $P_{(X,Y)}$ be the joint distribution and P_X, P_Y be the marginal distribution. The MI between feature X and Y is defined as:

$$I(X;Y) = D_{KL}(P_{(X,Y)} \| P_X \otimes P_Y) \tag{7}$$

where D_{KL} is the Kullback-Leibler divergence. $0 \leq I(X;Y) \leq H(X)$, where $H(X)$ is the entropy of feature X. $I(X;Y) = 0$ when X and Y are independent, which means feature X provides no information on identifying class Y. On the other hand, $I(X;Y) = H(X)$ when X is highly related to Y, which means X is the most informative feature on identifying class Y. Therefore, an important feature X can be identified if the $I(X;Y)$ reaches or exceeds a threshold δ.

4 Experiment Results

4.1 Datasets

To comprehensively evaluate the feature importance, we use five sophisticated DDoS attacks to attack a victim. The details are described as follows.

- SYN Flooding (SYN): An SYN flooding attack is a type of TCP state exhaustion attack that an attacker purposely exhausts the resources of SYN-Queue in the TCP connection. This is achieved by sending massive SYN requests to open half-opening TCP connection in the three-way-handshaking process and keep the corresponding final ACK packets to prevent the completion of the TCP connection [16]. The data we used comes from the Impact [2], and it contains 3,955,270 attack packets.

- DNS amplification (DNS) attack: The DNS amplification attack is a volumetric-based DDoS attack that the attacker overwhelms the victim's server using massive packets reflected from DNS servers. The attacker sends small requests to the DNS servers, and the servers could respond to larger replies. Those replies packets are targeted at the victim since the source IP address of the requests has been modified as the victim's address [14]. The data we used is from Impact, and it has 18,372,712 packets.
- Pulsing attack (Pulse): To avoid being detected, an attacker periodically sends attack packets by launching a pulsing attack. Compared to traditional attacks, the pulsing attack volume is significantly smaller, thus avoiding the abnormal detection [20]. The data is provided by Impact, which contains 2,665,797 packets.
- LowRate attack (Low): To conceal in benign traffic, the volume and attack rate of a low-rate DDoS attack is similar to benign traffic, hence evading the anomaly detection systems. The data comes from the Center for Applied Internet Data Analysis (CAIDA) [1], and we have 166,448 packets.
- Spoofing attack (Spoof): The spoofing attack is a sophisticated DDoS attack that the packet's information has been spoofed, especially the source IP address, to avoid being identified and traceback by detection systems. The data we used comes from the CAIDA, which provides us with 6,481,709 packets.

In this experiment, ISCX traffic is used as a victim attacked by the five DDoS attacks. The ISCX traffic comes from the Information Security Centre of Excellence (ISCX), which generating benchmark traffic for intrusion detection [3]. Since attack traffic still contains benign traffic, we merge the attack traffic and the last 300 s benign traffic into the real attack traffic, following the previous work [24]. We split the traffic into samples using a 2-s time window, and the details of the dataset are listed in Table 1. We extract 22 features used for DDoS attacks detection based on previous works [18,23,25] (shown in Table 2) and evaluate the feature importance using the real-world datasets.

Table 1. The details of the datasets.

Dataset	Packets	Duration	Samples
ISCX	11,709,971	29,135	14,567
SYN	3,955,270	300	150
DNS	18,372,712	300	150
Pulse	2,665,797	300	150
Low	166,448	300	150
Spoof	6,481,709	300	150

Table 2. The extracted features for DDoS attacks detection.

Feature	Description
F1. Pkt num	The total number of packets
F2. Ent pkt type	The entropy value of packet type
F3. Max pkt	The max length of packets
F4. Var pkt	The variance of packet length
F5. Ent pkt len	The entropy value of packet length
F6. Ent rate pkt len	The entropy rate of packet length
F7. ICMP num	The total number of ICMP packets
F8. ICMP ratio	The ratio of ICMP packets to all packets
F9. ICMP unreach num	The number of ICMP unreachable packets
F10. HTTP num	The total number of HTTP packets
F11. HTTP ratio	The ratio of HTTP packets to all packets
F12. DNS num	The total number of DNS packets
F13. DNS ratio	The ratio of DNS packets to all packets
F14. SYN num	The total number of SYN packets
F15. SYN ratio	The ratio of SYN packets to all packets
F16. ACK num	The total number of ACK packets
F17. ACK ratio	The ratio of ACK packets to all packets
F18. flow num	The total number of traffic flows
F19. Ent flow	The entropy value of traffic flow
F20. Ent rate flow	The entropy rate of traffic flow
F21. Ent IP src flow	The entropy value of IP source traffic flow
F22. Ent rate IP src flow	The entropy rate of IP source traffic flow

4.2   Evaluation

In this paper, we use six classifiers to evaluate the performance of the selected important features, which are K nearest neighbor (KNN) [10], Logistic Regression (LR) [15], Decision Tree (DT) [21], Deep Learning (DL) [17], support vector machine (SVM) [22] and Random forest (RF) [8]. Due to the different performance of the six classifiers when using the same features, we use the default parameters in sklean [5] and report the average result on the six classifiers as the final result. We use 10-fold cross-validation and F_1 score as the metric for each classifier due to the imbalanced data distribution is shown in Table 1.

4.3   Experiment Results

Traditionally an attacker launches a specific type of attack on a victim, while there is a trend that multi types of attacks are used simultaneously to explore the different vulnerabilities of the victim [23]. Therefore, we evaluate the feature importance in three scenarios: a specific type of attack detection, five simultaneous attacks detection, and attacks identification.

A Specific Type of Attack Detection. In this section, we evaluate the feature importance when a victim suffers a specific type of attack at a time. That is, the victim is respectively attacked by the five attacks. Our goal is to find out the most important features in a DDoS attack detection when a victim is attacked by a specific type of attack. We leverage AUC, DT, RF, and MI to calculate the feature importance for the five types of detection. Table 3 shows the feature importance details for each feature and the average results on the six classifiers using the selected features. The results show that the selected features with the six classifiers can achieve high classification performance.

Table 3. The feature importance of the four methods on the five attacks in the specific type of attack detection.

Method	AUC					DT					RF					MI				
Attack	DNS	Low	Pulse	Spoof	SYN	DNS	Low	Pulse	Spoof	SYN	DNS	Low	Pulse	Spoof	SYN	DNS	Low	Pulse	Spoof	SYN
F1	1.0	0.86	0.59	0.95	0.99	0.18	0	0	0	0	0.27	0.01	0	0.05	0.04	0.03	0.01	0	0.03	0.03
F2	0.89	0.79	0.62	0.53	0.86	0	0	0.05	0	0	0.01	0	0.01	0.01	0.03	0.02	0	0	0.02	0.03
F3	0.51	0.56	0.58	0.60	0.50	0	0	0	0.03	0.21	0.08	0	0.02	0.01	0.09	0	0	0	0.01	0.03
F4	0.52	0.57	0.61	0.76	0.79	0	0	0	0	0	0.19	0	0.01	0.01	0.02	0.03	0	0	0.02	0.02
F5	1.0	0.87	0.62	0.95	0.99	0	0	0	0	0.01	0.07	0	0.02	0.01	0.06	0.02	0	0	0.02	0.03
F6	0.99	0.85	0.58	0.94	0.99	0.69	0	0.01	0	0	0.05	0	0.01	0.03	0.04	0.04	0	0	0.01	0.04
F7	0.50	1.0	1.0	1.0	0.87	0	0.91	0	0.89	0	0.35	0.27	0.27	0.05	0	0.05	0.05	0.05	0.05	0.03
F8	0.50	0.99	0.99	0.99	0.87	0	0.03	0	0.01	0	0.23	0.15	0.12	0	0	0.05	0.05	0.05	0.05	0.02
F9	0.50	1.0	1.0	1.0	0.87	0	0	0.71	0.02	0	0.30	0.25	0.28	0.23	0.06	0	0.05	0.05	0.05	0.03
F10	0.53	0.53	0.53	0.53	0.99	0	0	0	0	0.45	0.01	0	0	0	0.08	0	0	0	0	0.04
F11	0.77	0.67	0.56	0.73	0.96	0	0	0	0	0	0	0	0	0	0	0.02	0.02	0	0	0.03
F12	0.55	0.55	0.55	0.55	0.91	0	0	0	0	0	0	0	0.03	0	0	0	0	0	0	0.02
F13	0.74	0.66	0.59	0.71	0.64	0	0	0.09	0	0	0.02	0.03	0	0	0.01	0	0	0	0	0.03
F14	0.60	0.79	0.66	0.60	1.0	0	0	0	0	0.02	0	0.02	0.03	0	0.13	0	0.02	0.01	0	0.04
F15	0.79	0.63	0.66	0.77	0.76	0	0	0	0	0	0	0	0	0	0	0.01	0.01	0	0.01	0.01
F16	0.59	0.62	0.58	0.74	0.99	0	0	0.01	0	0	0.04	0	0.01	0.02	0.06	0	0.01	0	0.02	0.03
F17	0.99	0.93	0.61	0.98	0.65	0	0.01	0.01	0	0	0.06	0.01	0.02	0.01	0.04	0.05	0	0	0	0.03
F18	0.51	0.70	0.60	1.0	1.0	0	0	0	0	0	0.05	0	0.01	0.12	0.08	0	0	0	0.04	0.03
F19	0.55	0.60	0.51	1.0	0.99	0	0	0.04	0	0	0.04	0	0.02	0.01	0.06	0.02	0	0	0.02	0.03
F20	0.99	0.87	0.59	0.88	0.95	0	0.04	0	0	0	0.01	0.01	0.01	0.03	0.02	0.04	0.01	0	0.01	0.04
F21	0.51	0.57	0.65	0.78	1.0	0	0.02	0	0.04	0	0.05	0	0.03	0.01	0.06	0.02	0	0	0.02	0.03
F22	0.99	0.84	0.64	0.93	0.95	0.11	0	0.02	0	0	0.05	0	0.01	0.04	0.06	0.04	0	0	0.01	0.03
Result	0.92	0.99	0.75	0.99	0.96	0.74	0.91	0.99	0.99	0.99	0.99	0.98	0.75	0.99	0.99	0.95	0.98	0.75	0.99	0.99

For the AUC method, a high AUC score of a feature infers that a binary classifier usually can achieve a high classification performance with that feature. We observe that the AUC scores of our features are considerably high; we consider a feature with AUC higher than 0.8 as an important feature, i.e., $\alpha = 0.8$. For example, in detecting DNS amplification attack when using AUC, these important features are F1, F2, F5, F6, F17, F20, and F22 (i.e., pkt num, ent pkt type, ent pkt len, ent rate pkt len, ACK ratio, ent rate flow and ent rate IP src flow). Similar results can be found in the detection of LowRate, Pulsing, Spoofing, and SYN attacks. For the DT method, since few features are selected by DT, to balance the number of features and effectiveness in the detection, we set the threshold β as 0.03. For the RF method, we choose $\gamma = 0.05$ as our threshold. For the MI method, the threshold δ is set as 0.03. We use the thresholds for each method in the rest of the paper. Note that the thresholds are determined as the balance between the feature importance and detection effectiveness in the experiments; other threshold values might be chosen based on expert knowledge.

Figure 1 shows the F_1 scores when using the selected features and using all features along with their ratio. The ratio represents the F_1 score percentage between the selected features and all features, and if the ratio is greater than 1, it indicates that the selected features outperform all features in classification performance. The results demonstrate that the selected features can achieve similar or even higher performance than all features used as the ratio is significant, which indicates that the selected features are the important features and using these features can improve accuracy compared all features used in the specific type of DDoS detection.

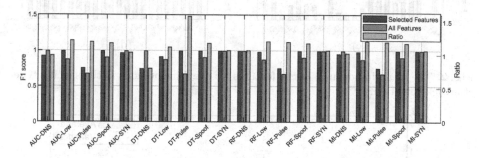

Fig. 1. The F_1 scores when using the selected features and using all features in the specific type of attack detection.

Since the above features are the important features in the given attack detection, and they vary according to the specific attack detection, we analyze the overall feature importance in all detection to investigate the overall important features. Especially, a feature can be identified as an overall important feature if the mean feature importance score on the five attacks detection reaches or exceeds the threshold. Figure 2 shows the mean scores of the feature importance for the four methods in the five attacks detection. We still use the above thresholds, and the details of selected features are shown in Table 4.

We evaluate the detection performance using the overall important features and report the average results of the five specific types of attack detection. Figure 3 shows the average and variance of the performance when using the overall important features. One can see that the features selected by DT, which are pkt num, max pkt, ICMP num, ICMP unreach num, HTTP num, flow num, perform best with the highest average and lowest variance of F_1 scores, which are 0.93 and 0.08, respectively. Followed by the AUC and RF methods, MI performs worst since the F_1 scores on DNS and SYN are only 0.55 and 0.68, respectively.

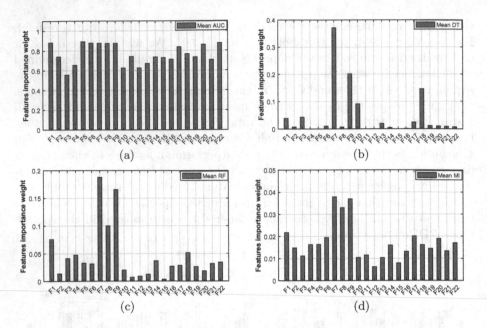

Fig. 2. The mean importance of the features for the four methods in the specific type of attack detection.

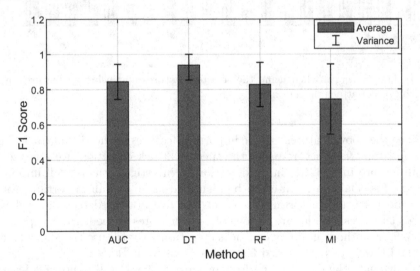

Fig. 3. The average and variance of F_1 scores for the four methods in the specific type of attack detection.

Therefore, the feature set selected by the DT method can be used as the overall features in the five attacks detection.

Table 4. Feature selection using the four methods.

Methods	Specific type				Mixed type			
	AUC	DT	RF	MI	AUC	DT	RF	MI
F1. Pkt num	✓	✓	✓		✓			✓
F2. Ent pkt type								
F3. Max pkt		✓						
F4. Var pkt								✓
F5. Ent pkt len	✓				✓		✓	
F6. Ent rate pkt len	✓				✓		✓	✓
F7. ICMP num	✓	✓	✓	✓	✓	✓	✓	✓
F8. ICMP ratio	✓		✓	✓	✓			✓
F9. ICMP unreach num	✓	✓	✓	✓	✓	✓	✓	✓
F10. HTTP num	✓						✓	✓
F11. HTTP ratio								
F12. DNS num								
F13. DNS ratio								✓
F14. SYN num							✓	✓
F15. SYN ratio								
F16. ACK num								✓
F17. ACK ratio	✓				✓			
F18. Flow num		✓	✓					✓
F19. Ent flow							✓	
F20. Ent rate flow	✓				✓			✓
F21. Ent IP src flow								
F22. Ent rate IP src flow	✓				✓		✓	✓

Mixed Type Attacks Detection. Here we examine the feature importance in the five mixed attacks scenario. We assume that the victim is attacked by the five attacks at the same time. Figure 4 shows the feature importance evaluated by the four methods in the five mixed attacks detection. Specifically, when using the AUC method, the features, which are F1 pkt num, F5 ent pkt len, F6 ent rate pkt len, F7 ICMP num, F8 ICMP ratio, F9 ICMP unreach num, F17 ACK ratio, F20 ent rate flow and F22 ent rate IP src flow, are identified as the most important features in the classification (shown in Fig. 4a). Figure 4b shows the feature importance using the DT method in the mixed attack detection. It clearly illustrates that the selected important features are F7 ICMP num and F9 ICMP unreach num. Particularly, the importance of F7 ICMP num can reach 0.967. Figure 4c and 4d illustrate the feature importance using the RF and MI method, respectively, and the selected features are listed in Table 4.

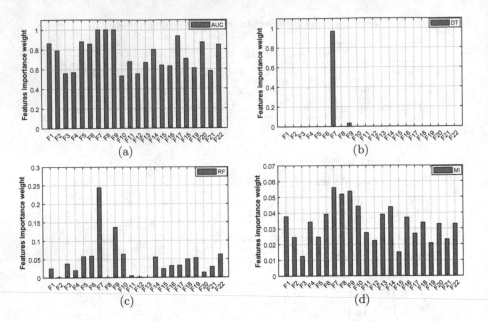

Fig. 4. The importance of the features for the four methods in the mixed attacks detection.

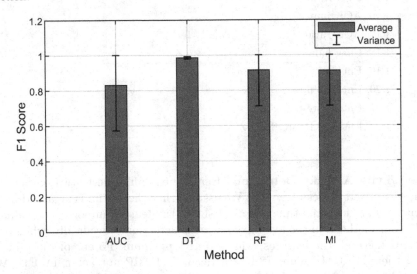

Fig. 5. The average and variance of F_1 scores for the four methods in the mixed type of attack detection.

We further evaluate the classification performance on the selected important features for each method and conduct comparison experiments to exploit the most important features. Figure 5 shows the average and variance F_1 scores of the four selected feature sets on the six classifiers. It clearly shows that the features selected by DT can achieve the most stable performance, i.e., the highest average and the lowest variance F_1 scores, which are 0.98 and 0.065, respectively. RF and MI have the similar performance, which are slightly worse than DT, by approximately 7% in the average F_1 score. AUC is the worst and the average F_1 score is only 0.82 since LR and SVM perform worse in which the F_1 scores are both only 0.49. Therefore, we can see that the features selected by DT, which are F7 ICMP num and F9 ICMP unreach num, generally perform best in the five mixed attacks detection.

Attacks Identification. In the above experiments, we analyze the important features in detecting attacks regardless of the type, i.e., label the attack as 1 for each binary classification; while in this section we attempt to find the important features in identifying the attack type, i.e., label the attack from 1 to 5, then this task is a multi-class classification. We apply the DT and RF methods to rank the feature importance and the results are shown in Fig. 6. Note that AUC cannot use in this task since it only works in the binary classification. In this experiment, features F7, F9, F10, F18, and F21 (ICMP num, ICMP unreach num, HTTP num, flow num, and ent IP src flow) are selected as the important features when using the DT. The average F_1 score using the selected features is 0.90, increasing 5% compared to all features used. On the other hand, features F7, F8, F9, F16, F18, F19, and F21 (ICMP num, ICMP ratio, ICMP unreach num, ACK num, flow num, ent flow, and ent IP src flow) are identified as the important features for the RF method. The average F_1 score using the selected features is 0.88, increasing 3% compared to all features used. We can see that the selected features are the important features in identifying the attack types.

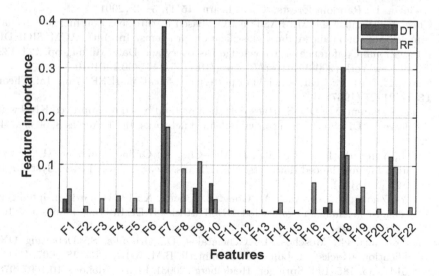

Fig. 6. The feature importance using DT and RF in the attack identification.

5   Conclusion

In this paper, we conduct a comprehensive evaluation on the feature's importance in DDoS attacks detection. 22 popular features are extracted and evaluated by four feature selection methods. The important features have been evaluated and selected in the specific, mixed types of attacks detection and attacks identification scenarios. Based on intensive evaluation with 6 real-world datasets, the results show that six popular classifiers have better performance on these selected features than all extracted features. These features, such as packet number, ICMP number, ICMP ratio and ICMP unreachable number, can be used to design more effective methods in the future.

References

1. Center for Applied Internet Data Analysis (CAIDA). https://www.caida.org/data/passive/ddos-20070804_dataset.xml. accessed 8 Jun 2021
2. Information marketplace for policy and analysis of cyber-risk & trust. http://www.impactcybertrust.org. Accessed 8 Jun 2021
3. Information security centre of excellence. https://www.unb.ca/cic/datasets/ids-2017.html. Accessed 8 Jun 2021
4. Netscout's 14th annual worldwide infrastructure security report. https://www.netscout.com/report/. Accessed 8 Jun 2021
5. scikit-learn. https://scikit-learn.org/stable/. Accessed 8 Jun 2021
6. Battiti, R.: Using mutual information for selecting features in supervised neural net learning. IEEE Trans. Neural Netw. **5**(4), 537–550 (1994)
7. Bradley, A.P.: The use of the area under the ROC curve in the evaluation of machine learning algorithms. Pattern Recognit. **30**(7), 1145–1159 (1997)
8. Breiman, L.: Random forests. Mach. Learn. **45**(1), 5–32 (2001)
9. Chen, X., Wasikowski, M.: FAST: a ROC-based feature selection metric for small samples and imbalanced data classification problems. In: 14th ACM SIGKDD International Conference on Knowledge Discovery and Data Mining, pp. 124–132. ACM, New York (2008). https://doi.org/10.1145/1401890.1401910
10. Cover, T., Hart, P.: Nearest neighbor pattern classification. IEEE Trans. Inf. Theor. **13**(1), 21–27 (1967)
11. Dong, S., Sarem, M.: DDoS attack detection method based on improved KNN with the degree of DDoS attack in software-defined networks. IEEE Access **8**, 5039–5048 (2020)
12. Hu, J., Yang, H., Lyu, R., King, I., Man-Cho, A.: Online nonlinear AUC maximization for imbalanced data sets. IEEE Trans. Neural Netw. Learn. Syst **29**(4), 882–895 (2018)
13. Jia, Y., Zhong, F., Alrawais, A., Gong, B., Cheng, X.: FlowGuard: an intelligent edge defense mechanism against IoT DDoS attacks. IEEE Internet Things J. **7**(10), 9552–9562 (2020)
14. Kambourakis, G., Moschos, T., Geneiatakis, D., Gritzalis, S.: Detecting DNS amplification attacks. In: Lopez, J., Hämmerli, B.M. (eds.) CRITIS 2007. LNCS, vol. 5141, pp. 185–196. Springer, Heidelberg (2008). https://doi.org/10.1007/978-3-540-89173-4_16
15. Kleinbaum, D.G., Klein, M.: Logistic Regression. Springer, New York (2002). https://doi.org/10.1007/b97379

16. Kumar, P., Tripathi, M., Nehra, A., Conti, M., Lal, C.: SAFETY: early detection and mitigation of TCP SYN flood utilizing entropy in SDN. IEEE Trans. Netw. Serv. Manag. **15**(4), 1545–1559 (2018)
17. LeCun, Y., Bengio, Y., Hinton, G.: Deep learning. Nature **521**(7553), 436–444 (2015)
18. Liu, Z., Cao, Y., Zhu, M., Ge, W.: Umbrella: enabling ISPs to offer readily deployable and privacy-preserving DDoS prevention services. IEEE Trans. Inf. Forensics Secur. **14**(4), 1098–1108 (2019)
19. Oo, K.K., Ye, K.Z., Tun, H., Lin, K.Z., Portnov, E.M.: Enhancement of preventing application layer based on DDOS attacks by using hidden semi-Markov model. In: Zin, T.T., Lin, J.C.-W., Pan, J.-S., Tin, P., Yokota, M. (eds.) Genetic and Evolutionary Computing. AISC, vol. 387, pp. 125–135. Springer, Cham (2016). https://doi.org/10.1007/978-3-319-23204-1_14
20. Rasti, R., Murthy, M., Weaver, N., Paxson, V.: Temporal lensing and its application in pulsing denial-of-service attacks. In: 2015 IEEE Symposium on Security and Privacy, San Jose, CA, USA, pp. 187–198 (2015). https://doi.org/10.1109/SP.2015.19
21. Safavian, S., Landgrebe, D.: A survey of decision tree classifier methodology. IEEE Trans. Syst. Man Cybern. Syst. **21**(3), 660–674 (1991)
22. Suykens, J.A., Vandewalle, J.: Least squares support vector machine classifiers. Neural Process. Lett. **9**(3), 293–300 (1999)
23. Wang, A., Chang, W., Chen, S., Mohaisen, A.: Delving into internet DDoS attacks by botnets: characterization and analysis. IEEE/ACM Trans. Netw. **26**(6), 2843–2855 (2018)
24. Xiang, Y., Li, K., Zhou, W.: Low-rate DDoS attacks detection and traceback by using new information metrics. IEEE Trans. Inf. Forensics Secur. **6**(2), 426–437 (2011)
25. Yu, S., Zhou, W., Doss, R., Jia, W.: Traceback of DDoS attacks using entropy variations. IEEE Trans. Parallel Distrib. Syst. **22**(3), 412–425 (2011)
26. Zheng, J., Li, Q., Gu, G., Cao, J., Yau, D.K.Y., Wu, J.: Realtime DDoS defense using COTS SDN switches via adaptive correlation analysis. IEEE Trans. Inf. Forensics Secur. **13**(7), 1838–1853 (2018)
27. Zhou, L., Liao, M., Yuan, C., Zhang, H.: Low-rate DDoS attack detection using expectation of packet size. Secur. Commun. Netw. **2017**, 14 (2017)
28. Zhou, L., Sood, K., Xiang, Y.: ERM: an accurate approach to detect DDoS attacks using entropy rate measurement. IEEE Commun. Lett. **23**(10), 1700–1703 (2019)

Adaptive Fault Resolution for Database Replication Systems

Chee Keong Wee[1]([✉]), Xujuan Zhou[2], Raj Gururajan[2], Xiaohui Tao[2], and Nathan Wee[3]

[1] Digital Application Services, eHealth Queensland, Brisbane, QLD, Australia
[2] School of Business, University of Southern Queensland, Darling Heights, QLD, Australia
{Xujuan.Zhou,Raj.Gururajan,Xiaohui.Tao}@usq.edu.au
[3] Dialog Information Technology, South Brisbane, QLD, Australia

Abstract. Database replication is ubiquitous among organizations' IT infrastructure when data is shared across multiple systems and their service uptime is critical. But complex software will eventually suffer outages due to different types of circumstances and it is important to resolve them promptly and restore the services. This paper proposes an approach to resolve data replication software's through deep reinforcement learning. Empirical results show that the new method can resolve software faults quickly with high accuracy.

Keywords: Database management · Data replication · Reinforcement learning · Fault resolution

1 Introduction

Data replication is a common and important requirement across many organizations and this service is performed by a wide range of software tools that can extract and load data among the multitude of databases. There are various types of data sharing methods but the most common practices are; Extract-Transform-Load (ETL) for Business Intelligent and Decision Support Systems, Extract-Load-Transform (ELT) for Data warehousing centric system, and Near Real-time replication for reporting and disaster recovery purposes [1, 2]. It is imperative to the success of the organization that the data replication service' uptime must remain high at 99.9% [3]. But these data replicating software and the environment that they work with, are complex and can encounter operational faults that can cause disruption. Most of them can be attributed to configuration changes, permission and privilege issues, software bugs, patching, etc. They can be caused by external factors such as issues from operating systems, network connectivity, authentication facility, storage etc. [4]. Therefore, it is important to identify the root cause of these faults and resolve them as soon as possible to minimize replication downtime. It will take a group of administrators of different expertise to resolve the faults [5]. Currently, there isn't much research done in the field of data replication's fault management approach using machine learning [6]. So, we propose a novel approach that uses reinforcement learning to conduct fault resolution tasks in this field of Data replication technology. This paper

© Springer Nature Switzerland AG 2022
B. Li et al. (Eds.): ADMA 2021, LNAI 13087, pp. 368–381, 2022.
https://doi.org/10.1007/978-3-030-95405-5_26

is an extension to a published research that conducted fault detection and diagnosis approaches on the same field [7].

2 Current Fault Resolution Approaches

Once the faults in the data replication environment have been identified and diagnosed [7], the next phase is to resolve them as quickly as possible. Fault resolution for complex software systems is conducted manually by IT administrators and they are laborious and time-consuming [8]. Resolve faults on the software require a systematic approach that covers information gathering and troubleshooting tasks [9]. The IT administrators need to acquire the knowledge of how the software operates, what are its elements' property and configuration should be to support the software and the various type of deviations that the software service may have deviated [10]. The troubleshooting process requires error identification, followed by error diagnosis and apply corrective action to resolve the service [11]. In complex software, many interconnected elements work together cohesively, so if one element suffered a fault, it will have a ripple effect that will impact the other elements and thus creating more outages [12]. But in the current industry, several IT administrators are required to cover a multitude of software. This causes significant delays and thus impact the time taken for restoring any faults. A survey that is like the fault diagnosis is made with the IT administrators from the industry [13]. Similar topics are covered using the Delphi method [14] on the approach of resolving software faults [15]. Manual approach - This is the general approach for all IT administrators to resolve any faults encounters on the systems with their working professional experiences using a combination of logical reasoning and information gathering [9]. External support/best practice - the IT administrator's manual approach forms the first level support for any system's fault but in the event when there are faults that are harder to resolve in-house, external parties will be engaged as the next level of support [16]. Decision rule-based scripting - these are used in current existing topical systems that are either handcrafted by the internal IT administrators or software vendors. They use a series of conditions and logic to apply solutions that are prescribed to topical detected and diagnosed faults [17]. These implementations have some scalability challenges, and they require well-experienced IT administrators to manage and update their logics constantly to keep them relevant [9].

Machine-learning algorithms - this approach has gained significant research in academia; it is gaining gradual adoptions in the industry. The neural network and Markov decision process are common algorithms that have gained significant use to resolve software system faults. It is especially useful when the state-space model between faults and solutions is high and conventional condition-based scripting is not feasible [16].

3 Adaptive Fault Resolution (FR) Module Design

To meet the challenge of an adaptive fault resolution for the data replication environment, we have proposed a novel approach as shown in Fig. 1. It is designed to mimic the function of a human IT administrator that evolved in his/her skill and knowledge through a series of interactions with the DRE and learn which corrective steps work best for each fault's situation, through the guidance of a teaching module. Referencing the research made on the DRE's fault diagnostics part [7] and to Fig. 1, the Fault Resolution (FR) module acts resolving the faults against DRE after it receives the inputs from the System Diagnostics (SD) module [13] on the service outages, and it uses the same architecture as Fault Diagnostics (FD) module [7].

The FR is based on the following outlines: 1) there is a finite number of corrective actions that can be taken to resolve a finite number of faults in the DRE [18]. Fixing the cascaded service faults requires some insights into the software element's attributes and function, where a series of appropriate actions is chosen by the FR module to restore the elements' function [19]. 2) It may take one or more correction iteration before the faults can be resolved [19]. 3) In the event if the faults cannot be resolved, then the system should be notifying the IT administrators for assistance [19]. 4) The FR module's architecture is adaptive and flexible for new changes and unfamiliar events that the FDR has not encountered before [19]. While most of the scenario has been anticipated, some have not been covered. Therefore, in the event when an unplanned scenario occurs, the FR module can adapt to the new challenges. It learns to overcome them and update its knowledge base, thus increase in its expertise. Figure 1 shows an overview of the FR within the FDR system.

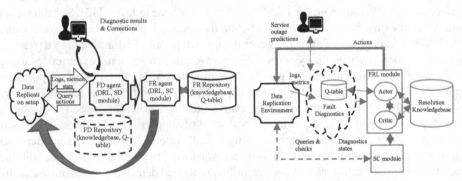

Fig. 1. Adaptive faults resolution overview   **Fig. 2.** Faults resolution agent's architecture and workflow

3.1 Diagnostic Reinforcement Learning (DRL) for FR Module

Figure 2 shows the workflow of the FR module and how it works with the FD module on the DRE. It is like the FD design, and it uses the Actor-Critic reinforcement learning model [20]. After the FD module passed the service outage information as input to the FR which in turn perform a function approximator to predict the best corrective action based on Eq. 1. This forms the Actor part of the DRL model. Besides the FR module is another module called the System Correction (SC) module which looks up detailed system diagnostics information based on the service outage information and tries to determine the exact course of corrective actions to take. These actions are UNIX scripts that contain commands for each of the elements within the specific software that perform some changes, be it altering the configuration, modifying the parameters, reconstitute some files or alter the state of the processes.

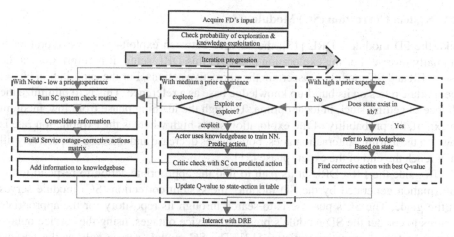

Fig. 3. DRL different phases of learning for the FR module

The SC module forms the DRL's critic which is used to validate the action of the FR as shown in Fig. 2. There are 3 phases of learnings for the DRL as depicted in Fig. 3. 1) Early learning phase; starts with little or no a-prior knowledge on what actions to take for the given FD's service outage input [13]. At this stage, the FR cannot predict anything useful, so it relies on the SC module to guide it. The SC took in the correcting diagnostics information in response to the service outage inputs and derive the list of possible corrective actions. The FR module then applies these actions onto the faulted DRE and receive a new state. If the fault or error persists, this routine will repeat until the problem is either resolved or the number of fault resolution attempts has failed a limit of retries, then it alerts the IT administrator for assistance. 2) Middle learning phase; After it has gathered enough knowledge between the service outage input and the fault resolution actions, the DRL's actor will use this information to train its NN and tries to predict the corrective actions for new service outages input. There is a high possibility that the predicted outcomes will have a high level of error, so the validation process will gauge between the predicted results and those from the SC module. The state-action relationship of both the service outage versus the corrective actions is assigned with a Q-value, and this determines the quality of the actions for a given state. As the knowledgebase grows, it is expected the minibatch for the NN training will be bigger and thus helps in its prediction accuracy. 3) High learning phase. when it reaches this phase, the DRL within the FR module would have considered reaching an expert level. It would have known all the state-actions relations that are associated with the DRE and be competent enough to predict accurate corrective actions for it. This is regarded as the exploitation of the DRL's rich build-up of knowledge where it can provide a very quick turnaround time in providing solutions quickly without invoking any action on the SC module. This is considered exploitation of its rich expert knowledge base. However, it also performs a probability calculation to determine whether it should continue to rely on its knowledge base or take a chance to explore for potential newer actions.

3.2   System Correction (SC) Module

Like the FD module's DRL [13], the balance between exploitation vs exploration is mutually inverse. For the exploration phase, in this DRL setup, it is referred to as the use of FR and SC module to ascertain the corrective actions. For the exploitation phase, the module relies on its build-up knowledge base as a reference. This is to minimize the chance of getting stuck in local optima. Through the learning phase from low, medium to expert, the probability of the exploration starts high whereas the exploitation rate is low. As the learning interaction goes, both phases decrease and increase respectively till they reach the end of the expert phase [21].

To guide the FR's DRL in its path to find the appropriate action to respond to the information generated by the SD module, the system correction (SC) module serves as the guide. The SC's purpose is to search through its repository for the appropriate actions to correct the SD module's predicted service outages, using the service outage related system diagnostics statistics [13]. The SC module serves only as the passive reference to validate the FR module's output and it does not play the proactive role as the intent of the FR module is to be trained up to a level that it knows the corrective actions to take for any given service outages event. For a certain software element's faults, there are multiple corrective solutions to use and at times, it requires more than one corrective action before their faults can be resolved. However, instead of randomly running through every combination of the corrective actions, the SC module chooses the appropriate actions, much like the equivalent of having an expert IT administrator guiding the junior on the appropriate action to take for a given identified fault. Referring to Fig. 1, The SC module receives the FD module's service outage matrix, and it can use the knowledgebase to lookup for the corresponding system diagnostics detailed statistics [13]. Each entity in the system diagnostics statistics is related to a vector of corrective action (CA) for that software element's attributes and function. The correlations have pre-determined like an IT troubleshooting guide except that the guide recommends a series of checks to determine the actions whereas the fault-correction matrix bypasses the checks and prescribe the actions.

The SC module comprises a multitude of libraries of external OS-based commands that interact with the software elements and make changes. These libraries are comprehensive and are maintained following each software's groups domain such as Oracle DB, Shareplex, network and OS. Each of the scripts that are intended to make the corrective changes have been crafted as a response specifically for each unique software element's functions and they are indexed for reference. The rationality of mapping the diagnosed faults to specific actions is derived from the fact that in any typical fault resolving scenario, the troubleshooting workflow passes the system information through various conditions and checks to decide whether a certain course of actions is to be taken and what specific commands or changes are needed. But when such system faults arise, the end goal is to use one or more appropriate corrective actions against the software element in the hope to rectify them or restore their function, it is a 1 : n relationship between faults and corrective actions. Examples of Some of the actions incurred are; 1) altering the state of the system processes through start-up or shutdown, 2) increase space availability for the system's directories, 3) correcting the setting of the privileges of the system's process, files, accounts that they operate from, 4) setting the values of the configurations and parameters that they are using, operating or initialize from, 5) ensuring network card operations' status for network connectivity, 6) unlocking the user accounts or regranting the appropriate privileges, 7) restoring the original baseline copy of the system and network files onto the Unix's/etc. folders and, 6) enabling the replication queues back to operation. This holds the flags of activation to match the library of corrective action scripts in a 1 : m relationship as shown in the matrices in Eq. (1).

$$Diagnostics\ matrix = \begin{bmatrix} oraf_1 \\ oraf_2 \\ \dots \\ oraf_n \end{bmatrix} \begin{bmatrix} spxf_1 \\ spxf_2 \\ \dots \\ spxf_n \end{bmatrix} \begin{bmatrix} nwf_1 \\ nwf_2 \\ \dots \\ nwf_n \end{bmatrix} \begin{bmatrix} osf_1 \\ osf_2 \\ \dots \\ osf_n \end{bmatrix},$$

$$corrective\ matrix = \begin{bmatrix} oraV_1 \\ oraV_2 \\ \dots \\ oraV_n \end{bmatrix} \begin{bmatrix} spxV_1 \\ spxV_2 \\ \dots \\ spxV_n \end{bmatrix} \begin{bmatrix} nwV_1 \\ nwV_2 \\ \dots \\ nwV_n \end{bmatrix} \begin{bmatrix} osV_1 \\ osV_2 \\ \dots \\ osV_n \end{bmatrix}$$

$$(1)$$

Where, the *ora*, *spx*, *nw*, and *os* identify the software groups as Oracle DB, Shareplex, network, and operating system. The suffix, f, identifies the specific software's diagnosed faults and, V, refers to the corrective actions vectors that have m dimensions.

3.3 Representation and Correlation of Diagnosed Faults to Corrective Actions

For the FDR design, a software element can have multiple types of faults and there is a list of corresponding corrective actions. Starting from the FD module, it produced the predicted outcome of the service outage (SO) information of the DRE's state for both the users and the FR module [13]. Each SO has its corresponding System Diagnostic (SD) statistics which has all the specific errors found. The FR module is then based on the SO information to predict the course of corrective actions for the troubled DRE, and the corrective actions are obtained from the external library that has a list of pre-built system commands and OS scripts for the various software elements. It is important to map each specific software elements' fault to those corrective actions that have been predetermined to restore their function. For example, the oracle DB user account may have been locked or lack the system privilege, so the appropriate list of actions is a multitude of commands that range from unlocking the account, granting additional space quota, granting system privilege, to recreating the account. Table 1 illustrates the relationship between the two state-space of diagnosed faults and corrective actions. Sometimes, a single software entity outage can cause multiple faults. For example, Oracle instance outage can attribute to other problems such as loss of database to the Shareplex, inability to read Oracle DB's logfiles by the Capture process, and Oracle DB's account checks. The table below illustrates this complex relationship hypothetically. The scope is narrowed down to the major and more significant form of changes that the corrective actions are developed for, which involves services' start-stop, parameters, and configuration changes, plus privilege and resources allocation.

The software DRE is segregated into 4 tiers: OS, network, database, and Shareplex. The DRL uses the Q-value is used to define the best course of corrective action matrix.

Referring to Table 2, for an example of resolving a common fault like a locked DB account, only the action of unlocking will be required. Therefore, the action for the fault with the vector of actions is required to enable the necessary activation of the commands to unlock it. The following table illustrates this relationship. Each array has a tuple of *<action flag, script id>* where action flag stipulates for activation, and the script id identifies the commands for the software element.

Table 1. Example of diagnosed faults correlation to corrective actions

Diagnosed faults	Corrective actions	Service fault#	OracleDB Action1 (script1.cmd)	Action2 (script2.cmd)	Action3 (script3.cmd)	Shareplex Action1 (script4.cmd)	Action2 (script5.cmd)	Action3 (script6.cmd)	Network Action1 (script7.cmd)	Action2 (script8.cmd)	Action3 (script9.cmd)	Linux OS Action1 (script10.cmd)	Action2 (script11.cmd)	Action3 (script12.cmd)
OracleDB	Fault1 (process, servces)	2	1	0	0	0	0	0	0	0	0	0	0	0
	Fault2 (operation, privileges)	3	0	0	1	0	0	0	0	0	0	0	0	0
	Fault3 (configuration, parameters)	4	0	0	0	0	0	0	0	0	0	0	0	0
Shareplex	Fault1 (process, servces)	2	0	0	0	1	1	0	0	0	0	0	0	0
	Fault2 (operation, privileges)	1	0	0	0	0	0	1	0	0	0	0	0	0
	Fault3 (configuration, parameters)	3	0	0	0	0	1	0	0	0	0	0	0	0
Network	Fault1 (process, servces)	6	0	0	0	0	0	0	0	0	1	0	0	0
	Fault2 (operation, privileges)	1	1	0	0	0	0	0	0	0	0	0	0	0
	Fault3 (configuration, parameters)	2	0	0	0	0	0	0	1	0	0	0	0	0
Linux OS	Fault1 (process, servces)	4	0	0	0	0	0	0	0	0	0	1	0	0
	Fault2 (operation, privileges)	2	0	0	0	0	0	0	0	0	0	0	0	1
	Fault3 (configuration, parameters)	1	0	0	0	0	0	0	0	0	0	0	0	0

Table 2. Association of corrective actions to diagnosed faults for specific software elements.

Oracle's diagnosed faults ID and description	Oracle DB corrective actions flag array	Corresponding action vector to external commands
1 = locked user account	[1,0,0,0,0]	Unlock user account.
2 = incorrect password	[0,0,0,1,0]	Grant space quota.
3 = not enough space	[0,1,0,0,0]	Grant more privilege.
4 = insufficient privilege	[0,0,1,0,0]	Reset password.
5 = user does not exist	[0,0,0,0,1]	Create the user account.

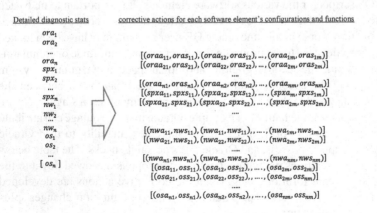

Detailed diagnostic stats   corrective actions for each software element's configurations and functions

ora_1
ora_2
...
ora_n
spx_1
spx_2
...
spx_n
nw_1
nw_2
...
nw_n
os_1
os_2
...
$[os_n]$

$[(oraa_{11}, oras_{11}), (oraa_{12}, oras_{12}), ..., (oraa_{1m}, oras_{1m})]$
$[(oraa_{21}, oras_{21}), (oraa_{22}, oras_{22}), ..., (oraa_{2m}, oras_{2m})]$
....
$[(oraa_{n1}, oras_{n1}), (oraa_{n2}, oras_{n2}), ..., (oraa_{nm}, oras_{nm})]$
$[(spxa_{11}, spxs_{11}), (spxa_{12}, spxs_{12}), ..., (spxa_{1m}, spxs_{1m})]$
$[(spxa_{21}, spxs_{21}), (spxa_{22}, spxs_{22}), ..., (spxa_{2m}, spxs_{2m})]$
....
$[(nwa_{11}, nws_{11}), (nwa_{11}, nws_{11}),, ..., (nwa_{1m}, nws_{1m})]$
$[(nwa_{21}, nws_{21}), (nwa_{22}, nws_{22}),, ..., (nwa_{2m}, nws_{2m})]$
.....
$[(nwa_{n1}, nws_{n1}), (nwa_{n2}, nws_{n2}),, ..., (nwa_{nm}, nws_{nm})]$
$[(osa_{11}, oss_{11}), (osa_{12}, oss_{12}),, ..., (osa_{2m}, oss_{2m})]$
$[(osa_{21}, oss_{21}), (osa_{22}, oss_{22}),, ..., (osa_{2m}, oss_{nm})]$
.....
$[(osa_{n1}, oss_{n1}), (osa_{n2}, oss_{n2}),, ..., (osa_{nm}, oss_{nm})]$

This can be summarized as; $d_{tn} = a_{tnm}$

Where d is the diagnosed faults, t is type software group, n is the number of software element faults, *a* is the corrective action array, m is the number of array's action flags position, $d \in D$ and $a \in A$, where d is the element of all diagnosed faults of set D, a is the element of all corrective actions of set A. the array of corrective action, *a,* is a list of tuples, each with an identification and a numerical reference to the specific entries in the correction external libraries of scripts and OS commands.

3.4 Prioritization of the Software Groups' Action

Not all the software in the DRE is regarded equally. Some can function independently without the need of others while others depend heavily on others to conduct their purpose and service. There is a different level of dependencies stacked hierarchically, starting from the top where one Shareplex operates on top of all the software and IT infrastructure, followed by the oracle DB that requires both networks and operating systems to support its service, but it is not dependent on Shareplex. In the DRE's fault resolution process, there are two extreme scenarios. In the best-case scenario, the fault is a minor and isolated incident that can be resolved by a single action. Such as the database account for Shareplex is locked the only corrective action needed is to unlock it. The service outage information to represent this will be a straight vector that contains no errors except with one value to depict the specific error, e.g. service outage information = [0,1,0,0.....0,0,0,0]. The action required is the corresponding array of software elements' corrective actions array which points to the respective external system commands. But in the worst-case scenario, this happens when a major software element in the DRE fails and that impact the rest of the other elements that depend on it. We proposed to perform corrective actions only to the most important groups of the software elements from the top level down and observe the effect on the rest of the other discovered faults. It is a sequence of succession in solving each software group in stages. This problem-solving process is not a single one-off but requires several iterations to assess just how effective the change will be against the problematic DRE before the next course of action is decided.

3.5 Cost Function and Q-Values for FR Module

The accuracy's measurement of each DRL's NN prediction is derived from finding the absolute differences in value between the predicted corrective actions values against those that are produced by the SC modules. Refer to Eq. (2), if the cost values of the predictions are high, then more work is required in building up the knowledge base and retrain the NN for the DRL. It also determines the confidence level in the FR module to predict the corrective action accurately and this reduces the dependency on the SC module.

$$\text{Cost} = |a_{predict} - a_{actual}| \qquad (2)$$

For a given input state of the service outage and based on the consideration of the software group's priority plus the best number of actions needed, the DRL will select the best course and how it does that is based on the reward that takes in the software group's priority and the number of actions it should take, given the assumption that the corrective actions can indeed resolve the faults as in Eq. (3).

$$Q - values = g_s * h_s \tag{3}$$

where g is the software group's priority in which the faults have occurred, h is the total actions used, s is the service outage state's identification.

For example, if there are faults in the SO matrix [<OracleDB>, <Shareplex>, <network>, <OS>], then the best choice of action is to resolve the OS' fault first based on its priority. Once the action has resolved the OS's fault, the focus is turned onto the Network's, and this keeps repeating onto the OracleDB and eventually the Shareplex's. However, if the applied action for a particular software group managed to resolve one set of faults but the DRE's state return with another fault of the same group, then the FR module's focus will not move and keep trying to resolve. Therefore, the values for g are 1 = Shareplex, 2 = OracleDB, 3 = Network, 4 = OS. Table 3 illustrated this sequence of considerations. As it resolved them, it calculates the cost or reward for the action to the state and builds up a hierarchical structure of actions vs service outage states like Fig. 2. The FR module's process solves each of the software groups' faults in the proposed hierarchical order.

4 Empirical Analysis

This section describes the test for the FR module against the DRE. The purpose is to determine the effectiveness of the proposed FR module in prescribing the best corrective actions for the DRE based on the service outage information that the FD module has determined about the DRE under simulated faults.

Table 3. Samples of DRE's software groups service outage fault & their corrective actions

Function	Attributes	Commands	Reason and Corrective actions	Corrective actions	Diagnosed Fault vectors	Corrective action vectors
1. OracleDB	**= [0, 0, 0, 0, 0, 0, 0, 0, 0, 0]**					
memory process 0~0~0	Check for DB1's smon Check for DB2's smon Check for DB1's pmon Check for DB2's pmon	if [$(ps aux|grep -i ora_smon_DB1|grep -v grep|wc -l) -eq 1]; then echo 0; else echo 1; fi if [$(ps aux|grep -i ora_pmon_DB1|grep -v grep|wc -l) -eq 1]; then echo 0; else echo 1; fi if [$(ps aux|grep -i ora_smon_DB2|grep -v grep|wc -l) -eq 1]; then echo 0; else echo 1; fi if [$(ps aux|grep -i ora_pmon_DB2|grep -v grep|wc -l) -eq 1]; then echo 0; else echo 1; fi	Oracle instance is not active, start it up Pmon, smon are together. Either both are up or both are down DB1 and 2	export ORACLE_SID=DB1 && echo "startup;"|sqlplus -s "sys/password as sysdba" export ORACLE_SID=DB2 && echo "startup;"|sqlplus -s "sys/password as sysdba"	[22,0,0,0,0,0,0, 0,0] [0,0,1,1,0,0,0, 0,0,0,0]	[1,0,0,0,0,0,0,0 ,0,0,0] [0,0,1,0,0,0,0,0 ,0,0,0]
2. Shareplex = [1, 0, 0, 0, 0, 0, 0, 0, 0, 0, 0, 0, 0, 0, 1, 0, 0, 0, 1]						
main processes 1~0~0	Check if sp_cop process is up Check if sp_ocap process is up Check if sp_opst_mt process is up Check if sp_xport process is up Check if sp_ordr process is up Check if sp_mport process is up	if [$(pidof -s sp_cop) > 1]; then echo 0; else echo 1; fi if [$(pidof -s sp_ocap) > 1]; then echo 0; else echo fi if [$(pidof -s sp_opst_mt) > 1]; then echo 0; else echo 1; fi if [$(pidof -s sp_xport) > 1]; then echo 0; else echo 1; fi if [$(pidof -s sp_ordr) > 1]; then echo 0; else echo 1; fi if [$(pidof -s sp_mport) > 1]; then echo 0; else echo 1; fi	When sp_cop is down, all the rest will be done too; start up sp_cop	echo password|su - splx -c $MDIR/startup.sh	[1,1,1,1,1,1,0, 0,0,0,0,0,0,0,0, ,0,0,0]	[1,0,0,0,0,0,0,0 0,0,0,0,0,0,0,0, 0,0]

The experiments are run on two Virtual Machines running on Linux OS and both have Oracle DB and Shareplex installed on them. Each VM has 4GB of RAM with 100GB of hard disk storage. The version of the Oracle software is 12 Enterprise edition and the 9.1 for the Shareplex. The network protocol that both VMs use is TCPIP. The DRE is set to the baseline where all the software works normally as expected. Each fault that belongs to the specific software is introduced in the DRE which will then yield information that the FD module will detect and predict the possible service outage, which in turn, is input into the FR module that will predict the best possible corrective actions based on its trained knowledge to score the best rewards. The FR module is expected to prescribe action for the following software element's faults in response to the service outage input regarding its associated system diagnostics information. Referring to Table 4 which is a test case with a list of common faults, and the corresponding action to rectify them. The priority for the FR module is to resolve the OS, followed by the network, OracleDB, and Shareplex in a hierarchical inter-dependent arrangement.

4.1 Test Results

There are two groups of results that are generated by the FR. One is from the SC module where it responds to the diagnostics information with a series of corrective actions and the outcomes of the DRE states. The other is the prediction performance and outcome of the DRL-NN in response to various diagnostics information from the DRE. These results are obtained through the process of introducing a series of known faults into the DRE and the FR module is executed against it.

4.2 FR Module - SC's Results

The SC is used prevalently when the entire FR's learning phase is at the early and middle stages. Table 4 showed the outcomes from the SC when a list of the known faults is injected into the DRE. The FR module used the diagnosed information from FD and derive the appropriate corrective actions based on the hierarchical order of the software group and the strategy is to solve that software of higher importance first and work its way down. The result showed the state of the DRE once the faults are executed and followed by the new state when the corrective action is executed (Fig. 4).

The SC did have several unsuccessful attempts to rectify the faults which are highlighted in orange. And those actions have yielded some positive changes in the DRE's diagnostics information are represented in green. The SC progress is considered rulebased which most decision-based system management system is based on and it showed the inefficiency involved. But this step is important to the overall FDR system as it forms the explorative phase where SC experience the different combination of ordered random actions against the environment's states, mapping what actions works against each type of DRE's state.

Table 4. SC's results in response to injected faults

```
#####################################
fault count= 0 fault cmd= export ORACLE_SID=DB1 && echo "shutdown immediate;"|sqlplus -s "sys/password as sysdba"
#####################################
DRE_current_state         = [0,0,0,0,0,0,0,0,0,0,0,0,0,0,1,0,0,0,1,0,1,1,0,0,1,0,1,0,1,0,1,0,1,0,0,0,0,0,0,0,0,0,0]
index= 19  correct cmd= export ORACLE_SID=DB1 && echo "startup;"|sqlplus -s "sys/password as sysdba"
single_element_corrective_action= [0,0,0,0,0,0,0,0,0,0,0,0,0,0,0,0,0,0,1,0,0,0,0,0,0,0,0,0,0,0,0,0,0,0,0,0,0,0,0,0,0]
DRE_new_state             = [0,0,0,0,0,0,0,0,0,0,0,0,0,0,0,0,0,0,0,0,0,0,0,0,0,0,0,0,0,0,0,0,0,0,0,0,0,0,0,0,0]
CHANGE reward = 1
resolved
#####################################
fault count= 1 fault cmd= export ORACLE_SID=DB2 && echo "shutdown immediate;"|sqlplus -s "sys/password as sysdba"
#####################################
DRE_current_state         = [0,0,0,0,0,0,0,0,0,0,0,0,0,0,0,0,0,1,0,0,1,1,0,1,0,1,0,1,0,1,0,1,0,0,0,0,0,0,0,0,0,0]
index= 21  correct cmd= export ORACLE_SID=DB1 && echo "startup;"|sqlplus -s "sys/password as sysdba"
single_element_corrective_action= [0,0,0,0,0,0,0,0,0,0,0,0,0,0,0,0,0,0,0,1,0,0,0,0,0,0,0,0,0,0,0,0,0,0,0,0,0,0,0,0,0]
DRE_new_state             = [0,0,0,0,0,0,0,0,0,0,0,0,0,0,0,0,0,1,0,0,1,1,0,1,0,1,0,1,0,1,0,1,0,0,0,0,0,0,0,0,0,0]
SAME reward = 0
DRE_current_state         = [0,0,0,0,0,0,0,0,0,0,0,0,0,0,0,0,0,1,0,0,1,1,0,1,0,1,0,1,0,1,0,1,0,0,0,0,0,0,0,0,0,0]
index= 22  correct cmd= export ORACLE_SID=DB2 && echo "startup;"|sqlplus -s "sys/password as sysdba"
single_element_corrective_action= [0,0,0,0,0,0,0,0,0,0,0,0,0,0,0,0,0,0,0,0,0,1,0,0,0,0,0,0,0,0,0,0,0,0,0,0,0,0,0,0,0]
DRE_new_state             = [0,0,0,0,0,0,0,0,0,0,0,0,0,0,0,0,0,0,0,0,0,0,0,0,0,0,0,0,0,0,0,0,0,0,0,0,0,0,0,0,0]
CHANGE reward = 1
resolved
........................
```

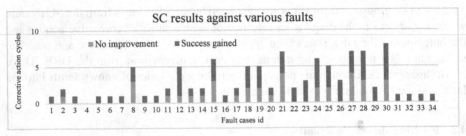

Fig. 4. FR-SC progress results against various faults

4.3 FR's Efficacy Test Results

The outcome is to validate how effective is the FR's final stage of prescribing the optimal corrective actions based on its NN model after it has learned via using the SC to decipher and execute corrective actions iteratively to resolve the detected faults. Two groups of faults are to be tested: known and unknown. For known faults, these have been predetermined and through the series of faults-corrective actions matrix relationship, scripted system commands that are present in the external libraries and detectable in the FD-SD's detecting routine. The performance measure is the percentage of fault correcting success that the FR can achieve over the step that it needs to resolve. The FR-SC may take numerous iterations of applying corrective actions that may be ineffective for a given DRE's state before arriving at one final effective one. The FR-NN should be able to predict the conclusive and effective one for a similar state directly. Table 5 showed the results using FR-NN to predict the best corrective actions that can yield positive rewards against the same series of fault injections.

Table 6 showed the results from the various efficacy tests, scoring 100% for all the registered or known faults. While the plan is to anticipate all possible faults that can and will happen in any complex environment, there is always a chance that some unplanned and unknown faults that can occur and the FR's fault-corrective action matrix has no provision for.

Table 5. SC's results in response to injected faults

```
######################################
fault count= 0 fault cmd= export ORACLE_SID=DB1 && echo "shutdown immediate;"|sqlplus -s "sys/password as sysdba"
######################################
DRE_current_state        = [0,0,0,0,0,0,0,0,0,0,0,0,0,0,1,0,0,0,1,0,1,1,0,0,1,0,1,0,1,0,1,0,1,0,0,0,0,0,0,0,0,0,0,0,0]
index= 19  correct cmd= export ORACLE_SID=DB1 && echo "startup;"|sqlplus -s "sys/password as sysdba"
single_element_corrective_action= [0,0,0,0,0,0,0,0,0,0,0,0,0,0,0,0,0,0,0,1,0,0,0,0,0,0,0,0,0,0,0,0,0,0,0,0,0,0,0,0,0,0]
DRE_new_state            = [0,0,0,0,0,0,0,0,0,0,0,0,0,0,0,0,0,0,0,0,0,0,0,0,0,0,0,0,0,0,0,0,0,0,0,0,0,0,0,0,0,0]
CHANGE reward = 1
resolved
######################################
fault count= 1 fault cmd= export ORACLE_SID=DB2 && echo "shutdown immediate;"|sqlplus -s "sys/password as sysdba"
######################################
DRE_current_state        = [0,0,0,0,0,0,0,0,0,0,0,0,0,0,0,0,1,0,0,1,1,0,1,0,1,0,1,0,1,0,1,0,0,0,0,0,0,0,0,0,0]
index= 22  correct cmd= export ORACLE_SID=DB2 && echo "startup;"|sqlplus -s "sys/password as sysdba"
single_element_corrective_action= [22,0,0,0,0,0,0,0,0,0,0,0,0,0,0,0,0,0,0,0,0,0,1,0,0,0,0,0,0,0,0,0,0,0,0,0,0,0,0,0,0,0,0]
DRE_new_state            = [22,0,0,0,0,0,0,0,0,0,0,0,0,0,0,0,0,0,0,0,0,0,0,0,0,0,0,0,0,0,0,0,0,0,0,0,0,0,0,0,0,0]
CHANGE reward = 1
resolved
.................
```

Table 6. FR module's efficacy test results

Software groups	Occurrences/combination/ service specifics	Total	outcomes
network	Network files, listeners	2	2 resolved
oracledb	privileges, accounts	4	4 resolved
oracledb	Oracle processes	4	4 resolved
Shareplex+ oracledb	Access, privileges	2	2 resolved
Shareplex	Sp_cop processes	5	5 resolved
Shareplex	Queues and services	5	5 resolved
shareplex	Accounts	2	2 resolved

In such instances, external intervention is required. While the above results have indicated the efficacy of the FR's SC and DRL-NN components, the next step is to differentiate the efficiency between the two components. Figure 5 showed the number of corrective action cycles that each of them took against the series of faults. For easier faults such as id #1, #3, #5 and #9, both SC and DRL-NN performed the same number of corrective action cycles. However, for more complex ones like fault id #8, #18, #21 or #30, the SC had to perform more cycles following its internal logic before resolving them. The NN can pick those actions that can yield a positive outcome for the faults and managed to resolve them under few cycles. That is far more efficient as compared to SC's process. Fig. 6 shows the difference in the time taken by both SC and DRL in deriving the solutions for each of the encountered faults.

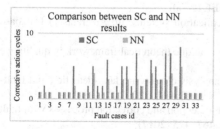

Fig. 5. Corrective action cycles result between SC and NN

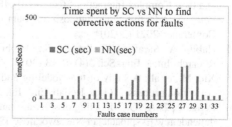

Fig. 6. Comparison of time taken to find corrective actions between SC and DRL-NN

5   Conclusion

The results have shown the feasibility of using Deep reinforcement learning for managing enterprise database's replication system fault resolution. Its flexibility has proven to cover a wide range of software, services and interdependent configurations under the different operating circumstances, and therefore able to scale both vertically and horizontally to meet an enterprise IT data replication environment's challenge.

References

1. Mukherjee, R., Kar, P.: A comparative review of data warehousing ETL tools with new trends and industry insight. In: 2017 IEEE 7th International Advance Computing Conference (IACC). IEEE (2017)
2. Sabtu, A., et al.: The challenges of extract, transform and loading (ETL) system implementation for near real-time environment. In: 2017 International Conference on Research and Innovation in Information Systems (ICRIIS). IEEE (2017)
3. Milani, B.A., Navimipour, N.J.: A systematic literature review of the data replication techniques in the cloud environments. Big Data Res. **10**, 1–7 (2017)
4. Tabet, K., et al.: Data replication in cloud systems: a survey. Int. J. Inform. Syst. Soc. Change (IJISSC) **8**(3), 17–33 (2017)
5. Iacob, N.: Data replication in distributed environments. Annals Econ. Ser. **4**, 193–202 (2010)
6. Van Aken, D., et al.: Automatic database management system tuning through large-scale machine learning. In: Proceedings of the 2017 ACM International Conference on Management of Data. ACM (2017)
7. Wee, C.K., Nayak, R.: Adaptive fault diagnosis for data replication systems. In: Australasian Database Conference 2021 (2020)
8. Hoffer, J., Ramesh, V., Topi, H.: Modern Database Management. Prentice Hall, Upper Saddle River (2015)
9. Liu, Y., et al.: A general modeling and analysis framework for software fault detection and correction process. Softw. Test. Verification Reliab. **26**(5), 351–365 (2016)
10. Jia, R., Abdelwahed, S., Erradi, A.: Towards proactive fault management of enterprise systems. In: 2015 International Conference on Cloud and Autonomic Computing. IEEE (2015)
11. Pavlo, A., et al.: Self-driving database management systems. In: CIDR (2017)
12. Sterritt, R., et al.: Exploring dynamic Bayesian belief networks for intelligent fault management systems. In: SMC 2000 Conference Proceedings. 2000 IEEE International Conference on Systems, Man and Cybernetics. Cybernetics Evolving to Systems, Humans, Organizations, and their Complex Interactions (cat. no. 0). IEEE (2000)
13. Wee, C.: Adaptive fault diagnosis for data replication systems. In: Australasian Database Conference 2021 (2020)
14. Habibi, A., Sarafrazi, A., Izadyar, S.: Delphi technique theoretical framework in qualitative research. Int. J. Eng. Sci. **3**(4), 8–13 (2014)
15. Xie, M., et al.: A study of the modeling and analysis of software fault-detection and fault-correction processes. Qual. Reliab. Eng. Int. **23**(4), 459–470 (2007)
16. Peng, R., ZhAi, Q.: Modeling of software fault detection and correction processes with fault dependency. Eksploatacja i Niezawodność **19**, 467–475 (2017)
17. Maiyya, S., et al.: Database and distributed computing fundamentals for scalable, fault-tolerant, and consistent maintenance of blockchains. Proc. VLDB Endowment **11**(12), 2098–2101 (2018)

18. Hu, J., et al.: Disaster preparedness backend database to read and write separation technology research. In: 2020 2nd International Conference on Computer Communication and the Internet (ICCCI). IEEE (2020)

19. Wee, C.K., Nayak, R.: Adaptive data replication optimization based on reinforcement learning. In: 2020 IEEE Symposium Series on Computational Intelligence (SSCI). IEEE (2020)

20. Haarnoja, T., et al.: Soft actor-critic: off-policy maximum entropy deep reinforcement learning with a stochastic actor. In: International conference on machine learning. PMLR (2018)

21. Wee, C.K., Nayak, R.: Adaptive database's performance tuning based on reinforcement learning. In: Pacific Rim Knowledge Acquisition Workshop. Springer (2019)

22. Ziv, J., Lempel, A.: A universal algorithm for sequential data compression. IEEE Trans. Inf. Theory 23(3), 337–343 (1977)

An Adjustable Diversity Metric for Multimodal Multi-objective Evolutionary Algorithms

Weiwei Zhang[1]([⊠])(ID), Yan Fan[1](ID), Ningjun Zhang[2](ID), and Weizheng Zhang[1](ID)

[1] Zhengzhou University of Light Industry, Zhengzhou, China
[2] Zhengzhou Institute of Science and Technology, Zhengzhou, China

Abstract. The performance of multimodal multi-objective evolutionary algorithms (MMEAs) is determined by not only the convergence to the Pareto front in the objective space, but also the distribution spread to the Pareto set in the decision space. Comparing with the performance matrix applied in the objective space, the performance assessment in the decision space should pay more attention to the distribution spread of solutions. This paper presents a novel diversity metric (PSCR) to reveal the distribution spread of a solution set to the pareto set in the decision space. In addition, in order to avoid the influence of boundary individuals, the grid-partition method is adopted. Through adjusting the scale of the grid, the proposed PSCR could evaluate the MMEAs on both coarse-grained and fine-grained way. The test is carried out on 6 test functions and the reasonable range of parameters is discussed. Moreover, the results of 21 experiments were measured with metrics, and PSCR was compared with other metrics. It was proved that PSCR could not only accurately measure the performance of the algorithm, but also had a higher degree of differentiation than the other metrics.

Keywords: Multimodal multi-objective optimization · Metric · Diversity

1 Introduction

In practical world applications, many optimization problems involve more than one conflicting objectives to be optimized, which are defined as multi-objective optimization problems (MOPs) [1,2]. For MOPs, there is only a unique Pareto optimal solution in decision space mapping to one point in Pareto front (PF). However, there may be multiple Pareto optimal solutions subsets (PSs) with the same PF in practical MOPs. In other words, multiple unique PSs in decision space are mapped to the uniform PF in objective space. This kind of multi-objective optimization problem is called multimodal multi-objective optimization problems (MMOPs) [3]. Therefore, a solution set to the MMOPs should not only approach the Pareto front in the objective space as close as possible but also cover the multiple Pareto set in the decision space.

© Springer Nature Switzerland AG 2022
B. Li et al. (Eds.): ADMA 2021, LNAI 13087, pp. 382–392, 2022.
https://doi.org/10.1007/978-3-030-95405-5_27

The output of the multi-objective optimization algorithm is generally a solution set close to the Pareto optimum. The multi-objective optimization evaluation metrics uses a special processing mechanism to quantify this solution set into a simple and effective value, which in turn intuitively reflects the merit of the solution set. Recently, a variety of evaluation metrics have been used to evaluate the diversity and convergence of multi-objective optimization algorithms, which are divided into three main classifications: (1) metrics evaluating only diversity (GD [4], MPFE [4]); (2) metrics evaluating only convergence (CL_μ [5], NDC_μ [5], Spacing [6]); (3) metrics evaluating both diversity and convergence(IGD [7], HV [8]). In particular, the indicators that evaluate diversity can be subdivided into two categories: (1) those that bias the evaluation of evenness (CL_μ, UD [9], NDC_μ, Spacing); (2) those that bias the evaluation of spread (OS [6], OS_k [6], MS [10], PD [11]). Due to the specificity of multimodal multi-objective optimization problems in decision space, evaluation metrics need to measure the diversity and convergence of solution sets in decision space and objective space. However, the above evaluation metrics are applied to measure the capability of multi-objective optimization algorithms and don't directly measure multimodal multi-objective optimization algorithms.

With the deepening of research, many works have been done on the MMOPs, including the benchmark functions [12], multimodal multi-objective evolutionary algorithms (MMEAs), and applications [13]. However, the performance assessment matrixes [14] to the MMOPs have not drawn enough attention. The performance to assess an algorithm is usually evaluated by convergence and diversity of the obtained solutions. The combination of evenness and spread reflects the diversity [15]. For MMOPs, both the diversity and convergence of the objective space and the decision space need to be considered. However, the algorithms that perform well in objective space are not always performed well in decision space. Therefore, the best approach is to come up with metrics that can measure one quality of performance in the decision space.

To this end, a novel diversity metric to evaluate the spread of solutions in the decision space for MMEAs is proposed in this paper. In this diversity metric, a grid partitioning method is introduced that adjusts the grid size according to the parameter control so that the target space is girded with different precision. The spread of the population distribution is measured with a coarse-grained measure. And fine-grained is adopted to improve the measurement accuracy. Consequently, the grid-partition method is adopted, the measurement accuracy is adjusted with grid size. It is experimentally proven to correctly and efficiently reveal the coverage degree of the obtained solution to the pareto set in the decision space.

The rest of this paper is shown below. Section 2 reviews related works. The proposed metric is then described in detail in Sect. 3. The experimental results and relevant discussions are given in Sect. 4. At last, Sect. 5 concludes this paper.

2   Related Works

To measure the nature of the solution set in the decision space, different evaluation metrics have been proposed on the basis of performance metrics for multiobjective evolutionary algorithms. IGD in decision space (IGDX) is proposed by Zhou [14] to measure the closeness between the PS obtained by the algorithm and the true PS. The smaller the value of IGDX, the closer the solution set obtained by the algorithm is to the reference point set. However, when the solution of the algorithm is also in the true PS and is not close to or coincides with the reference point, the value of IGDX will not reflect the proximity of the solution. Consequently, IGDX is not a very good metric for multimodal multiobjective optimization. Yue modified maximum spread (MS) and proposed cover rate (CR) [16], which measures the spread of the obtained solutions. And combined CR and IGDX to propose Pareto Sets Proximity (PSP) [16]. CR can only measure the spread of a solution set in the decision space. Therefore, the PSP still has the same issue as IGDX. In addition, CR only considers the maximum and minimum value of each dimension. It is well known that PS spreads as a piecewise manifold structure [17], so it is inappropriate to calculate the cover rate only based on the boundary points. The inverted generational distance multimodal (IGDM) [18] is a composite metric that simultaneously measures both convergence and diversity in the decision space and the objective space. The value of IGDM depends on the reference sets and sampled on the PF and the PS. Because different choices of reference points usually result in different IGDM values for an approximate solution set. Besides, IGDM has a new parameter $d_{\max}$, this is a penalty value set by the user. Different choices of $d_{\max}$ are also results in different of IGDM values for solution sets. If $d_{\max}$ is too large, the performance of an optimizer will be significantly affected by the fact that it has not found any Pareto optimal solution. On the other hand, if $d_{\max}$ is too small, it will be difficult to distinguish the differences between the optimizers.

3   Proposed Metric of PSCR

The Pareto-optimal Set Cover Rate (PSCR) is a modification from a grid-partitioning method called Number of Distinct Choices (NDC_{μ}), which was used to evaluate the diversity of solutions in the objective space. Here, the grid-partition method is applied to the decision space. The main idea is to check if the obtained solution covers the same grids which the true Pareto set covers. Therefore, the lower and upper bound of true Pareto set are considered as the boundary which is shown as the red board in Fig. 1(a). Then the $d-dimensional$ space is partitioned into μ^d number of grids, where $\mu = \{\mu^1, \cdots, \mu^d\}$ is the pre-defined integers, $v^d = 1/\mu^d$ is the side length of each grid. Under the certain smoothness assumptions, the PS could be viewed as piecewise continuous manifold [19]. It is reasonable to normalize every dimension to the range of $[0,1]$, and hereafter set the number of grids of each dimension to the same constant $\mu^1 = \cdots \mu^D = \mu$. Obviously, the length $v^1 = \cdots = v^D = v \in (0,1)$ would be the same as well. After partition, each of the grids corresponds to a hyper-cube region in $d-dimensional$, which is denoted as T_μ. Let $NT_\mu(q)$ denotes whether or not there is a point p falls into the region $T_\mu(p)$. Accordingly, let Ps denotes the obtained Pareto Set, and Ps^* presents the true Pareto Set. $NT_\mu(p,q)$ denotes whether or not both the obtained solution and the true Pareto Set are falling into the same region, where $p \in Ps$ and $q \in Ps^*$. Hereafter, PSCR is defined as Eq. (1).

$$PSCR = \frac{\sum_{l_d=0}^{v-1} \cdots \sum_{l_1=0}^{v-1} \underset{p\in Ps, q\in Ps*}{NT_\mu}(p,q)}{\sum_{l_d=0}^{v-1} \cdots \sum_{l_1=0}^{v-1} \underset{q\in Ps*}{NT_\mu}(q)} \qquad (1)$$

where $NT_\mu(q) = \begin{cases} 1, \exists q \in T_\mu(q) \\ 0, \text{otherwise} \end{cases}$ and $NT_\mu(p,q) = \begin{cases} 1, \exists p, q \in T_\mu(p,q) \\ 0, \text{otherwise} \end{cases}$

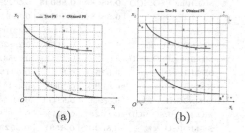

(a)   (b)

Fig. 1. The description of the proposed PSCR in the decision space, wherein Fig. 1(b) is the extension of Fig. 1(a) in the decision space (Color figure online)

It is worth noting that the obtained solutions may be very close to but out of the boundary of the true PS, such as the point A and B in Fig. 1(b). Both of them would be missed if only the solutions inside the red board are considered. Therefore, the bound is extended v to both sides of every dimensions shown as Fig. 1(b). In this way, the number of grids will become $\mu+2$, and the length is still v.

4   Experiment

4.1   Experimental Setting

In order to verify the effectiveness of the proposed PSCR, four state-of-the-art algorithms including DN-NSGAII [3], MO_Ring_PSO_SCD [16], NNIA [20], SS-MOPSO [21] are researched on 11 benchmark functions [16]. To allow a fair comparison, the population size N, the maximum fitness evaluations $fitcount$ of all the algorithms are set to $100 * d$ and $5000 * d$. Due to space reasons, six of the test functions are shown here, each of which has its own characteristics.

4.2   Analysis of the Performance Metrics

In the proposed metric PSCR, there introduced a key parameter μ which may influence the evaluation results. As to the setup of μ, it is more like the resolution which shows the coarse-grained comparison when it is small and fine-grained comparison when it is large. Table 1 gives the calculated PSCR values with μ equals to 5, 10, 20, and 40 respectively. The distribution of the true PS (the blue line) and the obtained PS (the red stars) by different algorithms are shown in Fig. 2.

Table 1. The PSCR with different μ by four algorithms

Function	Algorithm	PSCR			
		$\mu = 5$	$\mu = 10$	$\mu = 20$	$\mu = 40$
MMF1	NNIA	0.77778	0.66304	0.46696	0.30341
	DN-NSGAII	0.77778	0.59783	0.43172	0.30341
	MO_Ring_PSO_SCD	**0.88889**	**0.88043**	0.5022	0.33437
	SS-MOPSO	**0.88889**	**0.88043**	**0.59912**	**0.36842**
MMF2	NNIA	0.625	0.53333	0.42105	0.31481
	DN-NSGAII	0.5	0.43333	0.29825	0.25
	MO_Ring_PSO_SCD	0.6875	0.7	0.52632	0.35185
	SS-MOPSO	**0.875**	**0.8**	**0.63158**	**0.42593**
MMF5	NNIA	0.82759	0.70652	0.45133	0.30606
	DN-NSGAII	0.68966	0.52174	0.34956	0.25455
	MO_Ring_PSO_SCD	**0.86207**	0.80435	0.52655	0.30303
	SS-MOPSO	**0.86207**	**0.8587**	**0.59292**	**0.35455**
MMF7	NNIA	0.84211	0.76923	0.60833	0.39545
	DN-NSGAII	**0.94737**	0.80769	0.56667	0.37727
	MO_Ring_PSO_SCD	**0.94737**	0.88462	**0.69167**	0.41364
	SS-MOPSO	**0.94737**	**0.96154**	0.675	**0.47273**
SYM-PART simple	NNIA	0.33333	0.26667	0.2381	0.25
	DN-NSGAII	0.66667	0.53333	0.52381	0.55556
	MO_Ring_PSO_SCD	1	0.73333	0.80952	0.69444
	SS-MOPSO	1	**0.8**	**0.85714**	**0.94444**
Omni-test	NNIA	0.21739	0.22619	0.15084	0.15358
	DN-NSGAII	0.19565	0.17857	0.13408	0.12287
	MO_Ring_PSO_SCD	0.41304	0.30952	0.1676	0.07167
	SS-MOPSO	**0.56522**	**0.5119**	**0.30726**	**0.19454**

When μ is set to 5, the same PSCR is obtained by different algorithms on four test functions (MMF1, MMF5, MMF7, SYM-PART simple), which means that the performance of the algorithm is not highly differentiated. When μ is set to 10, it would be a lot better. MO_Ring_PSO_SCD and SS-MOPSO get the same PSCR value on MMF1, which is acceptable. In addition, when μ is set to 10, 20 and 40, PSCR shows consistency on almost benchmark functions except MMF7. According to the analysis of population distribution diagram, the reason you get different test results on the three test functions as the parameters change in the $[10, 40]$ range is because the solutions is not uniformly distributed in the decision space, $NT_\mu\,(p,q)$ and $T_\mu\,(p,q)$ change irregularly with the increase of μ. Also, only one measurement of the metric is accidental, and multiple tests are needed to truly reflect the performance of the algorithm.

In order to analyze the parameters of solution PSCR more intuitively. Take the MMF2 as an example. According to the distribution of and the obtained PS, SS-MOPSO can get a well-uniform solution set. We find that the solutions obtained by MO_Ring_PSO_SCD are missing in some regions on PS, but in most regions, the distribution of solutions is uniform enough. For NNIA and DN-NSGAII, the solutions are not well distributed. First of all, although the solutions obtained by NNIA are evenly distributed on one PS, only very few individuals can be found on the other PS. Secondly, although DN-NSGAII found some individuals in the two PS, the distribution of the solutions was very uneven and a large number of solutions clustered together. Therefore, the divergence performance of NNIA solution is better than that of DN-NSGAII. According to the above analysis, it is consistent with the results measured by PSCR.

Therefore, it would be an operable way to set to a small value at first to reduce computational complexity, and then increase the value of μ when the PSCR could not distinguish the differences. Apparently, it is not good to set μ as too large or too small. Given the condition of normalization to the considered space, 10 to 20 would be recommended. From the above analysis, μ is set to 10 in the rest of the experiments by default.

4.3   Results on Comparison by Different Metrics

For the distribution of the solutions shown in the figure, the Table 2 is evaluated with different metrics. The results of all the metrics are discussed below.

First of all, the value of CR is close to 1 on almost all benchmark functions. However, there are also unsatisfactory cases. And take MMF7 as an example. The solution obtained by NNIA has a large area that is not searched in the decision space, which is significantly worse than other algorithms. And in that case, CR still be close to 1. In addition, CR acquired by NNIA on SYM-PART simple is close to 0 and clearly inferior to other algorithms. By observing the distribution of the solutions, it is obviously unreasonable for CR to be so poor even though NNIA does not get ideal results on SYM-PART simple. The main reason for the above two situations is that CR pays too much attention to boundary points, which is misleading to evaluate the performance of the algorithm.

IGDX and IGDF are modified by IGD. By analyzing the experimental results, the algorithm obtained good IGDX usually performs poorly on IGDF. NNIA scored the best IGDF on 10 test functions, of which 6 had the worst IGDX. SS-MOPSO got the best IGDX on 11 test functions, but none of them performed well in the objective space. By analyzing the Fig. 2, IGDX and IGDF can distinguish the performance of the algorithms correctly.

PSP is combined CR with IGDX. For the analysis of Table 2, PSP and IGDX show consistency in the differentiation of algorithms. When the boundary point be found, CR is usually close to 1. At this time, PSP has been little impacted by CR and greatly affected by IGDX. When the boundary point hasn't been

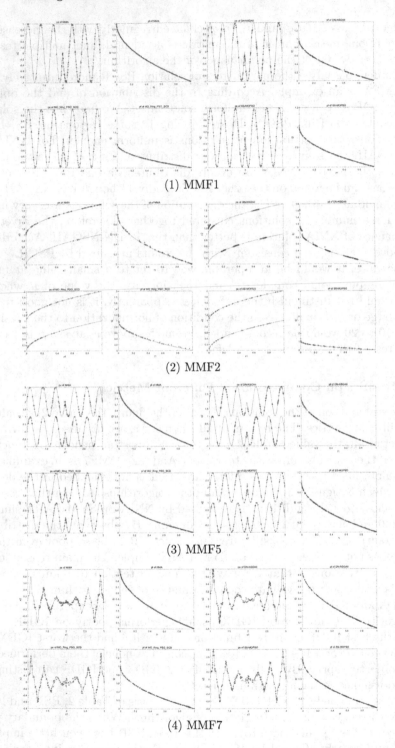

(1) MMF1

(2) MMF2

(3) MMF5

(4) MMF7

Fig. 2. The distribution of the true PS and the obtained PS by different algorithms (Color figure online)

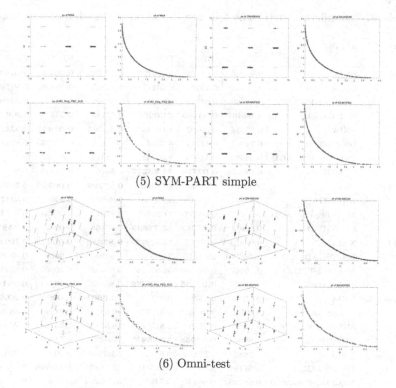

(5) SYM-PART simple

(6) Omni-test

Fig. 2. (*continued*)

found, CR approximates to 0. At the moment, PSP will be greatly affected by CR. Because the PSP is heavily influenced by CR, the simple combination of CR is unreasonable.

HV is another indicator except IGDF used to evaluate the objective space. Except for Omni-test, they showed consistency on the other benchmark functions in Table 2. According to the distribution of the solutions in the objective space on these two benchmark functions, solutions with better evenness may get better IGDF, and solutions with better convergence may get better HV.

SS-MOPSO, measured by both PSCR and CR, showed the best spread. And it is observed from Table 2 that the proposed PSCR has higher degree of differentiation than the other metrics, which means it's easier to distinguish algorithms. It is worth noting that the CR measured DN-NSGAII achieves the best value on MMF7 and SYM-PART simple, which is different from other metrics for testing the diversity of decision space. On the other hand, PSCR does very well on these benchmark functions. MO_Ring_PSO_SCD, measuring by PSCR, get the best value on SYM-PART rotated. According to the analysis of 3.2, this is due to PSCR is influenced by μ. After a large number of test experiments, the performance of the algorithms can still be reflected correctly by PSCR.

Table 2. The different metrics by four algorithms on six benchmark functions

Function	Algorithm	Metric					
		CR	IGDX	PSP	HV	IGDF	PSCR
MMF1	NNIA	0.98866	0.08473	11.66777	**0.87295**	**0.00249**	0.66304
	DN-NSGAII	0.99411	0.1029	9.66137	0.86905	0.00496	0.59783
	MO_Ring-PSO_SCD	0.99389	0.04915	20.22112	0.86996	0.00393	**0.88043**
	SS-MOPSO	**0.99467**	**0.04143**	**24.00917**	0.87143	0.00323	**0.88043**
MMF2	NNIA	0.92614	0.09193	10.07434	**0.85397**	0.01441	0.53333
	DN-NSGAII	0.74041	0.11341	6.5284	0.82191	0.04575	0.43333
	MO_Ring-PSO_SCD	0.94673	0.11025	8.58743	0.83311	0.02362	0.7
	SS-MOPSO	**0.96126**	**0.02776**	**34.63257**	0.84763	0.01585	**0.8**
MMF5	NNIA	0.99502	0.1139	8.73593	**0.87296**	0.00256	0.70652
	DN-NSGAII	0.98817	0.15511	6.37055	0.86991	0.0039	0.52174
	MO_Ring-PSO_SCD	0.99427	0.08453	11.76207	0.87075	0.00354	0.80435
	SS-MOPSO	**0.9964**	**0.07242**	**13.75892**	0.87168	0.00322	**0.8587**
MMF7	NNIA	0.94836	0.05956	15.92275	**0.87313**	**0.00243**	0.76923
	DN-NSGAII	**0.99779**	0.04147	24.05941	0.86984	0.00397	0.80769
	MO_Ring-PSO_SCD	0.99263	0.02689	36.92126	0.87034	0.00404	0.88462
	SS-MOPSO	0.9947	**0.02235**	**44.50239**	0.86943	0.00441	**0.96154**
SYM-simple	NNIA	0.07803	6.75768	0.01155	**16.66014**	**0.00919**	0.26667
	DN-NSGAII	**0.99953**	3.08761	0.32372	16.64345	0.01294	0.53333
	MO_Ring-PSO_SCD	0.99573	0.17109	5.81988	16.53517	0.03769	0.73333
	SS-MOPSO	0.99949	**0.07958**	**12.55938**	16.63277	0.01309	**0.8**
Omni-test	NNIA	0.7883	1.37463	0.57346	**52.79859**	0.0071	0.22619
	DN-NSGAII	0.97194	1.5333	0.63389	52.79857	**0.00696**	0.17857
	MO_Ring-PSO_SCD	0.98725	0.63921	1.5445	52.59294	0.038	0.30952
	SS-MOPSO	**0.99853**	**0.26392**	**3.78345**	52.72465	0.02251	**0.5119**

4.4 Discuss

According to the analysis in the above experimental, the following conclusions can be drawn. Firstly, PSCR can completely evaluate the spread of the decision space. When the decision-maker wants to obtain the performance of the solutions in the aspect of spread in the decision space, PSCR can be used to evaluate. Second, PSCR has higher degree of differentiation than the other metrics, that is, it is more effective in distinguishing algorithm performance. Thirdly, PSCR is a based grid-partitioning method and the spread of solutions is tested not only in the boundary region, but also in the entire feasible region. Granularity seems to be divided according to the degree of fineness of feasible regions. As μ gets bigger, the feasible regions are divided into more small regions. The setting of μ values should be discussed in detail when working on different test problems. A reasonable μ value is set on the basis of ensuring that the performance of the algorithm can be distinguished. Generally, PSCR is desirable to measure the spread of the solutions.

5   Conclusion

In this paper, a novel diversity metric (PSCR) designed for the aim of evaluating the performance of MMEAs. It could reveal the coverage degree of the obtained solution to the pareto set in the decision space. The method based on the grid-partition is adopted to explore the distribution of solution set in different grids in the feasible region. Through adjusting the scale of the grid, the proposed PSCR could evaluate the MMEAs on both coarse-grained and fine-grained way. And it has higher degree of differentiation than the other metrics. A larger PSCR value is considered to be a better spread of obtained solutions. Subsequently, a large number of experimental results have proved that PSCR is applicable. In the following research, the relationship between evenness and spread of solutions is attempted to be explored to propose more effective metrics for MMOPs.

Acknowledgment. The paper is supported by the National Natural Science Foundation of China (No. 51905494, 61501405), Funding program for key scientific research projects of universities in Henan province (No. 20A520004), science and technology key project of Henan province (No. 212102210154), Training plan of young backbone teachers in Colleges and universities of Henan Province (No. 2019GGJS138).

References

1. Deb, K., Pratap, A., Agarwal, S., et al.: A fast and elitist multiobjective genetic algorithm: NSGA-II. IEEE Trans. Evol. Comput. **6**(2), 182–197 (2002)
2. Trivedi, A., Srinivasan, D., Sanyal, K., et al.: A survey of multiobjective evolutionary algorithms based on decomposition. IEEE Trans. Evol. Comput. **21**(3), 440–462 (2016)
3. Liang, J., Yue, C., Qu, B.: Multimodal multi-objective optimization: a preliminary study. In: 2016 IEEE Congress on Evolutionary Computation (CEC), pp. 2454–2461 (2016)
4. Van Veldhuizen, D.A., Lamont, G.B.: On measuring multiobjective evolutionary algorithm performance. In: Proceedings of the 2000 Congress on Evolutionary Computation. CEC00 (Cat. No. 00TH8512), pp. 1: 204–211(2000)
5. Wu, J., Azarm, S.: Metrics for quality assessment of a multiobjective design optimization solution set. J. Mech. Des. **123**(1), 18–25 (2001)
6. Schott, J.R.: Fault Tolerant Design Using Single and Multicriteria Genetic Algorithm Optimization. cellular immunology (1995)
7. Zhou, A., Jin, Y., Zhang, Q., et al.: Combining model-based and genetics-based offspring generation for multi-objective optimization using a convergence criterion. In: 2006 IEEE International Conference on Evolutionary Computation, pp. 892–899(2006)
8. While, L., Hingston, P., Barone, L., et al.: A faster algorithm for calculating hypervolume. IEEE Trans. Evol. Comput. **10**(1), 29–38 (2006)
9. Tan, K., Lee, T., Khor, E.: Evolutionary algorithms for multi-objective optimization: performance assessments and comparisons. Artif. Intell. Rev. **17**(4), 251–290 (2002)
10. Zitzler, E., Deb, K., Thiele, L.: Comparison of multiobjective evolutionary algorithms: empirical results. Evol. Comput. **8**(2), 173–195 (2000)

11. Wang, H., Jin, Y., Yao, X.: Diversity assessment in many-objective optimization. IEEE Trans. Cybern. **47**(6), 1510–1522 (2016)
12. Yue, C., Qu, B., Yu, K., et al.: A novel scalable test problem suite for multimodal multiobjective optimization. Swarm Evolut. Comput. **48**, 62–71 (2019)
13. Yue, C., Liang, J., Qu, B., et al.: Multimodal multiobjective optimization in feature selection. In: 2019 IEEE Congress on Evolutionary Computation (CEC), pp. 302–309 (2019)
14. Zhou, A., Zhang, Q., Jin, Y.: Approximating the set of Pareto-optimal solutions in both the decision and objective spaces by an estimation of distribution algorithm. IEEE Trans. Evol. Comput. **13**(5), 1167–1189 (2009)
15. Tian, Y., Cheng, R., Zhang, X., et al.: Diversity assessment of multi-objective evolutionary algorithms: performance metric and benchmark problems. IEEE Comput. Intell. Mag. **14**(3), 61–74 (2019)
16. Yue, C., Qu, B., Liang, J.: A multiobjective particle swarm optimizer using ring topology for solving multimodal multiobjective problems. IEEE Trans. Evol. Comput. **22**(5), 805–817 (2017)
17. Zhang, Q., Zhou, A., Jin, Y.: RM-MEDA: a regularity model-based multiobjective estimation of distribution algorithm. IEEE Trans. Evol. Comput. **12**(1), 41–63 (2008)
18. Liu, Y., Yen, G., Gong, D.: A multimodal multiobjective evolutionary algorithm using two-archive and recombination strategies. IEEE Trans. Evol. Comput. **23**(4), 660–674 (2018)
19. Schütze, O., Mostaghim, S., Dellnitz, M., et al.: Covering Pareto sets by multilevel evolutionary subdivision techniques. In: International Conference on Evolutionary Multi-Criterion Optimization, pp. 118–132 (2003)
20. Gong, M., Jiao, L., Du, H., et al.: Multiobjective immune algorithm with nondominated neighbor-based selection. Evolut. Comput. **16**(2), 225–255 (2008)
21. Qu, B., Li, C., Liang, J., et al.: A self-organized speciation based multi-objective particle swarm optimizer for multimodal multi-objective problems. Appl. Soft Comput. **86**, 105886 (2020)

Cybersecurity Analysis via Process Mining: A Systematic Literature Review

Martin Macak[1](✉)(iD), Lukas Daubner[1](iD), Mohammadreza Fani Sani[2],
and Barbora Buhnova[1]

[1] Faculty of Informatics, Masaryk University, Brno, Czech Republic
{macak,daubner,buhnova}@mail.muni.cz
[2] Process and Data Science Chair, RWTH-Aachen University, Aachen, Germany
fanisani@pads.rwth-aachen.de

Abstract. The digitalization of our society is only possible in secure software systems governing ongoing critical processes. The understanding of mutual interdependencies of events and processes is crucial for cybersecurity. One of the promising ways to tackle these challenges is process mining, which is a set of techniques that aim to mine knowledge from processes. However, it is unclear how process mining can be practically used in the context of cybersecurity. In this work, we investigate the potential of applying process mining in cybersecurity and support research efforts in this area via collecting existing applications, discussing current trends, and providing promising research directions. To this end, we have conducted a systematic literature review covering all relevant works between 2014 and 2020.

Keywords: Process mining · Cybersecurity · Literature review

1 Introduction

The advancement of digitalization in modern society has fuelled the role of cybersecurity in various domains of critical information infrastructures, such as healthcare or transportation, where potential problems could result in injuries or loss of lives. Nowadays, the key challenge of effective cybersecurity assurance is the rapid advancement of information technology, with new types of threats and unprecedented discrepancies emerging daily. Existing security techniques are designed for the discovery and prevention of a specific type of problem, and hence having difficulties in adapting to new threats [5,37].

The security threats themselves develop over time within complex processes in which minor vulnerabilities (e.g., software bugs, weak separation of authenticated spaces) combine with human errors (e.g., credentials leaks) into major problems that are challenging to detect in their early stages [41]. Hence, the investigation of security threats is still largely manual [59] or is addressed with specialized domain-specific techniques [55,60]. The behavior of entities is often

© Springer Nature Switzerland AG 2022
B. Li et al. (Eds.): ADMA 2021, LNAI 13087, pp. 393–407, 2022.
https://doi.org/10.1007/978-3-030-95405-5_28

encoded into a mathematical model that might be hard to manipulate, abstract, or complex, making it hard to respond to the security threats adequately [27].

Process mining [2] is a set of techniques that could be promising in addressing the aforementioned challenges. In contrast to traditional data-centric approaches (like data mining) and process-centric approaches (such as BPM analysis), process mining involves both data and end-to-end processes in the analysis [1] to the benefit of final results [28,30]. For example, process mining techniques are used to examine when and how a process deviated from the nominal process model or how a bottleneck activity ultimately results in a delay. They are designed to discover, monitor, and enhance processes by extracting knowledge from event data (i.e., *event logs*). Process mining has already proven successful in many domains, aiding with challenging tasks such as fraud detection [45], robotic process automation [29], or learning analytics [42]. In [48], it is explained why process mining can be beneficial for advanced analysis, with several use cases.

The benefits of process mining make it a promising candidate to address the challenges in cybersecurity analysis—using its techniques, we might be able to detect unexpected behavior [15], identify issues [3], detect deviations [62], or verify whether the system conforms to the designed process [50] more effectively. Furthermore, it is able to provide an overview of alerts in the system, detect malware in a system, detect frauds, or verify user behavior. Its value lies in cybersecurity situations with uncertainty about the processes underlying system behavior, reconstructed based on the observed events in the system.

Currently, there is no comprehensive systematic literature review that would help understand where and how process mining could help to deal with cybersecurity issues. Therefore, this paper aids researchers and practitioners in the cybersecurity area via conducting a literature review of research papers using process mining for cybersecurity. The research approaches are grouped by their research directions to give insight into the current progress of process-mining usage in each one of them. We identify the techniques that are used for this purpose, together with their properties, and discuss possible research directions.

The paper is structured as follows. Section 2 contains a background of process mining. Afterward, Sect. 3 provides an overview of literature reviews on process mining. Section 4 contains the research questions and methodology of review. All found papers are presented in Sect. 5. Summary of the review and research questions are addressed in Sect. 6. Section 7 discusses the threats to the validity of our review. Finally, Sect. 8 concludes the paper.

2   Background

Process mining techniques are categorized in 1) *process discovery*, which aims to find a descriptive model of the underlying process from event logs, 2) *conformance checking*, i.e., monitoring and inspecting whether the real execution of the process conforms to the reference model, and 3) *process enhancement*, which improves and enriches a process model based on the related event data [2].

Process discovery aims to find a descriptive model that represents the process described in the event log. It has been first discussed in [21], which describes discovery methods in the context of software engineering processes. However, it was limited to sequential processes. There are several process discovery algorithms proposed in the literature such as Inductive miner [38] and DecMiner [36] that are able to capture and depict concurrent behaviors in the event log.

The purpose of conformance checking is to decide whether the execution of the process conforms to the corresponding process model [16]. Early techniques used token-based replay to detect non-fitting cases. They replayed a trace of events in a Petri net and produced some diagnostics based on the computed replay [2]. For example, Conformance Checker [51] introduced two metrics: fitness and appropriateness. Fitness measures the degree to which the process model can replay the traces from the log. Appropriateness measures the simplicity, precision, and generalization of the model.

Process enhancement techniques aim to improve or extend an existing process model using information extracted from the process described in an event log [2]. It is important when the model does not reflect reality accurately. An example of process improvement is [23], where the authors repair the given model, increasing its fitness with respect to the given event log. In process extension, a new perspective is added to the process model, such as an organizational or time perspective. The approach in [13] uses the organizational perspective to enhance the model by roles of the activity originators. On the other hand, in [33], the time perspective is used.

3 Related Work

Several literature reviews on the usage of process mining were performed. Typically, they are domain-specific, like healthcare [49,58] and education [11]. A notable multi-domain systematic literature review [54] aims to map the applications of process mining. The authors identified 19 application domains and described the main contribution of process mining in the most published areas, i.e., healthcare, ICT, manufacturing, education, finance, and logistics. Notably, security was placed in eighth place, thus not discussed in detail.

In the cybersecurity domain, there is no comprehensive review of process mining available yet. For example, the recent literature survey [22] provides only a foundation for future research regarding process mining utilization for privacy and confidentiality. Another partial work in cybersecurity area can be found in the review [39] focused on security in Process-Aware Information Systems, where process mining is only one of many methods considered. Moreover, as the review covered results from 1993 to 2012, the recent works are missing. An overview of the usage of process mining for security in the public sector domain published between 2000 and 2016 [34] was performed. Based on this review, the author provides a set of dominant topics, challenges, and future research directions. The paper, however, explicitly considers only the public sector domain. In contrast, our work expands this, including more recent publications and a wider spectrum of domains.

Fig. 1. The strategy of the review with the number of publications.

4   Methodology

The goal is to review recent research in cybersecurity employing process mining and discover research gaps in this area. To this end, we formulate a strategy to guide this study based on an existing guideline for systematic literature reviews [35]. It includes a search in major digital libraries, snowballing, and manual searching. The methodology is visualized in Fig. 1. To mitigate threats to validity, we followed the recommended strategy [63] described in Sect. 7.

Research questions. We formulated the following research questions (RQs) to guide the search, inclusion and exclusion criteria, and the result assessment.

RQ1: What are the research directions in which the process mining is used to ensure cybersecurity? The aspects of cybersecurity are usually considered within broader application domains such as networking, banking, or critical infrastructures. Here, the goal is to identify the research directions with utilization or active research in process mining to ensure cybersecurity.

RQ2: Which process mining techniques and approaches are utilized to ensure cybersecurity? As mentioned, process mining is a collection of different techniques, which can be used in numerous ways. The goal is to identify those commonly utilized, rarely considered, and those that are not used in cybersecurity. Concretely, the focus is placed on the used technique, target period, usage of expert knowledge, and automation of the analysis.

RQ3: What are the current gaps and possible research directions in the usage of process mining for cybersecurity? Here, we aim to combine the outcomes of the first two RQs to assess opportunities for researchers and available methods for practitioners. Mainly in comparison to the general utilization of process mining.

Primary Collection. To establish a base collection of papers, we searched in several digital libraries, specified in Fig. 1. The search string corresponds to *("process mining") AND (cybersecurity OR security)*, with results limited to the recent English-written research over the time period from 2014 to 2020.

Filtering. The primary collection contains many irrelevant false positives, which were filtered out in two steps. Firstly, only the paper title, abstract, keywords, and conclusion are considered. In the second step, a full text is read.

Filtering is based on specified criteria to maintain validity. A paper is kept if and only if it conforms to at least one inclusion criterion, and it is discarded if it conforms to at least one exclusion criterion or neither of them. In the case of multiple related papers from the same authors (i.e., follow-up of the same idea, but not a new topic), only the most recent or the most extensive is kept.

The *inclusion criteria* are that the work: (1) deals with the detection, analysis, modeling, recovery, or avoidance of cyberattack, malware, or fraud; (2) focuses on cybersecurity-related processes; (3) is concerned with anomalous behavior regarding cybersecurity.

The *exclusion criteria* are that the work: (1) does not utilize process mining; (2) does not consider software systems as the primary target of the approach; (3) is not a full paper (i.e., abstract, chapter fragment, or encyclopedia article).

Snowballing. The last stage is the inclusion of relevant papers referred by those in the collection. Additional papers are included based on a non-systematic search using scientific search engines like Google Scholar and consultation with domain experts. The filtering criteria are maintained during snowballing as well.

Classification. An important part of processing the papers was to classify them based on their research directions. The chosen approach was to identify representative keywords from the text and cluster them by a common topic. Any ambiguity was solved through discussion. The directions and keywords are: security of Industrial Control Systems (*ICS, SCADA, smart grids*), security of smartphones (*mobile, phone, Android*), web-application security (*web, information system, website*), network traffic security (*DNS, IDS*), attack inspection (*attack inspection, identification, extraction, observation*), outlier user behavior (*outlier, behavior*) and fraud detection (*fraud detection*).

5   Process Mining Used for Cybersecurity

This section discusses the works using process mining for cybersecurity in the individual identified research directions. Table 1 contains all the reviewed research papers. It shows the research directions the process mining approach is applied, the main target period of the analysis, used process mining approaches, whether the technique requires expert knowledge, which might affect its usability. Lastly, it shows whether the model analysis is performed manually or automatically.

5.1   Security of Industrial Control Systems

An industrial control system (ICS) is responsible for production, monitoring, and control. From the process mining techniques, the process discovery [10] and the combination of discovery and conformance checking [47] are used in this field.

Specifically, Bernardi et al. [10] studied the detection of anomalous behavior in energy usage from smart meter readings. They used process mining to discover the behavior of customers over time. In addition to process discovery, Myers et al. [46] used the conformance checking method. They firstly investigate the suitability of process-mining discovery algorithms for the detection of cyberattacks in ICS. Then they evaluate the most suitable process discovery

Table 1. Cybersecurity papers included in the review.

Paper	Research direction	Target period	PM Type[a]	Expert knowledge	Model analysis
[10]	Security of ICSs	Past	PD	✓	Automatically
[47]	Security of ICSs	Past	PD & CC	✓	Automatically
[8]	Security of smartphones	Past	PD	✓	Automatically
[17]	Security of smartphones	Past	PD	✓	Automatically
[31]	Security of smartphones	Past	PD & CC	✓	Automatically
[15]	Network traffic security	Past	PD	✓	Manually
[4]	Network traffic security	Past	PD	✓	Manually
[18]	Network traffic security	Present	PD & CC	✓	Both
[19]	Web-application security	Past	PD	✓	Automatically
[52]	Web-application security	Past	PD & CC	✓	Automatically
[9]	Web-application security	Past	PD & PE	✓	Manually
[62]	Web-application security	Past	PD & CC & PE	✓	Manually
[57]	Attack inspection	Past	PD	✓	Manually
[7]	Attack inspection	Past	PD	✗	Automatically
[43]	Attack inspection	Past	PD	✓	Manually
[44]	Outlier user behavior detection	Past	PD & CC	✓	Both
[27]	Outlier user behavior detection	Past	PD	✓	Manually
[40]	Outlier user behavior detection	Present	PD & CC & PE	✓	Automatically
[56]	Outlier user behavior detection	Present	CC	✓	Automatically
[53]	Outlier user behavior detection	Past	CC	✓	Automatically
[3]	Outlier user behavior detection	Past	CC & PE	✗	Automatically
[26]	Fraud detection	Past & Present	CC	✓	Automatically
[12]	Fraud detection	Past & Present	CC	✓	Automatically
[32]	Fraud detection	Past	PD & CC	✓	Automatically
[6]	Fraud detection	Past	CC	✓	Manually

[a] PD—process discovery, CC—conformance checking, PE—process enhancement

algorithm by comparing the number of detected anomalous cases, trace fitness, and time. Based on this paper, in their later work [47], they introduced a method for identifying anomalies in ICS and SCADA device logs.

5.2   Security of Smartphones

Similar to the ICS domain, the comparison of discovered models was also considered in smartphones for malware detection [8,17]. In addition, conformance checking is being used for the detection of a specific attack [31].

The approach for malware detection and phylogeny analysis in smartphone applications was proposed by Bernardi et al. [8], applying process discovery on systems calls to characterize the application behavior. Phylogenic analysis and malware family detection were also performed by Cimino et al. [17], using process discovery to obtain temporal logic formulae for formal model verification.

The process data from activity logs of Android devices were also used by process mining analysis by Hluchy and Habala [31], who applied conformance checking in addition to process discovery. From the phone logs, they chose OS-generated information about specific performed actions, browser history, and network connection log.

5.3   Web-Application Security

Several publications were focused on information systems (IS), social networks, or the security of other web applications. We observed both the utilization of automatic analysis [19,52] and manual analysis [9,62].

In [52], the authors proposed the approach for detecting abnormal user behavior in social network websites to prevent cybercrime. Firstly, they discover a model from normal user behavior using genetic process mining. Then, they identify the abnormal behavior of users by conformance checking technique.

Compagna et al. [19] proposed a tool named *Aegis* that improves the security of web applications by enforcing security policies. This tool uses process mining to discover workflow models of the target application from sets of user actions that occurred while interacting with web applications.

The security of web applications, specifically web IS, was also improved in work by Bernardi et al. [9], which utilizes process mining and model-driven engineering. Similarly, Zerbino et al. [62] proposed a process mining methodology in which the deviations in IS audit are detected.

5.4   Network Traffic Security

In the network traffic security direction, process discovery techniques are dominant. They are usually paired with manual analysis, where the discovered visual model is analyzed by an expert [4,15]. Similar to the previous directions, the analysis of the past is still prevalent, yet one approach focuses on real-time [18].

Bustos-Jiménez et al. [15] proposed an approach for the detection of unexpected behavior in DNS operations. Their focus is on the visual detection of a spam attack on DNS servers. Another approach that used visual analysis was proposed by Alvarenga et al. [4], who applied the process mining discovery technique on logs of alerts from Intrusion Detection Systems to create visual models.

The approach of Coltelese et al. [18] performs analysis in real-time. Using conformance checking, they aim to filter the IoT attacks that need to be handled by security operators while at the same time providing them the global attack model that updates automatically using online process discovery.

5.5   Attack Inspection

The works within the direction of attack inspection examine how the specific attack is performed. They all use process discovery for the analysis of past events.

Viticchie et al. [57] used process mining for the investigation of the process of the attacks on a small application. The process model was discovered from the annotated texts, describing the attack strategy of the participants. It was used to construct the attack process for the detailed investigation.

Macak et al. [43] took a different point of view that focuses on the unintentional insider attack vector identification. Process discovery is used on the event logs produced by the game platform, which simulate the working environment for players and several social engineering attacks.

The other approach in this domain is aiming for the inspection and detection of ransomware. Bahrani and Bidgly [7] created event logs from harmless applications and ransomware families. Then, for each software, they discovered a process model that can be used by a classification algorithm to identify ransomware. Thanks to this, no expert knowledge is required to use this approach.

5.6   Outlier User Behavior Detection

Multiple works have focused on the outliers in user behavior. They can be divided into two categories: approaches that take advantage of expert knowledge [27,40, 44,56] and those that do not [3]. In the works incorporating expert knowledge, two approaches can be seen. Either the security is focused as a primary goal [3], or the focus is to filter outliers for a better process model [20,24].

Genga and Zannone [27] designed a methodology for behavior analysis using process mining and applied it to a real event log, while Macak et al. [44] focused on the behavior analysis of insiders in organizations.

Li et al. [40] proposed an online monitoring framework for process interaction between collaborative sub-processes based on token-replay conformance checking to detect undesired behavior. Likewise, Salnitri et al. [53] utilized a conformance checking method to identify the security deviations in process executions.

A system for the online analysis presented by Talamo and Arcieri [56] utilizes real-time compliance checking for operational support of distributed business processes, which handle sensitive data. Here, the security is improved by reducing the human intervention in Service Desk through automation.

Alizadeh et al. [3] proposed an auditing approach that can identify the previously undiscovered deviations. It combines data and process perspectives to detect non-conforming user behavior with conformance checking.

5.7   Fraud Detection

The significant direction of process mining in the cybersecurity context is fraud detection, typically using conformance checking together with expert knowledge.

Fazzinga et al. [25] proposed a framework for the classification of event log traces as potential security breaches like frauds and misuses. They use process discovery to create a security breach model. Then they classify the incoming traces based on conformance checking. This approach was validated in their subsequent work [26].

Security breaches were also the aim of the work of Böhmer and Rinderle-Ma [12], who proposed an anomaly detection strategy in process execution events to prevent security breaches and frauds. They include the control flow, time, and resource perspective into one anomaly detection approach.

Baader and Krcmar [6] were also using process mining techniques for fraud detection. Specifically, they present a method for reducing the number of false positives in this detection. They combine the red-flag approach and process mining for the identification and visualization of possible undesired process instances.

In particular, Huda et al. [32] proposed a method for the identification of process-based frauds in a credit application. After discovering a process model, they perform conformance checking analysis to check skipped events.

6   Results

[RQ1] What are the research directions in which the process mining is used to ensure cybersecurity?

Within our review, we have identified 35 approaches and structured them according to the direction of the research problem they are addressing. Namely: security of ICS, security of smartphone devices, web application security, network traffic security, attack inspection, outlier user behavior, and fraud detection. Although this division is by no means perfect, it gives a useful understanding of the direction of process mining research in cybersecurity.

The most popular research approaches (regarding the number of publications) are directed towards detecting outliers – user behavior and frauds. Next is a direction aimed at networking, including websites, information systems, and other technologies primarily focused on communication, corresponding to overall cybersecurity trends. The research in the remaining directions is rather sparse.

Domains, generally dominant in process mining in general, were surprisingly not found among the results. These include healthcare, manufacturing, education, finance, and logistics. Thus, we assume that despite their general popularity, the utilization of process mining techniques has not yet been properly explored for cybersecurity. Alternatively, they could be employing general domain non-specific techniques and thus not published mentioning a particular domain.

[RQ2] Which process mining techniques and approaches are utilized to ensure cybersecurity?

Based on the discovered papers, most works are focused on analyzing past events, while the real-time analysis is mostly limited to outlier user behavior [40,56] and fraud [12,26] detection. However, we noticed a trend that many papers targeting the past mention the possibility of real-time application, which is not demonstrated or left for future work. Single paper utilizing online process discovery was found [18], while the rest uses real-time conformance checking.

Several patterns regarding the process mining methods were identified. Process discovery and conformance checking techniques are dominant. On the other hand, process enhancement was rarely used [3,9,40,62]. An interesting trend is the combination of process discovery and conformance checking in several papers [31,32]. A typical scenario is to generate a reference model using process discovery and then apply conformance checking for new cases. Otherwise, either process discovery [10] or conformance checking [53] is used.

In many papers, expert knowledge is needed to analyze the data. Yet, there are exceptions, like a paper [7] using process mining for ransomware classification in application software and paper [3] aimed at outlier detection.

Regarding the analysis, the majority of the papers analyze the obtained model automatically, partly because the process mining technique is very often used as a part of a more sophisticated method [7, 17]. However, there exist papers that utilize only manual analysis based on the discovered model. In this case, the goal is to employ visual analytics to discover unexpected anomalies [4, 15].

[RQ3] What are the current gaps and possible research directions in the usage of process mining for cybersecurity?

Research gaps and possible research directions can be observed in multiple aspects. The most obvious gap is using process mining in cybersecurity within domains, where it is commonly utilized for other applications (e.g., healthcare, manufacturing, education, and logistics). A possible research direction is analyzing current events, providing online process discovery and conformance checking. This approach aligns with the frequent topic of real-time analysis, where process mining is an ideal candidate. However, models found in papers are almost always static and based on past events. Furthermore, it would be beneficial to use process mining prediction methods to take steps before an imminent cyberattack.

Finally, as the number of publications is very sparse, there are likely many uninvestigated use cases of process mining in cybersecurity. Namely, considering the critical infrastructures which need to have a strong defense against cyberattacks. Such attacks might take advantage of seemingly minor vulnerabilities combined into malicious processes. Furthermore, process mining might be valuable in the analysis and diagnostics of already running or legacy systems, where streaming-based process mining techniques [14, 61] can be used in this regard.

7   Threats to Validity

To mitigate the threat to **construct validity**, we chose six popular digital libraries for primary collection, believed to cover the most high-quality publications. We used snowballing to reduce the possibility of missed relevant works.

The threat to **internal validity** was mitigated by the division of filtering into multiple phases, each performed by a different researcher. Furthermore, a sample of 10% of papers filtered out in the first phase was re-examined by a different researcher to avoid bias.

The biggest threat to **external validity** is the limitation to the up-to-date papers over the last six years, from 2014 to 2020. The restriction was motivated by the focus on the most recent trends and applications. Furthermore, the year 2014 corresponds to a local peak in the number of publications in the Dimensions dataset (https://app.dimensions.ai/), showing a slight change of trend.

Finally, the threat to **conclusion validity** was mitigated by formulating the review strategy. While some trends and research gaps could have been missed, we believe that the value of the provided summary is primarily in the overview of the existing body of knowledge in applying process mining in the area of cybersecurity. Therefore, we aim to facilitate the understanding of existing attempts in the area and its characteristics, making it easier for the reader to see where they can build on the existing approach and where they need to build their own.

8 Conclusion

We conducted a systematic literature review of research papers that use process mining for cybersecurity. While the process mining techniques have been used for this purpose, the coverage is still rather limited. As such, there is much potential in cybersecurity applications of process mining. We identified seven major research directions, discussed how they fit in the overall landscape, and presented how they apply process mining techniques. Based on this review, we pointed out a set of possible process mining research directions that can be taken to tackle the state-of-the-art challenges in cybersecurity. Primarily, we would encourage the research community to investigate the domain of critical information infrastructures, which might benefit significantly from more advanced techniques for cybersecurity. Additionally, real-time analysis of systems has a strong potential to utilize the advantages of process mining techniques, beneficial in advanced detection and prevention of cyberattacks.

Acknowledgements. This research was supported by ERDF "CyberSecurity, CyberCrime and Critical Information Infrastructures Center of Excellence" (No. CZ.02.1.01/0.0/0.0/16_019/0000822).

References

1. van der Aalst, W.: Using process mining to bridge the gap between BI and BPM. Computer **44**(12), 77–80 (2011)
2. van der Aalst, W.: Process Mining: Data Science in Action, 2nd edn. Springer Publishing Company, Incorporated (2016)
3. Alizadeh, M., Lu, X., Fahland, D., Zannone, N., van der Aalst, W.: Linking data and process perspectives for conformance analysis. Comput. Secur. **73**, 172–193 (2018)
4. de Alvarenga, S.C., Barbon, S., Miani, R.S., Cukier, M., Zarpelão, B.B.: Process mining and hierarchical clustering to help intrusion alert visualization. Comput. Secur. **73**, 474–491 (2018)
5. Asghar, M.R., Hu, Q., Zeadally, S.: Cybersecurity in industrial control systems: issues, technologies, and challenges. Comput. Netw. **165**, 106946 (2019)
6. Baader, G., Krcmar, H.: Reducing false positives in fraud detection: combining the red flag approach with process mining. Int. J. Acc. Inf. Syst. **31**, 1–16 (2018)
7. Bahrani, A., Bidgly, A.J.: Ransomware detection using process mining and classification algorithms. In: 16th International ISC Conference on Information Security and Cryptology, pp. 73–77 (2019)
8. Bernardi, M.L., Cimitile, M., Distante, D., Martinelli, F., Mercaldo, F.: Dynamic malware detection and phylogeny analysis using process mining. Int. J. Inf. Secur. **18**(3), 257–284 (2019)
9. Bernardi, S., Alastuey, R.P., Trillo-Lado, R.: Using process mining and model-driven engineering to enhance security of web information systems. In: IEEE European Symposium on Security and Privacy Workshops, pp. 160–166 (2017)

10. Bernardi, S., Trillo-Lado, R., Merseguer, J.: Detection of integrity attacks to smart grids using process mining and time-evolving graphs. In: 14th European Dependable Computing Conference, pp. 136–139 (2018)

11. Bogarín, A., Cerezo, R., Romero, C.: A survey on educational process mining. Wiley Interdisc. Rev.: Data Mining Knowl. Disc. **8**(1) (2018)

12. Böhmer, K., Rinderle-Ma, S.: Multi-perspective anomaly detection in business process execution events. In: OTM Confederated International Conferences on the Move to Meaningful Internet Systems, pp. 80–98. Springer (2016). https://doi.org/10.1007/978-3-319-48472-3_5

13. Burattin, A., Sperduti, A., Veluscek, M.: Business models enhancement through discovery of roles. In: CIDM, pp. 103–110 (2013)

14. Burattin, A., van Zelst, S.J., Armas-Cervantes, A., van Dongen, B.F., Carmona, J.: Online conformance checking using behavioural patterns. In: Business Process Management, pp. 250–267. Springer International Publishing, Cham (2018). https://doi.org/10.1007/978-3-319-98648-7_15

15. Bustos-Jiménez, J., Saint-Pierre, C., Graves, A.: Applying process mining techniques to DNS traces analysis. In: 33rd International Conference of the Chilean Computer Science Society, pp. 12–16 (2014)

16. Carmona, J., van Dongen, B., Solti, A., Weidlich, M.: Conformance Checking. Springer (2018). https://doi.org/10.1007/978-3-319-99414-7

17. Cimino, M.G., De Francesco, N., Mercaldo, F., Santone, A., Vaglini, G.: Model checking for malicious family detection and phylogenetic analysis in mobile environment. Comput. Secur. **90**, 101691 (2020)

18. Coltellese, S., Maggi, F.M., Marrella, A., Massarelli, L., Querzoni, L.: Triage of IoT attacks through process mining. In: OTM Confederated International Conferences "On the Move to Meaningful Internet Systems", pp. 326–344. Springer (2019). https://doi.org/10.1007/978-3-030-33246-4_22

19. Compagna, L., dos Santos, D.R., Ponta, S.E., Ranise, S.: Aegis: automatic enforcement of security policies in workflow-driven web applications. In: Proceedings of the 7th ACM Conference on Data and Application Security and Privacy, pp. 321–328. ACM (2017)

20. Conforti, R., La Rosa, M., ter Hofstede, A.H.: Filtering out infrequent behavior from business process event logs. IEEE Trans. Knowl. Data Eng. **29**(2), 300–314 (2016)

21. Cook, J.E., Wolf, A.L.: Automating process discovery through event-data analysis. In: Proceedings of the 17th International Conference on Software Engineering, pp. 73–82. ACM (1995)

22. Elkoumy, G., et al.: Privacy and confidentiality in process mining-threats and research challenges. arXiv preprint arXiv:2106.00388 (2021)

23. Fahland, D., van der Aalst, W.M.: Model repair-aligning process models to reality. Inform. Syst. **47**, 220–243 (2015)

24. Sani, M.F., van Zelst, S.J., van der Aalst, W.M.: Applying sequence mining for outlier detection in process mining. In: OTM Confederated International Conferences "On the Move to Meaningful Internet Systems", pp. 98–116. Springer (2018). https://doi.org/10.1007/978-3-030-02671-4_6

25. Fazzinga, B., Folino, F., Furfaro, F., Pontieri, L.: Combining model-and example-driven classification to detect security breaches in activity-unaware logs. In: On the Move to Meaningful Internet Systems. OTM 2018 Conferences, pp. 173–190. Springer (2018). https://doi.org/10.1007/978-3-030-02671-4_10

26. Fazzinga, B., Folino, F., Furfaro, F., Pontieri, L.: An ensemble-based approach to the security-oriented classification of low-level log traces. Expert Syst. Appl. **153**, 113386 (2020)
27. Genga., L., Zannone., N.: Towards a systematic process-aware behavioral analysis for security. In: Proceedings of the 15th International Joint Conference on e-Business and Telecommunications - Volume 1: BASS, pp. 460–469. INSTICC, SciTePress (2018)
28. van Genuchten, M., Mans, R., Reijers, H., Wismeijer, D.: Is your upgrade worth it? process mining can tell. IEEE software **31**(5), 94–100 (2014)
29. Geyer-Klingeberg, J., Nakladal, J., Baldauf, F., Veit, F.: Process mining and robotic process automation: a perfect match. In: Proceedings of the Dissertation Award, Demonstration, and Industrial Track at BPM 2018, pp. 124–131 (2018)
30. Ghasemi, M., Amyot, D.: From event logs to goals: a systematic literature review of goal-oriented process mining. Requirements Eng. **25**(1), 67–93 (2020)
31. Hluchý, L., Habala, O.: Enhancing mobile device security with process mining. In: IEEE 14th International Symposium on Intelligent Systems and Informatics, pp. 181–184 (2016)
32. Huda, S., Ahmad, T., Sarno, R., Santoso, H.A.: Identification of process-based fraud patterns in credit application. In: 2nd International Conference on Information and Communication Technology, pp. 84–89 (2014)
33. Jaisook, P., Premchaiswadi, W.: Time performance analysis of medical treatment processes by using disco. In: 13th International Conference on ICT and Knowledge Engineering (ICT & Knowledge Engineering 2015), pp. 110–115. IEEE (2015)
34. Kelemen, R.: Systematic review on process mining and security. In: Central and Eastern European e— Dem and e— Gov Days 2017 (2017)
35. Kitchenham, B., Charters, S.: Guidelines for performing systematic literature reviews in software engineering (2007)
36. Lamma, E., Mello, P., Montali, M., Riguzzi, F., Storari, S.: Inducing declarative logic-based models from labeled traces. In: Business Process Management. pp. 344–359. Springer, Berlin Heidelberg (2007). https://doi.org/10.1007/978-3-540-75183-0_25
37. Leander, B., Causevic, A., Hansson, H.: Cybersecurity challenges in large industrial IoT systems. In: 24th IEEE International Conference on Emerging Technologies and Factory Automation, pp. 1035–1042 (2019)
38. Leemans, S.J.J., Fahland, D., van der Aalst, W.M.P.: Discovering block-structured process models from event logs containing infrequent behaviour. In: Business Process Management Workshops, pp. 66–78. Springer International Publishing (2014). https://doi.org/10.1007/978-3-319-06257-0_6
39. Leitner, M., Rinderle-Ma, S.: A systematic review on security in process-aware information systems - constitution, challenges, and future directions. Inf. Softw. Technol. **56**(3), 273–293 (2014)
40. Li, C., Ge, J., Li, Z., Huang, L., Yang, H., Luo, B.: Monitoring interactions across multi business processes with token carried data. IEEE Trans. Serv. Comput. 1 (2018)
41. Liu, L., De Vel, O., Han, Q., Zhang, J., Xiang, Y.: Detecting and preventing cyber insider threats: a survey. IEEE Commun. Surv. Tutorials **20**(2), 1397–1417 (2018)
42. Macak, M., Kruzelova, D., Chren, S., Buhnova, B.: Using process mining for git log analysis of projects in a software development course. Educ. Inf. Technol. 1–31 (2021)

43. Macak, M., Kruzikova, A., Daubner, L., Buhnova, B.: Simulation games platform for unintentional perpetrator attack vector identification. In: Proceedings of the IEEE/ACM 42nd International Conference on Software Engineering Workshops, pp. 222–229 (2020)
44. Macak, M., Vanat, I., Merjavy, M., Jevocin, T., Buhnova, B.: Towards process mining utilization in insider threat detection from audit logs. In: 7th International Conference on Social Networks Analysis, Management and Security, pp. 1–6 (2020)
45. Mardani, S., Shahriari, H.R.: A new method for occupational fraud detection in process aware information systems. In: 10th International ISC Conference on Information Security and Cryptology, pp. 1–5 (2013)
46. Myers, D., Radke, K., Suriadi, S., Foo, E.: Process discovery for industrial control system cyber attack detection. In: ICT Systems Security and Privacy Protection, pp. 61–75. Springer International Publishing, Cham (2017). https://doi.org/10.1007/978-3-319-58469-0_5
47. Myers, D., Suriadi, S., Radke, K., Foo, E.: Anomaly detection for industrial control systems using process mining. Comput. Secur. 78, 103–125 (2018)
48. Reinkemeyer, L.: Process Mining in Action: Principles. Use Cases and Outlook, Springer Nature (2020)
49. Rojas, E., Munoz-Gama, J., Sepulveda, M., Capurro, D.: Process mining in healthcare: a literature review. J. Biomed. Inform. 61, 224–236 (2016)
50. Rosa, N.S., Campos, G.M., Cavalcanti, D.J.: Lightweight formalisation of adaptive middleware. J. Syst. Archit. 97, 54–64 (2019)
51. Rozinat, A., van der Aalst, W.M.: Conformance checking of processes based on monitoring real behavior. Inf. Syst. 33(1), 64–95 (2008)
52. Sahlabadi, M., Muniyandi, R., Shukur, Z.: Detecting abnormal behavior in social network websites by using a process mining technique. J. Comput. Sci. 10, 393–402 (2014)
53. Salnitri, M., Alizadeh, M., Giovanella, D., Zannone, N., Giorgini, P.: From security-by-design to the identification of security-critical deviations in process executions. In: International Conference on Advanced Information Systems Engineering, pp. 218–234. Springer (2018). https://doi.org/10.1007/978-3-319-92901-9_19
54. dos Santos Garcia, C., Meincheim, A., Junior, E.R.F., Dallagassa, M.R., Sato, D.M.V., Carvalho, D.R., et al.: Process mining techniques and applications - a systematic mapping study. Expert Syst. Appl. 133, 260–295 (2019)
55. Senator, T.E., Goldberg, H.G., Memory, A., Young, W.T., Rees, B., Pierce, R., et al.: Detecting insider threats in a real corporate database of computer usage activity. In: Proceedings of the 19th ACM/SIGKDD International Conference on Knowledge Discovery and Data Mining, pp. 1393–1401 (2013)
56. Talamo, M., Povilionis, A., Arcieri, F., Schunck, C.H.: Providing online operational support for distributed, security sensitive electronic business processes. In: International Carnahan Conference on Security Technology, pp. 49–54 (2015)
57. Viticchié, A., Regano, L., Basile, C., Torchiano, M., Ceccato, M., Tonella, P.: Empirical assessment of the effort needed to attack programs protected with client/server code splitting. Empirical Softw. Eng. 25(1), 1–48 (2020)
58. Williams, R., Rojas, E., Peek, N., Johnson, O.A.: Process mining in primary care: a literature review. Stud. Health Technol. Inform. 247, 376–380 (2018)
59. Yen, T.F., et al.: Beehive: large-scale log analysis for detecting suspicious activity in enterprise networks. In: Proceedings of the 29th Annual Computer Security Applications Conference, pp. 199–208. ACM (2013)

60. Young, W.T., Goldberg, H.G., Memory, A., Sartain, J.F., Senator, T.E.: Use of domain knowledge to detect insider threats in computer activities. In: 2013 IEEE Security and Privacy Workshops, pp. 60–67 (2013)
61. van Zelst, S.J., van Dongen, B.F., van der Aalst, W.M.: Event stream-based process discovery using abstract representations. Knowl. Inf. Syst. **54**(2), 407–435 (2018)
62. Zerbino, P., Aloini, D., Dulmin, R., Mininno, V.: Process-mining-enabled audit of information systems: methodology and an application. Expert Syst. Appl. **110**, 80–92 (2018)
63. Zhou, X., Jin, Y., Zhang, H., Li, S., Huang, X.: A map of threats to validity of systematic literature reviews in software engineering. In: 23rd Asia-Pacific Software Engineering Conference, pp. 153–160 (2016)

Identification of Stock Market Manipulation with Deep Learning

Jillian Tallboys[✉], Ye Zhu, and Sutharshan Rajasegarar

School of Information Technology, Deakin University, Geelong, VIC, Australia

Abstract. Anomaly detection is a common and critical data mining task, it seeks to identify observations that differ significantly from others. Anomalies may indicate rare but significant events that require action. Market manipulation is an activity that undermines stock markets worldwide. This paper shares five large real-world, labelled data sets of anomalous stock market data where market manipulation is alleged to have occurred. Cutting edge deep learning techniques are then shown to successfully detect the anomalous periods. An LSTM based method with dynamic thresholding is particularly promising in this domain as it was able to identify contextual local anomalies in the data quickly, taking seconds to score two years of trading data for each stock, which can often be a challenge for deep learning approaches.

Keywords: Anomaly detection · Time series · Deep learning · Stock market

1 Introduction

Anomaly detection, seeks to identify observations that differ significantly from others in a data set. An anomaly is best defined as *"an observation that deviates so significantly from other observations as to arouse suspicion that it was generated by a different mechanism"* [10]. Depending on the domain, these anomalies can represent adverse actions like fraud, mechanical failure [21] or illness [4].

In time series data there are broadly three kinds of anomalies: **Point anomaly**, where a single observation has an unusual value [7]; **Collective or segment anomaly**, where a number of observations are considered anomalous as a group but do not individually have usual values [5]; **Contextual or Local anomaly**: observations are only anomalous relative to neighbouring data points but not an anomaly relative to all other observations [12].

Identifying anomalies in a time series is a significant challenge, as the data has the inherently complex characteristics of seasonality, periodicity, trend and irregularity [10]. This problem is further complicated by:

– the lack of labelled data suitable for training supervised methods, which even when available, can be impractical for large data sets with high frequency observations [12]

© Springer Nature Switzerland AG 2022
B. Li et al. (Eds.): ADMA 2021, LNAI 13087, pp. 408–420, 2022.
https://doi.org/10.1007/978-3-030-95405-5_29

– even if labelled, by their nature anomalies are rare and this gives rise to a highly unbalanced classes in the data set [12]

Deep learning approaches are a subset of Machine Learning techniques that are based on artificial neural network architectures. These approaches have been used for both regression and classification problems across many domains such as computer vision, speech recognition and language processing. Their broad application is due to their ability to automatically discover complex features without extensive domain knowledge [11]. Given time series' data complex characteristics, it is no surprise these techniques are being explored to detect anomalies.

Although there has been extensive prior work on anomaly detection, approaches for time series data are less often considered. However, there has been a growing body of work that considers anomaly detection for time series data using deep learning approaches across many domains. Identifying anomalies in stock markets could benefit from such approaches, as anomalies periods that may be associated with market manipulation [6]. With around 33 million trades per month on the Australian Stock Exchange [1], effective and efficient identification of activities that may indicate market manipulation is necessary.

This paper will focus on techniques for unsupervised time series anomaly detection. Unsupervised approaches assume no a priori knowledge of anomalies, no normal baselines for comparison and no clear segmentation possible (e.g. no strong periodic patterns say for example as in an electrocardiogram signal) [5]. This most accurately represents real-life scenarios where it is impractical to label large volumes of streamed data (including stock market price data) [11]. However, to enable comparison between methodologies, the data sets used in such papers contain known anomalies. These are identified by human experts or synthetically added by algorithm.

Further, an efficient anomaly detection approach needs to be able to:

1. Detect anomalies quickly, that is it does not take long to train or score the observations, which can be a challenge with deep learning approaches.
2. Detect different types of anomalies, at a minimum, it should be able to identify point and contextual anomalies as these are most common in this use case.

In the next section, this paper will outline traditional and cutting-edge approaches. Then five large real-world, labelled data sets of anomalous stock market data will be shared and discussed, contributing to the field as such data is rarely publicly available. Next, this paper demonstrates that market manipulation is able to be detected using two cutting-edge deep learning approaches, TadGAN and LSTM with Dynamic Thresholding, and with results compared with a more traditional ARIMA approach. This paper will then evaluate the results and suggest improvements and identify any drawbacks in using the candidate methods.

2   Related Work

Artificial Neural Networks have been used since 1988 to predict stock returns and have shown to be advantageous as they are numeric, data-driven and adaptive with a higher capacity for noisy, nonlinear data [22]. With deep learning these advantages have been enhanced as deep nonlinear topologies can be built to better fit highly nonlinear functions [22]. Anomalies may indicate market manipulation, which is of great interest to markets and regulators. However, there has not been much research on applying deep learning approaches to identifying anomalies in stock markets. This section contains a summary of the small number of papers found from the last five years.

In Islam et al. [8], their ANOMALOUS algorithm is trained on historical stock volume data of US companies that had been identified from litigation as prominent illegal insider trading cases. In their ANOMALOUS algorithm, they used a LSTM (long short-term memory) RNN (recurrent neural network) to predict a future window of transaction volume. To identify the anomalies, Normalised Cross Correlation was used to measure the similarity of the signals. Unfortunately, comparisons to other approaches were not shared.

Wang et al. [20] propose a RNN-based ensemble learning (RNN-EL) framework. This takes a multi-dimensional approach and combines features from trading records and company characteristics from the China Securities Regulatory Commission, which have been labelled using prosecuted cases. Their results show the method outperforms the 8 comparison machine learning and statistical approaches by 29.8% in terms of AUC value.

In contrast to the above supervised approaches, Leangarun et al. [9] have developed an unsupervised approach using LSTM-GANs (generative adversarial networks). Based on LSTM to learn normal behaviour, the discriminator network of GANs detects the anomalies. They synthesised and injected anomalous observations into the data. It achieved 68.1% accuracy on unseen market data, identifying "pump-and-dump" manipulations. This approach seems quite promising as it takes the LSTM architecture as a base, which seems to be the best choice for time series data.

From the works above, it appears that deep learning techniques tend to be superior to more traditional statistical and machine learning techniques for identifying anomalies in time series. This is shown particularly in Munir's et al. work [10], comparing a wide range of techniques. In particular, LSTM and GAN architectures seem to be particularly successful, given this TadGAN and LSTM with Dynamic Thresholding have been tested with stock market data in Sect. 3.4.

While identifying market manipulation is a concern to markets and regulators, it appears most of the work using deep learning approaches on stock market data focuses on forecasting and prediction rather than identifying anomalies. There is a gap here in the research, as only a small number of papers identifying market manipulation apply deep learning techniques, and they mostly rely on supervised techniques with labelled data. Labelled data is difficult and costly to produce, and may limit the model's application in that it is only trained on identified cases of known manipulation. In the next section, we identify five real-world cases of alleged market manipulation to be used to test the selected approaches.

3   Stock Market Manipulation Identification

This paper will determine if deep learning techniques can be utilised to identify anomalies that may signify market manipulation in stock market trading data. It will compare two promising techniques for unsupervised learning - TadGAN and LSTM with Dynamic Thresholding with a statistical approach, ARIMA. These will be tested on stock market data with real market manipulation anomalies labelled for comparison purposes. The algorithms will also be assessed on their efficiency, their speed and the breadth of anomaly types identified, as well as their accuracy. This paper will identify any drawbacks in using these approaches to identify stock market manipulation. The approach taken is summarised in Fig. 1.

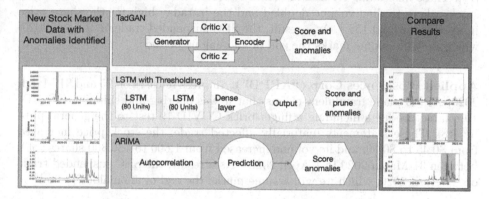

Fig. 1. Five new data sets were sourced and known anomalies were identified, these were then fed to the selected approaches and results were compared.

3.1   New Stock Market Data for Anomaly Detection

Stock market regulators such as the Australian Investment and Securities Commission (ASIC) and the Securities & Exchange Commission in the US seek to ensure the markets they regulate are fair, strong and efficient [2]. This includes administering and enforcing the law against misconduct. Both ASIC and the SEC publicly share details of recent cases on their official websites, asic.gov.au and sec.gov. These were searched with phrases such as "market manipulation" as well as "pump and dump". A "pump and dump" occurs when stocks are quickly sold while a stock's price is high based on false or misleading statements [8].

Unfortunately, there were only a few results available on ASIC and insufficient information was publicly available on the exact dates and impacts of the stock manipulation. The SEC, however, provide significant detail including copies of the court filings. These documents include dates of the suspicious trades or inaccurate announcements. The SEC has also released a bulletin, warning investors of COVID-19 related "pump and dump" scams, and included a list of stocks suspended from trade on suspicion of releasing information was inaccurate or unreliable [19]. From this, four recent cases were selected, including two where charges were laid.

In addition, in early 2021 there was much media attention paid to a social media lead "short squeeze" (a type of pump and dump manipulation) on the US retailer, GameStop. This has also been included for experimentation.

A summary of each stock is provided in Table 1 and a chart of each time series with the market manipulation noted is shown at Fig. 2.

Turbo Global Partners, Inc. ("TRBO"). This case involves two COVID-19 related fraudulent press releases issued on 30 March and 3 April 2020 by TRBO [17]. These misleading releases materially affected the trading market for TRBO stock, where trading volume doubled and the intraday high for the share price jumped by around 15%[1]. As a result, the SEC suspended trade on 9 April 2020, which we will assume marks the end of anomalous period[2].

Applied Biosciences Corp ("APPB"). In press releases on 25 and 31 March 2020, APPB made fraudulent claims that it was offering and shipping COVID-19 related products including a finger-prick COVID-19 test to the general public [18]. These statements materially affected trade, the stock price increased from $0.45 to $0.80, and its volume increased from 1,600 to 136,300 shares sold, between 31 March 2020 to 1 April 2020[3]. As a result, the SEC suspended trade on 13 April 2020, which we will assume marks the end of anomalous period[4].

Aethlon Medical, Inc. ("AEMD"). On 7 February 2020 trade was suspend for AEMD. This was due to potentially inaccurate information relating to the viability of the company's product to treat the coronavirus and unusual market activity by third-party promoters since 22 January 2020. No charges to date have been laid[5].

No Borders, Inc. ("NBDR"). From 11 March 2020, NBDR made potentially misleading social media statements and press releases about it's COVID-19 specimen collection kits and personal protective equipment products being available for distribution in the United States. The SEC suspended trade on 3 April 2020. No charges to date have been laid[6].

---

[1] https://www.sec.gov/litigation/complaints/2020/comp-pr2020-111-turbo.pdf.
[2] https://www.sec.gov/litigation/suspensions/2020/34-88609-o.pdf.
[3] https://www.sec.gov/litigation/complaints/2020/comp24977.pdf.
[4] https://www.sec.gov/litigation/suspensions/2020/34-88627-o.pdf.
[5] https://www.sec.gov/litigation/suspensions/2020/34-88142-o.pdf.
[6] https://www.sec.gov/litigation/suspensions/2020/34-88549-o.pdf.

GameStop ("GME"). Users from the online community r/wallstreetbets on Reddit.com executed a short squeeze on GME in January 2021. These actions rapidly increased GME's stock price and caught the attention of the SEC, the US government and the media. On 11 January 2021, GME appointed three new directors to its board which was well received by the market. By 13 January 2021, the stock price had risen by 50% to $31.40 a share and this generated interest on r/wallstreetbets, particularly posts by an individual investor, Keith Gill, who had previously shared his analysis of the stock as undervalued. On 19 January 2021, Citron Research (a stock research firm) called GME buyers 'suckers' on Twitter, momentum grew for GME on r/wallstreetbets driving the price up another 50%. The momentum in GME stocks continued, with prices reaching $354.83 after a tweet by Elon Musk on 26 January 2021 [16].

The rising price put some hedge funds in a precarious position. Citron Capital and Melvin Capital, two firms who shorted GME, closed their positions on 27 January 2021 taking significant losses. As a result, a number of trading platforms restricted trades involving GME. By 29 January 2021, lawmakers and the SEC publicly made statements and the price fell to $112.25. The price remained volatile but trended down to $53.33 a share by 4 February 2021 [16].

While the SEC has not categorised the influence of Reddit users as market manipulation [16], the short squeeze on GME is an interesting anomaly for investigation. For this research, we will focus on the time period between 11–29 January 2021.

3.2 Source

These five stocks were used to test if such anomalies are detectable and compare the efficacy of the approaches. Data for these stocks were retrieved via the yfinance library in Python. This library uses the Yahoo! Finance API and returns daily stock data (open, high, low, close and volume) for the selected period. For this research, data for 24 months before the identified market manipulation was selected, and data to 12 months after where available (N.B. given the recency of GME's anomalies, only three months of data after the anomaly was available).

3.3 Anomalies

Real anomalies were manually flagged as followed based on court filings and media reporting as summarised in Table 1.

Table 1. Real anomaly dates

Stock	TRBO	APPB	AEMD	NBDR	GME
Anomaly start	30-Mar-20	25-Mar-20	22-Jan-20	11-Mar-20	11-Jan-21
Anomaly end	9-Apr-20	13-Apr-20	7-Feb-20	3-Apr-20	29-Jan-21

It is to be expected that other anomalies will be present in the data, representing normal market responses to the company's behaviour (e.g. changes in leadership, profit announcements). In a practical application of the approach, the detected anomalies should be cross checked with a service that provides a feed of such announcements (e.g. Bloomberg).

3.4 Approaches Applied

The following approaches were applied to each data set.

TadGAN. The approach described in Geiger et al. [5], uses a Generative Adversarial Network (GAN). GANs are often used in image recognition, where a neural network is used to generate a fake image with random noise (the Generator) to fool another neural network who distinguishes between the real a fake images (the Critic). In their paper, this process is leveraged for time series where the generator trains on the observed data and is used to reconstruct the time series. The z-scores of both the error between the real and reconstructed time series as well as the Critic outputs are used to score anomalies. A threshold of 4 standard deviations from the mean initially identifies anomaly windows, which are then pruned to minimise false positives. The code for this approach is available in a Python library called Orion[7]. A summary of the underlying GAN architecture used in the TadGAN approach is shown in Fig. 1.

By default, TadGAN takes inputs with sequences of length 100, the latent space is 20-dimensional and the batch size is 64. It uses a 1-layer bidirectional LSTM with 100 hidden units as Encoder, while the Generator uses a 2-layer bidirectional LSTM with 64 hidden units. A 1-D convolutional layer is used for Critics [5]. Epochs, the number of times the full data set is cycled through the model, were trialed at 35 and 70. The window size, sets the size of the sub-segments, was set at the default of 100 as this parameter is not tunable in the current Orion library implementation.

LSTM with Dynamic Thresholding. The approach described by Hundman et al. [7], uses an LSTM to make predictions and a nonparametric, unsupervised approach to find an error threshold to identify both point and contextual anomalies. LSTMs contain a weighted self-loop that enables them to consider both the recent and more long-term dependencies in the data. This makes them a robust approach to highly complex temporal data. The threshold that is found in the approach considers the smoothed errors from the LSTM prediction, and includes a pruning step that ensures only the anomalies that cause the greatest change in the mean and standard deviation of the smoothed errors are flagged. The code for this approach has also been implemented in the Orion library.

By default, the LSTM with Dynamic Thresholding takes inputs with sequences of length 250 and a batch size of 64. The architecture includes two

---

[7] https://github.com/signals-dev/Orion.

LSTM layers with 80 hidden units each, then a dense layer with one unit which is used to predict the next time step value [7].

A summary of this approach is shown in Fig. 1. Epochs were trialed at 35 and 70. The window size was tested at 10 and 250.

ARIMA. Autoregressive Integrated Moving Average (ARIMA) is a statistical technique commonly used in time series analysis and anomaly detection [3]. This makes it a useful benchmark for comparison of the two methods above. It predicts future values from autocorrelations, and uses point-wise prediction errors that exceed the confidence band to detect anomalies [5]. The implementation from the Orion library has been applied. The window size was tested at 10, 100 and 250.

3.5 Environment

The approaches were applied in Google Colaboratory, a hosted Jupyter notebook service with 2 Intel(R) Xeon(R) CPU @ 2.30 GHz and 13 GB of RAM. The Adam optimiser was used for all approaches.

4 Results and Discussion

In both Geiger et al. [5] and Hundman et al. [7], the following approach is used to the calculation of evaluation metrics:

- True positive (TP) if the real anomaly overlaps with any detected anomaly window
- False negative (FN) if the real anomaly does not overlap with any detected anomaly window
- True negative (TN) if the real anomaly overlaps with any detected anomaly window
- False positive (FP) if detected anomaly window does not overlap with any real anomaly

While this approach does penalise false positive windows, it is somewhat lenient as a true positive is granted if the real anomaly falls anywhere in the detected window. In the Orion library a stricter, weighted approach to evaluation is available. In this approach, each window is considered in a window to window comparison and then weighted by duration [5]. This penalises the approach when the detected window is larger (or smaller) than the real anomaly. Both the overlapping and weighted metrics described above have been included in the evaluation in the calculation of the following metrics: $F1 = \frac{2 \cdot Precision \cdot Recall}{Precision + Recall}$, where $Precision = \frac{TP}{TP+FP}$ and $Recall = \frac{TP}{TP+FN}$.

In most cases, all approaches were able to correctly identify the anomalous area. However, the ARIMA approaches tended to provide a smaller detection window and so had a higher weighted F1, Precision and Recall scores than the LSTM with Dynamic Thresholding or TadGAN approaches.

Table 2. Best approach for each data set

Stock	Best approach	F1-score	Elapsed time
TRBO	ARIMA, Window Size = 250	0.14	24.7 s
APPB	ARIMA, Window Size = 250	0.16	24.5 s
AEMD	LSTM, Epochs = 35, Window Size = 10	0.09	19 s
NBDR	ARIMA, Window Size = 250	0.33	23.7 s
GME	ARIMA, Window Size = 100	0.27	27 s

The best approaches and their respective parameter settings for each data set are shown in Table 2, while Fig. 2 visualises this output.

From the results, it appears deep learning approaches work well to identify anomalies in stock market data. However, a more traditional statistical approach, ARIMA outperforms the deep learning approaches in terms of speed and more specifically identifying the anomalous period. That said, ARIMA did not perform well identifying the contextual/local anomaly in the AEMD data set.

For the AEMD data set the best approach was LSTM with Dynamic Thresholding. This approach shows real promise in that it was successfully able to detect the real anomaly being of the contextual/local anomaly type (see Fig. 2). In this data set the volumes during the period of alleged market manipulation are not as extreme as two other periods in the time series, which relate to positive company announcements regarding FDA approvals [13] and clinical trials [14]. This is an important feature as stocks can be quite volatile and responsive to forces that are not market manipulation such as announcements that may affect future profits (as in this case).

In terms of speed, ARIMA over all was the fastest approach to apply with the elased time of less than a minute for each run, followed by LSTM with Thresholding with no more than 3 min 9 s elasped while TadGAN took up to 15 min 20 s depending on the number of epochs and the data set used.

It should be noted that while the detected segments appear large and the weighed scores are low, identifying market manipulation is like searching for a needle in a haystack given the high volumes of stocks and data. Currently, regulators such as the SEC and ASIC rely on tip-offs from the public which are then investigated [15]. In a practical application, this type of model would feed into a detection system and be collated with other data sources for human investigation. For example, if an anomalous period coincided with a merger announcement (which would be available from a regulatory system) it could be disregarded by investigators. Further, the anomaly dates specified only relate to actions that can be proven but the market manipulation may have started earlier.

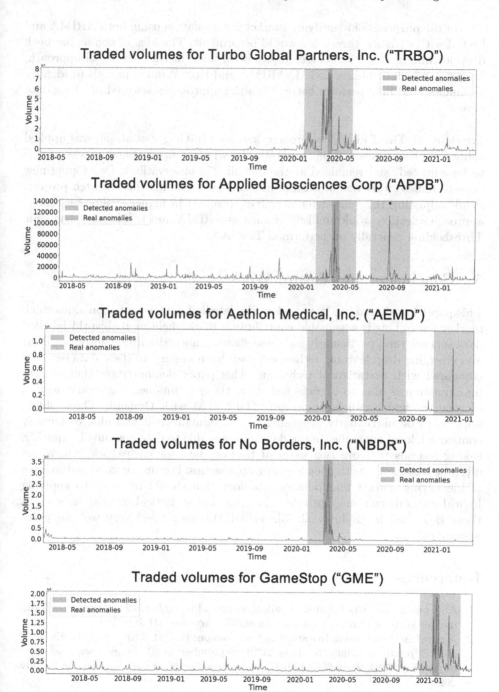

Fig. 2. Best results for each data set

For the purposes of identifying market manipulation using both ARIMA and LSTM with dynamic thresholds would be prudent. The idea of combining both deep learning and statistical techniques is outlined in Buda et al. [3] approach, DeepAD, which combines LSTM, ARIMA and Holt-Winters models to identify anomalies, and may perform better than the approaches selected on these data sets.

Limitations. The TadGAN approach described in Geiger et al. [5], was applied using the Orion library. Unfortunately, the window size parameter was unable to be adjusted, and remained at the default 250 observations. Developing new code to remedy this was unfeasible in the time frame for this research project. While adjusting this parameter may have resulted in higher evaluation scores, approach selection would unlikely change as ARIMA and LSTM with Dynamic Thresholding generally outperformed TadGAN.

5 Conclusion and Future Work

This paper has shared five large real-world, labelled data sets of anomalous stock market data. This is a valuable contribution to the field as real-world labelled data sets are rare, particularly for those showing allegedly illegal activities. New and emerging deep learning techniques have been applied to these data sets and compared with a statistical technique. This paper demonstrates that market manipulation is able to be detected using these techniques, with vary degrees of accuracy which can be improved. The LSTM with Dynamic Thresholding appears to be particularly promising in this domain as it was able to identify contextual/local anomalies in the data and was able to detect anomalies quickly, taking seconds to score two years of trading data for each stock, which can often be a challenge with deep learning approaches. For future work on the issue of identifying market manipulation consideration should be given to applying hybrid methods combing both deep learning and statistical techniques, such as those described in Buda et al. [3], as ARIMA performed very well on point anomalies.

References

1. ASX Operations Pty Limited: Trading volumes. https://www2.asx.com.au/about/market-statistics/trading-volumes#monthly. Accessed 04 July 2021
2. Australian Securities & Investments Commission: Report REP 666 ASIC Enforcement Update: January to June 2020, September 2020. https://www.asic.gov.au/media/5788492/rep666-published-22-september-2020.pdf. Accessed on 04 July 2021
3. Buda, T.S., Caglayan, B., Assem, H.: DeepAD: a generic framework based on deep learning for time series anomaly detection. In: Phung, D., Tseng, V.S., Webb, G.I., Ho, B., Ganji, M., Rashidi, L. (eds.) PAKDD 2018. LNCS (LNAI), vol. 10937, pp. 577–588. Springer, Cham (2018). https://doi.org/10.1007/978-3-319-93034-3_46

4. Fu, A.W., Leung, O.T.-W., Keogh, E., Lin, J.: Finding time series discords based on Haar transform. In: Li, X., Zaïane, O.R., Li, Z. (eds.) ADMA 2006. LNCS (LNAI), vol. 4093, pp. 31–41. Springer, Heidelberg (2006). https://doi.org/10.1007/11811305_3

5. Geiger, A., Liu, D., Alnegheimish, S., Cuesta-Infante, A., Veeramachaneni, K.: TadGAN: time series anomaly detection using generative adversarial networks (2020)

6. Golmohammadi, K., Zaiane, O.R.: Time series contextual anomaly detection for detecting market manipulation in stock market. In: 2015 IEEE International Conference on Data Science and Advanced Analytics (DSAA), pp. 1–10 (2015)

7. Hundman, K., Constantinou, V., Laporte, C., Colwell, I., Soderstrom, T.: Detecting spacecraft anomalies using LSTMs and nonparametric dynamic thresholding. In: Proceedings of the 24th ACM SIGKDD International Conference on Knowledge Discovery & Data Mining, July 2018

8. Islam, S.R., Khaled Ghafoor, S., Eberle, W.: Mining illegal insider trading of stocks: a proactive approach. In: 2018 IEEE International Conference on Big Data (Big Data), pp. 1397–1406 (2018)

9. Leangarun, T., Tangamchit, P., Thajchayapong, S.: Stock price manipulation detection using generative adversarial networks. In: 2018 IEEE Symposium Series on Computational Intelligence (SSCI), pp. 2104–2111 (2018)

10. Munir, M., Chattha, M.A., Dengel, A., Ahmed, S.: A comparative analysis of traditional and deep learning-based anomaly detection methods for streaming data. In: 2019 18th IEEE International Conference on Machine Learning and Applications (ICMLA), pp. 561–566 (2019)

11. Munir, M., Siddiqui, S.A., Dengel, A., Ahmed, S.: DeepAnT: a deep learning approach for unsupervised anomaly detection in time series. IEEE Access 7, 1991–2005 (2019)

12. Pang, G., Shen, C., Cao, L., Hengel, A.V.D.: Deep learning for anomaly detection. ACM Comput. Surv. 54(2), 1–38 (2021)

13. PRNewswire: Aethlon Announces FDA Approval of IDE Supplement for COVID-19 Patients, June 2020. https://finance.yahoo.com/news/aethlon-announces-fda-approval-ide-131900535.html. Accessed 22 May 2021

14. PRNewswire: Aethlon Medical Announces First Patient Treated in First-in-Human Clinical Trial of HEMOPURIFIER® in Head and Neck Cancer, December 2020. https://finance.yahoo.com/news/aethlon-medical-announces-first-patient-130200071.html. Accessed 22 May 2021

15. Ramonas, A.: Covid-19 scam crackdown prompts spike in SEC trading suspensions, July 2020. https://news.bloomberglaw.com/securities-law/covid-19-scam-crackdown-prompts-spike-in-sec-trading-suspensions. Accessed 22 May 2021

16. Thorbecke, C.: GameStop timeline: a closer look at the saga that upended wall street, February 2021. https://abcnews.go.com/Business/gamestop-timeline-closer-saga-upended-wall-street/story?id=75617315. Accessed 25 Apr 2021

17. U.S Securities and Exchange Commission: SEC Charges Companies and CEO for Misleading COVID-19 Claims, May 2020. https://www.sec.gov/news/press-release/2020-111. Accessed 25 Apr 2021

18. U.S Securities and Exchange Commission: SEC Charges Companies for Misleading COVID-19 Claims, May 2020. https://www.sec.gov/litigation/litreleases/2020/lr24819.htm. Accessed 15 June 2021

19. U.S Securities and Exchange Commission: Investor Alert 2021 — Look out for coronavirus-related investment scams, February 2021. https://www.sec.gov/oiea/investor-alerts-and-bulletins/ia_coronavirus. Accessed on 25 Apr 2021

20. Wang, Q., Xu, W., Huang, X., Yang, K.: Enhancing intraday stock price manipulation detection by leveraging recurrent neural networks with ensemble learning. Neurocomputing **347**, 46–58 (2019)
21. Wang, Z., Pi, D., Gao, Y.: A novel unsupervised time series discord detection algorithm in aircraft engine gearbox. In: Gan, G., Li, B., Li, X., Wang, S. (eds.) ADMA 2018. LNCS (LNAI), vol. 11323, pp. 202–210. Springer, Cham (2018). https://doi.org/10.1007/978-3-030-05090-0_18
22. Yu, P., Yan, X.: Stock price prediction based on deep neural networks. Neural Comput. Appl. **32**, 1609–1628 (2020). https://doi.org/10.1007/s00521-019-04212-x

Fuzzy Kolmogorov Complexity Based on Fuzzy Decompression Algorithms and Its Application to Fuzzy Data Mining
(Preliminary Report)

Tomoyuki Yamakami[✉]

Faculty of Engineering, University of Fukui, 3-9-1 Bunkyo, Fukui 910-8507, Japan

Abstract. We propose a new practical fuzzification of classical Kolmogorov complexity to measure the minimum amount of fuzzy algorithmic information needed to produce generic fuzzy data and we then cultivate the foundation of such a fuzzification. In this work, we view Kolmogorov complexity as a measure indicating the size of the maximally compressed data, from which the best possible decompressor algorithmically recovers the original data. As such decompressors, we use a generalized model of deterministic fuzzy Turing machines of Yamakami [SCIS 2014 & ISIS 2014, pp. 29–35] and introduce the notion of fuzzy Kolmogorov complexity of generic fuzzy data based on this computational model. As a direct application to data-mining issues, such as clustering and classification, we provide a set of new practical information distances induced by our notion of fuzzy Kolmogorov complexity.

1 Background and Main Contribution

We first review the basic notions of fuzzy computation and Kolmogorov complexity as the necessary background of this paper.

1.1 Fuzzy Data and Fuzzy Turing Machines

Real-life data are prone to contain a certain degree of "fuzziness". This "fuzziness" notion was first discussed in 1965 by Zadeh [34,35] and then dealt with computationally, followed by innovative ideas of the introductions of various computational models that were intended to capture the notation of "fuzzy algorithms" [25,35]. In contrast to fuzzy objects, standard (or classical) objects with no fuzziness are generally referred to as *crisp* objects. A piece of fuzzy data thus expresses a set of crisp data with associated "possibility" degrees. We wish to pay our special attention to the fuzzification of real-life, practical computational problems. To cope with those complex problems, a certain degree of abstraction of "fuzziness" is necessary and numerous methods have been proposed in the past literature to express "fuzziness" inside of the problems. To solve various forms of such "fuzzified" problems, a standard computational model of Turing

© Springer Nature Switzerland AG 2022
B. Li et al. (Eds.): ADMA 2021, LNAI 13087, pp. 421–436, 2022.
https://doi.org/10.1007/978-3-030-95405-5_30

machine has been adapted to capture fuzzy computation as well. Those machines are generally known as *fuzzy Turing machines*.

A good mathematical model for fuzzy Turing machine must have a reasonable fuzzification of classical Turing machine and it must perform a computation of reasonably-fuzzified configurations (or instantaneous descriptions). Numerous variations of such fuzzy Turing machine have been proposed and studied in the past literature [1,4,16,18,20,25,32]. The models of [25,29,30] are fuzzy analogues of nondeterministic Turing machines. Li [18] discussed their deterministic variant and showed the existence of universal fuzzy Turing machines. Yamakami [32], in contrast, introduced another computational model of fuzzy Turing machine (see Sect. 2.3 for its precise definition) and also an equivalent circuitry model, called *generic fuzzy circuits*, to solve various types of generic fuzzy problems (including fuzzy decision problems, fuzzy search problems, and fuzzy optimization problems) over more complex fuzzy instances (or fuzzy data sets), expressed as a more generalized notion of "fuzzy string." This is a natural fuzzification of classical string in a more general setting than the ones used in, e.g., [21], in which languages are fuzzified but strings are not fuzzified. A collection of fuzzy data in the form of such (generic) fuzzy strings are used as a fuzzy instance given to fuzzy decision problems. The formulation of fuzzy strings for fuzzy problems looks quite complicated but it is general enough to handle a wide range of real-life fuzzified computational problems. On the contrary, in [21], fuzzy languages (which are fuzzified languages) were used as a centerpiece of discussions on the fuzzy computability. Throughout this paper, we restrict our interest within this generalized model of fuzzy Turing machine as a basis to the main issue of (generic) fuzzy Kolmogorov complexity.

In the subsequent subsection, we will quickly review the notion of (classical) Kolmogorov complexity and a precursor [6] to our introduction of (generic) fuzzy Kolmogorov complexity.

1.2   Kolmogorov Complexity and Applications to Data Mining

In mid-1960s, early ideas of capturing *algorithmic information* sprouted out [5,15,26] and numerous applications have been since then sought out in various scientific fields. A basis to the development of algorithmic information theory is the notion of *Kolmogorov complexity*, which measures the size of a shortest "program" that produces a target piece of data by an appropriate universal reference machine.

The notion of Kolmogorov complexity has inspired numerous distinctive notions and numerous variants of Kolmogorov complexity have been proposed in the past literature: accepting complexity, function complexity, instance complexity, logical depth, etc. For more details, refer to a textbook of Li and Vitányi [17]. This notion of Kolmogorov complexity has been adapted to different computational mechanisms, for instance, *quantum Turing machines*. Three quite different formulations of *quantum Kolmogorov complexity* were given in [3,11,27] to capture the essence of quantum algorithmic information. Vitányi's notion of quantum Kolmogorov complexity is based on classical description whereas the notion of Berthiaume et al. is based on quantum description. In the latter definition, the complexity is measured by the "size" of a shortest quantum program, which is the logarithm of the dimension of the quantum program (viewed as a vector).

Another variant of the Kolmogorov-complexity notion was expected to arise in the field of fuzzy algorithms and computation. A "moderate" definition of a fuzzification of Kolmogorov complexity, which is dubbed as *fuzzy Kolmogorov complexity*, was recently discussed by Dai [6] based on the crisp descriptions of "programs" used for a universal fuzzy Turing machine of Li [18]. The Kolmogorov-complexity approach based on universal fuzzy Turing machine is quite distinctive, in comparison with fuzzified entropy notions used in, e.g., [19, 23, 31] and no precise relationship is yet known between fuzzy entropy and fuzzy Kolmogorov complexity.

Kolmogorov complexity can be rendered from a viewpoint of *data compression/decompression*, for which we measure the size of the smallest compressed data so that a fixed reference machine, working as a decompressor, algorithmically recovers the original data from this compressed data. A growing number of works have been published recently to address the importance of algorithmic data compression/decompression in data mining (e.g., [14]). Data compression is also related to the principals of *minimum description length* [24] and *minimum message length* [28] in machine learning (e.g., [22]). Lately, this aspect of minimum compression size of streaming data was nicely expanded into one-way deterministic/quantum finite automata [8, 13, 33]. Those works, nevertheless, require no fixed universal reference machine to define the compression complexity of data and, consequently, they opened a door to the definition of Kolmogorov complexity for various types of machine models not limited to deterministic Turing machines. In this work, we intend to take this new approach and introduce a fuzzified notion of classical Kolmogorov complexity.

Earlier, Faloutsos and Megalooikonomou [10], for instance, argued that some important aspects of data mining, such as classification, clustering, forecasting, and outlier detection, are closely related to data compression and thus to the estimation of Kolmogorov complexity. For instance, searching for good distance functions (or similarity measures) is significantly useful for clustering and case-base reasoning. The purpose of fuzzy data mining in this paper is to mine useful "fuzzy" information from given fuzzy data sets, which are represented as generic fuzzy strings (see Sect. 2.2 for their definitions).

1.3   Our Distinctive Approach to Generic Fuzzy Kolmogorov Complexity and an Application to Fuzzy Data Mining

We are particularly interested in a generalized form of fuzzy data [32], which we call "generic fuzzy data" or just "fuzzy data" for readability in the rest of this paper. Toward a wider range of practical application of fuzzy Kolmogorov complexity, apart from Dai's [6] notion of "fuzzy languages[1]", we intend to fuzzificate "strings" and "lengths" of such strings in a more generalized fashion. Since our target is fuzzy algorithms working on those data sets, we first need to clarify what is a "(generic) fuzzy string" and what is the "fuzzy length" of such a fuzzy string in Sect. 2 and then introduce our notion of *fuzzy Kolmogorov complexity* in Sect. 3.

Apart from [6], this work uses the model of (generic) fuzzy Turing machine of [32] and attempts to introduce a more appropriate notion of fuzzy Kolmogorov complexity, which is useful for real-life, practical applications. In particular, we aim at applying this new notion to *fuzzy data mining*. With the heavy use of fuzzy Kolmogorov complexity, we take a new approach toward fuzzy data mining in Sect. 4. We strongly hope that fuzzy Kolmogorov complexity would pave a road to a systematic study of fuzzy algorithmic information theory.

2   Preparation: Basic Notions and Notation

Here, we provide basic terminology and describe the computational model of (generic) fuzzy Turing machine of [32]. We refer to, e.g., [12] for basic concepts of fuzzy arithmetic and [21] for fuzzy computation.

2.1   Numbers, Strings, and Fuzzy Data

Natural numbers are nonnegative integers and $\mathbb{N}$ expresses the set of all natural numbers. The set $\mathbb{N} - \{0\}$ is abbreviated as $\mathbb{N}^+$. Given two integers m, n with $m \leq n$, $[m, n]_{\mathbb{Z}}$ denotes the integer interval, which is the set $\{m, m+1, m+2, \ldots, n\}$. For a number $n \in \mathbb{N}^+$, in particular, $[1, n]_{\mathbb{Z}}$ is abbreviated as $[n]$. Furthermore, $\mathbb{Z}$, $\mathbb{Q}$, and $\mathbb{R}$ respectively denote the set of all integers, that of all rational numbers, and that of all real numbers. In particular, we write $\mathbb{Q}^{>0}$ for the set of all positive rational numbers. For a set A, $|A|$ expresses the *cardinality* of A. Given the unit real interval $[0, 1]$, we call a function η on $[0, 1]$ (i.e., $\eta : [0, 1] \to [0, 1]$) *well-behaved* if (i) $\eta(0) = 1$ and $\eta(1) = 0$ and (ii) η is strictly decreasing. We further set $[0, 1]^* = \bigcup_{k \in \mathbb{N}} [0, 1]^k$ and $[0, 1]^+ = \bigcup_{k \in \mathbb{N}^+} [0, 1]^k$, where $[0, 1]^0 = \emptyset$. Given a logical statement (or a predicate) P, the notation $[P]$ denotes 1 if P is true, and 0 otherwise.

An *alphabet* is a finite set of "symbols" or "letters". A *word* or a *string* over alphabet Σ is a finite sequence of symbols in Σ. The *empty string* is always expressed as λ. The notation Σ^* denotes the set of all strings over Σ and Σ^+ is set to be $\Sigma^* - \{\lambda\}$. The *length* of a string x is the total number of symbols in x and is denoted $|x|$. For a string $x = x_1 x_2 \cdots x_n$ of length n and for any number $i \in [n]$, the notation $x_{(i)}$ denotes the ith symbol x_i. For convenience, we also set $x_{(0)} = \lambda$. The notation $bin(n)$ denotes the *binary representation* of n. For

---

[1] Fuzzy strings, which were called fuzzy languages in [6], are limited to n-valued fuzzy subsets. The reader should not be confused with the terminology of this work and the ones in [6,18,21].

instance, $bin(0) = 0$, $bin(1) = 1$, $bin(3) = 11$, and $bin(9) = 101$. It follows that $|bin(n)| = \lceil \log_2(n+1) \rceil$ for any $n \geq 1$.

Given two binary strings x and y, the *(generalized) Hamming distance* $H(x, y)$ between x and y is the total number of locations $i \in [\min\{|x|, |y|\}]$ satisfying $x_{(i)} \neq y_{(i)}$, plus the absolute value of the length difference $||x| - |y||$. For instance, we obtain $H(011, 00) = 2$, $H(1011, 1010) = 1$, and $H(1101, 100) = 3$. The *normalized Hamming distance* $h(x, y)$ is $\frac{H(x,y)}{\max\{|x|, |y|\}}$. For example, we obtain $h(011, 001) = 2/3$, $h(011, 01) = 1/3$, $h(011, 00) = 2/3$, and $h(011, 1) = 3/3$.

With respect to a fixed relative distance function d from $\Sigma^* \times \Sigma^*$ to $[0, 1]$ for a certain alphabet Σ, for a string $r \in \Sigma^*$ and a number $\gamma \in [0, 1]$, the *distance ball around center* r *of radius* γ is the set $\text{Ball}_d(r, \gamma) = \{x \in \Sigma^* \mid d(x, r) \leq \gamma\}$.

Given a universe X, a *fuzzy (sub)set* of X is a map from U to the real unit interval $[0, 1]$. Such a set, say, A is also viewed as a subset of $\{(x, \gamma) \mid x \in X, \gamma \in [0, 1]\}$ by identifying "$(x, \gamma) \in A$" with "$\gamma = A(x)$". Conventionally, these two different viewpoints are used interchangeably. The value $A(x)$ is the *membership degree* of x to A. Succinctly, we write $\mathcal{F}(X)$ to denote the collection of all fuzzy subsets of X. Given a fuzzy set A and a number $\gamma \in [0, 1]$, the γ-*cut of* A is the set $\text{Cut}_\gamma(A) = \{x \in X \mid A(x) \geq \gamma\}$, the *support of* A is $\text{Supp}(A) = \{x \in X \mid A(x) > 0\}$, and the *core of* A is $core(A) = \{x \in X \mid A(x) = 1\}$. Moreover, A is said to *have a singleton core* $\bar{x}$ if $core(A) = \{\bar{x}\}$ and, in this case, we simply write $core(A) = \bar{x}$ instead. The *height of* A is $height(A) = \sup\{A(x) \mid x \in X\}$. A fuzzy set A is *normal* if $height(A) = 1$. A singleton core $\bar{x}$ of A with $A(\bar{x}) = 1$ is called the *modal value* of A. Given two universes X_1 and X_2, let $A \subseteq \mathcal{F}(X_1)$ and $B \subseteq \mathcal{F}(X_2)$. A *(generic) fuzzy function* from A to B, denoted by $f : A \to B$, satisfies that, for any fuzzy set $s \in A$, $f(s)$ is a fuzzy set in B.

A fuzzy set $\tilde{r} \in \mathcal{F}(\mathbb{R})$ is *convex* if, for any $\gamma \in [0, 1]$ and any $x, y \in \text{Cut}_\gamma(\tilde{r})$, $\alpha x + (1 - \alpha)y$ is in $\text{Cut}_\gamma(\tilde{r})$ for any $\alpha \in [0, 1]$. A *fuzzy integer entity* (resp., a *fuzzy real entity*) is a fuzzy subset of $\mathbb{Z}$ (resp., $\mathbb{R}$) that is normal and convex. A *fuzzy integer* $\tilde{n}$ is a fuzzy integer entity such that (i) there exists a unique integer $\bar{n}$ that is a singleton core of $\tilde{n}$ (i.e., $core(\tilde{n}) = \bar{n}$) and (ii) there exists a well-behaved function η on $[0, 1]$ such that $\text{Cut}_\gamma(\tilde{n}) \subseteq \text{Ball}_d(\bar{n}, \eta(\gamma))$ holds for every $\gamma \in [0, 1]$. Notice that $\bar{n}$ is the modal value of $\tilde{n}$. Similarly, a *fuzzy real number* is defined. For instance, triangular fuzzy numbers and Gaussian fuzzy numbers (see, e.g., [12]) are fit into our definition.

Following [7], we consider a quadruple of auxiliary operators: $\mu_1 : [0, 1]^2 \to [0, 1]$, $\mu_2 : [0, 1]^+ \to [0, 1]$, $\mu_3 : [0, 1]^+ \to [0, 1]$, and $\xi : [0, 1]^* \to [0, 1]$. These auxiliary operators are called *safe* if, for any finite nonempty ordered set A and any finite ordered set B, (1) $\mu_1(\alpha, \alpha) = \alpha$ for any $\alpha \in [0, 1]$, (2) $\mu_2(\{\alpha_r\}_{r \in A}) = \alpha$ if $\alpha_r = \alpha$ for all $r \in A$, (3) $\mu_3(\{\alpha_r\}_{r \in A}) = \alpha$ if $\alpha_r = \alpha$ for all $r \in A$, and (4) $\xi(\emptyset) = 0$ and $\xi(\{\alpha_r\}_{r \in B}) = \alpha$ if $\alpha_r = \alpha$ for any $r \in B$ [32].

2.2 Generic Fuzzy Strings and Fuzzy Mean Values

We first review the notion of (generic) fuzzy strings, which was discussed in [32] to handle a wide range of practical applications, for which multiple fuzzy data sets constitute an "input" to a (generic) fuzzy problem. The purpose of [32] was to express each of such (generic) fuzzy data sets as a term of "(generic) fuzzy string." This notion of fuzzy string, which is truly different from, e.g., [21], seems to be a more natural fuzzification of (crisp) strings over alphabet Σ in such a sense that a (crisp) string is expressed as a unique modal value of a (generic) fuzzy string with finite support. A *fuzzy decision problem* takes such fuzzy strings and determines whether or not those fuzzy strings satisfy a pre-determined requirement. Fuzzy decision problems were naturally identified with "(generic) fuzzy languages"[2] in [32].

A *fuzzy string entity* over alphabet Σ is a normal fuzzy subset s of Σ^*, expressed as $\{(x, s(x)) \mid x \in \Sigma^*\}$, and $s(x)$ is called the *precision degree of* x. With respect to a fixed distance measure d and a well-behaved function $\eta :$ $[0,1] \to [0,1]$, a *fuzzy string* over Σ is a fuzzy string entity s over Σ that satisfies the following condition: there exist a crisp string $\bar{s} \in \Sigma^*$ such that (1) Supp(s) is a finite set and (2) $\text{Cut}_\gamma(s) \subseteq \text{Ball}_d(\bar{s}, \eta(\gamma))$ for any $\gamma \in [0,1]$. The requirement (2) implies that $\bar{s}$ is a singleton core of s. Let $F\Sigma^*$ denote the set of all (possible) fuzzy strings over Σ. In particular, a fuzzy string over $\{0,1\}$ is succinctly called a *fuzzy binary string*. Since Supp(s) is finite, there are two numbers $n_*, n^* \in \mathbb{N}$ such that $n_* \leq |x| \leq n^*$ holds for any string $x \in \text{Supp}(s)$. The requirement (1) aims at developing practically-efficient (e.g., polynomial time) algorithmic procedures to solve various fuzzy computational problems with fuzzy data sets. We say that s *has fixed length* n if $|x| = n$ holds for any crisp string x in Supp(s). The notion of fuzzy string heavily depends on the choice of (d, η), and therefore numerous variations of fuzzy strings may appear side by side when handling a given fuzzy problem. In Sect. 3.2, for instance, we will discuss a variant of $F\Sigma^*$ to deal with "fuzzy encodings" of two or more fuzzy strings.

For a fuzzy string s in $F\Sigma^*$, the *fuzzy length* of s is a fuzzy integer entity in $\mathcal{F}(\mathbb{N})$ satisfying $\ell(s)(n) = \bigvee_{x \in \Sigma^n} s(x)$ for any $n \in \mathbb{N}$. Note that Supp $(\ell(s))$ is finite since so is s. When s is a crisp string, $\ell(s)(|s|) = 1$ follows and, in this case, we naturally identify $\ell(s)$ with $|s|$. As a quick example, consider the following fuzzy binary string: $s = \{(1011, 0.5), (101, 1), (010, 0.1),$ $(011, 0.3), (110, 0.8), (10, 0.7), (1, 0.2)\}$. For this s, its fuzzy length $\ell(s)$ is $\{(4, 0.5), (3, 1), (2, 0.7), (1, 0.2)\}$ with the modal value of 3.

Section 3 will require a total order on all fuzzy integers having finite supports. In this respect, for any two fuzzy integers s and t with finite supports, we write $s \succeq_k t$ exactly when $\sum_{n \in \mathbb{N}} n \cdot s(n)^k \geq \sum_{n \in \mathbb{N}} n \cdot t(n)^k$ holds. The value $\sum_{n \in \mathbb{N}} n \cdot s(n)^k$ is conveniently called the *k-th fuzzy mean* of s. In particular, to express the fuzzy mean of the fuzzy length $\ell(s)$ of s, we succinctly write $\mathcal{E}_k(s)$. Given a set S of fuzzy integers and an element $r \in S$, r is called the *minimum* in S if $s \succeq_k r$ holds for all elements $s \in S$. For the previous example of $\ell(s)$, we obtain $\mathcal{E}_1(s) = 6.6$, $\mathcal{E}_2(s) = 5.02$, and $\mathcal{E}_3(s) = 4.194$. Moreover, it follows that $\lim_{k \to \infty} \mathcal{E}_k(s) = 3$. For readability, we write $\mathcal{E}(s)$ for $\mathcal{E}_1(s)$ and $\succeq$ for $\succeq_1$.

---

[2] The reader should not be confused with the terminology of this work and the terminology used in [6,18,21].

2.3   Generic Fuzzy Turing Machine

Turing machines are well-regarded as a mathematical model of algorithmic procedures in order to solve given computational problems. For numerous fuzzified problems, various fuzzy Turing machines have been proposed to solve them. Here, we intend to describe the fundamental model of (generic) fuzzy Turing machine introduced in [32] to resolve various types of fuzzy computational problems that take (generic) fuzzy strings as inputs. In particular, for the reader's sake, we wish to describe deterministic fuzzy Turing machines in a very general form as was given in [32]. An underlying idea of the introduction of such a general form of fuzzy Turing machine in [32] is to provide a unified medium to deal with a variety of "fuzzy data" that have appeared in real-life circumstances, not limited to a specific fuzzification of languages as in, e.g., [21]. Major deviations from deterministic fuzzy Turing machine of Li [18] are two folds: the choice of fuzzy transition function together with a deterministic requirement and an introduction of *fuzzy interference* of fuzzy configurations.

A (single-tape) *deterministic fuzzy Turing machine* (abbreviated as a DFTM) is formally a triplet $\langle M, \Xi, I \rangle$, where M has the form $(Q, \Delta, \{\vdash, \dashv\}, \Sigma, \Gamma, \delta, q_0, F)$, $\Xi = (\mu_1, \mu_2, \mu_3, \xi)$ is a quadruple of safe auxiliary operators, and I is a target pair $(F\Theta_1, F\Theta_2)$. Furthermore, Q is a finite set of inner states, Δ is an input alphabet, Σ is an input/work tape alphabet, Γ is an output alphabet, $\delta : (Q - F) \times \check{\Sigma} \to \mathcal{F}(Q \times \check{\Sigma} \times \Gamma \times D)$ with $\check{\Sigma} = \Sigma \cup \{\vdash, \dashv\}$ and $D = \{0, \pm 1\}$ is a fuzzy transition function, q_0 is the initial (inner) state in Q, and F is a set of finial (inner) state with $F \subseteq Q$. The fuzzy transition function δ must satisfy the *deterministic requirement*: (*) for any pair $(q, \sigma) \in Q \times \check{\Sigma}$, the fuzzy set $\delta(q, \sigma)$ is normal and has a singleton core. For convenience, we also express δ as a function from $(Q - F) \times \check{\Sigma} \times Q \times \check{\Sigma} \times \Gamma \times D$ to $[0, 1]$. Since Ξ and I are fixed, it is convenient for us to call M (instead of $\langle M, \Xi, I \rangle$) a DFTM. For convenience, $\mathcal{DFTM}$ denotes the set of all valid DFTMs for a fixed pair (Ξ, I).

A *(crisp) configuration* of M is of the form $uqv\natural w$ for $u, v \in \Sigma^*$, $q \in Q$, and $w \in \Gamma^*$, where $\natural$ is a designated separator. Let $CONF_M$ denote the set of all possible (crisp) configurations of M. A *fuzzy configuration* (or a *fuzzy instantaneous description*) is an element of $\mathcal{F}(CONF_M)$. The time evolution of fuzzy configurations is described in the following way. A fuzzy configuration $conf_0$ at time 0 is defined as $conf_0(upv\natural w) = s(x) \cdot [upv\natural w = q_0\tilde{x}\natural\lambda]$ for any configuration $upv\natural w$ of M, where $\tilde{x} = \vdash x \dashv$ and s is a fuzzy input. A fuzzy configuration $conf_{i+1}$ at time $i + 1$ is defined recursively by its *possibility degree* $conf_{i+1}$ $(u'pv'\natural w') = \mu_2(\{\ell_0(q, \sigma), \ell_{+1}(q, \sigma), \ell_{-1}(q, \sigma)\}_{(q,\sigma) \in (Q-F) \times \check{\Sigma}})$, where $\ell_0(q, \sigma) = \mu_1(conf_i(u\tau q\sigma \tau_3 v\natural w), \delta(q, \sigma, p, \tau_2, \eta, 0))$, $\ell_{+1}(q, \sigma) = \mu_1(conf_i(uq\sigma \tau_2 \tau_3 v\natural w), \delta(q, \sigma, p, \tau_1, \eta, +1))$, and $\ell_{-1}(q, \sigma) = \mu_1(conf_i(u\tau_1 \tau_2 q\sigma v\natural w), \delta(q, \sigma, p, \tau_3, \eta, -1))$. A *fuzzy computation* of M on the fuzzy input s is a series $(conf_0, conf_1, conf_2, \ldots)$ of fuzzy configurations.

Let $FIN_M(t, s)$ denote the set of all crisp strings of the form uqv with $q \in F$, $u, v \in \Sigma^*$, and $|uv| \leq t$. We define the *possibility degree* of the final configuration $uqv\natural w$ at time t as $final_M(t, uqv\natural w) = \mu_3(\{conf_i(uqv\natural w)\}_{i \in [0,t]_\mathbb{Z}}) \cdot [q \in F]$. The *(global) running time* of M on the fuzzy input s is a unique number $t \in \mathbb{N}$ for which (1) there exists a final configuration $u'q'v'\natural w'$ satisfying $conf_t(u'q'v'\natural w') > 0$ and (2) $conf_i(uqv\natural w) = 0$ for any configuration $uqv\natural w$ and all $i > t$. We say that M *outputs* b *on input* s *in time* t if b is a fuzzy string entity over Γ and satisfies $b(w) = \xi(\{final_M(t, uqv\natural w)\}_{uqv \in FIN_M(t,s)})$ for any $w \in \Gamma^*$. To express this b, we intend to write $M(s)$. In general, b may not have a finite support. Nevertheless, in later sections, we will consider only DFTMs whose outputs are limited to fuzzy strings (and thus finite support).

In the case of time-unbounded computation, we naturally expand the above definitions by unlimiting the number t of steps in the following way. Let $FIN_M(s) = \bigcup_{t \in \mathbb{N}} FIN_M(t, s)$ and define $final_M(uqv\natural w) = \mu_3(\{conf_i(uqv\natural w)\}_{i \in \mathbb{N}}) \cdot [q \in F]$ and $b(w) = \xi(\{final_M(uqv\natural w)\}_{uqv \in FIN_M(s)})$.

2.4 Fuzzy Interference of Crisp Computation Paths

In quantum computation, its computation paths (which are treated in a classical fashion with extra values called amplitudes) can interfere with one another when reaching the same configurations at the same time, influencing the overall probability of observing each final configuration at the end of the computation. In analogy to such quantum interference, on a run of a DFTM on a given fuzzy input, its fuzzy computation may generate numerous crisp computation paths in general and they may possibly reach the same configurations at the same time with various possibility degrees. Depending on the choice of safe auxiliary operators, all these possibility degrees collectively make a direct contribution to a unique overall possibility degree of each configuration at each step. We dare to call this phenomenon *fuzzy interference* in a way similar to the aforementioned quantum interference.

3 Generic Fuzzy Kolmogorov Complexity

3.1 Foundations of Fuzzy Kolmogorov Complexity

A basis to the introduction of "moderate" fuzzy Kolmogorov complexity of Dai [6] is the existence of a "universal" fuzzy Turing machine constructed by Li [18] in a way similar to universal quantum Turing machine [2].

In the rest of this paper, we fix the "standard" quadruple of safe auxiliary operators as follows. With the t-norm $\vee$ and $\wedge$, we define $\mu_1(\alpha, \beta) = \alpha \wedge \beta$. For any nonempty ordered set A, let $\mu_2(\{\alpha_r\}_{r \in A}) = \mu_3(\{\alpha_r\}_{r \in A}) = \bigvee_{r \in A} \alpha_r$. For any ordered set B, let $\xi(\emptyset) = 0$ and $\xi(\{\alpha_r\}_{r \in B}) = \bigvee_{r \in B} \alpha_r$ if $B \neq \emptyset$. Moreover, as a distance function d mapping $\Sigma^* \times \Sigma^*$ to $[0, 1]$, we use the relative Hamming distance h defined in Sect. 2.1. We also restrict η to polynomial functions of the specific form $\eta(\gamma) = 1 - \gamma^k$ for all real numbers $\gamma \in [0, 1]$, where k is an appropriate constant in $\mathbb{Q}^{>0}$ independent of γ. If s is a fuzzy string, then it must satisfy $Cut_\gamma(s) \subseteq Ball_h(\bar{s}, \eta(\gamma))$ for any $\gamma \in [0, 1]$; that is, $s(x) \geq \gamma$ implies $h(x, \bar{s}) \leq 1 - \gamma^k$. By choosing $\gamma = s(x)$, we derive $s(x)^k + h(x, \bar{s}) \leq 1$ as a requirement for s.

Example 1. We assert the existence of a DFTM M_{id} satisfying $M_{id}(s) = s$ for any binary string entity s. For this purpose, we define such an *identity machine* M_{id} as follows. On a fuzzy input string s given to an input tape, M_{id} copies any crisp string x written on the input tape onto an output tape, symbol by symbol, with possibility degree 1. More precisely, we define M_{id}'s transition function δ as $\delta(q_0, \vdash, q_1, \lambda, +1) = 1$, $\delta(q_1, \sigma, q_1, \sigma, +1) = 1$, and $\delta(q_1, \dashv, q_f, \lambda, 0) = 1$ for $\sigma \in \{0, 1\}$. For any other entry $(q, \sigma, p, \tau, \eta, d)$, we set $\delta(q, \sigma, p, \tau, \eta, d) = 0$. It then follows that $M_{id}(s)(x) = s(x)$ for all $x \in \Sigma^*$.

It is possible to construct a universal fuzzy Turing machine if we restrict the transition functions of DFTMs as in [18]. However, we avoid weakening the power of DFTMs in such a way. Instead, we take a recent approach of [8, 13, 33] toward the "decompression complexity," which expresses the size of the maximally compressed data that can be algorithmically recovered by the best possible decompressor of bounded size. In this paper, we want to use bounded-size fuzzy decompressors. For this purpose, we first clarify the meaning of the "size" of a DFTM.

Definition 2. *The* size *of a DFTM* $M = (Q, \Delta, \{\vdash, \dashv\}, \Sigma, \Gamma, \delta, q_0, F)$ *is set to be* $|Q|^2 |\Sigma|^2 |\Gamma| |D|$*, which is roughly the domain size of* $\delta : (Q - F) \times \check{\Sigma} \times Q \times \check{\Sigma} \times \Gamma \times D \to [0, 1]$*. We write* $size(M)$ *to express this value* $|Q|^2 |\Sigma|^2 |\Gamma| |D|$*. Throughout the rest of this paper, we intend to use the notation* $\mathcal{DFTM}^{\leq c}$ *to denote the set of all DFTMs* M *of size at most* c*.*

In what follows, let us define the *fuzzy Kolmogorov complexity* (abbreviated as FKC) of a fuzzy binary string s based on size-bounded fuzzy decompressors and then cultivate in Sect. 3.3 its foundations by proving various basic properties of FKC. Recall from Sect. 2.2 that the fuzzy length of a fuzzy string s is the fuzzy integer $\ell(s)$ and that $\succeq$ is the total ordering over all fuzzy integers. Given any nonempty set P of fuzzy strings, a fuzzy string p is said to be *the shortest* in P if $\ell(p)$ is the minimum among the set $\{\ell(q) \mid q \in P\}$ with respect to $\succeq$.

In a similar idea to quantum Kolmogorov complexity [3, 27], we use "approximate" generation of a target fuzzy string s instead of "precise" generation of s. Given two fuzzy sets A and B, we define $\|A - B\| = \sum_{x \in \Sigma^*} |A(x) - B(x)|$. We say that A *approximates* B to within ε, denoted $A \approx_\varepsilon B$, if $\|A - B\| \leq \varepsilon$.

Definition 3. *Let* M *denote an arbitrary DFTM and let* $\varepsilon > 0$ *be any constant. Let* s *and* w *be two fuzzy binary strings. The* (generic) fuzzy Kolmogorov complexity *of* s *on DFTMs of size at most* c *conditional to* w *with* difference factor ε*, denoted by* $FC_\varepsilon^{\leq c}(s \mid w)$*, is the fuzzy mean* $\widetilde{\mathcal{E}}(s)$ *of the fuzzy length* $\ell(p)$ *of a shortest fuzzy string* p *for which there exists a DFTM* $M \in \mathcal{DFTM}^{\leq c}$ *satisfying* $M(p, w) \approx_\varepsilon s$*. This* M *is referred to as the* (best) decompressor *for* s*. When* w *is the crisp empty string* λ*, we simply write* $FC_\varepsilon^{\leq c}(s)$ *instead of* $FC_\varepsilon^{\leq c}(s \mid \lambda)$ *and it is called the* (unconditional) fuzzy Kolmogorov complexity *of* s *on DFTMs of size at most* c *with difference factor* ε*. The* length-conditional fuzzy Kolmogorov complexity *of fuzzy string* s *is of the form* $FC_\varepsilon^{\leq c}(s \mid \ell(s))$*.*

It is obvious by the definition that, if $\varepsilon' \geq \varepsilon$ and $c' \geq c$, then $FC_{\varepsilon'}^{\leq c'}(s) \leq FC_{\varepsilon}^{\leq c}(s)$ holds for any fuzzy string s.

The DFTM M in Definition 3 works as a decompressor, which reconstructs s from a maximally compressed fuzzy data p. Note that, because of the use of individual DFTMs M, instead of a fixed "universal" DFTM, we can avoid any discussion on the *self-delimiting* property of the underlying reference machines.

3.2 An Encoding Scheme of Fuzzy Strings

It is often necessary to combine two or more fuzzy data sets and treat them as a single set of fuzzy data. To treat two or more different fuzzy strings in the same framework, it is useful to discuss how to merge two or more fuzzy strings and encode them into a "single" fuzzy string. Consider two fuzzy strings $s = \{(x, s(x)) \mid x \in \Sigma^*\}$ and $w = \{(y, w(y)) \mid y \in \Sigma^*\}$. Let $\bar{s}$ and $\bar{w}$ denote the singleton cores of s and w, respectively. Hereafter, we intend to define an appropriate encoding $\langle s, w \rangle$ of s and w.

The desired fuzzy encoded string $\langle s, w \rangle$ is defined in the following way. Let $x = x_1 x_2 \cdots x_n$ and $y = y_1 y_2 \cdots y_m$ be two nonempty crisp binary strings with $x_i, y_j \in \{0, 1\}$ for all indices i and j. We first define a crisp encoding $\langle x, y \rangle_c$ of the strings x and y, where the subscript "c" stands for "crisp". In the case of $n \leq m$, we define $\langle x, y \rangle_c = 1^{|bin(n)|} 0 bin(n) 0 xy$. In the case of $n > m$, by contrast, we define $\langle x, y \rangle_c = 1^{|bin(m)|} 0 bin(m) 1 xy$. It then follows that $|\langle x, y \rangle_c| = |x| + |y| + 2\lceil \log(\min\{|x|, |y|\} + 1) \rceil + 2$. Therefore, we obtain $|\langle x, y \rangle_c| \geq |x| + |y| + 2$. Finally, we set the fuzzy encoded string $\langle s, w \rangle$ to be the fuzzy set $\{(\langle x, y \rangle_c, \gamma_{xy}) \mid x, y \in \Sigma^+, x \in \mathrm{Supp}(s), y \in \mathrm{Supp}(w), \gamma_{xy} = s(x) \wedge w(y)\}$. We use the new notation $F\Sigma_2^*$ to denote the set of all fuzzy encoded strings.

Next, we introduce a new distance between two fuzzy encoded strings. Given strings $x, y, z \in \Sigma^+$, we define $h_2(\langle x, y \rangle_c, \langle u, v \rangle_c) = \frac{1}{2}(h(x, u) + h(y, v))$.

We see how to define $\langle s, w \rangle$ in the following quick example.

Example 4. In this simple example, we consider two fuzzy strings $s = \{(10, 0.5), (101, 1), (100, 0.7), (110, 0.2), (1111, 0.3)\}$ and $w = \{(00, 0.1), (011, 1), (010, 0.6), (101, 0.3), (0111, 0.8)\}$. Notice that $\bar{s} = 101$ and $\bar{w} = 011$. Note that $\ell(s) = \{(2, 0.5), (3, 1), (4, 0.3)\}$ and $\ell(w) = \{(2, 0.1), (3, 1), (4, 0.8)\}$. Take $\eta(\gamma) = 1 - \gamma^2$. To see that s and w are fuzzy strings, we check that $s(x)^2 + h(x, \bar{s}) \leq 1$ and $w(y)^2 + h(y, \bar{w}) \leq 1$ for any $x \in \mathrm{Supp}(s)$ and $y \in \mathrm{Supp}(w)$. Since $\mathscr{E}(s) = 5.2$ and $\mathscr{E}(w) = 6.4$, we conclude that $s \preceq w$. The fuzzy encoded string $u = \langle s, w \rangle$ is a fuzzy set composed of the elements $(\langle x, y \rangle_c, s(x) \wedge w(y))$ for $x \in \{10, 101, 100, 110, 1111\}$ and $y \in \{00, 011, 010, 101, 0111\}$. For instance, we obtain $\langle 110, 0111 \rangle_c = 11001110110111$, $u(\langle 110, 0111 \rangle_c) = 0.2$, and $h_2(\langle 110, 0111 \rangle_c, \bar{u}) = \frac{11}{24}$.

We claim that, for any two fuzzy strings s and w, the fuzzy encoded string $\langle s, w \rangle$ is indeed a fuzzy string with respect to h_2 and $\eta(\gamma) = 1 - \gamma^k$.

Lemma 5. *For any two fuzzy strings s and w, $\langle s, w \rangle$ is also a fuzzy string with respect to h_2 and $\eta(\gamma) = 1 - \gamma^k$.*

Proof. Let s, w be any fuzzy strings. Recall that h is the relative Hamming distance. Note that $\text{Cut}_\gamma(s) = \{x \mid s(x) \geq \gamma\}$, $\text{Cut}_\gamma(w) = \{y \mid w(y) \geq \gamma\}$, $\text{Ball}_h(\bar{s}, \eta(\gamma)) = \{x \mid h(x, \bar{s}) \leq \eta(\gamma)\}$, and $\text{Ball}_h(\bar{w}, \eta(\gamma)) = \{y \mid d(y, \bar{w}) \leq \eta(\gamma)\}$. Since s and w are fuzzy strings, it follows that $\text{Cut}_\gamma(s) \subseteq \text{Ball}_h(\bar{s}, \eta(\gamma))$ and $\text{Cut}_\gamma(w) \subseteq \text{Ball}_h(\bar{w}, \eta(\gamma))$.

Let $u = \langle s, w \rangle$ and $\bar{u} = \langle \bar{s}, \bar{w} \rangle_c$. We want to show that $\text{Cut}_\gamma(u) \subseteq \text{Ball}_{h_2}(\bar{u}, \eta(\gamma))$. Note that $\text{Cut}_\gamma(u) = \{\langle x, y \rangle_c \mid u(\langle x, y \rangle_c) \geq \gamma\}$ and $\text{Ball}_{h_2}(\bar{u}, \eta(\gamma)) = \{\langle x, y \rangle_c \mid h_2(\langle x, y \rangle_c, \bar{u}) \leq 1 - \gamma^k\} = \{\langle x, y \rangle_c \mid h(x, \bar{s}) + h(y, \bar{w}) \leq 2(1 - \gamma^k)\}$.

From $s(x)^k + h(x, \bar{s}) \leq 1$ and $w(y)^k + h(y, \bar{w}) \leq 1$, it follows that $\frac{1}{2}(s(x)^k + w(y)^k) + \frac{1}{2}(h(x, \bar{s}) + h(y, \bar{w})) \leq 1$. Since $s(x)^k \wedge w(y)^k \leq \frac{1}{2}(s(x)^k + w(y)^k)$, we obtain $u(\langle x, y \rangle_c)^k + h_2(\langle x, y \rangle_c, \bar{u}) \leq 1$. It then follows that, if $x \in \text{Ball}_h(\bar{s}, \eta(\gamma))$ and $y \in \text{Ball}_h(\bar{w}, \eta(\gamma))$, then $\langle x, y \rangle_c \in \text{Ball}_{h_2}(\bar{u}, \eta(\gamma))$.

As for extracting s out of $\langle s, w \rangle$, we remark that, by its definition, $\langle s, w \rangle$ preserves the values of all membership degrees associated with s (as well as w) in a collective way. Let $\log \ell(s) = \{(\log n, \gamma) \mid (n, \gamma) \in \ell(s)\}$.

Lemma 6. *For any two fuzzy strings $s, w \in F\Sigma^*$, $\mathscr{E}(\langle s, w \rangle) \leq \mathscr{E}(s) + \mathscr{E}(w) + O(\max\{mean_1(\log \ell(s)), mean_1(\log \ell(w))\})$, where $mean_1(n)$ denotes the 1-mean of a fuzzy integer n.*

3.3 Fundamental Properties of FKC

Based on our new notion of FKC, we intend to explore basic properties of FKC. The purpose of this section is to confirm that our new FKC satisfies standard properties of classical Kolmogorov complexity. We begin with the following form of *invariance relations*.

Lemma 7. *For any two constants $c > 0$ and $\varepsilon \geq 0$, there exist two constants $c' \geq c$ and $\varepsilon' \geq \varepsilon$ such that, for any two fuzzy strings s and w, the following statements hold. Let $\Delta = \min\{\log FC_\varepsilon^{\leq c}(s), \log FC_\varepsilon^{\leq c}(w)\}$.*

1 $FC_\varepsilon^{\leq c'}(s \mid w) \leq FC_\varepsilon^{\leq c}(s)$ and $FC_0^{\leq c}(s) \leq \mathscr{E}(s)$.
2 $FC_{\varepsilon'}^{\leq c'}(s) \leq FC_\varepsilon^{\leq c}(w) + FC_\varepsilon^{\leq c}(s \mid w) + O(\Delta)$.
3 $FC_{\varepsilon'}^{\leq c'}(s \mid w) \leq FC_\varepsilon^{\leq c}(s \mid u) + FC_\varepsilon^{\leq c}(u \mid w) + 2\Delta + 2$.

For two fuzzy strings s and w, we conveniently write $FC_\varepsilon^{\leq c}(s, w)$ instead of $FC_\varepsilon^{\leq c}(\langle s, w \rangle)$. We next show the *subadditivity property* of FKC.

Lemma 8. *For any two constants $c > 0$ and $\varepsilon \geq 0$, there exist two constants $c' \geq c$ and $\varepsilon' \geq \varepsilon$ such that, for any fuzzy strings $s, u, w \in F\Sigma^*$, each of the following statements holds. Let $\Delta = \min\{\log FC_\varepsilon^{\leq c}(s), \log FC_\varepsilon^{\leq c}(w)\}$.*

1 $FC_\varepsilon^{\leq c'}(s) \leq FC_\varepsilon^{\leq c}(s, w)$.
2 $FC_\varepsilon^{\leq c'}(s, w) = FC_\varepsilon^{\leq c}(w, s)$.
3 $FC_{\varepsilon'}^{\leq c'}(s, w) \leq FC_\varepsilon^{\leq c}(s) + FC_\varepsilon^{\leq c}(w \mid s) + 2\Delta + 2$.

There is a subtle but potentially essential difference between classical Kolmogorov complexity and its fuzzy counterpart, FKC. For instance, given $n \in \mathbb{N}^+$, the set $A_n = \{\langle x, y \rangle_c \mid C(x,y) \leq n\}$ can be recursively enumerated; however, its fuzzy counterpart $\tilde{A}_n = \{\langle s, w \rangle \mid FC_{\tilde{\varepsilon}}^{\leq c}(s,w) \leq n\}$ may not be recursively enumerated because there are uncountably many pairs $\langle s, w \rangle$ to consider. To circumvent this situation and demonstrate further fundamental properties of FKC, we need to confine our interest within *rational* possibility degrees of DFTMs. This is possible because, as shown in Lemma 9, we can approximate the outcomes of any DFTM by such a possibility-degree restricted DFTM.

For our purpose, we define $F\Sigma_{\mathbb{Q} \cap [0,1]}^*$ to be the set $\{s \in F\Sigma^* \mid \forall x \in \Sigma^* [s(x) \in \mathbb{Q} \cap [0,1]]\}$. We write $\mathcal{DFTM}_{\mathbb{Q} \cap [0,1]}^{\leq c}$ for the subset of $\mathcal{DFTM}^{\leq c}$ in which each DFTM uses only (transition) possibility degrees taken from $\mathbb{Q} \cap [0,1]$.

Lemma 9. *For any two constants $c > 0$ and $\varepsilon \geq 0$, there exists two constants $c' \geq c$ and $\varepsilon' \geq \varepsilon$ such that, for any DFTM M in $\mathcal{DFTM}^{\leq c}$, there exists another DFTM N in $\mathcal{DFTM}_{\mathbb{Q} \cap [0,1]}^{\leq c'}$ for which $M(s) \approx_\varepsilon N(s)$ for any fuzzy string s.*

Proof. The construction of the desired N can be done by approximating each (transition) possibility degree of M by an appropriately chosen number in $\mathbb{Q} \cap [0,1]$. The proof for $M(s) \approx_\varepsilon N(s)$ is done by induction on the number of steps of M.

Lemma 10. *For any two constants $c > 0$ and $\varepsilon \geq 0$, there exist three constants $c' \geq c$, $e > 0$, and $\varepsilon' \geq \varepsilon$ such that, for any two fuzzy strings $s, w \in F\Sigma_{\mathbb{Q} \cap [0,1]}^*$, it follows that $FC_{\tilde{\varepsilon}}^{\leq c}(s,w) \geq FC_{\tilde{\varepsilon}'}^{\leq c'}(s) + FC_{\tilde{\varepsilon}'}^{\leq c'}(w \mid s) - e \log FC_{\tilde{\varepsilon}}^{\leq c}(s,w)$.*

Proof. We show this lemma by contradiction. Our proof closely follows [17, Section 2.8]. Assume the following: there exist constants $c > 0$ and $\varepsilon \geq 0$ such that, for any constants $c' \geq c$, $\varepsilon' \geq \varepsilon$, and $e \geq 0$, a certain pair (s, w) of fuzzy strings satisfy that $FC_{\tilde{\varepsilon}'}^{\leq c'}(w \mid s) > FC_{\tilde{\varepsilon}}^{\leq c}(s,w) - FC_{\tilde{\varepsilon}'}^{\leq c'}(s) + e \log FC_{\tilde{\varepsilon}}^{\leq c}(s,w)$. Take a sufficiently large number e and fix (s, w) that satisfies the above inequality. We wish to estimate the value $FC_{\tilde{\varepsilon}}^{\leq c}(s)$ step by step. Let $n = FC_{\tilde{\varepsilon}}^{\leq c}(s,w)$. We set $A_n = \{\langle u, v \rangle \mid u, v \in F\Sigma_{\mathbb{Q} \cap [0,1]}^*, FC_{\tilde{\varepsilon}}^{\leq c}(u,v) \leq n\}$. Note that, because $F\Sigma_{\mathbb{Q} \cap [0,1]}^*$ is a countable set, we can recursively enumerate all elements of A_n (in a classical sense) when we are given $bin(n)$ as an input. To each element $\langle u, v \rangle$, we can assign a unique DFTM M in $\mathcal{DFTM}_{\mathbb{Q} \cap [0,1]}^{\leq c}$ and a unique fuzzy input p such that M starts with p and approximates $\langle s, w \rangle$ and $\tilde{\ell}(p)$ is the smallest with $\tilde{\ell}(s) \leq n$. Since this assignment is one-to-one, $|A_n|$ must be upper-bounded by 2^{n+c}.

We further define $A_n(u) = \{v \mid \langle u, v \rangle \in A_n\}$ for each fuzzy string u and we consider the set $A_n(s)$. Note that $A_n(s)$ can be recursively enumerated from $(s, bin(n))$. In such an enumeration of $A_n(s)$, since $w \in A_n(s)$, assume that w is the kth element. Let us consider the following DFTM N: on input $(s, \langle bin(n), bin(k) \rangle_c)$, N recovers w in a fuzzy fashion and outputs it. This implies that $FC_{\tilde{\varepsilon}'}^{\leq c'}(w \mid s) \leq |\langle bin(n), bin(k) \rangle_c| \leq \log |A_n(s)| + 2 \log n + 2(\log \log |A_n(s)| +$

$\log \log n) \leq \log |A_n(s)| + 3 \log n$ for appropriate constants $c' \geq c$ and $\varepsilon' \geq \varepsilon$. It then follows that $\log |A_n(s)| > FC_{\bar{\varepsilon}}^{\leq c}(s, w) - FC_{\bar{\varepsilon}'}^{\leq c'}(s) + (e - 3) \log n$. For simplicity, we write α for the right-hand side of this inequality and then define $B = \{u \mid |A_n(u)| > 2^{\alpha}\}$. Clearly, $s \in B$. Since $\{\langle u, v \rangle \mid u \in B, v \in A_n(u)\}$ is a subset of A_n, $|B|$ must be upper-bounded by $|A_n| / \min\{|A_n(u)| : u \in B\}$, which is at most $|A_n|/2^{\alpha} \leq 2^{n+c-\alpha}$. Since B is also recursively enumerable, we assume that s is the k'th element in this enumeration. Consider the DFTM N' that takes an input $\langle\langle bin(n), bin(\alpha)\rangle_c, bin(k')\rangle_c$, recovers s, and outputs it. This implies that $FC_{\bar{\varepsilon}'}^{\leq c'}(s) \leq |\langle\langle bin(n), bin(\alpha)\rangle_c, bin(k')\rangle_c| < 2 \log n + 2 \log \alpha + n - \alpha + c < FC_{\bar{\varepsilon}'}^{\leq c'}(s)$. This is obviously a contradiction.

By combining Lemma 7(3) and Lemma 10, we can draw the following equality.

Corollary 11. $FC_{\bar{\varepsilon}}^{\leq c}(s) + FC_{\bar{\varepsilon}}^{\leq c}(w \mid s) = FC_{\bar{\varepsilon}}^{\leq c}(w) + FC_{\bar{\varepsilon}}^{\leq c}(s \mid w) + O(\log FC_{\bar{\varepsilon}}^{\leq c}(s, w))$.

4   Applications of Fuzzy Kolmogorov Complexity to Fuzzy Data Mining

We seek direct applications of fuzzy Kolmogorov complexity (FKC), defined in Definition 3, to known issues regarding *fuzzy data mining*. In the past literature (e.g., [10,14]), classical Kolmogorov complexity (or its compression-complexity variant) has been used to solve certain issues in data mining. Many data-mining algorithms are laden with numerous parameters and thus tend to cause unwanted results, including the reporting of spurious patterns and the overestimation of obtained patterns (see, e.g., [14] for more discussions). The use of Kolmogorov complexity helps us design parameter-light or even parameter-free algorithms in a quite general setting.

In this work, we seek for a new method of searching for fuzzy correlations among given data sets and searching for good fuzzy distance functions. Many data-mining algorithms in practice rely on certain forms of similarity/dissimilarity measures used as core subroutines in solving data-mining tasks ranging over authorship attribution, stemmatology, music classification, network traffic, etc. (see, e.g., [17]). A key idea of solving clustering issues in search of centers of various clusters in a given data set (see, e.g., [9]) is to use an appropriately-chosen similarity/dissimilarity measure. Such a measure is actually a metric,[3] which indicates an information distance between two pieces of data. The information distance is used to help extract certain specific features out of vast data.

---

[3] A nonnegative function $g : \Sigma^* \times \Sigma^* \to \mathbb{R}$ is called a *metric* if (i) g satisfies the identity property (i.e., $g(x, y) = 0$ iff $x = y$), (ii) g is symmetric, and (iii) g satisfies the triangle inequality.

For given fuzzy data, we intend to introduce fuzzy information distances solely based on FKC. In particular, we target two types of normalized information distances and formulate their fuzzifications. Given two fuzzy strings s and w, the *fuzzy information distance* is defined as $E_{1,\varepsilon}^{\leq c}(s,w) = FC_{\varepsilon}^{\leq c}(s \mid w) + FC_{\varepsilon}^{\leq c}(w \mid s)$. Moreover, the *fuzzy max distance* $E_{2,\varepsilon}^{\leq c}(s,w) = \max\{FC_{\varepsilon}^{\leq c}(s \mid w), FC_{\varepsilon}^{\leq c}(w \mid s)\}$. For each index $i \in \{1,2\}$, the normalized version $e_{i,\varepsilon}^{\leq c}(s,w)$ of $E_{i,\varepsilon}^{\leq c}(s,w)$ is set to be $\dfrac{E_{i,\varepsilon}^{\leq c}(s,w)}{\max\{FC_{\varepsilon}^{\leq c}(s), FC_{\varepsilon}^{\leq c}(w)\}}$. Note that $e_{i,\varepsilon}^{\leq c}(s,w)$ is a real number in $[0,1]$.

With an appropriate use of basic properties of FKC discussed in Sect. 3.3, we can show that all measures $e_{i,\varepsilon}^{\leq c}(s,w)$ for $i \in \{1,2\}$ are indeed metrics.

Theorem 12. *The measures $e_{1,\varepsilon}^{\leq c}$ and $e_{2,\varepsilon}^{\leq c}$ are metrics (up to an additive logarithmic term).*

Proof. Here, we consider only $e_{2,\varepsilon}^{\leq c}$. By its definition, it is nonnegative. It also follows that $e_{2,\varepsilon}^{\leq c}(s,w) = e_{2,\varepsilon}^{\leq c}(w,s)$. The triangle inequality will be shown by case studies as follows. For simplicity, we write α for $\max\{FC_{\varepsilon}^{\leq c}(s), FC_{\varepsilon}^{\leq c}(w)\}$, β for $\max\{\alpha, FC_{\varepsilon}^{\leq c}(u)\}$, and Δ for $\min\{\log FC_{\varepsilon}^{\leq c}(s), \log FC_{\varepsilon}^{\leq c}(w)\}$.

(i) Consider the case of $FC_{\varepsilon}^{\leq c}(u) \leq \alpha$. From this, it follows that both $\max\{FC_{\varepsilon}^{\leq c}(u), FC_{\varepsilon}^{\leq c}(s)\}$ and $\max\{FC_{\varepsilon}^{\leq c}(u), FC_{\varepsilon}^{\leq c}(w)\}$ are upper-bounded by α. By Lemma 7(3), we obtain $FC_{\varepsilon'}^{\leq c'}(s \mid w) \leq FC_{\varepsilon}^{\leq c}(s \mid u) + FC_{\varepsilon}^{\leq c}(u \mid w) + O(\Delta)$. From this, it follows that $\max\{FC_{\varepsilon}^{\leq c}(s \mid w), FC_{\varepsilon}^{\leq c}(w \mid s)\} \leq \max\{FC_{\varepsilon}^{\leq c}(s \mid u) + FC_{\varepsilon}^{\leq c}(u \mid w), FC_{\varepsilon}^{\leq c}(w \mid u) + FC_{\varepsilon}^{\leq c}(u \mid s)\} + O(\Delta)$. The last "max" term is further upper-bounded by $\max\{FC_{\varepsilon}^{\leq c}(s \mid u), FC_{\varepsilon}^{\leq c}(u \mid s)\} + \max\{FC_{\varepsilon}^{\leq c}(w \mid u), FC_{\varepsilon}^{\leq c}(u \mid w)\} + O(\Delta)$. By dividing the both-hand sides of this inequation by α together with our assumption, we obtain the desired triangle inequality.

(ii) Consider the case of $FC_{\varepsilon}^{\leq c}(u) > \alpha$. Without loss of generality, we further assume that $FC_{\varepsilon}^{\leq c}(s) \geq FC_{\varepsilon}^{\leq c}(w)$. Let $\tau = FC_{\varepsilon}^{\leq c}(u) - FC_{\varepsilon}^{\leq c}(s)$. By Corollary 11, we obtain $FC_{\varepsilon}^{\leq c}(u \mid s) = FC_{\varepsilon}^{\leq c}(s \mid u) + \tau + O(\log \beta)$. From $FC_{\varepsilon}^{\leq c}(s \mid w) \leq FC_{\varepsilon}^{\leq c}(s \mid u) + FC_{\varepsilon}^{\leq c}(u \mid w) + O(\Delta)$ by Lemma 7(3), we divide the both-hand sides by $FC_{\varepsilon}^{\leq c}(s)$ and add τ to both the numerator and the denominator. We then obtain $FC_{\varepsilon}^{\leq c}(s \mid w)/FC_{\varepsilon}^{\leq c}(s) \leq FC_{\varepsilon}^{\leq c}(s \mid u)/FC_{\varepsilon}^{\leq c}(u) + FC_{\varepsilon}^{\leq c}(u \mid w)/FC_{\varepsilon}^{\leq c}(u)$.

References

1. Bedregal, B.C., Figueira, S.: On the computing power of fuzzy Turing machines. Fuzzy Sets Syst. **159**, 1072–1083 (2008)
2. Bernstein, E., Vazirani, U.: Quantum compelxity theory. SIAM J. Comput. **26**, 1411–1473 (1997)
3. Berthiaume, A., van Dam, W., Laplante, S.: Quantum Kolmogorov complexity. J. Comput. System Sci. **63**, 201–221 (2001)
4. Castro, J.L., Delgado, M., Mantas, C.J.: A new approach for the execution and adjustment of a fuzzy algorithm. Fuzzy Sets Syst. **121**, 491–503 (2001)

5. Chaitin, G.: On the length of programs for computing finite binary sequences. J. ACM **13**, 547–569 (1966)
6. Dai, S.: Fuzzy Kolmogorov complexity based on a classical description. Entropy 22, article 66 (2020)
7. Doostfatemeh, M., Kremer, S.: New directions in fuzzy automata. Int. J. Approx. Reason. **38**, 175–214 (2005)
8. Doty, D., Moser, P.: Feasible depth. In: Cooper, S.B., Löwe, B., Sorbi, A. (eds.) CiE 2007. LNCS, vol. 4497, pp. 228–237. Springer, Heidelberg (2007). https://doi.org/10.1007/978-3-540-73001-9_24
9. Elkan, C.: Using the triangle inequality to accelerate k-means. In: Proceedings of ICML 2003, pp. 147–153. AAAI Press (2003)
10. Faloutsos, C., Megalooikonomou, V.: On data mining, compression, and Kolmogorov complexity. Data Min. Knowl. Disc. **15**, 3–20 (2007)
11. Gács, P.: Quantum algorithmic entropy. J. Phys. A: Math. Gen. **34**, 6859–6880 (2001)
12. Hanss, M.: Applied Fuzzy Arithmiteic: An Introduction with Engineering Applications. Springer, Berlin (2010)
13. Jordon, L., Moser, P.: On the difference between finite-state and pushdown depth. In: Chatzigeorgiou, A., et al. (eds.) SOFSEM 2020. LNCS, vol. 12011, pp. 187–198. Springer, Cham (2020). https://doi.org/10.1007/978-3-030-38919-2_16
14. Keogh, E., Lonardi, S., Wei, L., Ratanamahatana, C.A., Lee, S.H., Handley, J.: Compression-based data mining of sequential data. Data Min. Knowl. Disc. **14**, 99–129 (2007)
15. Kolmogorov, A.: Three approaches to the quantitative definition of information. Probl. Inform. Transm. **1**, 1–7 (1965)
16. Lee, E.T., Zadeh, L.A.: Note on fuzzy languages. Inf. Sci. **1**, 421–431 (1969)
17. Li, M., Vitányi, P.: An Introduction to Kolmogorov Complexity and Its Applications, 3rd edn. Springer-Science, New York (2008)
18. Li, Y.: Fuzzy Turing machines: variants and universality. IEEE Trans. Fuzzy Syst. **16**, 1491–1502 (2008)
19. Luca, A.D., Termini, S.: Entropy of L-fuzzy set. Inform. Control **24**, 55–73 (1974)
20. Moniri, M.: Fuzzy and intuitionistic fuzzy Turing machines. Fundamenta Informaticae **123**, 305–315 (2013)
21. Mordenson, J.N., Malik, D.S.: Fuzzy Automata and Languages: Theory and Applications. Chapman and Hall, London, U.K. (2002)
22. Needham, S., Dowe, D.: Message length as an effective Ockham's razor in decision tree induction. In: Proceedings of AISTATS 2001, pp. 216–223 (2001)
23. Pal, N., Pal, S.: Higher order fuzzy entropy and hybrid entropy of a fuzzy set. Inf. Sci. **61**, 211–221 (1992)
24. Rissanen, J.J.: Modeling by the shortest data description. Automatica **14**, 465–471 (1978)
25. Santos, E.S.: Fuzzy algorithms. Inform. Control **17**, 326–339 (1970)
26. Solomonoff, R.A.: A formal theory of inductive inference, part I. Inform. Control **7**, 1–22 (1964)
27. Vitányi, P.M.: Quantum Kolmogorov compelxity based on classical descriptions. IEEE Trans. Inform. Theory **47**, 2464–2479 (2001)
28. Wallace, C.S., Boulton, D.M.: An information measure for classification. Comput. J. **11**, 185–195 (1968)
29. Wang, H., Qiu, D.: Computing with words via Turing machines: a formal approach. IEEE Trans. Fuzzy Syst. **11**, 742–753 (2003)

30. Wiedermann, J.: Characterizing the super-turing computing power and efficiency of classical fuzzy Turing machines. Theor. Comput. Sci. **317**, 61–69 (2004)
31. Yager, R.: On the measure of fuzziness and negation, part I: membership in the unit interval. Int. J. Gen. Syst. **5**, 221–229 (1979)
32. Yamakami, T.: The world of combinatorial fuzzy problems and the efficiency of fuzzy approximation algorithms. In: Proceedings of the Joint Conference of SCIS 2014 and ISIS 2014, pp. 29–35. IEEE (2014). arXiv: 1509.03057
33. Yamakami, T.: Quantum logical depth and shallowness of streaming data by one-way quantum finite-state transducers (preliminary report). In: Proceedings of UCNC 2021. LNCS, vol. 12984, pp. 177–193. Springer (2021)
34. Zadeh, L.A.: Fuzzy sets. Inform. Control **8**, 338–353 (1965)
35. Zadeh, L.A.: Fuzzy algorithms. Inform. Control **12**, 94–102 (1968)

Author Index

Printed in the United States
by Baker & Taylor Publisher Services

Printed in the United States
by Baker & Taylor Publisher Services